FOURTH EDITION

TEACHING *by* PRINCIPLES

AN INTERACTIVE APPROACH TO LANGUAGE PEDAGOGY

H. DOUGLAS BROWN
San Francisco State University

HEEKYEONG LEE
Monterey Institute of International Studies

Teaching by Principles: An Interactive Approach to Language Pedagogy, Fourth Edition

Pearson Education, 10 Bank Street, White Plains, NY 10606

Staff Credits: The people who made up the **Teaching by Principles, Fourth Edition**, team—representing editorial, production, design, photo/text rights, and manufacturing—are Tracey Cataldo, Rosa Chapinal, Aerin Csigay,Warren Fischbach, Nancy Flaggman, Linda Moser, Joan Poole, and Robert Ruvo.

Cover design: Warren Fischbach
Cover image provided by: Christian Delbert/Shutterstock
Project management and text composition: Kelly Ricci/iEnergizer Aptara®, Inc.
Text font: 10.5/12.5, ITC Garamond Std
Text credits: Please see page 667.

Library of Congress Cataloging-in-Publication Data

Brown, H. Douglas
Teaching by principles : an interactive approach to language pedagogy/
H. Douglas Brown, San Francisco State University;
Heekyeong Lee, Monterey Institute of International Studies. — Fourth edition.
pages cm
Includes bibliographical references and indexes.
ISBN 978-0-13-392585-2
1. Language and languages--Study and teaching. I. Lee, Heekyeong. II. Title.
P51.B7754 2015
418.0071--dc23

2014047746

ISBN 10: 0-13-392585-4
ISBN 13: 978-0-13-392585-2

Printed in the United States of America
5 17

CONTENTS

PREFACE

For those of you who used the third edition of *Teaching by Principles*, you'll notice some refreshing changes in this fourth edition.

I'm delighted that Dr. Heekyeong Lee of Monterey Institute of International Studies joined me as a coauthor for this edition. Her special interests in the subfields of sociopolitical issues, pedagogical grammar, technology, and the emerging construct of agency have added new dimensions to the current edition. And with her years of experience in language teacher education in several contexts, she has been an ideal partner in creating this latest edition.

You'll also discover significant changes, updates, additions—and a few deletions—here that appropriately reflect the growth of this burgeoning field of second language (L2) teacher education. Those changes are detailed below.

Finally, they say you should never judge a book by its cover, but we hope that the image of a lighthouse on this cover is symbolic of the mission of language teachers (and learners) around the globe. Through mutually intelligible linguistic exchanges, we are becoming better able to train a shining beacon on the open seas of international cooperation, cultural understanding, and global partnerships. Perhaps that same light has already steered us clear of the treacherous rocky shoals of social, political, and military conflict. But a quick glance at world headlines tells us we language users around the world still face many challenges in reaching peaceful negotiation in the stormy seas of injustice, violence, and hatred.

PURPOSE AND AUDIENCE

The purpose and audience of the fourth edition of *Teaching by Principles* (*TBP*) remain much the same:

- *TBP* is a synthesis of the state of the art of language teaching.
- *TBP* focuses on the key ingredient of communicative language teaching: interaction.
- *TBP* primarily addresses the needs of those in teacher education programs who seek information and expertise in language teaching.

- *TBP* also serves as a refresher course, or a handbook, for those who have had experience in teaching.
- *TBP* addresses teachers of all languages (with some preference for English), in many different contexts, including "second" and "foreign" language situations, and teaching in virtually every conceivable cultural, political, and geographical context.
- *TBP* is designed to be read, studied, and enjoyed by those with little or no previous work in linguistics, psychology, or second language acquisition (SLA).
- *TBP* helps teachers to build a repertoire of classroom techniques that are firmly embedded in well-established principles of SLA.

Most of these principles are treated comprehensively in the companion to this volume, *Principles of Language Learning and Teaching* (*PLLT*) (H. D. Brown, 2014) now in its sixth edition. Those who use *TBP* in their teacher-training program could benefit from (a) having first read *PLLT*, or (b) using *PLLT* as a concurrent or supplementary text. However, *TBP* can be used effectively without its companion, because major principles are summarized here in the early chapters.

PRINCIPAL FEATURES

The major features of the previous editions of *TBP* are retained:

- A comprehensive course in L2 teaching methodology with classroom applications throughout.
- A practical focus grounded in fundamental principles of SLA.
- Reader-friendly prose that speaks to teachers in plain, understandable language, yet with references to related research.
- A step-by-step approach to teaching language interactively that helps the novice teacher to become confident in directing collaborative, student-centered, communicative classrooms.
- A set of questions for reflection at the beginning of each chapter to center the reader on issues and topics to be covered.
- End-of-chapter topics for discussion, action, and research, many of which model an interactive classroom by providing tasks for pairs and small groups.
- Suggestions for further reading at the end of each chapter, annotated to facilitate informed choices of supplementary reading.

IMPROVEMENTS IN THE FOURTH EDITION

A number of improvements have been made in this edition:

1. **New chapters.** Several chapters have undergone major restructuring.
    - Chapter 4 (Teaching by Principles) has a new look, with eight principles representing a trimmer set of foundation stones for teaching.

Research on SLA in the last decade casts new light on the field, yielding new findings, new insights, and new perspectives. Many of the original twelve principles from the third edition are retained, but the reframing better represents key findings of the last decade.

- Chapter 5 (Agency in Language Learning) is completely new. Agency now serves as a prime example of one of the eight principles, described and applied to classrooms.
- Chapter 8 (Sociopolitical Contexts) is rewritten to reflect the tremendous quantity and quality of recent research on the interrelationship of language, society, ethnicity, culture, politics, and educational philosophy.
- Chapter 12 (Technology) has been reconstructed from the ground up. With the mushrooming advances in technology, from the ubiquitous possession of smartphones around the globe to apps available to every language learner, technology reaches into every aspect of people's lives. This growth is now reflected in this chapter.
- Chapter 19 (Teaching Grammar and Vocabulary) has undergone a major reworking to reflect recent advances in form-focused instruction.

2. **Previous chapters deleted or replaced.** A growing profession is reflected in new chapters, but growth means pruning, and so some chapters from the third edition have been deleted and their content distilled into other chapters.
    - Chapter 5: In the last edition, the featured principle was intrinsic motivation, which is now incorporated into Chapter 4 and other chapters.
    - Chapters 13 and 14: The two chapters on interaction and group work have been combined into a new Chapter 13.
    - Chapter 16: Strategies-based instruction is now a part of Chapter 4 and other chapters.
    - Chapter 17: The integration of the various skills is now interspersed into Chapters 15 through 18.
3. **Questions for reflection.** At the beginning of each chapter, questions serve as advance organizers and a preview of the topics coming up in the chapter.
4. **Tips for teaching.** When a set of practical guidelines lends itself to the kind of list that a reader might want to flag for later reference, boxes with a "tips" icon have been inserted. Collectively, these tips can add up to handy strategies for improving one's pedagogy.
5. **Classroom Connections.** In all but two chapters, occasional "classroom connections" have been added to spur the reader to think about the practical classroom implications and applications of a concept, principle, or research finding. These can also serve as class discussion topics or as pair/group work activity.
6. **Glossary.** Throughout *TBP*, certain specialized concepts and terms have been boldfaced when presented for the first time. In virtually all of these

instances, the term is contextually defined as it is presented. To aid in later references to such terms, a glossary listing all these terms is now included.

7. **Updated references.** In the eight years since the 2007 edition was published, the field of language pedagogy has made some significant advances that are reflected in every chapter of the book. The result is the addition of over 400 new bibliographic references in this edition! Also noticeable are new and updated suggestions for further reading at the end of each chapter.

ACKNOWLEDGMENTS

This fourth edition of *Teaching by Principles* is a collective product of decades of instruction and research in language pedagogy by both of us. During that time, it has been our pleasure and challenge to teach and to learn from hundreds of students in our courses. We're grateful for those inquisitive minds—now scattered across the country and around the world—whose insights are well represented here.

We're especially grateful for the exceptionally helpful reviews we received on the third edition, resulting in ideas, concepts, insights, and references that are now woven into the present edition. Thanks to all of you: Suresh Canagarajah, Pennsylvania State University; Carol Chapelle, Iowa State University; Kathleen Graves, University of Michigan; Loretta Gray, Central Washington University; Mark James, Arizona State University; Joseph Lee, Ohio University; John Murphy, Georgia State University; Caroline Payant, University of Idaho; and Suzanne Scott, California State University, Humboldt.

We're also indebted to teachers, colleagues, authors, and co-researchers in many countries of the world whom we have had the privilege of knowing, reading, consulting, and befriending over the years. We learn so much from the exchanges of ideas and issues and stories from these contacts!

Published books are always a product of teamwork, and we appreciate our collaboration with editors, artists, marketers, and managers at Pearson Education in White Plains, New York, all of whom helped to give birth to this revision.

Last but by no means least, we are both grateful for the amazing support that our respective spouses (that is, one spouse for each of us!) have given over the years. A great big thank you to Ferenc and to Mary, who magnanimously put up with our need for long hours of uninterrupted focus for our research and writing activity. This support and nurture on the home front is a loving affirmation of our work!

H. Douglas Brown
Lincoln, California
January 2015

PART I

FOUNDATIONS FOR CLASSROOM PRACTICE

The five chapters of this first part of *Teaching by Principles* provide background information that will facilitate the comprehension of subsequent chapters by defining terms, concepts, and issues in the field. Here is a quick overview:

- **Chapter 1, Getting Started,** gives readers a picture of a typical language lesson. A lesson is described, then readers are probed in the form of questions to look at the choices that the teacher made in carrying out the planned events of the class hour.
- **Chapter 2, A Century of Language Teaching,** offers a historical survey of language teaching trends and methods in the twentieth century.
- **Chapter 3, Contextualizing Communicative Approaches,** is a sweeping description of current "post-method" approaches in the spirit of communicative language teaching (CLT) principles.
- **Chapter 4, Teaching by Principles,** is a detailed description of eight foundational principles for the rest of the book, and upon which teachers can systematically build classroom lessons and techniques.
- **Chapter 5, Agency in Language Learning,** elaborates on what we see as a central principle of language teaching. It illustrates the complexity of any single principle and the multiple possible implications and applications of such a principle to practical considerations in the language classroom.

CHAPTER 1

GETTING STARTED

Questions for Reflection

- How does a typical language lesson unfold and what are its component parts?
- How do teachers transition from one component to another in a language lesson?
- As an observer of a class, what should you look for?
- What are some of the *choices* that a teacher makes, minute by minute, in delivering a planned lesson?

Welcome to the language teaching profession! Helping your students to learn an additional language will guarantee you more than your fair share of challenges, growth, joy, and fulfillment.

Challenges await you at every turn in your professional path. The discipline of language pedagogy is full of perplexing questions about how people learn foreign languages successfully.

Opportunities for *growth* abound because, for as long as you continue to teach, you will never run out of new questions, new possibilities, new ways of looking at your students, and new ways of looking at yourself.

The *joy* of teaching lies in the vicarious pleasure of witnessing your students' attainment of broader and broader vistas of linguistic proficiency and in facilitating the creation of a community of learners in your classroom.

And, ultimately, few professions can offer the *fulfillment* of knowing that your seemingly insignificant work really can make a difference in a world in need of communication that transcends national borders and interests.

You may be a little apprehensive about what kind of teacher you are going to be. What will it be like to be in front of a classroom full of expectant ears and eyes, hanging on my every word and action, ready and waiting to pounce on me if I make a false move? How will I develop the composure and poise that I've seen modeled by "master" teachers? Will I be able to take the sea of theoretical information about second language acquisition that I have studied and transform it into practical classroom applications? How do I plan a lesson? What do I do if my lesson plan falls apart? Where do I begin?

Before you ask any more questions, which might at this stage overwhelm you, sit back for a moment and tell yourself that you can indeed become a teacher who will fully meet the challenges ahead and who will grow in professional expertise, thereby opening the doors of joy and fulfillment. This textbook is designed to help you take that developmental journey one step at a time.

The first step in that journey is to come with us into a language classroom and observe what happens. Take special note, as the lesson unfolds, of each choice that the teacher makes: choices about how to begin the lesson, which activity will come next, how long to continue an activity, whom to call on, whether to correct a student, and so on. Everything a teacher says and does in the classroom is the result of conscious or subconscious choices among many alternatives. Many of these choices are—or should be—the result of careful consideration of underlying principles of second language learning and teaching.

A CLASSROOM OBSERVATION

The classroom we are about to enter is in a private language school in Seoul, Korea. Inside the classroom, a course in English as an Additional Language* (EAL) is taking place. The 14 students in the course are young adults, most of whom are recent college graduates and now are working in businesses in Seoul. This is an intermediate level class; most of the students "graduated" into the class after completing the beginner's level. The goal of the course is for students to be able to use English in their occupations, for future international travel, and to a minor extent in their local context (television, movies, pop culture, Internet). A few might eventually proceed to more advanced levels of English for job-related or academic purposes.

The course focuses on integrative skills (combining the four skills of listening, speaking, reading, and writing). The main textbook being used is *Top Notch: English for Today's World*, Second Edition, Level 2 (Saslow & Ascher, 2011). At this stage, two weeks into the course, the students are still not completely confident in their speaking ability, but can engage in simple social conversations and make some practical requests. Their listening ability varies but the teacher is able to appropriately adapt the textbook material to their level. They are quite good readers, having had English classes in their university studies. Their writing is modestly accurate at the sentence level using basic grammar, but rhetorical factors involved in composing an essay remain a challenge.

The lesson we are about to observe centers on the topic of "movies and entertainment." The *functional focus* of the lesson is:

- Discussing preferences, likes, and dislikes

The *formal objectives* of the lesson are:

- Students will comprehend and produce "would rather" in meaningful sentences;
- Students will use a number of terms to categorize types of movies.

---

* *English as an Additional Language* (EAL) is used in this book as a *generic* acronym to refer to instruction of English to speakers of other languages in any country under any circumstance. It subsumes both *ESL* (English in English-speaking countries) and *EFL* (English in non-English-speaking countries.)

The teacher, Ms. Choi, a native of Seoul, has about five years of teaching experience, and holds a certificate in Teaching English to Speakers of Other Languages (TESOL) from a local university in Seoul. Her English is excellent, partly the result of spending two years in Canada as a high school student while her father was assigned work there for his electronics company. She is confident, poised, and shows a great deal of empathy for her students. They seem to appreciate her warmth.

The lesson we are about to observe is reasonably well planned and executed, and characteristic of current communicative language teaching methodology. However, it is not necessarily "perfect" (are there ever any perfect lessons?), so what you are about to see may have a few elements that you or others could take issue with. Please remember this as you read on and, if you wish, take note of aspects of the lesson that you might question. Then compare these notes with the comments following the lesson description.

We take our seats in the rear of the classroom and observe the following sequence of activities.

1. Ms. Choi (T) begins the 50-minute class hour on this Monday evening with some small talk commenting on the weather, her own weekend's activity hosting a family friend from Canada, and a movie that several students (Ss) saw (in English) over the weekend.
2. As she engages them in small talk, she marks attendance in her class roster.
3. She then asks the Ss to think of some movies they have seen recently, either in English or subtitled. She asks them not to name any movies that have been dubbed (into Korean). Ss volunteer movie titles, somewhat hesitantly at first, but come up with a list that the T puts on the board:

Captain Phillips
Gravity
The Wind Rises (Kaze Tachinu)
The Amazing Spiderman 2
The Other Woman
Godzilla
Twelve Years a Slave
Guardians of the Galaxy
Frozen
Despicable Me 2
The Best Exotic Marigold Hotel
Endless Love

4. At this point the T stops and writes "Categories" on the board and then writes the following movie types or categories on the board:

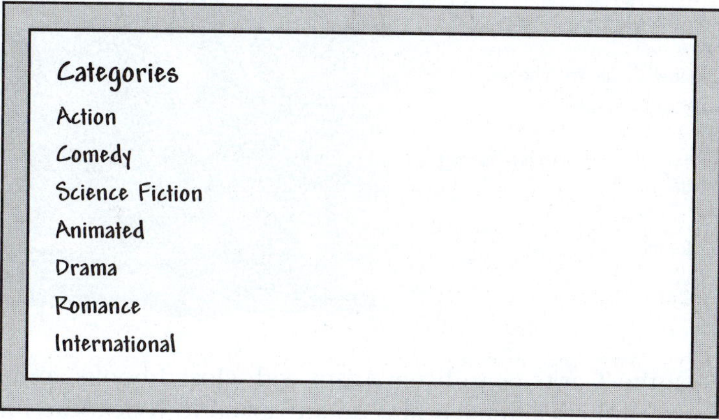

Categories
Action
Comedy
Science Fiction
Animated
Drama
Romance
International

5. She then asks Ss to volunteer what each word means. One by one, Ss slowly venture "definitions" for *comedy*, *science fiction*, and *romance* with synonyms such as "funny, comic, make me laugh" for the first, "future, fantasy" for the second, and "love" for the third. They seem to have difficulty defining others. Ss eventually fall into silence.
6. Seeing that definitions may be too difficult for Ss to create, the T takes a different tack. She provides her own definitions verbally, and as some Ss nod their heads in apparent understanding, she says, "Okay, now, does everyone understand the meaning of each of these categories?" A few more heads nod, and the T moves on.
7. The T then says, "Now, take out a sheet of paper and write down the names of all the movies that are up on the board, and then, with a partner, decide what kind of movie each one is, and write the category beside the name of the movie." She quickly pairs up Ss. Ss write the movies down, and proceed to engage in the pair work. The T walks around listening and checking on the pairs.
8. Next, the T asks Ss to report the movie categories. There is some disagreement among pairs, and most thought some movies belonged to two categories (*Captain Phillips*, for example, was thought to be both action and drama).
9. Now, says the T, "I want you to turn to page 19 in your books and listen to a dialogue on my CD player. Just listen this first time." The following dialogue is then presented on the CD:

A: What would you rather see—a classic or a new release?

B: It doesn't matter to me. You choose.

A: Well, what would you say to a documentary?

B: Hmm. To tell you the truth, I'm not that big on documentaries.

A: What about a comedy?

B: That works for me.

10. Next, the T asks Ss to listen again with closed books, and this time, with pauses in between each line, Ss are asked to repeat the line chorally. This procedure is repeated twice.
11. The T then asks Ss to turn back to page 18 of their textbook, in which examples are given for the grammatical construction *would rather* in both statements and questions. The T asks Ss to quickly skim the sample statements and questions, reproduced below:

State preferences with <u>would rather</u> / <u>would rather not</u> and the base form of a verb.

She'**d rather see** a less violent film.
We'**d rather not see** a horror film.

I / He / We / They	**'d rather**	**see** a musical. / **not go out** tonight.

Use <u>than</u> with <u>would rather</u> to contrast preferences.

I'**d rather rent** a movie **than** go to the theater.
They'**d rather go** to a Woody Allen film **than** a Martin Scorsese film.

Questions

Would you **rather see** *Casablanca* or *Wall-E*?
Which **would** they **rather see**—a comedy or a drama?
What **would** you **rather do**—see a play or a movie?

Short answers

Would you rather stay home? Yes, **we would.** NOT Yes, ~~we'd rather~~.
Would you like to see a movie? Actually, we'**d rather not.** We're too busy.

12. The T engages in some explanation of the structure, pointing out, for example, that the phrase "would rather" is similar to saying "prefer." She also provides a rough Korean translation of the construction, and gives a brief explanation in Korean before reverting back to English. Ss remain attentive but silent.
13. Next, the T says, "Now I want all of you to take your lists of the movies that we discussed (the ones on the board) and make a grid like this":

Movie	Category	Would you rather see it?
Captain Phillips		
Gravity		
The Wind Rises (Kaze Tachinu)		
The Amazing Spiderman 2		
The Other Woman		
Mandela: Long Walk to Freedom		
Twelve Years a Slave		
Guardians of the Galaxy		
Frozen		
Despicable Me 2		
The Best Exotic Marigold Hotel		
Endless Love		

14. In the next few minutes the T explains the next task:
Class, now I want you to write in the category or categories of each movie. [pause while students write] Now, everyone stand up and move around the room and talk to as many people as you can. Choose two movies each time to compare, and ask your classmate, "Would you rather see—name one movie—or—name another movie?" Then, write the name of the person you talk to in the third column beside the movie they would rather see. Okay? Make sure your partner answers you in a complete sentence! [pause] So, your partner must say, "Yes, I'd rather see—your partner names one movie" or something like, "Actually, I don't care." Does everyone understand? [Ss look a little confused, so the T translates the directions into Korean and then models in English as follows]:

Kyung-mi, you would say to Nam-hee, "Would you rather see *Gravity* or Endless Love?" Nam-hee, you might answer, "I'd rather see *Gravity*." Kyung-mi, then you would write the name of Nam-hee in the second column by *Gravity*. Then Nam-hee, you can ask Kyung-mi a similar question, and write the answer down. Then you move on to a new partner. Okay?

But, listen carefully! If you don't have a preference, just answer, "It doesn't matter to me." And in that case pick another pair of movies to compare until your partner gives you a definite preference. [pause] Okay, do you understand now?

15. After a little more clarification in Korean, Ss nod in agreement, and the T tells them to start their multiple interviews. This exercise lasts for about 15 minutes as Ss enthusiastically engage in the task.

16. When the T calls them back together, she tallies the number of students who responded affirmatively to each movie, and in an unscientific poll, announces what appears to be their favorite movie. "It's a tie between *Gravity* and *The Best Exotic Marigold Hotel*!"
17. With the time that's left (about 5 minutes) the T asks Ss to complete the grammar practice exercise on page 19 in which they write responses to 6 questions or statements, such as "I'd love to see a drama tonight" and "Would you like to see a comedy?" Their responses range from "I'd rather not" and "It doesn't matter to me" to "Actually, I'd rather see an action movie."
18. As time runs out, and students gather papers together to exit the classroom, the T tells Ss to complete their written exercise as homework, and to try to see an English movie sometime before the next class (in one week's time).

ANALYZING THE LESSON

You've just observed a relatively effective class hour in which the teacher competently planned a lesson around a textbook lesson, managed most segments of the hour without major problems, and carried out the activities with some warmth and enthusiasm. This may seem like a simple accomplishment, but let's think about the preparation, classroom management, and intuitive decisions that lie "behind the scenes."

What you have just witnessed is the product of a teacher's experience and intuition grounded in reasonably sound principles of learning and teaching. For every tiny moment of that classroom hour, certain choices were made, choices that may or may not be justified by research on second language learning and teaching. Think about those choices as you contemplate the numerous pedagogical questions that arise out of each numbered "statement" that follows.

1. Why the small-talk (vs. just getting straight to the lesson)? What teaching principle justifies such an opening? Why did the T comment on a movie that students saw on the weekend as part of the small talk? How long should such chatter continue?
2. Why did the T mark attendance while engaging in the small talk? It apparently didn't interfere with the small talk—how did the T manage to do two things at once? Why didn't she just call out names and have Ss say "here"? Is there another way to check attendance more interactively, involving student responses?
3. The textbook began with the dialogue (see #9) that this T chose to insert later. Why do you suppose she didn't start with that dialogue? Was her choice a better segue from the initial small talk that began the class? What purpose was served by asking Ss to come up with names of movies themselves at the outset? Why didn't the T just provide a list of her own?

And if she simply wants names of movies, why restrict the list to movies in English? What purpose did that serve? She chose to write the names of movies on the board—what purpose did that list serve?

4. Here she initiated the names of the categories. What would have happened if she had asked the Ss to create that list on their own? The title of this lesson, indicated in the textbook, is "Discuss preferences for movie genres." Why do you think that the T wrote "categories" on the board instead of the term "genres"?
5. Why did the T ask Ss for definitions? Wouldn't it be more efficient for the T to provide them? What purpose was served by urging them to create their own definitions? When Ss had some difficulty with defining, they tended to become more silent. Why was that? Was it a good idea for the T to ask Ss individually to come up with definitions of the words?
6. At this point it was apparent that T felt the task was over Ss' heads—what led her to that determination? Was it a good idea to switch to providing definitions herself at that point? She then asked if everyone understood, and after seeing some heads nodding affirmatively, she assumed they understood. Is such a question appropriate in this situation? Do you think the Ss really understood? What alternatives might she have employed to carry out that informal assessment?

Notice, before you move on, that each question implies that a choice was exercised by the teacher. Among dozens of possibilities for teaching this lesson on movies, categories, and the *would rather* construction, Ms. Choi has chosen, either consciously or subconsciously, a particular set of activities, a particular order, and a particular tone for each. A relatively straightforward lesson is supported by a plethora of principles of learning and teaching. To further complicate matters, some of those principles are disputable. For example, when should a teacher simply *give* information to Ss (#6) versus urging "discovery learning" by the Ss? The context does not always clearly dictate the resolution.

7. She now sets in motion some pair work for Ss. This exercise did not come from the textbook; it was her own innovation, only distantly resembling one in the textbook. Why do you suppose she chose not to follow the book here? What would be an ideal seating arrangement for doing such pair work? What should the T consider for pairing up students for a classroom task? Were her pair work directions clear? Some teacher guidelines suggest modeling such pair work—why didn't she do so? What do you suppose she was listening for as she walked around the classroom during this pair work? Do you think any Ss spoke Korean during the pair work? If so, what might the T have said or done?
8. What purpose did the reporting and processing serve? When there was disagreement on which category a movie belonged to, what do you think she did? What would you have done?

9. The T chose at this point to play the opening dialogue for the lesson. Did the background of the first 10–15 minutes of class provide enough context and interest for the Ss? What advantages and disadvantages do professionally recorded audio sound bites offer in a classroom in this context? The dialogue isn't terribly exciting; is that okay for the purposes of this lesson? What do you think of the T's pre-listening instruction for the Ss? Is there anything the T could have said or done differently before playing the CD?
10. Choral drilling is a commonly used technique in language teaching. Was it appropriate and useful here for this particular group of Ss? How do you think the T mentally justified its use? Why didn't the drill continue for several more repetitions?
11. This is one of the moments in the lesson that the T turns Ss' focus to form—particularly grammatical structure. Does the textbook segment (from page 18 of the book) sufficiently explain the structure?
12. Is the T's explanation justified at this point? Or should Ss just intuitively get a "feel" for the would rather structure? Could the T have done anything differently to help Ss understand the meaning of the target form? And what do you think about providing some explanation, as the T did, in Korean? Why did she choose to so then, and was the language switch justified? What would be the role of using Ss' L1 in this particular situation? She seemed to be "lecturing" to Ss here; should she have asked explicitly for some kind of response from the Ss? Or should they have had some more choral or quasi-communicative practice at this point?
13. The grid is an adaptation of a similar one in the textbook, but the T added the feature of using it in face-to-face interviews. Why did she choose to have another communicative activity here instead of following the textbook's suggestion of having Ss listen to some movie reviews on the CD and write in their recommendations?
14. The whole-class mingling activity seems simple enough on the face of it, but Ss had a little difficulty initially figuring out the process. Were the T's directions sufficient and clear, once she was able to follow up after the looks of confusion? Was her use of the L1 appropriate and useful here? What could she have done to make this stage of the activity clearer?
15. What is the objective of this activity? It's clear what Ss are being asked to do: frame questions, respond to them, and record the responses. They seemed enthusiastic about the activity—why? Why was an activity with fairly routine grammatical practice met with enthusiasm? Were those 15 minutes put to good purpose?
16. Why do you think the T tallied Ss' responses? Did the informal tally serve the objectives of the activity or simply offer some interest? What purpose was served by announcing the result of the tally: the most popular movie?

17. It's possible that this last activity was squeezed into too short a time frame. Was that okay? When a T runs out of time at the end of a lesson, what should he or she do? What purpose did a writing activity (as opposed to the other three skills) serve here?
18. Sometimes these last-second comments are lost in the shuffle of students getting ready to leave the classroom. Was some purpose nevertheless accomplished? When the T asked Ss to see an English movie as "homework," should she have given some guidance to them about what to do while seeing the movie?

A final question: As you look back over the lesson you've just observed, do you think the initial objectives were accomplished? Is there anything you think you might have done differently? Remember, you're dropping in on a class that is ongoing, so it may not be possible to completely judge the effectiveness of this lesson without the context of preceding and following lessons.

You've now skimmed through some of the many questions that one could ask about why certain choices were made about how to teach this lesson. Some of the answers are relatively standard, with few disagreements. Other answers would find even the best of teachers arguing the merits and demerits of the teacher's choices. But the answers to all these questions can be found, in one form or another, in the huge stockpile of second language acquisition research and collective experience of language teachers around the world. And many those answers will appear in the chapters ahead of you in this book.

★ ★ ★ ★ ★

Your goal, as you continue this journey, is to make the connections between research/theory/principles, on the one hand, and classrooms/teaching/practice on the other. By making those connections as you learn to teach, you will perhaps avoid some of the pitfalls of haphazard guesswork and instead engage in teaching that is informed by research and theory, or put another way, teaching by *principles*.

FOR THE TEACHER: ACTIVITIES (A) & DISCUSSION (D)

1. **(A)** A good activity for the beginning of a course on teaching methodology is to ask the members of small groups of three or four to talk about who was the "best" teacher they ever had. In the process, each should specify why that teacher was the best. As each group reports back to the whole class, make a chalkboard list of such reasons, which should reveal some attributes for all to emulate. (This activity also serves the purpose of (a) getting students to talk early on, and (b) giving students in the class a chance to get to know each other. To that end, group reports could include brief introductions of group members.)

2. **(A)** On page 8, it was noted that teachers are constantly making *choices* in the course of a class hour. Assign to pairs two or three of the numbered items through #18. Ask them talk about (a) what the teacher chose to do, (b) why she made that choice, and (c) what alternative choices she could have made. Make sure they refer to the second matched set of items in which certain questions were posed, and try to answer the questions. Ask the pairs to report their conclusions to the whole class, and encourage others in the class to ask questions.
3. **(D)** If it's feasible to do so, arrange for your students to observe an L2 class in a convenient location. Alternatively, show a video of a class. At this stage, try asking them to observe the class without a checklist or agenda, and ask them to just get a feel for the *dynamics* of the classroom. If, as they observe, some questions come up about why the teacher made certain choices, ask them to jot down those questions. After all have had a chance to make this observation, ask them to describe what they saw and what questions occurred to them as they observed.
4. **(D)** As an extra-class assignment, ask students to find some currently popular textbooks in EAL (or other L2) and spend some time leafing through them, without a specific agenda—just noting things that they like and don't like about each. Ask them to share their impressions with the rest of the class.
5. **(A)** An alternative to #4 above is to secure enough copies of various L2 textbooks from whatever sources your institution may have. Distribute a different textbook to each of however many pairs are feasible in your class size. Ask the pairs to brainstorm features that they like and dislike, and to report these to the rest of the class. Some possible features for them to observe (you could list these on the board or distribute them in a small handout): layout, illustrations, color, attractiveness, exercises, adequate small group work, stimulation of authentic communication, distribution of focus on form (grammar, vocabulary, etc.) versus focus on meaning/communication. You might add your own features. Ask a few of the pairs to report to the rest of the class on the *ease* or *difficulty* of evaluating a textbook.

FOR YOUR FURTHER READING

Brown, H. D. (2014). *Principles of language learning and teaching* (6th ed.). White Plains, NY: Pearson Education.

This course in second language acquisition (SLA) is a comprehensive survey of issues and principles of SLA as they apply to language teaching. It is designed as a recommended textbook to accompany or precede *Teaching by Principles*.

Celce-Murcia, M., Brinton, D., & Snow, A. M. (Eds.). (2014). *Teaching English as a second or foreign language* (4th ed.). Boston, MA: National Geographic Learning.

We recommend referring to this anthology of 40 chapters on L2 teaching methodology, including current summaries of research on key topics in SLA. It could serve as a useful companion volume to this one.

Saslow, J., & Ascher, A. (2011). *Top notch: English for today's world.* White Plains, NY: Pearson Education.

This text, referred to in the current chapter, is one of many possible samples of courses that would be useful to look at. If you are not familiar with how such courses are organized and presented, skimming through a course like this will give you a backdrop for the chapters to follow here in *Teaching by Principles.*

CHAPTER **2**

A CENTURY OF LANGUAGE TEACHING

Questions for Reflection

- What is the historical timeline of language teaching methodology?
- What is the difference between an *approach* and a *method*?
- How are teaching methods *derived* from a theory of SLA?
- How do methods, in turn, *contribute* to our knowledge of SLA?
- What are the distinguishing characteristics of various methods? Which of those attributes continue to be valid approaches and techniques today?
- How does a *communicative* approach differ from the succession of methods of the twentieth century?

An informative step toward understanding what language teaching is all about is to turn back the clock a little over a hundred years. Looking at the historical cycles and trends that have brought us to the present day will help you analyze the class session you just observed in Chapter 1. For the better part of this chapter we focus on methods as the identifying characteristics of many decades of language teaching efforts. How do methods of teaching reflect various trends of disciplinary thought? How does current research on language learning and teaching help us to distinguish, in our history, between passing fads and "the good stuff"? These are some of the questions we'll address here.

In Chapter 3, our historical overview culminates in a close look at the current state of the art in language teaching. Above all, you will come to see how language pedagogy is now more aptly characterized by a number of widely researched "approaches" rather than by competing, context-restricted methods. Those approaches will be described in detail, along with some of the current professional jargon associated with it.

As you read on, you will encounter references to concepts, constructs, issues, and models that are normally covered in a course in second language acquisition (SLA). Whether or not you have already taken or are currently taking such a course, you may wish to consult our companion volume, *Principles of Language Learning and Teaching*, Sixth Edition (Brown, 2014), or a book like Mitchell, Myles, and Marsden's (2013) *Second Language Learning Theories*, which summarizes current topics and issues in SLA. Throughout this book we will refer occasionally to certain chapters of the *Principles* book (*PLLT*) for background review or reading.

WHAT DO WE MEAN BY METHOD?

For the century spanning the mid-1880s to the mid-1980s, the language-teaching profession may be aptly characterized by a series of methods (or perhaps pedagogical trends) that rose and declined in popularity. Some practitioners in this time period hoped to define the *ultimate* method, one that would be generalizable across widely varying audiences, contexts, and languages (Richards & Rodgers, 2001). Historical accounts of the profession tend to describe a succession of methods, each of which was more or less discarded as a new method took its place (Larsen-Freeman & Anderson, 2011). Before turning to that history of language teaching, let's explain what we mean by **method**.

Over five decades ago Edward Anthony (1963) described method as the second of three hierarchical elements: An **approach**, according to Anthony, was a set of assumptions dealing with the nature of language, learning, and teaching. **Method** was described as an overall plan for systematic presentation of a language course based on a selected approach. **Techniques** were the specific activities manifested in a curriculum that were consistent with a method and therefore were in harmony with an approach as well.

In Anthony's terms, a teacher may, for example, at the approach level, affirm the ultimate importance of learning in a relaxed state of mental awareness just above the threshold of consciousness. The method that follows might resemble Suggestopedia (a description follows in this chapter). Techniques could include playing baroque music while reading a passage in the foreign language, getting students to sit in the yoga position while listening to a list of words, or having learners adopt a new name in the classroom and role-play that new person.

Today, Anthony's (1963) terms are still in relatively common use among language teachers, but with a multitude of varying definitions. Just two decades after Anthony's publication, for example, Richards and Rodgers (1982) proposed to call Anthony's method a *design*, and his technique a *procedure*. They still maintained the importance of the "interrelation of theory and practice"(p. 154), in which assumptions, beliefs, and theories about the nature of language and language learning lay at the foundation of classroom practice, but the terminology, in some ways, only muddied the waters.

What followed were a few decades of arguments about the irrelevance of methods in the "narrow, pejorative sense" (Bell, 2007, p. 141) in which they were touted in the 1960s and 1970s. Eventually, with the proclamation of a **postmethod** era, language teachers were encouraged to focus on a "pedagogy of particularity" (Kumaravadivelu, 2001, p. 538), that is, a sensitivity to learners, goals, context, and social milieu.

Then even more recently, Larsen-Freeman and Anderson (2011), were quite comfortable with using the term method to mean "a coherent set of principles linked to certain techniques and procedures" (p. xvi). In so doing, they echoed Bell's (2007) endorsement of method as "techniques which realize a set of principles or goals" and that offer "practical solutions to problems in a particular teaching context" (p. 141).

Classroom Connections

In your experience taking an L2 course, how would you describe your teacher's *method*? Was it clearly identifiable? Was it unified? Cohesive? Did you experience activities or techniques that you felt were grounded in a plausible *approach*, that is, justifiable from what we know about effective language teaching?

What did we learn from this checkered history and its accompanying lexicographic confusion? That *principled* language teaching involves an essential link between what we know about SLA in its variety of contexts and the practical everyday techniques that characterize our language classrooms. We'll return to a full development of this all-important connection in the next chapter.

Meanwhile, to avoid any further confusion in this book, we'll use some common terms in the following way:

Methodology. Pedagogical practices in general (including theoretical underpinnings and related research). Whatever considerations are involved in "how to teach" are methodological.

Approach. Theoretical positions and beliefs about teaching, language, language learning, learners, institutional and societal factors, purposes of a course, and the applicability of all to a specific educational context.

Method. A set of classroom specifications for accomplishing linguistic objectives. Methods tend to identify teacher and student roles, linguistic and subject-matter objectives, sequencing, and materials.

Curriculum. Specifications for carrying out a particular language program. Features include a primary concern with linguistic and subject-matter objectives, sequencing, and materials to meet the needs of a designated group of learners in a defined context. (The term **syllabus** is used more commonly in the United Kingdom to refer to what is usually called a curriculum in the United States.)

Technique (also commonly referred to by other terms). Any of a wide variety of exercises, activities, procedures, or tasks used in the language classroom for realizing lesson objectives.

CHANGING WINDS AND SHIFTING SANDS

We now return to our historical sketch. A glance through the past century or so of language teaching will give an interesting picture of how varied the interpretations have been of the best way to teach additional languages. As disciplinary schools of thought—psychology, linguistics, and education, for example—have come and gone, so have language-teaching methods waxed and waned in popularity. With the many theoretical positions that have been proposed over the last hundred years, it should come as no surprise to discover a wide variety of these methods, some in total philosophical opposition to others.

Albert Marckwardt (1972, p. 5) saw these "changing winds and shifting sands" as a cyclical pattern in which a new method emerged about every quarter of a century. Each new method broke from the old but took with it some of the positive aspects of the previous practices. A good example of this cyclical nature of methods is found in the "revolutionary" Audiolingual Method (ALM) (a description follows) of the mid-twentieth century. The ALM borrowed tenets from its predecessor, the Direct Method, by almost half a century while breaking away entirely from the Grammar Translation Method. Within a short time, however, ALM critics were advocating more attention to thinking, to cognition, and to rule learning, which to some smacked of a return to Grammar Translation!

What follows is a sketch of these changing winds and shifting sands.

THE "EARLY" YEARS

Classical and Grammar Translation Methods

For centuries, there were few if any theoretical foundations of language learning upon which to base teaching methodology. In the Western world, foreign language learning in schools was synonymous with the learning of Latin or Greek. Latin, thought to promote intellectuality through "mental gymnastics," was until relatively recently held to be indispensable to an adequate education. Similarly, in Asian countries, foreign language courses consisted of a focus on reading various languages, attained through translation and attention to rules and definitions of words (Chan, Chin, & Suthiwan, 2011). This genre of pedagogy came to be called the **Classical Method**: teacher centered, with memorization of grammatical rules and vocabulary, translations of texts, and written exercises.

As other languages began to be taught in educational institutions in the eighteenth and nineteenth centuries, the Classical Method was adopted as the chief means for teaching foreign languages. Little thought was given at the time to teaching someone how to speak the language; after all, languages were not being taught primarily to learn oral/aural communication, but to learn for the sake of being "scholarly" or for gaining reading proficiency. Because there was little if any theoretical research on SLA in general or on the acquisition of reading proficiency, foreign languages were taught as any other skill was taught.

By the late nineteenth century, the Classical Method came to be known as the **Grammar Translation Method**. There was little to distinguish Grammar Translation from centuries-long foreign language teaching practices beyond a focus on grammatical rules as the basis for translating from the second to the native language. Remarkably, the Grammar Translation Method withstood attempts at the turn of the twentieth century to "reform" language-teaching methodology (see below), and to this day it is practiced in too many educational contexts. Prator and Celce-Murcia (1979, p. 3) listed major characteristics of Grammar Translation:

Characteristics of the Grammar Translation Method

- Classes are taught in the students' L1.
- Attention is given to lists of isolated vocabulary and grammar rules.
- Reading is given almost exclusive focus, with related grammatical analysis.
- Translation exercises (usually from the L2 to the L1) are performed.
- Little or no attention is given to oral production.

Classroom Connections

Have you taken a language course that followed, even partially, Grammar Translation methodology? If so, how successful were you in learning the language? Why or why not? If not, can you imagine any "redeeming" value in Grammar Translation methodology in today's language courses?

It's ironic that this method has until very recently been so stalwart among many competing models. It is "remembered with distaste by thousands of school learners, for whom foreign language learning meant a tedious experience of memorizing endless lists of unusable grammar rules and vocabulary and attempting to produce perfect translations of stilted or literary prose" (Richards & Rodgers, 2001, p. 6). On the other hand, one can understand why Grammar Translation remains attractive. It requires few specialized skills on the part of teachers. Tests of grammar rules and of translations are easy to construct, can be objectively scored, and don't require fluent knowledge of the L2 by the test designer or teacher.

However, as Richards and Rodgers (2001) pointed out, "it has no advocates. It is a method for which there is no theory. There is no literature that offers a rationale or justification for it or that attempts to relate it to issues in linguistics, psychology, or educational theory" (p. 7). As you continue to examine language-teaching methodology in this book, you will understand more fully the "theorylessness" of the Grammar Translation Method.

Gouin's Series Method

The history of "modern" foreign language teaching may be said to have begun in the late 1800s with François Gouin, a French teacher of Latin with remarkable insights. History doesn't normally credit Gouin as a founder of language-teaching methodology because, at the time, his influence was overshadowed by that of Maximilian Berlitz, the popular German founder of the Direct Method. Nevertheless, some attention to Gouin's unusually perceptive observations about language teaching helps us to set the stage for the development of language-teaching methods for the century following the publication of his book, *The Art of Learning and Studying Foreign Languages*, in 1880.

Gouin had to go through a very painful set of experiences in order to derive his insights. Having decided in mid-life to learn German, he took up residency in Hamburg for one year. But rather than attempting to converse with the natives, he decided upon arrival in Hamburg to *memorize* a German grammar book and a table of the 248 irregular German verbs—all in the isolation of his room! He did this in a matter of only ten days, and hurried to "the academy" (the university) to test his new knowledge. "But alas!" he wrote," I could not understand a single word, not a single word!" (Gouin, 1880, p. 11). Undaunted, he rememorized his grammar and verbs, only to fail again.

In the course of the year in Germany, Gouin memorized books, translated Goethe and Schiller, and even memorized 30,000 words in a German dictionary, all in the isolation of his room, only to be crushed by his failure to understand German afterward. Only once did he try to "make conversation" as a method, but this caused people to laugh at him, and he was too embarrassed to continue that method. At the end of the year Gouin, having reduced the Classical Method to absurdity, was forced to return home, a failure.

But there was a happy ending. After returning home, Gouin discovered that his three-year-old nephew had, during that year, gone through the wonderful stage of child language acquisition in which he went from saying virtually nothing at all to becoming a veritable chatterbox of French. How was it that this little child succeeded so easily, in a first language, in a task that Gouin, in a second language, had found impossible? The child must hold the secret to learning a language! So Gouin spent a great deal of time observing his nephew and other children and came to the conclusion that language is a means of *thinking* and of representing reality!

 **Classroom Connections**

From what you know about child (L1) language acquisition, what are some of the key characteristics of child language acquisition? What attributes of that process do you think are directly applicable to *adult* L2 classes? Which aspects are not plausibly applicable?

So Gouin set about devising a teaching method that would follow from these insights. And thus the **Series Method** was created, a method that taught learners *directly* (without translation) and conceptually (without grammatical rules and explanations) a "series" of connected sentences that are easy to perceive. The first lesson of a foreign language taught a series of linked sentences such as "I walk to the door. I stop at the door. I stretch out my arm. I take hold of the handle." And other sentences followed, all with an unconventionally large number of grammatical properties, vocabulary items, word orders, and complexity. This is no simple lesson! Yet Gouin was successful with such lessons because the language was easily understood, stored, recalled, and related to reality.

Unfortunately, Gouin was a man ahead of his time, and his brilliant insights were largely lost in the shuffle of Berlitz's popular Direct Method. But as we look back now over more than a century of language-teaching history, we can appreciate the contributions of this most unusual language teacher.

The Direct Method

Either the world wasn't ready for the Series Method or Gouin wasn't a good businessman. So it took none other than contemporary Maximilian Berlitz (1887) to capitalize (literally) on naturalistic approaches to language learning in the form of the now well-known **Direct Method.** The basic premise of the Direct Method was that foreign language learning should be more like first language learning—lots of oral interaction, spontaneous use of the language, no translation between first and second languages, and little or no analysis of grammatical rules. Richards and Rodgers (2001, p. 12) summarized the principles of the Direct Method.

Characteristics of the Direct Method

- Instruction was conducted exclusively (directly) in the L2.
- Oral communication and listening skills were taught in small classes.
- Methodology consisted mainly of modeling and practice.
- Everyday, easily identified vocabulary was used.
- Grammar was taught inductively.

The Direct Method enjoyed considerable popularity in the United States and Europe at the turn of the nineteenth and twentieth centuries. As its popularity increased, it soon became known as the Berlitz Method, and to this day "Berlitz" is a household word with language schools thriving in every country of the world. Today, from Bucharest to Beijing to Buenos Aires, little storefront Berlitz language schools—teaching every conceivable language—can be found with ease.

Despite its success in private enterprise, the Direct Method did not take well in public education, where the constraints of budget, classroom size, time, and teacher background made such a method difficult to use. Moreover, its success may have been more a factor of the skill and personality of the teacher than of the methodology itself. So, for public education worldwide, the Direct Method was not as practical as Grammar Translation or methods that only emphasized reading skills.

The Audiolingual Method

Up through the middle of the twentieth century, Grammar Translation and reading methods prevailed in educational institutions worldwide, with few if any attempts to teach oral communication (Bowen, Madsen, & Hilferty, 1985). Then, in an ironic twist, one of the most visible of all language teaching "revolutions" in the modern era, the **Audiolingual Method** (ALM), burst into the headlines. Ironic, because much of the ALM borrowed tenets of the then half-century-old Direct Method!

An offshoot of what started as a United States military-sponsored program during World War II to teach oral proficiency in other languages, the ALM spread into broader educational contexts as a means to teach long neglected aural/oral skills. Characteristic of these courses was a great deal of oral activity—pronunciation drills, pattern practice, and exercises in rudimentary conversations—with virtually none of the grammar and translation found in traditional classes. By the 1950s the ALM—in a variety of offshoots that highlighted oral-aural activity—was widely used globally (Rivers, 1964) as air transportation "shrank" the world and ushered in an era of convenient travel, a greater awareness of other languages and cultures, and an immediate communicative use for foreign languages.

The ALM was firmly grounded in the linguistic and psychological theory of the era. Structural linguists of the 1940s and 1950s were engaged in what they claimed was a "scientific descriptive analysis" of various languages. Teachers and course developers saw a direct application of such analysis to the pattern practice drills that were the hallmark of the University of Michigan's English Language Institute (Fries, 1945). At the same time, behavioral psychologists advocated conditioning and habit-formation models of learning that were perfectly married with the "mim-mem" (mimicry-memorization) drills of audiolingual methodology.

The characteristics of the ALM may be summed up in the following characteristics (adapted from Prator & Celce-Murcia, 1979).

Characteristics of the Audiolingual Method

- Most language material was presented directly, with as little use of the students' L1 as possible.
- New material was usually presented in (spoken) dialogue form.
- Mimicry, memorization, and overlearning of language patterns were emphasized, with an effort to get students to produce error-free utterances.
- Grammatical structures were sequenced by means of contrastive analysis.
- Grammar and vocabulary were taught by inductive analogy and contextualized in dialogs.
- Great importance was attached to pronunciation.
- Courses capitalized on the use of tapes, language labs, and visual aids.

Classroom Connections

Have you experienced ALM-type drills in language courses that you have taken? Were they effective? Did you ever feel they were overused? Judging from your experiences learning or teaching an L2, how much drilling do you think is appropriate to use in a classroom? What aspects of SLA does drilling help to reinforce?

For a number of reasons, the ALM enjoyed many years of popularity, and even to this day, adaptations of the ALM are found in contemporary methodologies. For example, many language courses advocate occasional, quick repetition drills to acquaint students with the phonology of the L2. The ALM was firmly rooted in respectable theoretical perspectives of the time. And "success" could be overtly experienced by students as they practiced dialogs in off-hours.

But the popularity was not to last forever. In an eloquent book-length criticism, Rivers (1964) exposed numerous misconceptions of the ALM and cited its ultimate failure to teach long-term communicative proficiency. We discovered that language was not really acquired through a process of habit formation and overlearning, that errors were not necessarily to be avoided at all costs, and that structural linguistics did not tell us everything about language that we needed to know. But in the shifting sands of methodological change, language teachers ultimately reaped some positive benefits from the ALM.

THE "DESIGNER" METHODS ERA

One benefit was a collective challenge to the profession to inject new life into language classrooms full of weary students reciting endless drills, sometimes with no awareness whatsoever of the meaning of their "prefabricated patterns." The profession needed some spice and verve, and innovative minds from the mid-1960s to the 1970s were up to the challenge.

This time period was historically significant on two counts. First, perhaps more than at other moment in modern language-teaching history, research on second language learning and teaching grew from an offshoot of linguistics into a discipline in its own right. As more and more scholars specialized in SLA studies, our knowledge of how people learn languages inside and outside the classroom mushroomed. Second, in a spirited atmosphere of pioneering research, a number of innovative methods were conceived. These "designer" methods, to borrow a term from Nunan (1989a, p. 97), soon were marketed by entrepreneurs as the latest (and greatest?) applications of the multidisciplinary research findings of the day.

Today, as we look back at these methods, we can applaud their creators for innovative flair, for an attempt to rouse the language-teaching world out of its audiolingual slumber, and for stimulation of even more research as we sought to discover why they were, in the end, *not* the godsend that their inventors and marketers hoped they would be. The scrutiny that the designer methods underwent has enabled us today to refine current communicative approaches to language teaching.

Community Language Learning

In the 1950s, psychologist Carl Rogers (1951) proposed a "person-centered" view of education that placed the focus on *learners*, in opposition to the teacher-centered viewpoints that had dominated educational philosophy. Inspired by Rogers, Charles Curran (1972, 1976) regarded students as a *community* of learners and raised our awareness of the social dynamics of classrooms. As students and teacher joined together in a *team* effort, participants lowered their defenses and potential anxiety by means of a supportive classroom community. The key was for teachers not to be perceived as a threat, but rather, as *counselors*, to assist learners to reach their goals in a non-defensive atmosphere. Curran's Counseling–Learning model of education was extended to language learning contexts in the form of **Community Language Learning (CLL).**

While particular adaptations of CLL were numerous (LaForge, 1971), the basic methodology was explicit. The group of clients (for instance, beginning learners of English), having first established in their native language (say, Japanese) an interpersonal relationship and trust, are seated in a circle with the counselor (teacher) on the outside of the circle. When one of the clients wishes to say something to the group or to an individual, he or she says it in the native language

(Japanese) and the counselor translates the utterance back to the learner in the second language (English). The learner then repeats the English sentence as accurately as possible. Another client responds, in Japanese; the utterance is translated by the counselor into English; the client repeats it, and the conversation continues. If possible, the conversation is recorded for later listening, and at the end of each session, the learners inductively attempt together to glean information about the new language. If desirable, the counselor might take a more directive role and provide some explanation of certain linguistic rules or items.

Affectively, CLL was an attempt to put the philosophy of Carl Rogers into action and to overcome some of the threatening affective factors in a language classroom: the all-knowing teacher, making blunders in the L2 in front of classmates, competing against peers. The counselor allowed the learner to determine the topic and tenor of conversation and to analyze the foreign language inductively. And in some cases learners ended up spontaneously helping each other.

There were some practical and theoretical problems with CLL. The counselor-teacher could become too nondirective, leaving the student to a time-consuming and sometimes fruitless struggle. While some intense inductive processing is a beneficial component of SLA, the initial grueling days and weeks of floundering in CLL might have been alleviated by a more directive approach. And the success of CLL depended largely on the translation expertise of the counselor. A mistranslation could lead to unnecessary confusion.

Today, virtually no one uses CLL in a language curriculum. It was soon discovered that CLL was far too restrictive for institutional language programs. However, the principles of forming a classroom community, learning by discovery, creating student-centered classrooms, and developing student autonomy all remain viable in their application to language classrooms. As is the case with virtually any method, the theoretical underpinnings of CLL may be creatively adapted to your own situation.

 **CLASSROOM CONNECTIONS**

In language classes that you have taken, to what extent did you feel threatened by the teacher or by your classmates? How do you think a teacher could lessen or soften those threats? On the other hand, would you like to learn a language completely inductively in a CLL classroom? In a context that you're familiar with, what would you think might be problematic in using CLL?

Suggestopedia

Other new methods of the era were not quite as strictly affective as CLL. **Suggestopedia**, for example, was a method that was derived from Bulgarian psychologist Georgi Lozanov's (1979) contention that the human brain could process great quantities of material if given the right conditions for learning, among which are a state of relaxation and giving over of control to the teacher.

Drawing on insights from Soviet psychological research on extrasensory perception and from yoga, Lozanov's Suggestopedia (Larsen-Freeman & Anderson, 2011, p. 71 prefer to call it *Desuggestopedia*) capitalized on relaxed states of mind for maximum retention of material. Music, especially Baroque music with its 60 beats per minute and its specific rhythm, created the kind of "relaxed concentration" that led to efficient retention due to an increase in alpha brain waves and a decrease in blood pressure and pulse rate.

In applications of Suggestopedia to L2 learning, Lozanov and his followers experimented with the presentation of vocabulary, readings, dialogs, roleplays, drama, and a variety of other typical classroom activities. These "concert sessions" were carried out in soft, comfortable seats, accompanied by soft music that induced relaxed states of consciousness.

Suggestopedia was criticized on a number of fronts. Suggestopedia became a business enterprise of its own, and it made promises in the advertising world that were not completely supported by research. Scovel (1979) questioned the validity of Lozanov's data, which reported astounding results. The practicality of using Suggestopedia was an issue in settings where music and comfortable chairs were not available. More serious was the reliance on memorization for language learning (Scovel, 1979) during the concert sessions.

On the other hand, other researchers, including Schiffler (1992), offered a more moderate position, advocating the advantage of states of relaxation for learning. In the final analysis, through this method we may have been prodded to believe in the power of the human brain, to experiment with induced states of relaxation in the classroom, and more specifically to try using music as a way to get students to sit back and relax.

Classroom Connections

How might you see aspects of Suggestopedia applied to an L2 course that you have taken, or taught, or might some day teach? Besides music, what are some other ways to induce states of relaxation in a classroom? To what extent is it worth trying such techniques in a classroom?

The Silent Way

Like Suggestopedia, the **Silent Way** rested on more cognitive than affective arguments for its theoretical sustenance. While founder Caleb Gattegno was said to be interested in a "humanistic" approach (Chamot & McKeon, 1984, p. 2) to education, much of the Silent Way was characterized by a problem-solving approach to learning. Richards and Rodgers (2001, p. 81) summarized the theory of learning behind the Silent Way as the facilitation of learning though:

- encouraging inductive learning by discovery
- engaging in problem solving, using new language material
- relating (mediating) physical objects to the new language

Discovery learning, a popular educational trend of the 1960s (Bruner, 1961), advocated less learning "by being told" and more learning by discovering for oneself various facts and principles. Ausubel's (1968) subsumption theory (*PLLT*, Chapter 4) could also be said to underlie Silent Way methodology. Gattegno (1972) believed that learners should develop independence, autonomy, and responsibility. At the same time, learners in a Silent Way classroom had to cooperate with each other in the process of solving language problems. And for physical props, the Silent Way typically utilized a set of small colored rods of varying lengths and a series of colorful wall charts.

Oddly, the teacher was silent much of the time, thus the name of the method. Teachers were to resist their instinct to spell everything out in black and white and to come to the aid of students at the slightest downfall. They had to "get out of the way" while students worked out solutions. The teacher provided single-word stimuli or short phrases and sentences, once or maybe twice, and then the students refined their understanding of meanings and pronunciation among themselves, with minimal corrective feedback from the teacher.

In one sense, the Silent Way was too harsh a method and the teacher too distant to encourage a communicative atmosphere. Silent Way practitioners often found that students needed more guidance and overt correction than the method advocated. And because the rods and charts wore thin after a few lessons, teachers ended up introducing other materials, at which point the Silent Way classroom looked like any other language classroom.

And yet, some underlying principles of the Silent Way were valid. All too often we're tempted as teachers to provide everything for our students, neatly served up on a silver platter. We could benefit from injecting healthy doses of discovery learning into our classroom activities and from providing less teacher talk than we usually do to let the students work things out on their own. In recent years, for example, we have come to appreciate the value of students' *self-correction* stimulated by a teacher's feedback (Ellis & Collins, 2009).

Total Physical Response and the Natural Approach

You will recall from earlier in this chapter that well over a century ago, Gouin designed his Series Method on the premise that language associated with a series of simple actions will be easily retained by learners. Much later, psychologists developed the "trace theory" of learning in which it was claimed that memory is increased if it is stimulated, or "traced," through association with motor activity. It was this very idea that James Asher (1977) capitalized on in developing the **Total Physical Response** (TPR).

TPR drew in part on principles of child language acquisition, namely, that children learning their L1 appear to do a lot of listening before they speak, and that their listening is accompanied by physical responses (reaching, grabbing, moving, looking, and so forth). Asher was also convinced that language classes were often the locus of too much anxiety, so he wished to devise a method that was as stress-free as possible, where learners would not feel overly self-conscious and defensive. The TPR classroom, then, was one in which students did a great deal of listening and acting.

Typically, TPR heavily utilized imperatives, even into more advanced proficiency levels: *Open the window*, *Close the door*, *Stand up*, *Pick up the book*, *Give it to John*, and so on. More complex syntax could be injected: *Draw a rectangle on the chalkboard*, *Walk quickly to the door and hit it*; or more humorously: *Walk slowly to the window and jump*, (Asher, 1977, p. 55). Interrogatives also were used effectively: *Where is the book? Who is John?* Eventually students would feel comfortable enough to venture verbal responses to questions, then to ask questions themselves, and to continue the process.

The **Natural Approach**, a method undergirded by similar principles, was inspired by Asher's (1977) advocacy of a *comprehension-based* approach, but developed somewhat later in the early 1980s. Krashen and Terrell (1983) felt that learners would benefit from delaying production until speech "emerges," that learners should be as relaxed as possible in the classroom, and that a great deal of communication and "acquisition" should take place, as opposed to analysis. Their Natural Approach advocated the use of TPR activities at the beginning level of language learning when "comprehensible input" is essential for triggering the acquisition of language.

The Natural Approach was aimed at developing everyday language communication skills—conversations, shopping, listening to the radio, and the like. The initial task of the teacher was to provide comprehensible input, that is, spoken language that is understandable to the learner or just a little beyond the learner's level. Learners were not prodded to speak until they feel ready to do so. The teacher was the source of the learners' input and the creator of an interesting and stimulating variety of classroom activities—commands, games, skits, and small-group work.

Classroom Connections

Have you ever taken a language course that used TPR or Natural Approach techniques? If so, how effective were they? How would you feel about being in a class in which you were never *asked* by your teacher to speak, and you spoke only when you were ready to do so?

Neither method dominated language classrooms around the world (Richards & Rodgers, 2001). Both seemed to be especially effective in the beginning levels of language proficiency, but lost their distinctiveness as learners advanced in their competence. Further, after students overcame the fear of speaking out, classroom conversations and other activities proceeded as in almost any other communicative language classroom. The most controversial aspects of the Natural Approach were its advocacy of a "silent period" (delay of oral production) and its heavy emphasis on comprehensible input (Gibbons, 1985).

On the other hand, like every other method we have encountered, TPR and the Natural Approach offered new insights to the language teaching profession. Basing methods on healthy doses of listening to a new L2 eventually prodded SLA researchers to examine the crucial role of *input* in learning an L2. The de-emphasis on nonstop oral production, a reaction to the ALM, helped us to design language courses with carefully structured *listening comprehension* components. In later proposals for more communicative methods, we saw the importance of meaningful language that students could relate to the *real world*. And, of course, the *anxiety* experienced by learners in many language courses was a factor that both methods attempted to reduce.

Innovative methods such as the above "designer" methods expose us to principles and practices that you can sift through, weigh, and adapt to multiple contexts. Your responsibility as a teacher is to choose the best of what others have experimented with and then adapt your insights to your own situation. Those insights and intuitions can become a part of your own principled approach to language teaching.

THE DAWNING OF A NEW ERA

As the innovative methods of the 1970s were being touted by some and criticized by many, some significant foundations for future growth were being laid in the form of a number of emerging approaches that were built solidly on research findings in what was still the budding new field of SLA. From grassroots SLA conclaves and late night discussions at conferences, the field mushroomed in the 1970s and 1980s into a professional discipline that soon boasted worldwide conferences, presentations in every corner of the earth, and volumes of articles, books, dictionaries, and encyclopedias. Out of this vibrant incipient field of study came some distinctive methodological options that were later to catapult language teachers and researchers into the twenty-first century with principle-based, enduring innovations.

Notional-Functional Syllabuses

One of the most fruitful movements of the late twentieth century was embodied in what came to be known as the **Notional-Functional Syllabus**, or more commonly the **Functional Syllabus**. Beginning with the work of the Council of Europe (Van Ek & Alexander, 1975) and later followed by numerous interpretations of "notional" syllabuses (Wilkins, 1976), Notional-Functional Syllabuses (NFS) began to be used in the United Kingdom in the 1970s.

The distinguishing characteristics of the NFS were its attention to functions (see *PLLT*, Chapter 9) as the organizing elements of English language curriculum, and its contrast with a structural syllabus in which sequenced grammatical structures served as the organizers. Reacting to methods that attended too strongly to grammatical form, the NFS focused on the pragmatic purposes to which we put language. As such, it was not a method at all. It was closer to what we have called approach, but it was more specifically focused on curricular structure than any of its predecessors.

Notions, according to Van Ek and Alexander (1975), are both general and specific. General notions are abstract concepts such as existence, space, time, quantity, and quality. They are domains in which we use language to express thought and feeling. Within the general notion of space and time, for example, are the concepts of location, motion, dimension, speed, length of time, and frequency. *Specific notions* correspond more closely to what we have become accustomed to calling "situations." Personal identification, for example, is a specific notion under which name, address, phone number, and other personal information are subsumed. Other specific notions include travel, health and welfare, education, shopping, services, and free time.

The *functional* part of the NFS corresponded to language functions. Curricula were organized around such functions as identifying, reporting, denying, accepting, declining, asking permission, and apologizing. Van Ek and Alexander listed some seventy different language functions.

CLASSROOM CONNECTIONS

One of the challenges of the NFS was finding the appropriate *sequence* of functions in a curriculum that stretched across possibly many weeks. What kinds of criteria can you think of that would underlie a sequence? Frequency of occurrence? Usefulness? Grammatical complexity? Intuition? How might such criteria vary depending on the *context* of the L2 class?

The NFS quickly provided popular underpinnings for the development of communicative textbooks and materials in English language courses. The functional basis of language programs has continued to the present day. In Saslow and Ascher's (2011) *Top Notch* series, for example, the following functions are covered in the first several lessons of a beginner's textbook:

- Introducing self and other people
- Exchanging personal information
- Asking how to spell someone's name

- Asking about the location of places
- Giving and getting directions
- Identifying and describing people
- Talking about time

A typical unit in textbooks like this includes a blend of conversation practice with a classmate, interactive group work, role-plays, grammar and pronunciation focus exercises, information-gap techniques, Internet activities, and extra class interactive practice.

The NFS was, strictly speaking, a curriculum. While it was clearly a precursor to Communicative Language Teaching (see below), as a curriculum (syllabus) it still presented language as an *inventory* of functional units. Therefore, the danger that the NFS could simply be "structural lamb served up as notional-functional mutton" (Campbell, 1978, p. 18) was ever-present. However, the NFS set the stage for bigger and better things. By attending to the functional purposes of language, and by providing contextual (notional) settings for the realization of those purposes, it provided a link between a dynasty of methods that were declining and a new era of language teaching.

Communicative Language Teaching

In 1972, Dell Hymes published an essay on communicative competence, which may have been the coining of the now household phrase in SLA. Almost a decade later, Canale and Swain (1980) delivered their seminal 50-page treatise on the theoretical bases of communicative competence (CC). In brief, they proposed four major components of CC (Canale & Swain, 1980; Canale, 1983):

Canale and Swain's (1980) Components of Communicative Competence

- **Grammatical**. Knowledge of and ability to use the forms of language.
- **Discourse**. Knowledge of and ability to comprehend and produce stretches of language across sentences in both oral and written modes.
- **Sociolinguistic**. Applying sociocultural contexts to communication, including participants' roles, information they share, and the function of a communicative act.
- **Strategic**. Use of verbal and nonverbal tactics to accomplish a communicative goal, including compensation for breakdowns.

About that same time a cluster of publications spelled out the practical ramifications of a communicative approach to language teaching (Widdowson, 1978; Brumfit & Johnson, 1979; Breen & Candlin, 1980; Littlewood, 1981;

Savignon, 1983). Soon **Communicative Language Teaching** (CLT) was a byword in language teaching. With these and a plethora of other publications, the language teaching profession was to undergo a slow but solid revolution—from grasping at a method here and there to a research-based, virtually universal understanding of basic tenets of effective communicative language pedagogy.

Today CLT continues to be recognized globally as what is best described as a broadly based *approach* (not a method) to language teaching that interweaves a cluster of principles and foundation stones of SLA. CLT extends beyond the merely grammatical elements of communication into the social, cultural, and pragmatic features of language. It is an approach that encourages "real-life" communication in the classroom. It aims to develop linguistic fluency, and not just the accuracy that once consumed its methodological predecessors. CLT promotes classroom practices that equip students with tools for generating unrehearsed language performance "out there" when they leave the womb of the classroom. CLT seeks to facilitate lifelong language learning among students that extends well beyond classroom activities. Learners are partners in a cooperative venture. And CLT-based classroom practices seek to intrinsically spark learners to reach their fullest potential.

It is difficult to offer a formal definition of an approach as all-encompassing as CLT. From the earlier seminal works in CLT (cited above) up to more recent work (Savignon, 2005, 2007; Harmer, 2007; Larsen-Freeman & Anderson, 2011; Ur, 2012; Brown, 2014; Celce-Murcia, Brinton, & Snow, 2014) we have interpretations enough to send us reeling. For the sake of simplicity and directness, in the chart below we offer seven interconnected characteristics as a description of CLT, drawn from all the above sources:

Characteristics of Communicative Language Teaching

1. **Overall goals.** CLT suggests a focus on *all* of the components (grammatical, discourse, sociolinguistic, and strategic) of communicative competence. Goals therefore must intertwine the organizational (grammatical, discourse) aspects of language with the pragmatic (sociolinguistic, strategic) aspects.
2. **Relationship of form and function.** Language techniques are designed to engage learners in the pragmatic, authentic, functional use of language for meaningful purposes. Organizational language forms are not the central focus, but remain as important components of language that enable the learner to accomplish those purposes.
3. **Fluency and accuracy.** A focus on students' "flow" of comprehension and production and a focus on the formal accuracy of production are seen as complementary principles.

At times fluency may have to take on more importance than accuracy in order to keep learners meaningfully engaged in language use. At other times the student will be encouraged to attend to correctness. Part of the teacher's responsibility is to offer appropriate corrective feedback on learners' errors.

4. **Focus on real-world contexts.** Students in a communicative class ultimately have to use the language, productively and receptively, in unrehearsed contexts outside the classroom. Classroom tasks must therefore equip students with the skills necessary for communication in those contexts.
5. **Autonomy and strategic involvement.** Students are given opportunities to focus on their own learning process through raising their awareness of their own styles (strengths, weaknesses, preferences) of learning and through the development of appropriate strategies for production and comprehension. Such awareness and action will help to develop autonomous learners capable of continuing to learn the language beyond the classroom and the course.
6. **Teacher roles.** The role of the teacher is that of facilitator and guide, not an all-knowing font of knowledge. The teacher is an empathetic "coach" who values the best interests of students' linguistic development. Students are encouraged to construct meaning through genuine linguistic interaction with other students and with the teacher.
7. **Student roles.** Students are active participants in their own learning process. Learner-centered, cooperative, collaborative learning is emphasized, but not at the expense of appropriate teacher-centered activity.

These seven characteristics underscore some major departures from earlier methods and approaches. Structurally (grammatically) sequenced curricula were a mainstay of language teaching for centuries. CLT suggests that grammatical structure might better be subsumed under various pragmatic categories. A great deal of use of authentic language is implied in CLT, as learners attempt to build fluency—but not at the expense of a healthy focus on accuracy. In communicative classrooms, students are encouraged to deal with unrehearsed situations under the guidance, but not control, of the teacher. The importance of learners' developing a strategic approach to acquisition is a turnabout from earlier methods that never broached the topic of strategies-based instruction. And, finally, a teacher's facilitative role and students' collaborative roles in CLT are the product of two decades or more of slowly recognizing the importance of learner initiative in the classroom.

CLT has not been without some drawbacks. The authenticity implied in CLT continues to pose challenges for non-native speaking teachers whose own ability may be less than fluent (Kramsch, 2006; Kumaravadivelu, 2006a). However, with more widespread current access to technological media (video, television, audio, Internet, computer software, smart phones, and the social media), both teachers and students can benefit from language input well beyond the teacher and (printed) course material.

A related criticism of CLT centered on its "Western" origins and questions about its relevance in non-Western cultures, especially those in which nondirective, student-centered cooperative learning might be quite alien (Bax, 2003; Harmer, 2007). In recent years, however, a whole host of research from Asian, African, and Middle-Eastern countries has begun to show a positive turn-around from earlier years of skepticism (Littlewood, 2011). Pham (2007) noted that "while teachers in many parts of the world may reject the CLT techniques transferred from the West, it is doubtful that they reject the *spirit* of CLT" (p. 196).

Classroom Connections

What do you think underlies the criticism that CLT is too Western a concept for some cultures? If an educational system presumes the essentially *authoritarian* role of the teacher, do you think CLT necessarily undermines that authority (and power)? How can a teacher still be in *control* of a classroom yet offer collaborative, student-centered activities?

Another issue involves the frequent mismatch between CLT goals and standardized testing, in which the latter does not always successfully incorporate communicative features (McNamara & Roever, 2006). Assessment methods have, over the last two decades or so, qualitatively improved their communicative validity, but many students around the world are still perplexed by having to face the dreaded "examination day" and its discrete-point, grammar-based test questions (Brown & Abeywickrama, 2010).

Finally, one can easily argue that now, after almost half a century of seeing the term CLT incorporated into virtually every language methodology textbook, the term has lost its meaning (Bax, 2003; Harmer, 2003; Spada, 2007). With a multiplicity of definitions coupled with a "postmethod" (See Chapter 3) malaise at the beginning of the twenty-first century, CLT was deemed by some to be too watered down to be a viable construct (Bax, 2003). Others, most notably Littlewood (2011), argued that "the value of CLT as an 'umbrella term' should not be underestimated. . . . CLT still serves as a valuable reminder that the aim of teaching is not to learn bits of language but to improve students' ability to communicate" (p. 542).

Littlewood (2011) then continued with an eloquent case for fruitful research and development within a CLT framework, or what he calls a "transnational ideoscape" in which CLT is not so much a specific set of practices as it is an "ideational landscape that provides a location for deepening and extending the 'cosmopolitan conversation' about second language pedagogy" (p. 552).

★ ★ ★ ★ ★

Chapter 3 describes many of the manifestations of CLT that have been advocated and used in classrooms over the last few decades. All of these options are in keeping with the spirit of CLT, but are not separate methods. Rather, they address a multiplicity of contexts, situations, and specializations, reflecting the complexity of the "state of the art" as we know it today.

As an aid to your recollection of the characteristics of some of the methods reviewed earlier, you may wish to refer to Table 2.1 (pp. 36–37), in which the various methods described in this chapter are summarized.

Looking back over almost one and a half centuries of meandering history, you can no doubt see the cycles of changing winds and shifting sands alluded to earlier. In this remarkable succession of changes, we learned something in each generation. We did not allow history simply to deposit new dunes exactly where the old ones lay. So our cumulative history has taught us to appreciate the value of "doing" language interactively, of the emotional (as well as cognitive) side of learning, of absorbing language automatically, of consciously analyzing it only when useful and appropriate, and of pointing learners toward the real world where they will use English communicatively.

FOR THE TEACHER: ACTIVITIES (A) & DISCUSSION (D)

Note: For each of the "Classroom Connections" in this chapter, you may wish to turn them into individual or pair-work discussion questions.

1. **(D)** Because this chapter refers to some basic principles and research findings that are normally covered in a course in second language acquisition (SLA), you may wish to review such material (see Brown, 2014) as you discuss this chapter. For example, varied theories of learning are implied in all the methods just reviewed; the role of affective factors in second language acquisition is highlighted in some methods; conscious and subconscious (or focal and peripheral) processing assumes various roles, depending on the method in question. If you feel that your students encountered concepts or issues that they need to brush up on in order to comprehend this chapter, consider making some time for a thorough review.
2. **(A)** Ask your students to look back at the lesson observed and described in Chapter 1. Divide the class into pairs, and ask them to brainstorm *any* aspects of the lesson in Chapter 1 that are examples of *any* of the methods described in this chapter—or that they think might have been "inspired" by a method. As they report their findings to the rest of the class, ask them to justify their comparisons. If appropriate, list their findings on the board.

3. **(D)** Ask the class for specific examples of the three levels of *approach*, *method*, and *technique* in any class activities or tasks that they have recently observed or taught themselves. For example, if they cite a group work information gap exercise that requires small groups to solve a set of problems collaboratively, what principles are at work at the approach level, what if any method is being used, and what specific techniques are used to carry out the task? You might want to list their ideas on the board for further discussion.
4. **(D)** Richards and Rodgers (2001, p. 7) said Grammar Translation "is a method for which there is no theory." Is this too harsh a judgment? Ask students if they agree with the "theorylessness" of Grammar Translation and to justify their opinion.
5. **(A)** Consider the Series Method, the Direct Method, and the Audiolingual Method. Assign a different method to each of several small groups. Ask each group to list the theoretical foundations (assumptions about language, learning, and teaching) on which the method rested and share findings with the whole class. Consider listing their responses on the board.
6. **(A)** Assign the four "designer" methods (CLL, Suggestopedia, the Silent Way, and TPR/Natural Approach) to separate small groups of students. The groups' task (which may require some extra-class research beyond what is provided in this chapter) is to specify (as much as possible from the information given) the following descriptors (adapted from Larsen-Freeman & Anderson, 2011, p. 9) for the method assigned to them:

   a) The overall goals of the method
   b) The roles of teacher and students
   c) The nature of teacher-student and student-student interaction
   d) The ways in which students' feelings and emotions are handled
   e) The language skills that are emphasized
   f) The role of the native language of students
   g) The way the teacher responds to student errors
   h) The way assessment is accomplished

   Each group can then report their findings to the rest of the class. Students may find it useful to see the information in chart form (on the blackboard or developed into a computer-generated chart) like others in this chapter. An alternative to this exercise would be to assign it as extra-class work to be performed by students on their own. In this case, you might assign just *one* method per student.
7. **(D)** Ask your students to suggest what novel approaches were brought to the L2 teaching profession with the Notional-functional Syllabus. What did Campbell (1978) mean by saying we should beware of "structural lamb served up as notional functional mutton"?

Table 2.1 Characteristics of Methods

Method	Theoretical Foundations	Goals	Learner-Teacher Roles
Grammar-Translation	Classical assumptions about education as a "discipline" Learning a foreign language is the mark of educated persons	Vocabulary memorization Grammar rules Translation of passages Reading proficiency	Teacher as controller
Series and Direct Methods	L2 and L1 learning similarity Meaningful associations	Oral fluency Conversation ability	Teacher-directed Learners respond to modeled language
Audiolingual Method (ALM)	Habit formation through repetition Primacy of oral communication	Oral communication skills Pronunciation Fluency (within limited stretches of discourse)	Highly teacher-directed Learners respond to modeled language Learners practice target language on their own
Community Language Learning (CLL)	Whole-person, counseling-learning model of education Class members bond as a community Inductive learning	Oral communicative proficiency	Teacher is a counselor Teacher is a source of information Learner is a client Learners progress from dependence to independence
Suggestopedia	Relaxed states of consciousness create low anxiety Power of "suggestion"	Oral communication Conversational exchange Reading ability Acquisition of vocabulary	Highly teacher-directed Teacher initiates "concert" sessions and oral models Learners acquire subconsciously
Silent Way	Discovery learning Use of mediating physical objects Problem-solving approach	Oral communication Conversational exchange Reading ability Acquisition of vocabulary	Highly teacher-directed Teacher is mostly "silent" Learners are responsible for initiating clarification questions
Total Physical Response (TPR) and The Natural Approach	L1 and L2 learning are similar Comprehension-based approach Language connects with physical action	Listening comprehension Oral communicative skills	Teacher-directed Learners respond to modeled language Learners collaborate to perform simple routines

Typical Activities	Strengths	Weaknesses
Explaining rules Memorizing vocabulary Translating reading passages	Reading proficiency Become familiar with the written form of a language	No oral practice or fluency Reliance on memorization No SLA research to undergird it
Repeating teacher models Practicing dialogues, whole class	Cognitive associations Real-world relevance Common survival language is practiced	Limited in scope Learner creativity is not encouraged Writing not emphasized
Repeating teacher-modeled prescribed dialogues Oral pattern practice Pronunciation drilling Practicing memorized dialogues in pairs	Emphasis on oral language Building learner confidence Use of taped dialogues provides models	Little room for creativity Emphasis on error-free production Writing/reading not emphasized
Learners initiate desired language in their L1 Teacher provides translation into the L2 Learners request linguistic rules/information	Burden is on the learner to initiate language Learners decide topics Class builds community collaboratively Teacher is a resource	No set curriculum, so progress is dependent on student initiative Tedious, trial-and-error process Overly nondirective
"Concert" session with music in background Learners listen quietly in state of relaxation Repetition drills, role plays, dialogue practice	Low-anxiety situations Relaxation states offer optimal reception Appreciation of literary texts	Highly structured curriculum Over-reliance on assumptions about relaxation Wears thin after the first few weeks
Teacher modeling of target language items Use of colored objects, charts, diagrams Learners collaborate to refine understanding	Learning by discovery facilitates autonomy & collaboration Learners are not "spoon fed"	Teacher can become too distant Tedious, trial-and-error process Wears thin after the first few weeks
Imperative commands given to learners Learners respond with actions Role plays	Low-anxiety situations Physical-linguistic connections Learners not forced to speak too early Community building	Advocacy of "silent period" Overemphasis on physical actions, imperatives Wears thin after the first few weeks

8. **(A)** Ask pairs to look at the seven features used as a general definition of CLT in the list on page 31 and to brainstorm some practical classroom examples of each of the seven factors. Should any characteristics be added to the list? Or changed?
9. **(A)** Have students observe an ESL class and use the seven characteristics of CLT as a gauge of how closely the lesson approximates CLT. Ask students to share their observations in small groups.
10. **(D)** Ask students to review the cycles of "shifting sands" since Gouin's time. Table 2.1 on pages 36–37 may help to refresh memories. How did each new method borrow from previous practices? What did each reject in previous practices? On the board, you might reconstruct the historical progression in the form of a time line with characteristics listed for each "era." If time permits, try to determine what the prevailing *social, intellectual,* and *political* mood was when certain methods were flowering. For example, the ALM was a product of a post-WWII military training program and flourished during an era when scientific solutions to all problems were diligently sought. Are there some logical connections here?

FOR YOUR FURTHER READING

Richards, J., & Rodgers, T. (2001). *Approaches and methods in language teaching* (2nd ed.). Cambridge, UK: Cambridge University Press.

Larsen-Freeman, D., & Anderson, M. (2011). *Techniques and principles in language teaching* (3rd ed.). Oxford, UK: Oxford University Press.

Both volumes offer detailed summaries of the methods described in the present chapter. They analyze each method with a focus on teacher goals, roles of the teacher, the nature of student-teacher interaction, undergirding theories of language and culture, assessment, and other topics.

Wilkins, D. (1976). *Notional syllabuses.* London, UK: Oxford University Press.

An informative historical perspective on the early conception of the Notional-Functional Syllabus, precursor to CLT.

Brumfit, C., & Johnson, K. (1979). *The communicative approach to language teaching.* Oxford, UK: Oxford University Press.

Littlewood, W. (2011). Communicative language teaching: an expanding concept for a changing world. In E. Hinkel (Ed.), *Handbook of research in second language teaching and learning: Volume II* (pp. 541–557). New York, NY: Routledge.

A perspective on CLT is offered in the form of Brumfit and Johnson's detailed summary of communicative principles and practice in 1979, then in more recent reflections by Littlewood in 2011. You will note some interesting developments over the 30 years in between.

CHAPTER 3

CONTEXTUALIZING COMMUNICATIVE APPROACHES

Questions for Reflection

- What does the concept of "postmethod" imply in a historical context?
- Why has the dichotomizing of "theory" and "practice" been dysfunctional?
- What does it mean to be an "informed eclectic" in choosing and evaluating techniques for a communicative L2 course?
- What are the characteristics and contexts of a variety of *general* communicative approaches to methodology?
- What are some of the more *specific* contexts in which communicative approaches apply?

The history of language teaching described in the previous chapter, characterized by a succession of methodological milestones, had changed its course by the mid-1980s. Ironically, the methods that were such strong signposts of a century-old history were no longer the benchmarks that they once were. The profession had learned some profound lessons from its past journeys.

We became cognizant of the paramount importance of incorporating a communicative component into our language courses. We had learned to be cautiously eclectic in making informed choices of teaching practices that were solidly grounded in the best of what we knew about L2 learning and teaching. And perhaps more importantly, we became acutely aware of a multiplicity of *contexts* for L2 teaching, which brought with it myriad adaptations, applications, and localized approaches—all within the spirit of Communicative Language Teaching (CLT).

A look back today over several decades of these communicative approaches, techniques, and related research boggles the mind! In a mushrooming of research and classroom practices, we seem to have addressed every imaginable audience, age, proficiency level, and special purpose for L2 learning. And we have not ignored the importance of localizing language teaching to country, institution, socioeconomic level, political motive, and social-psychological variables at play in the teaching-learning dialogue.

In this chapter we'll address a good deal of this contextualization of language teaching by examining a variety of *methodological options* within the framework communicative approaches. Of course, in the process, we may omit one or two of your favorites, but we will at least have provided a picture of the amazing diversity of this field!

But first, let's take a look at the philosophical foundations undergirding the many manifestations of CLT approaches since the mid-1980s.

THE POSTMETHOD CONDITION

We seem to have an infatuation with "post" conditions, perhaps an indication of the human yearning to "get over" our past and look optimistically into the future. You may have heard enough about post-colonial, post-modern, post-structural, post-behavioral, post-cognitive, and even *post-linguistic* (Nelson & Kern, 2012) conditions, and more! But there is one more "post" condition that we cannot ignore here.

The notion of a **postmethod** era of language teaching was a concept that arose around the turn of the twenty-first century that described the need to put to rest the limited concept of method as it was used in the previous century. David Nunan (1991b), noting that there may never be a "method for all," summed it up nicely: "The focus in recent years has been on the development of classroom tasks and activities which are consonant with what we know about second language acquisition, and which are also in keeping with the dynamics of the classroom itself" (p. 228).

Kumaravadivelu (2001) was even more specific in calling for a "pedagogy of particularity," that is, being "sensitive to a particular group of teachers teaching a particular group of learners pursuing a particular set of goals within a particular institutional context embedded in a particular social milieu" (2006, p. 538). Others (Brown, 1993; Clarke, 1994; Richards & Rodgers, 2001) had earlier expressed the need for soundly conceived pedagogical approaches that attended to the particularities of contexts.

Was the proclamation of a postmethod condition merely a matter of semantic quibbling? Maybe. Bell (2003) astutely observed that we have too many definitions attached to the word method, and attempted to clear the muddied waters by differentiating method with a lowercase *m*, any of a wide variety of classroom practices, from Method with an uppercase *M*, "a fixed set of classroom practices that serve as a prescription" (p. 326). What are we to make of the confusion? Happily, Larsen-Freeman and Anderson (2011), among others, remain comfortable with maintaining the notion of methods (with a small *m*) as long as we are clear about the referent.

So perhaps by now the profession has attained a modicum of maturity where we recognize that the diversity of language learners in multiple worldwide contexts demands an eclectic blend of tasks, each tailored for a specified group of learners studying for particular purposes in geographic, social, and political contexts.

Classroom Connections

Imagine a language course that announced it was following a particular method, let's say, TPR or Suggestopedia. In such a course, how *different* would the actual adaptation of that method be across varying contexts? For example, a "traditional" teacher-centered institution or system versus a school that had more "open" definitions of teacher roles? Children versus adults? Academic language versus survival skills?

THE DYSFUNCTION OF THE THEORY-PRACTICE DICHOTOMY

The now discarded concept of Method (with a capital *M*) as a discrete set of unified techniques designed to apply to multiple contexts, carried with it, in some opinions (Clarke, 1994; Kumaravadivelu, 2006a), an implicit assumption about the relationship between what we have customarily called "theory" and "practice." *Theory*, in both philosophical and scientific inquiry, implies an organized set of hypotheses presumed to explain an observed phenomenon. In language teaching, an application of a theory may come in the form of a methodological set of practical options that follow from the theory.

All too often in our history of L2 teaching, we have seen the theory-building part of the formula carried out by researchers who may have been only distantly familiar with the practicalities of classroom teaching. Likewise, the *practice* part of the formula was thought to be the province of classroom teachers who accepted (or rejected) the theorist's pronouncements about the how's and why's of SLA. The relationship between the theorist and practitioner was—and in some cases, still is—similar to that of a producer of goods and a consumer.

Mark Clarke (1994) eloquently argued against such a relationship in analyzing the *dysfunction* of the theory-practice relationship. He and others since then (Richards & Rodgers, 2001; Nunan, 2003; Kumaravadivelu, 2006a; Larsen-Freeman, 2012) offered strong arguments against perpetuating this "misleading dualism" (Hedgcock, 2002, p. 308). Not only does such an understanding promote the notion of "a privileged class of theorists and an underprivileged class of practitioners," (Kumaravadivelu, 2006b, p. 166), but it also connotes a separation of researchers and teachers, and at worst, a one-way communication line from the former to the latter.

Recent work in the language teaching profession shows a marked departure from the artificial dichotomy of theory and practice (Murphy & Byrd,

2001; McKay, 2006; Alsagoff et al., 2012; Celce-Murcia, Brinton, & Snow, 2014; Graves, 2014). In this mode of viewing the profession, teachers *are* researchers and are charged with the responsibility of *reflecting* on their own practice (Murphy, 2014). Calls for "action research" and "classroom-based research" (Bailey, 2014) reflect a new and healthier "reconfiguring [of] the relationship between theorizers and practitioners" (Nelson & Kern, 2012, p. 47).

It has become increasingly inauthentic for researchers with PhDs to generate ideas from the "ivory tower" without experiencing them in person in the classroom. Likewise, more and more teachers are engaging in the process of systematic observation, experimentation, analysis, and reporting of their own experiences in classrooms around the world. More detail on the language teacher as *researcher* is offered in Chapter 22 of this book.

As you continue to read on in this and following chapters, it's important to view yourself as a capable observer of your own and others' practice. You need not think of theorists as people that are removed from the arena of classroom reality, nor of teachers as anything less than essential participants in a dialogue.

AN INFORMED ECLECTIC APPROACH

It should be clear from the foregoing that as both an informed and eclectic teacher, you think in terms of a number of possible pedagogical options at your disposal for tailoring classes to particular contexts. Your *approach*, or rationale for language learning and teaching, therefore takes on great importance. Your approach includes a number of basic principles of learning and teaching (such as those that will be elaborated in Chapter 4) on which you can rely for designing and evaluating classroom lessons. Your approach to language-teaching methodology is a theoretically well-informed global understanding of the process of learning and teaching. It is inspired by the interconnection of all your reading and observing and discussing and teaching, and that interconnection underlies everything that you do in the classroom.

But your approach to language pedagogy is not just a set of static principles "set in stone." It is, in fact, a dynamic composite of well-informed beliefs that change across time (as you learn more and more about the art of teaching) and that adapt themselves to whatever *situated contexts* in which you are teaching. The interaction between your approach and your classroom practice is the key to effective, authentic teaching.

If you have little or no experience in teaching and are perhaps now in a teacher education program, you may feel you cannot yet describe your own approach to L2 learning and teaching. On the other hand, you might just surprise yourself at the intuitions you already have about pedagogical foundations.

Look at the list below of a number of questions you may need to consider in designing a lesson. On the basis of what you know so far about SLA and teaching, and for a particular context you're familiar with, which side of a continuum of possibilities would you generally lean toward, and why? And what contextual variables might influence a change away from your general inclination?

Questions to Ponder in Designing and Teaching L2 Lessons

1. Should the course focus on meaning or form or both?
2. Will analysis or intuition benefit my students more?
3. As a teacher should I be tough and demanding or gentle and empathetic?
4. Should I directly correct students' errors or try to get them to self-correct?
5. Should a communicative course give more attention to accuracy or fluency?

Were you able to respond to these items? For example, the first item offers a choice between "meaning" and "form" for a focus. While you might lean toward meaning because you know that too much focus on form could detract from communicative acquisition, certain classroom techniques or tasks might demand a focus on formal aspects, such as grammar, phonology, or lexicon. Or your context (say, a test preparation course that helps students to pass a grammar test) might dictate your emphasis.

Classroom Connections

Suppose you're teaching in an educational context or culture in which teachers must not appear too empathetic lest students lose their respect for you. How would that modify your answer to item #3 above? What other contexts of teaching (age, skill level, culture, purpose) can you think of that would dictate an adaptation of your approach?

If you could make a choice within each item, it indicates that you do indeed have some intuitions about teaching, and perhaps the rudiments of an approach. Your approach is guided by several key factors. Consider the following list.

FACTORS CONTRIBUTING TO YOUR *APPROACH* TO LANGUAGE TEACHING

- the particular needs and goals of your students
- your own experience as a learner in classrooms
- whatever teaching experience you may already have had
- classroom observations you have made
- books you have read
- previous courses in the field

But more importantly, if you found that in almost every choice you wanted to add something like "but it depends on . . .," then you are on the way toward developing an *informed* approach to language learning and teaching. Your approach to language teaching must always account for specific contexts of teaching, or what Kumaravadivelu (2001) called a pedagogy of "particularity," as mentioned earlier. Rarely can we say with absolute certainty that a methodological set of techniques applies to all learners in all contexts for all purposes.

GENERAL APPROACHES

In the remainder of this chapter we will take you on a "tour" of language teaching options that represent the diversity of L2 pedagogy across the globe. All of our brief "stopovers" provide sketches of methodological approaches that can quite plausibly be subsumed under the rubric of CLT. Moreover, all of the approaches are *current*, in that they are being practiced, in a variety of interpretations, in L2 teaching today.

Some approaches are more *general* in nature: They are being used across many different contexts, countries, institutions, ages, and proficiency levels. Task-based language teaching, for example, is broadly applicable to an enormous variety of contexts. Other approaches are more *specific*: Certain identifiable contextual factors must be present for them to be of utility in a language program. Thus, workplace L2 teaching obviously is limited to a restrictive audience and purpose.

We turn first to the more broadly applicable approaches.

Learner-Centered Instruction

> When Gary Adkins walked into the first class hour of his advanced French grammar and reading class as a junior in college, his classmates quietly sat in their seats, stone faced, eyes fixed on the teacher. Professor Bouchard, in silence, sternly eyed the newest student, who took his seat as quickly as possible. Attendance was duly recorded, and with dispatch, the professor described the course, the prerequisites (mainly having completed second-year French), course requirements, and the grading system.
>
> "Any questions?" he asked, still sternly eyeing the students, but nary a person dared to stick a neck out.
>
> "Good. Now open your books to page 3, where you will find our first reading passage. Monsieur Adkins, read the first paragraph aloud."
>
> Trembling, unprepared, Gary read the paragraph. Quite well, he thought. Professor Bouchard had another opinion.
>
> "Monsieur Adkins, you must read more loudly next time. You mispronounced several words, and you must learn to read with more emphasis. . . . Now, Mademoiselle Allen, translate the first paragraph into English."

About this time Gary wondered why he had to be born into a family whose name began at the top of the alphabet! Miss Allen had similar thoughts as she stumbled through the translation, with a performance riddled with errors, causing Professor Bouchard to embark on a tirade about the intricacies of the present and past perfect tenses in French. You can imagine how the rest of the class hour went, and how thankful every student was when the bell rang—and how especially thankful were those whose last name began with "z"—they did not have to "recite" on this day!

Teacher-centered instruction has been with us for centuries, if not millennia. The teacher controls everything; students speak only when asked to; the teacher is an authority who is not to be questioned. But around the middle of the twentieth century, this model began to erode as educators probed new models of pedagogy. In the words of Weimer (2013), students "needed to find their way past self-doubt, awkwardness, and the fear of failure to a place where they could ask a question in class, make a contribution to a group, and speak coherently in front of peers" (p. 5). By the end of the twentieth century, **learner-centered instruction** was a catchword for a new model of education across many disciplines. Language teaching soon proved to be an ideal subject matter to put the forward-thinking model into practice, as aptly demonstrated in Nunan's (1988) manual describing curriculum design that incorporated collaboration between student and teacher.

Learner-centered instruction turned teacher-centered models "upside down" by playing down the all-knowing, authoritative role of the teacher, and giving opportunities to students to participate in a classroom without fear of being scolded or belittled by a teacher. Some of the hallmarks of learner-centered teaching included the following:

Characteristics of Learner-Centered Instruction

- a focus on learners' needs and goals
- understanding individual differences among learners in a classroom
- gauging the curriculum to learners' styles and preferences
- creating a supportive, nonfearful, nondefensive atmosphere
- offering students choices in the types and content of activities
- giving some control to the student (e.g., group work)

Because language teaching often presupposes a classroom where students have very little language proficiency with which to *negotiate* with the teacher, teachers may be wary of giving learners the "power" associated with a learner-centered approach. Such reluctance may not be necessary for two reasons. First, by conducting a formal or informal *needs assessment* at the beginning of a course, teachers can be relatively well-directed in the first few sessions of a class. Second, even in beginning level classes, teachers can still adhere to the goals of a curriculum while giving students opportunities to "try out" language.

In learner-centered classrooms, teachers are not being asked to relinquish *all* control, only to allow for student innovation, creativity, and eventually their autonomy. All of these efforts help to give students a sense of "ownership" of their learning and thereby add to their sense of *agency* and *identity*.

 **CLASSROOM CONNECTIONS**

Your students are in the first week or so of a beginning language class, and their ability is limited to a few words and phrases. How might what you say and do, what students say and do, and some of the activities all reflect a learner-centered approach? Remember, your students are beginners with limited language. Can yours still be a learner-centered classroom?

Task-Based Language Teaching

One of the most prominent perspectives within the CLT framework is **Task-Based Language Teaching** (TBLT). Ellis (2003) asserted that TBLT is at the very heart of CLT by placing the use of tasks at the core of language teaching. In Nunan's (2014) words, "CLT addresses the question *why?* TBLT answers the question *how?*" (p. 458). While there is a good deal of variation among experts on how to describe or define a **task**, Peter Skehan's (1998a, p. 95) concept of task still captures the essentials. The following lists the attributes of a successful task.

Characteristics of Effective Tasks

- meaning is primary
- there is a communication problem to solve
- there is a relationship to comparable real-world activities
- task completion has some priority
- the assessment of the task is in terms of outcome

Perhaps more simply put, "a task is an activity which requires learners to use language, with emphasis on meaning, to attain an objective" (Bygate, Skehan, & Swain, 2001, p. 11). A task may comprise several techniques. For example, a problem-solving task may include the techniques of grammatical explanation, teacher-initiated questions, small group-work, and an oral reporting procedure. Tasks are usually "bigger" in their ultimate ends than techniques.

Task-based teaching makes an important distinction between **target tasks**, which students must accomplish beyond the classroom, and **pedagogical tasks**, which form the nucleus of the classroom activity. Target tasks are not unlike the functions of language that are listed in Notional-Functional Syllabuses (see Chapter 2, here, and Chapter 8 of *PLLT*). For example, "giving personal information" is a communicative function for language, and an appropriately stated target task might be "giving personal information in a job interview." Notice that the task specifies a context.

Pedagogical tasks include any of a series of techniques designed ultimately to teach students to perform the target task. The ultimate pedagogical task usually involves students in some form of simulation of the target task itself (say, through a role-play simulation in which certain roles are assigned to learners). More elaborate tasks might involve planning an itinerary for a trip (Larsen-Freeman & Anderson, 2011, p. 149), which requires consulting transportation routes, ascertaining hotel rates, deciding on the best sights to see, and mapping out daily schedules.

Classroom Connections

Suppose you have been asked to teach a unit to intermediate-level learners (choose any context) in which the ultimate task was for small groups to each present an advertisement for a tour of Antarctica. What are some of the pedagogical tasks that might be important to include as steps toward the ultimate goal of the unit?

Pedagogical tasks are distinguished by their specific objectives that cumulatively point beyond the language classroom to the target task. They may, however, include both formal and functional techniques. A pedagogical task designed to teach students to give personal information in a job interview might, for example, involve

1. exercises in comprehension of *wh-* questions with *do*-insertion ("When do you work at Macy's?").
2. drills in the use of frequency adverbs ("I usually work until five o'clock.").
3. listening to extracts of job interviews.
4. analyzing the grammar and discourse of the interviews.
5. modeling a typical interview protocol.
6. role-playing a simulated interview with students in pairs.

While you might be tempted to consider only the ultimate task (#6) as the one fulfilling the criterion of pointing beyond the classroom to the real world, all of the techniques build toward enabling the students to perform the final technique.

A task-based curriculum, then, specifies what a learner needs to do with the English language in terms of target tasks and organizes a series of pedagogical tasks intended to reach those goals. An important criterion in task-based curricula is pedagogical soundness in the development and sequencing of tasks. The teacher and curriculum planner are called upon to consider communicative dimensions such as goal, input from the teacher, interaction, teacher and learner roles, and assessment (Ellis, 2003; Skehan, 2003; Nunan, 2004, 2014; Kumaravadivelu, 2006b).

Task-based instruction is not a new method. Rather, it puts task at the center of one's methodological focus. It views the learning process as a set of communicative tasks that are directly linked to the curricular goals they serve, the purposes of which extend beyond the practice of language for its own sake.

Research on task-based learning has pursued the following objectives (Van den Branden, 2006; Samuda & Bygate, 2008; Kim 2009; Robinson, 2011):

- identifying types of tasks that enhance learning (such as open-ended, structured, teacher-fronted, small group, and pair work)
- defining task-specific learner factors (for example, roles, proficiency levels, and styles)
- examining teacher roles and other variables that contribute to successful achievement of objectives
- specifying task complexity

Task-based instruction is a perspective within a CLT framework that urges you to carefully consider all the techniques that you use in the classroom in terms of a number of important pedagogical purposes:

Characteristics of Task-Based Language Teaching (TBLT)

- Tasks ultimately point learners beyond the forms of language alone to real-world contexts.
- Tasks specifically contribute to the communicative goals of learners.
- Their elements are carefully designed and not simply haphazardly or idiosyncratically thrown together.
- Their objectives are well specified so that you can at some later point accurately determine the success of one task over another.
- Tasks engage learners, at some level, in genuine problem-solving activity.

Theme-Based Instruction

When language courses are organized around meaningful situations or topics, they may be said to be **theme-based**, sometimes referred to as **topic-based** curricula. Theme-based instruction provides an organizing framework for a language course that transcends formal or structural requirements in a curriculum. Theme-based curricula can serve multiple interests of students in a classroom and can offer a focus on *content* while still adhering to institutional requirements for, let's say, coverage of grammatical criteria. Brinton (2013) puts theme-based teaching under the rubric of content-based language teaching (to be discussed below), but cautiously notes that there are variations in interpretation of the model (p. 4).

So, for example, an intensive English course for intermediate pre-university students might deal with topics of current interest such as public health, environmental awareness, or world economics. In the classroom students read articles or chapters, view video programs, discuss issues, propose solutions, and carry out writing assignments on a given *theme*, but the primary focus of the curriculum is not on *content* (e.g., medicine, business, science workplace)

Numerous current L2 textbooks, especially at the intermediate to advanced levels, offer theme-based courses of study. Challenging topics in these textbooks engage the curiosity and increase motivation of students as they grapple with an array of real-life issues ranging from simple to complex and also improve their linguistic skills across all four domains of listening, speaking, reading, and writing.

Consider just one of an abundance of topics that have been used as themes through which language is taught: *environmental awareness and action*. With this topic, you are sure to find immediate intrinsic motivation—we all want to survive! Here are some possible theme-based activities:

- Use environmental statistics and facts for classroom reading, writing, discussion, and debate.
- Carry out research and writing projects.
- Have students create their own environmental awareness material.
- Arrange field trips.
- Conduct simulation games.

In these activities, all four skills are actively in use. Students can get excited about solutions to real problems, some of which may be uncomfortably "close to home." They can use language for genuine communicative purposes, and are actively involved in learner-centered collaboration. And they can absorb a surprising number of "required" linguistically based curricular objectives.

Experiential and Project-Based Learning

In yet another of the many facets of CLT-inspired perspectives on language teaching, **experiential learning** offers a dimension that may not necessarily be implied in the concepts already discussed here. Experiential learning, also known as **project-based learning**, highlights giving students *concrete experiences* in which they must use language in order to fulfill the objectives of a lesson (Eyring, 1991; Stoller, 2006). Both models include activities that contextualize language, integrate skills, and point toward authentic, real-world purposes, as in the following examples:

Examples of Experiential and Project-Based Activities

- hands-on projects (e.g., constructing a diorama)
- field trips and other on-site visits (e.g., to a factory or museum)
- research projects (e.g., the value of solar power)
- extra-class dinner groups (e.g., learning about Vietnamese cuisine)
- creating a video advertising a product (e.g., organic fruit)

Experiential learning emphasizes the psychomotor aspects of language learning by involving learners in physical actions into which language is subsumed and reinforced. Through action, students are drawn into a utilization of multiple skills. The educational foundations of experiential learning lie in the advantages of "learning by doing," discovery learning, and inductive learning.

Classroom Connections

Imagine a unit in an L2 that involves advanced adult students in a research project on nuclear nonproliferation (disarming countries of nuclear weapons). What might some of the objectives (across all four skills of listening, speaking, reading, and writing) be for such a unit? What pedagogical tasks could you see being used in this unit?

A specialized form of experiential learning that is still used in some circles is the **Language Experience Approach** (LEA) (Van Allen & Allen, 1967), an integrated-skills approach initially used in teaching native language reading skills, but more recently adapted to second language learning contexts. With widely varying adaptations, students' personal experiences (a trip to the zoo, a movie, a family gathering at a park, etc.) are used as the basis for discussion, and then students, with the help of the teacher, write about the "experience," which is preserved in the form of a "book." The benefit of the LEA is in the intrinsic involvement of students in creating their own stories rather than being given other people's stories. As in other experiential techniques, students are directly involved in the creative process of fashioning their own products, and all four skills are readily implied in carrying out a project.

Strategies-Based Instruction

Ever since Paolo Freire (1970) and others introduced the concept of student *responsibility* for their own achievement of outcomes, educational theory has done an about-face across disciplines. In L2 pedagogy, one of the key foundation stones of successful instruction is enabling students to "learn how to learn." That is, learners become **autonomous** through becoming aware of their own strengths and weaknesses and taking action in the form of strategic involvement in learning. (In the Chapter 4, we will expand on the principles of autonomy and investment.)

Implied in all the CLT-inspired approaches described so far in this chapter is the centrality of the learner. One of the most powerful ways that learners can "seize the day" in their journey to success is through what come to be called **strategic investment**. The learning of any skill involves a certain degree of investment of one's time and effort. Every complex set of skills—like learning to play a musical instrument or a sport—is acquired through a combination of observing, focusing, practicing, monitoring, correcting, and redirecting.

Learning an L2 is no different. A language is probably the most complex set of skills one could ever seek to acquire; therefore, an investment is necessary in the form of developing multiple layers of strategies for getting that language into one's brain. Building into your pedagogy ways for students to achieve this kind of strategic autonomy has come to be known as **strategies-based instruction** (SBI), also called *learning strategy training* (Larsen-Freeman & Anderson, 2013) as well as *learner development/training* (Wenden, 1998, 2002).

Several decades ago research began to show that successful learners engaged in certain practices that distinguished them from unsuccessful learners (Rubin & Thompson, 1982; Oxford, 1990). Among other characteristics, good language learners take charge of their own learning, seeking out opportunities to use the language, experiment with the L2, make guesses, use production tricks, allow errors to work for them, and learn from their mistakes.

In order for learners to become self-driven independent learners beyond the classroom, they must be fully *aware* of their own strengths, weaknesses, preferences, and styles, and be able to capitalize on that metacognition through the use of appropriate action in the form of strategic options. The importance of *awareness-raising* in language learning is well documented (Chamot, 2005; Cohen, 2011; Oxford, 2011). When learners are aware of their own capacities and limitations, they can efficiently adopt pathways to success that capitalize on strengths and compensate for weaknesses.

The effective implementation of SBI in language classrooms involves several steps and considerations (see Brown, 2014 for details):

1. stimulating awareness within learners of preferred styles
2. linking style to strategy with "strategic" techniques
3. providing extra-class assistance for learners

Stimulating Awareness

Most L2 learners are unaware of their own styles, preferences, and ways of addressing various problems. If they are aware, certainly very few have ever made the connection between these styles and learning an L2. So, what are some practical steps you can take toward awareness raising? Consider the following possibilities as a start.

Stimulating Awareness of Learners' Styles

- ask students to fill out informal self-checklists
- administer formal personality and cognitive style tests
- involve students in readings (e.g., Brown, 2002b) about styles
- introduce (define) and discuss various styles
- encourage "good" learning styles among learners

 **CLASSROOM CONNECTIONS**

Have you ever been in an L2 course in which the teacher has talked about or encouraged you to become aware of your styles (strengths, weaknesses, preferences)? As a teacher, how would you use a style awareness checklist? How might you introduce your students to various styles?

Among awareness-raising possibilities is attention to **multiple intelligences** in L2 learning. As summarized in *PLLT*, Chapter 4 (Brown, 2014), Gardner's (1983, 1999, 2004) model of intelligence includes at least eight types of intelligence, which has led educators to view a number of forms of "smartness" that learners can manifest. A learner who is strong, for example, in interpersonal intelligence may thrive in the context of group work and interaction, while a student who has high spatial intelligence will perform well with plenty of charts, diagrams, and other visuals. Most educators who follow an MI approach advocate the use of a multiplicity of types of activities and techniques in order to appeal to as wide a swath of learners as possible (Armstrong, 1994). Christison (2005) offered a compilation of 150 different activities for language learners, each emphasizing a specific intelligence, coded for age and proficiency level.

Linking Style and Strategy in the Classroom

Recent research has linked styles and strategies and discussed classroom implications of such connections (Cohen, 2011; Oxford, 2011; Wong & Nunan, 2011; Brown, 2014). Among the various suggestions in these sources for engaging in SBI is the concept of taking into account a student's style that may be working *against* him or her and gauging classroom techniques that will address those needs. Consider some ways to accomplish this in the Tips box (from Brown, 2014) on the next page.

Purpura (2014) adds a further dimension to strategy training by considering the various *stages* of processing that learners go through. For example, processing new input involves a comprehending process that consists of attending, decoding, noticing, and clarifying. The same strategies to be applied at this stage are far different from those at, say, response preparation and generation (output), which come only after intake, storage, and retrieval have taken place. Others (Brown, 2002b; Oxford, 2011) have built on this observation by distinguishing among strategies for comprehension and production, remembering, monitoring, and sociocultural awareness, among many other subcategories.

Compensating for Styles That May Be Working *Against* Learners

To lower inhibitions

Guessing games and communication games
Role plays, skits, and songs
Group and pair work
Humor, fun, laughter, enjoyment
Students share their fears in small groups

To encourage risk taking

Praise students for making sincere efforts to try out language
Use fluency exercises where errors are not corrected at that time
Extra-class collaborative projects

To build students' self-confidence

Tell and show students that you believe in them
Students make lists of their strengths
Students enumerate goals accomplished

An increasing number of L2 textbooks are offering guidelines and exercises for strategy awareness and practice within the stream of a chapter. Brown's (2000) *New Vistas* series for ESL learners offered examples of embedding strategy work within the exercises of a textbook. In another series of textbooks (Sarosy & Sherak, 2006), for academic listening, students' attention is drawn to cues for listening accurately to a lecture, for example, by attending to language that signals sequences of points, the "big picture," and a new idea or topic. Similarly, Chamot, O'Malley, and Kupper (1992) included strategy training modules in each unit.

Providing Extra Class Assistance

A third step toward building students' strategic awareness and awareness can be implemented beyond the classroom. Teachers can issue challenges to students to implement certain strategies that have been practiced in the classroom, and bring reports of their successes back to share with classmates. Self-help study guides (Marshall, 1989; Rubin & Thompson, 1994; Brown, 2002) tend to have short, easy-to-understand chapters with information, anecdotes, tips, and exercises that will help learners to use strategies successfully beyond the language classroom. Excellent opportunities for authentic communication are available in the social media, and even though texting, tweeting, blogging, and Facebook posts are replete with nonstandard language, strategic investment may still reap benefits.

We will be spiraling TLT, SBI, and other CLT-inspired approaches into numerous examples in the rest of this book, as we look at more specific pedagogical basics in the chapters to come. We have so far just provided a sketch of the variety of outgrowth in the last few decades of the CLT "era."

Other Collaborative Approaches

Several other pedagogical approaches in the latter part of the twentieth century featured collaboration, interaction, and cooperation among learners in the classroom. We'll take a brief look at three such models, all within the principles of CLT, variations of which are present in many L2 classrooms today.

Cooperative learning, as opposed to viewing learners as individuals on a solitary quest for success, incorporated principles of learner-centered instruction. As students work together in pairs and groups, they share information and come to each other's aid. They are a "team" whose players must work together in order to achieve goals successfully. According to the research (Oxford, 1997; McCafferty, Jacobs, & DaSilva, 2006), in such a milieu, learners typical show heightened self-efficacy and identity, lowered anxiety, and in their communities of practice are able to nurture relationships among classmates.

Included among some of the challenges of cooperative learning are accounting for individual learning styles, personality differences, and possible over-reliance on the first language (Crandall, 1999). Further, virtually any models that feature *collaboration*—in which students and teachers work together to pursue goals—promote communities of learners that cut across the usual hierarchies of students and teachers, necessitating a cautious approach in cultures with strong power distance norms between teachers and students (Oxford, 1997, p. 443).

It almost goes without saying that communicative classrooms by definition are interactive. The extent to which *intended* messages are received is a factor of both one's production and the listener's/reader's reception. Most meaning, in a semantic sense, is a product of negotiation, of give and take, as interlocutors attempt to communicate. Thus, the communicative purpose of language compels us to create opportunities for genuine *interaction* in the classroom. An interactive course exhibits the following features, to name a few:

Characteristics of Interactive Language Teaching

- doing a significant amount of pair work and group work
- receiving authentic language input in real-world contexts
- producing language for genuine, meaningful communication
- performing classroom tasks that prepare Ss for actual language use beyond the classroom
- practicing oral communication through the give and take and spontaneity of actual conversations
- writing to and for real audiences, not contrived ones

The theoretical foundations of interactive learning lie in what Long (1985, 1996) described as the **interaction hypothesis** of second language acquisition (see *PLLT*, Chapter 10). Long and others have pointed out the importance of input *and* output in the development of language. As learners interact with each other through oral and written discourse, their communicative abilities are enhanced.

Another example of a collaborative approach was found in **whole language education,** which emphasized the interconnections between oral and written language. Interpretations and variations of this model were so divergent, however, that its impact soon waned (Rigg, 1991; Edelsky, 1993). Nevertheless the model offered three important insights that are worthy of mention.

- Language is not the sum of its many dissectible and discrete parts.
- Integrate the four skills (listening, speaking, reading, and writing).
- Language is a system of social practices that both constrain and liberate.

These insights underscore some key principles of L2 pedagogy. First, L1 acquisition research shows us that children begin perceiving "wholes" (sentences, emotions, intonation patterns) well before "parts." Teachers might therefore help their students attend to such wholes, resisting the temptation to build language only from the bottom up. Second, because the four skills are interrelated, beware of assuming that the skills are easily separable. And finally, in the words of Edelsky (1993, p. 548), whole language education is a perspective "anchored in a vision of an equitable, democratic, diverse society." Part of our job as teachers is to empower our learners to seize their *agency*, and to master whatever social, political, or economic forces might otherwise constrain them.

Classroom Connections

Edelsky (1993) made quite a jump from *whole language* to the *social* nature of language and language learning. In your learning of an L2, to what extent do you feel that you learned a "system of social practices"? If so, were you aware of such learning at the time? What are some examples of *social practices* that you as a teacher might include in your curriculum? How can you as a teacher help your students to be *empowered* through learning an L2?

SPECIFIC APPROACHES

All the above general approaches may to a great extent be implemented in any language course regardless of context. In the next few descriptions of CLT-based approaches in this chapter, we will focus on models that are more limited in their applicability and feasibility. Certain conditions must apply in order to render them relevant and viable. Some contextual constraints are age-related or institutionally determined, others vary by course goals or proficiency, and still others are embedded in sociopolitical and sociocultural constraints. Let's look at some of these options.

Content-Based Language Teaching

> Yaling is a Chinese child of eight who completed second grade in China and now, as her parents have just moved to Japan, she finds herself in a new country learning a new language. There is no special Japanese language class in Yaling's new elementary school in Osaka, so her parents place her in a regular third grade class, hoping that her intelligence, determination, and outgoing personality will pay off. Ultimately, Yaling manages, with a fair amount of difficulty in the first few months, to learn third grade subject matter as she simultaneously acquires Japanese.

Yaling was lucky. Parental support and better than average intelligence propelled her along. Others might have benefitted from some form of **content-based language teaching** (CBLT) to assist in the process of concurrently learning subject matter and a new language. CBLT can come in many forms and interpretations, and sometimes the definitions and boundaries among CBLT and its "cousins" are blurred by "competing claims in the literature" (Brinton, 2013, p. 1). So, it may be easier to think of CBLT as "an umbrella term for a multifaceted approach to second or foreign language teaching that...shares a common point of departure—the integration of language teaching aims with content instruction" Snow (2014, p. 439).

More specifically, according to Brinton, Snow, and Wesche (1989, p. vii), CBLT refers to "the concurrent study of language and subject matter, with the form and sequence of language presentation dictated by content material." Such an approach contrasts sharply with many practices in which language skills are taught virtually in isolation from substantive content. When language becomes the medium to convey informational content of interest and relevance to the learner, then learners are pointed toward matters of meaningful concern. Language takes on its appropriate role as a vehicle for accomplishing a set of content goals.

A surge of interest in CBLT in the late twentieth century resulted in widespread adoption of content-based curricula around the world, as chronicled by Brinton (2003), Stoller (2004), Schleppegrell et al. (2004), and others. Content-based classrooms have the potential of yielding an increase in intrinsic motivation and empowerment, because students are focused on subject matter that is important to their lives. And as they center their interest on mastery of subject matter, they are concurrently acquiring linguistic ability.

The challenges of CBLT range from a demand for a whole new genre of textbooks and other materials to the training of language teachers to teach the concepts and skills of various disciplines, professions, and occupations. Allowing the subject matter to control the selection and sequencing of language items means that you have to view your teaching from an entirely different perspective. You are first and foremost teaching science or math, for example, and secondarily teaching language. So you may have to become a double expert! Some team-teaching models of content-based teaching alleviate this potential drawback by linking subject-matter teachers and language teachers. Such an undertaking is what Brinton, Snow, and Wesche (1989) describe as an **adjunct model** of content-based instruction.

Can content-based teaching take place at all levels of proficiency, even beginning levels? While it is possible to argue, for example, that certain basic survival skills are themselves content-based and that a beginning level class could therefore be content-based, such an argument extends the content-based notion beyond its normal bounds. CBLT usually pertains to academic or occupational instruction over an *extended* period of time at intermediate-to-advanced proficiency levels. Talking about renting an apartment one day, shopping the next, getting a driver's license the next, and so on, is certainly useful and meaningful for beginners, but would more appropriately fall into the category of a *task-based* or *theme-based* curriculum, as discussed above.

Classroom Connections

At the beginning of this section, Yaling's adjustment at the age of 8 into a Japanese elementary school system was described. If you were her third-grade teacher, what kinds of assistance could you give to Yaling in her first few weeks of the school year? How might you involve parents, technology, or other students in your quest to help her to master the *content* of the curriculum?

Immersion and Sheltered Models

Over the years CBLT has been linked with several related models of education that, because of their uniqueness, deserve separate mention here.

Immersion models of language teaching began half a century ago in Canada and the United States with programs that sought more intensive instruction in French and Spanish, respectively, for native-English-speaking children in elementary school. Immersion models typically provide the majority of subject-matter content through the medium of the L2, thus the name "immersion." According to years of documentation (Tedick, Christian, & Fortune, 2011), immersion programs have been highly successful, with children performing on a par with their monolingual counterparts and becoming functional bilinguals by the end of elementary school. Immersion models have since sprung up in other countries: China, Hong Kong, Hungary, Finland, and Spain, among others (Snow, 2014).

Sheltered models of education involve "the deliberate separation of L2 students from native speakers of the target language for the purpose of content instruction" (Snow, 2014, p. 441). For L2 students whose language proficiency is not quite able to handle subject-matter content in the L1 of the educational system, they provide opportunities for them to master content standards with added language assistance. In such cases, the teacher of a school subject (say, science or history) modifies the presentation of material to help L2 learners process the content. Pre-teaching difficult vocabulary, suggesting reading comprehension strategies, explaining certain grammatical structures, and offering form-focused feedback are among techniques that have shown to be helpful (Echevarria, Vogt, & Short, 2012).

Bilingual Education

Among the multiplicity of communicative approaches to L2 instruction that have appeared over the last several decades is a cluster of models all of which may be classified as bilingual approaches. However, that "cluster" contains so many variations that some caution is in order, lest bilingual education be thought of as a single approach.

McGroarty and Fitzsimmons-Doolan (2014) define **bilingual education** as an approach in which "two languages are used as media of classroom instruction for the same group of students so that students receive some of their instruction in one language and some in the other, with the proportion of each language varying according to program type, instructional goals, and various contextual influences" (p. 503).

Researchers and practitioners alike are careful to explain the many forms that bilingual education has taken in elementary school, secondary school, and higher education, as well as in the context of language-majority and language-minority students (Kroon & Vallen, 2010; Garcia, 2013). Options at the elementary level, for example, can range from *early-exit*, or *transitional* programs (students are placed for a limited number of years in a bilingual classroom, until they are *mainstreamed*), to *developmental*, or *maintenance* programs (the child's L1 is maintained throughout the duration of the program). At the higher education level, language for specific purposes (see below) and content-based immersion programs may also fall into the category of bilingual education.

Worldwide, bilingual education has been shown to be effective in many contexts (Baker, 2011), in spite of the many forms and models it has taken over the years. Unfortunately, in the United States bilingual education has been highly politicized, and with inaccurate data reported by self-interests, "often based on ignorance and misunderstanding" (McGroarty & Fitzsimmons-Doolan, 2014, p. 513), it has faced strong opposition. Elsewhere there is better news. The Council of Europe's Common European Framework of Reference (CEFR), for example, representing 48 countries, supports multilingualism as a group right, a means for political cohesion, and cross-cultural understanding (Baetens Beardsmore, 2009; Huhta, 2013). We'll return to this issue in Chapter 8.

Workplace and Vocational L2 Instruction

The last couple of decades of the twentieth century saw a surge of interest in language instruction within the context of the workplace: factories, restaurants, hotels, retail stores, and offices, to name a few examples. **Workplace L2 instruction** offers distinct advantages by tailoring language to the specific linguistic needs of carrying out one's duties "on the job." Workers engaged in housekeeping services in hotels, for example, can in an hour or two a week of classroom instruction learn to comprehend basic vocabulary (e.g., towel, sheet, pillow), useful phrases ("I need an extra towel"), produce appropriate responses ("I'll bring an extra pillow"), and even read simple messages left by hotel guests ("Please repair the air conditioning") (Holloway, 2013).

CLASSROOM CONNECTIONS

You have no doubt experienced moments when a worker in a hotel you're staying in says something (maybe in a language you don't know, or maybe just in your L1, but with an accent that's hard to understand) you cannot decipher. Judging from those experiences, what are some words or phrases that you might teach those workers in order to communicate with customers?

Administrative challenges are sometimes an obstacle in that businesses are asked to provide instruction as part of the paid contract of a worker. Employees themselves may need to be convinced of the benefits of going to classes. And of course, instructors need to be paid and classroom space provided at the job site. Offsetting such potential obstacles are the ultimate "soft skills" (etiquette, customer relations) acquired by workers, which has been shown to raise the self-efficacy of employees as well as the company's reputation for service (Johns & Price, 2014).

Workplace programs intersect with what has come to be known as **vocational L2 instruction**, all of which may be subsumed under the category or languages for special purposes (see the next section). Many vocational programs differ in that they are part of an adult education program that provides pre-employment language training, and this typically includes basic academic language skills. Because students are anticipating entering the job market, interviewing and other skills for gaining employment are included in the curriculum. In English-speaking countries, **Vocational English as a Second Language (VESL)** courses typically combine basic literacy education with specialized occupational contexts, are geared toward a single occupation or multiple occupations, and are gauged for several levels of language ability (Johns & Price, 2014).

Languages for Specific Purposes

Workplace and vocational approaches to L2 instruction are forms of what is generically referred to as **languages for specific purposes (LSP)**, or in the case of English, **English for specific purposes (ESP)** (Master, 2005). This genre of L2 instruction is commonly associated with higher education, and has offshoots in **English for academic purposes (EAP)** (Hamp-Lyons, 2011), as well as in specialized English courses in, for example, the fields of science and technology (EST), business and economics (EBE), and medicine (EMP), in the case of international students studying in English-speaking countries.

You have no doubt experienced differences in the use of language, especially in vocabulary choice and discourse conventions, depending on the subject matter involved. A laboratory report of a chemistry experiment carries with it certain expectations in form and function, and those often bear little resemblance to a marketing analysis for a manufacturing company. Once learners have progressed beyond intermediate stages in their L2, they are usually both prepared and motivated to accomplish tasks in a chosen vocation or profession.

In the words of Johns (2010, p. 318), "in LSP, the *authentic* world must be brought to the students, and they must learn to interact with the language as it is spoken or written in target situations." Those target situations are the specific disciplines being pursued by students. Some of the advantages of LSP may be obvious, notably, acquiring knowledge and skills of one's chosen field of study along with developing the linguistic ability needed for such an accomplishment. A less immediately obvious advantage lies in the concept of *identity* (to be discussed further in the next two chapters). "LSP students' identities are both negotiated and developed as they increase their participation in particular communities of practice" (Paltridge & Starfield, 2011, p. 107). Such a view provides a richer conceptualization of students as potential members of a larger community, learning to participate more significantly in shifting power relationships (Belcher & Lukkarila, 2011).

As LSP courses and models have evolved over the last five decades, several important offshoots of LSP have emerged. The growth of research on *genre* analysis (the study of linguistic and discourse variations in text types) has led to **genre-based pedagogy** (Paltridge, 2001; Johns, 2002, 2010; Hyland, 2004; Tardy, 2013). Such an approach could present students with common genres in a wide variety of professional or occupational communities: e-mails, memos, letters, minutes of meetings, research reports, abstracts, texting, and blogging, for example. More specifically, genre-based pedagogy focuses students on discipline-specific genres, such as laboratory reports, travel brochures, financial reports, drug dosage precautions, essays, or newspaper articles.

Classroom Connections

Let's say you have been asked to teach a unit to advanced L2 students in a marketing course on "writing travel advertisements." What are some of the words, phrases, and discourse styles that you would need to include, in order for your students to be able to construct such a genre?

Corpus-Based Teaching

Let's look at one more approach, which could easily be subsumed under LSP, but because of the widespread applications of corpus research, it deserves a special category.

Corpus analysis (also known as **corpus linguistics**) is a computerized approach to linguistic research that stores and analyzes written and/or spoken texts in electronic form (Conrad, 2005). Corpora can be looked at in terms of syntax, lexicon, discourse, along with varieties of language, genres, dialects, styles, and registers (Johns, 2002; Silberstein, 2011). In written form, corpora can be classified into academic, journalistic, or literary prose, among others, and spoken corpora have been classified into conversations of many kinds: everyday conversation among friends, theater/television scripts, speeches, and even classroom language (Biber & Conrad, 2001; Conrad, 2005; McEnery & Xiao, 2011).

Within the broad scope of LSP, **corpus-based teaching** has added many advantages for curriculum and textbook writers as well as teachers in their daily methodological routines. Among the many corpora available today, subcategories include genres such as academic presentations, lectures, interviews, and textbooks, along with study group discussions, office hour conversations, and academic word lists (Paltridge & Starfield, 2011; Keck, 2013). This kind of research has clear benefits as it provides at one's fingertips (literally!) hundreds of millions of instances of words, phrases, and collocations all classified within a linguistic context of co-occurring words before and after the target item. At times social or discourse *contexts* may be difficult to discern, but recent developments have even been able to add certain contextual features into corpus studies (Paltridge & Starfield, 2011).

The benefits of corpus analysis extend well beyond LSP. Curriculum designers and materials developers in all contexts have access to *naturally* occurring language subcategorized into specific varieties, styles, registers, and genres. In lieu of "inventing" possibly inauthentic phrases, collocations, and sentences to illustrate linguistic specifications, these materials can present "real" language (McEnery & Xiao, 2011). A case in point is Walker's (2012) textbook on academic English vocabulary, which is based on the standard corpus-based

Academic Word List in which lexical and grammatical factors are linked and vocabulary presented in *context*. Similarly, Chapelle and Jamieson (2008) have offered useful "tips" that teachers can use in incorporating corpus research into language classrooms. (See Chapter 12 in this book for further discussion of the use of technology in L2 classrooms, including the use of corpus data.)

Classroom Connections

Log onto the *Longman Spoken and Written English Corpus* pearsonlongman.com/Dictionaries/corpus/index.html and look up some entries of your choice, but try some less common words to limit the number of instances. You could look up "genre" or "immersion," for example. Using the collocations you find there, design a few fill-in-the-blank exercises for intermediate to advanced students of English.

A methodological approach that has been considerably buoyed by the recent surge of corpus analysis is Michael Lewis's (1993, 1997, 2000) **Lexical Approach**. Building on the hypothesis that the essential building blocks of language are words and word combinations, Lewis maintained that one can do almost anything in a language with vocabulary, and therefore emphasized lexical phrases, or **collocations**, as central to a language course. Phrases like *not so good, how's it going,* and *I'll be in touch* are useful patterns for a learner to internalize along with predicable collocations like *do my homework, . . .the laundry, . . . a good job*, and *make. . . some coffee, . . . my bed, . . . a promise.*

A lexical emphasis has some obvious advantages. It remains somewhat unclear, however, how such an approach differs from other approaches (which certainly allow for a focus on lexical units). Nor is it clear how "an endless succession of phrase-book utterances, 'all chunks but no pineapple,'. . . can be incorporated into the understanding of a language system" (Harmer, 2001, p. 92).

In this chapter we have presented most of the major communicative approaches being used worldwide today. As you read further in this book, and as we focus more specifically on classroom lessons and activities, we'll be illustrating many of these approaches in concrete examples.

Meanwhile, a word of warning: Virtually all of the approaches and models described here might appear to be "buzzwords" or even "designer" models, in the same way that methods were depicted in the previous chapter. We claim that is *not* the case, however, because the approaches described here are the product of well-researched, time-tested, globally relevant methodological practices. In the next chapter, we invite you to discover why we think so, as we present basic *foundational principles* of language teaching on which each of the models can be evaluated and appraised. See for yourself!

FOR THE TEACHER: ACTIVITIES (A) & DISCUSSION (D)

Note: For each of the "Classroom Connections" in this chapter, you may wish to turn them into individual or pair-work discussion questions.

1. **(D)** Ask your students for concrete examples of the dysfunction of dichotomizing *theory* and *practice*. What's wrong with trained, expert researchers carrying out studies on SLA even if they have never taught in an L2 classroom? How is a teacher supposed to carry out systematic research if he or she has never been trained to do so? How might researchers and teachers productively cooperate?
2. **(D)** Review the notion that one's overall *approach* to language teaching can directly lead to curriculum design and lesson techniques, without necessarily subscribing to a *method*, as the term was used in the previous chapter. Ask your class how they might now understand the term *methodology* to refer to pedagogical *practice* in general? Alternatively, ask them to verbalize the difference between *method* and *methodology*.
3. **(A)** Divide your class into groups of 3 or 4 each and ask them to share any "horror" stories they have experienced in L2 classes that were (like the example of "Gary" on page 45) so authoritarian, strict, scary, or intimidating that they stifled learner-centered spontaneity and creativity. Then ask them to suggest how they might have *changed* that climate if they were teaching that class today. Ask for brief group oral reports of a few of their stories.
4. **(A)** In pairs, have students write down a few phrases to describe each of the following *general* CLT approaches:
   - learner-centered instruction
   - task-based language teaching
   - theme-based instruction
   - experiential/project-based learning
   - strategies-based instruction

   Ask them to share with their partner some examples from personal experience (learning or teaching) of approaches they have just defined. Then solicit a few examples to be reported to the class as a whole.
5. **(A)** In the same pairs, assign to each pair one of the 6 different *specific approaches* discussed in the last part of this chapter. Then have them brainstorm a few phrases to describe their approach, write their findings on the board, and provide a brief oral explanation to the rest of the class. The purpose of this activity is simply to review the many approaches covered in the

chapter. If any students have learned or taught an L2 within any of the models, ask them to briefly describe and evaluate their experience.

6. **(A)** In anticipation of Chapter 4, in which readers will encounter eight principles of language learning and teaching, ask students to brainstorm, in small groups, some assertions about language learning that one might include in a description of an approach to language teaching. For example, what would they say about the issues of age and acquisition, inhibitions, how to best store something in memory, and the relationship of intelligence to second language success? Direct the groups to come up with axioms or principles that would be relatively stable across many acquisition contexts. Then, as a whole class, list these on the board.

FOR YOUR FURTHER READING

Lee, J., & VanPatten, B. (2003). *Making communicative language teaching happen* (2nd ed.). New York, NY: McGraw-Hill.

A practical resource offering a comprehensive view of classrooms operating under the principles of CLT. Topics include teaching listening comprehension, grammar, spoken language, reading, and writing, all within a communicative framework.

Nunan, D. (2014). Task-based teaching and learning. In M. Celce-Murcia, D. Brinton, & A. Snow (Eds.), *Teaching English as a second or foreign language* (4th ed., pp. 455–470). Boston, MA: National Geographic Learning.

A concise summary of basic concepts of TBLT, its conceptual underpinnings, and a variety of practical classroom examples of TBLT in action.

Huhta, A. (2013). Common European framework of reference. In C. Chapelle (Ed.), *The encyclopedia of applied linguistics* (pp. 740–746). London, UK: Blackwell Publishing Ltd.

A concise introduction to the widely used Common European Framework of Reference (CEFR). This chapter is a synopsis of the history of CEFR, its functional, communicative basis, and recent research on its applications in numerous countries and contexts.

Celce-Murcia, M., Brinton, D., & Snow, A. M. (Eds.). (2014). *Teaching English as a second or foreign language* (4th ed.). Boston, MA: National Geographic Learning.

Most of the CLT approaches described in this chapter are explained in some detail across the chapters of this volume. A useful guide to research summaries, practical applications, and bibliographic references in each approach.

CHAPTER 4

TEACHING BY PRINCIPLES

Questions for Reflection

- What is meant by a *principle* of SLA? How do principles underlie an overall *approach* to language teaching?
- What are some of the key principles of SLA (eight are suggested in this chapter)?
- Among the eight principles, what are some related concepts or constructs that also form foundations for your teaching?
- What are some practical *implications* and *applications* of each of the eight principles?
- How would one prioritize the eight principles? How does one's context of teaching and learning determine which principles are more (or less) applicable?

So far in this book you have observed a classroom in action, examined a century of language-teaching history, and taken a look at major constructs that undergird current practices in language teaching. In the process, you already may have felt a little bewildered by the complexity of our profession. You may be asking questions like, "With all the options available, how can I make informed choices about what to do in the particular context of my classroom?" or, "How can I put into practice a cautious, enlightened eclectic approach?"

In order to sort through those questions and find some plausible answers, it's important for you to consider elements that are at the core of language pedagogy: foundational principles that can form the building blocks for your own theoretical rationale. For teachers, such principles comprise their *approach* to language teaching (discussed in Chapters 2 and 3).

In *Principles of Language Learning and Teaching* (Brown, 2014, hereafter referred to as *PLLT*), it was noted that the last few decades of research produced a complex storehouse of information on second language acquisition (SLA) and teaching. There are still many mysteries about SLA that lead us to be *cautious*, but there is a great deal that we do know about the process. We can be quite certain that among all the *eclectic* pedagogical options available, many of a teacher's choices can be grounded in established principles of language learning and teaching, and thereby be *enlightened*. You will be better able to see why you have chosen to use a particular classroom technique (or set of techniques), to carry it out with confidence, and to evaluate its utility after the fact.

You may be thinking that such a principled approach to language teaching sounds only logical. How could one proceed otherwise? Well, we have seen many a novice language teacher who would simply like to have "101 recipes for Monday morning teaching." Unfortunately, this sort of quick-fix approach to teacher education will not give you that all-important ability to comprehend when to use a technique, with whom it will work, how to adapt it for your audience, or how to judge its effectiveness.

We'll now take a broad, sweeping look at eight overarching principles of second language learning that interact with sound practice and on which your teaching can be based. These principles form the core of an approach to language teaching, as discussed in the previous chapter. There is no magic about the number eight. The previous edition of *Teaching by Principles* described twelve principles; Rod Ellis (2014) named ten; Tom Scovel (2001) cited five; but Bernard Spolsky (1989) named seventy! We have chosen eight for the sake of simplicity and inclusiveness.

Before we embark on a description of the eight principles, a special note is warranted for readers and instructors who have used the previous editions of *Teaching by Principles*. Times have changed. New findings and new approaches demand reconceptualizations. So, in this edition, not only will you find the number of principles reduced to eight, but you will also see some new concepts that must now be included in a comprehensive framework for teaching additional languages. All of the "old" principles are still here, but many are incorporated into broader, more powerful constructs.

The ordering of the eight principles is not random. The rationale is to move from the more cognitive psychological and individual principles to transactions of the self in relation to others, and finally to the learner as an agent within a cultural milieu. Of course, no single principle is discretely contained in a "box," unaffected by one or more of the principles. All eight categories have areas of overlap with their counterparts.

A further note: It may be helpful, as you are reading, to check referenced sections of *PLLT* (Brown, 2014) to refresh your memory of certain terms and background information.

AUTOMATICITY

John Hersch is an accomplished pianist. He has played in night clubs and orchestras, and most recently accompanies a 120-voice chorus. When he looks at a musical score and prepares to play it, he doesn't have the cognitive or physical time to cogitate on every note and marking. He not only takes in multiple bits of musical information simultaneously, but he also "translates" that information into movement of fingers across the keyboard. The result? Beautiful, harmonic sounds of piano strings. But when John was first learning to play the piano, all that instantaneous input and output was by no means **automatic**. That complex ability developed over time with hours of daily practice.

Learning music and learning language have much in common, not the least of which is that both require the development of automaticity for successful learning. Children learning additional languages are classic examples of developing automatic skills "naturally," in untutored contexts (see *PLLT*, Chapter 3) with little or no analysis of the **forms** (e.g., grammar, phonology, vocabulary) of language. Through an inductive process of exposure to language input and opportunity to experiment interactively with output, they appear to learn languages without overtly noticing language forms. They do, however, focus very effectively on the **function** (meaning) of their linguistic input and output.

For adults, **automaticity** is sometimes impeded by overanalysis of language forms, which become too focal (DeKeyser & Criado, 2013; McLaughlin, 1990), too much the center of attention. In order to cognitively manage the incredible complexity and quantity of language systems, they need to develop strategies of high-speed, automatic processing in which language forms are on the periphery of attention. For pianist John Hersch, his remarkable ability was the result of, in his words, "not *thinking about* the music so much, and just playing the piano *for fun*."

For L2 learning, the Principle of Automaticity highlights the importance of meaningful use of the new language through communicative interaction; efficient movement away from a capacity-limited control (McLaughlin, 1990) of a few bits and pieces to a relatively unlimited automatic mode of processing language, often referred to as **fluency**; and an optimal degree of focusing on forms of language that encourages learners to **notice** errors in their output, utilize a teacher's feedback, and, when appropriate, to respond in some way (Leow, 2013; Schmidt, 1990).

The Principle of Automaticity may be summarized as follows:

> Efficient second language learning involves a timely progression from *control* of a few language forms to fluid and error-free *automatic* processing (in both production and comprehension) of a relatively unlimited number of language forms. Development of fluency—usually through extensive long-term practice—is aided by a primary focus on meaning, purpose, and interaction, and a secondary but optimal amount of attention to language forms.

Notice that this principle does *not* say that the road to automaticity is paved with unceasing, relentless communicative activities in which form-focus is a "no-no." In fact, adults can especially benefit greatly from a modicum of focal processing of rules, definitions, and guided practice (DeKeyser & Criado, 2013). The other side of the coin is that adults might take a lesson from children by speedily overcoming our propensity to pay too much focal attention to the bits and pieces of language and by effectively moving language forms to the periphery, using language in authentic contexts for meaningful purposes. In so doing, automaticity is built more efficiently.

What does this principle, which commonly applies to adult instruction, mean to you as a teacher? Here are some practical possibilities:

Guidelines for Maintaining Automaticity in L2 Classrooms

1. Make sure that a major proportion of classroom activity is focused on the use of language for purposes that are as authentic as a classroom context will permit. Examples include task-based activity, group and pair work, and involvement in topics that are relevant to students' lives.
2. Practice exercises and explanations dealing with grammar, vocabulary, phonology, discourse, and other forms have a place in the adult classroom, but don't overwhelm your students with a focus on form. Short, five-minute grammar-focus exercises, for example, may be more helpful than long explanations or "lectures" from you.
3. When you focus your students on form, your goal is to help them to notice forms, to modify or correct errors when appropriate, and ultimately to incorporate that information into their language use. Error correction, for example, is more effective if students are made aware of an error and/or are encouraged to self-correct.
4. Fluency activities, in which you deliberately do not focus on forms, may help students to attend to meaning or to accomplishing a task, and to "unblock" their overattention to form. A classic writing example is freewriting, in which students are asked to write about a topic of interest with virtually no attention, at this stage, to correctness.
5. Automaticity is a slow and sometimes tedious process; therefore, you need to exercise patience with students as you slowly help them to achieve fluency. Don't expect your students to become chatterboxes overnight in their new language!

TRANSFER

Doug had been a tennis player for over two decades when one of his friends invited him to play racquetball. "It should be an easy sport for you," suggested his buddy, reasoning that both are racquet sports. In the first few games, Doug found that indeed certain abilities transferred relatively quickly: meeting the ball squarely, following through, positioning feet correctly, being ready for your opponent's next play. Even some of the strategic aspects of the game, figuring out the other guy's weaknesses and playing to one's own strengths, transferred positively. But there was some negative transfer: the side wall kept getting in the way, the ball bounced quite differently, and playing off three and sometimes four walls was disconcerting.

The Principle of **Transfer** plays a dominant role in learning an additional language. A historical look at research on language learning in the middle of the twentieth century reveals an obsession with transfer, especially from the first to the second language, known as **interlingual transfer** or **interference**. Some went so far as to claim that any difficulty in learning an L2 could be *equated* to the differences between a learner's first and second languages (Banathy, Trager, & Waddle, 1966).

It was not long before evidence mounted against the *predictability* of interference (Whitman & Jackson, 1972). Learner language manifested enough variation to dispute such claims of certainty, and further, when three or four or more languages were in question, the task of predicting became impossible. More recently, partly because transfer can work *both* ways, the SLA field has been using **cross-linguistic influence** as a more appropriate term to capture the relationship of two *or more* languages in contact (Jarvis & Pavlenko, 2008; Jarvis, 2013). The difference between today's emphasis on *influence*, rather than prediction, is important (Oostendorp, 2012) to capture the range of syntactic, lexical, discourse, and pragmatic interference that can occur.

In the 1960s and 1970s, **intralingual transfer** (within the L2), also known as **overgeneralization**, became a hot topic, especially in analyzing sources of error in learners' output, and in describing **interlanguage** of learners. These basic tenets of human learning undergirded a massive stockpile of research and helped propel SLA research into new unexplored territory. (See *PLLT*, Chapter 9.)

But strictly *linguistic* transfer is, in some ways, only a small piece of the psychology of learning an L2. Transfer is an all-encompassing principle that reaches across physical, cognitive, affective, and sociocultural domains. Virtually all learning is the product of transfer. We can define the term simply as the application of knowledge, skill, or emotion acquired in one situation to new situations. And transfer can be positive (advancing toward an objective) or negative (interfering with such advancement).

Closely related to the principle of transfer is a recent emphasis in cognitive psychology on what has come to be known as **embodied cognition** (Damasio, 2003; Gibbs, 2006). From this perspective, an organism's sensorimotor capacities, body, and environment play crucial roles in the development of cognitive (and linguistic) abilities. In other words, we are not merely thinking and feeling organisms, but our physical interactions with the world—our motor systems—are large determiners of the extent and diversity of our cognitive and linguistic competence. Embodied cognition offers an enlightening re-focus on the physical abilities that so preoccupied behavioral psychologists back at the turn of the twentieth century.

James (2006, 2010, 2012) demonstrated the importance of transfer in a number of academic contexts: general language skills to subskills (e.g., writing in general to writing for research purposes); certain skills (e.g., reading) to others (e.g., writing); earlier language courses to specific subject matter areas (e.g., engineering, business); and, of course, transfer from the classroom to real-world contexts. Likewise, **content-based instruction** (Snow, 2014) is successful because students are immersed in tasks and skills that are relevant to their lives and/or livelihood. Research on **dynamic systems theory** (DST), reminds teachers of the many, complex interconnections that learners make as their language abilities grow (Larsen-Freeman, 2012), all the result of transfer as learners connect one learning moment with another.

Half a century ago, cognitive psychologists revolutionized educational psychology by stressing the importance of **meaningful learning** (as opposed to **rote learning**) for long-term retention (Ausubel, 1963). That is, new material to be learned that is "attached" to existing cognitive structure (associated) will be more efficiently lodged. Transfer underlies all meaningful learning. For example, if a task in a group activity puts learners into a familiar context (such as the movies in Chapter 1), new grammatical, lexical, and discourse forms will be more easily embedded into students' L2 competence. And in learning to read and write, **schema theory** encourages students to relate existing knowledge, of both content and skills, to new material.

The Principle of Transfer may be summarized as follows:

> Because L2 learners naturally seek to transfer existing knowledge/ability to new knowledge or ability, efficient (and successful) learning will result from a process of making meaningful associations between a learner's existing knowledge, skills, and emotions and the new material to be learned.

Here are some classroom implications of the Principle of Transfer:

Guidelines for Maximizing Transfer in L2 Classrooms

Capitalize on the power of transfer by anchoring new material to students' existing knowledge and ability. If topics and contexts for tasks are associated with something students already know, then linguistic features will be more easily learned.

1. Become acquainted with your students' backgrounds, interests, personalities, occupations, hobbies, likes and dislikes, and ground classroom activities on those individual characteristics.
2. When introducing new grammar, vocabulary, or discourse features, review previously learned material on which the new material is based through brainstorming or clustering activities. Use graphic organizers (e.g., charts, diagrams, concept maps) to help students see the relevance to the new material.

3. As you teach one skill area—say, listening—connect what students are learning to other skills such as speaking or reading.
4. Avoid the pitfalls of rote learning. Don't overdo grammar explanations, drills, activities that have no clear purpose, and tasks that are unclearly understood by students. Base your teaching as much as possible on content that learners can identify with, as opposed to grammar-driven teaching.

REWARD

Here's a story about an experiment in the power of rewards (Kohn, 1990). Teenage girls were given the task of teaching some games to younger children. One group of "teachers" was simply given the teaching task, with no mention of a reward to be given. The other group was told that they would receive a free ticket to the latest "hot" movie for successfully completing the task. Results: The first group did their task faster, with greater success, and reported more pleasure in doing so than the second group!

Skinner (1938) and others demonstrated the strength of rewards in both animal and human behavior (see *PLLT*, Chapter 4). Virtually everything we do is predicated on the anticipation of a reward, whether physical, mental, emotional, or social. So what can we make of the above example? Does it contradict the reward principle? Not if you consider the *source* of rewards.

In Kohn's (1990) study, the first group of girls reported an **intrinsic motive** to succeed. They simply wanted the pleasure and satisfaction of having their young kids learn the game. No one promised them anything, and their internal drive to succeed shone through. The second group reported being more focused on getting the movie ticket, that is, on an **extrinsic motive** administered by someone else, and less on the results of their instruction (see *PLLT*, Chapter 6).

Psychologists (e.g., Maslow, 1970) and linguists (e.g., Dörnyei & Ushioda, 2011) have for many decades acknowledged not only the power of rewards, but also the power of intrinsically driven behavior. Classroom techniques have a much greater chance for success if they are self-rewarding in the perception of the learner: The learners perform the task because it is fun, interesting, useful, or challenging, and only secondarily because they anticipate some cognitive or affective rewards from the teacher.

The implications of intrinsically and extrinsically driven behaviors for the classroom are more complex than they might seem. At one end of the spectrum is the effectiveness of a teacher's praise for correct responses ("Very good, Maria!" "Nice job!"), grades or "gold stars" to indicate success, smiles and affirmation from classmates, and other public recognition. At the other end, students need to see clearly *why* they are performing something along with its relevance to their long-term goals in learning, so that they are not dependent on external rewards. The ultimate goal is for students to engage in **self-determination**—to *choose* to make an effort because of what they will gain, in either the short or long run (Deci & Ryan, 2002).

The Reward Principle can be stated as follows:

> Human beings are universally driven to act, or "behave," in anticipation of a reward. The most powerful rewards are those that are intrinsically motivated: The behavior stems from needs, wants, or desires within oneself and is self-rewarding.

The key to making the reward principle work in the language classroom is to create an optimal blend of extrinsic (teacher-administered) rewards, especially for the minute-by-minute routine of a classroom, and intrinsically-driven rewards that become embedded in a student's journey toward language proficiency. How do you do that? Consider the following tips:

Guidelines for Implementing the Reward Principle in L2 Classrooms

1. Provide an optimal degree of immediate verbal praise, encouragement, and acknowledgment of "good work" as a short-term reward, just enough to keep them confident in their ability.
2. Capitalize on the energy of cooperative group work in which students are given opportunities to communicate with each other and ultimately to feel proud of their accomplishments. Encourage students to reward each other with compliments and supportive action.
3. Display enthusiasm and excitement yourself in the classroom. If you are dull, lifeless, bored, and have low energy, you can be almost sure that it will be contagious.
4. Encourage learners to see the intrinsic, long-term rewards in learning an L2 by pointing out what they can do with the language, the benefits of being able to use it, jobs that require it, and so on. As you utilize content-based activities, you will help students to become linguistically involved with interesting, relevant subject matter.
5. Give your students some choices in types of activities, content, or subject matter so that they feel some "ownership" of their language development. Encourage students to discover for themselves certain principles and rules, rather than simply giving them an answer.

SELF-REGULATION

> When Kathy accepted a two-year English teaching position in Turkey, she made a point, in the three months before relocating from her home in the United States, of studying as much Turkish as possible. In an online short course, she learned a lot "about" Turkish and managed to internalize a couple of dozen survival phrases. Upon arrival in Ankara, she was pleased that she could understand and speak a few phrases. But that didn't last long. She very soon felt a bit "lost" in everyday Turkish, and decided to benefit from her previous learning of Spanish (in Bolivia) and Japanese. She was a highly organized person and determined to make the best of her residence in Turkey. She made elaborate plans, set daily and weekly goals, and monitored her progress. By the end of the first year, her self-determination had paid off. She was comfortable in most conversations and was able to read Turkish newspapers. Success!

Four decades ago, Rubin (1975) named fourteen characteristics of "good" language learners. They all placed responsibility on the learner to take action, to "take charge" of their learning, to create opportunities for using the language, to utilize a variety of strategies, and to organize information about language. All of this advice still holds! Oxford (2011) noted that the key to successful language learning is **self-regulation**, "deliberate goal-directed attempts to manage and control efforts to learn the L2" (p. 12). One of the key foundation stones of effective L2 pedagogy today is to create a climate in which learners develop **autonomy**, "the capacity to control one's learning" (Benson, 2001, p. 290), and self-regulation is cited as a key ingredient of autonomy (Benson, 2007).

Such an approach is a far cry from the days when students entered a classroom, sat down dutifully at their desks, and waited in silence for the teacher to tell them what to do. Worse, those directives might have been to translate a passage, memorize a rule, or repeat a dialogue. Today, autonomy is now almost universally manifested in the classroom in the form of allowing learners to do things like setting personal goals, developing awareness of strategic options, initiating oral production, solving problems in small groups, and practicing language with peers.

Further, thanks to a stockpile of research, our language curricula now recognize the crucial goal of helping learners to use the language *outside* of the classroom. Teachers encourage learners to "take charge" of their own learning, and to chart their own "pathways to success" (Brown, 2002b; Benson, 2003). Such self-regulation of course means that learners are encouraged to take *responsibility* for their learning as they develop a battery of **strategies** for intake, organization, compensation, output, uptake, and social interaction. (See *PLLT*, Chapter 5.) They are proactive *agents* (see Principle 8) in determining their ultimate success.

Is the Principle of Self-Regulation a culturally loaded concept? Does it undermine the authority of the teacher within an educational system that reveres the role of the teacher? Possibly, but Schmenk (2005) suggested using some caution in making assumptions across cultural contexts and to account for "specific cultural backdrops and impacts" (p. 115) in promoting self-regulation and autonomy in the language classroom. Once those accommodations have been appropriately addressed, you should by no means refrain from helping your students to participate actively in linguistic exchange and to continue their learning beyond the walls of your classroom (Crookes, 2013; Norton & Toohey, 2004).

Briefly, the Principle of Self-Regulation states:

> Mastery of an L2 will depend to a great extent on learners' ability to proactively take charge of their learning agenda, to make deliberate, goal-directed efforts to succeed, and to achieve a degree of autonomy that will enable them to continue their journey to success beyond the classroom and the teacher.

Consider the following classroom implications of this principle:

Guidelines for Maximizing Self-Regulation in L2 Classrooms

1. Learners at the beginning stages of a language will be somewhat dependent on the teacher, which is natural and normal. But teachers can help even beginners to develop a sense of autonomy through guided practice, strategy training (Wenden, 2002), and allowing some creative innovation within limited forms.
2. As learners gain confidence and begin to be able to experiment with language, implement activities in the classroom that allow creativity but are not completely beyond the capacity of students.
3. Encourage students to set some goals for their self-regulated learning: a number of vocabulary words to learn (and try out) each week; watch a TV show in English x times every week; speak English outside the classroom x times per week; write a story in English; and so on.
4. As much as possible, help your students to become aware of their own preferences, styles, strengths, and weaknesses, so that they can then take appropriate [self-regulated] action in the form of strategies for better learning. Self-regulation might be aided by checklists, and action can ensue as a choice on the part of the learner.

5. Share with your students what you believe are some of the "secrets" of your success in language learning. What strategies did you use that might also be helpful for your students? You could encourage risk-taking strategies, using nonverbal signals, avoidance tricks, methods for remembering vocabulary, and the list goes on. (See *PLLT*, Chapter 5.)
6. Pair and group work and other interactive activities that are focused on tasks provide opportunities for students to practice language, and to be creative in their choices of vocabulary, grammar, and discourse.
7. Praise students for trying language that's a little beyond their present capacity. Provide feedback on their speech—just enough to be helpful, but not so much that you stifle their creativity
8. Suggest opportunities for students to use their language (gauged for their proficiency level) outside of class. Examples include movies, TV, various social network avenues (Facebook, Twitter, etc.), the Internet, books, magazines, and practicing with each other.

IDENTITY AND INVESTMENT

Heekyeong, born and raised in Korea, started learning English when she was in middle school. By the time she went to college in Korea, she had excelled in English and successfully pursued a major in English. Her identity at this point was still predominantly Korean. She then relocated to Canada, and, after completing her PhD a decade later, lived and worked in Italy, then moved to New York, and now lives and works in Monterey, California. After these experiences, who is this Korean-Canadian-American with a bit of Italian thrown in? What is her cultural and emotional identity? Is there a dominant side of her, or is the "real" Heekyeong comprised of bits and pieces of everywhere she has lived?

In the 1970s the budding field of SLA was introduced to a seminal construct in the form of research on the notion that one's linguistic ability was intertwined with one's sense of worth, self-esteem, and self-efficacy. The explanatory power of **language ego** (Guiora et al., 1972) provided a refreshing new psychological contribution to our understanding of the affective nature of L2 learning, stimulated a diversity of pedagogical applications, and paved the way for several decades of spin-off research. (See *PLLT*, Chapter 6.)

It made perfect sense. Learning an additional language can be threatening for even the most confident learners, and risking making an utter fool of yourself in the L2 takes intestinal fortitude. "You are what you speak," said Frank Smith (1975) over four decades ago, and no one to this day can deny how one's ability to "hold your head up high" is bound up in one's linguistic utterances in *both* an L1 and an L2. We *transact* ourselves chiefly through language.

The concept of language ego also meshed well with an increasing emphasis on emotion and **affect** in SLA research and teaching. The 1970s were revolutionary in the incorporation of the affective domain into theories of SLA (Brown, 1973; Scovel, 1978), as strictly cognitive theories fell short of involving the "whole person" in the enterprise of learning an additional language. Forty years later, we're seeing a refocus on affect and emotion as SLA research experiences an "affective turn" (Pavlenko, 2013) following a period of intense interest in the social dimensions of SLA.

Today the language ego concept is more elegantly refined and expanded into what Norton (2013) and others have described as **identity**: the extent to which L2 learners do not perceive themselves merely as individual entities but, more importantly, as "an integral and constitutive part" (p. 522) of the social world to which they are connected. And even more poignantly, identity research brings to light the dynamics of power—and powerlessness—inherent in every learner's journey toward belonging to a community. Further, while the language ego construct viewed the "real me" as possessing a unique, fixed, constant core, the identity concept "depicts the individual as diverse, contradictory, dynamic, and changing over historical time and social space" (Norton, 2013, p. 522).

Identity, then, is more than just a core concept; it is also a principle that has far-reaching implications. On one end of the spectrum is the call for *self-regulated* learners to accurately understand themselves as they become *aware* of their personal strengths and weaknesses, likes and dislikes, and preferences in **styles** of learning, thinking, acting, and communicating. (See *PLLT*, Chapter 5.)

On the way to the other end of the continuum is a rich and diverse cluster of social factors at work in the L2 learning process, where learners are considered to be members of historical collectivities, who appropriate the practices of a given community. The completeness of learners' participation in that community is partly predicated on their **investment** in the long and often winding road to success (Norton & Gao, 2008). While investment involves commitment and motivation in the traditional sense (Dörnyei & Ushioda, 2011), more importantly, learners are seeking to increase the "value of their cultural capital" (Norton, 2013, p. 3)

An L2 learner's cultural capital will always be a factor of power relationships in a classroom, community, culture, and country (Canagarajah, 2004). Such relationships include race, ethnicity, religion, gender, age, sexual orientation, status, economic wealth, and the list goes on. This web of intertwining power issues plays into what Anderson (1991) called **imagined communities**, that is, a community as *perceived* by a learner, or more simply, the *mental image* of a socially constructed community. For example, nationalism is viewed as an affinity to an "imagined" construct of variables that presumably define a country, whether or not in fact such constructs can be empirically identified.

With that introduction to the related concepts of identity and investment, consider the following summary of the principle:

> Learning to think, feel, act, and communicate in an L2 is a complex socio-affective process of perceiving yourself as an integral part of a social community. The process involves self-awareness, investment, agency (see Principle #8), and a determination, amidst a host of power issues, to frame your own identity within the social relationships of a community.

What does all this say by way of some tips for the classroom teacher?

Guidelines for Optimizing Identity and Investment in L2 Classrooms

1. Overtly display a *supportive attitude* to your students. While some learners may feel quite helpless in this new language, remember that they are capable adults struggling with the acquisition of the most complex set of skills that any classroom has ever attempted to teach. Your patience, affirmation, and empathy need to be openly communicated.
2. Give your students credit for the many abilities and talents they already have, even though they feel somewhat incapacitated as they struggle with a new language. Try to incorporate those talents and skills into your teaching. Recognizing and using some of their artistic, musical, or sports-related skills will help to build self-confidence and worthiness as they seek to invest their time and effort in the L2 learning process.
3. Consider the fragility of students who are not only seeking membership in an imagined community, but who may also experience a considerable degree of *powerlessness*—in the classroom with the teacher "in charge," in a culture whose mores are not clearly perceived, or in a context in which race, classism, ethnocentricity, and other factors are at play.
4. Factor in learners' *identity* development in your decisions about whom to call on, when and how to give corrective feedback, how to constitute small groups and pairs, and how "tough" you can be with a student.
5. Give your students opportunities to make *choices* as much as your curriculum will permit. Students who can choose exercises, topics, time limits, homework, and even silence will be more apt to make an *investment* in their learning, and hence develop responsibility.

INTERACTION

Frenchman François Gouin (1880), the inspiration behind the "Series Method" of foreign language teaching, learned a painful lesson at the age of about 40. Determined at his "ripe old" age to learn German, he went to Hamburg for a year of residence. But for months on end this shy man shut himself in the isolation of his room, engaged in a rigorous regimen of memorizing huge quantities of German vocabulary and grammar. Occasional ventures into the streets to practice German resulted in so much embarrassment for François that all such attempts to relate to the locals were abruptly terminated with further closeting to memorize more German. At the end of the year, he returned to France, a failure. But wait! On his return home, François discovered that this three-year-old nephew had, during that same year, gone from saying virtually nothing to becoming a veritable chatterbox in his native French! François concluded that **interaction** was the key to acquisition . . . and the rest is history.

Our progression of principles has been guided by a sense of movement from factors that are more individual and cognitive in their nature to those that conceive of L2 learning as a primarily social phenomenon with affective and cultural overtones. The Principle of Interaction clearly centers on the latter. It is not a skill that you learn in the isolation of your room, as poor François Gouin discovered.

For some time now, L2 researchers have been focusing on a construct known as **willingness to communicate** (WTC), "a state of readiness to engage in the L2, the culmination of processes that prepare the learner to initiate L2 communication with a specific person at a specific time" (MacIntyre et al., 2011, p. 82). Observations of language learners' *un*willingness to communicate, for many possible reasons including anxiety, fear, and other affective factors, have led us to emphasize classroom activity that encourages learners to "come out of their shells" and to engage communicatively in the classroom. MacIntyre et al. (2011) also describe WTC as a socially constructed and dialogic process, rather than merely an internal attribute, highlighting the significance of perceived competence, error correction, and subtle features in particular social contexts.

The concept of WTC continues to be applicable across many cultures (Yashima, 2002). Many instructional contexts do not encourage risk-taking; instead they encourage correctness, right answers, and withholding "guesses" until one is sure to be correct. However, most educational research shows the opposite: task-based, project-based, open-ended work, negotiation of meaning, and a learner-centered climate are more conducive to long-term retention and intrinsic motivation.

As learners progress in their development, they gradually acquire the **communicative competence** (Canale & Swain, 1980) that has been such a central focus for researchers for decades (Hymes, 1972; Canale & Swain, 1980; Savignon, 1983, 2005). As learners engage in the meaningful use of the L2, they incorporate the organizational, pragmatic, strategic, and psychomotor components of language.

The key to communication, and ultimately to automatic production and comprehension of the L2, lies in what Long (2007) called the **interaction hypothesis**: Interactive communication is not merely a component of language learning, but rather the very *basis* for L2 development. In a strong endorsement of the power of interaction in the language curriculum, van Lier (1996, p. 188) devoted a whole book to "the curriculum as interaction." Here, principles of awareness, autonomy, and authenticity lead the learner into Vygotsky's (1978) **zone of proximal development** (ZPD), that is, the stage between what learners can do on their own and what can be achieved with the support and guidance of a knowledgeable person or instructor. Learners are led, through the **scaffolding** support of teacher, materials, and curriculum, to construct the new language through socially and culturally **mediated** interaction. (See *PLLT*, Chapter 10.)

Long's interaction hypothesis has pushed L2 pedagogical practices into a new frontier. It has centered us on the language classroom not just as a place where learners of varying abilities and styles and backgrounds mingle, but also as a place where the contexts for interaction are carefully *designed*. It has focused teachers on creating optimal environments and tasks for **collaboration** and **negotiation** such that learners will be stimulated to create their own **community of practice** (Lave and Wenger, 1991) in a *socially constructed* process.

The Principle of Interaction may be stated as follows:

> Interaction is the basis of L2 learning, through which learners are engaged both in enhancing their own communicative abilities and in socially constructing their identities through collaboration and negotiation. The primary role of the teacher is to optimally scaffold the learner's development within a community of practice.

What teaching implications can be drawn from the Principle of Interaction?

GUIDELINES FOR MAXIMIZING INTERACTION IN L2 CLASSROOMS

1. Give ample verbal and nonverbal assurances to students, affirming your belief in the student's ability.
2. Sequence (scaffold) techniques from easier to more difficult. As a teacher you are called on to sustain self-confidence where it already exists and to build it where it doesn't. Your activities in the classroom would therefore logically start with simpler techniques and simpler concepts. Students then can establish a sense of accomplishment that catapults them to the next, more difficult, step.
3. Create an atmosphere in the classroom that encourages students to try out language, to venture a response, and not to wait for someone else to volunteer language.

4. Provide reasonable challenges in your techniques—make them neither too easy nor too hard.
5. Help your students to understand what calculated risk-taking is, lest some feel that they must blurt out any old response.
6. Respond to students' attempts to communicate with positive affirmation, praising them for trying while at the same time warmly but firmly attending to their language.

LANGUACULTURE

Katsu took the bold step at the age of 45 of taking a leave of absence from his high school English teaching job in Japan to pursue a master's degree in California. Upon leaving California and returning to Japan, Katsu writes about his three years in the United States:

"When I first arrived in California, I was excited! Many things were different: food, the way people talked, friendly professors, the bad transportation system, people not so punctual. It was great, though, and after living in Japan for many years, I looked forward to studying in the USA.

"After a few months, my view changed. First of all, I was much older than most of my classmates, but I felt like they treated me as equal. They didn't respect my age. I also had a lot of experience teaching, but my experience didn't seem very important to my teachers. Because I was student again, I was in kind of a position of low status. Also, I found American women very aggressive. I think expression is 'in your face.' I was surprised about professors, very casual, treated students like equal, maybe too friendly.

"But when I got back to Japan, I was surprised! My family said, 'you have changed, you act like an American!' I think now I am confused, but I hope I will soon adjust to Japanese culture."

Katsu learned firsthand what it meant to adapt to a new culture, and found that while he was surprised at some American culturally related issues, he himself went through a minor metamorphosis that became apparent on his return to Japan. Language and culture are intricately intertwined, and often an L2 is so deeply rooted in a culture that it is not quickly and easily discerned or internalized by a learner. Agar (1994) used the term **languaculture** to emphasize the inseparability of language and culture. "The *langua* in languaculture is about discourse, not just about words and sentences. And the *culture* in languaculture is about meanings that include, but go well beyond, what the dictionary and grammar offer" (p. 96).

How does one come to "belong" to a culture? How does a learner's identity (see Principle 5) evolve in the process of developing communicative ability in an L2? Gaining skill in the *interaction* discussed in Principle 6 very intimately involves connecting language and culture. Can learners be taught to be **interculturally competent**?

Culture is a complex, dynamic web of customs and mores and rules that involves attitudes, values, norms, and beliefs that are *imagined* to be shared by a community. Cultural parameters include such dimensions as individualism (vs. collectivism), power, gender roles, age, time orientation, religion, and the list goes on (Matsumoto & Juang, 2013). Learning a second culture usually involves some effort to grasp the importance of shared cultural dimensions such as politeness, humor, slang, and dialect. More specifically, and perhaps more *authentically*, what books, music, movies, sports teams, celebrities, scandals, and electronic gadgets does everyone seem to be talking and tweeting about?

In a learner's process of socially constructing an identity either within (in the case of learning the L2 in the country that uses the L2) a culture or "outside" that culture, he or she will to some degree develop an **orientation** to the new context—and then integrate into or adapt to the culture (Gardner & Lambert, 1972; Dörnyei & Ushioda, 2011). Courses in SLA commonly incorporate cultural dimensions in their functional syllabuses, providing contexts for the forms of language to be utilized.

Here's a statement of the Languaculture Principle:

> Whenever you teach a language, you also teach a complex system of cultural customs, values, and ways of thinking, feeling, and acting. As learners redefine their identities as they learn an L2, they can be aided by a direct approach to acknowledging cultural differences, an open affirmation of learners' struggles, of the value of their "home" culture, and of their self-worth in potential feelings of powerlessness.

Classroom applications include the following:

Guidelines for Incorporating Languaculture into L2 Classrooms

1. Discuss cross-cultural differences with your students, emphasizing that no culture is "better" than another, but that cross-cultural understanding is an important facet of learning a language. Give illustrations of intercultural misunderstanding through (if possible) humorous anecdotes.
2. Include among your techniques certain activities and materials that illustrate the connection between language and culture, especially those that are more salient for your particular context.
3. Teach your students cultural connotations that will enable them to increase their interactive use of the L2, including politeness, humor, slang, "small talk," devices to keep a conversation going, and how to disagree with someone but still respect their right to an opinion.

4. Screen your techniques for material that may be culturally offensive.
5. Stress the importance of the L2 as a powerful tool for adjustment in a new culture.

AGENCY

Seong-jin is a twenty-three-year old Korean man enrolled in an intensive ESL program in a Canadian university. He is in a high-intermediate writing class that aims to help students develop English language skills for academic or professional purposes. He values good writing skills and aspires to be a good writer in the future. He enjoyed free-writing tasks when he had just started the English program at a beginning level and he found himself enjoying creative writing.

However, since he advanced to the high-intermediate class, he's been struggling with two conflicting discourses – a conventional way of writing an academic essay and his preferred personal writing style, which is to express his feelings freely. He recounts how he finds it very difficult to write an essay, such as an argumentative essay, in a formal academic style:

"I like writing based on my intuition. I don't like writing based on logic and by adding references. There always has to be a fixed structure. You have to write a positive argument with example sentences first and then a negative argument with example sentences. At the end then, you have to come up with "solution" stating what the best argument is. This is a sort of what they consider as a good writing sample."

It is obvious that he is aware of what is expected by his writing teacher in the assignment of writing an argumentative essay. However, he says:

"Yeah, but I don't like to do that. My writing then becomes the same as all the other students. I don't like to follow the same form as others."

We can all at some level identify with Seong-jin's plight, as reported by Lee and Maguire (2011). From early childhood we experience demands for structure imposed by "outside" agents: parents, teachers, peers, and social mores. We yearn to "breathe free" and function autonomously. For Seong-jin, perhaps his frustration with conforming to academic writing conventions is a product of his own creative urge to "be" himself, to express himself freely, and to realize his identity as a participant in his Canadian community of practice. His **agency** is at stake.

The Principle of Agency is our final principle in the list of eight for a number of reasons. First, it's a superb instance of a concept that is emblematic of the more recent "social turn" (Ortega, 2009) in SLA research, extending our horizons well beyond psycholinguistic, cognitive-interactional models that characterized much of the research of the last half of the 20th century. Second, agency provides an ample stockpile of pedagogical implications for the classroom teacher in concrete methodological terms. And finally, it's a construct that is so comprehensive in scope that it subsumes all the other principles we've described thus far—so sweeping, in fact, that the next chapter of this book will take a detailed look at agency as a prime example of how principles are embodied in our teaching.

In simple terms, agency refers to "people's ability to make choices, take control, self-regulate, and thereby pursue their goals as individuals, leading potentially to personal or social transformation" (Duff, 2012, p. 417). When learners capitalize on their role as an agent, they can make specific efforts to take on new roles and identities within their communities of practice and sociocultural milieu. Vygotsky (1978) reminded us that children gain agency as they acquire cognitive and linguistic abilities that enable them eventually to function autonomously.

The implications for the L2 classroom are myriad, as you will see in the next chapter. In some ways, agency is a further refinement of Maslow's (1970) hierarchy of needs, which garnered a great deal of attention in educational circles. As learners slowly develop the basic sustaining factors of belongingness and affirmation (by teachers and peers), they are enabled to reach for the ultimate goal of **self-actualization**. The difference between Maslow's self-actualization and current sociocultural concept of agency lies in the *ongoing* role (from the earliest stages) of agency as a means to achieve social transformation.

The Principle of Agency helps to frame a surprising number of other principles and constructs in SLA (Yashima, 2013). At the core of *motivation* is agency: the act of making *choices* in acts of self-determination. **Self-efficacy** theory emphasizes the importance of a learner's self-appraisal, a foundation stone of agency. Our *self-regulatory* processes, with the ultimate utilization of *strategies* and eventual achievement of *autonomy*, are all intertwined with agency. Even the *scaffolding* and *mediation* involved in successful L2 pedagogy are essential pathways to learners fully assuming their agency.

Finally, and perhaps most poignantly, from a "critical" perspective, Norton (2013) and Yashima (2013) both emphasized the crucial role of agency within the various power structures of one's social milieu. As Canagarajah (2013a) noted, agency helps us "go beyond the monolithic notions of culture and power" (p. 204) in intercultural communicative contexts of globalization and migration. In recent years we have seen more research on L2 learning by immigrants and refugees, and by those who are in "subtractive" roles in a society (where the L2 is seen as superior in some way to a learner's heritage language). Such contexts often involve learners in a struggle to appropriate a new language and to fight social constraints as they negotiate an identity (Yashima, 2013, p. 5).

Briefly stated, the Principle of Agency can be summed up as follows:

> Agency, which lies at the heart of language learning, is the ability of learners to make choices, take control, self-regulate, and thereby pursue their goals as individuals within a sociocultural context. Teachers are called on to offer appropriate affective and pedagogical support in their students' struggle for autonomy, development of identities, and journey toward empowerment.

Pedagogical implications and practical classroom applications are spelled out in detail in the next chapter. There, we focus exclusively on this powerful and foundational principle of SLA, *agency*, and all its concomitant influences on successful acquisition of additional languages.

The eight principles that have just been reviewed (listed for your convenience in Table 4.1) are some of the major foundation stones for teaching practice. While they are not by any means exhaustive, they can act for you as major theoretical insights on which your methodology can be based.

With these eight principles, you should be able to evaluate a course, a textbook, a group of students, and an educational context, and to determine solutions to pedagogical issues in the classroom. You should be able to assess the strengths and weaknesses of lessons you've observed or lessons you plan to teach. In short, you should be able to frame your own *approach* by considering the extent to which the eight principles inform your understanding of how languages are successfully learned and taught.

We hope you have gained from this discussion the value of undergirding your teaching with sound principles that help you to understand why you choose to do something in the classroom: what kinds of questions to ask yourself before the fact about what you are doing, how to monitor yourself while you are teaching, how to assess after the fact the effectiveness of what you did, and then how to modify what you will do the next time around.

Table 4.1 Principles of language learning and teaching

Principles	Related Constructs
1. Automaticity	attention, processing, noticing form and function, fluency
2. Transfer	cross-linguistic influence, interference, interlanguage, dynamic systems, meaningful learning, skill acquisition, embodied cognition
3. Reward	motivation (intrinsic & extrinsic)
4. Self-Regulation	autonomy, self-awareness, strategies, self-determination
5. Identity and Investment	language ego, imagined community, emotion and affect, styles
6. Interaction	willingness to communicate, feedback, communicative competence, collaboration negotiation, scaffolding, mediation, ZPD
7. Languaculture	communities of practice, intercultural competence, acculturation, language-culture connection
8. Agency	empowerment, self-actualization, self-efficacy

FOR THE TEACHER: ACTIVITIES (A) & DISCUSSION (D)

1. **(A)** All of the eight principles summarized in this chapter are important. Ask your students, in pairs or small groups, to *prioritize* them, placing two or three principles at the top of the list. Then, have the groups compare their top three with others in the class. They may discover how difficult it is to choose only three to be at the top of the list.
2. **(A)** Have any principles been left out that should have been included? Ask small groups to brainstorm their thoughts, name any such principles (or concepts), and justify their inclusion in such a list. Then ask each group to share its conclusions with the rest of the class, perhaps by writing their ideas on the board. Encourage your students to ask questions of each other.
3. **(A)** Direct students back to Chapter 1, in which a lesson was described in detail. Notice that in the second part of the chapter, numbered sets of questions were raised regarding the lesson that was described. Assign one or more of those 18 sets to pairs. Ask each pair to (a) determine which principles in this chapter *justified* the teacher's choice in each case, and (b) decide whether any aspects of that lesson should have been *altered* on the basis of any one or more principles. Ask pairs to share their thoughts with the rest of the class.
4. **(D)** Ask students to look back at Chapter 2, in which a number of methods were descriptive of a brief history of language teaching. Make a chalkboard list of the methods to stimulate a class discussion of the extent to which each method can be *justified* by certain principles described in this chapter, and then, conversely, *criticized* by other principles.
5. **(A)** The eight principles given here form elements of a *theory* of second language learning and teaching (see *PLLT*, Chapter 10). Ask your students, as extra-class work on their own, to write a brief one-page synopsis of what each would state as their own personal *theory of language learning and teaching*, using as many of the principles (and other concepts) as possible that are articulated in this chapter. If time permits, you might ask a few students to volunteer to read their statements when they complete the assignment. Note: Make sure they save these statements to read again at the end of the course.
6. **(D)** If possible, try to arrange for your students to observe an L2 class, and as a checklist, use the eight principles (plus other concepts described here) to determine which principles supported various activities. In some cases a principle may explain why students are successfully achieving lesson objectives; in other cases a principle might articulate why objectives were *not* reached. Ask students to report their insights back to the class.

FOR YOUR FURTHER READING

Mitchell, R., Myles, F., & Marsden, E. (2013). *Second language learning theories* (3rd ed.). Oxford, UK: Routledge.

This book provides an accessible alternative to *PLLT* in its survey of current theories and issues in the field of second language acquisition. It serves as a vantage point from which to view the backdrops to the eight principles presented in this chapter.

Richards, J.C. (2002). Theories of teaching in language teaching. In J. Richards & W. Renandya (Eds.), *Methodology in language teaching: An anthology of current practice* (pp. 19–25). Cambridge, UK: Cambridge University Press.

Richards puts theories of teaching into an unusual and thought-provoking framework of four categories: science-research based, theory-philosophy, values-based, and art-craft conceptions.

Allwright, D., & Hanks, J. (2009). *The developing language learner: An introduction to exploratory practice.* New York, NY: Palgrave MacMillan.

The authors present an innovative approach to understanding the role of learners as practitioners of learning and the role of teachers as practitioners of teaching. Through the narratives of learners and teachers from around the globe, it offers how exploratory practice can engage learners as practitioners and eventually enhance their learning process.

Alsagoff, L., McKay, S., Hu, G., & Renandya, W. (Eds.). (2012). *Principles and practices for teaching English as an international language.* New York, NY: Routledge.

As research on learning and teaching languages has now become a global concern, with contributions to the field in many countries around the world, this anthology helps the reader to gain a perspective on English teaching in many contexts, especially those in which English is not a predominant L1.

Pavlenko, A. (2013). The affective turn in SLA: From "affective factors" to "language desire" and "commodification of affect." In D. Gabrys-Barker & J. Brelska (Eds.), *The affective dimension in second language acquisition* (pp. 3–28). Clevedon, UK: Multilingual Matters.

An interesting affective emphasis is offered in this well-researched article that gives you both a historical perspective as well as information on the recent "revival" of the affective domain as a key to language success.

CHAPTER **5**

AGENCY IN LANGUAGE LEARNING

Questions for Reflection

- What is agency?
- How does self-efficacy affect learner agency?
- What does the notion of embodiment tell us about the relationship between cognitive development and social environment?
- What can we learn from neurobiological research on emotion regarding how our brain works in decision-making processes?
- Why is it important to understand learner agency in the sociopolitical process of L2 learning?
- How can teachers foster agency in language learners?

"Language learning is anchored in agency, as all of life is. Teaching, in its very essence, is promoting agency." (Leo van Lier, 2011b, p. 391)

In the previous chapter, we saw that agency fulfills and incorporates several important principles and related constructs in language education such as motivation, self-regulation, autonomy, identity, interaction, and cultural relevance. In this line of thinking, embracing and promoting learner agency is a fundamental principle of language classroom pedagogy. Agency is the key to understanding who language learners are and why they think and act the way they do. It is the basis for making sense of the complexity of classroom practices, reflecting on those practices, and organizing them into a coherent system.

In this chapter, we'll offer a theoretical framework for the principle of learner agency by explaining how agency is embodied in many of the key constructs, approaches, and strategies discussed in the language education literature as well as the rest of the book. And we'll challenge you to consider some of the practical methodological implications of agency in the L2 classroom.

The term **agency,** which we define broadly as the ability to take action with intention has long appeared in social science but has only recently become part of the main theoretical constructs of applied linguistics and SLA (Yashima, 2013). Influenced by the behaviorist tradition in which humans are treated as passive beings, language learners in the mainstream SLA literature once were considered as "processing devices" that simply receive input and produce predictable output. Over the last few decades there have been rigorous investigations into learner behavior and performance beyond controlled classrooms looking into the social world of language learners. In such investigations, the learners are described as agents who are aware of their actions and behaviors and take control over their learning processes. As human beings, they are volitional, social, evaluative, and make conscious decisions using their target languages through appropriation and/or resistance (Duff, 2012).

The first part of this chapter gives a brief review of how human agency has been conceptualized in various disciplines such as psychology, neuroscience, sociology, and literary study. We then show how this body of literature has influenced SLA, particularly in the area of research on individual differences. Finally, we provide some examples of how the principle of learner agency can be applied to classroom routines such as lesson planning, executing, evaluating, and materials development.

APPROACHES TO UNDERSTANDING AGENCY

Agency is a complex and multifaceted construct, so it is a daunting task to come up with an operational definition. However, defining agency is crucial since "the particular ways in which [scholars] conceive of agency have implications for understanding of personhood, causality, action, and intention" (Ahearn, 2001, p. 112).

In this section we introduce various theoretical approaches to examining human agency that have influenced SLA and language education over the last few decades. Also, there are many constructs related to agency that have been extensively researched, such as self-efficacy, motivation, self-regulation, autonomy, and identity. These terms may appear to imply phenomena similar to agency, and some even consider them as synonyms (van Lier, 2008). The following discussions outline a subset of that literature.

CLASSROOM CONNECTIONS

Review the traditional language teaching methods described in Chapter 2 (the Grammar Translation Method, Direct Method, Audiolingual Method, Suggestopedia, Total Physical Response, etc.). How does each method describe the role of language learners in their learning process? To what extent does each method encourage learners to exercise agency and to promote their "ability to take action with intention"?

Agency and Self-Efficacy

American psychologist Albert Bandura conducted extensive research on human agency particularly through the examination of **self-efficacy**. According to Bandura (2001), the core of motivation is agency, the act of making choices with self-determination. Human agency has four core features including intentionality, forethought, self-regulation, and self-reflectiveness.

Agency is manifested in human actions done intentionally. It informs an individual's future course of action and his or her proactive commitment to future actions (Bandura, 2001). Forethought of agency can be expressed in numerous ways. People exercise forethought, set goals for themselves, anticipate the likely consequences of actions, and avoid detrimental effects. Through the exercise of forethought, people "motivate themselves and guide their actions in anticipation of future events and outcomes" (Bandura, 1986, p. 7).

Anticipated material and social outcomes are not the only rewards influencing human behavior. Agency motivates, monitors, and regulates individuals' execution of decisions made and actions planned. People exercise self-direction keeping in mind personal standards and regulate their behaviors by self-evaluative outcomes. Agency also enables individuals to examine their metacognitive capability to reflect on the adequacy of one's thoughts and actions. According to Bandura (1986), "perceived self-efficacy plays a pivotal role in the self-regulation of motivation through goal challenges and outcome expectations" (p. 10).

For understanding this anticipatory self-guidance of human agency, the notion of self-efficacy is relevant. Bandura (1997) defines self-efficacy as an individual's perceptions of "one's capabilities to organize and execute the courses of action required to produce given attainments" (p. 3). Individuals construct outcome expectations from observed conditional relations between environmental events in the world around them, and the outcomes produced by their actions (Bandura, 1986). Self-efficacy has been investigated as a predictor of successful academic achievement (Schunk, 1991, 1996). Higher self-efficacy correlates to individuals' greater persistence when facing difficulties, leading them to exert more effort and make better use of learning strategies. On the other hand, students with low self-efficacy may choose not to participate in a learning activity because they perceive themselves to be lacking in the ability to succeed in it (Matthews, 2010).

Agency can be exercised not only directly by an individual but also by proxy or collectively. Bandura (2001) notes that on many occasions people do not have direct control over the social conditions and institutional practices that affect their everyday lives. In these circumstances, they seek their well-being, security, and valued outcomes through the exercise of proxy agency, as in the cases of children to parents, marital partners to spouses, citizens to their legislative representatives. Collective agency manifests itself when individuals pool their resources and work together successfully through performing their roles as the members of a group and coordinating activities with a high sense of efficacy (Bandura, 2000).

Let's consider an example of the connection between agency and self-efficacy.

> Pavinee, who has excelled in her high-school English classes, wishes to continue to "perfect" English in a language school in rural "up-country" Thailand. She has strong aspirations of then enrolling in a teacher education program in Chiang Mai to become an English teacher, but her parents and other family members have different aspirations for her. They believe she should marry the man they have selected for her, settle down, have children, and be a good wife.
>
> Pavinee's self-efficacy is hampered by family pressure, and as a result she is beginning to feel powerless to determine her own future, to continue her English studies, and pursue her dreams. She feels like her agency has been coopted by her family. Her intentions and ability to self-regulate are diminished by outside pressure. She asks her English teacher (proxy agency) for advice on building the strength she needs to pursue her goals.

Classroom Connections

If you were Pavinee's teacher, how would you advise her? How would you help her to regain her self-efficacy and seize the agency that she desperately wants? Have you ever felt that outside forces are diminishing your ability to exercise agency? In general, what can teachers do to help learners to "seize the day"?

Agency, Rewards, and Motivation

Motivation, one of the most researched constructs in the field of psychology, has in the context of L2 learning long been regarded as fundamental for successful language learning. Considering the principle of reward discussed in Chapter 4, you may wonder what causes language learners to be driven to act on learning and how one can sustain such drive. Understanding the role of agency in human motivation may give us insight into such questions.

From a behavioral perspective, motivation can be defined as "the anticipation of reinforcement." There is no question that a large portion of what we do is motivated by an anticipated reward. From eating to exercising to studying and even to altruistic acts of ministering to others, there is "something in it for me." The emotional overtones of the more intangible rewards must not be ignored. Cookies, hugs, and laughter are all payoffs worth striving for. Successful learners are conscious of potential rewards for taking a certain action, and decide to "go for it" expecting to gain those rewards. The question, then, is where the source of such motivation comes from.

Classroom teachers often use motivation as a catch-all term to make sense of why some students succeed and why others don't. To a certain extent, this was "proved" by Gardner and Lambert (1972) when they reported empirical evidence indicating that high levels of motivation in L2 learners were correlated with high achievement test results. The key constructs in the work of Gardner and Lambert, integrative and **instrumental** motivational **orientations**, have been used widely for explaining why people learn languages. Gardner (1985) in his socio-educational model particularly emphasized the importance of **integrative orientation**, which refers to learners' interests in getting to know about the people and culture of the target language. An instrumental motive, on the other hand, is driven by more practical value and advantages gained from learning the target language.

In their proposal for the self-determination theory, Deci and Ryan (1985, 2002) describe motivation as coming from inside individuals, implying that motivation has to be regulated by learners themselves, rather than regulated by others, in order to be sustained. The researchers view that humans are innately inquisitive and volitional beings without needing external incentives. They seek out challenges that direct personal growth. Intrinsically motivated actions derive from the desire of a person to accomplish something for his or her own pleasure, while external motivators, designed to control a person, can pressure a person to think, feel, or behave in a specific way.

Extrinsically driven behavior may give the person a feeling of being controlled and lead to loss of *autonomy*. In his notion of the "autonomy of self-reward," Bruner (1962) argued that one of the most effective ways to help both children and adults to think and learn is to free them from the control of external rewards and punishments. One of the principal weaknesses of extrinsically driven behavior is its addictive nature. Once captivated, as it were, by the lure of an immediate prize or praise, we can become dependent on those tangible rewards, even to the point that their withdrawal can extinguish the desire to learn.

For classroom teachers, intrinsic motivation is important because it is a crucial element in the cognitive, social, and physical development of humans, and leads to high-quality learning. It is crucial to know what factors do not undermine but enhance intrinsic motivation. More autonomous intrinsic motivation is associated with greater engagement, better performance, less dropping out, higher quality learning, and greater psychological well-being, among other outcomes.

Classroom Connections

According to Ryan and Deci (2000), in order to promote a high level of intrinsic motivation, learners need to experience "satisfaction of the needs both for competence and autonomy" (p. 58). What could language teachers do to help students feel self-confident and autonomous in daily classroom routines?

The research shows that one type of extrinsic reward can indeed have an effect on intrinsic motivation: the positive feedback that learners perceive as a boost to their feelings of competence and self-determination (Dörnyei, 2009). No other externally administered set of rewards has a lasting effect. So, for example, sincerely delivered positive feedback in a classroom, seen by students as a validation of their own personal autonomy, critical thinking ability, and self-fulfillment, can increase or maintain intrinsic motivation.

Acknowledging that motivation entails a complex and multifaceted nature, researchers in SLA have been trying to find better ways to describe motivation in learning languages. For example, Dörnyei (2005, 2009) proposed the "L2 Motivational Self System," drawing on learners' perspectives about themselves in the future. *The ideal self* refers to the person one hopes to become, and *the ought-to self* indicates the attributes that one believes one ought to possess to meet those expectations. The assumption is that if becoming fluent in a target language is essential to one's *ideal* or *ought-to self*, students will be greatly motivated to learn the language because they want to "reduce the discrepancy between current- and future-self states" (Ushioda, 2013a, p. 3764).

Another notable development in L2 motivation research is Ushioda's (2009) "person-in-context relational view" of motivation. Ushioda notes that L2 motivation is dynamic and can be mediated socially. It has strong relationship with learner identity and agency because one's sense of identity and agency depends on actions carried out not only on his or her own but also under the control of others (e.g., peers and teachers). External factors (e.g., teacher instructional strategies, materials, or particular behaviors) and experiences (e.g., travel, intercultural encounters) influence (either positively or negatively) L2 learners' engagement, persistence, and success in their learning processes.

Motivation is not located solely within the individual but is socially distributed, created within cultural systems of activities involving the mediation of others (Rueda & Moll, 1994). Ushioda (2013a) calls for viewing motivation as a "process rather than a measurable cause or product" (p. 3) and an "integral part of the evolving organic and adaptive system of cognitive, affective, and contextual processes shaping language learning" (p. 5).

Dörnyei and Ushioda (2009, 2011) have called for capturing a complex **dynamic systems** perspective on L2 learner motivation rather than the positivist psychometric cause-effect approach to what "moves" L2 students to learn. In Lamb's (2004) study, for example, L2 learners were highly motivated but exercised their agency to *choose* to be a speaker of English as a lingua franca rather than to be a member of communities of English native speakers as assumed in the traditional notion of integrative motivation (Gardner & Lambert, 1972).

Ushioda (2013a) warns that a cause-and-effect approach to identifying external factors of motivation may overlook the important complexity of the dynamic development of motivation. We need to consider why "the same classroom setting, learning tasks, teacher behaviors, and strategies may affect the motivation of its learners in different ways" (Ushioda, 2013a, pp. 3764–3765). Relevant pedagogical implications are discussed further in Chapters 8 and 11.

Consider this example of agency and motivation.

> Raoul and Alberto are cousins, both English learners in the same high school class in Guadalajara, Mexico, and have been classmates for about three months. Raoul is highly involved in self-determining his future in English as an L2, spends extra-class time using English on the Internet, watching movies, and tweeting and texting in English. Alberto, on the other hand, does just enough to "get by" in English, and really sees little use for English once he's out of high school and in the work force in his home town.
>
> What aspects of motivation and agency could account for the difference between these two learners? Interviews revealed that Raoul aspired to entering a university in the United States and eventually earning an MBA to return to Guadalajara and work in his father's importing business, which had been languishing over the last few years. He wasn't highly social, but interviewers felt he was polite and respectful. Alberto was the opposite in personality: social, fun-loving, "a class clown," and had no special plans for his life after high school, beyond picking up a job locally.

Classroom Connections

Considering the interconnections between motivation and agency discussed in this section, what further questions would you like to ask Raoul and Alberto about their English learning? Would you do something to spur Alberto to greater interest? How might you redirect Alberto to appreciate his English class more . . . or should you do so?

Agency and Embodiment

Many seasoned teachers may believe that for their students "learning by doing is the best way to learn," and therefore plan their lessons to enable students to engage in a variety of activities. To consider a rationale behind such a belief, it may be useful to look at the connection between cognition, body, and human action. In particular, we draw on the notion of **embodied cognition**, also known as **situated cognition**, to discuss the relationship between the mind and action and how this relationship can be relevant to human agency.

Over 100 years ago, John Dewey (1896) argued that all human activity involves embodied coordination. All human learning begins "not with a sensory stimulus, but with a sensorimotor co-ordination . . . the real beginning is with the act of seeing; it is looking, and not a sensation of light" (Dewey, 1896, pp. 137–138). In other words, perception and action are not causally connected in a linear way. Making sense of perceptual experience and response happens as the individuals engage in the very action. For instance, when looking at a chair we perceive not just the shape of the chair itself but also an object signaling the possibility of one's sitting in it. Perception and embodied action are inseparable as we explore and perceive visual objects anticipating potential affordable actions (Gibbs, 2006).

According to Gibbs (2006), perception is "the ability to derive meaning from sensory experience to guide adaptive behavior" (p. 42). Agency can manifest in the active process of *perceptual learning*, that is, learning to perceive particular features and meanings (i.e., affordances) in the environment. Individuals' perception of affordances is relative to the perceiving object. Cultural connection also comes into play in this learning process because individuals may perceive the affordances differently depending on their prior **languaculture** (Agar, 1994). This type of learning goes beyond the cognitive development through information processing. As van Lier (2008) stresses, it involves "a whole-person, body and mind, socially situated process" (p. 180).

In other words, agency is a prerequisite of "real" learning, involving cognition, emotion, and physical movement in a sociocultural, historically situated context. Taking a sociocognitive approach to SLA, Atkinson (2011) views cognition as *adaptive intelligence,* which is "an open biological system to align with the environment" (p. 144). This alignment with the environment takes on agency because such alignment is "socially situated, adaptive behavior, [and] a process of continuously and progressively fitting oneself to one's environment" (Atkinson, 2010, p. 611). From this point of view learning is more about figuring out how to align oneself with the social world than extracting knowledge from it.

When the notion of embodiment is applied to language instruction, language is viewed as a reflection of "the human perceptual system and human understanding of the spatial-physical-social world we inhabit" (Tyler, 2008, p. 459). In other words, language is not simply stored inside the brain; rather it is a multisensory and multimodal experience involving motor patterns as well as auditory and visual information.

Consider some practical examples of embodiment in L2 classrooms; first, a study by Lindstromberg and Boers (2005):

> The researchers showed that actual physical movement (e.g., acting out word meanings) in the learning of action verbs was effective for Dutch-speaking college students to increase their English vocabulary. When these students were asked to enact or mime manner-of-movement verbs (e.g., sway and hurl), which is a key feature of the TPR method (see Chapter 2), they demonstrated better retention and more accurate interpretation than those who were only asked to explain.

Another study employed a drama-based approach to L2 instruction (Haught & McCafferty, 2008):

> The findings confirmed that gesture, body language, and intonation are all a part of the learning process and contribute to embodied language learning. Six adult ESL students participated in a semester-long workshop entitled 'English through Drama' and exhibited improvement in their fluency while attending the workshop. The researchers concluded that drama is an effective multimodal teaching approach because it can create a context in which L2 learners embody language (both verbal and nonverbal) and culture through taking on another identity and having them engage in recursive practice.

Further support for the benefit of embodied action on cognitive development is from the field of **haptics**, the study of "touch and the human interaction with the external environment though touch" (Minogue & Jones, 2006, p. 316). This area of research focuses on how human beings interact with the environment through the sense of touch, and eventually how haptic perception might affect student learning and help them gain useful information.

For instance, in their series of experiments with 308 college students on haptic recognition, Kiphart, Auday, and Cross (1988) suggest that human beings' capacity to process information by touch may be superior to the visual and auditory sensory systems. Many science educators believe that simulations and virtual models involving haptic feedback are powerful tools for advancing and applying science knowledge (Linn, 2003). Although little empirical research has been produced to shed light on how haptic modality might be beneficial, most researchers note that *active touch* should be emphasized when haptics is examined in an educational setting (Minogue & Jones, 2006). For example, having students *consciously choose* to examine the properties of an object may increase their motivation and attention to learning (Sathian, 1998). More information and discussion on the use of technology in relation to haptics are in Chapter 12.

 **CLASSROOM CONNECTIONS**

What pedagogical implications of the notion of embodiment can you think of, particularly if you are to teach *content-based* language courses? What are some common classroom activities that draw on the various manifestations of embodiment?

Cognition, Emotion, and Agency

When agency means *the ability to take action with intentionality*, it is important to understand how the brain works when an individual takes such an action, what roles the brain plays in taking further actions, and what that action does to the brain in response. Cognitive neuroscience, especially brain studies using functional Magnetic Resonance Imaging (fMRI) and related methods, has increasingly been influential and has provided multiple levels of analysis and a deeper understanding of the human mind as a complex organic system (Ryan, 2007). In particular, recent advances in neurology suggest that cognitive processes such as learning, attention, memory, and decision-making are greatly affected by the processes of *emotion*. In other words, emotion plays a fundamental role in reasoning and decision-making (Damasio, 2003; Immordino-Yang & Damasio, 2007).

The importance of emotion in human cognitive functioning has long been emphasized in the fields of psychology and language education but only by a handful of scholars. Vygotsky (1962) observed the close connection between cognition and emotion and stressed the importance of the affective and volitional tendency of the human mind in the development of the thought process. This part of Vygostky's work has seldom been explored. In the early 1970s, when most SLA researchers were preoccupied with the cognitive mechanisms of learner language development, Brown (1973) called for rigorous investigations on the affective domain in L2 education, as he saw its equal importance to uncover the ultimate key to successful learning.

Although there has been recent increasing attention to emotion in the neurosciences and cognitive psychology (e.g., Damasio, 1994, 2003; Barrett, 2009; Scherer, 2009), the fundamental significance of emotion in language learning has been marginalized in most SLA textbooks and encyclopedias (Pavlenko, 2013). In fact, up until the late 1980s the field of brain research has also ignored the critical role of emotion in influencing social behaviors and the process of making logical and rational decisions (Damasio, 1994).

Antonio Damasio (1994, 2003) reported intriguing results from his research on the neuroscience of emotions. His neurological patients, whose frontal lobe and the ventromedial prefrontal cortex were damaged, show "compromised" social behaviors such as being insensitive to others' emotions, unable to learn from their mistakes, having difficulty in making appropriate decisions, and not feeling embarrassed after violating social and ethical rules. On the other hand, these patients displayed no loss of knowledge and were able to cogently explain social and logical rules that guide one's future plans and behaviors. Damasio (2003) concludes that the patients' logic and knowledge could be intact, but "factual knowledge about social behavior requires the machinery of emotion and feeling to express itself normally" (p. 151).

Based on the findings from the studies with brain-damaged people, Immordino-Yang and Damasio (2007) propose an important hypothesis for education: that is, emotion plays a critical role in "bringing previously acquired knowledge to inform real-world decision making in social contexts" (p. 5). In other words, emotion is a critical factor for the maximum **transfer** (see Chapter 4) of acquired knowledge to novel situations and for helping learners decide when and how to apply what they have learned previously.

This is also a crucial point for the principle of agency. Emotion is what makes people enable to engage in sound decision making with a repertoire of know-how and actions that would allow people to respond appropriately in different social situations. Simply focusing on accumulating knowledge and skills does not guarantee that students will be able to use them appropriately in their real life. In other words, emotion should be grounded in every learning setting in order for a learner to exercise agency as a desirable member of a community of practice. To ignore the importance of students' emotions is to fail to appreciate a critical force in students' learning, which, in turn, is to "fail to appreciate the very reason that students learn at all" (Immordino-Yang & Damasio, 2007, p. 9).

Neurobiological findings help us understand how beliefs and emotions have a major impact on the success or failures of learning process, and how emotions and learning are influenced by the process of the biological brain interacting with our senses and the physical world. Pavlenko (2005, 2013) notes that cross-linguistic variations in lexical encoding may lead to inter-group differences in terms of how people perceive and categorize emotional events, which bring challenges to the L2 learning process. Pavlenko and Driagina's (2007) study showed that L2 learners with lower levels of proficiency seem to experience difficulties in using the L2 emotion lexicon and may end up drawing on L1 emotion categories to express themselves in the L2. Once they have internalized the L2 emotion lexicon, some L2 users manifest their agency by keeping two sets of emotional categories and perform according to the constraints of their respective languages. Others may experience L2 influences on their L1 emotion categories and notice the conceptual shift, starting to "forget" particular concepts and distinctions, or may even choose not to use one of the two languages (Pavlenko, 2013).

 **Classroom Connections**

What are some examples of the "L2 emotion lexicon"? In learning an L2, have you experienced difficulty in using the L2 emotion lexicon to express your feelings in the L2? What are some examples in your experience? How would you as a teacher help your students to "internalize" the L2 emotional lexicon?

Agency in a Sociopolitical Context

Given the intricate relationship among agency, emotion, and decision-making in language use and language learning, we now move to a consideration of how this complex relationship may manifest itself in the real world, that is, in its connection to sociopolitical contexts.

Learner agency in a sociopolitical context and its importance in language education are strongly connected with how language learners have traditionally been viewed in mainstream SLA research. For quite some time SLA researchers have been preoccupied with the internal mechanisms of *interlanguage* rather than language learners themselves for their main research focus. In fact, as Duff (2012) argues, the participants in SLA research often have been described as "interlanguage speakers, fossilized L2 users, immigrants, limited (English) proficient speakers, refugees, non-native speakers, heritage-language learners, [or] generation 1.5 learners" (p. 410). The language learners' multiple social roles, identities, unique characteristics, and agency were considered to be of less importance to our understanding of SLA.

Since the emergence of the *social turn* (Block, 2003) in SLA, however, a great deal of attention has been placed on the analysis of sociocultural and political context in which additional language learners' experiences take place. Their roles as social beings and the ways they perceive their L2 worlds, experiences, and themselves are examined. In particular, what actions they decide to take, thus, the manifestation of agency, has been a focal point in the analysis of their learning trajectories. Influenced by sociocultural theory and poststructuralism, a number of studies have shown the significant role of learner agency in L2 identity research focusing on appropriation, negotiation, and resistance in dynamic and diverse language development (McKay & Wong, 1996; Norton, 2000; Duff, 2002; Pavlenko & Blackledge, 2004; Block, 2007).

Agency has been a popular concept for L2 researchers who aim to understand learner autonomy in situated L2 learning and how the learners' roles as social beings shape their learning paths (e.g., Norton Peirce, 1995; McKay & Wong, 1996; Harklau, 2000; Norton, 2000). L2 learning takes place as learners increase their participation in target communities of practice (Lave & Wenger, 1991) in which their engagement can be facilitated or constrained. In these studies, learner agency refers to "learners' ability to make choices, take control, self-regulate and pursue their goals as individuals" (Duff, 2012, p. 417).

Unequal relations of power between language learners and target language speakers often are the center of the discussion. Norton (2000) proposed the notion of "investment" to complement the conventional notion of motivation, which refers to "the socially and historically constructed relationship of learners to the target language, and their often ambivalent desire to learn and practice it" (p. 10). According to Norton, learners invest in learning a target language hoping that they will acquire certain types of symbolic and material resources that will promote their social, political, and economic status in their communities of practice.

Understanding learner agency within the identity approach to SLA is useful for explaining how some seemingly intelligent and highly motivated students would not want to speak/write or cannot speak/write in a classroom or a particular community of practice. According to Norton (2000), identity refers to "how a person understands his or her relationship to the world, how that relationship is constructed across time and space, and how the person understands possibilities for the future" (p. 5). An investment in learning a new language is not simply obtaining knowledge and a set of skills. It is an investment in one's identity, which often becomes a process of struggle as multiple identities are constantly negotiated and re-negotiated through interaction with others (Norton, 2013).

In this locus of struggle, L2 learners may exert their agency by resisting undesirable identities imposed on them and striving for constructing a new one that they prefer and aspire to in their future. Let's illustrate with an example from Norton (2000) that described immigrant women in Canada:

> Eva, one of the five participants in the study, was highly invested in learning English because she hoped to have better relationships with her co-workers (i.e., symbolic resources) and to enhance job possibilities (i.e., material resources), which in turn would increase her self-confidence. Initially positioned as an "ESL immigrant," she resisted and repositioned herself as a "multilingual resource," capitalizing on her Polish and Italian language skills, and came to be considered as a respected individual by her co-workers.

Another example comes from McKay and Wong (1996):

> In a study of Chinese adolescent immigrant students in the United States, the researchers found that students' investment in different language skills (e.g., listening, speaking, reading, and writing) can be highly selective depending on their identities and values in those skills. One of their participants, Michael, showed strong agency in resisting and counteracting his position as an "ESL student" imposed by school staff and teachers.

Further discussion on agency and identity in sociocultural, political, and institutional contexts continues in Chapter 8.

ENACTING THE PRINCIPLE OF AGENCY IN L2 CLASSROOMS

Facing a current globalizing world in which a massive number of people constantly travel, migrate, and communicate with others physically and virtually, we realize that mobility and diversity are common features of the world of L2 learners. In fact, these learners may live in what Blommaert (2010) refers to as *super-diversity* spaces, highly diversified geographical and social spaces due to the multilateral flow of people, ideas, and commodities across borders. In these spaces, multilingual users choose or mesh their languages, values, and emotions based on a variety of resources and constraints. Therefore, human agency becomes essential to maneuver their dynamic and complex lives.

How can we language teachers help them develop negotiation strategies for constructing their new norms and identities that would align harmoniously with their desirable environment? How can we foster their agency in their language learning and use? We share just a few ideas here:

Encourage Learners to *Do* Language

Let's first reflect on how we see what language is. In the framework of the principle of agency, we view language as something we use to do things—engaging in actions and activities (Gee, 2011). Therefore, language is not a conduit that merely conveys information and is not a "transparent vehicle carrying only referential meaning" (Goodwin, 1990, p. 4). Language is viewed as a form of social action, a cultural resource, and a set of sociocultural practices (Schieffelin, 1990).

Agency is then situated in a particular context and is something that "learners *do*, rather than something that learners *possess*" (van Lier, 2008, p. 171).

Language researchers and teachers may become too focused on input and/or output and on drills and exercises for the correct uptake of target forms, while giving little attention to the manifestations of learner agency. Agency should be at the center of planning, executing, reflecting, evaluating, and re-planning classroom instruction (see Chapters 9, 10, 11). Teachers should create opportunities in which students can do something in their L2 in authentic real-life contexts so that they use language as social practice and accomplish tasks. A few examples are:

Promoting Agency in the Classroom Through Authentic Real-Life Activity

- Reading Yelp reviews to find a restaurant in a new town
- Ordering take-out food for a movie party
- Returning a purchased item at a customer service desk
- Writing an e-mail to request a reference letter
- Complaining to a neighbor about a barking dog
- Evaluating different car commercials on TV

It should be noted that agency is not a *precursor* to that context but rather *emerges* from the social, political, and cultural dynamics of a specific place and time (Desjarlais, 1997). Whether or not agency is actually promoted in a particular situation depends on factors such as learners' choice, giving them the right to speak, responsibility for their actions, and stimulating debate to express their opinions (van Lier, 2008).

Allow Learners' *Voice* to Develop

Teachers need to support learners when they wish to express their **voice,** ideas, and opinions. As mentioned earlier, agency can be executed by individuals, groups, and communities (Bandura, 2001). For example, a whole class tries to negotiate workload or a deadline with the teacher as they speak from a "we" perspective (van Lier, 2008). Teachers can create an opportunity for students to work as individuals (e.g., organize their work schedule using Google calendar) as well as in groups (e.g., conduct a group project through cooperative learning). The key is to let their *voice* be heard in their use of language. Voice can be defined as infusing one's words with one's own feelings, thoughts, and identity (Bakhtin, 1981). Teachers can find ways for students to express their emotions, transfer their prior knowledge and skills, and choose and enact their desirable identities in their target language.

 **CLASSROOM CONNECTIONS**

Most L2 learners would contend that at the very beginning stages of learning an L2, they cannot very adequately express their *voice* (by infusing words with "feelings, thoughts, and identity"). Do you agree? At what stage in learning an L2 did you feel you could begin to express your voice in the L2? What were the keys to reaching that level of L2 development? As a teacher, how would you help learners just to *begin* to express their voice? For example, might one's voice be expressed by just raising a hand to object/reject something?

Iida (2010) proposes teaching haiku to help L2 writers develop and express their voice, which eventually leads to their construction of identity. Through the process of expressing personal experiences in haiku and reading and commenting on the quality of their classmates' haiku, they also become aware of the relationship between the writer and the reader. While reading published haiku (e.g., see hsa-haiku.org) and those composed by peers, students are encouraged to respond to the following questions (Iida, 2010, p. 31):

- What is the theme?
- What is the context?
- What is happening in the poem?
- What does the writer want to tell you in the haiku?
- What is your impression from this haiku?

While freely exchanging different interpretations of a haiku and discussing them in groups, students should be encouraged to explore why they feel one way or the other about the haiku. The peer writers should also explain what they intend to express in their haiku.

Promote Perceptual Learning and Affordances

Classrooms should provide language **affordances** (action possibilities) as opposed to merely offering language input. According to Lantolf and Thorne (2006), agency also refers to "the ability to assign relevance and significance to things and events" (p. 143), that is, the ability to perceive affordances. Affordance indicates not the amount of input available but the *opportunities for meaningful action* that the situation affords. It is a reciprocal relationship between an organism and a particular feature of the environment that signals a possibility for action (van Lier, 2000). Agency becomes part of crucial features of handover and takeover in *scaffolding* (see more on scaffolding in Chapter 13).

When developing materials, it is important for teachers to capitalize on learners' cultural and linguistic backgrounds, abilities, and aspirations, as well as on other aspects of their identity that are important to them (artistic, academic, etc.). It is also important to include suitable topics and projects/assignments for their interests and life goals based on the data from needs assessments (see Chapter 9). The analysis of student needs is very important because an oversimplified understanding of learner background can lead to stereotyping L2 students, and eventually promote a "one-size-fits-all" model. Lee (2008) warns that "grouping and categorizing L2 students simply based on their cultural origin neglects the complexity of individuals' different identities and meaning-making processes" (p. 110).

Classroom Connections

In your own learning of an L2, in what ways were you able to seize "opportunities for meaningful action"? Did you feel you were exercising *agency* when you took those actions? How might you help your own students to use their unique identities to individualize projects or assignments that would provide *affordances*?

Teachers may focus on the ways learners can actively *perceive* affordances in their learning environment, capitalizing on their individual knowledge, skills, and experience. For example, perceptual learning can be facilitated through meaningful interaction in an authentic social context in which students draw on multimodal affordances of all senses (e.g., visual, auditory, and haptic) such as texts, symbols, gestures, photos, music, and videos. Various technology devices (computers, portable laptops, tablets, smartphones, etc.) can be used to provide such an opportunity in which students express themselves to take an action – express their ideas and identities through text, emoticons, photos, or video clips (see relevant examples in Chapter 12).

Guide Students to Develop Self-Regulating Strategies

From a psychological viewpoint, agency is an individual property that influences learning behaviors such as self-determination and self-regulation. The construct of *self-regulation* encompasses both the external manifestations of learning strategies and the psychological processes behind them, such as maintaining commitment and self-evaluation (Dörnyei, 2005). *Self-regulatory learning strategies* are "actions and processes directed at acquisition of information or skills that involve agency, purpose, and instrumentality perceptions by learners" (Zimmerman, 1990, p. 5).

These strategies involve a self-feedback system and a decision making process to fit an appropriate strategy with a task or objective through self-evaluation (see Chapter 21). From a sociocultural perspective, this self-regulatory process is enhanced by teachers' and peers' support, crucial to learners' ability to activate their agency. The process is interdependent, and is mediated by a particular social situation. Learners should be encouraged to exert their agency and to be aware of the responsibility for one's own actions vis-à-vis the environment. Teachers should draw on open-ended and content-oriented questions rather than closed- and rule-driven questions (see Chapters 13 and 19).

Teachers can guide students in developing self-regulating strategies by first having them become aware of what self-regulated learners usually do, as outlined by Oxford (2011) or the characteristics of "good language learners" (see *PLLT*, Chapter 5). It may be helpful to introduce students to strategic techniques (see *PLLT*, Chapter 5, p. 136, and Chapter 3 in this book), in order to maintain their self-regulatory learning processes.

However, as Ushioda (2009) emphasized, teachers must be aware of the complexity of viewing their students as "persons-in-context," as opposed to hastily taking a predictive inclination, in understanding the process of successful language learning. Teachers need to take a holistic approach in guiding, facilitating, and assessing self-regulatory (or autonomous) learning, such as analyzing students' narrative accounts and paying attention to the cycle of how they relate themselves to their social worlds through their perceptions, actions, and interpretations (van Lier, 2007; Lamb, 2011).

SUMMARY GUIDELINES FOR ENACTING AGENCY IN L2 CLASSROOMS

- Encourage learners to "do" language.
- Allow learners' *voice* to develop.
- Promote the development of *affordances* (action possibilities).
- Offer opportunities for *perceptual* learning.
- Guide students to develop self-regulating strategies.
- Treat students as "persons in context".

FOR THE TEACHER: ACTIVITIES (A) & DISCUSSION (D)

Note: For each of the "Classroom Connections" in this chapter, you may wish to turn them into individual or pair-work discussion questions.

1. **(A)** Divide the class into small groups of three or four and ask them to look at the English lesson in Chapter 1. Then, assigning segments of the lesson to different groups, ask them to consider whether or not what happened could have promoted or demoted students' *agency* during the

lesson. What aspects of agency did you draw on in your analysis? What might be the ingredients that perhaps would indicate more or less agency?

2. **(A)** Divide the class into pairs or groups, and ask them to share personal experiences in their own L2 learning of when their emotional state affected the process of their decision-making and action-taking. Then have them share what they think a teacher could do to counteract the negative effects of emotion.
3. **(A)** Assign students to write a journal entry about their memorable L2 learning events (either positive or negative). Then, have them bring their journal entries to class and exchange them, in small groups, with their peers. Ask students to find instances in which a particular *experience* or *interpretation* reflected the author's *identity* or sense of *agency*. Ask them to discuss any possible factors that may have influenced the learner's perception and evaluation of the experience. Ask for volunteers to share their findings with the whole class.
4. **(D)** Ask the class to brainstorm various classroom seating arrangements that would be conducive to the emergence of students' agency. Prompt them with the suggestion of "desks all facing the front" and "desks in concentric circles," and ask for some other suggestions, and list them on the board. Then, as a review of concepts presented in this chapter, ask them to identify what *specific aspects* of agency might be promoted.
5. **(A)** Pair students up and ask them to share the extent to which they developed self-regulating strategies when learning an L2. What were some of those strategies? Were they encouraged by the teacher? How did using those strategies give you a sense of *agency*?
6. **(D)** Review the factors in the final section of this chapter that were suggested as guidelines for enacting agency. Ask students to volunteer any experiences they have had in learning an L2 that promoted (or demoted) their own sense of agency. Ask the rest of the class to comment on why those instances promoted/demoted agency.

FOR YOUR FURTHER READING

Duff, P. (2012). Identity, agency, and SLA. In A. Mackey & S. Gass (Eds.), *Handbook of second language acquisition* (pp. 410–426). London, UK: Routledge.

A brief yet comprehensive review article on the issues of identity and agency in L2 development. It offers useful discussions about historical and current perspectives on identity and agency discussed in SLA and sociolinguistic research.

van Lier, L. (2008). Agency in the classroom. In J. Lantolf & M. Poehner (Eds.), *Sociocultural theory and the teaching of second languages* (pp. 163–186). London, UK: Equinox.

An excellent discussion on the notion of agency and its role in L2 learning and teaching from both theoretical and practical points of view. With the extracts from classroom discourse, the author illustrates how learner agency may manifest itself and be enacted or even silenced in relation to identity, perceptions, action, and emotion. Pedagogical implications for action-based curricula also are presented.

Dörnyei, Z., & Ushioda, E. (Eds.). (2009). *Motivation, language identity, and the L2 self*. Bristol, UK: Multilingual Matters.

An edited volume containing a diverse range of conceptual and empirical views on motivation, identity, and the L2 self. The authors attempt to explore the complex relationships between the self and L2 motivation from a dynamic systems perspective.

Fogle, L. W. (2012). *Second language socialization and learner agency: Adoptive family talk*. Bristol, UK: Multilingual Matters.

An examination of language use, language learning, and identity construction within transnational adoptive families, with a focus on how learners achieve agency in L2 socialization processes and how agency informs L2 learning and cultural maintenance.

Murray, G., Gao, X., & Lamb, T. (Eds.). (2011). *Identity, motivation, and autonomy in language learning*. Bristol, UK; Buffalo, NY: Multilingual Matters.

An exploration of the complex relationship between identity, motivation, and autonomy in language learning. Thought-provoking discussions include the constructs of agency, metacognition, imagination, beliefs, and self, followed by pedagogical implications.

Arnold, J., & Murphey, T. (Eds.). (2013). *Meaningful action: Earl Stevick's influence on language teaching*. Cambridge, UK: Cambridge University Press.

An exploration of the importance of meaningful action for language teaching and learning, drawing on the influence of Earl Stevick's work. It offers insight into how learners can engage in activities appealing to sensory and cognitive processes, and how meaning is constructed by learners' internal characteristics and their relationship with others, such as their teachers and peers.

PART II

CONTEXTS OF LEARNING AND TEACHING

One of the principal contributions of the last few decades of research and practice in L2 pedagogy is an increasingly complex set of descriptions of the multiplicity of *contexts* in which L2s are learned and taught. As more and more research corroborated the concept that all learners and all contexts are *not* the same, teaching methodology followed with explorations of how to identify an array of needs and how to meet them methodologically.

The three chapters of Part II describe some of the principal *contexts* of L2 learning and teaching. Following are brief descriptions of these chapters:

- **Chapter 6, Teaching Across Age Levels,** describes and provides guidelines for one of the most salient learner factors, age. Three general age-based categories are featured: children, *teens* (also known as *tweens*), and adults.
- **Chapter 7, Teaching Across Proficiency Levels,** treats another obvious contextual variable, proficiency level, with descriptions and applications for what are loosely labeled *beginning*, *intermediate*, and *advanced* levels of learning.
- **Chapter 8, Cultural and Sociopolitical Contexts,** surveys one of the most complex, fascinating, and enigmatic facets of L2 learning and teaching worldwide. Issues of culture, ethnicity, identity, agency, and situational politics are far-reaching and can have direct bearing on the success of a learner. Within those settings, *institutions* of learning are often a unique blend of culture, politics, and educational philosophy.

CHAPTER **6**

TEACHING ACROSS AGE LEVELS

Questions for Reflection

- What are the pertinent *age* factors to incorporate into designing lessons and courses?
- What are the unique characteristics of *children's* learning of additional languages, especially in classroom contexts?
- How do mental, emotional, and physical differences between *adults* and *children* affect teaching across age levels?
- What are some of the characteristics of students "in between" childhood and adulthood?
- What kinds of tasks and activities are appealing and challenging to teenagers?

Those of us who are language teacher educators are occasionally asked about how one can prepare to teach an L2. They might ask something like, "Since English is my native language, I won't have any problem teaching it as a second language, will I?" Or on the eve of their departure for another country (without the slightest clue of who their future students will be), "Can you recommend a good textbook for my students?" Or maybe even, "I'd like to learn how to teach Chinese. Can you recommend a good workshop?"

These questions may be buoyed by advertisements in the media that promise lifelong employment as an English teacher (in exotic places) if only you'll attend someone's weekend seminar and of course pay a hefty enrollment fee. So far in this book, you undoubtedly have begun to sense the complexity of teaching an L2, and you have begun to appreciate the array of questions, issues, approaches, techniques, and principles that must be included in any training as a language teacher—a complexity that cannot be covered effectively in a weekend workshop.

As you saw in Chapter 3, part of this complexity is brought on by the multiplicity of contexts in which languages are learned and taught. Even if you could somehow pack a suitcase full of the most current teaching resources, you would still have to face the question of *who* your learners are, *where* they are learning, and *why* they are learning.

This chapter begins to deal with contextual considerations in language teaching by addressing the learner variable of *age*. Chapter 7 then covers the variable of language proficiency (beginning, intermediate, and advanced). And Chapter 8 surveys some of the often thorny variables introduced by sociopolitical contexts of teaching, ranging from country to culture to institution. Each of these considerations is essential to weave into your choices of lesson organization, techniques and activities, and supporting materials.

TEACHING CHILDREN: THE YOUNGER, THE BETTER?

Popular tradition would have you believe that children are effortless L2 learners, and that the younger a child is when exposed to an L2, the better will be the outcome. The corollary to this belief is that children are superior to adults in their eventual success. On both counts, the SLA research offers counter-evidence (Singleton & Ryan, 2004; Singleton & Muñoz, 2011), which calls for some major qualifications of any statement about age and acquisition. Let's look at some of those caveats.

Effort. Children's widespread success in acquiring second languages belies a tremendous subconscious *effort* devoted to the task. As you may have discovered in other reading (see *PLLT*, Chapters 2 and 3), children exercise a good deal of both cognitive and affective effort in order to internalize both native and second languages. The difference between children and adults (that is, persons beyond the age of puberty) lies primarily in the contrast between the child's spontaneous, *peripheral* attention to language forms and the adult's tendency to give overt, *focal* awareness of and attention to those forms.

What is "success"? Adults are not necessarily less successful in their efforts. Studies have shown that adults, in fact, can be superior in a number of aspects of acquisition (Singleton & Muñoz, 2011). They can learn and retain a larger vocabulary. They can utilize various deductive and abstract processes to shortcut the learning of grammatical and other linguistic concepts. And, in classroom learning, their superior intellect usually helps them to learn faster than a child. So, while children's fluency and naturalness are often the envy of adults struggling with second languages, the context of classroom instruction may introduce some difficulties to children learning an L2.

Younger versus older children. The popular claim of "the younger the better" fails to differentiate very young children (say, four- to six-year-olds) from pre-pubescent children (twelve to thirteen) and a range of ages in between. There are actually many instances of six- to twelve-year-old children manifesting significant difficulty in acquiring a second language for a multitude of reasons (Garton, Copland, & Burns, 2011). Ranking high on that list of reasons are a number of complex personal, social, cultural, and political factors at play in elementary school education.

Teaching an L2 to school-age children, therefore, is not merely a matter of setting them loose on a plethora of authentic language tasks in the classroom. In fact, for some TESOL professionals (Shin, 2014), the challenge of teaching children warrants a separate acronym: TEYL (teaching English to young learners). Teacher reference books are devoted solely to the issues, principles, and methodology surrounding the teaching of children (Linse, 2005; Pinter, 2006; Curtain & Dahlberg, 2010).

Classroom Connections

Were you exposed to other languages as a child? What were the circumstances? If you were *taught* an L2 for even a few weeks in elementary school, what are your recollections of the experience? Before reading on in this chapter, think about what your *approach* would be to teaching an L2 to young children? What would your foundation stones be? What would you pay special attention to?

To successfully teach children a second language requires specific skills and intuitions that differ from those appropriate for adult teaching. Five categories may help give some practical approaches to teaching children.

Intellectual Development

> An elementary school teacher once asked her students to find a piece of paper and pencil and write something down. A little boy raised his hand and said, "Teacher, I ain't got no pencil." The teacher, somewhat perturbed by his grammar, embarked on a barrage of corrective patterns: "I don't have a pencil. You don't have a pencil. We don't have pencils . . . " Confused and bewildered, the child responded, "Ain't nobody got no pencils?"

Because children (up to the age of about eleven) are still in an intellectual stage of what Piaget (1972) called "concrete operations," we need to remember their limitations. Rules, explanations, and other even slightly abstract talk about language must be approached with extreme caution. Children are centered on the here and now, on the functional purposes of language. They have little appreciation for our adult notions of "correctness," and they certainly cannot grasp the metalanguage we use to describe and explain linguistic concepts. Considering children's cognitive development, here is some advice.

Guidelines for Teaching Children: Cognitive Development

- Don't *explain* grammar using terms like "present progressive" or "relative clause."
- *Rules* stated in abstract terms ("To make a statement into a question, you add a *do* or *does*") should be avoided.
- Some grammatical concepts, especially at the upper levels of childhood, can be called to learners' attention by showing them

certain *patterns* ("Notice the *ing* at the end of the word") and *examples* ("This is the way we say it when it's happening right now: 'I'm walking to the door'").

- Certain more difficult concepts or patterns require more *repetition* than adults need, but not to the point of boredom! Short, snappy drills may be very helpful.
- But when you do short drills, make sure your students understand the *meaning* and *relevance* of what they are reciting. Try to avoid scenes like the one with the little boy who had no pencil!

Attention Span

One of the salient differences between adults and children is attention span. It's important to understand what attention span means. Put children in front of a TV showing a favorite cartoon, or holding an iPad with the latest video game, and they will stay riveted for the duration! So, you cannot make a sweeping claim that children have short attention spans! But short attention spans do come into play when children have to deal with material that to them is tedious, useless, or overly difficult. Because language lessons at times can be difficult for children, your job is to make them interesting, lively, and fun. How do you do that?

Guidelines for Teaching Children: Attention Span

- Children are focused on the immediate *here and now*, so activities need to be designed to capture their immediate *interest*. Songs, games, sports, arts and crafts, and talking about *themselves* are examples.
- A lesson needs a *variety* of activities to keep interest and attention alive. On the other hand, they can maintain attention for quite a long time to certain activities that are highly fascinating.
- A teacher needs to be *animated*, lively, and enthusiastic about the subject matter. Consider the classroom a stage on which you are the lead actor. Your energy will be infectious. While you may think that you're overdoing it, children love this exaggeration, and it can keep spirits up and minds alert.
- A *sense of humor* will go a long way to keep children laughing and learning. Because children's humor is quite different from adults', remember to put yourself in their shoes.
- Children have a lot of natural *curiosity*. Make sure you tap into that curiosity whenever possible, and you will thereby help to maintain attention and focus.

Consider the following task that was used in an EAL class for children ages 8–10, an example of an activity that certainly held students' *attention* as they collaborated to complete the project.

> The teacher introduced a science project in which her class, in teams of four, made a volcano out of modeling clay (of various colors), then placed some baking soda, vinegar, and food coloring into the "crater" for a quite explosive effect! A lot of language was used: color terms, numbers (to measure amounts of baking soda and vinegar), requesting discourse, exclamations, negotiations, and more.

Sensory Input

Children need to have all five senses stimulated. Your activities should strive to go well beyond the visual and auditory modes that may be sufficient for an adult classroom.

Guidelines for Teaching Children: Sensory Input

- Pepper your lessons with *physical* activity, such as having students act out things (role-play), play games, sing songs, or respond to commands to do things like stand up, walk to the window, touch your elbow, etc.
- Projects and other *hands-on activities* will help children to internalize language. Examples include the science project described above, plus drawing pictures, working in groups on a poster or diorama, cooking foods (conditions permitting), dressing up for holidays, and performing a song for other classes.
- *Sensory aids* help children to internalize concepts. The smell of flowers, the touch of plants and fruits, the taste of foods, and liberal doses of audiovisual stimuli like videos, photos, and music are all important elements in children's language teaching.
- Remember that your own *nonverbal language* is important because children will attend very sensitively to your facial expressions, gestures, and other elements of your body language.

Classroom Connections

To what extent did the "volcano" project described above follow the guidelines for keeping children's *attention span* as well as providing *sensory input*? What specific *language* objectives could be achieved in the task? If you were to follow up this task with some *form-focused* reminders for the children, what might they be? An example: "What words for *colors* did you learn/use?" Be sure to keep children's ages in mind in these comments.

Affective Factors

A common myth is that children are relatively unaffected by the inhibitions that adults find to be a block to learning. Not so! Children are often innovative in language forms but still have a great many inhibitions. They are extremely sensitive, especially to peers: What do others think of me? What will so-and-so think when I speak in this other language? Children are in many ways even more fragile than adults. Their egos are still being shaped, and therefore the slightest nuances of communication can be negatively interpreted. Teachers need to help them to overcome such potential barriers to learning.

Guidelines for Teaching Children: Affective Factors

- Help your students to laugh *with* each other at various mistakes that they all make.
- Be patient and *supportive* in order to build self-esteem by complimenting them on their work and accomplishments. At the same time be *firm* in your expectations of students.
- Elicit as much *oral participation* as possible from students, especially the quieter ones, to give them opportunities to try out newly introduced language.

Authentic, Meaningful Language

Children are focused on what this new language can actually be used for here and now. They are less willing to put up with language that doesn't hold immediate rewards for them. Your classes can ill afford to have an overload of language that is neither authentic nor meaningful.

Guidelines for Teaching Children: Authenticity

- Be real; be *genuine.* Show that you truly *enjoy* them. Children are good at sensing when adults are "going through the motions" or bored with their own job. Enthusiastically embrace children as if they are your own!
- Language needs to be firmly *context embedded.* Story lines, familiar situations and characters, real-life conversations, meaningful purposes in using language—these will establish a context within which language can be used and thereby improve attention and retention. *Context-reduced* language in abstract, isolated, unconnected sentences will be much less readily tolerated by children's minds.

- Capitalize on the interrelationships among the various skills (listening, speaking, reading, and writing) for reinforcement. *Integrate* at least two skills whenever possible. If language is broken into too many bits and pieces, students may not see the relationship to the whole.

Let's take a look at a lesson, developed by Taiwanese English teacher Vera Chen for 8- to 9-year-old children in Taiwan learning English. As you go through the lesson, think about the extent to which some of the above principles and tips for teaching children are applied.

Context: Private language school in Taiwan

Students: Ages 8-9 years old; L1 Taiwanese, Mandarin

Class level: Low-intermediate conversation class

Number of students: 12

Length of class: 60 minutes

In the previous class:

Introduced:

1. past tense verbs (mostly regular verbs and a few irregular ones)
2. Q & A: *What did you do yesterday?*
   I played basketball.

Today's lesson:

1. Review past tense verbs from the previous class
2. Introduce some new regular past tense verbs
3. Introduce more irregular verbs
4. Q & A: *What did* ________ *do last night/yesterday morning/last Monday?*
   He/She ________.

A. Warm-up

Review past tense verbs:

1. Students shout out verbs.
   T writes verbs on the board and makes a sentence orally:
   For example: *play → played (Say: I played basketball yesterday.)*
   go → went (Say: I went to a mall yesterday.)
2. Students pair up. (a stronger S with a not-so-strong S)
3. Students in the class ask T, "What did you do yesterday?"
   T says, *"I went for a walk yesterday."*

Pairs go to the board, circle "go -> went," each S repeats what the T said:
"I went for a walk yesterday."
Pairs continue this process.
Note: T switches from <u>yesterday</u> to <u>last night</u>, <u>yesterday morning</u>, etc.
T draws a clock and calendar and colors the time period to help Ss understand: last night, yesterday morning, etc.

4. T asks Ss randomly (starts with stronger Ss), *"What did you do?"*
   S1, *"I watched TV."*
   S2, *"I go see a movie."*
   T, *"I <u>went</u> to see a movie."*

B. Introduce: What did [<u>a third person</u>] do last night?

Introduce: What did [he/she] do last night?

1. Ss mingle and ask each other.
   T shouts, "Stop!" and randomly picks one S and asks about his partner, *"What did Daniel do last night?"*
   S answers, *"He played computer games last night."*
2. T writes the following on the board.
   "What did [name of student] do last night?"
   "He/She ________ last night."
3. Ss go back and mingle. T stops Ss a few more times.
4. T asks each S about their partner for a wrap up.

C. Practice/Drill

1. T gives each S a card with a picture printed on it. For example,
   Picture. 1 Jeremy

2. Reminder: T calls Ss' attention to the board:
   "What did [name of student] do last night?
   "He/She _________ last night."

3. Ask a S come up to the front and do the demo with T.
   Make sure every S sees the picture printed on the card.
   T shows the card to the S doing the demo (and the whole class) and asks,
   "What did Jeremy do last night?"
   S answers, "He cooked last night."

4. T asks Ss if there are any questions regarding what they should do and say with their pictures.

5. Ss mingle with their cards, asking each other questions using the past tense. T listens in randomly as Ss do this activity.

D. Wrap up

1. T uses PowerPoint slides and projector to show the exact same pictures handed out to Ss earlier.

2. T asks Ss randomly about each picture.
   "What did _________ do last night/yesterday morning/last Monday?"

3. T then introduces new pictures in the PowerPoint slides encourages Ss, in pairs, to ask each other questions based on the new set of pictures.

4. Note: If the T considers Ss are ready, T adds multiple people in the pictures and introduces sentences like:
   Jeremy cooked dinner with Karen last night.
   Daniel played baseball with Robert yesterday.
   Stephanie saw a movie with Susan last Saturday.

F. Extra-class assignment

Practice past tense verbs with a friend or a brother/sister.

Classroom Connections

In what way were the five categories (described above) manifested in Vera Chen's lesson? Did it suit the children's level of intellect? Were the students able to *use* examples of the past tense (vs. hearing rules and explanations)? Was the length of each activity appropriate for their attention spans? Was there appropriate sensory input? Did the teacher stimulate authentic, meaningful language?

TEACHING ADULTS: THE "ADULT ADVANTAGE"?

Although many of the tips for teaching children can apply in some ways to teaching adults, the latter age group poses some different, special considerations for the classroom teacher. Adults have superior cognitive abilities that can make them more successful in certain classroom endeavors. Their need for sensory input can rely a little more on their imaginations ("imagine" smelling a rose vs. actually smelling a rose). Their level of shyness can be equal to or greater than that of children, but adults usually have acquired a self-confidence not found in children. And, because of adults' cognitive abilities, they can at least occasionally deal with language that isn't embedded in a "here and now" context (Smith & Strong, 2009; Eyring, 2014).

Adults also bring *life experiences* to the classroom, which gives them background schemata as a backdrop for the situations introduced in a curriculum. It means they can bring a rich array of skills, strategies, and convictions to bear on the tasks that the language course asks them to carry out. Spalding (2013), commenting on the "fun" aspect of teaching adults, quips: "My students have told me where you can buy a fake Social Security card . . . and what life is like in a refugee camp in Thailand [and] about underground clubs and high school race riots. My students have taught me more than I could have learned in a hundred lifetimes" (p. 13).

Let's look more specifically at the adult student.

Abstract thinking ability. Adults are better able to understand a context-reduced segment of language. Authenticity and meaningfulness are, of course, still highly important, but with adults a teacher can take temporary digressions to dissect and examine isolated linguistic properties.

Attention span. Adults have longer attention spans for material that may not be intrinsically interesting to them.

Self-confidence. Adults often bring a modicum of general self-confidence into a classroom, so their egos may be somewhat stronger, but we should never underestimate the emotional fragility of adults.

Vocational interests. Adult learners, especially those in their college years and beyond, are more able to focus on their vocational future, and will derive motivational intensity from such vision.

From those four observations, here's some advice for teaching adults.

GUIDELINES FOR TEACHING ADULTS

- Beware of *too much* abstract explanation of grammar and vocabulary. Keep adults focused primarily on meaning, secondarily on form.

- Even though adults cannot express complex thinking in their new language, they are nevertheless intelligent adults with mature cognition and adult emotions. Show *respect* for the deeper thoughts and feelings that may be "trapped" for the moment by an inability to express oneself in the L2.
- Don't treat adults in your class like children by calling them "kids," using "caretaker" talk (the way parents talk to children), or talking "down" to them. And if *discipline* is necessary, treat them like the responsible adults they are.
- Yes, adults have longer attention spans than children, but it's still important to keep your activities moving along at a *lively pace.*
- Give your students as many opportunities as possible to make *choices* (to enact their *agency*) about what they will do in and out of the classroom. That way, they can more effectively make an *investment* in their own learning process.
- Give them opportunities to *share their stories.* Even at lower ability levels, asking them to talk or write or ask questions about their lives, past and present, can enrich the meaningfulness of learning the L2.
- Tap into your students' *vocational* or avocational interests as much as possible in your choice of topics, issues, questions, and discussions in the classroom. For adults in their twenties and beyond, extra-class field trips, Internet exploration, interviews, and projects can help boost relevance and investment.

Classroom Connections

The task (on page 119) described by Richards and Burns (2012) is designed for adults at a high beginning to intermediate level. In this example of Task-Based Language Teaching, to what extent were characteristics of adults' (vs. children's) learning characteristics taken into account? Did the task capitalize on the "adult advantage"? Depending on the context, what do you think you might have done differently with this same task?

Sample Listening Task

The following exercise, designed for high beginning to intermediate English learners, involves teacher-student discussion, explanation, and an interactive listening task cued by an audio recording. The latter uses a simple handout (to accompany item #4 below) that asks students to identify who is speaking and what is being requested in each exchange.

Activity 6.2	***Who? Where? and What?***
Level	Beginner–Intermediate
Handout	Page 180
Tip	Establish appropriate purposes for listening.
Description	Understanding the difference between interactional and transactional speech can be very helpful for students, particularly when they are interacting with people they are not familiar with.

1. Talk with students about interactional speech (in which the focus is on establishing a comfortable zone of interaction with others) and transactional speech (where the focus is on what is said or done).
2. Explain that they will hear six short transactional interactions involving two or three speakers (husband, wife, flight attendant). Their task is to identify who is speaking and what the person is requesting.
3. Play the recording and model the first interaction to demonstrate what learners should do.
4. Have students complete the activity for interactions 2–6.
5. Check answers with the class (use the transcript for this).

Teaching notes:

- With lower-level learners, use the visuals provided and ask students to guess what the request will be about. With higher-level learners, the task is more interesting and challenging without the visuals.
- As an extension, ask learners to identify which of the interactions are more informal (the ones involving the husband and wife).

TEACHING "IN BETWEEN"

Ask a teacher of 11- to 14-year-old children how easy that job is! Invariably, the answer will express a blend of both challenge and joy. The *challenge* is in recognizing and appreciating the enormous physical, mental, and emotional changes occurring at this age, which, ironically, is intertwined with the *joy* of stretching these wonderful, growing young people. It takes a special person to be able to manage, entertain, and instruct a classroom full of adolescent kids!

Does a child suddenly cease to be a child one day and become an adult? Of course not. But while research on SLA typically focuses on either children or adults, often in contrast, few research findings are available for L2 learning at this age, perhaps because of the enigma of teaching adolescents (Legutke, 2012). So, we do well to consider some of the variables that apply in teaching the "in-betweens." The *Urban Dictionary* describes 10- to 14-year-old girls as *tweens*, "too old for toys, too young for boys," which may only begin to touch on the characteristics of this age.

The tweens (boys, too!) are in an age of transition and self-consciousness. Intellectually, they are developing their abstract thinking ability, and in L2 learning are becoming capable of using conscious, explicit strategies. Their *intelligence* is broadening, becoming more comprehensive and integrated (Gardner, 2011), and they can process underlying principles that are beneath the surface (Sternberg, 2007). Their sense of *identity* is wrapped up in the turmoil of adolescent relationships, bonding with a circle of friends, giggling over in-jokes, figuring out who they are, and relating to the opposite sex—whose physical changes are both a pleasure and an enigma (Slavin, 2011). All of which can make concentration in the classroom a significant challenge (Ur, 2012, p. 265).

More specifically, let's look at some of what we know about adolescents, and then relate that knowledge to some practical advice.

Intellectual capacity. In Piaget's (1955, 1970) terms, the onset of abstract operational thought (age 11) means more sophisticated intellectual processing. Complex problems can be solved with logical thinking. Linguistic metalanguage (e.g., grammatical explanations) can now have some impact. However, *over*-analysis may be as ineffective as it is on adults.

Attention spans. While attention spans are lengthening, with many diversions present in a teenager's life, those potential attention spans can easily be mitigated as the learner focuses on self, appearance, sexuality, being accepted, a weekend party, and perhaps the temptation, when they think the teacher isn't looking, to sneak in text-message exchanges on their smart phones!

Identity. Factors surrounding ego, self-image, and self-efficacy are at their pinnacle. Teens are ultra-sensitive to how others perceive their changing physical and emotional selves along with their mental capabilities. A further identity issue is found in a significant number of adolescent L2 learners who must become "language brokers"—interpreters and translators for parents and grandparents when the latter are not proficient users of the L2 (Tse, 1996; Villanueva & Buriel, 2010; Lee, Hill-Bonnet, & Raley, 2011).

With those three major domains in mind, consider the following advice as a beginning toward effectively teaching adolescents.

Guidelines for Teaching Young Teenagers

- When you use explanations, definitions, and other *metalanguage*, make them brief, to the point, and relevant to the communicative tasks at hand. Grammar points can be made by *analogy* more effectively than by a possibly stilted, academic monologue.
- Some of your activities can involve *critical thinking* (applying values and beliefs to controversial issues). For example, environmental topics such as waste and pollution can underlie interesting field trips, projects, and problem-posing discussions, including neighborhood "action" to put findings into practice.
- Make sure your lessons have *variety*, so that attention span is not an impeding factor. Remember, this is a classroom and not a movie or video game on their electronic tablets, so keep the pace at an appropriate clip.
- Appeal to your students' *immediate interests*. What music and music groups do your students like? What do they text each other about? What kinds of "gossip" do they enjoy? What sports or sports figures are they into? What TV shows, movies, or clothing styles capture their interests?
- Give them chances to talk about their own *likes and dislikes*. Fashions, actors, singers, and sports teams will usually stimulate opinions.
- Keep *self-esteem* high by affirming each learner's talents and strengths. Avoid embarrassing them by calling attention to their mistakes. When they do make errors/mistakes in the L2, use those instances as learning moments. And beware, an 11- or 12-year-old will *not* want to be called a "child" or treated as one!
- Encourage small-group work where risks can be taken more easily. In those groups, emphasize *cooperative teamwork*, and conversely, de-emphasize competition among classmates.

Now let's look at a sample activity designed by Claire Ballon Arnett for 13- to 14-year-old students in junior high school in California taking English as a Second Language (ESL) classes in addition to their regular school work. The students are predominantly immigrants from Spanish L1 countries. Students attend this 50-minute class twice a week to develop their English skills so that they can eventually "mainstream." The class consists of 14 students who are of low intermediate proficiency in English. The lesson focuses on speaking fluency, with reading and listening skills supporting this aim. As you read her lesson plan, think about the extent to which the activity takes into account the "tips" outlined above.

Lesson Outline

Setting: ESL junior high school students attending a public school in Monterey, California

Learner Background Information:

- Class size: 10-14
- Age: 13-14
- Students are from Spanish L1 background
- English proficiency level: Low Intermediate

Lesson Length: 50 minutes

Terminal objectives

Students will be able to:

- Obtain specific information from peers using wh-questions.
- Provide specific information to peers by responding to wh-questions.
- Share their opinions with peers using wh-questions.

Enabling objectives

Students will be able to:

- Gather information to make plans to see a movie by using wh-questions in an information gap activity.
- Respond to questions about movie listings by reading and paraphrasing their contents in an information gap activity.
- Give suggestions by using wh-questions, e.g., "How about . . . ?"

Materials and Equipment

1. Attendance sheet
2. Whiteboard and dry erase markers
3. Movie Listings Handout, 7 copies (see Appendix A)
4. Student B Handout, 7 copies (see Appendix B)
5. Movie Night Handout, 14 copies (see Appendix C)
6. Notebooks (Students have these)
7. Timer
8. Student dictionaries (Students have these)
9. Student journals (Students have these)

Time	Procedures/Teacher Actions	Materials/ Equipment
3–5 min.	**Introduction and Warm-up** • Make announcements. • Take attendance with the attendance sheet. • Free talk with Ss about any interesting things that have happened to them since last class. • Invite Ss to recall what we concluded at the end of the last class session.	• Attendance sheet
3–5 min.	**Schema Activation Pre-task (Whole Class)** • Introduce the topic of going to the movies. • Ask Ss to name things you need to know when picking a movie; write their suggestions on the whiteboard with dry-erase marker to make a mind-map. • Distribute the Movie Listings Handout to the Ss; have them share with their neighbor, two people to one handout. • Ask Ss to look over the listings and find some of the things from the mind-map on the listings.	• Whiteboard and dry-erase markers • Movie Listings Handout (7 copies)
5–8 min.	**Transition: Explaining the Main Task** • Tell Ss to make pairs with the person they are sharing the Movie Night Handout with. • Have Ss do rock paper scissors, winner chooses if they are A or B. • Explain the activity: Student A will have the Movie Listings Handout and Student B will have the Student B Handout. Tell Ss that they will have to work together and follow the directions on the Movie Night Handout. • Distribute the Student B Handout to all B's, and a Movie Night Handout to all students. • Call on a student to read the first line of directions on the Movie Night Handout, then have them pick another student to read the next line until all the directions have been read. • Have the Ss read aloud the words in the left-hand part of the table on the Movie Night Handout and double check their understanding of the words. • Check for understanding of instructions by asking for Ss to give an example of what they might ask to accomplish the task. • Give Ss 2 minutes with their notebooks to brainstorm some questions they might ask during the task.	• Student B Handout (7 copies) • Movie Night Handout (14 copies) • Notebooks (Ss have these)

Time	Procedures/Teacher Actions	Materials/ Equipment
5 min.	**Main Task (Pair work)** • Put 5 minutes on the timer and tell Ss to begin the Movie Night Handout task. • Move about the classroom and listen to Ss to make sure they are on task. • Contingency: If Ss have trouble with the movie listings, help them by explaining what the movies are about and paraphrase difficult movie titles. • When the timer runs out, announce "Time's up!"	• Timer • Movie Listings Handout (7 copies) • Student B Handout (7 copies) • Movie Night Handout (14 copies)
4–6 min.	**Debrief (Whole class)** • Get Ss feedback on the task by asking them to offer their impressions. • Ask Ss to talk at their tables for 1 minute about the strategies they used to pick a movie. • Have Ss give some examples of strategies they used to pick a movie. • Tell Ss they'll now repeat the task with new partners and with switched roles. • Tell Ss to think about the strategies their classmate's mentioned as they attempt their new role.	
5–7 min.	**If Ss are struggling with Main Task: Form practice (Whole class)** • Ask Ss to call out the wh-words they remember from last lesson and write them on the board. • Tell Ss to take a minute and discuss at their group tables a way they might ask the name of a movie title, Ex. "What is the movie called? "What is the movie's name?" Write Ss suggestions on the board and have Ss do choral practice of the Qs. • Ask Ss to discuss in groups a way they might find out which movie their friend wants to see, Ex. "What movie do you want to watch?" "Which movie do you want to see?" Draw Ss attention to do-insertion, have Ss practice as a class. • Give Ss a couple minutes to look at their Movie Night handout and brainstorm ways to ask similar questions for each row of the handout. • Proceed to Main Task Repetition, and do not do Second Debrief.	• Timer • Movie Listings Handout (7 copies) • Student B Handout (7 copies) • Movie Night Handout (14 copies)

Time	Procedures/Teacher Actions	Materials/ Equipment
	If Ss seem comfortable with Main Task: **Main Task Repetition (pair work)** • Tell Ss to trade roles and exchange their Movie Listings Handout and Student B Handout with each other. • Tell the new Student A's to move one seat to the left to form a new pair. • Ask Student A's to raise their hands, ask one to paraphrase what their role in the task is to check understanding. • Ask Student B's to raise their hands, ask one to paraphrase what their role in the task is to check understanding. • Put 5 minutes on the timer and tell Ss to begin. • Move about the classroom and listen to Ss to check if they are on task. • When the timer runs out, announce "Time's up!"	
6–8 min.	**Second Debrief: Focus on Form (Whole class)** • Ask Ss to give impressions on their second attempt at the task. Was it easier this time? Why? • Make a grid with these sections on the whiteboard: Movie title: Movie theater: Showtime: Length: Genre: Other • Ask for Ss to come up to the board and write an example of a question they asked to learn these pieces of information about the movie. • Draw attention to the Wh-questions that were elicited, discuss the forms with the class and help Ss identify which Qs were well formed. • Ask Ss to volunteer which movies they ended up choosing to see; ask how they decided on a movie and discuss the negotiation strategies they used.	• Whiteboard and dry-erase markers
5–7 min.	**Closing/Review** • Tell Ss to free write in their journals about something they learned today. • Dismiss Ss for the day. • Have Ss turn in their Movie Night handout as they leave class.	• Student journals

Appendix A: Movie Listings Handout

The handout consists of listings of five movies being shown in the Monterey-Salinas (California) area.

The five movies are;

The Hunger Games: Catching Fire
Frozen
The Nut Job
Ride Along
Jack Ryan: Shadow Recruit

The information, taken from website listings for each movie, consists of:

Name of movie
Length
MPAA rating
Stars and other cast members
Genre
Synopsis
Official website

Names of five theaters currently showing the movie
Theater address and phone number
Showtimes

Appendix B: Student B Handout

Below is your schedule for the day of the movie. Also keep in mind that theaters in Monterey are 5 minutes away and theaters in Salinas are 20 minutes away.

8:00–9:00	School
9:00–10:00	
10:00–11:00	
11:00–12:00	
12:00–1:00	
1:00–2:00	
2:00–3:00	
3:00–4:00	Club activities
4:00–5:00	
5:00–6:00	
6:00–7:00	
7:00–8:00	
8:00–9:00	
9:00–10:00	
10:00–11:00	Curfew

Appendix C:

Movie Night Handout

Name ___________________________

Date _________________

Directions: In pairs, decide on a movie to see together. Student A has the listings for five movies and Student B has a schedule. Talk together and pick a movie that will fit in Student B's schedule. You will have 5 minutes to pick a movie. You can't look at each other's papers, but you may use your student dictionaries to look up words.

Movie Title	*Example: Harry Potter and the Sorcerer's Stone* 1. 2.
Movie Theater	*Example: Century 20 Oakridge and XD* 1. 2.
Showtime	*Example: 6:20 pm* 1. 2.
Length	*Example: 101 minutes* 1. 2.
Genre	*Example: Comedy* 1. 2.

Classroom Connections

In Claire Ballon Arnett's lesson for 13- to 14-year-old students, how is age accounted for? Consider the overall topic, the type of activities that were used, the management of the classroom, the pacing of the lesson, the use of visuals and handouts, and teacher–student exchanges. How much of the lesson is age-*restricted* in some way? (Would it work for adults or much younger children?)

FOR THE TEACHER: ACTIVITIES (A) & DISCUSSION (D)

Note: For each of the "Classroom Connections" in this chapter, you may wish to turn them into individual or pair-work discussion questions.

1. **(A)** Divide your students into small groups of three or four and ask them to look at the English lesson that was described in Chapter 1. That was an adult class. Now, ask each group to discuss how they would go about teaching virtually the same *grammar* and *discourse* to children of, say, ages seven to eight. Would the general topic fit? Would the same grammatical and communicative goals apply? What would they do differently? Have the groups report their findings to the rest of the class.
2. **(A)** Divide the class into pairs or groups, assigning them to categories (a), (b), and (c) below. Ask them to brainstorm other considerations—beyond those mentioned in this chapter—that should be brought to bear on teaching an L2 to:

   (a) children **(b)** adults **(c)** "tweens."

   Have each pair/group share their thoughts with the rest of the class, possibly writing their added factors on the board.
3. **(D)** Ask your students to share any experiences they have had *learning* an L2 in a classroom as a child or adolescent. Did the teacher effectively take into account the factors that have been listed in this chapter? If anyone in the class has *taught* children, ask them to recount that experience. Encourage students to ask questions of the student that is sharing an experience.
4. **(A)** Divide your class into pairs or groups, and assign one of the four categories below to each. Their task is to describe in their own words what the *differences* are between children and adults in the four categories:

   (a) ego-fragility, inhibition, and self-doubt

   (b) ability to learn faster (or more slowly)

   (c) ability to process corrective feedback (noticing and uptake)

   (d) appropriate age-related topics.

   Ask them to provide examples of each of these factors. Then have them report their insights to the rest of the class.
5. **(D)** Engage the class in a discussion about whether one should *teach* language to children at all. Aren't their innate capacities sufficient without having to be instructed? What would happen if children (in a context you specify) were just "exposed" to English with no classroom? What would they gain? What would they lose? You might want to debate this issue, with some class members arguing for the "no-classroom" position and others defending the contention that language classes for children can be beneficial.
6. **(A)** Assign pairs to make a series of three *observations* of L2 classes: one pair goes to an elementary school, another to a middle or junior-high

school, and a third to a class for adults. Each observer should take careful note of the following:

- topic or subject matter of the lesson
- teacher talk and student talk
- variety and type of techniques
- discipline or behavior problems
- physical activity and sensory input
- apparent motivation and interest

After the observation, have each pair share their findings, especially what insights were garnered about teaching at the different age levels.

FOR YOUR FURTHER READING

Crandall, J., & Shin, J. (2013). *Teaching young learners English.* Boston, MA: Heinle ELT.

Pinter, A. (2006). *Teaching young language learners.* Oxford, UK: Oxford University Press.

Both of these practically oriented books consist of a variety of classroom activities suitable for young children, ranging in age from preschool to ten. Activities are thematically organized, either by skill area or by topic. In both, some general comments are made about the issues and principles of teaching children at various ages.

Legutke, M. (2012). Teaching teenagers. In A. Burns & J. Richards (Eds.), *The Cambridge guide to pedagogy and practice in second language teaching* (pp. 112–127). New York, NY: Cambridge University Press.

In this article the author focuses on numerous issues and challenges involved in teaching students who fall "in between" children and adults. Some of the joys of teaching this age group are included.

Eyring, J. (2014). Adult learners in English as a second/foreign language settings. In M. Celce-Murcia, D. Brinton, & A. M. Snow (Eds.), *Teaching English as a second or foreign language* (4th ed., pp. 568–583). Boston, MA: National Geographic Learning.

Smith, A., & Strong, G. (Eds.). (2009). *Adult language learners: Context and innovation.* Alexandria, VA: TESOL.

Instructional practices that are especially useful for adults are presented by numerous authors on a variety of topics, including podcasts, e-portfolios, team teaching, field trips, role plays, and drama.

Pawan, F., & Sietman, G. (Eds.). (2008). *Helping English language learners succeed in middle and high schools.* Alexandria, VA: TESOL.

For a focus on "in-betweeners" and secondary school learners, this edited volume provides helpful information about how to link subject matter with language instruction at this level, along with summaries of related research.

CHAPTER 7

TEACHING ACROSS PROFICIENCY LEVELS

Questions for Reflection

- What is language *ability?* What does it mean to be *proficient* in a language?
- What are the characteristics of what are commonly thought to be "beginning," "intermediate," and "advanced" levels?
- How do the types and complexity of tasks and activities differ across classes of beginning, intermediate, and advanced students?
- How do the concepts of accuracy, fluency, comprehensibility, grammaticality, and sociolinguistic appropriateness apply to teaching different levels of ability?

Introductions at language teacher conferences often go something like this:

"It's nice to meet you, too. What level do you teach?"

"Mostly high-intermediate students in our adult education program. How about you?"

"Well, almost all my students in the refugee program are pretty much beginners, maybe a few high-beginners."

"Oh, I'm sure that's a challenge!"

The terms "beginning," "intermediate," and "advanced" are among the first descriptors we use for our students, but ironically, they are slippery terms. Take a university language institute in the United States, for example, and the "beginning" level will usually have students who already know several hundred English words, are able to engage in a rudimentary conversation, and can read simple texts. In a high school French class in Korea, "beginners" are mostly *true* beginners.

So, a certain sense of relativity must be taken into account when these terms are used, as context usually implies fuzzy lines of distinction. But is there a standard set of guidelines by which levels of ability may be *uniformly* understood? The answer is a qualified yes, in the form of a number of lists of standards, competencies, guidelines, frameworks of reference, or proficiency levels—the terminology varies depending on whose list you're consulting. So, as we look at teaching at various levels of ability in this chapter, let's first try to come to an understanding of what we mean.

DEFINING PROFICIENCY LEVELS

Over the last half-century or more, many definitions of ability levels have appeared in the form of guidelines, standards, and other criteria. While such indices are obviously useful for assessment purposes, they have also served as means for gauging curriculum levels, including concise statements of goals and objectives. Among the dozens—or hundreds—of such lists available across the globe, we'll take a look at several of the more prominent ones.

FSI/ILR Levels

In the United States, one of the first official sets of competencies was compiled in the 1960s by the United States Foreign Service Institute (FSI) to address the need for standards of oral proficiency for government workers in other countries. Up to that time, phrases like "fluent in French" and "excellent German" were subjective terms that were not uniformly applied. In 1968, after several years of research and validation, the FSI, in cooperation with the Interagency Language Roundtable (ILR), released descriptions of levels of proficiency for its newly adopted FSI Oral Interview (Lowe, 1988).

The FSI Oral Interview is a carefully designed set of structured tasks that elicit pronunciation, fluency and integrative ability, sociolinguistic and cultural knowledge, grammar, and vocabulary. The test-taker is judged to possess speaking proficiency that falls into one of the specified levels. "FSI levels" quickly became common parlance among English language teachers and researchers. Conversations among colleagues in the diplomatic corps went something like, "Oh, wow, you're a 3+ already? I'm still at a 2 and hoping to reach 2+ by the end of the year." And everyone seemed to know exactly what that meant! Even with these sweeping descriptions of levels, we were able to better understand a learner's progression from beginning to advanced ability.

Table 7.1 (page 132) lists, in general terms, the six levels (from 0 to 5), now referred to simply as ILR Speaking Proficiency Levels. By adding the "+" symbol to the scale, eleven different sublevels are defined. For detailed descriptors of each of the eleven levels, visit govtilr.org or search for *Interagency Language Roundtable, ILR Scale.*

 **CLASSROOM CONNECTIONS**

In the speaking proficiency levels described above, what is your first-glance thought about the lines of distinction among the different levels? In an L2 that you have studied, what do you think your speaking level is? Think about someone you know who is "fairly fluent" in an L2—what would you say is his or her level? How can you judge that from just these descriptors? How would you use these descriptors in your teaching? Are they useful in assessing your students?

Table 7.1 Summary of ILR Speaking Proficiency Levels

Level	Description
0	Unable to function in the spoken language.
0+	Able to satisfy immediate needs using rehearsed utterances.
1	Able to satisfy minimum courtesy requirements and maintain very simple face-to-face conversations on familiar topics.
1+	Able to initiate and maintain predictable face-to-face conversations and satisfy limited social demands.
2	Able to satisfy routine social demands and limited work requirements.
2+	Able to satisfy most work requirements with language usage that is often, but not always, acceptable and effective.
3	Able to speak the language with sufficient structural accuracy and vocabulary to participate effectively in most formal and informal conversations on practical, social, and professional topics.
3+	Often able to use the language to satisfy professional needs in a wide range of sophisticated and demanding tasks.
4	Able to use the language fluently and accurately on all levels normally pertinent to professional needs.
4+	Speaking proficiency is superior in all respects, usually equivalent to that of a well-educated, highly articulate native speaker.
5	Speaking proficiency is functionally equivalent to that of a highly articulate, well-educated native speaker and reflects the cultural standards of the country where the language is spoken.

IELTS Band Scale

Over the years, the British Council has invested a great deal of effort and expertise in teaching English worldwide, and one its major language agencies is the International English Language Testing System (IELTS). Used in dozens of countries for academic, occupational, and business purposes, the IELTS assesses listening, speaking, reading, and writing. The IELTS Band Scale, not unlike the FSI levels, standardizes a system of tests and defines broadly based descriptors of ten different levels of ability.

Table 7.2 outlines those levels (ranging from 0 to 9), and in this case is designed to apply to any of the four skills. A complete list of descriptions is available at ielts.org or search for *IELTS Band Scale*.

In each of the above scales, you may be wondering how to identify beginning, intermediate, and advanced. Of course, the answer is, "it depends." The institutional context, the range represented by the population of students being targeted, and the ultimate purpose of the classifications all affect the sometimes arbitrary lines of division. Perhaps like colors of a rainbow, there is a gradual progression of hues that remain, even in experts' opinion, subjective.

Table 7.2 IELTS Band Scale

9	Expert User	Has full operational command of the language: appropriate, accurate, and fluent with complete understanding.
8	Very Good User	Has full operational command of the language with only occasional unsystematic inaccuracies and inappropriacies. Misunderstandings may occur in unfamiliar situations. Handles complex detailed argumentation well.
7	Good User	Has operational command of the language, though with occasional inaccuracies, inappropriateness and misunderstandings in some situations. Generally handles complex language well and understands detailed reasoning.
6	Competent User	Has generally effective command of the language despite some inaccuracies, inappropriacies and misunderstandings. Can use and understand fairly complex language, particularly in familiar situations.
5	Modest User	Has partial command of the language, coping with overall meaning in most situations, though is likely to make many mistakes. Should be able to handle basic communication in own field.
4	Limited User	Basic competence is limited to familiar situations. Has frequent problems in using complex language.
3	Extremely Limited User	Conveys and understands only general meaning in very familiar situations.
2	Intermittent User	No real communication is possible except for the most basic information using isolated words or short formulae in familiar situations and to meet immediate needs.
1	Nonuser	Essentially has no ability to use the language beyond possibly a few isolated words.
0	Did not attempt the test	No assessable information provided at all.

 **Classroom Connections**

What are the differences between the IELTS band scales and the previous FSI levels? Do the descriptions of the IELTS scales make it easier to pinpoint the level of L2 learners? Would you favor one system over the other? Is one system more applicable to an instructional setting than the other?

ACTFL Proficiency Guidelines

The American Council on Teaching Foreign Languages, one of the leading national organizations of foreign language pedagogy in the United States, publishes a multi-page, detailed description of proficiency levels in each of the four skills of listening,

Table 7.3 ACFTL Guidelines — Listening

Level	Description
Distinguished	Listeners understand speech that can be highly abstract, highly technical, or both, as well as speech that contains very precise, often low-frequency vocabulary and complex rhetorical structures.
Superior	Listeners can follow linguistically complex extended discourse such as that found in academic and professional settings, lectures, speeches, and reports.
Advanced	Listeners can understand the main ideas and most supporting details in connected discourse on a variety of general interest topics, such as news stories, explanations, instructions, anecdotes, or travelogue descriptions.
Intermediate	Listeners can understand information conveyed in simple, sentence-length speech on familiar or everyday topics.
Novice	Listeners can understand key words, true aural cognates, and formulaic expressions that are highly contextualized and highly predictable, such as those found in introductions and basic courtesies.

speaking, reading, and writing. The ACTFL Proficiency Guidelines, designed in 1986 as an adaptation of the FSI/ILR levels for the academic community, are a recognized proficiency standard in many language-teaching circles. The current version (published in 2012) of the Guidelines has been revised to reflect real-world assessment needs, to accentuate what the learner *can* do (as opposed to negative connotations of what the learner cannot do), and now includes an additional "distinguished" level above its "superior" level. Table 7.3 is a summary of descriptors for listening ability at the five major levels.

The separate descriptions in the Guidelines may be found by visiting actfl.org or searching for *ACTFL Proficiency Guidelines*. In approximately nine printed pages for each of the four skills, you can imagine the detail incorporated into each of the above sublevels. Within each level, for example, descriptions take into account six considerations: global tasks and functions, accuracy, content, context, sociolinguistic culture, and text types.

We'll give you an excerpt from the Guidelines of just one of the sublevels in one skill area, *speaking*, below. The Intermediate High level is preceded by a general description of Intermediate, followed by specifics for the highest of three Intermediate sublevels (ACTFL, 2012, p. 7).

ACTFL Guidelines—Speaking: Intermediate Level

Speakers at the Intermediate level are distinguished primarily by their ability to create with the language when talking about familiar topics related to their daily life. They are able to recombine learned material in order to express personal meaning. Intermediate-level speakers can ask simple questions and can handle a straightforward survival situation. They produce sentence-level language, ranging from discrete sentences to strings of sentences, typically in present time. Intermediate-level speakers are understood by interlocutors who are accustomed to dealing with non-native learners of the language.

Intermediate High

Intermediate High speakers are able to converse with ease and confidence when dealing with the routine tasks and social situations of the Intermediate level. They are able to handle successfully uncomplicated tasks and social situations requiring an exchange of basic information related to their work, school, recreation, particular interests, and areas of competence.

Intermediate High speakers can handle a substantial number of tasks associated with the Advanced level, but they are unable to sustain performance of all of these tasks all of the time. Intermediate High speakers can narrate and describe in all major time frames using connected discourse of paragraph length, but not all the time. Typically, when Intermediate High speakers attempt to perform Advanced-level tasks, their speech exhibits one or more features of breakdown, such as the failure to carry out fully the narration or description in the appropriate major time frame, an inability to maintain paragraph-length discourse, or a reduction in breadth and appropriateness of vocabulary.

Intermediate High speakers can generally be understood by native speakers unaccustomed to dealing with non-natives, although interference from another language may be evident (e.g., use of code-switching, false cognates, literal translations), and a pattern of gaps in communication may occur.

 **CLASSROOM CONNECTIONS**

Notice the added details in the ACTFL descriptions of high-intermediate L2 speakers. What has been added that wasn't in the previous two lists? How helpful are the added descriptors? How might you use the ACTFL descriptors in your instruction or in designing assessments?

The ACTFL Guidelines are not connected with any one proficiency test, as are the FSI/ILR levels and the IELTS band scales. Instead, they were created to guide any test-maker in the process of assessment. Today, numerous test designers utilize the Guidelines as a standard for assessment. While they were expressly not created for assessing achievement in any one curriculum, the Guidelines provide a number of useful checkpoints for curriculum development and revision. The description of each sublevel in terms of tasks, functions, discourse, pronunciation (in the case of speaking), grammar, and more, has contributed to textbook and course development worldwide.

You might be wondering if the ACTFL levels correspond to the FSI levels, and the answer is no. For example, the introduction to the ACTFL Guidelines suggests that their "superior" level is "roughly equivalent" to the ILR 3 range. Likewise, the IELTS scale presented earlier shows subtle differences across its levels, and so, the ten IELTS levels should *not* be considered to be equivalent to the eleven ACTFL levels. Test developers have measured these equivalences, and can offer comparative statistics across various tests and scales (Slagter, Surface, & Mosher, 2009).

The Common European Framework of Reference (CEFR)

We'll touch on one more set of guidelines that has worldwide use. Between 1989 and 1996 the Council of Europe compiled a framework for learning, teaching, and assessing that would apply to all L2 teaching across Europe. By the early 2000s, a Common European Framework of Reference (CEFR) was developed that focused on linguistic, sociolinguistic, and pragmatic competence (Council of Europe, 2001). Now widely used and respected across Europe and well beyond, the CEFR defines competences for *basic* users of a language, *independent* users, and *proficient* users, splitting each of those three categories into two subcategories.

The CEFR has been endorsed by most European countries along with other countries such as China, Korea, and the United States. It specifies competencies for listening, speaking, reading, and writing. Table 7.4 gives you general descriptors of competencies, not broken down into skill areas, across the six levels.

The CEFR does not stop with such generalities. Remarkably, some of the subcategories are very detailed; for example, under the main category of *discourse competence*, specifications are given for "flexibility" and "turn-taking," among others. Table 7.5 (page 138) spells out the competencies for *flexibility*.

 **Classroom Connections**

If you were a test administrator using the CEFR "flexibility" descriptors in Table 7.5 to identify an L2 learner's level, what kinds of questions would you need to ask in order to elicit the desired performance? If you were designing a textbook for, say, level B2, what kinds of situations, contexts, and tasks can you imagine you would design in order to teach the skills that are described?

Table 7.4 Common Reference Levels: Global Scale

Band	Level	Descriptor
C Proficient user	C2	Can understand with ease virtually everything heard or read. Can summarize information from different spoken and written sources, reconstructing arguments and accounts in a coherent presentation. Can express him/herself spontaneously, very fluently and precisely, differentiating finer shades of meaning even in the most complex situations.
	C1	Can understand a wide range of demanding, longer texts, and recognize implicit meaning. Can express him/herself fluently and spontaneously without much obvious searching for expressions. Can use language flexibly and effectively for social, academic and professional purposes. Can produce clear, well-structured, detailed text on complex subjects, showing controlled use of organizational patterns, connectors and cohesive devices.
B Independent user	B2	Can understand the main ideas of complex text on both concrete and abstract topics, including technical discussions in his/her field of specialization. Can interact with a degree of fluency and spontaneity that makes regular interaction with native speakers quite possible without strain for either party. Can produce clear, detailed text on a wide range of subjects and explain a viewpoint on a topical issue giving the advantages and disadvantages of various options.
	B1	Can understand the main points of clear standard input on familiar matters regularly encountered in work, school, leisure. Can deal with most situations likely to arise traveling in an area where the language is spoken. Can produce simple connected text on topics are familiar or of personal interest. Can describe experiences and events, dreams, hopes ambitions and briefly give reasons and explanations for opinions and plans.
A Basic user	A2	Can understand sentences and frequently used expressions related to areas of most immediate relevance (e.g., very basic personal and family information, shopping, local geography, employment). Can communicate in simple and routine tasks requiring a simple and direct exchange of information on familiar and routine matters. Can describe in simple terms aspects of his/her background, immediate environment and matters in areas of immediate need.
	A1	Can understand and use familiar everyday expressions and very basic phrases aimed at the satisfaction of needs of a concrete type. Can introduce him/herself and others and can ask and answer questions about personal details such as where he/she lives, people he/she knows and things he/she has. Can interact in a simple way provided the other person talks slowly and clearly and is prepared to help.

Table 7.5 CEFR Descriptors for Flexibility in Discourse Competence

	Flexibility
C2	Shows great flexibility reformulating ideas in differing linguistic forms to give emphasis, to differentiate according to the situation, interlocutor, etc., and to eliminate ambiguity
C1	As B2+
B2	Can adjust what he/she says and the means of expressing it to the situation and the recipient and adopt a level of formality appropriate to the circumstances. Can adjust to the changes of direction, style, and emphasis normally found in conversation. Can vary formulation of what he/she wants to say.
B1	Can adapt his/her expression to deal with less routine, even difficult, situations. Can exploit a wide range of simple language flexibly to express much of what he/she wants.
A2	Can adapt well-rehearsed memorized simple phrases to particular circumstances through limited lexical substitution. Can expand learned phrases through simple recombinations of their elements.
A1	No descriptor available.

Is it possible to line up all these scales and levels and find equivalences? The answer is a qualified yes, in that assessment data show concordances across all of the above scales, but not necessarily with pinpoint accuracy. The British Council publishes equivalencies between the IELTS band scores and CEFR levels that show that even the highest CEFR level of C2 is not precisely equivalent to an IELTS score of 9.0 (see Table 7.6). And as the table shows, lines of division in each case are somewhat fuzzy. More information is available at takeielts.britishcouncil.org or search *British Council IELTS*.

Table 7.6 IELTS and CEFR Equivalencies

IELTS	**CEFR**
9.0	
8.5	
8.0	C2
7.5	
7.0	
6.5	C1
6.0	
5.5	
5.0	B2
4.5	
4.0	B1

Are there commonalities that would enable lines of distinction to be drawn among beginning, intermediate, and advanced levels? Not exactly. You will notice that only one of the scales, the FSI levels, uses a three-part division of abilities. Others come close. The CEFR band scales A, B, and C are sometimes labeled basic, independent, and proficient, respectively. Sublevels are referred to by such terms as "breakthrough" and "threshold" (both with positive connotations of what the learner *can* do, rather than a list of deficiencies).

With some caution, we can continue to use beginning, intermediate, and advanced as labels for three general stages of development. A major caveat is that language ability is componential—not uniform across all modes of competence. For example, a learner might be at CEFR level B2 in pronunciation accuracy, A1 in grammatical ability, and A2 in conversational/discourse competence. Numerous other combinations are possible, of course.

With this backdrop, we'll now turn to the more practical issues of teaching across ability levels in the L2 classroom.

TEACHING BEGINNING LEVELS

Teaching beginners is considered by many to be the most challenging level of language instruction. Because students at this level have little or no prior knowledge of the target language, the teacher (and accompanying techniques and materials) becomes a central determiner in helping students to accomplish their goals. This can also be the most tangibly rewarding level for a teacher because the growth of students' proficiency is apparent in a matter of a few weeks. As noted above, CEFR quite appropriately refers to this level as "breakthrough," progressing to "waystage."

At the beginning or even "false" beginning (a discarded term for a stage in which a few survival phrases can be understood and spoken) levels, your students have minimal language "behind" them. You may therefore be tempted to go along with the popular misconception that the L2 cannot be taught directly, that you will have to resort to a good deal of talking "about" the second language in the students' L1. Such is clearly not the case, as beginning language courses have demonstrated for many decades. But you do have to keep in mind that your students' capacity for taking in and retaining new words, structures, and concepts is limited. Foremost on your mind as a teacher should be the presentation of material in simple segments that don't overwhelm your students.

The following ten factors—and the advice accompanying each—will help you to formulate an approach to teaching beginners. As you more fully grasp each factor, you will be able to design lessons and activities that are consistent with your approach.

1. Students' Cognitive Learning Processes

In those first few days and even weeks of language learning, the students' processing with respect to the L2 itself is operating with very few background schemata to rely on, that is, few existing cognitive "pegs" on which to "hang" new words and structures. With little or no automaticity in producing or comprehending the new language (DeKeyser & Criado, 2013), learners need to be led one small step at a time in these early stages, with adequate repetition of new material.

Even in the first few days of class, however, you can encourage your students to reach beyond simply repeating words and phrases to use practiced language for genuinely meaningful purposes. For example, getting information from a classmate whom a student does not know will require using newly learned language ("What's your name?" "Where do you live?"), but with a focus on the *purposes* to which the language is put, not on the forms of language. The forms themselves, although still in limited numbers, can begin to become automatic as students become immersed in the task of seeking genuine information.

Classroom Connections

At a beginning or high-beginning level, what other kinds of questions would you teach your students to ask in order to enable them to practice "getting information from a classmate"? How would you go about teaching your students to produce those questions and possible answers? What kinds of activities or role plays could be used to encourage students to use these exchanges?

2. The Role of the Teacher

Beginning students are highly dependent on the teacher for models of language, and so a teacher-centered or teacher-fronted classroom is appropriate for some of your classroom time. Students are able to initiate few questions and comments, so it is your responsibility to "keep the ball rolling." Still, your beginning level classes need not be devoid of a modicum of student-centered work. Pair work and group work (see Chapter 13) are effective techniques for taking students' focus off you as the center of attention and for getting them into an interactive frame of mind even at the most beginning level.

It follows that the degree of control of classroom time also leans strongly in the direction of the teacher at the beginning levels. In a second language context where instruction is carried out in the target language, virtually all of your class time will be teacher-controlled. Because students have no means, in the second language anyway, of controlling the class period, the onus is on you to plan topics, activity types, time-on-task, and so on. As students gain in their proficiency, they will be able to initiate questions and comments of their own that may then occasionally shift the locus of control. In a foreign language situation, where your students speak the same native language (and you speak it as well), some negotiation might be possible in the native language, allowing for a small amount of student control (see #3 below).

3. Teacher Talk

Your input in the class is crucial. All ears and eyes are indeed focused on you. Your own English needs to be clearly articulated. It is appropriate to slow your speech somewhat for easier student comprehension, but don't slow it so much that it loses its naturalness. And remember, you don't need to talk any louder to beginners than to advanced students if your articulation is clear. Use simple vocabulary and structures that are at or just slightly beyond their level.

Is it appropriate to use the students' L1? As noted above, in second language situations, especially multilingual classes, your use of a student's native language is seldom an issue. In foreign language situations, however, it becomes an option. It is important not to let your classes go to excess in the use of the students' native language. The rule of thumb here is usually to restrict classroom language to the L2 unless some distinct advantage is gained by the use of their L1, and then only for very brief stretches of time. Examples of such advantages include the following:

- negotiation of disciplinary and other management factors,
- brief descriptions of how to carry out a technique,
- brief explanations of grammar points,
- quick pointers on meanings of words that remain confusing after students have had a try at defining something themselves, and
- cultural notes and comments.

 **CLASSROOM CONNECTIONS**

When you were taking a beginning class in an L2, how much did the teacher talk, as opposed to setting the stage for students to talk? If he or she allowed considerable opportunity for student talk, how did that come about? If not, what could the teacher have done to talk less and allow students to talk more?

4. Authenticity of Language

Even at the beginning levels of L2 learning, it's important to present to students language that is as authentic as possible. Simple greetings and introductions, for example, are authentic and yet easily understood. Make sure utterances are limited to short, simple phrases. If at times such language appears to be artificial to *you* because of all the repetition needed at this stage, don't despair. Your students will appreciate the opportunity to practice their new language.

5. Fluency and Accuracy

Fluency is a goal at this level but only within limited utterance lengths. Fluency does not have to apply only to long utterances. The "flow" of language is important to establish, from the beginning, in reasonably short segments.

Attention to accuracy should center on the particular grammatical, phonological, or discourse elements that are being practiced.

In teaching speaking skills, it is extremely important at this stage that you be very sensitive to students' need to practice freely and openly without fear of being corrected at every minor flaw. On the other hand, you need to correct some selected grammatical and phonological errors so that students don't fall into the trap of assuming that "no news is good news" (no correction implies perfection). Pronunciation work (on phonemes, phonemic patterns, intonation, rhythm, and stress) is very important at this stage. Neglecting phonological practice now may be at the expense of later fluency. Your job, of course, is to create the perfect balance. Chapter 16 will deal in more detail with this balance.

6. Student Creativity

The ultimate goal of learning a language is to be able to comprehend and produce it in *unrehearsed* situations, which demands both receptive and productive creativity. But at the beginning level, students can be creative only within the confines of a highly controlled repertoire of language. Innovation will come later when students get more language under their control.

7. Activities and Tasks

Short, simple techniques must be used. Some mechanical techniques are appropriate—choral repetition and other drilling, for example. A good many teacher-initiated questions dominate at this level, followed only after some time by an increase in simple student-initiated questions. Group and pair activities are excellent techniques as long as they are structured and clearly defined with specific objectives. A variety of techniques is important because of limited language capacity.

8. Listening and Speaking Goals

Figure 7.1 (see pages 144–145) is a reproduction of the Scope and Sequence chart for Level 1 of *English Firsthand* (Helgesen, Brown, & Wiltshier, 2009). Notice that the listening and conversation functions for beginners are meaningful and authentic communication tasks. They are limited more by grammar, vocabulary, and length of utterance than by communicative function. It is surprising how many language functions can be achieved with very uncomplicated language.

9. Reading and Writing Goals

A glance at the Scope and Sequence charts in Figure 7.1 demonstrates typical goals for a beginning level course: reading and writing topics are confined to brief but nevertheless real-life written material. Advertisements, forms, and recipes are grist for the beginner's reading mill, while written work may involve forms, lists, and simple notes and letters. The most important contextual factor that you should bear in mind in teaching reading and writing to beginners is their literacy level in their own native language, an issue that is covered in Chapters 17 and 18.

10. Form-Focused Instruction (FFI)

As Figure 7.1 (pages 144–145) shows, a typical beginning level will deal at the outset with very simple verb forms, personal pronouns, definite and indefinite articles, singular and plural nouns, and simple sentences, in a presumed progression from simple to complex. However, in recent years grammatical *sequencing* has been shown to be problematic and highly dependent on context (Larsen-Freeman, 2014). So, even at beginning levels, complexity and difficulty cannot be objectively determined, as teachers are still "left to their own judgment on how to proceed" (Larsen-Freeman, 2014, p. 267).

Whether or not you choose to overtly "explain" grammar in the classroom is another issue (see Chapter 19 for more discussion). If you are teaching an L2 in a non-L2-speaking country, and your students all speak the same native language, you may—especially at this beginning level—profit from occasionally using their L1 to explain grammatical points. In other situations where you must rely only on the L2 in the classroom, grammatical explanations of any complexity could easily overwhelm the students. Therefore, an inductive approach to grammar with suitable examples and patterns will be more effective.

At this level some vocabulary items will be efficiently internalized through analogy and meaningful use in different contexts. Others may require simple definitions with synonyms, demonstration, or if appropriate, an L1 translation.

 **CLASSROOM CONNECTIONS**

When you were taking a beginning class in an L2, how much "explanation" of grammar did the teacher engage in? How useful was it in contributing to your growing ability to *perform* the L2? If it was useful, why? If not, what would you do differently now as a teacher?

TEACHING INTERMEDIATE LEVELS: BEYOND THE "PLATEAU"

The intermediate levels of SLA are quite tricky. Learners have progressed beyond novice stages to an ability to sustain basic communicative tasks, establish some minimal fluency, deal with a few unrehearsed situations, self-correct on occasion, use a few compensatory strategies, and generally "get along" in the language beyond mere survival.

But the journey to mastery is circuitous, with plenty of backsliding, and because progress is not as dramatic now, learners sense they are in linguistic doldrums, wondering if they will ever "make it." Learners know just enough to feel some *confidence*, but not enough to feel completely at ease. They may also become more conscious of *error* at this level, having internalized basic forms of the L2, but still retaining the discomfort of venturing into new "territory."

Figure 7.1 Scope and Sequence chart

TABLE OF CONTENTS

Unit Title & Theme	PREVIEW Vocabulary	LISTENING Listening targets	CONVERSATION Communication model	PAIRWORK Partner task for accuracy	LANGUAGE CHECK Grammar for communication	INTERACTION Group work for fluency	REAL STORIES Reading & writing personal stories
Unit **0** Welcome to *English Firsthand 1* pages 8–11	• Find someone who . . . • Getting started: Think about your learning. • It's up to you. • Get to know your teacher.						
Unit **1** *It's nice to meet you.* • Meeting people • Giving personal information pages 12–19	Hobbies and interests	Identify • names and locations • volunteer activities	Introducing yourself at a party	Exchange personal information	Simple present: Questions and answers *What **do** you **do**?* *I **am** a student.*	**GROUP TALK:** Find out about your classmates	"Let me introduce myself" Write about who you are
Unit **2** *Who are they talking about?* • Describing people • Talking about family pages 20–27	Appearance adjectives	Identify • physical features • related vocabulary	Describing friends	Identify people based on descriptions	Simple present: *be* vs. *have* *She **has** brown eyes.* *Her eyes **are** brown.*	**LINE-UP:** Describe your family, shadow partners	"The world's biggest family" Write about your family
Unit **3** *When do you start?* • Describing routines and schedules pages 28–35	Daily activities and routines	Understand • personal schedules • how often people do things	Making a date	Compare routines	Adverbs of frequency *I **always** sleep well.* *He is **usually** late.*	**GROUP TALK:** Talk about things you do	"A balanced life" Write about your daily schedule
Unit **4** *Where does this go?* • Talking about locations pages 36–43	Furniture, household furnishing, and locations	• Infer objects talked about • Identify locations in a room	Negotiating with a parent	Find differences between two rooms	Prepositions with *There is* and *There are* *There's a* *. . . light **over** the desk.* *. . . photo **above** the TV.*	**LINE-UP:** Describe a place that is special for you, shadow partners	"I love my room!" Write about your room
Unit **5** *How do I get there?* • Giving directions pages 44–51	Giving directions; stores and services	• Follow map directions • Identify direction phrases	Asking for directions	Give and understand map directions	*To, at, from, on, in* with directions ***Walk from** City Hall.* *Our office is **on** the right.*	**GROUP TALK:** Give directions to a taxi driver, shadow partners	"My farewell party!" Draw a map and write the directions
Unit **6** *What happened?* • Talking about the past pages 52–59	Important life events, past activities	Understand • situations and topics • time expressions	Talking about weekends	Talk about a trip you took	Past tense: Irregular verbs *Did you get up at six?* *No, I **overslept**.*	**GROUP TALK:** Talk about your experiences	"Unlucky day!" Write about your own good / bad day story
Review Unit **1** pages 60–63	*Slap* vocabulary game			*What we've learned together* mini-tasks		*Let's talk!* fluency game	

6

Figure 7.1 Scope and Sequence chart (*Continued*)

TABLE OF CONTENTS

Unit Title & Theme	PREVIEW Vocabulary	LISTENING Listening targets	CONVERSATION Communication model	PAIRWORK Partner task for accuracy	LANGUAGE CHECK Grammar for communication	INTERACTION Group work for fluency	REAL STORIES Reading & writing personal stories
Unit 7 *I'd love that job.* • Talking about types of jobs, job qualifications, and job skills pages 64–71	Occupations	Understand • job interests • reasons • decisions	Interviewing for a job	Exchange job skill information. Find the best person for the job	*Enjoy, like, good at* and *good with* *I **like** to go on hikes.* *I **enjoy** swimming.* *I'm **good at** math.*	MIXER: Ask questions and guess jobs	"Boxing is only my hobby." Write about your skills and dreams
Unit 8 *What's playing?* • Talking about entertainment • Inviting and suggesting pages 72–79	Entertainment	Identify • situations • times for entertainment events	Making a plan	Plan a "perfect day out"	Different verb patterns for invitations *Let's get a coffee.* *How about a coffee?*	MIXER: Play an invitation match game	"Welcome to E-cube." Write about a place you like
Unit 9 *What are you going to do?* • Talking about the future pages 80–87	Future plans and activities	Identify • vacation plans • activities	Looking forward to summer	Predict your partner's future	Future tense ***I'll give** her a call back.* ***I'm going to** meet him.*	GROUP TALK: Make predictions	"Our gap year" Write a one-year travel plan
Unit 10 *How much is this?* • Shopping pages 88–95	Clothing, electronics, and personal items	• Understand prices • Infer shopping decisions	Questioning a shop clerk	Buy and sell things at a flea market	Comparatives + intensifiers *My car's **faster** than yours.* *My car's **much faster**.*	GROUP TALK: Talk about shopping experiences and preferences	"Buy Nothing Day" Write a 3-day "spending diary"
Unit 11 *How do you make it?* • Describing processes pages 96–103	Processes	Identify • food words • cooking verbs	Asking a friend for advice	Learn and teach origami paper folding	Sequence markers + imperatives *First, mix the eggs.* *First we mixed the eggs.*	GROUP TALK: Guess processes from hints	"The best dancers" Write about something you can do
Unit 12 *Listen to the music.* • Talking about music pages 104–111	Opinions and music	• Rate the music • Imagine commercials	Giving opinions about music	Talk about your musical history and preferences	Simple past vs. present perfect ***Did** he **play** for a long time?* ***Has** he **played** for a long time?*	LINE-UP: Tell your life story and its soundtrack	"Silent Disco" Write about a trend in your country
Review Unit 2 pages 112–115	*Slap* vocabulary game			*What we've learned together* mini-tasks		*Let's talk!* fluency game	
Learning Appendix pages 116–143	• Interaction Progress Chart • Extra Listening • Vocabulary Maps • Grammar Explanations • Acknowledgements						

They are likely to feel that others expect them to be more proficient than they really are, thus raising *self-consciousness* even more.

As Richards (2008a) notes, a common experience at this stage is to feel that they have "reached a *plateau* in their language learning and do not perceive that they are making further progress" (p. 1). It's a time when many learners give up, feeling overwhelmed with the prospect of reaching fluency or mastery. However, a positive outlook views the plateau as a critical stage. It's a moment for renewed *motivation* to press on, a time to put more *effort* into the process of learning, and a stage in which learners must *believe* in their eventual success.

Richards (2008a) describes five characteristics of the plateau:

1. A gap between receptive and productive competence
2. Fluency that has progressed at the expense of accuracy
3. A limited vocabulary range.
4. Adequate production ability but speech that is unnatural.
5. Persistent, frequent language errors

Can you help your learners to deal with these issues and progress through the intermediate stage? Let's look at some practical suggestions under the rubric of the same ten topics of the previous section.

CLASSROOM CONNECTIONS

If you have experienced plateaus in your learning of an L2, what were they like? How did you manage to move beyond those plateaus? What are some specific things a teacher could do or say to help students move out of learning "doldrums"?

1. Students' Cognitive Learning Processes

At the intermediate stage some automatic processing has taken hold. Phrases, sentences, structures, and conversational rules have been practiced and are increasing in number, forcing the mental processes to automatize. We might think of automaticity as placing elements of language into the "hard drive" of one's neurological computers. Learners' immediately controlled "desktops" (limited in capacity) are too small to contain all the information we need. One of the teacher's principal goals at this level is to help students to continue to automatize the bits and pieces of language that might otherwise clutter the mind.

At this stage learners are also becoming accustomed to being weaned from the dependence of an L1, so the temptation to think in the L1 is lessened. Teachers can engage the students directly in the L2. Also, meaningful communication in the L2 is increasing, thus stimulating subsumption of material in ways that were not possible at the beginning level.

2. The Role of the Teacher

You are no longer the only initiator of language. Students should be encouraged to ask questions, make comments, and negotiate certain options in learning where appropriate. More student–student interaction can now take place in pairs, small groups, and whole-class activity.

Learner-centered work is now possible for more sustained lengths of time as students are able to maintain topics of discussion and focus. By its very nature, the intermediate level is richly diverse; that diversity can work to your advantage with carefully designed cooperative activities that capitalize on differences among students. Don't set equal expectations for all students, however, as abilities, especially speaking abilities, can vary widely.

3. Teacher Talk

Most of your oral production can be sustained at a natural pace, as long as your articulation is clear. Teacher talk should not occupy the major proportion of a class hour; otherwise, you are probably not giving students enough opportunity to talk. You should be using less of the native language of the learners at this level, but some situations may still demand it.

4. Authenticity of Language

At this level students sometimes become overly concerned about grammatical correctness and may want to wander into esoteric discussions of grammatical details. This penchant for analysis might get them too far afield from authentic, real language. Make sure they stay on the track, but still allow for some form-focused instruction.

Students may also be overly consumed with accent, thinking that they should strive for "perfect" pronunciation. Adults learning an L2 will almost never sound like a "native," and in this era of worldwide varieties of languages, nativelike accents are a non-issue. Your goal is to help your students develop clear articulation of fluent speech. Tell them that any "accent" is just part of their charm!

Classroom Connections

How important is it for a student to "sound like a native," whatever that means? Were you ever worried about attaining a very good or perfect accent in an L2 you were learning? If so, what did you do, or what could you do now as a teacher, to help students to set reasonable, attainable goals in learning the phonology of a language?

5. Fluency and Accuracy

The dichotomy between fluency and accuracy is a crucial concern here, as Richards (2008a) notes, more so than at either of the other ends of the proficiency spectrum. Some students are likely to become overly concerned about accuracy, possibly berating themselves for the mistakes they make and demanding constant corrections for every slip-up. Others may slide into a self-satisfied rut in which they actually become quite fluent, in the technical sense of the term, but in which they become very difficult to comprehend. Be on the lookout for both types of student and be prepared to offer individualized attention to each.

In general, fluency exercises (saying or writing a steady flow of language for a short period of time without any self- or other-correction at all) are a must at this level (Bohlke, 2014). They help to get students over the hump of always having to say or write everything absolutely correctly. You want them in due course of time to go through the "breakthrough" stage of language learning, often thought of as a stage after which a learner looks back and says, "Wow! I just carried on a whole conversation without thinking about my grammar!" A big part of your task with most students is to maintain their flow with just enough attention to error to keep them growing.

6. Student Creativity

The fact that some of this new language is now under control gives rise to more opportunities for the student to be creative. Interlanguage errors such as the following are a good indication of the creative application of a system within the learner's mind:

> Does John can sing?
>
> What means this?
>
> I must to make a lot of money.

Try to recognize this form of creativity as a positive sign of language development and of the internalization of a coherent system. At the same time, remember the fine line between accepting student creativity and allowing errors to be inadvertently reinforced (Richards, 2008a). When you hear persistent erroneous patterns in your students' production, make sure you help them to *notice* those errors and work on their eventual eradication.

 **CLASSROOM CONNECTIONS**

What are some ways to help students to *notice* errors without completely interrupting their attempts to communicate? How do you know if a student has noticed an error? What signals do they give, at the moment or later? How can you help them to self-correct their errors?

Students are also becoming more capable of applying their classroom language to unrehearsed situations. In some settings those situations may be more difficult to find, but through the various forms of technological and print media, applications to the real world, heretofore unrehearsed in the classroom, are available and should be encouraged.

7. Activities and Tasks

Because of the increasing language capacities of your students, techniques can increase in complexity. Common interactive techniques for intermediates include chain stories, surveys and polls, paired interviews, group problem solving, role-plays, storytelling, and many others.

8. Listening and Speaking Goals

The linguistic complexity of communicative listening-speaking goals increases steadily. Along with the creation of novel utterances, students can participate in short conversations, ask and answer questions, find alternative ways to convey meaning, solicit information from others, and more. The functions themselves may not be intrinsically more complex, but the forms they use are. (For more information on teaching listening and speaking, see Chapters 15 and 16.)

Students at this stage can often understand much more than they can produce, which can be frustrating. But it can also provide learning moments for students as they convert what they comprehend into productive performance.

9. Reading and Writing Goals

Increasing complexity in terms of length, grammar, and discourse now characterizes reading material as students read paragraphs and short, simple stories, and are beginning to use skimming and scanning skills. Writing is similarly more sophisticated. (For more information on teaching reading and writing, see Chapters 17 and 18.)

10. Form-Focused Instruction (FFI)

Grammar topics such as progressive verb tenses and clauses typify intermediate level teaching. Students can benefit from small doses of short, simple explanations of points in English. Whether through English or the native language medium, such overt attention to "sore spots" in grammar can, in fact, be exceedingly helpful at this stage. Students have been known to flounder in a sea of inductivity until one cogent tip from a teacher sets them back on a straight course. In the process of recounting a story, a student at this level said:

> She can kept her child.
>
> He must paid the insurance [premium].

When the teacher simply called attention to the apparent inconsistency, the student was able to *notice* the formation of modal auxiliaries in the past tense, and from that point on no longer made that error.

Keep grammatical metalanguage to an ideal minimum at this level; otherwise, your students will become English grammarians instead of English speakers. Remember, you are interested in grammar because that is where some of your training has been, but you don't need to make budding PhDs in linguistics out of your students! Overt grammatical explanation has its place, in the wings, if you will, as a prompter of sorts, but not as the dominant focus of student attention.

TEACHING ADVANCED LEVELS

As students move up the developmental ladder, they get closer and closer to their goals, developing fluency along with a greater degree of accuracy. With increasing confidence in their ability, they are able to handle most situations in which target language use is demanded. For many, reading and writing skills are also well developed. They may be said to be at a "clean up" stage, with a focus on cleaning up lingering issues. Primary attention is given to persistent errors, to refining their syntactic stockpile, to noticing sociolinguistic nuances, and to adding more sophisticated vocabulary. They are now "advanced" students.

All of the guidelines and standards described in the beginning of this chapter list as the *top* level a fully fluent, virtually error-free, completely capable user of the L2—so capable, in fact, that the ACTFL Guidelines describe the highest attainable level as "distinguished." And so distinguished are such users that many native speakers of the language do not measure up! It almost goes without saying, then, that there is no need even to conceive of an L2 course at these tip-top levels.

So, in turning to guidelines for teaching at "advanced" levels, we will focus here on what the ACTFL Guidelines describe as "advanced," what CEFR labels a B2 or "independent" user, and what IELTS calls "competent" to "good" users (levels 6–7). Remember, of course, the contextual variations in what an institution would call an "advanced" learner.

CLASSROOM CONNECTIONS

In your own words, how would you identify what **you** consider to be an advanced (as opposed to an intermediate) learner? What kinds of language elements would be appropriate to focus on at this stage? Try to think of some specific examples, either in your own experience or in others' experiences.

1. Students' Cognitive Learning Processes

As competence in language continues to build, students can realize the full spectrum of processing, assigning larger and larger chunks to automatic modes and gaining the confidence to put the formal structures of language on the periphery so that focal attention may be given to the interpretation and negotiation of meaning and to the conveying of thoughts and feelings in interactive communication. Some aspects of language, of course, need focal attention for minor corrections, refinement, and other "tinkering"; otherwise, teachers would almost be unnecessary. So your task at this level is to assist in the ongoing attempt to automatize language and in the delicate interplay between focal and peripheral attention to selected aspects of language.

2. The Role of the Teacher

On the surface, your job may appear easier with advanced students; you can sit back and let their questions and self-generated curiosity take over. In reality, the independence that students have acquired must be cleverly channeled into classroom routines that benefit most of the students most of the time. No mean task! The most common occurrence in advanced level teaching is that your class runs away with itself and you are left with only a quarter or half your plans fulfilled. So, while you want to take advantage of the self-starting personalities in your class, orderly plans are still important. A directive role on your part can create effective learning opportunities even within a predominantly learner-centered classroom.

3. Teacher Talk

Natural language at natural speed is a must at this level. Make sure your students are challenged by your choice of vocabulary, structures, idioms, and other language features. But, after all, they are still learning the language, so remember that they have not yet turned into native speakers. The amount of teacher talk should be commensurate with the type of activity. Make sure your students have ample opportunities to produce language so that your role as a provider of feedback takes prominence. For some of your students, this is the last chance to benefit from informed, systematic feedback on their performance; from here on out, they will be "out there" where people, out of politeness or respect, rarely give corrections.

Very little, if any, reliance on the students' native language is now justified. Discipline, explanations, and other more complex language functions can be carried out in English. Occasionally, a teacher of an advanced class will resort to a word or two (a definition, for example) in the native language in order to help a student who is "stuck."

4. Authenticity of Language

Everything from academic prose to literature to idiomatic conversation becomes a legitimate resource for the classroom. Virtually no authentic language material should be summarily disqualified at this stage. Certain restrictions may come to bear, depending on how advanced your class is, of course.

5. Fluency and Accuracy

At this level most, if not all of your students are "fluent" in that they have passed beyond the breakthrough stage and are no longer thinking about every word or structure they are producing or comprehending. A handful or two of problems still need attention. If errors are relatively rare, an occasional treatment from you or from peers may be quite helpful.

6. Student Creativity

The joy of teaching at this level is in those moments of student performance when you know that they are now able to apply classroom material to real contexts beyond. Make sure that students keep their eyes fixed on those goals. Be ever wary of classroom activity that simply ends right there in the classroom.

CLASSROOM CONNECTIONS

What are some examples of classroom activities or tasks that extend beyond classroom practice to the real world outside the classroom? What are some examples of activities at the advanced level—in reading or listening as a start—that could have practical follow-ups in a student's life beyond the language classroom?

7. Activities and Tasks

Techniques can now tap into a full range of sociolinguistic and pragmatic competencies. Typical of this level are activities like group debates and argumentation, complex role-plays, scanning and skimming reading material, determining and questioning author's intent, and writing essays and critiques. Often at this level students have specific purposes for which they are planning to use English. Focus on those purposes as much as possible.

8. Listening and Speaking Goals

At this level students can focus more carefully on all the sociolinguistic nuances of language. Pragmatic constraints are common areas needing work as students fine-tune their production and comprehension in terms of register, style, the status of the interlocutor, the specific context of a conversational exchange, turn-taking, topic nomination and termination, topic-changing, and culturally conditioned language constraints.

9. Reading and Writing Goals

Reading and writing skills similarly progress closer and closer to native-speaker competence as students learn more about such things as critical reading, the role of schemata in interpreting written texts, and writing a document related to one's profession (laboratory reports, records of experimental research findings, etc.).

10. Form-Focused Instruction (FFI)

The concern at the intermediate level for basic grammatical patterns now graduates to functional forms, sociolinguistic and pragmatic phenomena, and building strategic competence (see *PLLT*, Chapter 10). Linguistic metalanguage may now serve a more useful role as students perceive its relevance to refining their abilities. Your classes need not become saturated with explanations of form, but well-targeted form-focused instruction will often be extremely effective at this level.

 **Classroom Connections**

What are some examples of "well-targeted FFI" that take place at this level? Because it was described earlier as a "clean-up" phase of language learning, what are some examples in your L2 learning of forms that needed "cleaning up" and how, if at all, did that happen?

You have now had a chance to contemplate quite a number of variables that change as you teach lower or higher levels of proficiency. The age and proficiency variables are two extremely important issues to incorporate into any attempt to plan and conduct language lessons. Next, Chapter 8 will introduce some of the sociopolitical and institutional variables that come to bear on decisions that you make when you teach in a classroom.

FOR THE TEACHER: ACTIVITIES (A) & DISCUSSION (D)

Note: For each of the "Classroom Connections" in this chapter, you may wish to turn them into individual or pair-work discussion questions.

1. **(A)** Pair students up, and ask them to refer to the FSI/ILR levels (Table 7.1, p. 132) and *IELTS Band Scale* (Table 7.2, p. 133). For an L2 that each has studied, ask them to try a quick self-assessment using either or both of the two scales. How confident does each feel about their self-rating? Ask them to report back to the whole class on how they felt about such an informal self-rating.
2. **(A)** Ask the class to imagine they have been asked to do an oral interview of a speaker of English as a second language. Direct pairs or small groups to collaborate to design a set of specific questions to include in such an interview so that one could determine a *listening*

and/or *speaking* ACTFL level (see pages 134–135) of a learner. After groups have compared formats, set up a role-played interview for one or two of the small groups to perform for the rest of the class, perhaps in a language other than English.

3. **(D)** Ask your class if anyone has experienced an oral interview to determine their level, even if it's just a brief interview to determine placement into a course level. To what extent did any of those interviewers appear to use any of the FSI, IELTS, or ACTFL guidelines to determine their ability?
4. **(A)** Ask pairs to brainstorm how one would teach a class in which there are true beginners as well as "false" beginners. How would one keep the latter challenged without overwhelming the former? Have pairs share their ideas with the rest of the class.
5. **(A)** It was noted on page 147 that in some L2 situations, teachers might "negotiate" certain elements of classroom practices with students. Ask pairs to identify some classroom contexts and to figure out some specific examples of negotiation. How do those differ, depending on proficiency level? For example, at the very beginning level, what form does negotiation take and how does that differ from negotiation at an advanced level?
6. **(D)** Ask your students to volunteer ways that the concept of *fluency* (Bohlke, 2014) differs from very beginning levels to advanced? What are some typical fluency activities at lower levels? At advanced levels?
7. **(A)** Ten criteria were offered in this chapter for considering differences across proficiency levels. Pair up your students and assign one criterion to each pair, and ask them to (a) note differences *across* the three proficiency levels for each, and (b) illustrate each with a specific language example. Then ask pairs to share their thoughts with the rest of the class.
8. **(A)** If feasible, assign observations to your students that span classes from beginning to advanced, a few students assigned to each of as many levels as are available. Ask them to note the kinds of activities and tasks they observe. Then have them report back to the rest of the class with a list of activities. Board work would help everyone to focus on ability levels.

FOR YOUR FURTHER READING

American Council on the Teaching of Foreign Languages. (2012). *ACTFL proficiency guidelines*. www.actfl.org

The complete Guidelines describe proficiency levels for all four skills: speaking, listening, writing, and reading. They are available at the above referenced website: Go to "publications" and click on "proficiency guidelines."

Council of Europe. (2001). *Common European framework of reference for languages: Learning, teaching, assessment.* Cambridge, UK: Cambridge University Press.

An excellent description and analysis of CEFR's framework for language teaching. Many of the detailed sublevels of the CEFR framework are quoted and explained.

Richards, J. (2008a). *Moving beyond the plateau: From intermediate to advanced levels in language learning.* Cambridge, UK: Cambridge University Press.

A practical set of suggestions across a number of useful categories for dealing with intermediate level students, to help them move beyond a potential leveling out of ability.

Richards, J., & Burns, A. (2012). *Tips for teaching listening: A practical approach.* White Plains, NY: Pearson Education.

Useful practical classroom activities in this and other "Tips for Teaching" volumes in this series are all classified by their suggested proficiency level. A glance through this book will demonstrate differences across levels in the complexity of tasks.

CHAPTER **8**

CULTURAL AND SOCIOPOLITICAL CONTEXTS

Questions for Reflection

- What is the relationship between language and culture?
- What is the role of discourse and identity in understanding culture in L2 learning?
- What does the notion of *English as an international language* mean to language teachers in terms of their pedagogical decisions and practices?
- What are some advantages of nonnative English-speaking teachers (NNESTs)?
- How is *translingual* practice different from traditional bilingual practice?
- How does language policy influence a nation and its people at a micro- and a macro-level?

Age and proficiency are significant individual variables that affect every aspect of our lesson or curriculum. While they may be essential variables to keep in mind, however, another cluster of factors also emerges for the language teacher: second language (L2) culture, identity, and sociopolitical contexts. These domains intertwine in such a way that it is sometimes impossible to disentangle them and examine one without considering the other. Culture underlies all language learners' emotion, cognition, and their senses of who they are. Government policies and local politics are equally powerful influences on teachers' and students' daily lives, and finally, educational institutions are products of culture and policy, and indeed often are microcosms of one's sociopolitical milieu.

While this chapter will not attempt to treat all such issues in detail, they are nevertheless important aspects to consider whenever you step into a language classroom. The goal of the chapter is to discuss the social dimension of L2 learning with reference to the culture and identity of L2 learners in dynamic sociopolitical contexts.

LANGUAGE AND CULTURE

Culture is a way of life. It is the context within which we exist, think, feel, and relate to others. It makes us sensitive to matters of status, and helps us know what others expect of us and what will happen if we do not live up to their expectations. As noted in Chapter 4, Principle 7, when learning and teaching an additional language, we must be aware of the complex and dynamic relationship between language and cultural customs, values, and beliefs that are embedded in language practice.

In language education and applied linguistics, the term *culture* implies many different definitions and considerations. For example, Wintergerst and McVeigh (2011) explain that the so called "big C visible" culture refers to the literature, arts, architecture, history, and geography of the country in which a target language is spoken, whereas the "big C invisible" culture implies the native speakers' core values, beliefs, social norms, assumptions, and legal foundations. On the other hand, "little c visible" culture includes gestures, body language, use of space, dress, food, leisure life, and daily customs while "little c invisible" culture is related to popular opinions, viewpoints, preferences, or tastes.

Culture is highly important in the learning of a second or foreign language. Agar's (1994) notion of **languaculture** highlights the inseparable relationship between language and culture. He says, "culture is in language, and language is loaded with culture" (p. 28). In other words, the two are intricately interwoven so that one cannot separate them without losing the significance of either language or culture. Many researchers in applied linguistics (e.g., Hymes, 1996; Lantolf, 2011; Kramsch, 2013; Hinkel, 2014) also have emphasized the complex reciprocal development of the two.

Classroom Connections

What does *culture* mean to you? In what ways is your L1 "loaded with culture"? In your learning of an L2, what are some concrete examples of that L2 being "intricately interwoven" with the culture that the L2 represents? In what ways was your learning of an L2 and the L2 culture a "reciprocal development"? As a teacher, what are some ways to incorporate culture, especially the "invisible" aspects, into your instruction?

CULTURE, DISCOURSE, AND IDENTITY

Teaching culture is a complex task. It might be that during casual interactions with speakers of other languages, most people are not aware of the impact of the invisible culture of both interlocutors (Hinkel, 2014). Furthermore, culture is neither monolithic nor static. It is multiple, dynamic, and political (Kramsch, 2013). In order to understand the complex dynamic nature of culture, it is helpful to draw on the concepts of *discourse* and *identity*.

Sociolinguist James Gee refers to "Discourse" with a capital "D" as "ways of combining and integrating language, actions, interactions, ways of thinking, believing, valuing, and using various symbols, tools, and objects to enact a particular sort of socially recognizable identity" (2011, p. 29). Gee uses the term "identity" to mean "a *socially situated identity*, the 'kind of person' one is seeking to be and enact here and now" (2011, p. 30). A person might talk, act, and interact in such a way that he or she would get recognized as a corporate lawyer in one context, while this same individual in another context would talk, act, and interact completely differently to be a subservient spouse. According to Gee (2011), Discourse is inherently political as it distributes particular beliefs, assumptions, social goods, social relations of power, and hierarchical structure in society. A particular **discourse** can be used as an invisible "theory" to control people's minds as to what is a "normal" and "appropriate" way of thinking and behaving in a particular sociopolitical setting.

Consider the following account of Heekyeong's experience with literacy practices when she was in elementary school in Korea:

> When I was ten years old in elementary school, there was a huge nation-wide social campaign sponsored by the government (one of the military regimes in 1980s) called a "Social Purification Campaign." My school was one of the schools to try out a new school curriculum before it was actually implemented in other schools in the country. I was told that it was an "honor" for the school to be selected for the research. In fact, even crews of the national broadcasting company often visited my school to videotape our classroom activities for their news program.
>
> As a core member of the student organization I had several meetings with my teachers after the regular classes in order to discuss what kinds of activities students could do for that nation-wide campaign. The activities emerging from the discussion were keeping clean around oneself at school and on the street, and not being lazy about reporting "bad" people to the police in order to get rid of "the social harm," such as thieves, robbers, alcoholics, and the homeless around the neighborhood. The more specific literacy practices for the school kids were to hold competitions consisting of compositions or posters on the themes relevant to this campaign.
>
> As one of the leaders of the student committee of my elementary school, I actively participated in the meetings and competitions, and several times won the prizes for one of the best compositions and posters. I was very proud of myself at those times until I learned the truth when I entered university. I heard that the government at that time was formed by a military coup d'état, and under the same name of the campaign that I participated in, "Social Purification Campaign," the military regime brutally killed hundreds of people who were against them and sent a large number of homeless people away from the city to a concentration camp in a remote area.

Street (1994) notes that literacy is not simply a technical and neutral skill but is "imbued with relations of power and ideology and with deep cultural meanings about identity both personal and collective" (p. 20). In the case of Heekyeong's literacy practices in elementary school, the institution (government) had the power to dictate what the students should think and do in order to pacify the public for government actions. Only when a more democratic government came into the office did Heekyeong, who then was a college student, realize how powerful the former government propaganda was in that it infiltrated even her discourse practice in elementary school.

Classroom Connections

What are the differences among cultural identity, linguistic identity, and national identity? What is your identity, in these terms? What parts of your identity are influenced by your L1 culture? And your L2 culture? How would you recognize and/or capitalize on those separate identities in students in your L2 classroom?

Kumaravadivelu (2012) discusses two approaches to the conception of identity: a *modernist* view and a *postmodernist* view. From a modernist point of view (which was influential during the mid-17th to mid-20th century), the individual identity is defined by pre-existent and static societal norms. For example, individuals usually are identified with their affiliation to nation, ethnicity, race, religion, class, profession, gender, language, or family. This conception of identity tends to generalize individuals as stable beings based on characteristics externally imposed on them.

On the other hand, a postmodernist approach to understanding identity is very much based on its ongoing nature. It sees identity as "fragmented, not unified; multiple, not singular; expansive, not bounded" (Kumaravadivelu, 2012, p. 10). The primary contributors to the formation of identity are not only inherited traditions and features such as culture, historical backgrounds, and socioeconomic status, but also the individual's ability to exercise *agency*. Individuals' actions, words, or thoughts at certain times often are an internal compromise among several different voices and discourses. Identity is constantly changing and negotiated across time and space (Norton, 2013).

The idea that individuals' identities are constantly situated and constructed in their various sociocultural environments raises critical questions about an assumption that has long prevailed in the field of SLA. A dominant understanding about individual learners in SLA research has been that every person has an essential, unique, fixed, and coherent attribute such as German or Chinese, an international student or an immigrant, motivated or unmotivated.

For the last decade, however, an increasing number of researchers (e.g., Norton, 2000, 2013; Pavlenko & Blackledge, 2004; Ricento, 2005; Duff, 2012) have taken a sociocultural approach to understanding L2 learner identity. This approach recognizes and capitalizes the fact that the lives of individuals in L2 contexts involve a wide array of sociocultural roles and identities as students, as gendered and cultured individuals, as immigrants, as native speakers or non-native speakers, as individuals with political convictions, and as members of families, organizations, and societies at large.

The multiple identities and positions and roles are socially and culturally constructed based on various social relations of power that influence learners in positioning themselves in different social contexts (Norton, 2000). As discussed in Chapter 5, agency plays a crucial role in the particular positioning of L2 learners in their L2 practice. For example, Lee and Maguire (2011) illustrated that regardless of a teacher's explicit instruction about discursive practice (i.e., disciplinary cultural knowledge) in North American higher education, some international students may resist appropriating that knowledge and practice because it conflicts with their ideal L2 selves that are originally influenced by their preferred L1 *habitus* (Bourdieu, 1991).

Classroom Connections

In your L2 learning experiences, have you been a newcomer to your L2 social and cultural contexts? Were you ever asked to participate in a cultural or discursive practice that you did not agree with? If so, what conflicts and frustrations did you experience in your L2 practice and how did you deal with those challenges? How would you help your own students if they found themselves in the same situation?

CONTEXTS OF LANGUAGE LEARNING AND TEACHING

In some of our professional musing about teaching and learning, we interchange the terms **second** and **foreign** in referring to the context of English (and other L2) teaching. But some caution is warranted, particularly in relation to a curriculum or a lesson, because (a) the difference between the two is significant, and (b) this dichotomy has been overgeneralized in recent years.

The operational distinction between a *second* and a *foreign language* context is usually concerned with what is going on outside language classrooms. Once your students leave your class, which language will they hear in the hallways, out on the sidewalks, and in the stores? Second language learning contexts are those in which the classroom target language is readily available beyond the classroom. Teaching *English* in the United States or Canada clearly falls into this (ESL) category. Foreign language contexts are those in which students learn a language of other countries and do not have ready-made contexts for communication beyond their classroom. They may be obtainable through language clubs, special media opportunities, books, or an occasional tourist, but efforts must be made to create such opportunities. Teaching

English in China, Iraq, or Russia is almost always a context of English as a foreign language (EFL).

The seemingly clear dichotomy between ESL and EFL, however, has been criticized for its referential vagueness in the wake of increasing use of English worldwide for a variety of purposes (Nayar, 1997). For example, the contexts for English communication vary widely: in many places in the United States, monolingual English speakers abound; in countries such as India or Singapore, English is a second language widely used for education, government, and commerce; and in Scandinavian countries, English has no official status but is commonly spoken by virtually every educated person. Likewise, in countries where a language might be quickly judged as foreign (for instance, Spanish or Chinese in the United States, English in Japan), learners may find readily available potential for authentic use of the language in such venues as indigenous language communities and the media (Internet, TV, film).

With that fair warning, it is still useful to consider the pedagogical implications for a *continuum* of contexts ranging from high-visibility, ready access to the target language outside the language classroom to little access beyond the classroom door. In a typical second language context, students have a tremendous advantage. When you plan a lesson or curriculum in a context that falls into the second language category, students can capitalize on numerous opportunities. Here are some ways to seize this advantage:

Guidelines for Taking Advantage of L2 Communication Just Outside the Classroom

- Give homework that involves a specific speaking task with a person outside the classroom, listening to a radio or TV program, reading a newspaper article, or writing an e-mail to a peer or a company for an inquiry.
- Encourage students to seek out opportunities for using the language.
- Encourage students to seek corrective feedback from others.
- Have students keep a log or diary of their extra-class learning.
- Plan and carry out field trips (to a museum or an adjacent city, for example).
- Arrange a social “mixer” with native English speakers.
- Invite speakers into your classroom.

How about learning English in an EFL setting? Here are some guidelines to help you compensate for the lack of ready communicative situations outside the classroom.

Guidelines for Maximizing L2 Use in "Foreign" Language Contexts

- Use class time for optimal authentic language input and interaction.
- Don't waste class time on work that can be done as homework.
- Help students to see genuine uses for the L2 in their own lives.
- Provide extra-class learning opportunities, such as suggesting an L2-speaking movie or TV show, using the L2 on social media such as Facebook or Twitter, getting an L2-speaking conversation partner if available, doing outside reading (news magazines, books), or writing a journal or diary, in the L2, on their learning process.
- Form a language club and schedule regular activities.

GLOBALIZATION AND LANGUAGE EDUCATION

Closely related to the ESL/EFL distinction are the dynamic and diverse roles of English—among a few other languages including French, Spanish, and Portuguese—in the wake of post-colonialism and globalization. Let's look at English in particular here, especially as it is now a dominant global language.

English in a Globalizing World

There have been rigorous discussions about the changes English is going through as it has been used beyond the context of monolingual English native speakers. It is estimated that well over 1 billion people are currently using English. According to the British Council, 750 million of these learners are what traditionally are called English as a foreign language (EFL) speakers while approximately 375 million are English as a second language (ESL) speakers (Beare, 2010). Many models to represent the global use of English have been proposed such as World Englishes (Kachru, 1992, 2010; Kirkpatrick, 2007), English as an international language (McKay, 2002, 2012), and English as a lingua franca (Seidlhofer, 2004, 2011; Jenkins, 2009, 2011).

Classroom Connections

Does the term "English as a lingua franca" sound different from the commonly used term, "English as a *foreign* language"? What are the differences in context between the two? How would those differences manifest themselves in the classroom? Consider homework assignments, topics, and your student demographics. Which English or other L2 would be a goal for your students and your school?

Two issues have emerged for English teachers to contemplate (Kachru, 2010; McKay, 2012):

1. English is increasingly being used as a tool for interaction among nonnative speakers. Over 5 billion people of the world do not speak English as either their first or second language (Graddol, 2006). Most English language teachers across the globe are nonnative English speakers, which means that the norm is not monolingualism, but rather multilingualism.
2. English is not frequently learned as a tool for understanding and teaching American or British cultural values. Instead, English has become a tool for international communication in transportation, commerce, banking, tourism, entertainment, technology, diplomacy, research, publishing, and information sharing on the Internet.

In a nutshell, the ownership of English is no longer limited to English "native speakers" and their countries. As Alsagoff (2012) notes, we need to rethink "what it means to 'own' a language" (p. 109).

 **Classroom Connections**

In what ways do you think the notion of "native speaker" affects how your L2 is taught and learned? In what ways do textbooks and particular materials reflect the goal of becoming a "native speaker" (of English, for most readers here, or any target language)? In light of Alsagoff's (2012) comment above, how appropriate is such a goal? What are some concrete ways in which you can modify or change the idealized notion of "native speaker"?

English as an International Language

The multiplication of varieties of English poses some practical concerns for the teacher. One of those concerns is the issue of grammaticalness and correctness. What standard do you accept in your classroom? The practical issue boils down to the need for your open acceptance of the prevailing variety of English in use in the country where you're teaching, be it India, Nigeria, or the Philippines. It is certainly not necessary to think of English as a language whose cultural identity can lie only with countries like the United States, the United Kingdom, or New Zealand. Your students no doubt will be more interested in the practical, nonstigmatized uses of English in various contexts in their own countries than in imitating American or British English. They will *own* and use their English as an international language in their chosen global communities. In this context, English becomes a lingua franca (ELF), which is the common language of choice among speakers who come from different linguacultural backgrounds (Jenkins, 2009).

There is an important issue we need to consider, which has been and continues to be debated in language teaching circles: How important is it that a teacher of a language be a "native" speaker of that language? Take a look at the employment ads for language schools in newspapers in Taipei, Seoul, São Paulo, or any other city you choose, and you will find that roughly nine out of ten ads ask for "native speakers only." The assumption, of course, is that a native speaker will provide a "correct" model of English.

For many decades the English language teaching profession assumed that **native English-speaking teachers (NESTs),** by virtue of their ostensibly "superior" model of oral production, comprised the ideal English language teacher. However, this is a "comparative fallacy" (Bley-Vroman, 1983; Cook 1999), because L2 speakers are different from monolingual native speakers in their cognitive processes of accessing their knowledge of the L2 and L1. Additional language learners in the world can use more than one language; therefore, they have some degree of **bilingualism** or **multilingualism**. These bilingual or multilingual language learners do not fit into the description of an "ideal" native speaker. From this perspective, it is not right to compare L2 learners' competence to that of monolingual native speakers (Cook, 1999).

Cook (1999) proposed that we use the term "multicompetent language users" (p. 185) instead of nonnative speakers. "L2 user" refers to people who know and use a second language at any level of achievement while "L2 learner" implies people who learn a language without using it on daily or frequent uses (Cook, 2013). For instance, an American student who takes a Chinese course in Beijing becomes an L2 user of Mandarin when she steps out of the classroom immediately. On the other hand, a senior Chinese-American citizen who comes to an adult English class in New York tends to be an "L2 learner" when he returns to his home in Chinatown in Manhattan.

Classroom Connections

Based on Cook's distinction between "L2 user" and "L2 learner," what would be the appropriate category for students in your current or proposed language teaching context? If you call them "L2 learners," how would you help them become "L2 users"? What are the criteria for becoming a "multicompetent language user"?

NESTs and NNESTs

We have learned some important lessons from all the recent research on multicompetent language users. First, as we now recognize worldwide *varieties* of English (and other L2s), the monolingual native-speaker ideal of yesteryear no longer holds. Second, in those few situations that call for native-speaker models, we have an ample supply of those models through Internet, TV, and other spoken/written media, all readily accessible worldwide. Finally, and most importantly, NESTs are clearly and unequivocally *not* better teachers than NNESTs by virtue of their "native" language background. The most important qualification for a teaching position is *training* and *experience* in teaching languages.

Llurda (2009), among others (Braine, 1999; McArthur, 2001; Higgins, 2003), showed that **nonnative English-speaking teachers (NNESTs)** offer as many if not more inherent advantages. Not only are multiple varieties of English now considered legitimate and acceptable, but also teachers who have actually gone through the process of learning English possess distinct advantages over native speakers. Some of the advantages of NNESTs (adapted from Cook, 1999; Llurda, 2009) are listed below.

The "Nonnative-Speaker" Advantage

1. Serving as role models of successful L2 users.
2. Knowing their students' culture and L1 so they have a high level of awareness about crosslinguistic differences and cultural differences.
3. Familiarity with what it is like to learn the target language as an L2 and be more empathetic with students about their needs and challenges.
4. Providing efficient explanations about target forms, meanings, and uses.
5. Ability to simplify a target language for more comprehensible input.
6. Understanding the roles of target language and evaluate teaching approaches and materials for local suitability.

The emergence of English as an international language has had a profound impact on language teaching. In this multicultural and globalizing world where users of English in the "outer" and "expanding" circles (Kachru, 1992) outnumber those in the "inner" circle by a ratio of more than two to one, it becomes rather inappropriate to use such terms as "native" or "native-like" in the evaluation of their communicative competence (Savignon, 2005).

 **Classroom Connections**

How do you feel about the question, "Where are you from?" How would you answer that question? How easy is it for you to answer that question? How is being "from" somewhere different from what you consider to be your *identity*? As a teacher, what are some alternative questions you could ask of your students? How would those alternatives also encourage some elaboration by students?

Superdiversity, Transnational, and Translingual Practice

The current globalized societies, particularly in urban centers, have been facing a complex level of diversity in linguistic, cultural, and socioeconomic terms. The notion of diversity extends beyond the one variable of *ethnicity*. Vertovec (2007) introduces the term, **superdiversity**, which refers to a "diversification of diversity" (Hollinger, 1995) due to the multilateral flow of people, goods, and ideas across borders. He acknowledges that since the early 1990s, there has been a multiplication of variables that influence "where, how and with whom people live" (Vertovec, 2007, p. 1025) and it has become much more challenging to define boundaries among community, identity, and citizenship. It is true that more and more people these days cannot think of their identities based only on one language or culture. Their languages, cultures, and communities are no longer as "pure" and homogeneous as they used to be (Canagarajah, 2007). They are becoming *the citizens of the world*.

Canagarajah (2013) puts forward a thought-provoking framework for understanding **transnational** and **translingual** individuals' use of resources that is mobile, fluid, and hybrid. For instance, translinguals are able to align with multiple communities, treating languages as mobile, constructed, hybrid, and heterogeneous. Communication of people in superdiverse spaces goes beyond only words. Their practice meshes in transformative ways, involving diverse semiotic resources combining oral, written, pictorial, and design modes (e.g., Facebook, Twitter, online blogs, mobile phones).

To understand these translingual users' communicative practices, Canagarajah (2013) urges us to focus on their "code-meshing" instead of "code-switching" practices. While code-switching assumes different codes for different contexts, code-meshing provides for merging diverse codes in the same context. As translinguals bring "their diverse varieties of English to the interaction, they are developing conversational strategies to communicate with each other, shifting to a shared variety . . . [adopting] creative ways to negotiate the norms operating in different contexts " (pp. 5–6). The ultimate pedagogical goal here is to promote *pluralism* that "acknowledges the difference between cultures and identities while finding modes of social cohesion to accommodate the difference" (p. 195).

Taking this pluralism further, Canagarajah (2013) proposes a model of **dialogical cosmopolitanism**, which is "interactive and negotiated. It is not given, but is achieved in situated interactions. It is based on mutual collaboration, within an acceptance of everyone's difference. It enables self-awareness and self-criticism, as communities don't just maintain their difference and identity but further develop their cooperative disposition and values" (p. 196).

CLASSROOM CONNECTIONS

How would you implement Canagarajah's *dialogical cosmopolitanism* in your teaching practice? How would you teach students to develop tolerance for the language norms of others, while being creative in merging their own language resources with dominant norms for voice?

Intercultural Competence

There has been an increasing attention to the concept of **intercultural competence** in the field of language education and professional development in general. This trend reflects the importance of intercultural competence for successful language learning and completion of professional tasks. According to Byram (2000), interculturally competent persons are able to perceive cultures in relationship, both within and outside a society, and are able to interpret each culture in the perspective of the other. He or she is also "someone who has a critical or analytical understanding of (parts of) their own and other cultures—someone who is conscious of their own perspective, of the way in which their thinking is culturally determined, rather than believing that their understanding and perspective is natural" (p. 10).

As Blommaert (2013) notes, superdiverse social environments are intensely complex and put high demands on *register development* (p. 195) for those who live and act in them. In Europe, the concept of intercultural competence is discussed in relation to communicative competence with particular attention to social and political contexts (Kramsch, 2013). In superdiversity space, in which traditionally recognized boundaries of nation, language, race, gender, and class have been challenged, it has become much more important to develop intercultural competence (Kramsch, 2013).

LANGUAGE POLICY

A further contextual consideration at play in your language teaching is a set of sociopolitical issues in relation to policy: What *status* does your country give to the target language? Does your country have an official **language policy** toward the language? How does this policy or status affect the motivation and purpose of your students? Language policy and planning is extremely important because it has direct and substantial consequences for society, economics, education, and culture (Lo Bianco, 2013). Let's view these issues in the form of a controversy that has been debated in the United States.

The status of English in the United States is certainly not in question from a sociological or educational point of view. However, for a number of years the United States has experienced a language policy debate. At one end of the spectrum is the notion of "English Only," which advocates the exclusive use of the English language for all educational and political contexts and carries an implicit assumption that the use of one's "home" language will *impede* success in learning English.

In contrast, the concept of "English Plus," a movement representing many organizations, advocates programs in which students' home languages and cultures are valued by schools and other institutions, but in which ESL instruction is promoted and given appropriate funding. Many educational organizations including Teachers of English to Speakers of Other Languages (TESOL) and the American Association for Applied Linguistics (AAAL) support the latter policy (Wiley, 2013). The debate has polarized many Americans. On one side are those who raise fears of "wild and motley throngs" of people from other cultures creating a linguistic muddle. On the other extreme, linguistic minorities lobby for recognition in what they see as a white supremacist governmental mentality.

Classroom Connections

What would be the long-term consequences to American society if English-only policies prevailed and were incorporated into public schools? How would they impact heritage languages and the functionality of the United States in a globalizing world? In your learning of an L2, have you ever encountered people who feel the L2 should be made an "official" language to the exclusion of others? How would you respond?

Current sociopolitical trends in the United States have created a unique challenge for some college-level ESL programs. As more and more families immigrate into the United States, children are placed into elementary and secondary schools according to their achievement in their home countries. Without adequate ESL or bilingual instruction, they may get a "social pass" from one grade to the next without demonstrating mastery of the subject matter or the English proficiency necessary for that mastery. After a few years, they find themselves in the upper secondary school grades and in colleges, but with language skills inadequate for academic demands. They typically have gained the **basic interpersonal communication skills (BICS)** that enable them to get along well socially, but not the **cognitive academic language proficiency (CALP)** needed to progress through a college program. They fall into neither ESL nor native-language course categories in most colleges, and so specialized courses are sometimes developed to meet their special needs. Such courses stress study skills, reading strategies, academic listening skills, and techniques for successful academic writing.

Language policies and social climates may dictate the status accorded to native and second languages, which in turn, can positively or negatively affect attitudes and eventual success in language learning. Two commonly used terms characterize the status of one's native language in a society where a second language is learned. A native language is referred to as **subtractive** if it is considered to be detrimental to the learning of a second language. In some regions of the United States, for example, Spanish may be thought to be sociopolitically less desirable than English. A native Spanish-speaking child, sensing these societal attitudes, may feel "ashamed" of Spanish (or in some cases the parents feel ashamed) and the child must conquer those feelings along with learning English. **Additive** bilingualism is found where a language is held in prestige by the community or society. Children learning English in Montreal, Canada, for example, are proud of their native French language and traditions and therefore can approach the second language more positively, promoting linguistic and cultural diversity.

Classroom Connections

Bilingual parents of children growing up in the United States often so strongly desire their children to learn English that they discourage them from using the L1 in the home. In your L2 learning, have you felt that your experiences have been *subtractive*? If you are teaching in a context in which your students feel their home or heritage language and culture are "beneath" the L2 languaculture, how would you approach those students in your classroom? How might you help them to better appreciate their heritage language and culture?

By the end of the 20th century, attitudes toward bilingualism and multilingualism had changed significantly. Researchers in multilingual education (e.g., Hornberger, 2005; García, 2009; Creese & Blackledge, 2010) have taken a further step from the *additive* bilingual approach, calling for a pedagogy that is "rooted in the multilingual and multimodal language and literacy practices of children in schools of the twenty-first century" (García, 2009, p. 8). Cummins

(2001, 2007) found that children's knowledge and abilities acquired in one language can be available for the development of another; both languages can bolster each other in the process of developing students' cognitive knowledge and functions.

García and Sylvan (2011) proposed a dynamic multilingualism in which the goal is to help students to become global and responsible citizens understanding different cultures and languages beyond cultural boundaries. **Translanguaging** is a classroom manifestation to implement flexible multilingualism, similar to the principles of translingual practice proposed by Canagarajah (2013). Through translanguaging (e.g., code-switching or translating in reading, writing, discussing, note-taking, singing), bilingual students and teachers engage in multiple discursive practices in order to make sense of meanings and functions of target forms (García & Sylvan, 2011).

INSTITUTIONAL CONTEXTS

One of the most salient and relevant contexts of language teaching is the institution in which you are teaching. L2 classes are found in such a wide variety of educational establishments that textbook publishers have a hard time tailoring material for the many contexts. Even within one "type" of institution, multiple goals are pursued. For example, language schools in many countries are now finely tuned to offer courses in conversation, academic skills, language for specific purposes (LSP), workplace English, vocational/technical English, test-taking strategies, and other specializations.

Institutional constraints are often allied to the sociopolitical considerations discussed above. Schools and universities cannot exist in a social (or political) vacuum. Public elementary and secondary schools are subject to official national language policy issues. In the United States and other countries, the type of second language program offered in schools is a product of legislation and governmental red tape. Students' purposes in taking additional language classes at the higher education level may be colored by institutional policies, certification and degree requirements, instructional staffing, and even immigration regulations.

Elementary and Secondary Schools

Language policies and programs in elementary and secondary schools differ greatly from country to country. For instance, English learner programs in the United States, designed for school-age children whose native language is not English, vary not only by state but also by school districts, which may number in the hundreds in larger states. In EFL countries, English is sometimes a required secondary school subject and almost always one of several foreign language options. In certain countries (Norway and South Korea, for example) English is required in elementary schools.

A number of models are currently practiced in the United States for dealing with nonnative English-speaking students in elementary and secondary schools. Some of these models apply to other countries in varying adapted forms. A few of the models were described in Chapter 3; however, they are repeated here for your convenience, in the following summary (Richard-Amato, 2010; McGroarty & Fitzsimmons-Doolan, 2014).

1. **Submersion.** The first way of treating nonnative speakers in classrooms is really a lack of treatment: pupils are simply "submerged" in regular content-area classes with no special foreign language instruction. The assumption is that they will "absorb" English as they focus on the subject matter. Research has shown that sometimes they don't succeed in either English or the content areas, especially in subtractive situations. So, a few schools may provide a "pull-out" program in which, for perhaps one period a day, students leave their regular classroom and attend special tutorials or an ESL class.
2. **Immersion.** Here, pupils attend specially designed content-area classes. All the students in a class speak the same native language and are at similar levels of proficiency in English. The teacher not only is certified in the regular content areas but also has some knowledge of the students' first language and culture. Immersion programs are found more commonly in FL contexts than in L2 contexts. For example, the French immersion schools in Canada offer French as a subject to children (usually from grade 4) in Anglophone school districts. In most immersion programs, pupils are in an additive bilingual context and enjoy the support of parents and the community in this enriching experience.
3. **Sheltered English.** This is a specialized form of immersion program that has become popular in recent years. It differs from immersion in that students come from varying native language backgrounds and the teacher is trained in *both* subject-matter content *and* ESL methodology. Also, students often have a regular ESL class as part of the curriculum. At Newcomer High School in San Francisco, for example, newly arrived immigrants are given one year of sheltered instruction in which ESL-trained teachers combine content and ESL in every subject.
4. **Mainstream classes.** In some submersion programs, students first receive instruction in ESL before being placed into content areas. Once teachers and tests conclude that students are proficient enough to be placed into ongoing content classes, they are mainstreamed into the regular curriculum. We need to remember that this ESL instruction should be content-centered so that pupils will not be at a disadvantage once they are placed in an ongoing class.
5. **Transitional/Early-exit bilingual programs.** In the United States, three different forms of bilingual education—in which students receive instruction in some combination of their first and second languages—are in

common use. Transitional programs teach subject-matter content in the native language, combined with an ESL component. When teachers and tests determine that they are ready, students are transitioned into regular all-English classes. This has the advantage of permitting students to build early cognitive concepts in their native language and then cross over later to the dominant language. The major disadvantage is that students too often are mainstreamed before they are ready, before their academic and linguistic skills have been sufficiently built.

6. **Maintenance/Late-exit/Developmental bilingual programs.** Here, students continue throughout their school years to learn at least a portion of their subject matter in the native language. The goal of the program is to develop biliteracy skills of language-minority students. This has the advantage of stimulating the continued development of pupils' native languages and of building confidence and expertise in the content areas in both languages. Disadvantages include discouraging the mastery of English and the high cost of staffing maintenance classes in budgetary hard times.
7. **Enrichment bilingual programs.** A third form of bilingual education has students taking selected subject-matter courses in a foreign language while the bulk of their education is carried on in their native language. Students in such programs in the United States are not doing so for survival purposes, but simply to "enrich" themselves by broadening their cultural and linguistic horizons.

 **Classroom Connections**

What kinds of language education did you experience in your elementary or secondary school? How successful were those curricula? What made the methodology or subject matter successful or unsuccessful? What would you do to make them more effective if you were a teacher in one of those models?

Post-Secondary and Adult Education

At the next age level one finds a cluster of institutional English learning opportunities for adults who may or may not anticipate going on into college or university degree programs, but who nevertheless may need English for social or occupational purposes. Typical of these institutions are those classified as language schools (usually small proprietary schools exclusively focused on language instruction), adult education schools (in the United States, state- or city-sponsored centers for educational, vocational, and recreational classes), and community colleges (two-year, non-baccalaureate degree-granting institutions of higher education), and extended learning (also known as continuing education) programs affiliated with four-year colleges or universities. Included among the varieties of possible courses in such institutions are the following (Parrish, 2004; Eyring, 2014):

1. **Survival/Social** curricula run the gamut from short courses that introduce adults to conversational necessities to full-blown curricula designed to teach adults a complete range of language skills for survival in the context of the second culture. By definition, such programs would not progress beyond intermediate skill levels. These courses are frequently offered in night-school adult education programs and private language schools such as Berlitz Schools.
2. **Family Literacy** programs are designed to teach students whose native language reading/writing skills are either nonexistent or very poor. Learning to be literate in English while learning aural-oral forms as well requires energy and motivation on the part of students. Teachers need special training to teach at this challenging level.
3. **VESL** (Vocational ESL) targets those who are learning trades (carpenters and electricians, for example), arts (such as photography), and other occupations not commonly included in university programs. VESL courses may be offered in **technical schools** or **trade schools** (institutions exclusively dedicated to teaching various arts and trades, ranging from art, fashion design, and architecture, to carpentry, automotive mechanics, and masonry).
4. **Workplace ESL** programs may be housed in any one of the above named types of institutions, or in the workplace itself. These are courses specifically devoted to teaching language needed for designated professional or occupational purposes. They differ from VESL programs in that a course will usually be narrowly focused on one context, and often offered in the workplace itself. For example, programs around the world are offered for hotel workers (or, even more specifically, housekeepers in hotels), grocery store workers, computer industry employees, and employees in multinational corporations that use English for international communication.
5. **Civic Education** programs help immigrants prepare for citizenship exams and encourage them to vote and participate in their communities as citizens.

Institutions of Higher Education

English language teaching programs also exist, of course, in four-year colleges and universities and post-graduate universities. The types of programs listed below may also be found in two-year community colleges and language schools, referred to above. Following are three broad types of curricula that are designed to fit varying student goals:

1. **IEPs** (Intensive English Programs) are pre-academic programs designed for students—usually from non-English-speaking countries—who anticipate entering a regular course of study in an English-speaking college or university. Some such programs are "full-time" and quite rigorous: students attend classes for 20 to 25 hours per week, usually for a quarter or a semester. The focus varies in such programs from rather general language skills at the advanced-beginner level to advanced courses in reading, writing, study skills, and research.
2. **EAP** (English for Academic Purposes) is a term that is broadly applied to any course, module, or workshop in which students are taught to deal with academically related language and subject matter. EAP is common at the advanced level of pre-academic programs as well as in colleges and universities, especially courses in writing at the academic level and in oral production (giving presentations, speeches, and participating in oral discourse in the classroom).
3. **ESP** (English for Specific Purposes) programs are specifically devoted to professional fields of study. A course in English for Agriculture or in Business Writing would fall under the general rubric of ESP. Usually ESP courses are differentiated from VESL English in that ESP refers to disciplines in which people can get university majors and degrees, while VESL refers to trades and other certificate programs.

Institutional constraints sometimes are the biggest hurdle you have to cross. Once you have found ways to compromise with the system and still feel professionally fulfilled, you can release more energy into creative teaching. Many of these issues will be dealt with in future chapters.

FOR THE TEACHER: ACTIVITIES (A) & DISCUSSION (D)

Note: For each of the "Classroom Connections" in this chapter, you may wish to turn them into individual or pair-work discussion questions.

1. **(A)** Divide the class into pairs or groups, and ask them to talk with their peers who are new to their L2 social and cultural contexts about a particular cultural or discursive practice they may not agree with or share with other people in the same L2 discourse community. Have them talk about any conflicts and frustrations they have experienced in their L2 practice and how they dealt with those challenges.
2. **(D)** Ask your students, as extra-class work, to investigate the official policy on English (and, possibly, other second languages) in the government and educational system of your own country or a country of their choosing. When they return to class, ask them to report their findings. Are

there unofficial policies in business, educational, or social circles? Do they sustain or contradict the official stance?

3. **(A)** In small groups ask students to share experiences they have had taking an L2 from a teacher who was not a "native" speaker of the L2. Have them evaluate positive and negative aspects of those experiences.
4. **(A)** Pair students up and ask them to describe other instances of subtractive bilingualism (page 169). What could one do as a teacher to help students create a more positive outlook on their native and second languages?
5. **(A)** If possible, direct your students to observe different ESL classes that represent some of the models described on pages 171–172. Have them compare the differences and similarities in the programs and describe what seemed to be the most and the least effective elements in each program or class hour. Their findings might be shared with the rest of the class.
6. **(A)** Direct small groups to decide how they would deal with each of the following scenarios. In each case, make sure each group specifies a targeted context (country, culture, language policy, institutional program):
   a. Your administrator insists that you teach a highly form-focused class, because your students will have to pass a multiple-choice grammar and vocabulary/reading test at the end of the term. You're convinced that not only is a communicative approach appropriate, but you can *also* thoroughly cover the necessary grammar and vocabulary, and through CLT your students would get excited and motivated to learn.
   b. You are a NNEST teaching in a non-English-speaking country, and your students have complained that your pronunciation is not native-like (in spite of the fact that your English is "excellent," even if nonnative).
   c. You are teaching in a language school where you would like to share ideas with your teaching colleagues, but no one wants to talk with you because they say they're too busy (and you suspect they are a bit defensive about the "rut" they're in after teaching at the same place for many years). How could you get teachers to share ideas in a nonthreatening way?

FOR YOUR FURTHER READING

Hinkel, E. (2014). Culture and pragmatics in language teaching and learning. In Celce-Murcia, M., Brinton, D. M., & Snow, M. A. (Eds.), *Teaching English as a second or foreign language* (4th ed.) (pp. 394–408). Boston, MA: National Geographic Learning.

A chapter offering a concise introduction to varied complex issues in teaching language, culture, and pragmatics. The author presents helpful tips for classroom teachers.

Martin-Jones, M., Blackledge, A., & Creese, A. (2012). *The Routledge handbook of multilingualism*. Oxon, UK; New York, NY: Routledge.

A comprehensive survey of the field of multilingualism and discussions about a number of issues on sociopolitical context of language education from current critical perspectives.

Blommaert, J. (2010). *The sociolinguistics of globalization*. Cambridge, UK; New York, NY: Cambridge University Press.

A critical introduction to a theory of changing language in the age of globalization. It provides a convincing rationale for why we need to reconsider issues of locality, identity, repertoires, competence, and sociolinguistic inequality that may concern students in the classroom.

Canagarajah, S. (2013). *Translingual practice: Global Englishes and cosmopolitan relations*. New York, NY: Routledge.

A new way of looking at the use of English in a global context that reexamines the complex issues of world Englishes, multilingualism, and intercultural communication. The author proposes the notion of translingual practices as a means to open up constructive negotiation strategies for both language teachers and learners.

Alsagoff, L., McKay, S., Hu, G., & Renandya, W. (Eds.). (2012). *Principles and practices for teaching English as an international language*. New York, NY: Routledge.

As research on learning and teaching languages has now become a global concern, with contributions to the field in many countries around the world, this anthology helps the reader to gain a perspective on English teaching in many contexts, especially those in which English is not a predominant L1.

PART III

PRACTICAL CLASSROOM CONSIDERATIONS

Part III presents practical considerations involved in designing and implementing classroom lessons. From a survey of curriculum and lesson design in the early chapters, the focus shifts to implementing techniques, materials, and technology in the classroom, and then to practical guidelines for stimulating interaction and for the "nuts and bolts" of classroom management.

- **Chapter 9, Curriculum and Course Design,** sets the stage for many of the subsequent chapters by giving readers a picture of how courses, programs, and curricula are created, revised, and implemented.
- **Chapter 10, Lesson Planning,** offers—with the backdrop of the previous chapter—specific guidelines for lesson planning.
- **Chapter 11, Techniques, Textbooks, and Materials,** focuses on the myriad techniques (tasks, activities) that a teacher may implement, and on the textbooks and materials that support those tasks and activities.
- **Chapter 12, Technology in Language Learning and Teaching,** is an updated overview of the beneficial effects of technology, which permeates learners' daily lives, for L2 learning both within and beyond the classroom.
- **Chapter 13, Creating an Interactive Classroom,** breaks down, step by step, the process of generating and maintaining interaction in communicative L2 classrooms, from even beginning levels to advanced. Featured are practical steps toward creating successful pair and group work.
- **Chapter 14, Classroom Management,** addresses the down-to-earth issues of how to manage a group of students in an L2 classroom. Problems of discipline, physical features in the classroom, the teacher's "presence," poise, roles, styles, unplanned moments, and creating a "positive climate" are featured.

CHAPTER 9

CURRICULUM AND COURSE DESIGN

Questions for Reflection

- How do the concepts of *curriculum*, *syllabus*, *program*, and *course* differ and what are some recommended steps to take in planning each?
- How does one go about a systematic, stepwise process of designing a course?
- What are some recommended means to evaluate the extent to which a lesson is appropriately embedded in a course as well as in an overall curriculum?
- How does a *situation analysis* and a *needs analysis* contribute to specifying goals, developing a syllabus, choosing materials, creating assessments, and evaluating a course?
- Do course *design* and course *revision* involve similar principles and steps?

Do you remember the English classroom in Seoul, Korea that you "observed" in Chapter 1? What do you suppose *preceded* and *followed* that lesson? In what way was the lesson an important stepping stone from previously learned language to future linguistic competencies? It was part of a whole course in English learning, so how were the building blocks of the course put together? Was that course part of a planned curriculum or program—a sequence of courses designed to meet stated goals? And if so, where did those goals come from?

Now that you have the backdrop of historical roots of language teaching, major principles that inform language pedagogy, and an acquaintance with some of the contextual variables involved in L2 teaching, let's center our focus on *practical classroom methodological realities*. Those realities include, in the next few chapters, how courses and curricula are designed; planning lessons; choosing among techniques, textbooks, materials, and technological aids; creating interactive classrooms; and classroom management issues.

The first step in this plethora of practicalities is to take a look at curriculum and course design. If you're a novice teacher, you might be thinking that course development is way over your head! Just tell me how to design a lesson, you're thinking. Fair enough, but we would like to start with the big picture here—a synopsis of course design—so that you will possess at least a passing acquaintance with the place of a given lesson within the *larger framework* of a course and/or curriculum. Here, Kumaravadivelu's (2001) "pedagogy of particularity" is highly relevant, for no one would dream of planning a lesson in a vacuum, or of assuming that lessons are *not* embedded in a much larger picture.

DEFINING TERMS

We'll begin by defining some terms. In both the research literature and common parlance, there is some variation in the interpretation of related concepts. At times, *curriculum* is used synonymously with *syllabus, course,* and *program,* depending on which source you read (or listen to), and sometimes on whether you are using British or American English. For the sake of clarity in this book, we will opt for the following definitions, adapted from Graves (2000, 2014), J. D. Brown (2010), Nation and Macalister (2010), and Richards and Schmidt (2002):

Curriculum: The selection and structure of the goals, content, sequence, procedures, and assessment of a program or course. A curriculum may refer to *one course* (J. D. Brown, 2010, p. 341; Nation & Macalister, 2010), or it could consist of *more* than one course, so beware! A curriculum may also refer to *program,* but is usually distinguished by its explicitly specified educational processes. For example, San Francisco State University's American Language Institute's overall *program* includes a *curriculum* in English for Specific Purposes, composed of *courses* designed for students about to matriculate into the University.

Program: A broad term describing a collection of classes or courses offered within a single institution, sometimes leading to a certificate or degree. So, for example, Monterey Institute of International Studies offers a graduate *program* in Nonproliferation and Terrorism Studies, which consists of courses, research projects, lectures, and discussions.

Syllabus: The planned structure of a single course (within a program) that outlines specific course goals, requirements, readings, assessments, and scheduled assignments across the length of the course (Graves, 2000). In British English, curriculum and syllabus are often synonymous (Richards & Schmidt, 2002, p. 139). We will opt in this book for the common American English usage cited here. Example: The *syllabus* for the final seminar in the MA-TESOL program requires three periodic portfolio evaluations and a classroom presentation.

Course (or class): A time-limited educational experience, usually carried out in regular meetings (or communications with an instructor) with a limited number of students. Courses are explicit in their statement of prerequisite qualifications and are designed for a stated classification of matriculated students who are pursuing specific needs and goals. In an adult education program, for example, one might offer a *course* in intermediate reading-writing, the *syllabus* of which spells out details.

 **Classroom Connections**

In language courses that you have taken, think of examples of a curriculum, program, syllabus, and course, and in your own mind clarify differences among these concepts. With examples from an institution you know, try to sort out possible fuzzy lines of distinction among these common terms.

As you continue to read this chapter, we will for the most part focus on *course* design, which at some point will imply a *syllabus* as well. Also note that the concept of *curriculum* may also be appropriate!

OVERVIEW OF THE COURSE DESIGN PROCESS

The flowchart shown in Figure 9.1 paints a "picture" of the process of designing a course, a sequence of steps that will be explained in the subsequent sections of this chapter. In the center of the chart are the basic steps normally followed in designing a course. On each side are influential *interacting factors*. Toward the top, note that as goals are being defined and as a course is being conceptualized, institutional constraints and available materials and resources must be *simultaneously* analyzed in order to determine feasibility and to avoid wasted effort on impossible goals.

In the lower part of the flowchart, the training, experience, and ability of the teacher will interact with the process of lesson design and teaching the course itself. Then, as instruction is ongoing, formative assessment will have the effect of monitoring students' progress and gauging the effectiveness of various components of the course.

Finally, assessment of students and teacher not only provides information about successes, achieved goals, and areas that need further work, but will also lead to potential appropriate *revisions* of the course as well as possible previous (prerequisite) courses and subsequent courses that are designed to build on the present one. Notice that any proposed revisions might be implemented at any one or more of the successive stages of course development. Further, the assessment of a course could lead to changes in an entire program of courses.

A PERSONAL EXPERIENCE IN COURSE DESIGN

Before embarking on our synopsis of course development, here's an account of a request that Doug, one of the authors, received from a university in Central America that wanted San Francisco State University to offer a four-week summer "short course" in English.

Figure 9.1 Second language course development process

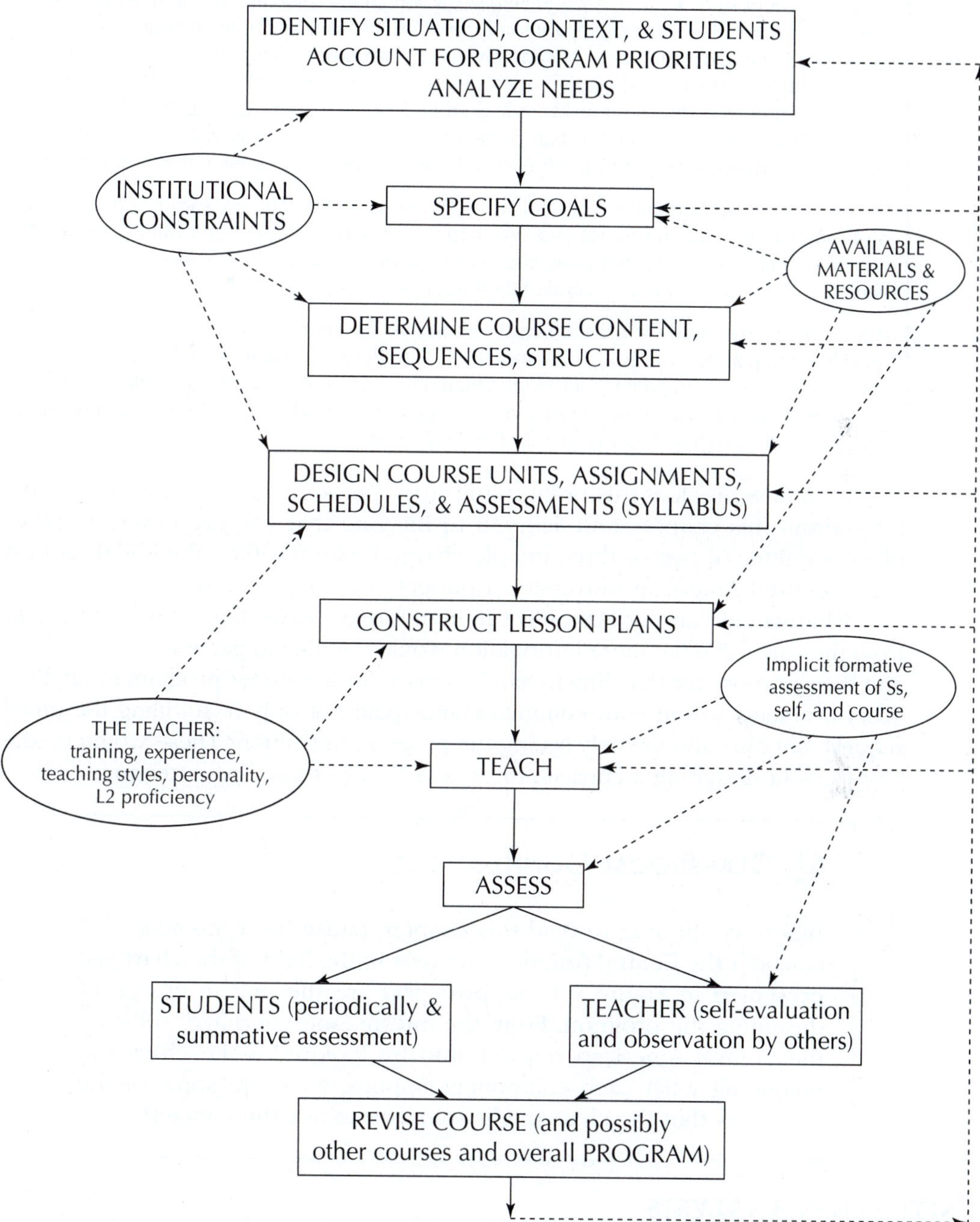

The primary contact proposed to send 45 students between the ages of 18 and 24 for a "rigorous, serious course in academic English" at a high intermediate to advanced level of proficiency. They also wanted preparation in the TOEFL®, as many of the prospective students intended to apply to American universities for further study. They wanted to reside in university dormitories and eat their meals there. And they wanted several weekday and/or weekend excursions to various sights in and around San Francisco, and asked for an activities leader to coordinate this part of the program. This, then, was in addition to the academic program, which was, by their request, to be five days a week, for 4–5 hours a day.

For reasons that are difficult to explain, we were not able to obtain any sort of verification of proficiency of the students in advance. We had no test scores, grades, or writing samples. A very brief preliminary questionnaire, filled out by about 15 students, provided minimal demographic data and broadly verified their interest in academic English.

It was now January and the program was proposed to start in mid-June, so we had to act quickly to prepare for this group; five months of lead time was minimal, but doable if communications could go back and forth efficiently. Our Central American contact asked for a proposed budget (which was a primary consideration in whether or not the program would happen), and a proposed curriculum for the 45 students.

We'll now break at this point in the story, before continuing in installments throughout this chapter, and ask you to imagine that you are now a member of a committee of two or three people charged with fulfilling the initial request of the Central American university: a budget and a curriculum.

What would you do? First, what more information would you need or desire from the contact? What more information would you like to get about the students and their purpose for traveling to San Francisco for a summer program in English? What problems would your committee anticipate not only in fulfilling the initial request, but also in ultimately seeing the program to fruition? These would be the first steps in designing a curriculum, so let's turn to those, in succession.

CLASSROOM CONNECTIONS

Before continuing to read this chapter, pause for a moment, and consider the Central American request in the light of the chart just presented in Figure 9.1. Suppose *you* are the one in charge of designing the program. From the information you have so far on the Central American request, and by looking at the chart and imagining what each component implies, what are some of the questions that the chart might spur you to ask the contact?

SITUATION ANALYSIS

The first—or perhaps among the first—steps in course design is an analysis of the setting, the audience, and needs of the students, otherwise known as a **situation analysis** (Richards, 2001), or in Nation and Macalister's (2010, p. 15) words **environment analysis**. Every effective course is undergirded by a consideration of the following factors:

1. **Educational setting.** Within what societal and cultural norms is the course situated? What is the institutional framework into which the course must be integrated? What are the broad instructional goals of the program? In general what is the structure of the program? What are the physical conditions (e.g., classrooms) and resources (labs, computers, AV, materials)? Who are the learners, in very general terms? Basic questions here look at the larger educational context within which a course is placed.
2. **Class characteristics.** How would you describe the class in terms of the homogeneity of learners, the size of the class, and its relationship to others that learners are taking?
3. **Faculty characteristics.** What are the qualifications of teachers—training, experience, methodological biases? What are the working conditions (hours of teaching, support services) for the faculty? To what extent is there collaboration among teachers?
4. **Governance of course content.** Who determines course content? To what extent can teachers choose content and/or adapt content as they perceive the need to do so?
5. **Assessment and evaluation requirements.** What stipulations are in force for assessing students for placement, diagnostic, or achievement purposes? What grading norms are in place? How, if at all, are courses evaluated and revised?

This preliminary but important step in course design takes a sweeping look at the broad parameters of the curriculum. If it's a new course you are about to design, one that is need of revision, or simply a course you're teaching and you need some background information, a situation analysis allows you to lay some foundation stones either for further development or for understanding the nature of a course.

NEEDS ANALYSIS

A second step in the process of developing or understanding a course centers on the needs that the course presumes to address. Richards (2001) is quick to point out that *needs* is not an easy concept to define. Depending on whom you ask, they are "wants, desires, demands, expectations, motivations, lacks, constraints, and requirements" (p. 54). A **needs assessment** (Graves, 2014, pp. 56–58) is an important precursor to designing the **goals** of a course in that it can identify the overall purposes of the course, "gaps" that the course is intended to fill, and the opinions of both course designers and learners about their reasons for designing/taking the course. As such, it is important to identify at least two types of needs: *objective* and *subjective*.

Objective needs are those that can be relatively easily measured, quantified, or specified with agreement by administrators (and possibly teachers) on what constitutes defined needs. Typically, objective needs are analyzed through test data (including learner language samples), questionnaire results, teacher reports, observations, and interviews of teachers and students. Information gathered will include the following:

- demographic data on learners, including language ability, interests, etc.
- needs expressed in terms of proficiency levels
- language skills to be addressed
- what learners need to *do* in English (target contexts for English use)

Subjective needs are often of equal or greater importance, as they focus on needs as seen through the eyes of the learners themselves. Granted, sometimes learners' perceived needs do not match their actual needs. For example, students often feel that they should spend lots of time studying grammar in a class, when in reality they may need more time in communicative activities. But it still is wise for a curriculum developer to ascertain all subjectively perceived needs in order to address them in the course itself. Subjective needs are more difficult to gather, but are typically sought through interviews, questionnaires, teachers' perceptions, observations, and the opinions of "experts." From these procedures, the following information may emerge:

- learners' attitudes toward the target language, culture
- expectations that students have of themselves, and of the course
- purposes that students perceive for studying English
- specific language skills that students wish to focus on
- preferences (styles, strategies) that students have about their learning

 **CLASSROOM CONNECTIONS**

If you had to research the **subjective** needs of students in a course you were asked to design, how would you go about gathering information on the above five criteria? From your experience learning or teaching an L2, what other subjective needs might be examined?

PROBLEMATIZING

Graves (1996, p. 5) suggests that an important feature of course design is the careful consideration of the potentially large number of things that can go "wrong" with one's best laid plans for a course. With all the societal, institutional, and pedagogical constraints already implied in simply *preparing* to design a curriculum, it may be obvious that problems are going to appear, and the better prepared you are to respond to such problems, the less likely it will be that insurmountable impediments will prevent the project from reaching its fruition. Problematizing a course, that is, anticipating impediments, issues, and other potential obstacles in advance, will save untold hours of effort that otherwise may be spent "patching up" the shortcomings later on.

Recently, Doug, one of the authors, had a graduate student of his propose to design a workplace curriculum for grocery store workers for whom English was a second language, and who were having difficulties communicating with customers, colleagues, and bosses. A number of immediate problems came up:

- Did the learners perceive their own need to learn certain skills in English?
- Were managers supportive of the effort?
- Would workers receive paid time to take the course?
- Would prospective students have to pay to attend the course?
- Would the overall administrator of the grocery store pay the teacher for her services?
- Would there be money to pay for materials?
- Was there a convenient space available for the class?

These and a host of other problems had to be addressed before the project could go forward, and many of them involved the slowly turning wheels of bureaucracy.

Classroom Connections

If you were approached by a group of employees in a workplace setting with a similar request, what other questions might you want to pose in an attempt to gather more information and preclude "problems" down the road?

Courses are usually successful because they have anticipated such problems in advance and have effectively determined realistic answers to them. Consider the following list as just scratching the surface of the process of addressing the challenges that face you in this particular task:

Questions to Address in Problematizing a Proposed Course

- What are institutional requirements and conditions that impact on the course?
- What administrative authorities must be brought into the process in order to obtain approval, budget, space, and staffing?

- What contradictions might exist between what learners want/need and institutional constraints?
- What budgetary constraints exist and how might a budget be effectively constructed for maximum efficiency and accomplishing of goals?
- Are there any problems surrounding faculty qualifications and availability that impact on the course?
- Are there conflicting expectations between administrator(s) and teachers on what the course can accomplish?
- What requirements for student assessment are in place and how can a teacher creatively work "within the system" to carry out appropriate assessments?

Before continuing with an enumeration of further steps in the process of course design, let's go back to the story of the proposed Central American program.

> The situation analysis proved to be the easiest part of the task. We had a readily available setting in the American Language Institute (ALI); we were familiar with academically bound international students and their needs; a course in academic English could easily be a spin-off of our existing courses; we had classrooms and resources. We knew the students would all be native Spanish speakers, a mix of men and women, and we were accustomed to classes of 15 students each, so the group would comprise three classes, each targeted at different proficiency levels (although here is where we eventually ran into some problems).
>
> A teacher pool was no problem. Current teachers at the ALI were happy about the prospect of summer employment and we easily planned for them to teach about 10 hours a week. We planned a collaborative effort in which teachers and one coordinator would meet almost daily to deal with course content during the program. We easily put achievement tests into place, and the students would be given the TOEFL® test at the end of the session.

Needs analysis presented serious problems:

> We wanted to get test scores ahead of time, to administer a self-check questionnaire to determine interests, and to obtain writing samples of students (speech samples were not available). For a number of logistical reasons virtually none of the above was possible to obtain, except for the very brief aforementioned questionnaire returned by 15 of the prospective students. As time was rapidly marching on, we were forced to anticipate needs on the basis of past experience with similar groups.

A further issue in the problematizing process arose when budgetary matters were discussed.

> We were informed that the initial figure that we proposed was too high and a request was made for a lower amount. We eventually agreed on a lower amount, but only by removing the activities leader and responsibility for the cultural aspects that initially were to be part of the whole package. We also had to dissociate what we had intended to be an interaction of language and culture in the course and plan a strictly academic program. Therein lay a further problem that arose later on!

With some consternation now about how successful the program was going to be, we nevertheless moved ahead to tackle the next steps: stating goals, objectives, materials, and course content.

SPECIFYING GOALS

The terms *goal* and *objective* are often interchanged in pedagogical literature, and depending on whom you consult, you might find some confusion in defining the two terms. For the sake of clarity and brevity here, we'll offer a distinction between the two terms that seems to conform to the majority of uses of the two terms. It is really quite a simple distinction.

Goals are rather broadly based aims and purposes in an educational context, and are therefore more appropriately associated with whole programs, courses, or perhaps sizable modules within a course. According to J. D. Brown (1995), goals are "general statements concerning desirable and attainable program purposes and aims" (p. 71).

Objectives, sometimes referred to as "subgoals" (Graves, 2014, p. 58), are much more specific than goals, both in their conception and in their context. Objectives usually refer to aims and purposes within the narrow context of a lesson or an activity within a lesson. They are "specific statements that describe particular knowledge, behaviors, and/or skills" (J. D. Brown, 1995, p. 73). Obviously there can be some gray area in between the two concepts, but they are essentially distinguished by the size and scope of the context in question.

Most curriculum experts agree that once a situation analysis and needs analysis have confirmed some of the general parameters of a course, goals need to be carefully stated in order to be certain about what the course will accomplish and what it will not. For the Central American program, to guide our thinking, we developed the following *speaking* goals for the lowest of the three levels we planned (we also had goals for listening, reading, and writing):

By the end of the course, students will be able to:

1. Participate in social conversations in English.
2. Speak with few hesitations and with only minor (local) errors.
3. Successfully apply some form-focused instruction to their speech.
4. Self-monitor their speech for potential errors.
5. Participate comfortably in pair, group, and whole-class discussions.
6. Give a simple oral presentation on a familiar topic.

These served as guidelines for determining course content, and eventually lesson objectives could be derived from these overall goals.

CLASSROOM CONNECTIONS

For an L2 course that you have either taken or taught, reconstruct the general goals of the course. Then, try to remember a specific lesson or unit within the course, and restate its objectives. How might the success of accomplishing those objectives be assessed?

CONCEPTUALIZING A COURSE SYLLABUS

The next *two* steps in many cases will be undertaken simultaneously or at least interactively: as you put together what most institutions call a *syllabus* (Robinson, 2009), it is often helpful to carry out a review of options in *materials* (textbooks and other resources) that are available. It would be unrealistic to draw up a prototype of your course with no consultation of the potential materials that might support the course. You could end up having to redesign a great deal of your course if you find that just the right materials don't exist!

So, how much time and effort should you spend on designing a syllabus before consulting the options for existing materials? This is a difficult question to answer because it depends on a number of factors, among which are time, expertise, money, and one's own need to offer the perfect course. Sometimes excellent courses are launched simply on the basis of an available textbook, and sometimes those curricula are unsuccessful. But it's also rare to design the perfect curriculum the first time around, and so perhaps with the revision process (the bottom box in Figure 9.1) a course can be redesigned quite successfully after a mediocre first run.

A communicative syllabus (function-focused as opposed to form-focused) should minimally consist of the following components:

COMPONENTS TO INCLUDE IN A COMMUNICATIVE SYLLABUS

1. Goals for the course (and possibly goals for modules within the course).
2. Suggested objectives for units and possibly for lessons.
3. A sequential list of functions (purposes), following from the goals, that the curriculum will fulfill. Such a list is typically organized into weeks or days.

4. A sequential list of topics and situations matched to the functions in #3.
5. A sequential list of grammatical, lexical, and/or phonological forms to be taught, again matched to the sequence of functions.
6. A sequential list of skills (listening, speaking, reading, writing) that are also matched to the above sequences.
7. Matched references throughout to textbook units, lessons, and/or pages, and additional resources (audio, visual, workbooks, etc.) to be used.
8. Possible suggestions of assessment alternatives, including criteria to be tested and genres of assessment (traditional tests, journals, portfolios, etc.).

In addition, depending on how detailed the syllabus ultimately gets, it is not unusual to see syllabuses that include outlines of lesson plans (especially if a teacher's manual is included with a textbook) and/or suggested activities. In such lesson plans, one will often find suggestions for extra-class ("homework") activity to assign to students.

How did we fare here in our plans for the Central American program?

> With only about eight weeks remaining before the arrival of students, we began to get some mixed messages from our contact about the "real" purposes of the program. It was looking less and less "academic" and more and more "cultural"; we learned that the prospective students might only be at a low intermediate level of English; and it looked like the initial proposed 45 students were now considerably fewer!
>
> We had neither time nor money available for course development, even though we clearly had the expertise. With a number of uncertainties entering into the planning of the program, we decided to conceptualize a course that was a hybrid of a published textbook series and our own ALI curriculum, with little further planning. This decision was expedient, and saved us from spending a lot of time in developing a course that might turn out to be the wrong course for a possible surprise audience!

SELECTING TEXTBOOKS, MATERIALS, AND RESOURCES

As noted above, the process of reviewing potential textbooks, materials, and resources, beyond those that you might design yourself, is one that ideally takes place in concert with conceptualizing the syllabus. Of great importance in this process is ascertaining that your *goals*—the outgrowth of a situation and needs analysis—are in central focus at all times. It is tempting to allow existing textbooks to drive your goals, but doing so can obviously lead you astray.

There are many different ways of approaching the process of reviewing textbooks and making a final decision. The following set of guidelines is a synthesis of factors drawn from several sources (J. Brown, 1995, p. 161; Cunningsworth, 1995; Richards, 2001, p. 258).

Criteria for Evaluating and Choosing Textbooks for a Course

1. Textbooks should correspond to overall program goals, learners' needs, and the course objectives.
2. Textbooks should reflect the purposes of the course and uses (present or future) that learners will make of the language.
3. Textbooks should correspond to the intended methodological philosophy of the course (in most cases, not dogmatically imposing a restricted "method").
4. The physical characteristics of the textbook (layout, illustrations, organization, variety) should be appealing to students.
5. The usefulness of the textbook's teacher's edition or notes should be accounted for, especially for less experienced teachers.
6. Consider logistical factors such as price, availability, auxiliary aids, workbooks, and website support.

For a more complete treatment of textbook evaluation and selection, see Chapter 11 of this book.

Beyond textbook selection, the ongoing process of locating and choosing *materials* is a crucial element in course planning. Some materials are available with the purchase of a course textbook (see guideline #6 above). Other materials are teacher-made (additional activities and exercises, handouts, charts, review sheets, etc.). Such personalizing of a curriculum is highly recommended in that such material can be specifically gauged for the particular audience, and it is a motivating factor for both teacher and students.

ASSESSMENT

Assessment of the students' attainment of objectives of lessons and units, and of the goals of the curriculum, may be offered in a wide array of possible formats. Traditional periodic tests such as quizzes, multiple-choice tests, fill-in-the-blank tests, and other somewhat mechanical test types, offer the possibility of a practical quick level-check of students' attainment. Mid-term and final examinations might include, along with some of the above techniques, short essays, oral production, and more open-ended responses. Alternatives in such assessment techniques are available in journals, portfolios, conferences, observations, interviews, and self- and peer-evaluation. Details on all these possibilities are described in Chapters 20 and 21 of this book.

Another category of assessment must not be overlooked. Suppose your students overwhelmingly failed to meet anticipated objectives? Or what if certain students whom you know to be "good" did not perform up to expectations?

In this and other instances of *student* assessment, teachers might benefit from "looking in the mirror" to ascertain if something in their *own* course and syllabus design, methodology, or assessment procedures should be modified.

 **CLASSROOM CONNECTIONS**

In the Central American program, assessment was limited to very brief end-of-course oral presentations and individual oral interviews. What would you use as criteria for *assessment* of the students if you were one of the teachers? Looking at the goals of the course presented earlier, and considering the oral communication scales presented earlier in Chapter 7, what components of oral production would you assess?

COURSE REVISION

Few courses are "perfect" the first time around. In fact, successful teachers will always look for ways to improve a course the next time it is taught. In embarking on a major step in course design, making it better the next time around, what are some of the steps you might follow in revising a course?

In what Nation and Macalister (2010, pp. 173–179) call "introducing change," four preliminary considerations will help you to revise a course:

1. **See the need for change.** The impetus for change is always stronger when it comes from within your conviction. You must envision the potential advantage of change in order to be intrinsically driven to effect the change.
2. **Determine the extent of change**. In most cases, a course will be improved with some minor "tweaking." Major revamping of the course could be an inefficient use of your time.
3. **Engage in realistic change.** A related factor is the matter of being practical in terms of your time, other courses surrounding yours, and the total program.
4. **Follow your own principled teaching**. Course revision is rarely successful if you have been forced out of your own principled approach to L2 teaching.

Next, review the steps you followed in course development and determine what aspects of that interconnected set of processes need to be evaluated. Here are some reminders of those design steps:

- appropriateness of the course *goals* (in meeting needs and purposes)
- adequacy of the *syllabus* to meet those goals

- textbooks and *materials* used to support the curriculum
- classroom *methodology*, activities, and procedures
- appropriate *orientation* of both teachers and students before the course
- the students' *motivation* and attitudes
- the students' *perceptions* of the course
- *monitoring* students' progress through (informal) assessment
- the students' *actual performance* as measured by (formal) assessments
- *institutional* support, including resources, classrooms, and environment
- *staff collaboration* and development before and during the course
- the place of your course within the total *program*

 **CLASSROOM CONNECTIONS**

Have you ever taught (or taken) a course that you thought went quite well, but when all the student assessment was completed, you were less than satisfied with the results, especially if too many students failed to meet the objectives? Speculating on what might not have been ideal in carrying out the course, which of the above steps do you think might emerge as the most crucial ones to examine in order to consider revising the course for a subsequent term?

A PERSONAL EXPERIENCE: THE REST OF THE STORY

Here's the rest of the story of the Central American program, all in the light of the last few sections of this chapter.

> As we approached the day of the students' arrival, we made sure all the physical arrangements were set: housing, transportation, ordering textbooks and copies of the institutional TOEFL® test, issuing contracts to teachers, reserving classroom space, and ascertaining that immigration regulations were being met. The latter almost cancelled the program, as the group had to "pull strings" with the U.S. immigration office in order to obtain visas, but at the last minute that crisis was averted (another long story).
>
> About two weeks before the arrival date, we were informed that there would be only 25 students in the program! This had a significant impact on our plan to offer three sections, and the outcome of that was to offer only two sections, with another budgetary (and curricular) adjustment. The day after the students arrived, we had a placement testing day and discovered that they were clearly of lower proficiency than we had initially expected; but even more significant was their almost unanimous desire not to undertake a strictly academic course. Instead, their wishes indicated a course in conversation and culture, with only a light treatment of reading and writing skills, and with a liberal number of hours each day to enjoy the beautiful city of San Francisco!

What were we to do with our prepared syllabus? An "emergency" meeting among the teachers and coordinator resulted in an amazing collaborative effort to revise the curriculum on the spot, and to meet together daily for the first two weeks and to share results of the previous day and to plan activities for the next. We were able to salvage some of the textbook lessons but the textbook proved to be marginally useful. Some of our own ALI curriculum was used to fill in certain gaps. Most of the four-week course was a daily process of creative design based on informal monitoring of student needs and their progress. We further arranged to have some cultural connections between class activity and afternoon and weekend tours. The TOEFL® prep part of the curriculum was reduced to two optional workshops.

At the end of the course, students' oral presentations and individual oral interviews showed marked improvement in their English skills. Some of this was no doubt attributable to their residence in San Francisco for the duration of the course. We also found through various program evaluative measures that the students loved the course, the teachers, and the setting. They self-reported that their needs were more than fulfilled. They left San Francisco with cherished memories and experiences they might never again encounter.

This story could happen to you, but with a little bit of luck and better predictions of needs, it will not. What could have happened to give this event a more educationally satisfying ending? Here were our conclusions:

1. Carry out a more accurate needs analysis.
2. Begin the planning process much earlier in the academic year in order to better reach the desired numbers of participants, to establish a more realistic budget, and to plan the course accordingly.
3. With more accurate pinpointing of needs and purposes of the course, the syllabus, textbooks, and other resources would have been appropriate, and we would have avoided the "emergency" patching together of a course.

This survey of course design is intended to give you a picture of what lies behind the daily lessons and activities that you might observe or carry out in the classroom. It's important to place every class period against the backdrop of the course in which it is embedded, and certainly the context of preceding and subsequent lessons. Without such a framework, from the point of view of the teacher, lessons might be inappropriately planned and executed, and from the point of view of an observer, inappropriately evaluated. We now turn to what many consider the "basic unit" of a course, the daily, time-framed set of activities designed to meet specific objectives: the lesson.

FOR THE TEACHER: ACTIVITIES (A) & DISCUSSION (D)

Note: For each of the "Classroom Connections" in this chapter, you may wish to turn them into individual or pair-work discussion questions.

1. **(D)** Ask your students for one or two examples of courses that the class is familiar with. Then, as a whole class brainstorm what the *situational*

context of the course is, and how such contextual variables are accounted for in the curriculum. Use the five points outlined in the section on Situation Analysis, on page 182, as a guideline for the discussion.

2. **(A)** Divide your class into small groups of 3 or 4. Ask them to look at the factors listed in the circles and ovals at the sides of the chart in Figure 9.1 (page 181): institutional factors, materials, teacher variables, and formative ongoing assessment. Ask each group to choose one course that everyone in the group is familiar with and brainstorm how the four factors have influenced (or should influence) the course. Have the groups share results with the whole class.
3. **(A)** Ask pairs to quickly enumerate examples of *objective* needs and *subjective* needs in a course that both members of the pair are familiar with. Then have pairs write the objectives on the board, report their findings briefly, followed by a whole class reflection on the relative importance of selected items.
4. **(D)** Among the members of the class, solicit examples of "problems" that have arisen, or might arise, in a course familiar to everyone, in the process of developing a curriculum. If any of your students have had personal experience developing a course, encourage them to share their thoughts.
5. **(D)** If possible, secure a digital file of an existing syllabus for a language course. See Graves (1996, 2000) and Murphy and Byrd (2001), for examples of course descriptions. Then, if your equipment permits it, convert the file to computer projected slides (e.g., PowerPoint), and go step by step through the course, asking your students to identify each of the eight elements of a course syllabus (see pages 188–189).
6. **(A)** Ask your students to bring any L2 textbooks they have to the next class period. Then, ask pairs to share their thoughts about the texts based on the criteria cited by Richards (2001) (page 190) or J. D. Brown's five categories. Ask pairs to share their thoughts with the rest of the class.
7. **(D)** On pages 191–192, twelve bulleted items are suggested as factors to consider in a program evaluation. Using those items, ask your class to briefly evaluate—on a scale of 5 (excellent) to 1 (poor)—the success of the Central American program that was synopsized in the chapter. Note that in some cases you have incomplete information about the program.

FOR YOUR FURTHER READING

Graves, K. (2000). *Designing language courses: A guide for teachers.* (2nd ed.) Boston, MA: Heinle & Heinle.

Nation, I. S. P., & Macalister, J. (2010). *Language curriculum design.* New York, NY: Routledge.

Both of these books serve as manuals for L2 curriculum development. They are comprehensive in scope and provide a wealth of information, ideas, guidelines, and practical examples.

Graves, K. (2014). Syllabus and curriculum design for second language teaching. In M. Celce-Murcia, D. Brinton, & M. A. Snow (Eds.), *Teaching English as a second or foreign language* (4th ed., pp. 46–62). Boston, MA: National Geographic Learning.

Brown, J. (2010). Second language curriculum development. In M. Berns (Ed.), *Concise encyclopedia of applied linguistics* (pp. 341–349). Amsterdam: Elsevier.

These two chapter-length treatments of course and curriculum development provide useful synopses of processes. Graves includes a number of practical examples of courses in her chapter, and J. Brown's entry includes a useful summary of important components and parameters of curriculum development.

Murphy, J., & Byrd, P. (Eds.). (2001). *Understanding the courses we teach: Local perspectives on English language teaching.* Ann Arbor, MI: University of Michigan Press.

This edited volume includes eighteen real-world accounts of courses that teachers have taught (and in some cases developed themselves). The accounts are classified into workplace, adult education, EFL, university credit courses, and pre-university noncredit courses.

CHAPTER **10**

LESSON PLANNING

Questions for Reflection

- What are some of the foundational factors that underlie lessons before you even start the actual planning process?
- What is the difference between lesson *goals* and *objectives,* and what are the specifications for well-framed objectives?
- What are performance-based objectives and why is it important to state objectives in terms of *performance*?
- What could we include among guidelines for planning a lesson?
- How can you evaluate the effectiveness of a lesson?

You now have a sense of the larger picture of course/curriculum design, so let's zoom in here on *lesson* planning. Most courses are presented in a number of units of varying lengths (usually from one to three weeks in a normal 15-week term), whose focus is defined by goals that ultimately contribute to overall goals. Such units commonly consist of a series of lessons: the building blocks of units and courses, time-defined, in-class sets of activities designed to accomplish one or more specific objectives.

The term **lesson** is popularly considered to be a unified set of procedures that cover a period of classroom time, usually ranging from 45 to 90 minutes. These classroom time units are administratively significant for teachers because they represent steps in a curriculum before which and after which you have a hiatus (of a day or more) in which to evaluate and prepare for the next lesson. Sometimes your whole life seems to be caught up in a never-ending process of lesson planning. But those lessons, from the point of view of your own and students' time management, are practical, tangible units of effort that serve to provide a rhythm to a course of study.

How do you go about planning a lesson? This chapter should give you some guidelines.

"BENEATH" THE LESSON PLAN

You cannot simply plunge into a lesson plan without considering the framework of a number of guiding, foundational factors. Purgason (2014) says "lesson planning is the process of taking everything we know about teaching and learning along with everything we know about the students in front of us, and putting it together to create a road map for what a class period will look like" (p. 362).

What are some of those interconnected elements? Let's look at the following factors (adapted from Purgason, 2014, pp. 362–363), arranged from macro-issues to more detailed considerations.

- Your own general philosophy of education
- Principles of L2 learning, such as those described in Chapter 4
- Specific SLA research findings on successful L2 acquisition
- The methodological options available to you (see Chapter 3)
- The geographical, cultural, and sociopolitical context of your classroom
- Institutional constraints, requirements, standards, and benchmarks
- The stages before and after a lesson—how it fits into the whole curriculum
- The particular focus and objectives for the lesson
- The students and the *uniqueness* of their community of practice
- The range abilities of students in your class

Classroom Connections

What is your "philosophy of education"? What are the ingredients that make for successful learning in the classroom? Besides the above list of underlying factors in lesson planning, what are some others that you think are important in guiding and determining how a lesson should unfold?

All of these factors will affect this "road map" you're about to construct for the class hour. It's important to allow these considerations to act as implicit, peripheral guidelines for your planning.

But now, if you're a beginning teacher you may be thinking, "Planning is taking so much time! I don't have enough hours in the day to do it well." Or as an experienced teacher, you may feel that it's too tedious to do all that planning (Woodward, 2001, p. 4). You might also feel that you shouldn't plan *too* much, lest the plans have to change! "How can I anticipate everything that will happen in this lesson?" What are you to do?

Harmer (2007, p. 364) suggests that teachers "need maps to help them through the landscape," and we would add that even road maps and sophisticated GPS navigators require occasional interpretation and adaptation by users. In due course of time, you will achieve a rhythm in the process of gauging optimal planning for lessons.

FORMAT OF A LESSON PLAN

While variations abound, seasoned teachers generally agree on what the essential elements of a lesson plan should be. For examples of each, turn to the sample lesson plan at the end of this chapter.

1. Goal

As you discovered in the previous chapter, a well-designed course will specify a number of **goals**. Each lesson in the course will in some way address those "big" overall purposes. A first step in a lesson, then, would be to acknowledge the way in which your lesson is designed to contribute to such goals. Sweeping goals may be generalized and cut across several lessons, but they provide a pedagogical context for you.

In the sample lesson plan at the end of the chapter, the goal is not explicitly stated, but rather is implied. The course in oral communication skills is designed to help students to communicate in "socially appropriate" ways (see the second terminal objective) and this lesson's focus is on imperatives.

2. Objectives

It's important to state clearly what you want students to gain from the lesson. Explicit statements help you to:

- be sure that you indeed know what it is you want to accomplish.
- preserve the unity of your lesson.
- predetermine whether or not you are trying to accomplish too much.
- evaluate students' success at the end of or after the lesson.

Objectives are most clearly captured in terms of stating what students will *do*—that is, what they will *perform*. What does this mean?

First, let's look at what *not* to do in designing objectives. Try to avoid vague, unverifiable statements like "Students will *learn about* the passive voice," or "Students will *practice* some listening exercises," or "Students will *discuss* the homework assignment."

CLASSROOM CONNECTIONS

What is meant by the phrase *performance objectives?* Before you read on, look at the three examples of *unacceptable* objectives above, and consider what's "wrong" with them. Why don't they qualify as appropriately framed objectives?

You would be unable to confirm the realization of these abstruse, loosely stated objectives that are unobservable. Note, however, that some language objectives are not overtly observable, and therefore you may need to depart from strictly behavioral terms for such objectives. Notably, comprehension objectives (listening, reading) are tricky because you cannot actually *observe* either. You're forced to rely on performance that demonstrates or confirms correct comprehension; in other words, you have to *infer* the acquisition of those objectives.

In stating objectives, you should be able to identify an overall purpose that you will attempt to accomplish by the end of the class period. It's also important to think in terms of what Richards and Bohlke (2011, p. 4) call "*meaningful* learning outcomes," which includes helping students to develop positive attitudes toward learning and, as much as possible, to take control of their own learning.

Beyond these global purposes of a lesson, other supportive objectives need to be stated as well, leading us to distinguish between two kinds of objectives. **Terminal objectives** are final learning outcomes that you will be responsible for assessing. **Enabling objectives** are interim steps within a lesson that build upon each other and ultimately lead to a terminal objective.

Consider the terminal and enabling objectives in the lesson plan at the end of the chapter:

Terminal objectives

Students will be able to:

- Give instructions and commands using imperatives
- Use imperatives in a socially appropriate manner

Enabling objectives

Students will be able to:

- Practice imperatives through an information gap activity
- Categorize giving imperative commands in terms of appropriateness
- Practice giving appropriate commands using imperatives through a situational activity

Depending on a wide variety of contextual factors, including your individual "artistry" as a teacher, your own enabling objectives might vary from what this teacher has chosen. The important element is to identify the specific tasks or activities you will employ in realizing the terminal objective.

Here's another set of terminal and enabling objectives for an intermediate integrated skills class in an adult education course in the USA.

> **Terminal objective**
>
> - Students will successfully request information about airplane arrivals and departures.
>
> **Enabling objectives**
>
> - Students will demonstrate comprehension of the lesson's ten listed new vocabulary items through accomplishment of the main task.
> - Students will show comprehension of an airline schedule by responding to a preliminary list of ten questions.
> - Students will produce questions with *when, where*, and *what time* in the main task.
> - Students will produce appropriate polite forms of requesting in the main task.
> - Students will successfully complete the main task of filling in an information gap exercise sheet containing an airline schedule that has missing information.

In both lesson plans, terminal and enabling objectives are clearly specified with explicit identification of the elements of the lesson that will accomplish given objectives. This way the teacher can, before teaching, be certain about the purpose of the lesson, and after the lesson is completed, make at least an informal assessment of the students' success.

Highly exacting enabling objectives that state outcomes in quantifiable terms are usually not practical for lesson planning purposes. So, to say "students will correctly respond to seven out of ten questions" may be overstepping the purpose of designing a lesson plan.

3. Materials and Equipment

It may seem a trivial matter to list materials needed, but good planning includes knowing what you need to take with you or to arrange to have in your classroom. It is easy, in the often harried life of a teacher, to forget to bring to class an audio player/recorder, laptop (for visual enhancement on a screen), a poster, some handouts you left on your desk at home, or the workbooks that students gave you the night before.

Notice the list of materials in our sample lesson plan. Using a YouTube video implies preparation in the form of technological aids and access to the video. Being forced by inadequate planning to skip that part of the lesson would diminish some of the verve of this lesson.

4. Procedures

At this point, lessons clearly have tremendous variation. However, as a very general set of guidelines for planning, you might think in terms of making sure your plan includes the following:

a. An opening statement or activity as a warm-up and ascertaining appropriate background knowledge on the part of the students
b. A set of activities and techniques in which you have considered appropriate proportions of time for whole class work, small group and pair work, teacher talk, and student talk
c. Closure—a brief "wind-down" time so the class hour doesn't end abruptly

 **CLASSROOM CONNECTIONS**

Think about some lessons from your experiences learning or teaching an L2, and recall some of the ways a class hour has *opened*, perhaps with small talk or a warm-up activity of some kind. What purposes do these few minutes of class time serve?

5. Assessment

Next, how can you determine whether your objectives have been accomplished? If your lesson has no assessment component, you can easily find yourself simply making assumptions that are not informed by careful observation or measurement. Now, of course, every lesson does not need to end with a quiz or a test, nor does evaluation need to be a *separate* element of your lesson. Informal assessment can take place in the course of most classroom activity. Some forms of assessment may have to wait a day or two until certain abilities have had a chance to build. Whatever manifestation your assessment takes, make sure, after students have sufficient opportunities for learning, that you have appropriately considered how you will (a) assess the success of your students, and possibly (b) make appropriate adjustments in your lesson plan for the next day.

6. Extra-Class Work

What we commonly call "homework" (but students don't necessarily do such work only at *home*) is more appropriately named **extra-class work**. If it is warranted, extra-class work needs to be planned carefully and communicated clearly to the students. With the widespread availability of media (Internet, social media, search engines, news programs, movies, and more—all literally at your students' fingertips on their mobile devices), you can almost always find applications or extensions of classroom activity that will help students do some learning beyond the class hour.

CLASSROOM CONNECTIONS

Whether you are teaching an L2 in the L2-speaking country (e.g., English in an English-speaking country) or not, global communications now allow various languages to be readily accessible. Consider some of the ways that you might use the Internet and other electronic media as a source for extra-class work for your students. Keeping in mind the ability level of your students, where and how might they access written and spoken input? What might you ask them to *do* with that input?

GUIDELINES FOR LESSON PLANNING

With the background of the basic elements of a lesson plan, we'll now take you on a step-by-step set of guidelines for lesson planning.

1. How to Begin Planning

In most normal circumstances, especially for a teacher without much experience, the first step of lesson planning will already have been performed for you: choosing what to teach. No doubt you will be—or already have been—given a textbook and told to teach from it, with either a suggestion or a requirement of how many chapters or units you should cover. As you look over the chapter you are to cover for a class hour, you might go through the following sequence:

GUIDELINES FOR BEGINNING THE PROCESS OF LESSON PLANNING

1. Assuming that you are already familiar with (a) the curriculum your students are following (see "Adapting to an Established Curriculum" in this section) and (b) the overall plan and "tone" of the textbook(s), look over the textbook chapter.
2. Based on what you perceive as (a) the goals of the curriculum and this course, and (b) the overall language needs being met, determine the topic and purpose of your lesson. You might want to consider this its *goal.*
3. With the goal mind, draft out one or two explicitly stated *terminal objectives* for the lesson.
4. Of the exercises that are in the course book, decide which ones you will do, change, delete, and add to, all based on the objectives you have drafted.

5. Draft out a skeletal outline of what your lesson will look like.
6. Carefully plan step-by-step procedures for carrying out the lesson, making revisions as needed. State the purpose(s) of each technique and/or activity as *enabling objectives.*

For teachers who have never taught before, it is often useful to write a script of your lesson plan in which your anticipated words are written down and followed by what you would expect students to say in return. Scripting out a lesson plan helps you to be more specific in your planning and can often prevent classroom pitfalls where you get all tangled up in explaining something or students take you off on a tangent. Writing a complete script for a whole hour of teaching is probably too laborious and unreasonable, but more practical and instructive (for you) are *partial* scripts that have the following components:

COMPONENTS OF A PARTIAL SCRIPT OF A LESSON PLAN

- introductions to activities
- directions for a task
- statements of rules or generalizations
- anticipated interchanges that could easily bog down or go astray
- oral testing techniques
- conclusions to activities and to the class hour

2. Variety, Sequencing, Pacing, and Timing

As you are drafting step-by-step procedures, you need to look at how the lesson holds together as a whole. Four considerations come into play here:

a. **Variety**. Is there sufficient variety in techniques to keep the lesson lively and interesting? Most successful lessons give students a number of different activities during the class hour, keeping minds alert and enthusiasm high.
b. **Sequencing**. Are your techniques or activities sequenced logically? Ideally, elements of a lesson will build progressively toward accomplishing the ultimate goals. Easier aspects usually will be placed at the beginning of a lesson; tasks that require knowledge gained from previous exercises will be sequenced appropriately.
c. **Pacing**. Is the lesson as a whole paced adequately? Pacing can mean a number of things. First, it means that activities are neither too long nor too short. You could, for example, have so many short activities that just as students are getting the "feel" for one activity, they get

bounced to the next. Second, you need to anticipate how well your various techniques "flow" together. You would not, for example, find a smooth flow in a class that had five minutes each of whole-class work, pair work, whole-class work, group work, pair work, whole-class work, etc. Nor would you normally plan two silent reading activities in a row. Third, good pacing also is a factor of how well you provide a transition from one activity to the next. An example:

T: Okay, you've just had a good chance to listen to the way a lecturer signals various segments of a class lecture. Now we're going to use this information to look at a reading passage about space exploration and figure out . . .

d. **Timing**. Is the lesson appropriately timed, considering the number of minutes in the class hour? This is one of the most difficult aspects of lesson planning to control. It's not unusual for new teachers to plan a lesson so tightly that they actually complete their lesson plan early, but after just a little experience it is more common that we don't complete our lessons within the planned time allotment. The latter is not a cardinal sin, for most likely it means you have given some time to students for genuine interaction and creative use of language. But timing is an element that you should build into a lesson plan: (a) if your planned lesson ends early, have some *backup activity* ready to insert; (b) if your lesson isn't completed as planned, be ready to gracefully end a class on time and, on the next day, pick up where you left off.

Classroom Connections

Offhand, what are some possible "backup activities" that you could insert at the end of a class hour to make productive use of a few extra minutes of time? Think about types of questions you could ask, quick games you could play, or media that you could use in such a case. Could these "five-minute activities" be generic enough that they could be inserted into virtually any lesson?

3. Contingency Panning

Closely related to the issue of appropriately timing your lesson is the problem of contingency planning (Purgason, 2014). What should I do if the lesson takes an unexpected tangent that throws me completely off track? We'll discuss this all-important matter in Chapter 14, Classroom Management (page 289), in what we're calling "unplanned teaching." But for lesson planning purposes it is always prudent to have a few of the above-mentioned *backup activities* (Purgason, 2014, pp. 371–372). Beyond that, your *flexibility* consists in understanding that a "plan" is just that, not a certainty. Coping with a variety of interruptions and unanticipated events is an essential aspect of the life of a teacher.

4. Gauging Difficulty

Figuring out in advance how easy or difficult certain techniques will be is usually learned by experience. It takes a good deal of cognitive empathy to put yourself in your students' shoes and anticipate their problem areas. Some difficulty is caused by tasks themselves; therefore, make your directions crystal clear by writing them out in advance (note the comments on "scripting" lessons, above). Writing them ahead of time allows you to be more objective in determining if everything is clear. And then, either give an example yourself or solicit an example of a subtask within a technique.

Another source of difficulty, of course, is linguistic. If you can follow the "reasonable challenge" principle of providing material that is just a little above, but not too far above, students' ability, the linguistic difficulty should be optimal. The main problem here lies in the heterogeneity of a classroom full of learners whose proficiency range is potentially quite broad. Individual attention, feedback, and small-group work can sometimes bring balance into the classroom.

5. Individual Differences

For the most part, a lesson plan will aim at the majority of students in class who comprise the "average" ability range. But your lesson plan should also take into account the variation of ability in your students, especially those who are well below or well above the classroom norm. You can take several steps to account for individual differences:

GUIDELINES FOR ACCOUNTING FOR INDIVIDUAL DIFFERENCES AMONG STUDENTS

- Design techniques that have a range of easy to difficult aspects or items.
- Solicit responses to easier items from students who are below the norm and to harder items from those above the norm.
- Try to design techniques that will involve all students actively.
- Use judicious selection to assign members of small groups so that each group has either (a) a deliberately heterogeneous range of ability or (b) a homogeneous range (to encourage equal participation).
- Use small-group and pair-work time to circulate and give extra attention to those below or above the norm (see Chapter 13 on group work design).

CLASSROOM CONNECTIONS

As a language learner have you ever felt that an activity or task is either too easy or too hard for you? If so, did the teacher offer any options? How, in general, would you as a teacher help to provide an optimal challenge to *all* of your students in your planned activities?

6. Student Talk and Teacher Talk

Give careful consideration in your lesson plan to the balance between student talk and teacher talk. Our natural inclination as teachers is to talk too much! As you plan your lesson, and as you perhaps script out some aspects of it, see to it that students have a chance to talk, to produce language, and even to initiate their own topics and ideas.

7. Adapting to an Established Curriculum

In the previous chapter, you were introduced to the steps involved in designing a curriculum. The assumption then, and in this chapter, is that your primary task is *not* to write a new curriculum or to revise an existing one, but to follow an established curriculum and *adapt* it to your particular group of students, their needs, and their goals, as well as your own philosophy of teaching.

As you plan lessons, your first concern is that each class hour must contribute to the goals that a curriculum is designed to pursue. But perhaps your institution has no curriculum spelled out in a document; in other words, it is a "textbook-driven" curriculum that, in practice, simply tells you to teach everything in a textbook. Or you may find only broadly stated specifications for the course you are about to teach somewhere in the description of the institution. At best, you would be presented with a document that clearly delineates the goals of the curriculum and offers suggestions on how to meet those goals in terms of weekly or even daily lesson objectives.

If you don't have such overall course goals, it might be feasible to devise some for yourself so that you can keep your course focused on attainable, practical ends. Where could you find such lists? Other course books at similar levels covering similar skills may offer a good starting point. Or you could consult one or more of the proficiency guidelines referenced in Chapter 7. Within the Internet listings of ACTFL, CEFR, and IELTS scales, you may find more than enough correspondence to your course. A practical and useful set of descriptors is available in ACTFL's "Can-Do" Statements at actfl.org.

As you formulate goals, incorporate the factors outlined in the previous chapter that contribute to curriculum planning:

- situation analysis (especially learner characteristics)
- needs analysis (especially learner factors and institutional factors)
- supporting materials and resources
- assessment requirements

By paying attention to the learner factors above, you will have a good chance of pointing your students toward pragmatic, communicative goals in which their real-life needs for English will be met. You will focus on the learners and their needs but temper those with the realities of your institution's needs. The latter will add some administrative practicality to your goals. After all, every educational institution is limited in some way in its capacity to deliver the very "best."

Your course goals might look like these goals of an advanced pre-university listening comprehension course:

American Language Institute, Level 48 Listening Comprehension

- Students will understand the teacher's instructions and demonstrate that understanding.
- Students will understand the teacher's explanations and show that comprehension.
- Students will understand classroom peers in discussions, activities, and oral reports.
- Students will understand academic lectures given by different speakers.
- Students will identify topics and topic development.
- Students will infer relationships among topics.
- Students will recognize different points of view.
- Students will identify key information as signaled by vocabulary.
- Students will recognize key information as signaled by stress and intonation.
- Students will identify key information as signaled by grammatical structure.

8. Classroom Lesson Notes

A final step in your lesson planning process is a very practical one: What sort of lesson notes will you actually carry into the classroom with you? If you have pages and pages of notes and reminders and scripts, you will never free yourself for spontaneity. Most experienced teachers operate well with about *one page* of a lesson outline and notes. Some prefer to put lesson notes on a series of index cards for easy handling. By reducing your plans to such a physically manageable minimum, you will reduce the chances of getting bogged down in all the details that went into the planning phase, yet you will have enough in writing to provide order and clarity as you proceed.

CLASSROOM CONNECTIONS

Some teachers, with experience, are artful enough to be able to walk into a classroom with as little as some notes on scraps of paper or some marginal notes in the textbook, and still conduct an excellent, well-paced, challenging lesson. What do you think your inclination would be in writing up classroom lesson notes? What are the advantages (and disadvantages) of a "minimalist" tendency as opposed to taking several pages of notes into the classroom with you?

Following is a summary of the facets of the lesson planning process that we have discussed:

GENERAL GUIDELINES FOR EFFECTIVE LESSON PLANNING

1. Begin with terminal objectives, a skeletal outline, and enabling objectives.
2. Include variety in your sequencing, pacing, and timing.
3. Account for unpredictable contingencies.
4. Gauge the difficulty level of aspects of your lesson.
5. Allow for individual differences among your students.
6. Stimulate student talk and minimize teacher talk.
7. Adapt to an established curriculum.
8. Make a few classroom lesson notes to guide you as you teach.

A SAMPLE LESSON PLAN

What follows here is a lesson plan designed by Safa Lateef for first-year college students attending a prerequisite English language class at Salahaddin University in Erbil, Iraq. The 25–30 students in the class range in age from 18 to 23. Their proficiency level is high-beginner to low-intermediate. Their L1s are Arabic and Kurdish.

In her introduction to the lesson plan Lateef noted that the lesson reflects principles of Task-Based Language Teaching (TBLT) with (a) pre-, main, and post-task phases; (b) a primary focus on meaning; and (c) at least one task that employs focus on form. Formative assessment is accomplished by informal observation of student performance during tasks and through the extra-class "homework" assignment.

Imperatives Lesson Plan

Target Audience and Context: *EFL students in Salahaddin University in Erbil, Iraq*

Learner Level: High beginner/Low intermediate

Class size: 25–30

Class length: 90 minutes

Terminal objectives

Students will be able to:

- Give instructions and commands using imperatives.
- Use imperatives in a socially appropriate manner.

Enabling objectives

Students will be able to:

- Practice imperatives through an information gap activity.
- Categorize giving imperative commands in terms of appropriateness.
- Practice giving appropriate commands using imperatives through a situational activity.

Materials

- YouTube video (youtube.com/watch?v=E_FzgtLVzbI)
- Whiteboard and markers
- Vocabulary matching handout (Appendix A)
- Fill-in-the-blanks handout (Appendix B)
- My favorite dance (Appendix C)
- Uses of commands handout (Appendix D)
- Application of commands in different situations handout (Appendix E)

Time and Materials	Procedures
3–5 min.	**Welcome** • Ask about Ss weekend, and how they spent it. • Take attendance.

25–27 min. Appendix A (Vocab. matching handout) YouTube video (youtube.com/watch?v=E_FzgtLVzbI) Appendix B (Fill-in-the-blanks handout)	**Pre-Task: Introduction/schemata activation** • Tell Ss they are going to watch a video on how to dance the Moonwalk so that they can see an example of giving commands in context. • Distribute a few snapshots from the video and ask Ss to predict how the Moonwalk is danced. Ask Ss which famous singer is associated with it. • Distribute vocabulary-picture match-up worksheet (Appendix A). • Ask Ss to work independently; give them 5–7 minutes. • Prompt a few Ss to share their answers and explain any difficult word. **Stimulus material: YouTube video** • Show entire video once through; have Ss just watch, so they have a general idea about the video. • Ask Ss if they understand the content of the video after watching it. • Distribute fill-in-the-blanks handout (Appendix B). Play video a second time through and ask Ss to complete worksheet as they watch the video. • Review the answers and ask Ss to keep the handout with their answers on it, as they will return to the handout later. • Direct students to compare Moonwalk to cultural Kurdish dance to further activate their cultural and content schemata.
20–23 min. Appendix C (My Favorite Dance)	**Main Task: Information gap activity** • Ask Ss to form pairs. Distribute Appendix C: My Favorite Dance. Have them take turns describing a favorite dance by giving instructions to their partner, using imperatives. As a reference, have them use the script from the video (provided in Appendix C). • Tell Ss that the dance could be from Iraqi/Kurdish culture. Some examples from Kurdish dance are: *Se peyi* dance, *Du peyi* dance, or *Hawrami* dance. • Ask each pair to share the description of their dance with another pair, after describing the dance. Student pairs guess each other's dances. • Ask Ss to take notes while working on this activity, as the teacher will randomly pick some pairs to share their favorite dance. • Allow the pairs 15 minutes to discuss and take notes. • Circulate the classroom for support.

20–23 min. Appendix B (Fill-in-the-blanks handout, again)	**Post-Task: Review of the main-task answers** • Pick some pairs to share their responses by describing or modeling the dance. Have a couple of pairs write their responses on the board. **Focus on Form** • As a class, review the language Ss just used. • Draw Ss' attention to the student-generated sentences on the board. • Ask Ss to compare these sentences with the completed script-gap (Appendix B) to notice the form and how it is used, and to notice their errors if they have any. • Invite Ss to correct any errors on the board. • Elicit the function of the imperatives used in the video (give commands) and during the main activity (give instructions). **Transition** • Ask students if they know some situations in which using imperatives specifically to give commands is appropriate and/or inappropriate. • Give students a few minutes to discuss with the person next to them. • Call on new volunteers to share responses.
20–23 min. Appendix D (Uses of command) Appendix E (Application of commands in different situations)	**Extended Post-Task: Register judgment activity** • Distribute Appendix D: Uses of command. • Ask Ss to circle yes, no, or maybe based on the appropriateness of the commands based on the situations. • Check their understanding of the activity directions. • Circulate the classroom for support. • After allowing them some time, open a discussion by inviting students to share and give reasons for their choice. **Application of the register judgment** • Distribute Appendix E: Application of commands in different situations. • Ask Ss to choose some of the situations from Appendix D to write a new imperative command for them. • Direct them to use *I need you* and *Let's* to soften the command. • Tell Ss that they can work alone. If they find the activity hard they can work with another student. • After 5–7 minutes solicit responses from those who haven't participated.
2–4 min.	**Closure: Application/Extra-class work** • Ask Ss to select an activity they are interested in (such as a sport, playing a game, or cooking). • Tell them to post their topic on the blog and write a short description about how to do/play/cook by using mainly imperatives.

Appendix A

Vocabulary Matching Handout

Student Name ______________________________

Directions: Write the correct word under each picture.

balance	trainers	step	slide
snap	swing	duplicate	lift

A	B	C	D
Lift			

E	F	G	H

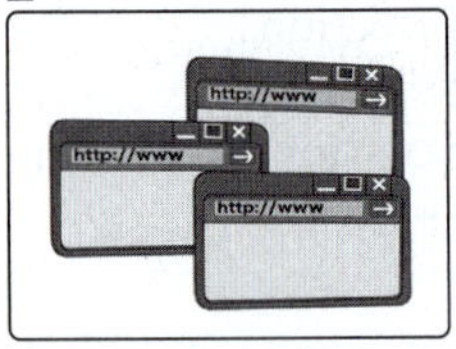

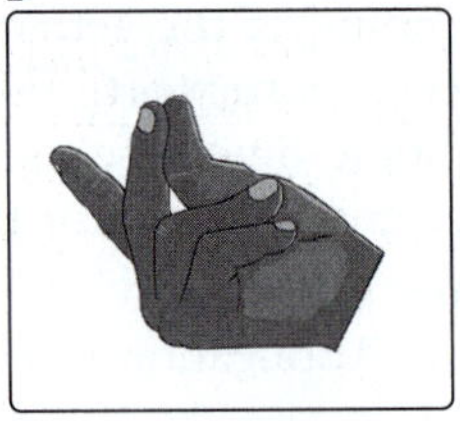

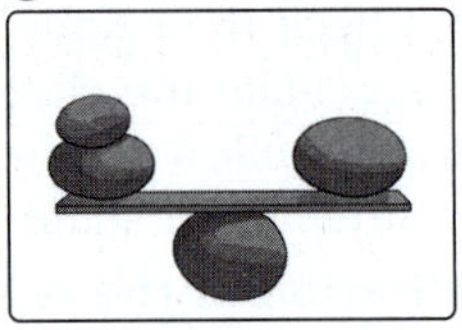

Appendix B

(youtube.com/watch?v=E_FzgtLVzbI)

Fill-in-the-Blanks Handout

Student Name ____

Directions: Watch the video and listen carefully to fill in the blanks on the script below:

Get out your white socks and __________ on your gloves. Ladies and gentlemen, the Moonwalk: Step one you will need smooth surface, soft dance shoes or trainers, and comfortable clothes. Step two, starting position with your back straight and your feet together pointing forward. Step three, the L position: Next, __________ your right leg and place the toes of your right foot down on the floor approximately a foot behind your left leg. Step four, balance: If you feel off balance you can __________ the width between your legs to create a wider center of gravity. Step five, the __________: __________ back onto your rear leg and slide the left heel back and into the floor so it finishes behind the right leg. At the end of the movement snap the heel of your left foot up off the floor. Top tip: the toes of both feet should never come off the floor even when the heels do. Step six, the __________: As you your left heel up off the floor, your right heel should simultaneously snap down onto the floor. Step seven, copy: From the finishing position of the last move, __________ the slide on the other foot. Step eight, the head: To help create the illusion of the move, __________ a head movement. As you slide your leg back slowly, move your head forward as if it is being left behind the movement and then pull it back towards the body as you switch to the other foot. Step nine, the arms: To make the step look better __________ your arms as if you are walking normally while keeping them in time with your legs movement. As your left leg slides back, your right arm should swing forward.

For Teacher's use: Answer key: 1. Put 2. Start 3. Lift 4. Increase 5. Slide; slide 6. Snap; snap 7. Duplicate 8. Add 9. Swing

Appendix C

My Favorite Dance

Student Name ____

Directions: Describe a favorite dance to your partner by giving instructions using imperatives.

The following script from the video handout is an example of the task:

Get out your white socks and put on your gloves. Ladies and gentlemen, the Moonwalk: Step one you will need a smooth surface, soft dance shoes or trainers, and comfortable clothes. Step two, starting position: start with your back straight and your feet together pointing forward. Step three, the L position: Next, lift your right leg and place the toes of your right foot down on the floor approximately a foot behind your left leg. Step four, balance: If you feel off balance you can increase the width between your legs to create a wider center of gravity. Step five, the slide: slide back onto your rear leg and slide the left heel back and into the floor so it finishes behind the right leg. At the end of the movement snap the heel of your left foot up off the floor.

Appendix D

Uses of Command

Student Name ______________________________

Directions: Circle yes if the imperative is appropriate in the situations below. Circle no if it is not appropriate, and circle maybe if you think it depends. Give reasons for your choice.

Yes No Maybe A student says to a teacher, "Give me my test."

Yes No Maybe A father says to his son, "Let's clean your room."

Yes No Maybe An office assistant says to her boss, "Please copy this for me."

Yes No Maybe A customer says to a taxi driver, "Keep the change."

Yes No Maybe A teacher says to his boss, "Give me my paycheck."

Yes No Maybe A police officer says to a driver, "Do not park here."

Yes No Maybe A students says to a classmate, "Don't worry about the test. Relax."

Yes No Maybe A librarian says to students, "Be quiet."

Yes No Maybe A boss says to a teacher, "I need you to begin your classes on time."

Adapted from: Badalamenti, V., & Henner-Stanchina, C. (2007). *Grammar dimensions: Instructor's manual* (2nd ed.). Boston, MA: Thomson Heinle.

Appendix E

Application of Commands in Different Situations

Student Name ______________________________

Directions: Choose five of the situations from Uses of Commands worksheet and write a different command for each situation. Use *I need you* and *Let's* to soften your commands.

1. **Situation**
   Customer to taxi driver

   Command
   Turn right at the next corner.

2. **Situation**

   Command

3. **Situation**

   Command

4. **Situation**

   Command

5. **Situation**

   Command

6. **Situation**

   Command

Adapted from: Pavlik, C. (2004). *Grammar sense.* Oxford: Oxford University Press.

 **CLASSROOM CONNECTIONS**

Formative assessment while teaching a lesson may be easier said than done. What kinds of mental (or written) notes do you think a teacher can make in order to assess the accomplishment of the three enabling objectives? How would you determine if students have accomplished each objective? If you think an objective may *not* have been accomplished, what would you do to help students meet the objective?

This chapter has focused specifically on the planning stage of classroom teaching. When you walk into the classroom, all that planning (you hope!) will work to your advantage. We turn in the next two chapters to an overview of materials—textbooks, technology, and other resources—that support the delivery of successful lessons.

FOR THE TEACHER: ACTIVITIES (A) & DISCUSSION (D)

Note: For each of the "Classroom Connections" in this chapter, you may wish to turn them into individual or pair-work discussion questions.

1. **(A)** Following are some curricular goals selected from academic English language programs:
   - Understand academic lectures
   - Write a business letter
   - Use greetings and "small talk"
   - Request information in a restaurant
   - Read informal essays

   Assign one goal to each of five small groups, and for each, instruct groups to (a) describe an audience for which the goal might be appropriate, then (b) transform the goal into *terminal* objective(s), and finally (c) brainstorm a number of *enabling* objectives that would have to be reached in order to accomplish the terminal objective. Have groups share their results with the rest of the class.
2. **(A)** Assign students in pairs to observe an L2 class in which they look for manifestations of *variety*, *sequencing*, *pacing*, and *timing*, or the lack thereof. Have them write down their observations and share them in the form of brief reports to the class.

3. **(D)** Accounting for individual differences is not as easy as it sounds. Ask students to describe some dimensions of student differences they have experienced or observed. How would one ensure, in each case, that students on both ends of the continuum are "reached" in some way? Small groups sometimes provide a means for bridging ability gaps. What are some other ways to account for individual differences?
4. **(A)** Have small groups look at the sample lesson plan (pp. 208–215) and use the six guidelines for lesson planning (pp. 202–203) to evaluate the plan. Should any changes be made? Conclusions should be shared with the rest of the class. Note: This could be a lengthy group discussion followed by reports, so allow plenty of time for full discussion in the groups.
5. **(A)** For extra-class work, ask students to transform the sample lesson plan (pp. 208–215) into some practical "lesson notes"—no more than one or two index cards perhaps—that they could carry into the classroom with them. When they report back, pair them up to briefly share their notes with a partner. Then, ask students as a whole class to share the following: What decisions did they have to make? On what basis did they decide to create notes the way they did?
6. **(D)** A *needs analysis* normally considers such questions as who the learners are, why they are learning English, in what context(s) they use it, and so on. Ask students to identify learners they are familiar with, and brainstorm a list of specific questions that one could use to analyze needs and, in turn, to determine how a curriculum or a set of lessons should be designed.
7. **(D)** Find a teacher's manual or instructor's edition of an L2 textbook, and choose one lesson. Duplicate the "Suggestions for Teaching" for the lesson, or present them on a laptop and projector. Ask students to use the principles cited in this and in previous chapters to evaluate those notes. How might the notes be changed to better reach objectives?

FOR YOUR FURTHER READING

Purgason, K. (2014). Lesson planning in second/foreign language teaching. In M. Celce-Murcia, D. Brinton, & M. A. Snow (Eds.), *Teaching English as a second or foreign language* (4th ed., pp. 362–369). Boston, MA: National Geographic Learning.

A practically oriented article that steps the reader through processes of designing and evaluating lesson plans, with a number of examples of lessons.

Woodward, T. (2001). *Planning lessons and courses.* Cambridge, UK: Cambridge University Press.

Written in reader-friendly style, this book-length treatment offers many examples of lesson plans along with practical suggestions for effective designing of lessons.

Richards, J., & Bohlke, D. (2011). *Creating effective language lessons.* Cambridge, UK: Cambridge University Press. (Available online at www.cambridge.org)

This 50-page booklet is available for free online (search by author and/or title) and downloadable. Like the above two references, it offers many practical examples that are easily applied to various courses.

CHAPTER 11

TECHNIQUES, TEXTBOOKS, AND MATERIALS

Questions for Reflection

- What are the distinguishing characteristics of technique, task, activity, procedure, and other similar terms (that seem to be synonymous)?
- What is the evolution of classroom techniques that led to our current understanding of communicative and task-based instruction?
- What are some widely used *techniques* that can be chosen to accomplish various purposes in the classroom?
- How might one evaluate the potential of a proposed *textbook*? By what guidelines? What are some tips for choosing and adapting a textbook?
- How can one analyze and evaluate potential *materials* to incorporate into a lesson?

With the backdrop of an overview of curriculum/course design and lesson planning, we turn now to the building blocks of those lessons: the techniques and materials and textbooks that you utilize in accomplishing your goals. The choices that you make about what to *do* in the classroom are informed and guided by what you know about learner characteristics, institutional structure, student needs and purposes, and of course the all-important set of lesson objectives that you have established.

TECHNIQUES REDEFINED

At the outset, it's important to ascertain that certain terms are well defined. In Chapter 2 (page 15), the term **technique** was introduced and defined, but it was noted in passing that some other commonly used terms have been used synonymously, including *task, activity, procedure, practice, behavior, exercise*, and even *strategy*. With the potential confusion arising from multiple terms, you will no doubt find it helpful to do some clarifying. Bear in mind, however, that experts in the field may have slightly differing points of view about the working definitions here.

Task

You may recall from Chapter 3, in a discussion of task-based instruction, that **task** usually refers to a specialized form of technique, or more appropriately a series of techniques, with real-world-related communicative goals. The common thread running through half a dozen definitions of task is its focus on the authentic use of language for meaningful communicative purposes beyond the language classroom.

Activity

A popular and loosely defined term, **activity** usually refers to a reasonably unified set of student behaviors, limited in time, preceded by some direction from the teacher, with a particular objective. Activities include role-plays, drills, games, peer-editing, small-group information-gap exercises, and much more. Because an activity implies some sort of active performance on the part of learners, it is generally *not* used to refer to certain teacher behaviors like saying "good morning," maintaining eye contact with students, explaining a grammar point, or writing a list of words on the chalkboard. Such teacher behaviors, however, can indeed be referred to as techniques (see below).

Procedure

Richards and Rodgers (2001) used the term **procedure** to encompass "the actual moment-to-moment techniques, practices, and behaviors that operate in teaching a language according to a particular method" (p. 26). Procedures, from this definition, include techniques, but the authors appear to have no compelling objection to viewing the terms synonymously. Thus, for Richards and Rodgers, this appears to be a catch-all term.

Practice, Behavior, Exercise, Strategy

In the language teaching literature, these terms, and perhaps some others, all refer in varying degrees of intensity to what is defined below as *technique*.

Technique

Even before Anthony (1963) discussed and defined the term, the language teaching profession generally accepted **technique** as a superordinate term to refer to various activities that either teachers or learners perform in the classroom. In other words, techniques include all tasks and activities. They are almost always planned and deliberate. They are the product of a choice made by the teacher. And, for your purposes as a language teacher, they can comfortably refer to the pedagogical units or components of a classroom session. You can think of a lesson as consisting of a number of techniques, some teacher-centered, some learner-centered, some production-oriented, some comprehension-oriented, some clustering together to form a task, and some as tasks in and of themselves. We now turn to examine these classroom components of focus or activity.

CATEGORIZING TECHNIQUES

Is it possible to describe parameters for categorizing techniques? To attempt to be exhaustive in such an effort would be unrealistic, as the number and variety of techniques is virtually unlimited. Bailey (2005), for example, suggests at least 100 techniques for teaching speaking. Linse (2005), Nunan (2005), and Helgesen and Brown (2007) together offer hundreds of different techniques for teaching young children, grammar, and listening, respectively. Other teacher reference books from virtually every major publisher collectively describe thousands of techniques for different ages, skills, and proficiency levels (Klippel, 1984; Claire, 1988; Shoemaker & Shoemaker, 1991).

How can one best conceptualize this multitude of techniques? Over the years, several rubrics have been used to classify techniques.

The Manipulation–Communication Continuum

Techniques can be thought of as existing along a continuum of possibilities between highly manipulative and very communicative. At the extreme end of the **manipulative** side, a technique is totally controlled by the teacher and implies a predictable response from students (Kurtz, 2011). Choral repetition and cued substitution drills are examples of oral techniques at this extreme. Other examples are dictation (listening/writing) and reading aloud.

At the **communicative** extreme, student responses are open-ended and unpredictable. Examples include storytelling, brainstorming, role-plays, discussions, small group work, and some games. Teachers are usually in a less controlled role here, as students become free to be creative with their responses and interactions with other students. However, keep in mind that a modicum of teacher control, whether overt or covert, should always be present in the classroom. In the words of van Lier (2007), "the dynamism (and tension) between the planned and predictable and the improvised and unpredictable is essential in the development of true action-based pedagogy, and I would argue, in all pedagogy" (p. 54).

It is most important to remember that the manipulation–communication scale does not correspond to the beginning-through-advanced proficiency continuum! For too many years the language-teaching profession labored under the incorrect assumption that beginners must have isolated, mechanical bits and pieces of language programmed into them (typically through repetition or memorization drills) and that only later could "real" communication take place. The CLT approach accentuates a diametrically opposed philosophy: *that genuine communication can take place from the very first day of a language class.*

The extent to which a communicative technique can sustain itself for long periods of time in the classroom will often be a factor of the overall proficiency level of your class. But even at the beginning level, students can engage in meaningful communication for significant stretches of time. Communicative techniques for beginners involve appropriately small chunks of language and build in some repetition of patterns for establishing fluency. On one of the very first days of class, for example, students can be taught to *ask* and *respond* to questions such as the following:

QUESTIONS TO STIMULATE COMMUNICATION AT BEGINNING LEVELS

- How are you?
- What's your name?
- Where do you live?
- How old are you (for children)?
- What do you do (for adults)?
- Do you have brothers (sisters, children, etc.)?
- What are their names?

At an intermediate level, students can get involved in a "mixer" in which they go around the room, getting information from, say, four or five other students. At the more advanced levels, a simple question or problem posed by the teacher can lead to sustained, meaningful student communication between student and teacher, in pairs, or in small groups.

Controlled versus Open-Ended Techniques

You may see teacher's manuals refer to another continuum that compares what appear to be the same concepts: controlled versus open-ended. The difference may be the extent to which the teacher "controls the flow of the discourse . . . and learners simply fill the discursive slots provided" (Kurtz, 2011, p. 137). Open-ended techniques allow teacher and student to "break through the communicative cocoon" (Kurtz, 2011, p. 133) and to *improvise* in the classroom. As van Lier (2007) noted, "lessons and tasks are planned, but there should always be an element of improvisation . . . in which new and unexpected things happen" (p. 53).

Here are a few generalizations:

Controlled	**Open-Ended**
T restricts communication	Ss are free to improvise
T elicits an intended response	Ss' responses are spontaneous
T emphasizes forms/structure	Ss focus on meaning/communication
T monitors Ss' responses	Ss are relatively unmonitored

In reality, techniques are rarely as black-and-white as these generalizations would have you believe. For example, many controlled techniques are manipulative, as described above. But controlled techniques sometimes have communicative elements. Or a technique may swing back and forth from controlled elements to more open-ended, which is why it is prudent to think of this continuum as various *aspects* of techniques.

Classroom Connections

Think about some of the techniques you have participated in as an L2 learner or used as a teacher. What are some examples of techniques that involve both controlled *and* open-ended aspects? Did you have opportunities to *improvise*? What are the advantages of controlled techniques for you and for the student? Open, communicative techniques? And what disadvantages might apply to each?

Mechanical, Meaningful, and Communicative Techniques

In the decades of the 1940s through the 1960s, language pedagogy was obsessed with drills, which occupied a good deal of class time. Current practice makes minimal—or we should say optimal—use of drilling.

By definition, a **drill** is a *mechanical* technique that focuses on a minimal number of language *forms* (grammatical or phonological structures) through repetition. Drills can be choral, with the whole class repeating in unison, or individual. And they can take several forms, ranging from simple repetition to various substitution formats. Here are some examples of the latter:

T: I went to the store yesterday. **Ss:** I went to the store yesterday.
T: Bank. **Ss:** I went to the bank yesterday.
T: In the morning. **Ss:** I went to the bank in the morning.

Mechanical drills have only one correct response from a student and have no implied connection with reality. What some have called **meaningful drills** (Paulston & Bruder, 1976) can add some reality, but may stretch the concept of drill too far:

T: The woman is outside. [*pointing out the window at a woman*] Where is she, Hiro?
S1: The woman is outside.
T: Right, she's outside. Keiko, where is she?
S2: She's outside.
T: Good, Keiko, she's outside. Now, class, we are inside. Hiroko, where are we?
S3: We are inside.

And the process may continue on as the teacher reinforces certain grammatical or phonological elements, but connects utterances to reality. This is more appropriately a case of what one could call *meaningful practice*, useful in virtually any communicative classroom.

Classroom Connections

Paulston and Bruder (1976) referred to some drills as meaningful. Do you believe a *drill* can be meaningful? Imagine a substitution drill in which the slots all referred to students in the classroom and adjectives to describe them (tall, short, pretty, smart). Would you be able to conduct a *meaningful* drill in this case?

A further extension of meaningful communicative practice is found in **form-focused** communicative practice that might go something like this, if you were trying to get students to practice the past tense:

T: Good morning, class. Last weekend I went to a restaurant and I ate salmon. Juan, what did you do last weekend?

Juan: I went to park and I play soccer.

T: Juan, you *play* soccer or you *played* soccer?

Juan: Oh . . . eh . . . I played soccer.

T: Good! Ying, did you go to the park last weekend?

Ying: No.

T: What did you do?

Ying: I went to a movie.

T: Great, and what did you do, Fay?

This exercise is an attempt to force students to use the past tense, but allows them to choose meaningful replies. Juan chose the safety of the teacher's pattern, while Ying, perhaps because she was more focused on communicative reality than on past tense formation, initially broke out of the pattern before returning. The previous exercise also illustrates how teachers might *control* interaction in the classroom, but not be as *manipulative* as they would be in drill. There are opportunities for students to venture out of a pattern if they wish, which is communicative, but not completely *open-ended*.

A final word about drills. A communicative approach to language teaching can make some use of drilling techniques, but only in moderation. A few short, snappy drills here and there, especially at the lower levels of proficiency, can be quite useful in helping students to establish structural patterns, rhythm, and certain pronunciation elements. But moderation is the key, especially if your drills are mechanical.

A TAXONOMY OF TECHNIQUES

A comprehensive taxonomy of common techniques for language teaching, adapted from Crookes and Chaudron (1991), is found in Table 11.1 (pages 226–227). Notice that three broad categories are used: controlled, semi-controlled, and open-ended. Bearing in mind the somewhat slippery concept of control referred to above, you may be able to gain a broad picture, from this taxonomy, of a range of classroom language-teaching techniques. In the chapters that follow, many of these techniques will be discussed with examples and analysis.

In a taxonomy such as this, not only will many techniques be somewhat difficult to categorize in terms of the control continuum, but some techniques will fit into more than one category. Consider the following "warm-up" activity for the first day of an intermediate-level class:

Warm-up

Divide the class in half. For one half of the class (Group A), ask each student to write his/her favorite (1) *sport*, (2) *singer*, and (3) *actor/movie star* on a piece of paper. The papers are collected and redistributed to the other half of the class (Group B) at random.

Then ask Group B to mingle with Group A in order to find the person whose favorites they have been given. They are told to ask yes-no questions about all three items on the piece of paper. Then, if they don't know their partner's name, ask their name. Examples are questions like: "Do you like baseball?" "Is Ben Affleck your favorite actor?" "What's your name?"

When everyone has found their partner, they introduce that student to the rest of the class, giving their name and their three favorites.

If time permits, repeat this activity by switching the roles of Groups A and B.

This exercise seems to fit into a number of possible categories. It involves *question-answer, referential* activity; there is *information exchange*; and in some ways either *problem solving* or *games* may fit here. The purpose in referring to such a taxonomy, therefore, is not to be able to pinpoint every technique specifically. Rather, the taxonomy is more of a help to you as:

- an aid to raising your awareness of the wide variety of available techniques.
- an indicator of how techniques differ according to a continuum ranging from controlled to open-ended.
- a resource for your own personal brainstorming process as you consider types of techniques for your classroom.

Table 11.1 Taxonomy of language-teaching techniques (adapted from Crookes & Chaudron 1991: 52–54)

Controlled Techniques

1. **Warm-up:** Mimes, dance, songs, jokes, play. This activity gets the students stimulated, relaxed, motivated, attentive, or otherwise engaged and ready for the lesson. It does not necessarily involve use of the target language.
2. **Setting:** Focusing in on lesson topic. Teacher directs attention to the topic by verbal or nonverbal evocation of the context relevant to the lesson by questioning or miming or picture presentation, possibly by tape recording of situations and people.
3. **Organizational:** Structuring of lesson or class activities includes disciplinary action, organization of class furniture and seating, general procedures for class interaction and performance, structure and purpose of lesson, and so on.
4. **Content explanation:** Grammatical, phonological, lexical (vocabulary), sociolinguistic, pragmatic, or any other aspects of language.
5. **Role-play demonstration:** Selected students or teacher illustrate the procedure(s) to be applied in the lesson segment to follow. Includes brief illustration of language or other content to be incorporated.
6. **Dialogue/Narrative presentation:** Reading or listening passage presented for passive reception. No implication of student production or other identification of specific target forms or functions (students may be asked to "understand").
7. **Dialogue/Narrative recitation:** Reciting a previously known or prepared text, either in unison or individually.
8. **Reading aloud:** Reading directly from a given text.
9. **Checking:** Teacher either circulating or guiding the correction of students' work, providing feedback as an activity rather than within another activity.
10. **Question-answer, display:** Activity involving prompting of student responses by means of display questions (i.e., teacher or questioner already knows the response or has a very limited set of expectations for the appropriate response). Distinguished from referential questions by the likelihood of the questioner's knowing the response and the speaker's being aware of that fact.
11. **Drill:** Typical language activity involving fixed patterns of teacher prompting and student responding, usually with repetition, substitution, and other mechanical alterations. Typically with little meaning attached.
12. **Translation:** Student or teacher provision of L1 or L2 translations of given text.
13. **Dictation:** Student writing down orally presented text.
14. **Copying:** Student writing down text presented visually.
15. **Identification:** Student picking out and producing/labeling or otherwise identifying a specific target form, function, definition, or other lesson-related item.
16. **Recognition:** Student identifying forms, as in Identification (i.e., checking off items, drawing symbols, rearranging pictures), but without a verbal response.
17. **Review:** Teacher-led review of previous week/month/or other period as a formal summary and type of test of student recall performance.
18. **Testing:** Formal testing procedures to evaluate student progress.
19. **Meaningful drill:** Drill activity involving responses with meaningful choices, as in reference to different information. Distinguished from Information exchange by the regulated sequence and general form of responses.

(Continued)

Semicontrolled Techniques

20. **Brainstorming:** A special form of preparation for the lesson, like Setting, which involves open-ended, undirected contributions by the students and teacher on a given topic, to generate multiple associations without linking them; no explicit analysis or interpretation by the teacher.
21. **Storytelling (especially when student-generated):** Not necessarily lesson-based, a lengthy presentation of story by teacher or student (may overlap with Warm-up or Narrative recitation). May be used to maintain attention, motivate, or as lengthy practice.
22. **Question-answer, referential:** Activity involving prompting of responses by means of referential questions (i.e., the questioner does not know beforehand the response information). Distinguished from Question-answer, display.
23. **Cued narrative/Dialogue:** Student production of narrative or dialogue following cues from miming, cue cards, pictures, or other stimuli related to narrative/dialogue (e.g., metalanguage requesting functional acts).
24. **Information transfer:** Application from one mode (e.g., visual) to another (e.g., writing), which involves some transformation of the information (e.g., student fills out diagram while listening to description). Distinguished from Identification in that the student is expected to transform and reinterpret the language or information.
25. **Information exchange:** Task involving two-way communication as in information-gap exercises, when one or both parties (or a larger group) must share information to achieve some goal. Distinguished from Question-answer, referential in that sharing of information is critical for the task.
26. **Wrap-up:** Brief teacher- or student-produced summary of points and/or items that have been practiced or learned.
27. **Narration/exposition:** Presentation of a story or explanation derived from prior stimuli. Distinguished from Cued narrative because of lack of immediate stimulus.
28. **Preparation:** Student study, silent reading, pair planning and rehearsing, preparing for later activity. Usually a student-directed or -oriented project.

Open-Ended Techniques

29. **Role-play:** Relatively open-ended acting out of specified roles and functions. Distinguished from Cued dialogues by the fact that cueing is provided only minimally at the beginning, and not during the activity.
30. **Games:** Various kinds of language game activity not like other previously defined activities (e.g., board and dice games making words).
31. **Report:** Report of student-prepared exposition on books, experiences, project work, without immediate stimulus, and elaborated on according to student interests. Akin to Composition in writing mode.
32. **Problem solving:** Activity involving specified problem and limitations of means to resolve it; requires cooperation on part of participants in small or large group.
33. **Drama:** Planned dramatic rendition of play, skit, or story.
34. **Simulation:** Activity involving complex interaction between groups and individuals based on simulation of real-life actions and experiences.
35. **Interview:** A student is directed to get information from another student or students.
36. **Discussion:** Debate or other form of grouped discussion of specified topic, with or without specified sides/positions prearranged.
37. **Composition:** As in Report (verbal), written development of ideas, story, or other exposition.
38. **A propos:** Conversation or other socially oriented interaction/speech by teacher, students, or even visitors, on general real-life topics. Typically authentic and genuine.

TEXTBOOKS

Many of your classroom activities involve the use of various forms of materials to support and enhance them. What would language classes be without books, pictures, charts, realia, and technological aids? Yes, you could have conversations, role-plays, discussions, and chalkboard work, but much of the richness of language instruction is derived from supporting materials. Today such materials abound for all levels and purposes.

What kinds of materials are available to you? How do you decide what will work and what won't? Is it worthwhile to create your own materials? If so, what sorts of things can be relatively easily made? We'll look at these and related questions here as we consider these all-important supporting elements in a lesson.

The most obvious and most common form of material support for language instruction comes through *textbooks*. Most likely, as a relatively new teacher, your first concern will not be to choose a textbook, but rather to find creative use for the textbook that has been handed to you by your supervisor. So, while your textbook may not be "perfect" in your estimation, your challenge is to make the very best use of the one you have: follow the guidelines that have been given in the textbook's teacher notes, adapt segments of the book to suit your context, and add other materials (see the next section of this chapter) to enhance your lessons.

 **CLASSROOM CONNECTIONS**

Think about an L2 class that you once took and a textbook that you remember fairly well. What was your impression of the textbook, overall? Was it boring, interesting, challenging, too easy? What characteristics of the book lead you to retain these current impressions?

Textbook Adaptation

Let's say you're preparing for tomorrow's lesson. If your textbook has teacher's notes (possibly in a separate teacher's edition), by all means consult them and use as many of the suggestions as you feel are appropriate. If there are no teacher's guidelines available, your task is more difficult, but not by any means insurmountable.

On pages 230–231 is a lesson from Unit 13 in Book 1 of *Worldview* (Rost, 2002), pitched for a high-beginning level class. You will see that this lesson, titled "How sweet it is!", focuses on vocabulary related to food and indirectly on noun quantifiers. The techniques in the lesson use the following categories in the taxonomy in Table 11.1:

Exercise 1: (1) Warm up; (2) Setting; (10) Question-answer, display; (16) Recognition; (9) Checking.

Exercise 2: (15) Identification; (11) Drill.

Exercise 3: (10) Question-answer, display; (24) Information transfer; (25) Information exchange; (14) Copying.

Exercise 4: (22) Question-answer, display; (25) Information exchange.

Exercise 5: (15) Identification.

Exercise 6: (25) Information transfer.

Exercise 7: (6) Narrative presentation; (22) Question-answer, referential; (25) Information exchange; (9) Checking.

Exercise 8: (15) Identification; (10) Question-answer, display.

Could you devise a plan (using the guidelines in the previous chapter) that would "teach" these eight exercises? Of course, each exercise has brief directions to students, but how would you contextualize the lesson for your audience and context? Let's say your objectives focus on

- vocabulary for food
- talking about food you like, and
- a message about unhealthy sweet food.

Here are just a few of the questions you might ask yourself in the lesson planning stage:

- Is Exercise 1 really the best way to begin this lesson? If they know these words, is this just a review?
- How will I direct students to perform Exercise 1? After the pairs have finished, what will the "reporting" process be?
- Is Exercise 2 too mechanical for my context?
- In Exercise 3, should I "teach" the word *sweet* first?
- Exercise 4 seems too complex for my high beginners. Should I just tell them about these two terms and then have a show of hands on those who feel they fall into one category or another? Or maybe at this point, they could take the lists of food in Exercise 3 and *talk about* what they like and don't like?
- Should I combine Exercises 5 and 6?
- Exercise 7 looks like it needs some background setting, and some directions for what students should do *while* they read—what they should look for in the article as they are reading. Maybe I should follow this with some oral whole-class questions to serve as a comprehension check (rather than Exercise 8)?

How sweet it is!

Vocabulary Food
Grammar Count and non-count nouns; *How much/How many*; Quantifiers: *much, many, a lot of*
Speaking Talking about foods you like

Lesson A

Getting started

1 *PAIRS.* **Match the photos with the words in the box.**

bread ___	butter _A_	cake ___	candy ___	cheese ___
chocolate ___	coffee ___	cookies ___	crackers ___	fruit ___
ice cream ___	milk ___	nuts ___	potato chips ___	soda ___

2 **Listen and check your answers. Then listen and repeat.**

3 *PAIRS.* **Which foods in Exercise 1 are sweet and which are not sweet? Write them in the correct column.**

Sweet	Not sweet
soda	cheese

13

Lesson **A**

Listening

4 *PAIRS.* **Do you know what the following word and phrase mean: *chocoholic* and *to have a sweet tooth*?**

5 **Listen to the interview and check (✓) the words from Exercise 1 that you hear.**

6 **Listen again. Are the sentences true or false? Write *T* or *F* next to each one.**

1. Lorraine eats some chocolate almost every day. T
2. Tae-Soon eats a lot of sweet things.
3. Gustavo eats a lot of cookies.
4. Gustavo buys a lot of potato chips.
5. Janice prefers salty food.

Reading

7 *PAIRS.* **Do you think sweet foods are healthy or unhealthy for you? Read the article and compare your answers.**

Short and Sweet

The Truth about Sweets

Are you crazy about sweets? How many cookies do you eat in a day? How much chocolate? How much soda do you drink? A lot of people love sweets. In fact, a lot of people eat and drink too many sweet things. And that's not good. It can lead to health problems.

If you eat a lot of cookies, ice cream, or cake—be careful. Doctors say that too many sweets are bad for your health. They say to eat a variety of foods: lots of fruits and vegetables, and smaller portions of bread, meat, and dairy. Then have a cookie or two for dessert.

Are two cookies enough to satisfy your sweet tooth? If not, try these suggestions: eat some fruit instead of a lot of chocolate or ice cream, drink some juice instead of soda, or eat a few nuts instead of some candy.

8 **Read the article again. Underline the word that makes each sentence true.**

1. A lot of people love **sweets / butter**.
2. Too many **cookies / vegetables** are bad for your health.
3. It's OK to eat one or two **cookies / cakes** for dessert.
4. It's good to eat some **fruit / chocolate** instead of ice cream.

- Instead of Exercise 8, should I consider a "mixer" in which I get students to line themselves up according to how much they like some of the foods listed in Exercise 1? That might wrap up this lesson with a focus on the message that sweet foods aren't all that healthy.

Classroom Connections

How would you answer all these questions about the lesson? What further questions would you ask in order to consider options for teaching this lesson?

The above questions are issues of textbook adaptation that you face almost every time you plan a lesson. You see to it that the way you present the textbook lesson is appropriately geared for your particular students—their level, ability, and goals—and is just right for the number of minutes in your class.

Textbook Selection

If your teaching situation allows you to *choose* a textbook, you have an exciting but complex task ahead of you. In fact, the number of questions that need to be asked about a textbook can be overwhelming. But once you have carried out a thorough investigation of textbooks using some kind of consistent evaluation procedure, you will be rewarded by having chosen a textbook that is an optimal fit for all of your criteria.

Table 11.2 (adapted from Garinger, 2002; Harwood, 2010; Ur, 2012; Byrd & Schuemann, 2014) provides a set of questions that can comprise practical criteria for either choosing a textbook for a course or evaluating the textbook you are currently using. The list is certainly not exhaustive, but it offers you a number of useful categories for consideration.

Classroom Connections

Think of an L2 textbook that you have recently encountered, then apply the questions in the textbook selection list in Table 11.2. How well does your book meet the criteria? Did any of the questions trigger some ideas you had not thought of before?

OTHER CLASSROOM AIDS AND MATERIALS

Most courses are designed, at the very least, around a textbook or preplanned sets of materials as issued by the program. But beyond the textbook, there are many options for additional materials, and the latter may be crucial in the

Table 11.2 Criteria for Textbook Selection and Evaluation

Program and Course

1. Does the textbook support the goals of the curriculum and program?
2. Is the textbook part of a series, and if so, is it at the appropriate level of your students?
3. Are a sufficient number of the course objectives addressed by the textbook?
4. Is the textbook gauged for learners at the appropriate age group, ability, purpose, and background?
5. Is the textbook attractive and motivating in its design and layout?
6. Is the textbook sensitive to the cultural background(s) of the students?

Approach

7. Are the roles of teacher and learners in concert with current knowledge about second language acquisition?
8. Do the sequencing, difficulty levels, pacing, and variety represented in the textbook reflect current knowledge about second language acquisition?
9. Does the approach challenge learners to use and develop their own strategies and to work toward autonomy?

Skills

10. Does the textbook account for a variety of learners' preferences and styles as they develop various skills?
11. Is the "mix" of skills presented in the textbook appropriate for the course?
12. Does the textbook provide learners with adequate guidance as they are acquiring these skills?

Techniques and Supplementary Materials

13. Do the techniques in the textbook promote learners' language development?
14. Is there a balance between controlled and open-ended techniques?
15. Do the techniques reinforce what students have already learned and represent a progression from simple to more complex?
16. Are the techniques varied in format so that they will continually motivate and challenge learners?
17. Does the textbook include supplementary photocopy-ready handouts, workbook, work sheets, assessments, audio or video disc, and/or web-based exercises?
18. Is there an accompanying teacher's guide?

Practical Issues

19. Is the textbook available and cost-effective?
20. Can the book be obtained in a timely manner? Is it available as an e-book?

overall success of a course. Those materials offer you an opportunity to fashion a course that is *unique*, that is tailored for your *particular* students at a particular time, and that has the kind of *verve* that inspires (and possibly entertains) your students.

An almost unlimited supply of materials is available (Tomlinson, 2011). We daily encounter signs, schedules, calendars, advertisements, menus, memos, notes, and more (see Chapter 20 for a long list of written texts). Visual and auditory aids are powerful aids in adding a multisensual flavor to classroom lessons. And with the current mushrooming of digital files, documents, photos, and videos, the number of relevant supporting materials is astronomical. Consider some of the possible types of materials that are at your fingertips:

Teacher resource books. Dozens of resource books are specifically designed to provide ideas for teachers. For example, books are available on speaking (e.g., Bailey, 2005); listening (Helgesen & Brown, 2007); reading (Nuttall, 1996; Anderson, 1999); grammar (Nunan, 2005); activities for children (Linse, 2005); and the list goes on.

Other student textbooks. Even a small library of student textbooks other than the one you are using will yield a book or two with some additional material that you can employ as supplementary material.

Realia. Realia are probably the oldest form of classroom aid. There is nothing like an "object" lesson. Objects—food items, cosmetics, household gadgets, tools, clothing—always add some significant reality to the classroom. Their effectiveness in helping students to connect language to reality cannot be underestimated. Realia are especially useful and important for teaching children who benefit from tangible objects that can stimulate kinesthetic connections.

Digital media. With smart phones, tablets, laptops, and all the supporting media that can be retrieved and stored on these devices, access to relevant materials is literally endless (Tomlinson, 2011). Many classrooms now include computer-projection equipment as standard, which makes both visual and audio display readily available. From YouTube videos, to photo-sharing sites, to sites that store tens of thousands of photos and clip art—all this and more is at the fingertips of both teachers and students. In the next chapter we'll touch on this aspect of teaching an L2 in the age of ubiquitous technology.

Self-made paper-based visual aids. With the dominance of digital media in our world today, you may think it's odd to consider some of the more traditional forms of visual aids. Posters, charts, and magazine pictures represent "old-fashioned" but surprisingly (and refreshingly) effective teaching aids. If you are artistically inclined, you might consider trying your hand at creating posters or charts for classroom use. Otherwise, a resource that many teachers find helpful is an assemblage of dozens of magazine pictures that you can file and cross-index. Start with a pile of fairly recent magazines and pick out pictures (photos, diagrams, advertisements, etc.) that show people or objects large enough to be easily seen by all students in a classroom setting. Mounting them on cardboard or laminating them will protect your pictures from wrinkling. You could create a similar *digital* indexed picture/video file, stored on a convenient hard drive available to you for ready wireless access.

Commercially available visual aids. Also keep your eye open for commercially available slides, photographs, posters, and other illustrations—again, in paper-based or digital form. Some publishers provide posters and charts to accompany textbooks, and most will include DVDs and web-based supplementary materials. Media resource centers in many institutions offer a diversity of materials.

 **Classroom Connections**

Look back at the "How sweet it is!" lesson on pages 230–231, and consider added *materials* that might enhance the lesson. What additional realia, visuals, or technological material would help to stimulate interest or add further challenges?

FOR THE TEACHER: ACTIVITIES (A) & DISCUSSION (D)

Note: For each of the "Classroom Connections" in this chapter, you may wish to turn them into individual or pair-work discussion questions.

1. **(A)** Ask pairs to review the differences among mechanical, meaningful, and quasi-communicative techniques, and illustrate with more examples. What is the place of mechanical drills in an interactive CLT course?
2. **(D)** Refer students to the taxonomy of techniques referred to in Table 11.1, and try to clarify any questions they might have about what each technique is.
3. **(A)** Divide a selection (of your choice) of the techniques in the taxonomy in Table 11.1 among pairs in the classroom, and have partners plan and then present a sample of their technique to the rest of the class.
4. **(A)** On page 229 some questions were asked about the eight exercises reprinted from the *Worldview* series. Ask pairs to devise a plan that would "teach" selected exercises. For example, how would you introduce such a lesson? How would you direct Exercise 1? Or treat the reading passage in Exercise 7? Of the techniques listed earlier in this chapter, which might be appropriate additions to these exercises?
5. **(A)** Refer your students to the criteria for textbook selection in Table 11.2 (p. 233). Ascertain that enough textbooks are available in your institutional library or reading room. Then pair students up and distribute one textbook to each pair. Then, assign extra-class work that asks them to use the list of criteria to evaluate their book. Upon completion of this task, have them make brief oral reports to the class about the textbooks they were assigned. Ask them to articulate any problems they had performing such an evaluation.

6. **(D)** With the whole class, brainstorm different digital/technological materials that could be used in a language classroom. Write all their suggestions on the board and discuss their feasibility.

FOR YOUR FURTHER READING

Garinger, D. (2002). *Textbook selection for the ESL classroom.* Washington, DC: Center for Applied Linguistics.

This brief report, available online at www.cal.org is a useful quick overview of the textbook selection process.

Byrd, P., & Schuemann, C. (2014). English as a second/foreign language textbooks: How to choose them—how to use them. In M. Celce-Murcia, D. Brinton, & M. A. Snow (Eds.), *Teaching English as a second or foreign language* (4th ed., pp. 380–393). Boston, MA: National Geographic Learning.

A concise resource for evaluating textbooks and for adapting them to one's own context. The chapter includes a checklist for textbook selection that could act as an alternative to Table 11.2 in this book.

Harwood, N. (Ed.) (2010). *English language teaching materials: Theory and practice.* Cambridge, UK: Cambridge University Press.

Tomlinson, B. (2011). *Materials development in language teaching* (2nd ed.). Cambridge, UK: Cambridge University Press.

Both volumes offer links between research on SLA and materials development and principles to follow in materials development. Harwood gives tips on materials development in languages for specific purposes (LSP) and Tomlinson provides a comprehensive overview of available electronic materials.

Ur, P. (2012). *A course in English language teaching* (2nd ed.). Cambridge, UK: Cambridge University Press.

Chapter 14 of this practical methodology textbook gives guidelines for coursebook evaluation and for materials development, with practical examples throughout.

CHAPTER **12**

TECHNOLOGY IN LANGUAGE LEARNING AND TEACHING

Questions for Reflection

- What are the key developments in the use of technology for L2 education?
- What are some benefits of integrating technology in L2 learning and teaching?
- What is expected in the technology standards for language teachers?
- How can we apply various technological tools to language classrooms?
- What are CALL and MALL and how do they differ?
- What are pedagogical issues that L2 teachers should consider in the applications of technology?

Many L2 teachers and students carry out their work with the help of technology, often referred to as **CALL** (Computer Assisted Language Learning). However, the term is used less and less these days as we see that many facets of our professional and personal lives involve active use of technology. Using technology has become an integral rather than a supplementary (as implied in the word "assisted") aspect of our daily living. In many teaching and learning contexts, working on computers with a wide range of software and having access to the Internet are as routine as pen and paper or the black- or whiteboard (Ur, 2012).

In particular, current elementary and secondary school students are regarded as digital learners and even referred to as "digital natives" (Prensky, 2001) because technology is ubiquitous in their academic world as well as in their daily social lives. These digital learners of the new generation are immersed in technologies such as computers, cell phones, MP3 players, and, even before entering school, videogames (Prensky, 2010). They have grown up surrounded and pampered by technology (e.g., watching cartoons on TV or a portable DVD player instead of playing with a stuffed toy), and as Tapscott (2009) notes, it may be that for them, "using the new technology is as natural as breathing" (p. 18).

These learners may process information in a fundamentally different way from older generations of learners in that they are "digitally wise" (Prensky, 2010) as they use new technological innovations to complement their learning strategies and compensate for cognitive limitations (Prensky, 2010). Considering this reality, what we need is not to assess whether or not [computer-mediated] practices are superior to classroom learning but to see that "many of the tools and practices are used by many learners naturally while they are using their foreign language" (Chapelle, 2013, p. 2). Therefore, it is essential for language teachers to incorporate technology use into their classroom practice.

In this chapter we'll first take a look at the historical development of technology use in language education, then consider some important issues for pedagogy, followed by examples of practical applications for teachers and learners.

HISTORICAL DEVELOPMENTS

The practice of using technology, as we currently define it, for language learning and teaching began in the 1960s. This historical development of CALL can be divided into three stages: behavioristic CALL, communicative CALL, and integrative CALL (Warschauer & Healey, 2009).

Computer-Assisted Language Learning (CALL)

Up until the late 1970s, CALL applications appeared only in universities taking on a behavioristic approach to language learning. The computer was regarded mainly as "a mechanical tutor which never grew tired or judgmental and allowed students to work at an individual pace" (Warschauer & Healey, 2009, pp. 79–80). In the 1980s, CALL continued to be used for skill practice but with more emphasis on communicative use of language, employing non-drill activities. The use of computers became more open and humanistic in the form of language games, puzzles, and reading and writing practice.

The third phase began in the 1990s with the development of the World Wide Web, known simply as the Internet. CALL began to be considered to be a key pedagogical tool as the Web grew exponentially and individual users participated in creating and changing new websites. The third phase of CALL involved interactive communication and collaboration via the Internet.

What has come to be known as **Web 1.0** is a tool that provides information, while **Web 2.0** is a tool to connect people (Wesch, 2007). Warschauer and Grimes (2008) observe:

> The earlier Web [1.0] allowed people to publish content, but much of that online material ended up in isolated information silos. The new Web's [2.0] architecture allows more interactive forms of publishing (of textual and multimedia content), participation, and networking through blogs, wikis, and social network sites (p. 2).

Web 1.0 tools are more static in content and users of the tools are *viewers* of such content (static webpages such as Britannica Online, directories, news sites, etc.). On the other hand, Web 2.0 tools are more active in content and users are also *creators* of such content (in blogs, wikis, social networking sites, etc.) (Maloney, 2007).

Web 2.0 is a more interactive version of Internet capabilities in which users are the creators of materials because the barrier of learning HTML has been eliminated (Sokolik, 2014). Learners employing Web 2.0 tools rather than Web

1.0 have greater potential for maximizing student learning and becoming active users of the target language through interaction and collaboration with others (Ormiston, 2011). In addition, the possibility of linking people enables learners to reach and to communicate with authentic speakers outside the classroom. Web 2.0 tools (e.g., Facebook, Twitter, YouTube, Vimeo, Skype, Google +, LinkedIn, Flickr, WordPress) enable students and instructors to have "more control than ever over classroom materials [. . . and . . .] support the current focus on authentic materials and communicative tasks" (Sokolik, 2014, p. 412).

It seems that Web 2.0 tools have immeasurable potential to create and realize a collaborative and interactive environment for students to promote their language learning in and outside of the classroom. Furthermore, now that a large part of our daily social discourse takes place via the Internet through such Web 2.0 tools, exposing students to these means of communication has become inevitable. Another important development in technology for education is the rise of mobile learning (m-learning). Sokolik (2014) observes that "Web 2.0 technologies are less and less platform-specific, meaning that they are available on laptops and mobile phones, as well as on an assortment of other connection tools such as tablet computers and e-book readers" (p. 412).

We'll now consider how Web 2.0 applications available in portable devices such as cell phones, MP3 players, tablets, and laptop computers promote authentic materials, collaboration, and communicative learning tasks.

Mobile-Assisted Language Learning (MALL)

Over the last decade there has been an exponential increase in the number of mobile phone users in many parts of the world. There were about 6.9 billion mobile subscriptions worldwide around mid-2014 (Sanou, 2014), which is "more than three times as many phones as personal computers" (Kukulska-Hulme, 2013, p. 1). Not only is Wi-Fi connection common in many public spaces, making the use of tablets and laptops a given, but also smart phone use has increased greatly, rendering access to all media virtually ubiquitous. For instance, in Japan most students possess a mobile phone, and smart phone users have become the norm rather than the exception (Wang & Smith, 2013). A majority of Japanese students surveyed by Thornton and Houser (2005) preferred to receive learning materials on mobile phones rather than PCs.

Wang and Smith (2013) describe three main reasons for this new development. First, the gap in the operational power functionalities between mobile and PC technology has narrowed. Smart phones connecting to Wi-Fi have the same connectivity as PCs have. However, smart phones give users far greater flexibility than do PCs because they can connect to the Internet through cellular data networks in addition to local Wi-Fi. The change is not just limited to the wireless environment; mobile phone hardware has seen exponential progress as well. The screen size of some smart phones has increased to "five inches or larger and the resolution has improved to around 1980x1080 pixels" (p. 117).

The ready availability of mobile devices and easy access to Wi-Fi connections multiply the possibilities for language learning "on the move," or what we now call **Mobile-Assisted Language Learning (MALL)**. It has provided educators greater freedom for extending learning outside traditional learning environments (Rosell-Aguilar, 2013). Mobile devices offer immediate access to the Internet and, thus, to an abundance of "apps" (applications) that for language learners may be more attractive alternatives compared to structured learning such as playing language games, watching movies in the L2, or listening to a radio. In particular, most mobile phones are now equipped with photo and video cameras, GPS (Global Positioning Services), Internet access, e-mail, Short Messaging Service (SMS), and Multimedia Messaging Service (MMS). Applications such as YouTube, Facebook, Skype, Twitter, and various multimedia resources are all accessible on mobile phones (Rosell-Aguilar, 2013).

An interesting new reality to note is that portable devices (mobile phones, MP3/MP4 players, smart phones, tablet PCs, e-book readers, etc.) have brought a "blurring of boundaries between daily life, entertainment, work, and learning and thus present a difficult challenge to conventional, orderly, formal ways of teaching and learning" (Kukulska-Hulme, 2013, p. 1). Gurung and Rutledge (2014) reported that digital natives seem to bring their digital habits of texting, listening to music, visiting social networking sites, and using computers into their classrooms without perceiving boundaries between their personal and educational engagement.

Furthermore, we should also note that the level of engagement in mobile-assisted learning may be superficial or casual rather than deep, probably due to the difficulty of working at length with a small screen and keyboard to do tasks. Ushioda (2013b) states the power of mobile technologies should also motivate learners to attain deeper and more sustained levels of engagement. Some of the limitations of implementing MALL, such as reduced screen sizes, virtual keyboarding, and one-finger data-entry, remain as challenges to teachers.

 **Classroom Connections**

What different approaches and strategies should you consider when using desktop computers, laptops, tablets, and mobile phones for your students and classroom applications? How do uses of computers/laptops differ, for classroom purposes, from uses of mobile "smart" phones?

BENEFITS OF TECHNOLOGY INTEGRATION

The amazing variety of available technologies can serve as useful tools for language learners and teachers. We'll first look at some of the *standards* for integrating technology that recently have been introduced, as an illustration of current expectations of language teachers' abilities in incorporating technology into their curricula. Then, we'll outline some *advantages* that can be provided by technological tools. By "technologies" we refer not only to Web-based tools like YouTube, Wikipedia, and Moodle, but also to independent software such as *Rosetta Stone* and *Adobe Connect Pro*.

TESOL Technology Standards

The TESOL Technology Standards (Healey et al., 2011) provide guidelines on what teachers are expected to teach and students to learn in the growing use of technology in the field of language education. It outlines what the technology standards are, their importance in CALL, and how they can be put into practice in different L2 educational contexts. Following are sample standards from Hubbard (2014):

Sample Technology Standards (Hubbard, 2014)

Goal 1, Standard 1: Language teachers demonstrate knowledge and skills in basic technological concepts and operational competence, meeting or exceeding TESOL technology standards for language learners in whatever situation they teach

This means that as a teacher you have to know at least as much about technology for language education as you—and the Learner Standards—expect your students to know.

Goal 2, Standard 4: Language teachers use relevant research findings to inform the planning of language learning activities and tasks.

Part of being a professional in any field involves understanding the research base of that field. To teach with technology you should know not only about research on second language learning pedagogy but also about research on integrating relevant technology into your class.

Goal 3, Standard 3: Language teachers evaluate the effectiveness of specific student uses of technology to enhance teaching and learning.

This means you gather information, formally or informally, and use it to reflect on whether a particular program, activity or task was helpful and what you might do to make it more effective the next time.

Goal 4, Standard 2: Language teachers regularly reflect on the intersection of professional practice and technological developments so that they can make informed decisions regarding the use of technology to support language learning and communication.

You keep up to date with new technology developments to see if they can make your teaching and your students' learning more effective. You are a lifelong learner.

Retrieved from http://www.stanford.edu/~efs/TESOL-2014.pdf

Opportunities for Interaction

Language learners can be exposed to various forms of interaction while using technology (Chapelle, 2013). Networking in online environments has become an increasingly popular form of social interaction. It allows users to express themselves, build profiles, form online communities of shared interests, and interact socially with others. In their social networks, they can engage in relationships, build friendships, and collaborate with others while enacting and constructing distinct identities (Lomicka & Lord, 2009; McBride, 2009). According to Celik (2012), however, many instructors tend to use the Internet for purposes of gathering data or for communication rather than for "enhancing learner-learner and learner-content interaction" (p. 10).

Technologies, especially Web 2.0 tools such as Facebook, Twitter, and LinkedIn, can help our students enhance social connections. In fact, online social networking has become almost necessary in their social lives as means of enacting individual and/or group identities and building useful connections. Communication with speakers of the students' target language can be done through synchronous or asynchronous written online chatting with local peers in the language class (Chun, 2008). In this way students, especially those who learn **LCTLs** (less commonly taught languages), can compensate for lack of contact with their L2 and extend their social interactions beyond the language classroom.

Klimanova and Dembovskaya (2013) conducted a study to investigate how L2 learners of Russian construct their online L2 identities as they engage with native speakers of Russian in a series of tele-collaborative tasks in the popular Russian social networking space, *VKontakte*. The researchers reported that their Russian learners in the study were "digitally wise L2 learners," as each took advantage of "social affordances that Internet mediation provides for L2 learning in order to legitimize his or her social power as an L2 speaker" (p. 70).

Through the frequent interaction with the authentic users of target language, students increase their proficiency. Research shows that online chatting can be helpful for vocabulary learning (Smith, 2004), raising learners' awareness of target language form as they type messages (Payne & Whitney, 2002), and promoting their exploration of cross-cultural communication strategies (Ware & Kramsch, 2005). Mills (2011) examined **social networking sites (SNSs)** in a French-as-a-foreign-language classroom and found that students developed the grammatical, functional, and linguistic objectives of their French language course. SNSs created authentic opportunities for learning, promoted learners' meaningful social interactions, and developed community memberships. These advantages are further discussed in the following sections.

CLASSROOM CONNECTIONS

Are you a member of any social networking sites? How often do you use them and for what purposes? How might your activities on those sites help you in learning languages if you are participating in them through the medium of your L2? What factors would you consider if you apply them for your own teaching?

Access to Authentic Linguistic Data and Use

While engaging in meaningful social interaction, students naturally tend to use their target language and gain access to authentic linguistic materials. One of the important functions of Web 2.0 sites is that users of the sites can create and contribute their own information (Chapelle, 2013).

It is true that the Internet has a plethora of resources available, and teachers need to carefully design lesson plans and activities and select appropriate materials. Of course, this can be quite time-consuming. However, as Warschauer and Kern (2000) noted, if we want to help students participate in new authentic discourse communities and become new members of their desired discourse communities that are increasingly located on-line, it seems appropriate to integrate relevant online resources with activities in the classroom. Positive results were reported by Kukulska-Hulme and Bull (2009), who showed that mobile learning helps "noticing" in second language learning.

Because learners can easily access the multimodal collection of linguistic and cultural information on the Web, teachers need to guide them on what and how to use such resources for the benefits of their learning. The wealth of authentic texts, video clips, online dictionaries, online grammar checkers, and corpus databases can be incorporated into classroom activities. Students can be encouraged to create their own websites, blogs, and online communities using **multimodal communication**, which can be turned into active project-based learning (Chapelle, 2013).

Enacting Agency and Identity

Another important aspect of Web 2.0 influences is that language learners' engagement in SNSs can facilitate the construction of their social identities. By creating virtual "subject positions" (Kramsch, 2009, p. 20) for themselves and choosing particular discursive patterns and symbolic resources in words, photos, videos, symbols, and other modalities (Chen, 2013), learners come to exercise agency. They make a decision on how they project themselves in relation to others in the SNS space, and how they want other users to perceive them in particular social networks. These are conscious efforts and intentional processes because the learners are aware that other users can read and react to their posts. Therefore, learners' participation in social networking sites represents the very "dynamic development of an individual's identities" (Chen, 2013, p. 145).

Classroom Connections

What are some of the typical "discursive patterns" that people use in social networking systems? How do those patterns compare with conventional language in the academic arena? For example, what are some of the "shortcuts" that are used for texting, and what traditional grammatical/spelling rules are "violated"? What would you say to students at an intermediate level who ask you why SNS communication doesn't follow the "rules"? Would you teach those students texting conventions?

In a study of learner identity and L2 use in SNSs, Pasfield-Neofitou (2011) focused on the informal use of SNS by native speakers of English and Japanese across two SNSs, Facebook (English-medium SNS) and Mixi (Japanese-medium SNS). The learners were asked to align themselves with a reference group and positioned themselves with various identities by selecting consciously different languages in the Japanese and English contexts. Pasfield-Neofitou (2011) reported that the learners' choices of language reflected their sense of ownership of a particular language and indexed their online identity as foreigners.

According to Tapscott (1998), digital natives thrive in independent and autonomous learning contexts due to their ingrained habits of seeking and retrieving information from various online sources and media (Tapscott, 1998). In fact, learners' use of technology for language learning occurs beyond the classroom. Their agency in the process of choosing appropriate resources to express themselves is crucial for their language development (Mills, 2011). MALL can provide instructional and learning environments that are self-paced and sensitive to individual differences and aspirations. Advanced learners can move quickly through assignments that represent too little challenge for them, while others can take the time they need to gain control over basic behaviors (Ranalli, 2013).

Opportunities for Cross-Cultural Learning

Digital learning environments can foster cross-cultural awareness and understanding through online videos, blogs, visual images, and photos, offering a rich storehouse of world history and cultural information. Blattner and Fiori

(2011) observed 15 students in an intermediate Spanish course and found that over the course of a semester, learners, through Facebook-mediated awareness-raising tasks, developed a linguistic repertoire and socio-pragmatic competence such as greetings and leave-takings.

According to Kukulska-Hulme (2013), location-specific learning is possible in MALL. Portable devices such as smart phones can detect a learner's current location and provide a context-specific and appropriate learning experience. For example, Comas-Quinn, Mardomingo, & Valentine (2009) carried out a mobile learning project to engage language learners in the creation of an online resource that focuses on a foreign culture. In this project, students used their mobile phones, digital cameras, and MP3 recorders to select and record samples of their encounters with foreign cultures. Students then sent or uploaded these encounters to a cultural blog to be shared with other group members for their comments and feedback.

PRINCIPLES FOR USING TECHNOLOGY IN LANGUAGE TEACHING

Given the possible advantages of using technological tools, it may be important to think about how to take technology-based language teaching approaches. What do we need to consider in terms of planning and carrying out dynamic interactions in online environments, which are different from those of face-to-face interaction? Let's consider some important principles to follow in integrating technology resources to enhance our teaching.

First, teachers need to acknowledge the fact that *the boundary between learning and playing (leisure time) is blurring*. Personal life, entertainment, professional work, and educational tasks are increasingly overlapping due to the ubiquitous presence of smart phones (Kukulska-Hulme, 2013). Digital learners have a tendency to blur the boundary between personal engagement and academic engagement (Gurung & Rutledge, 2014). For example, they may listen to music to stay focused on work and to avoid distracting classroom noises. While working on an assignment, they may constantly check e-mails and Facebook postings.

Second, *promote active and collaborative learning activities using technology*. Let the learners utilize their *digital wisdom* (Prensky, 2010) and let them use their personal digital knowledge and skill in order to complete assignments. Integrate project-based assignments that are beyond simple drills and exercises.

Third, *provide scaffolding when needed for successful task completion*. Monitoring students' activities and participation can be done not only by the instructor but also by the students themselves. In particular, in asynchronous online discussions, peer moderation can be effective for promoting quantity, diversity, and interaction among the participants (Xie, Yu, & Bradshaw, 2014). Peer moderation also has affective and cognitive benefits, especially regarding students' attitudes and motivation (Xie et al., 2006).

Next, *keep paragraphs concise and use bulleted lists for online reading texts*, especially on mobile devices. According to Agger (2008), online readers tend to skip large blocks of text, and shorter paragraphs and bulleted lists get more attention. Remember that in many communities around the world, mobile phones are more common than computers. Most smartphones may have more computing capacity than the desktop computers of the early 1990s (Sokolik, 2014).

Finally, teachers need to *be aware of the challenge of maintaining up-to-date information, knowledge, and resources available on the Internet.* For example, some websites or video clips available now can disappear later on, and some software programs mentioned today can be outmoded in a few months (van Lier, 2009). Also, where we are literate today will be defined by even newer technologies that have yet to appear (Leu, Everett-Cacopardo, Zawilinski, McVerry, & O'Byrne, 2013).

The list below summarizes these five guidelines for successful use of technology in the classroom.

PRINCIPLES FOR USING TECHNOLOGY IN THE L2 CLASSROOM

- Acknowledge the fact that the boundary between learning and playing (leisure time) is blurring.
- Promote active and collaborative learning activities using technology.
- Provide scaffolding when needed for successful task completion.
- Keep paragraphs concise and use bulleted lists for online reading texts, especially on mobile devices.
- Be aware of the challenge of maintaining up-to-date information, knowledge, and resources available on the Internet.

CLASSROOM CONNECTIONS

Besides the five principles discussed above, are there any other issues we should consider for using technology effectively in the classroom? What are some factors that would influence the benefits of technology use? What might be some examples of instances when *scaffolding* is needed to help your students complete a task successfully?

CLASSROOM APPLICATIONS

The possible applications of technology in a language classroom are seemingly endless. Every time teachers read a new article or book or attend a conference presentation, a novel idea is presented. What we present here are merely some examples of how to apply the tools.

Reading and Writing

The Internet offers a huge amount of reading material that can be used for class materials as well as for individual or collaborative work. A variety of **computer-mediated communication** (CMC) can encourage students to use the target language for authentic and meaningful purposes. Setting up a classroom website using a **course management system** (CMS) (if available in your institution) is a good starting point. CMSs offer an integrated set of tools to organize and deliver course materials, including sending e-mails to all your students in one message.

1. E-mail

E-mail may now be the most frequently and widely used means of communication for either formal or informal purposes. E-mail exchanges between students, between teachers and students, and between students and others outside the classroom involve composing, reading, and information/opinion sharing. If you want to keep class e-mails separated from your personal e-mails, it's a good idea to use other platforms such as Facebook for communicating with students (Sokolik, 2014).

2. E-book Readers and E-reserves

New devices for reading electronic books such as e-book readers and mobile telephones have increased exponentially. School libraries provide articles and book chapters on their e-reserves system. Short readings, links to useful websites, and assignment descriptions can be posted on the class CMS directly by the instructor and have all students access the list of readings at their convenience. Portable devices usually have integrated dictionaries, parallel texts, and tools for translation, which become very handy, especially for those who have a long daily commute (Kukulska-Hulme, 2013).

3. Wikis and Blogs

Wikis are websites with multiple hyperlinked pages but differ from blogs in the sense that content can be edited directly in the browser. Wikipedia is a collaboratively written encyclopedia using the wiki model. It can create a space in which students write information individually or as a group and other students add to it or amend it. Aydin and Yildiz (2014) used wikis to promote collaborative writing for EFL students. The writing tasks included three different wiki-based writing tasks such as argumentative, informative, and decision-making. The study concluded that argumentative tasks promoted more peer-corrections than did informative and decision-making tasks. Overall, the students perceived that their writing skills had improved.

Blogs are usually constructed by an individual writer who posts regular entries of ideas, events, photos, graphics, or embedded video links. Blog sites are usually interactive, allowing visitors to leave comments. Blog assignments can be used for all levels of students using free software platforms (WordPress.com, blogger.com, etc.). The writer can choose their blogs to be private or available to the public. While it is possible to receive messages from strangers, making the class blog public can encourage students to be more cautious about the quality of their writing (Sokolik, 2014).

Classroom Connections

If you are interested in using Wikis or blogs for your L2 teaching context, what tasks would you give your students for their reading and/or writing practice? What instructions should you give them when assigning those tasks? What might cause some difficulty for students?

4. Social Networking

The number of users of social networking sites (SNSs) such as Facebook, Twitter, and LinkedIn has seen tremendous worldwide growth. As of March 31, 2014, Facebook (2014) indicates that its monthly active users are 1.28 billion around the world, 1.01 billion mobile users, and 802 million daily users. Approximately 81.2% of Facebook's daily users are outside the United States and Canada. For learners born in the 1990s or later, virtual communication and connections play significant roles in their daily functions.

SNSs such as Facebook allow users to develop and maintain social connections and relationships both online and offline by participating in multimodal and multisensory affordances (e.g., profiles, status updates, shared links, synchronous chats, asynchronous messages, photo sharing) (Chen, 2013). More and more teachers have adopted social networks to communicate with their students as well as to use as a site for creating interesting course activities.

Mills's (2011) study shows how a Facebook project can be implemented in a foreign language classroom. Seventeen intermediate French students in an American college were asked to create Facebook accounts and profiles and interact three times a week in a Facebook community called *immeuble* (building). Each student created a fictitious character of her or his choice living in the same Parisian building and wrote in the first person about that character's daily experiences. Every week the instructor provided a series of themes for course content such as lodging in Paris, the Montmartre quarter, Parisian cuisine, love stories, and even murder mysteries. Along with the themes, students were also provided with grammatical, linguistic, and cultural objectives of the week. Writing assignments for students included the following (Mills, 2011, p. 350):

- a character self-portrait and description of the Montmartre quarter
- a description of a neighbor's apartment
- a memorable meal and dialogue with immeuble residents at a Parisian restaurant
- a narrative describing a murder mystery in the building

The examples of Facebook profiles for immeuble characters following customary Facebook entries, usually included biographic information, relationship status, and preferences of leisure activities including favorite TV shows, movies, and books.

Figure 12.1 is an example of students' posting interactions with their peer characters.

Students in Mills's study were observed to engage in a heated discussion while enacting their chosen character's identity. In a post-project survey the students expressed the value of participating in the Facebook project such as practicing their French, and learning and sharing different people's lives and ideas through mutual engagement in various real-life tasks (Mills, 2011).

Figure 12.1 Sample postings between student characters (Mills, 2011, p. 354)

Andre Manasse Je ne parle pas votre langue, mademoiselle... Et je n'apprécie pas ce dérangement très impoli!
27 Janvier, à 21:36 · Commenter · J'aime

Zoe Vasser Bjr Andre! Cav? Jj'aBIT pres de toi. Est'ce que tu m'e'D trouver mon cle stp? J'tapLDkej'pE! Rstp!
27 Janvier, à 11:46 · Commenter · J'aime

Listening and Speaking

High-speed connection and WiFi service have greatly improved the delivery of audio and video files over the Internet (Sokolik, 2014). As a result, there is a large number of online resources that offer great opportunities for students to practice listening and speaking skills.

1. Video Clips and Audio Podcasts

Videos are great materials for providing language input in a meaningful context. Popular websites such as YouTube, Vimeo, and TED Talks offer countless video clips in a variety of genres: music videos, documentaries, sports highlights, TV talk shows, commercials, soap operas, sitcoms, and so on. However, the video links are useless if there is no Internet connection in the classroom. In that circumstance, podcasts would be good alternatives for authentic listening materials in various topical areas such as academic lectures, talk-radio broadcasts, interviews, and audiobooks.

Listening opportunities have been expanded and become more flexible with advancements in the capabilities of mobile phones or MP3 and MP4 players. These devices allow the user to listen to music or podcasts while sitting in the car, working out in a gym, walking around the house and garden, or traveling (Demouy & Kukulska-Hulme, 2010).

CLASSROOM CONNECTIONS

What are some currently available websites in which you can find useful video clips and podcasts for your target language and target student population? What issues and principles should you keep in mind when using those materials? How could you use your L2 productively if you shared these materials either in person or online with a classmate?

2. Audio- and Video-Conferencing

Another promising popular technology is the carrying out of conferences over a digital microphone or a video camera installed in computers, smart phones, or portable tablet PCs. Voice-over Internet protocol (VoIP), so-called "Internet telephone," can be voice only or can integrate video. When the hardware is available, free software can be obtained from some Internet sites. The current top video conferencing software may include Skype, Google Hangouts, FaceTime (available free of charge), and Adobe Connect (with a fee-based service). With this technology teachers can provide students with one-on-one tutoring sessions as well as additional consultations from any location (Sokolik, 2014). It can also be used to invite guest speakers or native speakers of a target language who can speak with students in the classroom.

3. Portable Internet Devices with a Video Camera

A digital camera built into portable devices such as smart phones, iPads, and tablet PCs can be an excellent tool for dynamic classroom or take-home assignments. Lys (2013) conducted an investigation of the use and integration of iPads in an advanced German conversation class. The study explored how the use of iPads influenced the development of 13 American students' German oral proficiency from intermediate high to advanced low level (according to ACTFL descriptions). In this nine-week course, student participants spent about 24 minutes a week individually in video conversations on FaceTime, which was installed in their iPads. The required weekly recordings increased from a little over one minute at the beginning of the quarter to more than seven minutes for the last assignment. The linguistic complexity of the required tasks was scaffolded from simple to more complex so that students could feel comfortable and competent enough to produce increasingly longer speech samples.

The tasks were introduced to the students following the steps listed below (adapted from Lys, 2013, pp. 98–99):

1. Introduce the topic ("Where I live").
2. Watch a news segment about the living situation of German students (focus on content, vocabulary, and relevant language forms).
3. Discuss the segment using Glassboard (a social network application that is more private than other SNSs).
4. Talk about living situations during the FaceTime chat outside of class, using vocabulary and phrases that appeared in the news segment.
5. Take a video of your own house or apartment (or parts of it) with an iPad camera while describing each room.
6. Post the video assignments on a private YouTube channel for peer review and/or instructor feedback.

Based on the analysis of students' speeches from the video recordings divided by pre- and post-course language in terms of complexity of language and cultural content, Lys (2013) reported that the students' oral language proficiency increased over the nine-week period; and therefore, real-time conversational activities through FaceTime can be beneficial in students' oral proficiency development. In the post-course survey the students also expressed that increased opportunities for language practice using mobile technologies seemed to improve their confidence in using the target language.

Grammar and Vocabulary Practice

In general, users may agree on the limited functionality of a grammar-checker built into word processing software. For example, the software is not sophisticated enough to discern different genre conventions such as academic English for the humanities and for the natural sciences field (Sokolik, 2014). Online websites such as *Grammarly*, *PaperRater*, and *Ginger Grammar Checker* may give more sensitive feedback on English errors.

1. Online Grammar Exercises

Grammar Clinic is an online application that asks users to identify sentence-level errors (sentence fragments, run-on sentences, article use, verb use, noun use, preposition use, relative pronoun use, punctuation use, etc.) and to correct them. Users receive immediate feedback on their performance, and a short grammar handbook comes with the application. Li and Hegelheimer (2013) conducted a study in which ten intermediate-level ESL students in an American university participated in outside-class grammar exercises using Grammar Clinic for one semester. Their results showed that the students who used the mobile application improved their English writing and increased self-editing corrections.

2. Corpus and Concordance

With literally billions of linguistic corpus data now readily available, the process of **concordancing** (searching for words in context and **collocations**) has become relatively simple. A concordance is a "type of index that searches for occurrences of a word or combinations of words, parts of words, punctuation, affixes, phrases, or structures within a corpus and can show the immediate context of the search item" (Sokolik, 2014, p. 417).

Teachers can assign students to collect authentic discourse data (i.e., *corpora*) to examine how target language structure is used in particular contexts. By examining patterns emerging from the collocation data (lexical items and the words that typically appear together), students can become aware of appropriate usage of target forms within authentic contexts (Reppen, 2010). More discussion on vocabulary learning using online corpus data continues in Chapter 19.

CLASSROOM CONNECTIONS

Imagine that you have been assigned to teach a content-based English language course for academic purposes. Go to the site of *Michigan Corpus of Upper-Level Student Papers* (micusp.elicorpora.info) and find out what resources are available on the website. Do they appear to be useful for your teaching? If so, how would you use them for your classroom?

3. Mobile Devices

Innovative mobile devices can support the process of learning target forms effectively and meaningfully. A study by Wong et al. (2010) indicated that a combination of in-class and online discussions of the contexts of Chinese idioms using smart phones enhanced students' understanding of proper usage of the idioms. Kuo and Hooper (2004) reported the benefits of using mnemonics for learning Chinese characters, especially the effects of visual and verbal coding mnemonics using computers. Generating one's own relationship between a symbol and its meaning appears to be an effective strategy for remembering Chinese characters (Kuo & Hooper, 2004).

Yang and Xie (2013) implemented iPads for teaching Chinese idioms to Chinese heritage learners in an American university. The researchers investigated the effects of self-generated mnemonics on character learning—especially those for which the meaning cannot be guessed or in which the literal meaning of the four characters is far from the actual meaning (e.g., 落落大方 [luo-luo-de-fang] → (literal meaning: fall-fall-big-square; actual meaning: "very graceful": Yang & Xie, 2013, p. 14).

The students were asked to use iPads to do in-class reading with the help of a pop-up dictionary program embedded in the browser of the iPads. Then students posted questions, commented on each other's blog entries, and searched specific information related to the content (e.g., "the advantages and disadvantages of the Internet"). Below is the sequence of the tasks that students were required to follow (Yang & Xie, 2013, p. 15):

1. Provide the pronunciation and definition of each character in each idiom.
2. Provide the definition of each idiom.
3. Provide a visual illustration of each idiom.
4. Make up a story or sentences with the idioms.
5. Post comments on other groups' work on the class blog site (e.g., WordPress, Blogger, or Google Sites).

Examples of the products created by the students are on page 254 in Figure 12.2 (Yang & Xie, 2013, p. 17).

The students in this study practiced target language forms (i.e., idioms) in action enacting *embodied cognition*—working in pairs to generate meanings, present visual illustrations, and construct sentences with assigned idioms. Textual and visual illustrations of the idioms strengthened the learners' memory and understanding of the meanings as proven by the results of the students' post-test scores. Students were able to recall 40% of the idioms even two weeks after the post-test had been conducted (Yang & Xie, 2013).

★ ★ ★ ★ ★

The advantages and values of using technologies in L2 classrooms are endless. New technological tools and novel ideas about how to use them for language learning and teaching are being rapidly produced and developed. It is a huge challenge and almost impossible for classroom teachers to keep

Figure 12.2 Two examples of student artifacts: concrete (left) and abstract (right) (Yang & Xie, 2013, p. 17)

Concrete idiom
人头攒动 réntóu cuándòng
有很多人，像人山人海

海边人头攒动。
"The beach is full of people."

Abstract idiom
不屈不挠 bùqū bùnáo
不屈：will not crouch
不挠：will not submit

他很有力，有什么问题都不屈不挠。
"He was very strong and never submitted to any difficulty."

up with all the resources available out there and to select what may be the best materials to use. One very important thing to remember is that the ultimate goal of using those tools should be to help students become more independent learners and promote their agency for their own needs and aspirations.

FOR THE TEACHER: ACTIVITIES (A) & DISCUSSION (D)

Note: For each of the "Classroom Connections" in this chapter, you may wish to turn them into individual or pair-work discussion questions.

1. **(A)** With the whole class, make a list of technological tools and resources described in the classroom application (pp. 247–249). Ask students to add any additional tools and resources to the list. Then have students review the list individually and consider their familiarity with each application on three scales: very familiar; somewhat familiar; unfamiliar. Based on their familiarity, divide students into groups and ask them to brainstorm ways to incorporate technology that are not included in this chapter, and then to report their results to the rest of the class.

2. **(D)** After the group presentations (see #1 above), brainstorm any contingency plans they can think of for using the tools. Write their ideas on the board and discuss any relevance to their own learning and teaching experience.
3. **(D)** Ask your class to reflect on any privacy concerns in adopting social media as a classroom tool. Discuss codes of conduct for all participants in order to create a safe and pleasant web environment for its optimal use.
4. **(A)** Divide the class into five groups. Each group will identify tools, resources, and ideas for contingency plans that can be useful for teaching one of these five areas: (1) listening, (2) speaking, (3) reading, (4) writing, and (5) grammar and vocabulary. Ask students to present their group's ideas and discuss their feasibility and practicality.
5. **(A)** Create a *class blog* to archive all discussions and presentations on technology use from the classes. Ask students to post their reflections on any of the shared ideas. Encourage students to post new tools and resources they encounter in the future and share their reactions on the blog.
6. **(D)** As a way to encourage students to search for further resources and applications of technology, here is one example you can show: *Poll Everywhere* (polleverywhere.com) is an online service for audience response voting in real time with mobile phones. It allows users to submit their votes or comments and see the voting results instantly through a PowerPoint slide. It facilitates interaction in the audience and is a good alternative to paper-based polls and expensive audience response clickers. To learn about how it can be used, go to the demo video on *Vimeo* (vimeo.com/37674303).

FOR YOUR FURTHER READING

Chapelle, C. (2013). Instructional computer-assisted language learning. In C. A. Chapelle (Ed.), *The encyclopedia of applied linguistics* (pp. 2718–2721). West Sussex, UK: Wiley-Blackwell Publishing Ltd.

Heift, T., & Chapelle, C. A. (2012). Language learning through technology. In S. M. Gass & A. Mackey (Eds.), *The Routledge handbook of second language acquisition* (pp. 555–569). New York, NY: Routledge.

Both chapters provide concise overviews of key issues, research, resources, and pedagogical implications of technology in language education.

Kukulska-Hulme, A. (2013). Mobile-assisted language learning. In C. A. Chapelle (Ed.) *The encyclopedia of applied linguistics* (pp. 3701–3709). West Sussex, UK: Wiley-Blackwell Publishing Ltd.

A concise yet comprehensive overview of MALL and recent updates on its applications to language learning and teaching.

Sokolik, M. (2014). Digital technology in language teaching. In M. Celce-Murcia, D. Brinton, & M. A. Snow (Eds.), *Teaching English as a second or foreign language* (4th ed., pp. 409–421). Boston, MA: National Geographic Learning.

An overview of many uses of technology in language teaching with practical pedagogical tips.

Blake, R. J. (2013). *Brave new digital classroom: Technology and foreign language learning* (2nd ed.). Washington, DC: Georgetown University Press.

A summary of successful CALL projects showing how to implement technology in foreign and second language learning. A variety of recent online resources and their applications to language classrooms are also included.

Stanley, G. (2013). *Language learning with technology: Ideas for integrating technology in the language classroom.* Cambridge, UK, and New York, NY: Cambridge University Press.

A practical resource for teachers who are interested in concrete classroom activities for beginner to advanced levels of students, incorporating a wide range of up-to-date technologies.

Mills, N. (2011). Situated learning through social networking communities: The development of joint enterprise, mutual engagement, and a shared repertoire. *CALICO Journal, 28*, 345–368.

An interesting empirical study on the incorporation of Facebook in a French course with an overview of social networking tools in education and situated learning theory.

CHAPTER **13**

CREATING AN INTERACTIVE CLASSROOM

Questions for Reflection

- What general principles of *interaction* underlie the design of communicative lessons?
- What are some practical ways to *initiate* interaction among students?
- What kinds of *questioning strategies* can be adopted to elicit responses and communicative exchanges among students?
- What are some misconceptions about *group work* (that can tempt teachers to avoid group work)?
- What are some steps leading to the successful design, monitoring, and evaluation of group tasks and activities?

The quiet buzz of voices from the classroom echoes down the hallway. The thirty-some-odd students in an intermediate English class in a Bangkok high school are telling stories, joking, gossiping, and talking about the latest popular music. As the teacher walks in, the students fall silent, face forward, and open their textbooks in anticipation of another English lesson, another day of reciting, repeating, copying, reading aloud, and translating sentences.

But today their usual teacher is absent, and a substitute teacher sits down at the front of the class and asks the students to rearrange their desks into circles of four students each. Surprised, the students comply. Then the teacher speaks:

T: Kavin, what's your favorite movie?

S: [showing surprise, then some silence] I'm sorry. Please repeat.

T: What movie do you like best?

S: [long silence, furtive glances to classmates] Best?

T: Yeah, your favorite movie?

S: [more silence] I like best, ah, The Impossible movie.

T: The Impossible, uh-huh, okay. Arunee, what about you?

S: [embarrassed, giggles] About me?

T: Yeah, what do you think? What's your favorite movie?

S: Oh . . . , favorite movie is Lincoln.

T: Great. Now, Salinee, what's your favorite food?

This line of questioning continues for several minutes, with an increasing degree of ready participation by the students. Then the teacher changes the format a little:

T:	Now, Anchalee, ask Pravit what his favorite sport is.
Anchalee:	[silence] What your favorite sport?
Pravit:	Uh, soccer.
T:	Okay, Pravit, now ask Salinee a question.
Pravit:	[long silence] What sport you like?
Salinee:	Okay, Pravit, good try. Now, say it this way: "What is your favorite sport?"
Pravit:	What is favorite sport?

Slowly, the students warm up to asking each other questions. The teacher then asks students to talk in their circles of four, continuing to ask about favorite movies, songs, sports, and food. The students comply, at first hesitantly, then more confidently.

The teacher then asks the students to make four columns on a blank sheet of paper with the headings *Singer, TV program, Actress, Actor*. In the same circles of four, the teacher directs each group to fill in their sheets with the favorites of the other members of the group—in English! Initial silence is gradually replaced by exchanges of language in the groups as the teacher circulates and encourages some of the more reticent students to participate. The exercise ends with "reports" of findings from appointed group leaders.

The last few minutes of the class hour are spent with the teacher pointing out certain grammatical reminders ("His favorite movie is _____." "I like ____ best.").

EXPLORING INTERACTION

The class just described, whose students had been accustomed to recitation and mechanical output, just became—perhaps for the first time—interactive. The students not only connected language with their meaningful reality, but they were on the way to genuine interaction.

Interaction is an important word for language teachers. We listed interaction as one of our eight major principles in Chapter 4. In the era of communicative language teaching, interaction is, in fact, the heart of communication. We send messages, receive them, interpret them in a context, negotiate meanings, and collaborate to accomplish certain purposes. In Walsh's (2011) words, "Crucially, in a classroom, it is through language in interaction that we access new knowledge, acquire and develop new skills, identify problems of understanding, deal with 'breakdowns' in communication, and establish and maintain relationships" (p. 3).

Interactive Principles

Interaction is the collaborative exchange of thoughts, feelings, or ideas between two or more people. Storch (2013) notes that to *collaborate* means "to share labor," which involves "high mutuality" and a spirit of equality, both of which make interaction fruitful and productive. Theories of communicative competence emphasize the importance of interaction as human beings use language in various contexts to "negotiate" meaning, or simply stated, to get an idea out of one person's head and into the head of another person and vice versa.

Most of the eight principles listed and discussed in Chapter 4 form foundation stones for structuring a comprehensive understanding of interaction in the language classroom. Consider the following selected relationships:

Relationship of Interaction to Major Principles of SLA

- Interaction is enhanced by *automaticity*. The spontaneity of interactive discourse requires attention on meaning through fluent sending and receiving of messages.
- As students become engaged with each other in speech acts of fulfillment and *agency*, their deepest drives are *rewarded*. And as they more fully appreciate their own competence to use language, they can develop a system of *intrinsically motivated self-reward*.
- Interaction requires the use of *self-regulated* strategies both to make certain decisions on how to produce or interpret language, and to modify utterances when communication pathways are blocked.
- Interaction requires the learner to *invest* in the process of learning, and to express one's *identity* within a language community.
- The *cultural* components of interactive speech (and writing) require that interlocutors be thoroughly versed in the cultural nuances of language (*languaculture*).
- Through interaction, learners realize their *agency* as they express ideas, thoughts, and feelings and ultimately work toward *empowerment* within the communities of practice in which they are situated.

Interactive Teachers

An interactive teacher is by definition one who is fully aware of the **group dynamics** of a classroom. As Dörnyei and Murphey (2003) explained, the success of classroom learning is very much dependent on how students relate to each other, what the classroom environment is, how effectively students cooperate and communicate with each other, and, of course, what roles the teacher and learners play.

But it's important to remember that effective interaction within the dynamics of a classroom is a gradual incremental process. According to Vygotsky (1978), effective learning in students' "zones of proximal development" involves "[starting out with] firm leading and modeling on the part of the teacher and [shifting] as students internalize more and more of the processes and teachers learn how to let go" (Dörnyei & Murphey, 2003, p. 98).

Teachers can play many roles in the course of teaching. Rebecca Oxford et al. (1998) pointed out that teacher roles are often best described in the form of metaphor: teacher as *manufacturer*, teacher as *doctor*, teacher as *judge*, teacher as *gardener*, and others. In other metaphors that describe teacher roles, some are obviously more likely to pave the way to interaction.

Teacher as Controller

A role that is sometimes expected in educational institutions is that of controller, in charge of every moment of a lesson. Of course, some control on your part is an important element of structuring a lesson and successfully carrying out interactive techniques. But for interaction to take place, it's also important to create a climate in which *spontaneity* can thrive, *unrehearsed* language can be freely performed, and students are encouraged to *improvise*.

Teacher as Director

Some interactive classroom time can legitimately be structured in such a way that the teacher is like a conductor of an orchestra or a director of a drama. As students engage in either rehearsed or spontaneous language performance, it is your job to keep the process flowing smoothly and efficiently. The ultimate motive of such direction, of course, must always be to enable students eventually to engage in the real-life drama of improvisation as each communicative event brings its own uniqueness.

Teacher as Manager

This metaphor captures a teacher's role as one who plans lessons and who structures the longer segments of classroom time, but who then allows each individual to be creative within those parameters. A successful manager in any walk of life oversees progress toward goals, engages in ongoing evaluation and feedback, but gives freedom to each person to develop individual areas of expertise.

Teacher as Facilitator

A less directive role might be that of a guide, making learning easier for students and helping them to clear away roadblocks. The facilitating role requires that you step away from the managerial or directive role and allow students, with your guidance and gentle prodding, to find their own pathways to success. A facilitator capitalizes on allowing students to *discover* language through using it pragmatically.

Teacher as Resource

This is the least *directive* role. You are available for advice and counsel when the student seeks it, but generally that initiative comes from the student. Some degree of control, of planning, of managing the classroom is essential, but there are appropriate times when you can literally take a back seat and allow the students to proceed with their own linguistic development.

 **CLASSROOM CONNECTIONS**

Sometimes teachers take the role of *controller* a little too far and become "master controllers," micromanaging every moment of class time. On the other hand, being too *laissez faire* in a classroom can lead to chaos and to unfulfilled objectives. Reflecting on the methods discussed in Chapter 2, which ones call for more control and which ones might advocate *too* nondirective a role for the teacher?

In the lessons that you teach, you can appropriately assume all five of these roles on this continuum of **directive** to **nondirective** teaching, depending on the purpose and context of an activity. The key to interactive teaching is to strive toward the nondirective end of the continuum, gradually enabling your students to move from their roles of total dependence (upon you, the class activities, the textbook, etc.) to relatively total independence. The proficiency level of your class often determines which roles will dominate, but even at the lowest levels, some genuine interaction can take place, and your role must be one that, within understood limitations, releases your students to try things for themselves.

Interactive Students

So far we've looked almost exclusively at teachers. What might we add about the roles of interactive *students*?

A huge proportion of students who enter an L2 classroom feel anything *but* interactive, especially in the first few days of a beginning level. They don't know any words or phrases in the language (or very few). The teacher, on the other hand, is perceived to be omniscient, possessing fluent control of the L2 along with a vast storehouse of technical information about the language. Such perceptions may persist even into intermediate and advanced levels. "Who am I, a mere student, to venture to say anything in this language?"

In the rest of this chapter we will address these student self-perceptions, but meanwhile, consider these observations. Students in your classes will have many different "profiles": confident, anxious, motivated, risk-taking, reflective, impulsive, extroverted, introverted, self-starting, analytical . . . and the list of styles and personality types goes on. Your challenge is to discover those characteristics and, as much as possible, help students maximize traits that might work in their favor, minimize those that are working against them, and help them each to seize their *agency* in this new language. In fact, one of the ultimate purposes of creating an interactive classroom is to form a *community* of learners whose interactions serve as a vital motivating force in their language development.

Another way to look at interactive students is to recognize and encourage *student roles* that contribute to collaborative group interaction. Sarkisian (2010) suggests that functioning in groups is usually successful when the participants to do the following:

- take initiative (suggest options; change direction; provide new ideas)
- seek information (ask for facts; solicit opinions)
- question the group by asking for further clarification
- clarify when there is confusion or misunderstanding
- summarize to put contributions into a pattern

As we turn now to some very practical considerations of interaction in the communicative language classroom, you will see the importance of connecting *learner* roles and *teacher* roles.

INITIATING INTERACTION: QUESTIONING STRATEGIES

The most important key to creating an interactive language classroom is the initiation of interaction by the teacher. However nondirective your teaching style is, the onus is on you to provide the stimuli for continued interaction. These stimuli are important in the initial stage of a classroom lesson as well as throughout the lesson. Without such ongoing teacher guidance, classroom interaction may indeed be communicative, but it can easily fall prey to tangential chitchat and other behavior that is off-course from the class objectives.

Functions and Advantages of Teacher Questions

One of the best ways to develop your role as an initiator and sustainer of interaction is to develop a repertoire of questioning strategies. In second language classrooms, where learners often do not have a great number of tools for initiating and maintaining language, your questions provide necessary stepping stones to communication. Appropriate questioning in an interactive classroom can fulfill the following different functions (adapted from Christenbury & Kelly, 1983; Kinsella, 1991).

How do teacher questions stimulate interaction? Some guidelines

- Teacher questions give students the *impetus* and *opportunity* to produce language comfortably without having to risk initiating language themselves. It's very scary for students to have to initiate conversation or topics for discussion. Appropriately pitched questions can give more reticent students an affective "green light" and a structured opportunity to communicate in their second language.
- Teacher questions are useful devices to stimulate students to *practice* morphosyntactic, phonological, and discourse forms that are the focus of a lesson. Most of these questions are *display* questions (see below).
- Teacher questions can serve to initiate a *chain reaction* of student interaction. One question may be all that is needed to start a discussion; without the initial question, however, students will be reluctant to initiate the process.
- Teacher questions give the instructor *immediate feedback* about student comprehension. After posing a question, a teacher can use the student response to diagnose comprehension difficulties along with grammatical or phonological problem areas in the student's production.
- Teacher questions provide students with opportunities to find out what they think by hearing what they say. As they are nudged into responding to questions about, say, a reading or a film, they can discover what their own opinions and reactions are. This *self-discovery* can be especially useful for a prewriting activity.

Classroom Connections

Can you think of other advantages of teacher questions? What are some examples of a question starting a "chain reaction" of student interaction? How do teacher questions lead students to *discover* their opinions?

Display and Referential Questions

There are many ways to classify what kinds of questions are effective in the classroom. Perhaps the simplest way to conceptualize the possibilities is to think of a range of questions, beginning with **display** questions that attempt to elicit information *already known* by the teacher, all the way to highly **referential** questions that request information *not known* by the questioner.

Is there a place for both types of questions? The answer is a qualified yes. Display questions are useful to elicit certain desired grammatical, phonological, or discourse patterns from a student. So, for example, a teacher might ask, "Is it cloudy outside?" (when it's obvious from a glance out the window that it's bright and sunny) in order to elicit a negative or the word *sunny* ("No, it's not cloudy. It's sunny.") However, if possible, you might try to avoid "silly" display questions like "Is this a book?" (as you hold up what is obviously a book). In which case, to elicit production of the word *book*, an information question may be more effective ("What's this?").

Referential questions, in which the teacher can engage students with more "communicative authenticity" (Ur, 2012, p. 229), are much more likely to be genuinely meaningful. This kind of question involves real transfer of information and is in keeping with the tenets of CLT.

Classroom Connections

In your learning of an L2, did you ever feel that the teacher asked "silly" display questions, like, "Is this a pencil?" while holding up a book? Or are those questions really that silly? Is there a place for such teacher input in order to elicit certain words or structures from students?

Categories of Referential Questions

The list below provides seven categories of questions, mostly referential, with typical classroom question words associated with each category.

Categories of Teacher Questions (Adapted from Kinsella, 1991)

1. **Knowledge questions:** Eliciting factual answers, testing recall and recognition of information. Examples: Define, tell, list, identify, describe, select, name, point out, label, reproduce. Who? What? Where? When? Answer "yes" or "no."
2. **Comprehension questions:** Interpreting, extrapolating. Examples: State in your own words, explain, define, locate, select, indicate, summarize, outline, match.

3. **Application questions:** Applying information heard or read to new situations. Examples: Demonstrate how, use the data to solve, illustrate how, show how, apply, construct, explain. What is ____ used for? What would result? What would happen?
4. **Inference questions:** Forming conclusions that are not directly stated in instructional materials. Examples: How? Why? What did ____ mean by? What does ____ believe? What conclusions can you draw from ___ ?
5. **Analysis questions:** Breaking down into parts, relating parts to the whole. Examples: Distinguish, diagram, chart, plan, deduce, arrange, separate, outline, classify, contrast, compare, differentiate, categorize. What is the relationship between? What is the function of? What motive? What conclusions? What is the main idea?
6. **Synthesis questions:** Combining elements into a new pattern. Examples: Compose, combine, estimate, invent, choose, hypothesize, build, solve, design, develop. What if? How would you test? What would you have done in this situation? What would happen if . . . ? How can you improve . . . ? How else would you . . . ?
7. **Evaluation questions:** Making a judgment of good and bad, right or wrong, according to some set of criteria, and stating why. Examples: *Evaluate, rate, defend, dispute, decide which, select, judge, grade, verify, choose why. Which is best? Which is more important? Which do you think is more appropriate?*

All of these types of questions are useful if not essential in an interactive classroom. Even those that are more on the display end of the continuum are very useful in eliciting both content and language from students. Usually, the higher the proficiency level you teach, the more you can venture into the upper, referential end of the continuum. One interesting study of high intermediate pre-university ESL students (Brock, 1986) found that teachers who incorporated more referential questions into their classes stimulated student responses that were longer and more grammatically complex. Make sure, then, that you challenge your students sufficiently but without overwhelming them.

Classroom Connections

In your learning of an L2, to what extent did your teacher use a wide variety of referential questions? Why did Brock's (1986) study find that referential questions stimulated longer and more complex responses? That is, exactly what—in grammatical, discourse, or semantic terms—do responses to referential questions invoke?

Asking a lot of questions in your classroom will not by any means guarantee stimulation of interaction. Certain types of questions may actually impede interactive learning. Beware of the following (adapted from Kinsella, 1991):

How not to discourage interaction: Questions to avoid

- Too much class time spent on display questions—students can easily grow weary of artificial contexts that don't involve genuine seeking of information.
- A question that insults students' intelligence by being so obvious that students will think it's too obvious to bother answering.
- Vague questions that are worded in abstract or ambiguous language (for example, "Do you pretty much understand more or less what to do?").
- Questions stated in language that is too long, too complex, or too wordy for aural comprehension (e.g., "Given today's discussion, and also considering your previous experience, what are the potential developmental impacts on children in an educational system in which assessment procedures largely consist of multiple-choice, paper and pencil instrumentation?").
- Too many rhetorical questions (that you intend to answer yourself) that students think you want them to answer, then get confused when you supply the answer.
- Random questions that don't fall into a logical, well-planned sequence, disrupting students' thought patterns.

Other Means of Stimulating Interaction

Questioning strategies are certainly "the most common and universally used activation technique in teaching" (Ur, 2012, p. 228). And we could argue that they are also one of the most important teaching behaviors for you to master. What do you do and say to get students started, to prime them, to stimulate them to further communication? There are, of course, other teacher strategies that promote interaction. Consider the following:

Strategies for promoting interaction in the classroom

- Designing pair work and group work (details in the next section)
- Giving commands or directions ("Open your books," "Do the following exercise")

- Using organizational language ("Get into small groups")
- Reacting to students (praise, recognition)
- Responding genuinely to student-initiated questions
- Encouraging students to develop their own strategies (to stimulate self-regulation and autonomy)
- Following short lectures/brief teacher monologues with designed collaborative student tasks

Most of these strategies will be described in the upcoming chapters of this book. We now turn to the intricate process of managing what has come to be a hallmark of interactive language teaching: group work.

GROUP WORK: THE STANDARD BEARER OF CLT

The teacher of the community college ESL class of 20 students has just played a video produced by the National Geographic Society on ocean ecology. The language of this 10-minute mini-lecture was comprehensible, but the subject matter itself carried a heavy cognitive load. Now, the teacher asks the students to get into groups of four students each to answer a set of comprehension questions. His directions are: "Get into groups now and answer the questions on the handout." He then gives each student a handout with ten comprehension questions, such as, "What is the role of shrimp in ocean ecology?" and "According to the video, in what three ways are human beings dependent on the ocean for survival?"

The students comply with the first part of the directive by getting into previously arranged groups. Then, silence. Students spend three to four minutes silently reading the questions. Some students in some groups jot down answers to some of the questions. Others look up occasionally to see what other groups are doing or look at each other and then go back to studying the handout.

Finally, in one group a student says to another:

S1: You figure out number 3?
S2: Um, no, and you?
S1: No. How about number 6?
S2: Well, answer is "plankton," I think.

Whereupon the group falls back into silence and more individual work.

In another group, one student has apparently finished jotting down answers to the questions, and a second student says:

S3: You got them all?
S4: Yes, I think so.
S3: So, what you write down?
S4: Number 1 is . . .

And S4 continues to read off his answers one by one as other Ss in the group fill in the answers in silence.

A third group also queries one of their members, who appears to have all the answers. And the fourth group works on in silence; students occasionally glance at each other's papers, mumble a comment or two, and make emendations. Meanwhile the teacher has circulated around once to watch the students, responding only if a student initiates a question directly. He then returns to his desk to record attendance and grade some papers.

After about fifteen minutes, the teacher asks the class to report on their responses, question by question, with students individually volunteering answers. For each question the teacher asks if anyone disagrees, then indicates whether the answer is right or wrong, then asks if everyone in the class understands.

There is something wrong with this picture! If the fifteen-minute time period in which students were in small groups is group work, then the language-teaching profession is in serious trouble! The description you have just read demonstrates just about everything that you should *not* do in conducting group work techniques in your classroom.

 **CLASSROOM CONNECTIONS**

Before reading on, jot down (a) problems with the above lesson, and (b) what you think the teacher could have done with the same video to make a successful group activity following a ten-minute mini-lecture.

We'll now focus on group work as central to maintaining linguistic interaction in the classroom. In so doing, you will get some answers to questions such as: What are some of the myths about group work? What are the advantages of group work? What different kinds of tasks are appropriate for group work? What are some steps for implementing group work? What are some rules for successful group work?

MYTHS ABOUT GROUP WORK

Before presenting various steps and "how-to" suggestions about group work, let's take a quick look at some of the *mis*conceptions about group work.

Some teachers are reluctant to try group work. They feel that they'll lose control, or that students will just use their native language, or that students will just reinforce others' errors and so they shy away from it, none of which is necessarily true. The limitations or drawbacks to group work are all surmountable obstacles when group work is used appropriately.

Let's look at these limitations—or "myths"—and try to understand how to deal with them.

Myth #1: The Teacher Is No Longer in Control of the Class

In the following educational contexts, control could be perceived as an important issue:

- the institution requires a traditional, whole-class methodology
- in your cultural context, effective teaching is believed to be students quietly working in orderly fashion, speaking only when spoken to by the teacher
- large classes (of 50 or more students) make the managing of many small groups problematic
- discipline is a major issue (the assumption is that Ss will misbehave)
- you are an L2 speaker yourself with somewhat low confidence in your own ability in the L2

Despite these potentially adverse contexts, with careful attention to guidelines for implementation of group work, administrative or managerial dilemmas should be avoidable. As we noted earlier in this chapter, if control is thought of as predicting *everything* that is going to transpire in a class hour, then you do not want "control" because you will be thwarting the very nature of an interactive language classroom. Group work still allows you to play the roles of director, manager, facilitator, and resource.

Classroom Connections

Have you ever taken an L2 class in which you felt that the teacher was not very confident in his or her own ability to communicate in the L2? If you are asked to teach a language in which you're not highly proficient, what are some measures you can take to avoid situations in which you're "over your head"? Is it okay to *admit* to your students that you don't know certain words or that you feel your pronunciation isn't as good as it could be?

Myth #2: Students Will Use Their Native Language

There are situations when L1 use in the classroom can be advantageous. We'll touch on those contexts in the next chapter. Here, the concern is that use of students' native language might become a "crutch" or an easy way for students to avoid accomplishing the group task in the target language. No doubt we have all wished at times in our L2 classes that we could just code-switch to our own language. Now, obviously this temptation is more likely to occur in L2 settings where *one* L1 is used by students. When a multiple number of L1s are represented in a single classroom, students are less likely to fall back on their L1, unless a classmate also uses the same L1.

In both cases, you can take some steps toward encouraging target language use in groups. Judicious following of guidelines for implementation (see next section of this chapter) will help. If students feel that the task is too hard (or too easy), or that directions are not clear, or that the task is not interesting, or that they are not sure of the purpose of the task, then you may be inviting students to take shortcuts via their own language.

The most important factor, however, is setting the *climate* for group work. How can you do this? Here are some tips:

GUIDELINES FOR SETTING A POSITIVE CLIMATE FOR GROUP WORK

- Stress the importance of *practice* in the L2.
- Appeal to various *motivational* factors affecting them so that they can see some real uses for English in their own lives.
- Your own overt display of *enthusiasm* will help to set a tone for enjoyment.
- Remind your students of the *security* offered by the smaller groups. Get the groups to think of themselves as *teams*, and that in their groups, they can try out language without feeling that the whole class (and the teacher!) is watching and criticizing.
- For students who argue that the only reason they are in your class is to pass an *examination*, remind them that research has shown that people do better on tests if they dive into the language itself rather than just study test items. If they can be convinced that small groups help to build their intuitions about language, they may also understand that those intuitions will be their ally in a test situation.

Myth #3: Students' Errors Will Be Reinforced in Small Groups.

Another group work myth is the fear that students will reinforce each other's errors and the teacher won't get a chance to correct them. There is now enough research on errors and error treatment (Long & Porter, 1985; McDonough, 2004; Sheen & Ellis, 2011; Spada, 2011) to tell us that (a) levels of accuracy maintained in unsupervised groups are as high as those in teacher-monitored whole class work, and that (b) as much as you would like *not* to believe it, teachers' overt attempts to directly correct speech errors in the classroom have a negligible effect on students' subsequent performance.

Errors are a "necessary" manifestation of language development, and we do well not to become obsessed with their constant correction. Moreover, well-managed group work can encourage spontaneous peer feedback on errors within the small group itself. (For more on form-focused instruction, see Chapter 19.)

CLASSROOM CONNECTIONS

Why do you suppose students' errors produced in (unmonitored) groups do not get reinforced in the developing competence of listeners? Is there something you could do as a teacher to encourage students to monitor each other's errors? And could they then help each other—somewhat surreptitiously—to *notice* errors?

Myth #4: Teachers Cannot Monitor All Groups at Once.

Related to the issue of control is the sometimes misguided belief that a teacher should be "in on" everything a student says or does during the class hour. Interactive learning and teaching principles counter with the importance of meaningful, purposeful language and real communication, which in turn must allow the student to be creative. Yes, the effective teacher will circulate among the groups, listen to students, and offer suggestions and criticisms. But it is simply not necessary—for reasons cited in #3 above—to be a party to all linguistic intercourse in the classroom.

Myth #5: Some Learners Prefer to Work Alone.

It is true that many students, especially adult-age students, prefer to work alone because that's the way they have operated ever since they started going to school. As a successful manager of group work, you need to be sensitive to such preferences, acknowledging that some if not many of your students will find group work frustrating because they may simply want you just to give them the answers to some problem and then move on.

Help your students to see that language learning is not a skill where you can simply bone up on rules and words in isolation. Language is for communicating with people (whether through oral or written modes), and the more they engage in such face-to-face communication, the more their overall communicative competence will improve.

Myth #6: Diverse Student Learning Styles Complicate Group Work.

Sometimes **learning style** variations among students are magnified in small groups. Because the teacher isn't present within the group at all times controlling every move, individual differences may become more salient than they are in whole-class work. Following are some possible scenarios:

- A highly left-brain-oriented student is put off by the otherwise more right-brain members of the group.
- Quicker (impulsive) thinkers tend to blurt out their ideas, overwhelming the slower (reflective) thinkers.
- Impulsive learners get easily frustrated with the group process, which they perceive as circuitous.
- Competitive members of a group are reluctant to share information with others.
- "Talkative" students dominate the process.

CLASSROOM CONNECTIONS

Consider each of the above possible complications that could arise from a diversity of *learning styles* among students in groups. What are some possible solutions to each of these drawbacks? What would you say or do to either prevent or minimize them?

While such problems can and do occur in group work, virtually every problem that's rooted in learning style differences can be solved by careful planning and management. In fact, when group members know their task and know their roles in the group, learning style differences can be efficiently utilized and highly appreciated.

ADVANTAGES OF GROUP WORK

Group work is a generic term for a variety of techniques in which two or more students are assigned a task that involves collaboration and self-initiated language. **Pair work** is simply group work in groups of two, but usually involves less complex and briefer tasks. The collective practice of teachers shows that groups of three or four are usually optimal, and that any more than six defeat one of the major purposes for doing group work: giving students more opportunities to speak.

A look at the principles described in Chapter 4 readily reveals the benefits of interactive small groups for realizing *all eight* of those tenets. Let's explore those advantages.

Group Work Generates Interactive Language.

In so-called traditional language classes, teacher talk is dominant. Teachers lecture, explain grammar points, conduct drills, and at best lead whole-class discussions in which each student might get a few seconds of a class period to talk. Group work helps to solve the problem of classes that are too large to offer many opportunities to speak by increasing individual practice time.

Closely related to the sheer *quantity* of output made possible through group work is the variety and *quality* of interactive language. "They value each other's contributions, cooperate, learn from each other, and help each other" (Jones, 2007, p. 2). Small groups provide opportunities for student initiation, face-to-face give and take, practice in negotiation of meaning, extended conversational exchanges, and student adoption of roles that would otherwise be impossible.

Group Work Offers an Embracing Affective Climate.

A second important advantage offered by group work is the security of a smaller group of students where each individual is not so starkly on public display, vulnerable to what the student may perceive as criticism and rejection. Shy students become vocal participants in the process of forming a community of practice pursuing common goals. The sheer "friendliness" of a small group helps learners to feel more secure and therefore more capable of participating.

Group Work Promotes Learner Responsibility and Autonomy.

While a small group is an affirming context, it also by nature demands responsibility. Each student is an important element in contributing to the success of a task, and one cannot easily "hide" in such a context. Along with the responsibility of participating, students are developing the kind of autonomy they might not otherwise experience in exclusively whole-class work.

Group Work Is a Step Toward Individualizing Instruction.

Each student in a classroom has needs and abilities that are unique. Usually the most salient individual difference that you observe is a range of proficiency levels across your class and, even more specifically, differences among students in their speaking, listening, writing, and reading abilities. Small groups can help students with varying abilities to accomplish separate goals. The teacher can recognize and capitalize upon other individual differences (age, cultural heritage, field of study, cognitive style, to name a few) by careful selection of small groups and by administering different tasks to different groups.

Classroom Connections

What are some other advantages of group work, beyond the four described above? Could whole-class discussion generate the same advantages (except, perhaps, for the last one)?

IMPLEMENTING GROUP WORK IN YOUR CLASSROOM

As you saw in the ESL community college scenario described earlier, group work can fall apart if it is not carefully planned, well executed, monitored throughout, and followed up on in some way. We'll now look at practical steps to take to carry out successful group work in your classroom.

Classroom Language

One of the first considerations in implementing group work is to ascertain that your students have an appropriate command of **classroom language** with which to carry out the group task that you have in mind. Now, some group work is linguistically quite simple, and appropriately so for lower proficiency levels. But at the higher levels, in order to make sure that a group task is accurately understood by students, not only are clear directions important, but students must be able to carry out the discourse necessary to accomplish the task. This means that prior (either in the same lesson or in previous lessons) to the task, students have encountered the classroom language that the task presupposes.

Consider the following examples of expressions for agreeing and disagreeing (adapted from Sarosy & Sherak, 2006, p. 54):

Expressions of agreement and disagreement
To agree with others:
I agree with ______
That's a good point
I agree with ______'s point
Perhaps you're right about ______
To disagree with others:
I'm afraid I don't agree
I'm sorry, but I have to disagree
No, I don't think that's true
I see your point, but . . .

Classroom Connections

Acceptable discourse of disagreement varies from culture to culture. Some cultures are much more "in your face" and blunt, while others go out of their way to be so polite that frankness is almost absent. The above phrases may represent the latter frame of mind. How would you teach students from more confrontational cultures to use this degree of politeness?

There are other forms of classroom language that can make a difference in the success of a group task. Consider the following list (adapted from Sarosy & Sherak, 2006):

- Interrupting another student ("Excuse me . . .")
- Asking for clarification ("Sorry, what did you mean by _______?")
- Asking for more information ("Could you elaborate, please?")
- Supporting your opinion ("Let me tell you why . . .")
- Coming to a consensus ("Would you all agree to . . .?")
- Going over exercises with a partner ("Oh, I wrote something different")
- Giving oral feedback to peers' written work ("Have you thought about . . .?")

The important point here is *not* simply to assume your students have the necessary competence to perform the discourse required of a group task, without making sure those abilities are there. Once the necessary classroom language is in place, the task can proceed to its aims more efficiently.

Pair Work versus Group Work

So far, in looking at group work, differences between **pair work** and group work have not been emphasized. There are, in fact, some important distinctions. Pair work is more appropriate than group work for tasks that are (a) short, (b) linguistically simple, and (c) quite controlled in terms of the structure of the task. Appropriate pair activities (that are *not* recommended for groups of more than two) include the following:

Types of Activities Suitable for Pair Work

- practicing dialogues or doing drills with a partner
- simple question-and-answer exercises
- very brief (one minute or less) brainstorming activities
- checking written work with each other
- preparation for merging with a larger group
- any brief activity for which the logistics of assigning groups, moving furniture, and getting students into the groups is too distracting

Pair work enables you to engage students in interactive (or quasi-interactive) communication for a short period of time with a minimum of logistical problems. But don't misunderstand the role of pair work. It is not to be used exclusively for the above types of activity; it is also appropriate for many group work tasks (listed in the following section).

Classroom Connections

In the above list of pair work tasks, why are they not recommended for groups of more than two? What are some other examples of appropriate pair work tasks? What do you think is an appropriate time limit for pair work?

Group Work Techniques

The first step in promoting successful group work is to select an appropriate task. In other words, choose something that lends itself to the group process. Lectures, drills, dictations, certain listening tasks, silent reading, and a host of other activities are obviously *not* suitable for small-group work.

Typical group tasks are defined and briefly characterized below. For further examples and information, we recommend that you consult any of a wide variety of teacher resource books that offer a multitude of tasks for you to consider. (Some are listed at the end of this chapter.)

1. Games

A game could be any activity that formalizes a technique into units that can be scored in some way. Several of the group tasks outlined below could thus become games. Guessing games are common language classroom activities. Example:

> *Twenty Questions is easily adapted to a small group. One member secretly decides that he or she is some famous person; the rest of the group has to find out who, within twenty yes/no questions, with each member of the group taking turns asking questions. The person who is "it" rotates around the group and points are scored.*

2. Role-Play and Simulations

Role-play minimally involves (a) giving a role to one or more members of a group and (b) assigning an objective or purpose that participants must accomplish. Examples:

> *In pairs, student A is an employer and student B is a prospective employee. The objective is for A to interview B. In groups, similar dual roles could be assumed with assignments to others in the group to watch for certain grammatical or discourse elements as the roles are acted out.*
>
> *A group role-play might involve a discussion of a political issue, with each person assigned to represent a particular political point of view.*

Simulations usually involve a more complex structure and often larger groups (of 6 to 20) where the entire group is working through an imaginary situation as a social unit, the object of which is to solve some specific problem. Example:

> *All members of the group are shipwrecked on a "desert island." Each person has been assigned an occupation (doctor, carpenter, garbage collector, etc.) and perhaps some other mitigating characteristics (a physical disability, an ex-convict, a millionaire, etc.). Only a specified subset of the group can survive on the remaining food supply, so the group must decide who will live and who will die.*

CLASSROOM CONNECTIONS

Assuming that the "desert island" simulation would be successful at an intermediate to advanced level of language ability, what kinds of *grammatical structures* and *discourse features* would be appropriate to incorporate into the task, perhaps as a focus on form?

3. Drama

Drama is a more formalized form of role-play, with a preplanned story line and script. Longer, more involved dramatic performances have been shown to have positive effects on language learning, but they are time consuming and rarely can form part of a typical school curriculum. More practical would be to ask students in groups to prepare their own short dramatization of some event, writing the script and rehearsing the scene as a group. This may be more commonly referred to as a "skit." Example:

> *The City Council has just voted to ban the use of all leaf blowers in town, stating that they are noisy, gas-powered ones pollute the air, they spread allergens through the neighborhood, and often the result is that leaves are just blown into the streets or someone else's yard. Your group takes the roles of a City Council member, an environmental rights representative, the president of the local lawn and garden care union, and a homeowner. The task is to write the script for a roundtable conference among these four. The purpose is to practice the discourse of persuasion.*

4. Projects

For learners of all ages, but perhaps especially for younger learners who can greatly benefit from hands-on approaches to language, certain projects can be rewarding indeed. Example:

> *You are pursuing an environmental awareness theme in your class. Small groups are assigned to do different things: Group A*

creates an environmental bulletin board for the rest of the school; Group B develops fact sheets; Group C makes a three-dimensional display; Group D puts out a newsletter for the rest of the school; Group E develops a skit and presents it.

As learners get absorbed in purposeful projects, both receptive and productive language is used meaningfully.

5. Interview

A popular activity for pair work, but also appropriate for group work, interviews are useful at all levels of proficiency. At the higher levels, interviews can probe more complex facts, opinions, ideas, and feelings. At lower levels, interviews can be very structured, both in terms of the information that is sought and the grammatical difficulty and variety. The goal of an interview could at this level be limited to using requesting functions, learning vocabulary for expressing personal data, and producing questions. For example:

Students are directed to ask each other questions like: "What's your name?" "Where do you live?" "Who's your favorite singer?" Students then give appropriate responses, and venture into creative answers when they feel confident to do so.

6. Brainstorming

Brainstorming is a technique whose purpose is to initiate some sort of thinking process. It gets students' "creative juices" flowing without necessarily focusing on specific problems or decisions or values. Brainstorming is often put to excellent use in preparing students to read a text, to discuss a complex issue, or to write on a topic. Brainstorming involves students in a rapid-fire, free-association listing of concepts or ideas or facts or feelings relevant to some topic or context.

You are about to read a passage on future means of transportation. As a pre-reading technique, you have asked small groups to brainstorm (a) different forms of transportation, past and present, and (b) current obstacles to more efficient means of transportation. Each group's task is to make a composite list of everything they can think of within the category, without evaluating it.

In brainstorming, no discussion of the relative merits of a thought takes place; anything goes. This way, all ideas are legitimate, and students are released to soar the heights and plumb the depths, as it were, with no obligation to defend a concept. In whatever follow-up to brainstorming you plan, at that point evaluation and discussion can take place.

CLASSROOM CONNECTIONS

What instructions would you need to give to students prior to carrying out a brainstorming activity? What "rules" would you specify? Would you like to see this activity done in groups or as a whole class? Why?

7. Information Gap

These final four types of technique are quite commonly used in adult classes around the world and across the proficiency continuum.

Information-gap activities include a variety of techniques in which the objective is to convey or request information. The two focal characteristics of information-gap techniques are (a) their primary attention to information and not to language forms and (b) the necessity of communicative interaction in order to reach the objective. The information that students must seek can range from very simple to complex.

An example at more beginning levels:

> *Each member of a small group is given the objective of finding out from the others their birthday, address, favorite food, etc., and filling in a chart with the information.*

In intermediate classes:

> *You ask groups to collectively pool information about different occupations: necessary qualifications, how long it takes to prepare for an occupation, how much the preparation costs, what typical job conditions are, what salary levels are, etc.*

In advanced classes:

> *Small groups or pairs are asked to determine an author's inferred message when it's not overtly stated, or to make a list of actions one could take to remedy an ecological crisis.*

8. Jigsaw

Jigsaw techniques are a special form of information gap in which each member of a group is given some specific information and the goal is to pool all information to achieve some objective. Examples include the following:

> *Each of four members of a group is given the same job application form, but on each form different information is provided. As students ask each other questions (without showing anyone their own application form), they eventually complete all the information on the form.*

> *You provide maps to students in small groups, each student receiving different sets of information (location of the bank, park, grocery store, etc.). The goal for beginners is simply to locate everything correctly, and for intermediate learners to give directions on how to get from one place on the map to another, requiring a collaborative exchange of information in order to provide complete directions.*

One popular jigsaw technique that can be used in larger groups is known as a "strip story," which students always enjoy and find challenging:

> *The teacher takes a moderately short written narrative or conversation and cuts each sentence of the text into a strip of paper, shuffles the strips, and gives each student a strip. The goal is for students to determine where each of their sentences belongs in the whole context of the story, to stand in their position once it is determined, and to read off the reconstructed story.*

9. Problem Solving and Decision Making

Problem-solving group techniques focus on the group's solution of a specified problem. They might or might not involve jigsaw characteristics, and the problem itself might range from simple to complex:

> Simple: *Students must give directions on a map.*
>
> Moderately complex: *Groups must work out an itinerary from train, plane, and bus schedules.*

 **CLASSROOM CONNECTIONS**

Suppose you have assigned the task of having groups figure out how to travel from one city and country to a different city and country, with various transportation schedules to refer to. What grammatical and discourse features might you want to preteach (or review) at, say, an intermediate level?

> Quite complex: *Groups are asked to solve a mystery in a crime story or deal with a political or moral dilemma.*

Once again, problem-solving techniques center students' attention on meaningful cognitive challenges and not so much on grammatical or phonological forms.

Decision-making techniques are simply one kind of problem solving where the ultimate goal is for students to make a decision. Some of the problem solving techniques alluded to above (say, giving directions to someone and solving a mystery) don't involve a decision about what to do. Other problem solving techniques do involve such decisions. For example:

> *Students presented with several profiles of applicants for a job are asked to decide which person they would hire. On the "desert island" game (referred to earlier) a decision must be made. In a debate on nuclear disarmament, students might present several possible causes of escalation, but also decide what they would actually do to reduce the proliferation of nuclear weapons.*

10. Opinion Exchange

An opinion is a belief or feeling that might not be founded on empirical data or that others could plausibly take issue with. Opinions are difficult for students to deal with at the beginning levels of proficiency, but by the intermediate level, certain techniques can effectively include the exchange of various opinions. Many of the above techniques can easily incorporate beliefs and feelings. Sometimes opinions are appropriate; sometimes they are not, especially when the objective of a task is to deal more with factual, empirical information.

Moral, ethical, religious, and political issues are often sensitive, "hot" topics for classroom debates, arguments, and discussions. Students can get involved in the content-centered nature of such activity and thus pave the way for automatic processing of language itself. Here are a few such issues:

- *women's rights*
- *choosing a marriage partner*
- *widening of the gap between rich and poor (the "haves" and "have nots")*
- *sexual orientation, same-sex marriage*
- *privacy rights and government "snooping"*
- *censorship of selected access and information*
- *abortion and a woman's right to choose*
- *euthanasia (death with dignity)*
- *environmental crises (air, water, forests, atmosphere, oceans)*
- *chemical warfare*
- *nuclear nonproliferation*

A word of advice: You play an important and sensitive role when you ask students to discuss their beliefs or opinions, which may be deeply ingrained from childhood rearing, cultural traditions, or religious training. So, in these discussions a student might be offended by what another student says. In such exchanges, do everything you can to assure everyone in your class that, while there may be disagreement on issues, *all expressed opinions are legitimate,* and the person giving them is to be valued and respected, and not belittled or ridiculed. We'll touch more on this issue in Chapter 23.

 **CLASSROOM CONNECTIONS**

Suppose your class is engaged in a discussion of a sensitive topic like same-sex marriage or gay rights, and one or two students express very strong feelings on one side of the issue, to the point that they become highly emotional and adamant in their unwillingness to entertain other sides of the issue. What would you do to restore order? How would you show respect for the adamant students' right to their opinion, but also continue a discussion?

Planning and Initiating Group Work Tasks

One of the most common reasons for the breakdown of group work is an inadequate introduction and lead-in to the task itself. Too often, teachers assume that purposes are clear and directions are understood, and then have to spend an inordinate amount of time clarifying and redirecting groups. For example, teachers like to tell students to "discuss" something, *assuming* that everyone will easily jump into an exchange of ideas. When you say to your class, "Okay, everyone, get into pairs and discuss these ideas from the lecture you just heard," what does that *mean* to students?

Once you have selected an appropriate type of activity, your planning and initiating phases should include the following seven "rules" for implementing a group technique. Here, you are acting in the role of *director* or *manager*.

1. Introduce the Technique

The introduction may simply be a brief explanation. For example, "Now, in groups of four, you're each going to get different transportation schedules (airport limo, airplane, train, and bus), and your job is to figure out, as a group, which combination of transportation services will take the least amount of time." The introduction almost always should include a statement of the ultimate purpose so that students can apply all other directions to that objective.

2. Justify the Use of Small Groups for the Technique

If you think your students have any doubts about the significance of the upcoming task, then tell them explicitly why the small group is important for accomplishing the task. Remind them that they will get an opportunity to practice certain language forms or functions, and that if they are reluctant to speak up in front of the whole class, now is their chance to do so in the security of a small group.

3. Model the Technique

In simple techniques, especially those that your students have done before, modeling may not be necessary. But for a new and potentially complex task, it's important to be explicit in making sure students know what they are being asked to do. After students get into their groups, you might, for example, show them (possibly on a projector screen) four transportation schedules (not the ones they will see in their groups). Then select four students to simulate a discussion of meshing arrival and departure times; your guidance of their discussion will help.

4. Give Explicit Detailed Instructions

Now that students have seen the purpose of the task and have had a chance to witness how their discussion might proceed, give them specific instructions on what they are to do. Include

- a restatement of the purpose,
- rules they are to follow (e.g., Don't show your schedule to anyone else in your group. Try to use a specified grammatical structure, e.g., *if* clauses).
- a time frame (e.g., You have ten minutes to complete the task.)
- assignment of roles (if any) to students (e.g., The airport limo person for each group is the "chair." The airplane person will present your findings to the rest of the class. The train person is the timekeeper, etc.).

5. Divide the Class into Groups

This element is not as easy as it sounds. In some cases you can simply number off (e.g., 1, 2, 3, 4, . . .) and specify which area of the room to occupy. But to ensure participation or control you may want to *pre-assign* group composition in order to account for some of the following:

CATEGORIES TO CONSIDER FOR PRE-ASSIGNING GROUPS

- native language (especially in ESL classes with varied native language backgrounds)
- proficiency levels
- age or gender differences
- culture or subcultural group
- personality types
- cognitive style preferences
- cognitive/developmental stages (for children)
- interests
- prior learning experience
- target language goals

CLASSROOM CONNECTIONS

Considering *proficiency level* as a criterion for pre-assigning group composition, how would that play out? Would you put lower-proficiency students all together in *one* group? Or *mix* the abilities? What are the advantages of each of these approaches? How would you pre-assign groups according to *introversion* and *extroversion*?

In classes of fewer than thirty people, pre-assigning groups is quite manageable if you come to class with the pre-assignments, having thought through the variables that you want to control. Just put the group names up on the chalkboard and tell people to get into their groups.

6. Check for Clarification

Before students start moving into their groups, check to make sure they all understand their assignment. You might ask a question like, "Keiko, please restate the purpose of this activity," or, "What are you going to do first in your groups?"

One form of question that is *not* advisable is, "Does everyone understand?" Teachers are often tempted to assume that asking a blanket question like this provides an informal assessment of how well students comprehended something. Usually, whether students understood or not, a small minority of them will nod their heads affirmatively while the rest of the class shows no response. The few nodding heads must *not* be taken as a measure of comprehension by all.

7. Set the Task in Motion

This part should now be a relatively simple matter of saying something like, "Okay, get into your groups and get started on your task." Some facilitation may be necessary to ensure smooth logistics.

Monitoring the Task

Your job now becomes one of *facilitator* and *resource*. To carry out your role, you need to tread the fine line between inhibiting the group process and being a helper or guide. The first few times you do group work, you may need to establish this sensitive role, letting students know you will be available for help and that you may make a suggestion or two here and there to keep them on task, but that they are to carry out the task on their own. There may actually be a few moments at the outset where you do not circulate among the groups so that they can establish a bit of momentum. The rest of the time it's important to circulate so that, even if you have nothing to say to a group, you can listen to students and get a sense of the groups' progress and of individuals' language production.

GUIDELINES FOR MONITORING GROUPS

- Actively circulate through the groups.
- Show interest, but remember it's *their* group, not yours.
- Offer a few helpful comments, but don't dominate.
- Maintain a "fly on the wall" nondisruptive role.
- Keep your own verbal comments to a minimum.
- Divide your time as equally as possible among the groups.
- Correct students' errors only if an error is causing a crucial misunderstanding, or a student requests it.

Debriefing (Processing) the Task

Almost all group work can be brought to a beneficial close by some sort of whole class debriefing, once the group task is completed. This debriefing, or *processing*, as some would refer to it, has two layers:

1. Reporting on Task Objectives

If groups were assigned a reporter to present something to the class, or if the task implicitly lends itself to some discussion of the "findings" of the groups, then make sure that you leave enough time for this to take place. As reporters or representatives of each group bring their findings, you may entertain some brief discussion, but be sure not to let that discussion steal time from other groups.

This whole-class process gives each group a chance to perceive differences and similarities in their work. Some group work involves different assignments to different groups, and in these cases the reporting phase is interesting to all and provides motivation for further group work.

2. Focus on Form

Many—if not most—group tasks involve the use of certain grammatical or discourse features that are deliberately embedded into the task. An information gap task involving a map, for example, might be a way to stimulate *wh*- questions, certain vocabulary, directions, or polite requests. The debriefing phase is usually an appropriate time for the teacher to call attention to these formal features, reminding students of forms that seemed to cause errors as well as those that students produced correctly.

 **CLASSROOM CONNECTIONS**

Imagine your advanced beginner students have just completed a task involving map directions. How would you direct their attention to the various forms that you intended the task to elicit? For example, what if students seemed to have trouble forming *wh-* questions? What techniques would you employ to encourage them to notice certain features of these questions?

3. Establishing Affective Support

A debriefing phase also serves the purpose of exploring the group process itself and of bringing the class back together as a whole community of learners. If you or some students have questions about how smoothly the task proceeded, how comfortable people were with a topic or task, or problems they encountered in reaching their objective, now is an excellent time to encourage some whole-class feedback. This gives you feedback for your next group work assignment.

Ultimately, even a very short period of whole-class discussion reminds students that everyone in the room is a member of a team of learners and that the groups, especially if any intergroup competition arose, are but temporary artifacts of classroom learning.

It's possible that these last few sections on group work have been so explicit that you feel overwhelmed by the prospect of doing group work in your classroom. If so, that need not be the case! All of the guidelines and reminders and dos and don'ts included in this chapter will in time become a part of your subconscious, intuitive teaching behavior. You won't have to process every minute of your class hour in terms of whether you've done all the "right" things. In the meantime, just remember that conscientious attention to what makes for successful group work will soon pay off.

FOR THE TEACHER: ACTIVITIES (A) & DISCUSSION (D)

Note: For each of the "Classroom Connections" in this chapter, you may wish to turn them into individual or pair-work discussion questions.

1. **(D)** Ask your students to describe ways in which an interactive classroom differs from a "traditional" classroom. On the board, list the factors that they name and have students evaluate their validity.

2. **(D)** Ask the class the following: Of the five teacher roles described on pages 260–261, how would those roles change depending on (a) the proficiency level, (b) the age, and (c) the culture of students?
3. **(A)** Ask small groups to (a) brainstorm as many metaphors for *teachers* as possible (teacher as manufacturer, doctor, bus driver, gardener, etc.). Then have them (b) choose a few to describe by extending the metaphor. For example, the teacher as *gardener* must offer a *nurturing environment* for students as plants, considering the *climate* of context. Then have the groups each present one such extended metaphor to the rest of the class.
4. **(A)** If it's feasible to ask students to observe an L2 class, or if you have a video of a class, ask students to notice the kinds of *questions* the teacher asks, and write them down. How many were *display* questions, and how many were *referential* questions? How effective were both types of questions?
5. **(A)** Pair students up and ask each pair to list some specific examples of questions that *discourage* interaction and to discuss why they think those examples fail to promote interaction. Pairs will share their thoughts with other members of the class.
6. **(D)** What is "control"? How much is control an issue for teachers? How might one do group work and still stay in control? Specifically, at what points should a teacher relinquish control?
7. **(A)** Ask pairs of students to choose one of the examples of the eight categories of classroom language (adapted from Sarosy & Sherak, 2006) listed on page 275 and brainstorm *other phrases* used in English to accomplish the discourse function. Each pair can write the list on the board for a composite list of samples from the eight categories.
8. **(D)** On page 283, some criteria were listed for pre-assigning group membership. Ask your students to justify the use of those criteria—that is, under what circumstances and for what reasons would one pre-assign small-group membership? Are there other criteria?
9. **(A)** Direct pairs to think of other "sensitive" topics for opinion exchange (p. 281). Would some of them be too sensitive or personal to include in classroom discussion? Why? Pairs will then share their thoughts with the rest of the class.

FOR YOUR FURTHER READING

Jones, L. (2007). *The student-centered classroom.* New York, NY: Cambridge University Press.

In this 48-page "booklet" (available online at www.cambridge.org) the author gives numerous practical steps to creating and maintaining an interactive classroom.

Walsh, S. (2011). *Exploring classroom discourse: Language in action*. New York, NY: Routledge.

A comprehensive examination of classroom discourse including describing a number of approaches to recording and analyzing classroom interaction.

Long, M., & Porter, P. (1985). Group work, interlanguage talk, and second language acquisition. *TESOL Quarterly, 19,* 207–228.

In this seminal, ground-breaking article on group work, the authors examine myths about group work and encourage teachers to employ interactive small-group work. Most of the findings and observations of 30 years ago are still relevant today.

McDonough, K. (2004). Learner-learner interaction during pair and small group activities in a Thai EFL context. *System, 32,* 207–224.

Kim, Y. (2009). The effects of task complexity on learner-learner interaction. *System, 37*, 254–268.

Both articles report research on interaction in L2 classrooms, looking at the effectiveness of pair and small group activities (McDonough), and exploring the varied effects of task complexity on the amount and quality of interaction (Kim).

Storch, N. (2013). Collaborative language learning. In C. A. Chapelle (Ed.), *The encyclopedia of applied linguistics* (pp. 725–730). West Sussex, UK: Blackwell Publishing Ltd.

A summary of research on collaborative language learning that examines the theoretical bases for collaboration, how learners performing pair work take on various collaborative roles, and the link between dyadic interaction and language learning outcomes. A useful bibliography is attached.

CHAPTER 14

CLASSROOM MANAGEMENT

Questions for Reflection

- What *physical features* in the classroom environment will affect the success of a lesson?
- How can one monitor one's own *voice* and *body language* and make changes as necessary?
- What are some suggested guidelines for dealing with *unexpected*, unplanned moments, and turn them to one's advantage?
- What are some strategies for teaching *large* classes?
- How do a teacher's perceived *role* (as a teacher), personality, and preferred communication *styles* affect successful classroom management?
- How does one generate *energy* in the classroom and create a *positive* atmosphere?

Is teaching an art or a science? Are teachers born or made? Is the learning-teaching connection poetically or scientifically created? These questions commonly swirl about in the minds of educators, not so much as "either-or" questions but rather as "both-and" questions. You can no doubt easily agree that teaching is *both* an art and a science, that some innate ability complements learned teaching skills, and that with all of our best-laid lesson plans there still remains an intangible reliance on intuition and experience beneath most successful teaching.

As we take a careful look in this chapter at **classroom management**, you'll appreciate the interweaving of art and science. From the physical arrangement of a classroom, to teaching styles and philosophy, to classroom energy, art and science comingle in mysterious but satisfying ways. As you focus on identifiable, overtly observable skills, you open the door to the intangible—to the invisible sparks of energy that kindle the flames of learning.

GENERAL PRINCIPLES OF CLASSROOM MANAGEMENT

Let's first look at some of the fundamentals of classroom management that might apply to any classroom. Consider the following "keys" to effective classroom management (adapted from Marzano & Marzano, 2003).

 General Guidelines for Classroom Management

- **Establish clear teacher and student roles.** Learner-centered classrooms that involve student interaction and participation function efficiently only when it has been made explicit what your role as a teacher is, and how student participation fits into an organized class hour. Studies have found that, in general, students prefer teacher guidance and control over "permissive" approaches that have the potential of becoming chaotic (Chiu & Tulley, 1997).
- **Articulate unambiguous objectives and goals.** When students know what the ultimate purpose of lessons and tasks within the lesson are, they will more effectively develop intrinsic motives to succeed.
- **Be flexible.** As we noted in Chapter 10, it's obviously important to plan your lessons, but as Scrivener (2012) noted, plans have a way of going awry, so while you should indeed prepare for a lesson, you will need to be flexible in modifying and adapting your original plans.
- **Allow students some choice in activities and exercises.** Your planned activities and tasks are important ways to lead students toward reaching objectives, but within that structure, when students are given options to choose from, it increases their interest.
- **Take a personal interest in students.** Teachers sometimes have dozens of students that they teach every day, but the more you can see each one as a unique individual, worthy of your attention, the better. Informal conversations, compliments on good work, and awareness of personal backgrounds and situations can all contribute toward a fully functioning community of students.
- **Be fair to all students.** It's easy to have "favorites" in your classrooms, but it's important to treat every student with equal affection and attention. Otherwise, you set yourself up for discord and jealousies.
- **Exhibit enthusiasm and a positive attitude yourself.** The more you exude enthusiasm for classroom activities, the more this positive outlook with rub off on your students. There's nothing worse than teachers whose body language, demeanor, and words communicate apathy. The key is to *engage* your students (Wright, 2005), and you are the one to spearhead that engagement.
- **Challenge students of both higher and lower levels of ability.** One of the most challenging aspects of teaching is reaching *all* of your students, across a spectrum of ability, intelligence, and motivation. Some means of accomplishing this include a variety of activities, judicious assignment of groups, individual attention, and extra-class conferences.

The fundamentals of classroom management are not unique to the language teaching field, but the particular demands of communicative classrooms are a challenge for teachers. It's much easier to be teacher-fronted and completely in control than to release some of that control to students. The latter requires attentiveness to your role as both a manager *and* a facilitator (see Chapter 13, page 260).

THE PHYSICAL ENVIRONMENT OF THE CLASSROOM

One of the simplest principles of classroom management centers on the physical environment for learning, namely the classroom, and the *space* that students occupy (Wright, 2005). Consider four categories:

Sight, Sound, and Comfort

As trivial as it may first appear, in the face of your decisions to implement language-teaching principles in an array of clever techniques, students are indeed profoundly affected by what they see, hear, and feel when they enter the classroom. If you have any power to control the following, then it will be worth your time to do so:

CREATING AN OPTIMAL CLASSROOM PHYSICAL ENVIRONMENT

- Maintain a classroom that is neat, clean, and orderly in appearance.
- Erase chalkboards (whiteboards) before each class period.
- Arrange chairs are appropriately (see below).
- If the room has bulletin boards and you have the freedom to use them, take advantage of visual stimuli to interest students.
- As much as possible, keep the classroom free from external noises (machinery outside, street noise, hallway voices, etc.).
- If possible, see to it that acoustics within your classroom are optimal.
- Ensure efficient operation of heating/cooling systems (if applicable).

Granted, you may be powerless to control some of the above. We have experienced classrooms in tropical countries where there was no air conditioning, the concrete walls of the classroom echoed so badly you could hardly hear anyone, and jackhammers were rapping away outside! But if these factors can be controlled, don't pass up the opportunity to make your classroom as physically comfortable as possible.

Classroom Connections

What are some other factors that you might consider for creating or maintaining an environment in your classroom that is conducive to learning? What kinds of material would you consider putting on a bulletin board? What might you do about external noises, acoustics, and heating and cooling systems that are not under your direct control?

Seating Arrangements

You may have had the experience of walking into a classroom and finding the movable desks all lined up in columns (not rows) that are perpendicular to the front wall of the room. Neat and orderly, right? Yes, but . . . So what can you do?

If your classroom has movable desk-chairs, consider patterns of semi-circles, U-shapes, concentric circles, or—if your class size is small enough—one circle so that students aren't all squarely facing the teacher. If the room has tables with two to four students at each, try to devise configurations that make interaction among students feasible. Give some thought to how students will do small group and pair work with as little disruption as possible.

Should you determine who sits next to whom? Students may soon fall into a comfortable pattern of self-selection in where they sit, but is that always optimal for potential interaction? Not always. You may perceive the need to force a different "mix" of students. In some contexts where students come from varied native language backgrounds, the L2 will be more readily practiced if students of the same L1 are *not* sitting next to each other. And if some adjacent students are being disruptive, you may decide to selectively move a few people. Or you may wish to mix personality styles (e.g., introverts and extroverts) in seating groups. When assigning small groups, as noted in Chapter 13, you may need to do so with a certain plan in mind.

Chalkboard (Whiteboard) Use

The chalkboard—in many classrooms a whiteboard is used with erasable markers—is one of your greatest allies (Scrivener, 2012, p. 264). It gives students added visual input along with auditory. It allows you to illustrate with words and pictures and graphs and charts. It is always there and it is recyclable! So, take advantage of this instant visual aid by profusely using the board. At the same time, try to be neat and orderly in your board use, erasing as often as appropriate; a messy, confusing chalkboard drives students crazy.

Equipment

Many courses now assume that equipment is either built in to the classroom or readily available on portable carts. If you're using electrical equipment (say, a laptop computer, projection equipment, audio, or video player), make sure that the following issues are under control:

GUIDELINES FOR ASCERTAINING FUNCTIONING EQUIPMENT

- Check that the room's electrical outlets are within reach of the cord provided, or, if not, that an extension cord is on your equipment list.
- Make sure the equipment fits comfortably in the room.
- Confirm that everyone can see (and/or hear) the visual/auditory stimulus.
- Leave enough time before and after class to get the equipment and return it to its proper place.
- Try out equipment ahead of time to ascertain that it actually works.
- Familiarize yourself with how to operate it.
- There is an extra light bulb or battery or whatever else you'll need if a routine replacement is in order.

You would be surprised how many lesson plans go awry because of some very minor practicality surrounding the use of equipment.

CLASSROOM CONNECTIONS

If you have the ability to request equipment from your institution, what would be on your priority list? Compile such a list in your mind, ranked from your highest priority to lowest.

YOUR VOICE AND BODY LANGUAGE

Another fundamental classroom management concern has to do with *you* and the messages you send through your voice and through your body language.

One of the first requirements of good teaching is voice projection. You do not have to have a loud, booming voice, but you need to be heard by all the students in the room. When you talk, project your voice so that the person sitting farthest away from you can hear you clearly. If you are directing comments to a student in the first row sitting right in front of you, remember that in whole-class work, all the rest of the students need to be able to hear that comment. As you speak, articulate clearly; remember, these students are learning a new language, and they need every advantage they can get.

Should you slow down your normal rate of delivery? For beginning level classes, yes, but only slightly so, and not to the point that the rate of delivery is downright silly. Keep as natural a flow to your language as possible. Clear articulation is usually more of a key to comprehension than is slowed speech.

Your voice isn't the only production mode available to you in the classroom. Nonverbal messages are very powerful. In language classes, especially, where students may not have all the skills they need to decipher verbal language, their attention is drawn to nonverbal communication. Consider these pointers:

Toward Effective Teachers' Nonverbal Communication

- Let your body posture exhibit an air of confidence.
- Your face should reflect optimism, brightness, and warmth.
- Use facial and hand gestures to enhance meanings of words and sentences that might otherwise be unclear.
- Make frequent eye contact with all students in the class.
- Do not "bury yourself" in your notes and plans.
- Do not stand in one place for the whole hour.
- Move around the classroom, but not to the point of distraction.
- Follow the conventional rules of proxemics (distance) and kinesthetics (touching) that apply for the culture(s) of your students.
- Dress appropriately, considering the expectations of your students and the culture in which you are teaching.

Classroom Connections

In your own culture (or the culture you think you will be teaching in), what are the rules of proxemics, kinesthetics, eye contact, and other nonverbal factors? Are the standards for teachers the same as those for students? What about the dress codes for teachers and students? At what point does either teacher or student cross the line into inappropriateness?

UNPLANNED TEACHING: MIDSTREAM LESSON CHANGES

Now that you have considered some of the factors in managing the physical space and your physical self, imagine the following scenario:

> You have entered the classroom and begun your lesson. The warm-up has gone well. You have successfully (with clear, unambiguous directions) introduced the first major technique, which has to do with different countries' forms of government. Students are clear about why they are doing this task and have launched themselves into it.
>
> Then one student asks about the political campaign happening right now, a hot issue in the news. Another student responds, and then another, and before you know it, students are engaged in a somewhat heated debate about current political issues, and emotions are beginning to run high. This theme is related to your lesson, but the discussion is not what you had in mind. Nevertheless, students are all alert, interested, participating, and using fairly complex language in the process.

This scene is commonplace. What would you do now? Should you have cut off the conversation early and nipped it in the bud? Or were you wise to let it continue and to discard some other activities you had in mind? Classroom management involves decisions about what to do and when. Consider these possibilities:

- Your students digress and throw off the plan for the day.
- *You* digress and throw off the plan for the day.
- An unexpected but pertinent question comes up.
- Some technicality prevents you from doing an activity (e.g., a machine breaks down, or you suddenly realize you forgot to bring handouts that were necessary for the next activity).
- You are asked a question you don't know the answer to (e.g., a grammatical point).
- A student is disruptive in class.
- There isn't enough time at the end of a class period to finish an activity that has already started.

And the list could go on. In short, you are daily called upon to deal with the *unexpected*. You have to engage in what we'll call unplanned teaching that makes demands on you that were not anticipated in your lesson plan. One of the initiation rites that new teachers go through is experiencing these unexpected events and learning how to deal with them gracefully.

The key is *poise*. You will keep the respect of your students and your own self-confidence by staying calm, assessing the situation quickly, making a midstream change in your plan (if warranted), and allowing the lesson to move on.

Classroom Connections

In your own L2 learning, what unexpected, unplanned things do you remember happening? What did the teacher do? How did you react? What would you do if a machine (say, a computer projector) didn't work and you had a substantive part of the lesson planned for it? Or if a student asks you a question about the L2 that you can't answer?

TEACHING UNDER ADVERSE CIRCUMSTANCES

Under the category of "adverse circumstances" are a number of management concerns of a widely divergent nature. What is implied here is that no teaching-learning context is perfect. There are always imperfect institutions, imperfect people, and imperfect circumstances for you to deal with. How you deal with them is one of the most significant factors contributing to your professional success.

Teaching Large Classes

You're in a teaching methodology class discussing the problem of large classes. The instructor asks for suggestions about how to deal with large classes. You begin to list the kinds of adjustments you could make with classes of 50 to 75 students, when one of your classmates says that he once had to teach a really large class—with 600 students! As you try not to show too much shock, you respond by asking him how he would teach 600 people to swim in one swimming pool without displacing all the water in the pool!

What would you do in this situation? Ideally, language classes should be comprised of no more than twelve to fifteen students (LoCastro, 2001). They should be large enough to provide diversity and student interaction and small enough to give students plenty of opportunity to participate and to get individual attention. Unfortunately, with paltry educational budgets worldwide, too many language classes are significantly larger. Classes of 50 to 75 are not uncommon across the globe. While you need to keep reminding administrators (who too often may believe that languages are learned by rote memorization) of the diminishing returns of classes in excess of 25 or 30, you nevertheless may have to cope with the reality of a large class for the time being. Large classes present some problems (Shamim, 2012):

- Proficiency and ability vary widely across students.
- You tend to rely on lectures, videos, and other whole-class presentations.
- A good deal of group work might be unmonitored, and "reports" from groups may have to be randomly selected.
- Individual teacher-student attention is minimized.
- Student opportunities to speak to the whole class are lessened.
- Teacher's feedback on students' written work is limited.

Some solutions to these problems are available. Consider the following that apply to one or several of the above challenges:

Suggestions for Teaching Large Classes

- Try to make each student feel important (and not just a "number") by learning names and using them. Name tags or desk "plates" serve as reminders in the early days of the course.
- Assign students as much interactive work as possible, including plenty of "get-acquainted" activities at the beginning, so that they feel a part of a community and are not just lost in the crowd.
- Optimize the use of pair work and small-group work to give students chances to perform in English. In grouping, consider the variation in proficiency levels (see next section, below).
- Do more than the usual number of listening comprehension activities, using tapes, video, and yourself. Make sure students know what kind of response is expected from them. Through active listening comprehension, students can learn a good deal of language that transfers to reading, speaking, and writing.
- Use peer-editing, feedback, and evaluation in written work whenever appropriate.
- Give students a range of extra-class work, from a minimum that all students must do to challenging tasks for students with higher proficiency.
- Don't collect written work from all of your students at the same time; spread it out in some systematic way both to lighten your load and to give students the benefit of a speedy return of their work.
- Set up small "learning centers" in your class where students can do individualized work.
- Organize informal conversation groups and study groups.

Classroom Connections

What are some other solutions that might compensate for the disadvantages of very large classes? How might you "optimize" pair and group work? What is meant by "active" listening comprehension and what are some ways to encourage it? How might technology (online exercises; web-based activities; social media) help to maximize opportunities for communication in large classes?

Teaching Multiple Proficiency Levels in the Same Class

There is often a wide range of proficiency levels among students in the same class, especially in large classes, but even relatively small classes can be composed of students who in your estimation should not all be placed at the same level. In either case, you are faced with the problem of challenging the higher-level students and not overwhelming the lower-level students, and at the same time keeping the middle group well-paced toward their goals. We cannot simply teach to that middle group and hope to reach the rest of the students (Bell, 2012). Most of the time, the phenomenon of widely ranging competencies in your class is a byproduct of institutional placement procedures and budgetary limits, so there is little you can do to eliminate the students at either extreme. So, how do you deal with this? Here are some suggestions to consider:

SUGGESTIONS FOR TEACHING CLASSES WITH MULTIPLE PROFICIENCY LEVELS

- **Avoid overgeneralization of proficiency levels.** Blanket classification of students into "good" and "bad" students is a common mistake among teachers. In a set of skills as complex as language, it is often difficult to determine whether a student's performance is a factor of aptitude, ability, a "knack," or a matter of time and effort.
- **Individualize your techniques.** As much as possible, identify the specific skills and abilities of each student in your class so that you can tailor your techniques to their needs. Through diagnostic exercises and day-by-day monitoring of students, you may be able to pinpoint certain linguistic objectives and direct your students toward those.
- **Offer choices**. If students are given a choice in individual (written and extra-class) techniques that vary according to needs and challenges, you may be able to reach a wider range of students. Convey to your students that they *all* have challenges and goals to pursue and that if some students seem to be "ahead" of others, it is no doubt due to previous instruction, exposure, and motivation.
- **Use technological aids.** Take advantage of a multitude of stimuli available on the Internet. All proficiency levels can benefit from electronically delivered review and practice exercises, often suggested in textbooks and curricular materials.
- **Aim for the middle.** Gauge the complexity of your classroom teacher talk (instructions, explanations, lectures, etc.) for the middle of the range of proficiency in your class.

- **Vary group work tasks.** Group work offers opportunities for you to solve multiple-proficiency issues. Sometimes you can place students of varying ranges in the same group (and pitch your task accordingly), and at other times students of the same range in a group together. Both scenarios, of course, offer advantages and disadvantages.

 **Classroom Connections**

What are the advantages and disadvantages of assigning groups of (a) varying ranges in the same group and (b) placing students of more or less equal proficiency in the same group? Can you think of circumstances in which one method of placement would be favored over the other?

"Target Language Only" in the Classroom?

In language teaching circles across the globe, there has historically been an undercurrent of opinion that claims that one should never use native languages in the classroom. Such convictions may stem from methods like the Direct Method, which endorsed "target language only" practices in the classroom, and from an overreaction to Grammar Translation methodology that often saw little use at all of the target language. It is now clear from research and experience that "English only" prohibitions go too far (Harmer, 2007; Larsen-Freeman & Anderson, 2011; Hall & Cook, 2012; Ur, 2012).

On the other hand, especially in "foreign" language teaching contexts, an undue *over*use of the native language in the classroom remains an issue. Teachers who may not feel highly confident in their L2 proficiency are tempted to use more of the L1 than may be pedagogically advisable. And while students may welcome the chance to receive input in their L1, it might not fully challenge students to put forth the effort that they should.

Is there a middle ground? Your cultural, institutional, and methodological contexts will usually lead to a reasonable solution, or as Hall & Cook (2012, p. 271) noted, "*optimal* in-class own-language use." When students all share the same L1, a good deal of time is saved by using their L1 for some definitions, grammatical explanations, directions for a task, or cultural comments. A challenging context in such classes is in pair and group work: students will by nature revert to their L1 occasionally if they can "get away with it."

Classroom Connections

In your own culture, or in a culture that you might teach in some day, what guidelines for L1/L2 use can you think of that would be reasonable and effective in that context? How far would you go in giving explanations or directions in the students' L1 (assuming they all share the same L1)?

Some institutions pride themselves in advertising "direct" use of the target language in their classrooms and you will have to determine how and when such proscriptions should be broken. In "second" language contexts, with multiple languages represented in a single classroom, the issue is not as acute, but even here clusters of students from the same country may engage in native language chatter, and it's up to you to determine how to deal with those possibilities.

Harmer (2001) and Gebhard (2006) offer some guidelines for dealing with issues of whether or not, and when, to use native languages in the classroom. The following is an amalgamation of the two sources:

Guidelines for Using and Not Using L1s in the Classroom

- **Set clear guidelines.** Students need to know when L2 (target language) use is essential, when it is more or less "okay" to use the native language, and when it is counterproductive to use the native language.
- **Explain the value of using the L2.** Negotiate with students on why it is important for them to use the L2 in the classroom. If they understand the importance of practicing the L2, and the reasons for occasional uses of the L1, they will experience the "buy in" necessary for conforming to the negotiated standard.
- **Stimulate intrinsic motivation.** If students use the L2 because they themselves see the value in it, they will be less likely to use their native language. They will view use of the L2 in the classroom as an opportunity for practice and feedback from others.
- **Choose appropriate tasks.** Make sure your students are capable, at their level of the L2, of accomplishing the objectives of activities, and are therefore less tempted to "cheat" by using their native language. Sensitivity to their zone of proximal development (ZPD) (Vygotsky, 1978) will provide just enough challenge without overwhelming them.

- **Create in your classroom an L2 "atmosphere."** Especially in "foreign" language situations, if students are surrounded by posters, magazines, technological aids, software, and other realia that stimulate the use of the L2, they will be more likely to want to speak the L2 in the classroom.

Compromising with the "Institution"

Another adverse circumstance is one that most teachers have to deal with at some time in their careers: teaching under institutional conditions that do not meet their ideal standards or philosophy of education. Sometimes such circumstances focus on an individual in charge, a director or principal. And sometimes they center on administrative constraints that are beyond the scope and power of one individual. Some examples:

- classes that are far too large to allow for the kind of results that the administration expects (see above)
- physical conditions in the classroom that are counterproductive
- administratively imposed constraints on *what* you have to teach in your course (the curriculum, possibly in great detail)
- administratively imposed constraints on *how* you should teach (a specific methodology that you disagree with is required)
- courses that satisfy an institutional foreign language requirement, in which students simply want a passing grade
- courses that are test-focused rather than language-focused

Discipline

Volumes of research and practical advice have been written on the subject of classroom discipline. If all of your students were hard-working, highly motivated, active, dedicated, intelligent learners, discipline issues would be minimal. But the reality is that virtually every classroom atmosphere benefits from a clear understanding of behavior expectations. Without making this section a whole primer on discipline, we'll simply offer some pointers here and let you make the applications to specific instances.

GUIDELINES FOR MAINTAINING CLASSROOM DISCIPLINE

- **Authority.** Learn to be comfortable with your position of authority.
- **Fairness.** Gain the respect of your students by treating them all with equal fairness.

- **Codes of conduct**. Establish clearly and explicitly certain expectations regarding students' behavior in class, or what Harmer (2007, p. 156) calls a "code of conduct." Harmer suggested that if the code is established through negotiation with students, rather than as "rules" that you as the authority insist on, the democratically established code is more effective.
- **Expectations.** Emphasize the importance of conventions for turn-taking, respect for others, listening to other students, attendance issues (tardiness/absence policy), and extra-class obligations.
- **Firmness.** Be firm but warm in dealing with variances to these expectations.
- **Student dignity.** If a reminder, reprimand, or other form of verbal disciplinary action is warranted, do your best to preserve the dignity of the student (in spite of the fact that you may be quite frustrated) and the terms of any negotiated "rules."
- **Decorum.** Try, initially, to resolve disciplinary matters outside of class time (ask to see a student after class and quietly but firmly make your observation and let the student respond), so that valuable class minutes aren't spent focusing on one student.
- **Source of problems.** In resolving disciplinary problems, try to find the source of the problem rather than treating symptoms (for example, if a student isn't paying attention in class, it could be because of a lack of sleep caused by trying to work a late night shift, in which case you could suggest a different shift or a different time bracket for the English class).
- **Institutional support.** If you cannot resolve a recurring disciplinary problem, then consult your institution's counselor or administrator.

Classroom Connections

Suppose one (or two) of your students are disruptive in class. They talk while you're talking, distract other students, and seek attention to themselves with inappropriate gestures and language. What would you do—immediately, and over the long term?

Cheating

Cheating is a special disciplinary matter that warrants careful treatment. For the sake of definition, we will say *cheating* is a surreptitious violation of stated or implicit standards for responding to tests or other exercises.

The first step to solving a perceived problem of cheating is to ascertain a student's own perception: Did he or she honestly believe they were doing something wrong? There is a good deal of cultural variation in defining what is or isn't cheating, and for some, what you may think is cheating is merely an intelligent utilization of resources close at hand. In other words, if the answer that is written on the test is correct, then the means used to come up with the correct answer are justified. Once you have adequately ascertained a student's perception, then follow the disciplinary suggestions as a guide to a solution.

Minimizing opportunities to cheat—that is, prevention—may prove to be more fruitful than trying to tangle with the mixture of emotions that ensue from dealing with cheating after the fact. Why do students cheat? Usually because of pressure to "excel." So if you can lower that pressure (see Chapters 20 and 21), you may reduce the chance that someone will write notes on a fingernail or glance across the aisle. Remind students that you and the test are there to help them and to give them feedback, but if you don't see their "real" selves, you won't be able to help them.

If the classroom size permits, get students spread out as much as possible (this "elbow room" also promotes some physical relaxation). Then, consider an "A" and "B" form of a test in which items are in a different order for every other person, thereby making it more difficult for someone to spot an answer.

All these and even further adverse circumstances are part of the reality of teaching and ultimately of classroom management because they all impinge in some way on what you can do in your lessons. Your handling of such situations will almost always demand some sort of compromise on your part. You must, as a professional "technician" in this field, be ready to bring professional diplomacy and efficiency to bear on the varying degrees of hardship.

Classroom Connections

Consider the culture in which you are teaching, or another culture in which you may find yourself someday. Imagine a situation in which a student (whose past performance has been quite poor) has apparently copied answers on a test from another student (who is an "A" student) who was sitting in the next seat. What series of steps would you take to handle this situation?

One particularly thorny problem that is often categorized as cheating is *plagiarism*, copying another source in one's own essay without giving credit to the source. This issue is fraught with a variety of cultural norms, ranging from complete acceptability to forbidden practice. The best way to address this is to make it crystal clear to students what your expectations are, and to demonstrate those with illustrations of quotations and citations.

TEACHERS' ROLES AND STYLES

In these final sections on classroom management, we turn a little more centrally to the affective or emotional side of being and becoming a good teacher.

Roles

A teacher has to play many **roles**, as was pointed out in Chapter 13. Think of the possibilities: authority figure, leader, knower, director, manager, counselor, guide, and even such roles as friend, confidante, and parent. Depending on the country you are in, on the institution in which you are teaching, on the type of course, and on the makeup of your students, some of these roles will be more prominent than others, especially in the eyes of your students.

For growing comfortable and confident in playing multiple roles, two rules of thumb are to willingly accept the many ways that students will perceive you, and to be consistently fair to all students equally. Know yourself, your limitations, your strengths, your likes and dislikes, and then accept the fact that you are called upon to be many things to many different people. Then, as you become more comfortable with, say, being an authority figure, be consistent in all your dealings with students. There is something quite unsettling about a teacher who is a sympathetic friend to some students and a dispassionate authority figure to others. Such waffling in playing out your roles can set students against each other, with many feeling shut out from an inner circle of "teacher's pets."

Teaching Styles

Your **teaching style** is another affective consideration in the development of your professional expertise. Teaching style will almost always be consistent with your personality style, which can vary greatly from individual to individual. As you consider the teaching styles below, remember that each represents a continuum of possibilities:

Teaching Style Continua

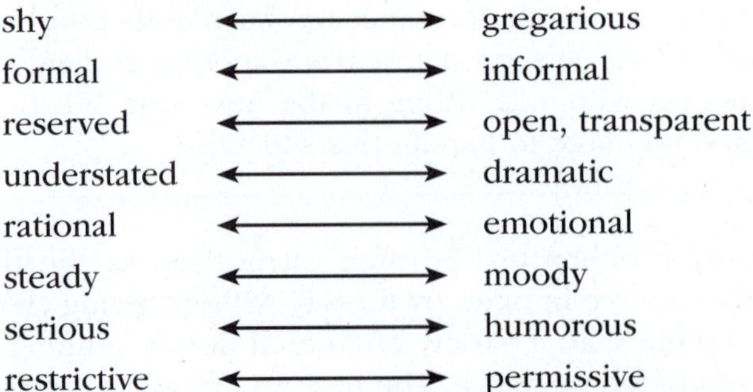

shy ⟷ gregarious
formal ⟷ informal
reserved ⟷ open, transparent
understated ⟷ dramatic
rational ⟷ emotional
steady ⟷ moody
serious ⟷ humorous
restrictive ⟷ permissive

Classroom Connections

Where do you place your*self* on these continua? Do you feel it is necessary to lean toward one end in order to be an effective teacher? In what ways might you describe yourself as somewhere in between each end of a continuum? In each case, consider any styles that you think you should change in order to be an effective teacher.

We have seen excellent teachers on both ends of these style continua. As you grow more comfortable with your teaching roles in the classroom, make sure your style of teaching is also consistent with the rest of you and with the way you feel you can be most *genuine* in the classroom; then, learn how to capitalize on the strengths of your teaching style. It's generally not very wise to force yourself into a stereotype that doesn't jibe with your most effective "self" in the classroom.

Cultural Expectations

Western cultures emphasize nondirective, nonauthoritarian roles and teaching styles in the right-hand column in the list above. One major consideration, therefore, in the effectiveness of playing roles and developing styles is the culture in which you are teaching and the culture of your students.

Listed in Table 14.1 are a number of cultural expectations of roles and styles as they relate to teachers and students and schools (adapted from Hofstede, 1986).

Table 14.1 Contrasting cultural expectations of teacher and student roles (Adapted from Hofstede, 1986)

• Teachers are expected to have all the answers.	• Teachers are allowed to say "I don't know."
• Teachers are expected to suppress emotions (and so are students).	• Teachers are allowed to express emotions (and so are students).
• Teachers interpret intellectual disagreement as personal disloyalty.	• Teachers interpret intellectual disagreement as a stimulating exercise.
• Teachers reward students for accuracy in problem solving.	• Teachers reward students for innovative approaches to problem solving.
• Students admire brilliance in teachers.	• Students admire friendliness in teachers.
• Students should speak in class only when called on by the teacher.	• Students are encouraged to volunteer their thoughts.
• Teachers should never lose face; to do so loses the respect of students.	• Teachers can admit when they are wrong and still maintain students' respect.
• Students expect the teacher to show them "the way."	• Teachers expect students to find their own way through self-discovery.

CLASSROOM CONNECTIONS

On which side of these opposites do you place your own philosophy of teaching? Are you "in between" on some factors? How would you deal with a situation in which your philosophy is quite different from that of your colleagues and students? Would you try to change your own philosophy, or that of your colleagues and students? If so, how would you accomplish that? If not, how would you reconcile the differences?

Wherever you find yourself teaching, the above forces will come into play as you attempt to be an effective teacher. If you feel that one column is more "you" than the other, then you should be cautious in developing a relationship with students and colleagues who may come from a different tradition. Always be sensitive to the perceptions of others, but then do what you feel is appropriate to gracefully negotiate changes in attitude. Be ready to compromise your ideal self to some extent, especially when you begin a teaching assignment. There is little to be gained by coming into a teaching post and alienating those around you. If you have convictions about what good teaching is, it pays to be patient in slowly reaching your goals. After all, you might learn something from *them*!

CREATING A POSITIVE CLASSROOM CLIMATE

The roles you play and the styles you develop will merge to give you some tools for creating a classroom climate that is positive, stimulating, and energizing.

Establish Rapport

Rapport is a somewhat slippery but important concept in creating positive energy in the classroom. Rapport is the relationship or connection you establish with your students, a relationship built on trust and respect that leads to students' feeling capable, competent, and creative. How do you set up such a connection? Consider the following guidelines:

STRATEGIES FOR ESTABLISHING RAPPORT

- Show interest in each student as a person.
- Give feedback on each person's progress.
- Openly solicit students' ideas and feelings.
- Value and respect what students think and say.

- Laugh with them and not at them.
- Work *with* them as a team, and not *against* them.
- Develop a genuine sense of vicarious joy when they learn something or otherwise succeed.

Balance Praise and Criticism

Part of the rapport you create is based on the delicate balance that you set between praise and criticism. Too much of either renders it less and less effective. Genuine praise, appropriately delivered, enables students to welcome criticism and to put it to use. Table 14.2 shows the contrast between effective praise and ineffective praise.

CLASSROOM CONNECTIONS

In an L2 class that you have taken, or one that you have taught, how was praise conveyed to students? How effective were various means of praising? How effective is a teacher's constant (but possibly mechanical) saying "good!" and "great!" to students? What are some alternatives to these generic and possibly overused words?

Table 14.2 Effective praise versus ineffective praise (adapted from Brophy 1981)

Effective Praise	Ineffective Praise
• shows genuine pleasure and concern	• is impersonal, mechanical, and "robotic"
• shows verbal and nonverbal variety	• shows bland uniformity
• specifies the particulars of an accomplishment, so students know exactly what was performed well	• is restricted to global comments, so students are not sure what was performed well
• is offered in recognition of noteworthy effort on difficult tasks	• is offered equally strongly for easy and difficult tasks
• attributes success to effort, implying that similar success can be expected in the future	• attributes success to ability, luck, or other external factors
• fosters intrinsic motivation to continue to pursue goals	• fosters extrinsic motivation to perform only to receive more praise
• is delivered without disrupting the communicative flow of ongoing interaction	• disrupts the communicative flow of ongoing interaction

Generate Energy

What is classroom "energy"? In some ways it's a force unleashed in a classroom, perhaps perceivable only through a "sixth sense," that's acquired in the experience of teaching itself. Energy is what you react to when you walk out of a class period and say to yourself, "Wow! That was a great class!" or "What a great group of students!" Energy is the electricity of many minds caught up in a cycle of thinking and talking and writing. Energy is an aura of creativity sparked by the interaction of students. Energy drives students toward higher engagement and participation (Wright, 2005). Students (and teachers) take energy with them when they leave the classroom and bring it back the next day.

How do you create this energy? Not necessarily by being dramatic or flamboyant, witty, or wise. Sometimes energy is unleashed through a quiet, reserved, but focused teacher. Sometimes energy forces gather in the communal intensity of students focused on possibly mundane tasks. We have found in our teaching that *interaction* and *collaboration* are keys to energy building—*engaged* students, whether in whole-class or small group settings—are often key ingredients.

But *you* are the key. Because students initially look to you for leadership and guidance, you are the one to begin to get the creative sparks flying. And by whatever means you accomplish this, you do so through solid preparation, confidence in your ability to teach, a genuinely positive belief in your students' ability to learn, and a sense of joy in doing what you do.

Classroom Connections

Think of some specific means of creating or nurturing energy in a classroom. What is it that you *say* (verbally) or *do* (nonverbally), or how do students intrinsically generate their own energy? How do you *build* energy through a class period?

Perhaps the art and the science of teaching converge on issues of classroom management. On the one hand, a good deal of the process of maintaining pace, rhythm, and energy in a class hour requires the artistic brush strokes of intuitive moment-by-moment decisions. When you have a classroom full of individuals with particular needs and moods and motivations, it's virtually impossible to predict everything that those individuals will do or say.

But on the other hand, your intuitions are informed by the collective experience and best practices of those who have gone before you in the form of guidelines and parameters for successful management. By combining those well-tested principles with your personal intuition, you can enter the non-predictabilities of the classroom arena with confidence and creativity.

FOR THE TEACHER: ACTIVITIES (A) & DISCUSSION (D)

Note: For each of the "Classroom Connections" in this chapter, you may wish to turn them into individual or pair-work discussion questions.

1. **(D)** Ask members of the class to volunteer stories about classes they have been in (or taught) where (a) something went wrong with the physical environment of the classroom, (b) some kind of unplanned or embarrassing moment occurred, or (c) some form of adverse circumstance took place. What did the teacher do? What *should* the teacher have done? Ask your students to brainstorm possible solutions.
2. **(A)** Consider some of the customary seating arrangements used in classrooms. Here are a few:

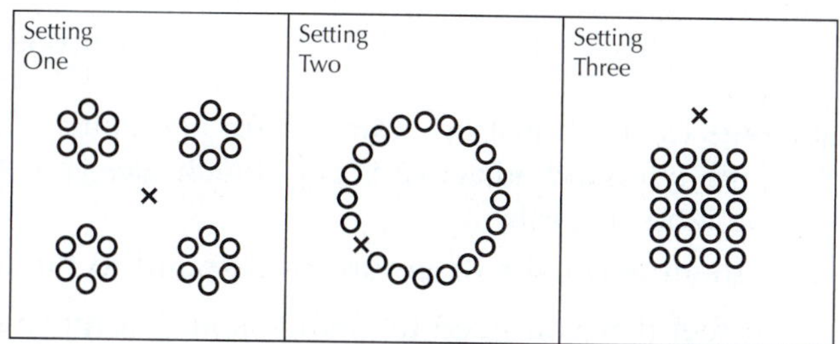

O = Student location × = Teacher location

Now, ask pairs to quickly brainstorm *other* seating arrangements that might work, and draw them on the board. Then have the whole class discuss the pros and cons of the suggestions from the point of view of classroom management.

3. **(A)** Assign different groups to (a) large-class issues and (b) multiple-proficiency issues. Direct them to look at the lists of suggested solutions, and to evaluate the extent to which the solutions are practical. Do they apply to actual classes that someone is familiar with? What further measures can be taken to maximize student learning in each of the two circumstances?
4. **(A)** Divide the class into groups of about four students each. Ask them to brainstorm solutions to the following situation, then report back to the rest of the class. What would they do? How would they—without losing their job—resolve the difference between what they believe students need and the demands of the director?

You have been assigned to teach English in a private language institute for adults in _____. The director insists that students will learn best through the Grammar Translation Method, mainly because that's the way he learned three foreign languages. He has in no uncertain terms demanded that you use this method, and the textbooks for the course are a grammar reference guide and a book of readings with vocabulary words listed at the end of each reading. Your class is a group of intermediate level young adults, all currently employed in various places around the city. They want to learn English in order to travel to English-speaking countries and read English on Internet-based media.

5. **(D)** Discuss the following questions with your class: What is cheating? How is it defined in various cultures? Has a classmate ever tried to cheat in a class in which you have been a student? What did the teacher do, if anything? What would you have done had you been the teacher?
6. **(A)** Ask your students to rate themselves on the continua of teacher styles on page 304. Use four categories in between the extreme of each factor for their rating by designing a chart something like this:

   shy 1 2 3 4 gregarious

   Direct students to check just one number for each pair of adjectives. Check #1 if the left-hand adjective is *very* much like you, #2 if it *somewhat* describes you, and so forth.

   Then, place them into pairs or groups to respond to the following:

   a. Do you feel that you need to change some of those natural styles when you enter a classroom?
   b. If not, why do you feel that your present styles are adequate?
   c. Are there any tendencies that might work against you?
   d. What should you do to prevent such a problem?

   Ask selected pairs/groups to share their findings.
7. **(A)** Arrange groups preferably with heterogeneous representations of people who are from or have knowledge of varied cultures. Consider the society your students are *now* in, and ask them to address the following questions:

   a. Where does that society fall on the list of continua describing cultural expectations of students?
   b. Would you add any other expectations to the list?
   c. Consider each factor and discuss specific ways in which you would deal with a conflict of expectations between your students and yourself.

   Ask selected pairs/groups to share their findings.
8. **(D)** Ask students in the class to volunteer, in their own words, a description of classroom "energy." Write the concepts on the board and ask the class to identify actions, techniques, tasks, or words of the teacher or the students that might help to "energize" the class.

FOR YOUR FURTHER READING

Scrivener, J. (2012). *Classroom management techniques.* Cambridge, UK: Cambridge University Press.

Underwood, M. (1991). *Effective class management.* London, UK: Longman.

Both of these practically oriented books provide details of classroom management issues in a number of categories, ranging from the physical environment of the classroom, to teacher roles, to discipline.

Bell, J. (2012). Teaching mixed level classes. In A. Burns & J. Richards (Eds.), *The Cambridge guide to pedagogy and practice in second language teaching* (pp. 86–94). Cambridge, UK: Cambridge University Press.

Shamim, F. (2012). Teaching large classes. In A. Burns & J. Richards (Eds.), *The Cambridge guide to pedagogy and practice in second language teaching* (pp. 95–102). Cambridge, UK: Cambridge University Press.

The two chapters in the same anthology offer practical guidelines on two common classroom management issues: missed level classes and large classes.

Wright, T. (2005). *Classroom management in language education.* New York, NY: Palgrave Macmillan.

A unique perspective is offered here in looking at the dimensions of time, space, engagement, and participation as key elements in managing language classrooms.

Marzano, R., & Marzano, J. (2003). The key to classroom management. *Educational Leadership, 61,* 6–13.

This article gives a concise set of guidelines for classroom management that may apply to any classroom context, not just L2 teaching. Specific suggestions are made for students with "special needs."

PART **IV**

TEACHING LANGUAGE SKILLS

It is crucial to recognize that by attending to the four skills in four separate chapters we are nevertheless strongly advocating the teaching of skills as *integrated and related modes of communication.* In most contexts of human communication we do not separate the skills, and it's clear that the activation of one skill (listening, for example) can be readily reinforced by the use of another skill (speaking, reading, and/or writing).

That being said, for practical purposes, Part IV systematically analyzes the unique factors and guidelines involved in teaching *each* of the four skills of listening, speaking, reading, and writing, respectively. The final chapter of this section examines the teaching of grammar and vocabulary. After all, the four skills inherently involve structure (grammar) and lexical items (vocabulary), along with lexicogrammar (the manner in which lexical items—words—convey grammatical structure and meaning), and discourse.

- **Chapter 15, Teaching Listening,** begins with some comments on the importance of integrating skills, then offers principles, issues, practical techniques, and assessment guidelines for teaching listening comprehension.
- **Chapter 16, Teaching Speaking,** follows much the same organization, with some guidelines ranging from pronunciation to conversation, and a section on treatment of speech errors.
- **Chapter 17, Teaching Reading,** follows a similar breakdown of both principles and practical techniques.
- **Chapter 18, Teaching Writing,** matches the previous three chapters in its balance of principles and practical classroom activities and tasks.
- **Chapter 19, Teaching Grammar and Vocabulary,** has been updated to include recent findings on approaches to incorporating *form-focused instruction* into L2 classes.

CHAPTER 15

TEACHING LISTENING

Questions for Reflection

- Why is the *integration* of two or more skills important in language pedagogy?
- What are the key issues and concepts in pedagogical research that are related to teaching listening comprehension?
- What makes listening difficult for students?
- How can language be classified into *types* of spoken language? And into micro- and macroskills? And what do learners "do" to perform listening?
- How can one design effective, principled techniques for teaching listening? How does one apply those principles to observing—and learning from—others' teaching?
- What are the basic principles and methods for assessing listening comprehension?

> Three people are on a train in England. As they approach what appears to be Wembley Station, one of the travelers says,"Is this Wembley?" "No," replies a second passenger, "it's Thursday." Whereupon the third person remarks,"Oh, I am too; let's have a drink!"

This little joke is an illustration of the importance of listening—or in this case *hearing*! Through reception, we internalize linguistic information without which we could not produce language. In classrooms, students always do more listening than speaking. Listening competence is universally "larger" than speaking competence. Is it any wonder, then, that in recent years the language-teaching profession has placed a concerted emphasis on listening comprehension?

Listening comprehension has not always drawn the attention of educators to the extent that it now has. Perhaps human beings have a natural tendency to look at speaking as the major index of language proficiency. Consider, for example, our commonly used query, "Do you speak Japanese?" Of course we don't mean to exclude comprehension when we say that, but when we think of L2 learning, we tend first to think of speaking. In the decades of the 1950s and 1960s, language teaching methodology was preoccupied with the spoken language, and classrooms full of students could be heard performing their oral drills. It was not uncommon for students to practice phrases orally they didn't even understand!

Recent decades have seen a welcome change in emphasis on the oral. We now understand that words and sentences carefully and slowly pronounced for classroom learners is *not* the real world. The latter, which students in classrooms must be ready to face, is "being able to identify words in the *acoustic blur* or normal conversational speech" (G. Brown, 2010, p. 157). This continues to be our current challenge, magnified by our awareness of the importance of context, culture, discourse, community, and other sociolinguistic variables.

INTEGRATING THE FOUR SKILLS

Before launching into a treatment of teaching listening, let's first make it crystal clear that the four skills are rarely if ever encountered as discrete skills, inseparable from the others. Listening frequently implies speaking, and in academic contexts possibly note-taking; speaking virtually always implies a listener; writing and reading are share obvious links; and the interconnections go on.

In L2 classrooms, we'll often find the following instances of integration:

- a pre-*reading discussion* of a topic to activate schemata, followed by either a *reading* or a *writing* task
- *listening* to a *spoken* lecture or monologue, accompanied by *note-taking* and followed by a *discussion*
- *writing* a response to a *reading* passage

 **CLASSROOM CONNECTIONS**

What other instances of the integration of at least two skills can you think of? How might that integration lead to reinforcing both (or all) the skills in question? Are there any disadvantages to such integration?

Does the integration of the four skills diminish the importance of the fundamentals of listening, speaking, reading, and writing? Not at all. If anything, the added richness of integration gives students greater motivation that converts to better retention of principles of effective speaking, listening, reading, and writing. And such integration can still utilize a strong, principled approach to the separate, unique characteristics of each skill.

You may be wondering why courses weren't always integrated in the first place. There are several reasons. In the pre-CLT era, the focus on the *forms* of language almost predisposed curriculum designers to segment courses into the separate language skills. Further, administrative considerations made it easier to program separate skills courses. And finally, certain languages for specific purposes (LSP) courses may still best be labeled by one of the four skills, especially at the high intermediate to advanced levels.

The integration of at least two of more skills is now the typical approach within a communicative, interactive framework. As Hinkel (2006, p. 113) noted, "In an age of globalization, pragmatic objectives of language learning place an increased value on *integrated and dynamic multiskill* instructional models with a focus on meaningful communication and the development of learners' communicative competence." The following observations support such models.

Advantages of Integrating Two or More Skills

1. Production and reception are two sides of the same coin.
2. Interaction involves sending *and* receiving messages.
3. By attending primarily to what learners can *do* with language, we invite any or all of the four skills that are relevant into the classroom arena.
4. One skill will often reinforce another.
5. Most of our natural language performance entails connections between language and the way we think and feel and act.

LISTENING COMPREHENSION IN PEDAGOGICAL RESEARCH

Now, bearing in mind the importance of the integration of skills, for the sake of simplicity we'll look at the four skills separately in the next four chapters. We return to our focus on listening.

A Historical Sketch

Listening as a major component in language learning and teaching first hit the spotlight in the late 1970s with James Asher's (1977) work on Total Physical Response (see Chapter 2). In TPR the role of comprehension was given prominence as learners were given great quantities of language to listen to before they were encouraged to respond orally. Similarly, the Natural Approach (again see Chapter 2) recommended a significant "silent period" during which learners were allowed the security of listening without being forced to go through the anxiety of speaking before they were "ready" to do so.

Such approaches were an outgrowth of a variety of research studies that showed evidence of the importance of input in second language acquisition (see *PLLT*, Chapters 9 & 10). Krashen (1985), for example, stressed the significance of comprehensible input, or the aural reception of language that is just a little beyond the learner's present ability.

About the same time, researchers were also discovering the significance of what learners actually *did* with input, perhaps through *noticing* certain features of language, but ultimately internalizing those elements in their long-term competence (Gor & Long, 2009; Goh, 2014). You can be "exposed" to great quantities of language, but what counts is the linguistic information that you ultimately glean from that exposure through conscious and subconscious attention, through cognitive strategies of retention, through feedback, and through interaction.

Classroom Connections

In your own learning of an L2, think of examples of your receiving input from your teacher (or from video or audio media) that you were not able to convert into your long-term competence. For example, let's say you experienced an activity on the past tense, then a few minutes later made mistakes on what you had just practiced. What were the reasons for your not being able to convert auditory input into long-term competence? How can you help your students to better *notice* and retain such information?

Meanwhile, pedagogical research on listening comprehension made significant refinements in the process of listening. Studies looked at the effect of a number of different contextual characteristics and how they affect the speed and efficiency of processing aural language. Rubin (1994) identified five such factors: text, interlocutor, task, listener, and process characteristics. In each case, important elements of the listening process were identified. For example, the listener characteristics of proficiency, memory, attention, affect, age, gender, background schemata, and even learning disabilities in the L1 all affect the process of listening (pp. 206–10).

In other research, attention was given to types of meaning involved in the act of comprehending language (Flowerdew & Miller, 2005). In this perspective, phonological, syntactic, semantic, and pragmatic knowledge are considered, along with nonverbal elements involved in most real-world (face-to-face) listening. Other studies have looked at the extent to which *first* language listening ability contributes to one's performance of second language listening, with the interesting suggestion by Vandergrift (2013) that if you're a good listener in your L1, you stand a good chance of doing well in L2 listening tasks.

Classroom Connections

What are the attributes of a "good" listener? Think about a range of elements—from phonological, to pragmatic, to contextual. In light of those factors, do you think good listeners in their L1 tend to also be successful listeners in an L2? If the presumed correspondence is not always true, what elements, if any, of listening in one's L1 might *not* carry over to the L2?

Research has also examined the role of strategic factors and of strategies-based instruction in listening comprehension (Mendelsohn, 1998; Vandergrift, 2003, 2004, 2013; Flowerdew & Miller, 2005; Rost, 2005; Hinkel, 2006). Studies tend to agree that listening, especially for academic and professional contexts, is a highly refined skill that requires a learner's attention to a battery of strategies for extracting meaning from texts (Flowerdew, 1994).

Myths and Pedagogical Objectives

All this research has helped to expose some important myths about listening, misconceptions that "have sprung up and influenced the way listening is taught" (Richards & Burns, 2012, p. ix). Let's briefly look at these misconceptions at the outset (adapted from Richards & Burns, 2012, and S. Brown, 2011):

Misconceptions about Teaching Listening

- Listening is a "passive" skill.
- Listening is a "one-way" process.
- Listening is an individual process.
- Listening skills are acquired subconsciously—students just "absorb" them.
- Listening equals comprehension.
- Listening and speaking should be taught separately.

As you read on in this chapter, you will discover why all these statements (which have at one time or another been claimed to be true) are indeed myths. We will look at how students can be active learners, combine listening performance with other skills, collaborate with other students in listening comprehension tasks, and ultimately improve their overall competence in the L2 through listening.

Classroom Connections

In each of the six myths above, why do you suppose they are believed by some to be true? In arguing against their authenticity, what principles or guidelines emerge in each case? For example, in the first myth, how can you make listening an *active* skill in the classroom?

Here are some specific objectives we will address in this chapter on teaching listening comprehension:

Pedagogical Questions about Teaching Listening

- What are listeners "doing" when they listen?
- What factors affect good listening?
- What are the characteristics of "real-life" listening?
- What are the many things listeners listen for?
- What are some principles for designing listening techniques?
- How can listening techniques be interactive?
- What are some common techniques for teaching listening?

AN INTERACTIVE MODEL OF LISTENING COMPREHENSION

Listening is not a "one-way street." It is not merely the process of a unidirectional receiving of audible symbols. One facet—the first step—of listening comprehension is the psychomotor process of receiving sound waves through the ear and transmitting nerve impulses to the brain. But that's just the beginning of what is clearly an interactive process as the brain acts on the impulses, bringing to bear a number of different cognitive and affective mechanisms.

The following seven processes—adapted from Clark and Clark (1977) and Richards (1983)—are all involved in comprehension. With the exception of the initial and final processes below, no sequence is implied here; they all occur if not simultaneously, then in extremely rapid succession. Neurological time must be viewed in terms of microseconds.

Listening Comprehension Processes

1. Decoding auditory sounds
2. Determining the function of the speech event
3. Activating schemata
4. Assigning literal meanings
5. Assigning intended meaning
6. Determining the demand for short- or long-term memory
7. Retaining essential information or meanings

Let's look at these seven processes in detail.

1. The hearer processes what we'll call "raw speech" and holds an "image" of it in short-term memory. This image consists of the constituents (phrases, clauses, cohesive markers, intonation, and stress patterns) of a stream of speech.

2. The hearer determines the type of speech event being processed (for example, a conversation, a speech, a radio broadcast) and then appropriately "colors" the interpretation of the perceived message. By attending to context and the content, for example, one determines whether the speaker wishes to persuade, request, exchange pleasantries, affirm, deny, inform, and so forth. Thus the *function* of the message is inferred.
3. The hearer recalls background information (or **schemata**; see Chapter 18 for more on this topic) relevant to the particular context and subject matter. A lifetime of experiences and knowledge is used to perform cognitive associations in order to bring a plausible interpretation to the message.

 **CLASSROOM CONNECTIONS**

Imagine you are about to present a short five-minute video to your intermediate level class on the topic of the top five recommended sights to see in your city. What might you do for about five or ten minutes to prepare the students for the video—to *pre-teach* the listening process? Use these first three processes to guide your thoughts.

4. The hearer assigns a *literal* meaning to the utterance, a process that involves semantic interpretation. In many instances, literal and intended (see item 5) meanings match. So, for example, suppose one of your students walks into your office while you are very busy with something and says she has a question for you, then says, "Do you have the time?" You might answer "yes" to the presumed literal meaning of the question. But then let's say a stranger sitting beside you on a bus looks at you and says, "Do you have the time?" Your appropriate response is not "yes" or "no" but rather "It's quarter to nine," which is appropriate for the metaphorical meaning of the question.
5. The hearer assigns an *intended* meaning to the utterance. The person on the bus intended to find out what time of day it was, even though the literal meaning didn't directly convey that message. How often do misunderstandings stem from incorrect assumptions that are made on the hearer's part about the intended meaning of the speaker? Such breakdowns can be caused by careless speech, inattention of the hearer, conceptual complexity, contextual miscues, psychological barriers, and a host of other performance variables.
6. The hearer determines whether information should be retained in *short-term* or *long-term* memory. Short-term memory—a matter of a few seconds—is appropriate in contexts that call for a quick oral response from the hearer. Long-term memory is more common when, say, you are processing information in a lecture. There are, of course, many points in between.

7. The hearer deletes the form in which the message was originally received. Exact words, phrases, and sentences in normal speech acts are quickly forgotten, "pruned" of cognitive "clutter." Instead, the important information, if any (see item 6 above), is retained conceptually. (See also *PLLT*, Chapter 4.)

CLASSROOM CONNECTIONS

In the video referred to in the above "classroom connections," what could you do *after* showing the video to help students to retain information in their long-term memory? Use points 6 and 7 above to guide your thinking.

It should be clear from the foregoing that listening comprehension is certainly an *active* undertaking (Goh, 2014), but more importantly an *interactive* process. After the initial reception of sound, we human beings perform at least six other major operations on that set of sound waves. In conversational settings, of course, further interaction takes place immediately after the listening stage as the hearer becomes speaker in a response of some kind.

All of these processes are important for you to keep in mind as you teach. They are all relevant to a learner's purpose for listening, to performance factors that may cause difficulty in processing speech, to overall principles of effective listening techniques, and to the choices you make of what techniques to use and when to use them in your classroom.

TYPES OF SPOKEN LANGUAGE

Much of our language-teaching energy is devoted to instruction in mastering English conversation. However, other forms of spoken language are also important to incorporate into a language course, especially in teaching listening comprehension. As you plan lessons or curricula, some simple categories (Nunan, 1991b) will guide your thinking:

Types of Spoken Language

A. Monologues

1. Planned/rehearsed/spoken from a written text or notes
2. Spontaneous/impromptu/unplanned

B. Dialogues

1. Interpersonal/social/conversational
2. Transactional/informational/factual

In monologues, when one speaker uses spoken language for any length of time, as in speeches, lectures, readings, news broadcasts, and the like, the hearer must process long stretches of speech without interruption—the stream of speech will go on whether or not the hearer comprehends. Planned as opposed to spontaneous monologues differ considerably in their discourse structures. Planned monologues (such as speeches and other prewritten material) usually manifest little redundancy and are therefore relatively difficult to comprehend. Spontaneous monologues (impromptu lectures and long "stories" in conversations, for example) exhibit more redundancy, which makes for ease in comprehension, but the presence of more performance variables and other hesitations (see below) can either help or hinder comprehension.

Dialogues involve two or more speakers and can be subdivided into those exchanges that promote social relationships (**interpersonal**) and those for which the purpose is to convey propositional or factual information (**transactional**). In each case, participants may have a good deal of shared knowledge (background information, schemata); therefore, the *familiarity* of the interlocutors will produce conversations with more assumptions, implications, and other meanings hidden between the lines. In conversations between or among participants who are *unfamiliar* with each other, references and meanings have to be made more explicit to assure effective comprehension. When such references are not explicit, misunderstandings can easily follow.

One could also have subdivided dialogues between those in which the hearer is a participant and those in which the hearer is an "eavesdropper." In both cases, the above conversational descriptions apply, but the major—and highly significant—difference is that in the latter the hearer is, as in monologues, unable to interrupt or otherwise participate vocally in the negotiation of meaning.

Classroom Connections

In interpersonal or transactional dialogues, what are some specific ways in which language forms and discourse differ, depending on whether the dialogue is among *familiar* or *unfamiliar* participants? Can you think of how *assumptions* about one's audience are manifested in language? How would you teach some of those examples?

Remember that in all cases these categories are really not discrete, mutually exclusive domains; rather, each dichotomy, as usual, represents a continuum of possibilities. For example, everyday social conversations can easily contain elements of transactional dialogues, and vice versa. Similarly, "familiar" participants may share very little common knowledge on a particular topic. If each category, then, is viewed as an end point, you can aim your teaching at appropriate ranges in between.

WHAT MAKES LISTENING DIFFICULT?

As you contemplate designing lessons and techniques for teaching listening skills, or that have listening components in them, a number of special characteristics of spoken language need to be taken into consideration. Second language learners need to pay special attention to such factors because they strongly influence the processing of speech, and can even block comprehension if they are not attended to. In other words, they can make the listening process difficult. The following eight characteristics of spoken language are adapted from several sources (Richards, 1983; Ur, 1984; Dunkel, 1991; Flowerdew & Miller, 2005).

1. Clustering

In written language we are conditioned to attend to the sentence as the basic unit of organization. In spoken language, due to memory limitations and our predisposition for "chunking," or clustering, we break down speech into smaller groups of words. Clauses are common constituents, but phrases within clauses are even more easily retained for comprehension. In teaching listening comprehension, therefore, you need to help students to pick out manageable clusters of words; sometimes second language learners will try to retain overly long constituents (a whole sentence or even several sentences), or they will err in the other direction in trying to attend to every word in an utterance.

2. Redundancy

Spoken language, unlike most written language, has a good deal of redundancy. The next time you're in a conversation, notice the rephrasings, repetitions, elaborations, and little insertions of "I mean" and "you know." Such redundancy helps the hearer to process meaning by offering more time and extra information. Learners can train themselves to profit from such redundancy by first becoming aware that not very new sentence or phrase will necessarily contain new information and by looking for the signals of redundancy. Consider the following excerpt of a conversation.

Jeff: Hey, Matt, how's it going?

Matt: Pretty good, Jeff. How was your weekend?

Jeff: Aw, it was terrible, I mean the worst you could imagine. You know what I mean?

Matt: Yeah, I've had those days. Well, like what happened?

Jeff: Well, you're not gonna believe this, but my girlfriend and I—you know Rachel? I think you met her at my party—anyway, she and I drove up to Point Reyes, you know, up in Marin County? So we were driving along minding our own business, you know, when this dude in one of those big ugly SUVs, you know, like a Hummer or something, comes up like three feet behind us and like tailgates us on these crazy mountain roads up there—you know what they're like. So, he's about to run me off the road, and it's all I can do to just concentrate. Then . . .

You can easily pick out quite a few redundancies in Jeff's recounting of his experience. Learners might initially get confused by this, but with some training, they can learn to take advantage of redundancies as well as other markers that provide more processing time.

3. Reduced Forms

While spoken language does indeed contain a good deal of redundancy, it also has many reduced forms and sentence fragments. Reduction can be phonological ("Djeetyet?" for "Did you eat yet?"), morphological (contractions like "I'll"), syntactic (elliptical forms like "When will you be back?" "Tomorrow, maybe."), or pragmatic (phone rings in a house, child answers and yells to another room in the house, "Mom! Phone!"). These reductions pose significant difficulties, especially for classroom learners who may have initially been exposed to the full forms of the English language.

4. Performance Variables

In spoken language, except for planned discourse (speeches, lectures, etc.), hesitations, false starts, pauses, and corrections are common. Native listeners are conditioned from very young ages to weed out such performance variables, whereas they can easily interfere with comprehension in second language learners. Imagine listening to the following verbatim excerpt of a sportsman talking about his game:

> But, uh—I also—to go with this of course if you're playing well—if you're playing well then you get uptight about your game. You get keyed up and it's easy to concentrate. You know you're playing well and you know . . . in with a chance then it's easier, much easier to—to you know get in there and—and start to . . . you don't have to think about it. I mean it's gotta be automatic.

In written form this looks like gibberish, but it's the kind of language we hear and process all the time. Learners have to train themselves to listen for meaning in the midst of distracting performance variables.

Everyday casual speech by native speakers also commonly contains ungrammatical forms. Some of these forms are simple performance slips. For example, "We arrived in a little town that there was no hotel anywhere" is something a native speaker could easily self-correct. Other ungrammaticality arises out of dialect differences ("I don't get no respect") that second language learners are likely to hear sooner or later.

5. Colloquial Language

Learners who have been exposed to standard written English and/or "textbook" language sometimes find it surprising and difficult to deal with colloquial language. Idioms, slang, reduced forms, and shared cultural knowledge are all manifested at some point in conversations. Colloquialisms appear in both monologues and dialogues. Contractions and other assimilations often pose difficulty for the learner of English.

6. Rate of Delivery

Virtually every language learner initially thinks that native speakers speak too fast! Actually, as Jack Richards (1983) points out, the number and length of pauses used by a speaker is more crucial to comprehension than sheer speed. Learners will nevertheless eventually need to be able to comprehend language delivered at varying rates of speed and, at times, delivered with few pauses. Unlike reading, where a person can stop and go back to reread, in listening the hearer may not always have the opportunity to stop the speaker. Instead, the stream of speech will continue to flow!

7. Stress, Rhythm, and Intonation

The prosodic features of the English language are very important for comprehension. Because English is a stress-timed language, English speech can be a terror for some learners as mouthfuls of syllables come spilling out between stress points. The sentence "The PREsident is INTerested in eLIMinating the emBARgo," with four stressed syllables out of eighteen, theoretically takes about the same amount of time to utter as "Dead men wear plaid." Also, intonation patterns are very significant (see Chapter 16) not just for interpreting straightforward elements such as questions, statements, and emphasis but for understanding more subtle messages like sarcasm, endearment, insult, solicitation, or praise.

8. Interaction

Unless a language learner's objective is exclusively to master some specialized skill like monitoring radio broadcasts or attending lectures, interaction will play a large role in listening comprehension. Conversation is especially subject to all the rules of interaction: negotiation, clarification, attending signals, turn-taking, and topic nomination, maintenance, and termination (see Chapter 8 of *PLLT*). So, to learn to listen is also to learn to respond and to continue a chain of listening and responding. Classroom techniques that include listening components must at some point include instruction in the two-way nature of listening. Students need to understand that good listeners (in conversation) are good responders. They know how to negotiate meaning (to give feedback, to ask for clarification, to maintain a topic) so that the process of comprehending can be complete rather than being aborted by insufficient interaction.

 **Classroom Connections**

In your own learning of an L2, which of these eight factors were the most challenging for you? For those most challenging areas, what, if anything, did your teacher do to help you to meet the challenge? What might you do in your teaching to help students to overcome these same difficulties?

A fourth-century Chinese proverb says it eloquently:

Not to let a word get in the way of its sentence
Nor to let a sentence get in the way of its intention,
But to send your mind out to meet the intention as a guest;
THAT is understanding.

MICROSKILLS AND MACROSKILLS OF LISTENING

In his seminal article on teaching listening skills, Jack Richards (1983) provided a comprehensive taxonomy of aural skills, which he called **microskills**, involved in conversational discourse. We have adapted Richards's original microskills into a list of micro- and **macroskills**, the latter to designate skills that are technically at the *discourse* level. The former pertain to skills at the *sentence* level. Such lists are useful in helping you to break down just what it is that your learners need to actually *perform* as they acquire effective listening strategies.

One might easily assume that micro- and macroskills are synonymous with *bottom-up* and *top-down processing* (the latter to be discussed later in this chapter). However, it is conceivable that teaching some sentence-level microskills might involve a top-down approach. For example, suppose you are teaching stress patterns or intonation (microskill #3), you might easily adopt a top-down approach in which you ask students to simply listen to a stretch of spoken language without specifically having them focus on the details of stress or intonation. Likewise, an activity involving recognition of cohesive devices (macroskill #11) might lend itself to a bottom-up approach in which specific devices are initially listed and explained, and only later provided in stretches of meaningful discourse.

Classroom Connections

Look at the list of seventeen micro- and macroskills, and think about others (besides #3 and #11) in which a *micro*skill could be approached from the "top down," and a *macro*skill could be taught through "bottom-up" processing.

Through a checklist of micro- and macroskills, you can get a good idea of what your techniques need to cover in the domain of listening comprehension. As you plan a specific technique or listening module, such a list helps you to focus on clearly conceptualized objectives. And in your evaluation of listening, these micro- and macroskills can become testing criteria. The items on page 327 comprise just such a checklist, adapted from Richards and other sources.

It is important to note that these seventeen skills apply to conversational discourse. Less interactive forms of discourse, such as listening to monologues like

Micro- and Macroskills of Listening Comprehension (Adapted from Richards, 1983)

Microskills

1. Retain chunks of language of different lengths in short-term memory.
2. Discriminate among the distinctive sounds of English.
3. Recognize English stress patterns, words in stressed and unstressed positions, rhythmic structure, intonational contours, and their role in signaling information.
4. Recognize reduced forms of words.
5. Distinguish word boundaries, recognize a core of words, and interpret word order patterns and their significance.
6. Process speech at different rates of delivery.
7. Process speech containing pauses, errors, corrections, and other performance variables.
8. Recognize grammatical word classes (nouns, verbs, etc.), systems (e.g., tense, agreement, pluralization), patterns, rules, and elliptical forms.
9. Detect sentence constituents and distinguish between major and minor constituents.
10. Recognize that a particular meaning may be expressed in different grammatical forms.

Macroskills

11. Recognize cohesive devices in spoken discourse.
12. Recognize the communicative functions of utterances, according to situations, participants, goals.
13. Infer situations, participants, goals using real-world knowledge.
14. From events, ideas, etc., described, predict outcomes, infer links and connections between events, deduce causes and effects, and detect such relations as main idea, supporting idea, new information, given information, generalization, and exemplification.
15. Distinguish between literal and implied meanings.
16. Use facial, kinesic, body language, and other nonverbal clues to decipher meanings.
17. Develop and use a battery of listening strategies, such as detecting key words, guessing the meaning of words from context, appealing for help, and signaling comprehension or lack thereof.

academic lectures, include further, more specific micro- and macroskills (Flowerdew, 1994; Blackwell & Naber, 2006; Sarosy & Sherak, 2006). Students in an academic setting need to be able to perform such things as identifying the structure of a lecture, weeding out what may be irrelevant or tangential, detecting the possible biases of the speaker, critically evaluating the speaker's assertions, and developing means (through note-taking, for example) of retaining the content of a lecture.

CLASSROOM CONNECTIONS

Which one or two microskills and one or two macroskills do you think present the *most* difficulty for L2 learners in general? What kinds of tasks or activities might help students to meet the challenges of acquiring those skills?

TYPES OF CLASSROOM LISTENING PERFORMANCE

With literally hundreds of possible techniques available for teaching listening skills, it will be helpful for you to think in terms of several kinds of listening performance—that is, what your students do in a listening technique. Sometimes these types of performance are embedded in a broader technique or task, and sometimes they are themselves the sum total of the activity of a technique.

1. Reactive

Sometimes you want a learner simply to listen to the surface structure of an utterance for the sole purpose of repeating it back to you. While this kind of listening performance requires little meaningful processing, it nevertheless may be a legitimate, even though a minor, aspect of an interactive, communicative classroom. This role of the listener as merely a "tape recorder" (Nunan 1991b, p. 18) is very limited because the listener is not generating meaning. About the only role that reactive listening can play in an interactive classroom is in brief choral or individual drills that focus on pronunciation.

2. Intensive

Techniques whose only purpose is to focus on components (phonemes, words, intonation, discourse markers, etc.) of discourse may be considered to be intensive—as opposed to extensive—in their requirement that students single out certain elements of spoken language. They include the bottom-up skills (see p. 260) that are important at all levels of proficiency. Examples of intensive listening performance include the following:

- Students listen for cues in certain choral or individual drills.
- The teacher repeats a word or sentence several times to "imprint" it in the students' mind.

- The teacher asks students to listen to a sentence or a longer stretch of discourse and to notice a specified element, such as intonation, stress, a contraction, or a grammatical structure.

3. Responsive

A significant proportion of classroom listening activity consists of short stretches of teacher language designed to elicit immediate responses. The students' task in such listening is to process the teacher talk immediately and to fashion an appropriate reply. Examples include

- asking questions ("How are you today?" "What did you do last night?")
- giving commands ("Take a sheet of paper and a pencil.")
- seeking clarification ("What was that word you said?")
- checking comprehension ("So, how many people were in the elevator when the power went out?").

4. Selective

In longer stretches of discourse such as monologues of a couple of minutes or considerably longer, the task of the student is not to process everything that was said, but rather to *scan* the material selectively for certain information. The purpose of such performance is not to look for global or general meanings, necessarily, but to be able to find important information in a field of potentially distracting information. Such activity requires field independence (see *PLLT*, Chapter 5) on the part of the learner. Selective listening differs from intensive listening in that the discourse is in relatively long lengths. Examples of such discourse include

- speeches
- media broadcasts
- stories and anecdotes
- conversations in which learners are "eavesdroppers."

Techniques promoting selective listening skills could ask students to listen for

- people's names
- dates
- certain facts or events
- location, situation, context, etc.
- main ideas and/or conclusion.

5. Extensive

This sort of performance, unlike the intensive processing (item 2) described above, aims to develop a top-down, global understanding of spoken language. For students in classrooms, extensive performance typically involves listening to lectures and other impromptu teacher monologues, commonly referred to as *academic listening*. Such listening may require the learner to invoke other interactive skills (e.g., note-taking, asking questions, discussion) for full comprehension (Flowerdew & Miller, 2014). However, sometimes conversations involve attending to "a long story," explanations, or descriptions, requiring the hearer to derive a comprehensive meaning or purpose.

6. Interactive

Finally, there is listening performance that can include all five of the above types as learners actively participate in discussions, debates, conversations, role-plays, and other pair and group work. Their listening performance must be intricately integrated with speaking (and perhaps other) skills in the authentic give and take of communicative interchange.

 **CLASSROOM CONNECTIONS**

The six types of listening performance listed here imply a gradual increase in language ability as you progress up the scale from 1 to 6. Nevertheless, under what circumstances in *advanced* levels would reactive (#1), intensive (#2), and responsive (#3) performance be beneficial? What are some examples of activities or tasks that are appropriate at this level?

PRINCIPLES FOR TEACHING LISTENING SKILLS

Several decades of research and practice in teaching listening comprehension have yielded some practical principles for designing classroom aural comprehension techniques. These principles should help you to create your own techniques and activities. Some of them, especially the second and third, actually apply to any technique; the others are more germane to listening.

1. Include a Focus on Listening in an Integrated-Skills Course

Assuming that your curriculum is dedicated to the integration of all four skills, remember that each of the separate skills deserves special focus in appropriate doses. It is easy to adopt a philosophy of just letting students "experience" language without careful attention to component skills. Because aural comprehension itself cannot be overtly "observed" (see item 4 below), teachers sometimes incorrectly assume that the input provided in the classroom will be converted into learners' long-term competence. The creation of effective listening techniques requires studied attention to all the principles of listening already summarized in this chapter.

2. Use Techniques That Are Stimulating and Motivating

Appeal to listeners' personal interests and goals. Because background information (schemata) is an important factor in listening, take into full account the experiences, goals, and abilities of your students as you design lessons. Also, remember that the cultural background(s) of your students can be both facilitating and interfering in the process of listening. Then, once a technique is launched, try to construct it in such a way that students are caught up in the activity and feel self-propelled toward its final objective.

3. Utilize Authentic Language and Contexts

Authentic language and real-world tasks enable students to see the relevance of classroom activity to their long-term communicative goals. If you introduce natural texts (conversations, media broadcasts, stories, speeches) rather than concocted, artificial material, students will more readily dive into the activity.

4. Include Pre-, While-, and Post-Listening Techniques

Learning to listen is not merely a matter of repeated listening, over and over, until the student "gets it." For classroom lessons that involve a focus on a major listening event (such as an audio/video presentation, a news broadcast, or a teacher's planned lecture), effective lessons have been found to include three major stages (Richards & Burns, 2012).

The first is a schemata-activating process that helps the learner to prepare for listening by checking vocabulary, ascertaining background knowledge that is essential for understanding, gaining a hint of what the topic is, and exploring any contextual factors that might otherwise make the listening difficult.

The second stage is one that can easily be neglected. You might assume that telling your students simply to "listen to the audio/video" that you're about to play is sufficient. Not true! Effective pedagogy will give students something to "do" *while* they are listening: for example, take notes, fill in a chart, note a sequence of events, listen for the main idea, listen for certain details. Remember, listening is an active process, so make sure your students are actively doing something while they listen.

Finally, what will students do *after* the presentation? We commonly think of questions or discussions to check comprehension, but this is only one form of post-listening activity that you can do. You might plan any of the following: a vocabulary or grammar check, difficulties that students had in comprehension (rapidity of speech, length, discourse complexity, content complexity), and/or extensions of the content of the listening passage to other related content. This phase might involve everything from processing a handout to a general discussion, to a debate.

5. Carefully Consider the Form of Listeners' Responses

Comprehension itself is not externally observable. We cannot peer into a learner's brain through a little window and empirically observe what is stored there after someone else has said something. We can only *infer* that certain things have been comprehended through students' overt (verbal or nonverbal) *responses* to speech. It is therefore important for teachers to design techniques in such a way that students' responses indicate whether or not their comprehension has been correct. Lund (1990) offered nine different ways that we can check listeners' comprehension:

Guidelines for Determining a Listener's Comprehension

- doing—the listener responds physically to a command
- choosing—the listener selects from alternatives such as pictures, objects, and texts
- transferring—the listener draws a picture of what is heard
- answering—the listener answers questions about the message
- condensing—the listener outlines or takes notes on a lecture
- extending—the listener provides an ending to a story heard
- duplicating—the listener translates the message into the native language or repeats it verbatim
- modeling—the listener orders a meal, for example, after listening to a model order
- conversing—the listener engages in a conversation that indicates appropriate processing of information

6. Encourage the Development of Listening Strategies

Most foreign language students are simply not aware of how to listen. One of your jobs is to equip them with listening strategies that extend beyond the classroom. Draw their attention to the value of such strategies as the following:

Strategies for Listening Comprehension

- looking for key words
- looking for nonverbal cues to meaning
- predicting a speaker's purpose by the context of the spoken discourse
- associating information with one's existing cognitive structure (activating background information)
- guessing at meanings
- seeking clarification
- listening for the general gist
- various test-taking strategies for listening comprehension

 **CLASSROOM CONNECTIONS**

When you were learning an L2, did you use any of the above strategies? Or did your teacher encourage them? How would you implement these strategies in lessons designed to help learners to improve their listening skills?

As you "teach learners how to learn" by helping them to develop their overall strategic competence (see Chapter 16), strategies for effective listening can become a highly significant part of their chances for successful learning.

7. Include Both Bottom-Up and Top-Down Listening Techniques

Speech-processing theory distinguishes between two types of processing in both listening and reading comprehension. **Bottom-up processing** proceeds from sounds to words to grammatical relationships to lexical meanings, and so on, to a final "message." **Top-down processing** is evoked from "a bank of prior knowledge and global expectations" (Morley, 1991a, p. 87) and other background information (schemata) that the listener brings to the text.

Bottom-up techniques typically focus on the "bits and pieces" of language, breaking language into component parts and giving them central focus. Top-down techniques are more concerned with the activation of schemata, with deriving meaning, with global understanding, and with the interpretation of a text. It is important for learners to operate from both directions because both can offer keys to determining the meaning of spoken discourse. But in a communicative, interactive context, you don't want to dwell too heavily on the bottom-up techniques, for to do so may hamper the development of a learner's all-important automaticity in processing speech.

LISTENING TECHNIQUES FROM BEGINNING TO ADVANCED

Techniques for teaching listening will vary considerably across the proficiency continuum. Chapter 7 has already dealt with general characteristics. Listening techniques are no exception to the general rule. Table 15.1 (pages 334–338) provides three lists of techniques for each of three proficiency levels. Each list is broken down into bottom-up, top-down, and interactive types of activity.

The importance of listening comprehension in language learning should by now be quite apparent. As we move on to look at speaking skills, always remember the ever-present relationship among all four skills and the necessity in authentic, interactive classes to integrate these skills even as you focus on the specifics of one skill area.

Table 15.1 Techniques for teaching listening comprehension (adapted from Peterson, 1991, pp. 114–121)

FOR BEGINNING-LEVEL LISTENERS

Bottom-Up Exercises

1. Goal: *Discriminating Between Intonation Contours in Sentences*

   Listen to a sequence of sentence patterns with either rising or falling intonation. Place a check in column 1 (rising) or column 2 (falling), depending on the pattern you hear.

2. Goal: *Discriminating Between Phonemes*

   Listen to pairs of words. Some pairs differ in their final consonant, and some pairs are the same. Circle the word "same" or "different," depending on what you hear.

3. Goal: *Selective Listening for Morphological Endings*

   Listen to a series of sentences. Circle "yes" if the verb has an -ed ending, and circle "no" if it does not.

   Listen to a series of sentences. On your answer sheet, circle the one (of three) verb forms contained in the sentence that you hear.

4. Goal: *Selecting Details from the Text (Word Recognition)*

   Match a word that you hear with its picture.

   Listen to a weather report. Look at a list of words and circle the words that you hear.

   Listen to a sentence that contains clock time. Circle the clock time that you hear, among three choices (5:30, 5:45, 6:15).

   Listen to an advertisement, select the price of an item, and write the amount on a price tag.

   Listen to a series of recorded telephone messages from an answering machine. Fill in a chart with the following information from each caller: name, number, time, and message.

5. Goal: *Listening for Normal Sentence Word Order*

   Listen to a short dialogue and fill in the missing words that have been deleted in a partial transcript.

Top-Down Exercises

6. Goal: *Discriminating Between Emotional Reactions*

   Listen to a sequence of utterances. Place a check in the column that describes the emotional reaction that you hear: interested, happy, surprised, or unhappy.

7. Goal: *Getting the Gist of a Sentence*

   Listen to a sentence describing a picture and select the correct picture.

8. Goal: *Recognize the Topic*

   Listen to a dialogue and decide where the conversation occurred. Circle the correct location among three multiple-choice items.

   Listen to a conversation and look at the pictured greeting cards. Decide which of the greeting cards was sent. Write the greeting under the appropriate card.

   Listen to a conversation and decide what the people are talking about. Choose the picture that shows the topic.

Table 15.1 Techniques for teaching listening comprehension (*Continued*)

Interactive Exercises

9. Goal: *Build a Semantic Network of Word Associations*

   Listen to a word and associate all the related words that come to mind.

10. Goal: *Recognize a Familiar Word and Relate It to a Category*

    Listen to words from a shopping list and match each word to the store that sells it.

11. Goal: *Following Directions*

    Listen to a description of a route and trace it on a map.

FOR INTERMEDIATE LEVEL LISTENERS

Bottom-Up Exercises

12. Goal: *Recognizing Fast Speech Forms*

    Listen to a series of sentences that contain unstressed function words. Circle your choice among three words on the answer sheet—for example: "up," "a," "of."

13. Goal: *Finding the Stressed Syllable*

    Listen to words of two (or three) syllables. Mark them for word stress and predict the pronunciation of the unstressed syllable.

14. Goal: *Recognizing Words with Reduced Syllables*

    Read a list of polysyllabic words and predict which syllabic vowel will be dropped. Listen to the words read in fast speech and confirm your prediction.

15. Goal: *Recognize Words as They Are Linked in the Speech Stream*

    Listen to a series of short sentences with consonant/vowel linking between words. Mark the linkages on your answer sheet.

16. Goal: *Recognizing Pertinent Details in the Speech Stream*

    Listen to a short dialogue between a boss and a secretary regarding changes in the daily schedule. Use an appointment calendar. Cross out appointments that are being changed and write in new ones.

    Listen to announcements of airline arrivals and departures. With a model of an airline information board in front of you, fill in the flight numbers, destinations, gate numbers, and departure times.

    Listen to a series of short dialogues after reading questions that apply to the dialogues. While listening, find the answers to questions about prices, places, names, and numbers. Example: "Where are the shoppers?" "How much is whole wheat bread?"

    Listen to a short telephone conversation between a customer and a service station manager. Fill in a chart that lists the car repairs that must be done. Check the part of the car that needs repair, the reason, and the approximate cost.

Top-Down Exercises

17. Goal: *Analyze Discourse Structure to Suggest Effective Listening Strategies*

    Listen to six radio commercials with attention to the use of music, repetition of key words, and number of speakers. Talk about the effect these techniques have on the listeners.

18. Goal: *Listen to Identify the Speaker or the Topic*

    Listen to a series of radio commercials. On your answer sheet, choose among four types of sponsors or products and identify the picture that goes with the commercial.

(*Continued*)

Table 15.1 Techniques for teaching listening comprehension (*Continued*)

19. Goal: *Listen to Evaluate Themes and Motives*

    Listen to a series of radio commercials. On your answer sheet are four possible motives that the companies use to appeal to their customers. Circle all the motives that you feel each commercial promotes: escape from reality, family security, snob appeal, sex appeal.

20. Goal: *Finding Main Ideas and Supporting Details*

    Listen to a short conversation between two friends. On your answer sheet are scenes from television programs. Find and write the name of the program and the channel. Decide which speaker watched which program.

21. Goal: *Making Inferences*

    Listen to a series of sentences, which may be either statements or questions. After each sentence, answer inferential questions such as "Where might the speaker be?" "How might the speaker be feeling?" "What might the speaker be referring to?"

    Listen to a series of sentences. After each sentence, suggest a possible context for the sentence (place, situation, time, participants).

Interactive Exercises

22. Goal: *Discriminating Between Registers of Speech and Tones of Voice*

    Listen to a series of sentences. On your answer sheet, mark whether the sentence is polite or impolite.

23. Goal: *Recognize Missing Grammar Markers in Colloquial Speech*

    Listen to a series of short questions in which the auxiliary verb and subject have been deleted. Use grammatical knowledge to fill in the missing words: ("Have you) got some extra?"

    Listen to a series of questions with reduced verb auxiliary and subject and identify the missing verb (does it/is it) by checking the form of the main verb. Example: "'Zit come with anything else? 'Zit arriving on time?"

24. Goal: *Use Knowledge of Reduced Forms to Clarify the Meaning of an Utterance*

    Listen to a short sentence containing a reduced form. Decide what the sentence means. On your answer sheet, choose the one (of three) alternatives that is the best paraphrase of the sentence you heard. Example: You hear "You can't be happy with that." You read: (a) "Why can't you be happy?" (b) "That will make you happy." (c) "I don't think you are happy."

25. Goal: *Use Context to Build Listening Expectations*

    Read a short want-ad describing job qualifications from the employment section of a newspaper. Brainstorm additional qualifications that would be important for that type of job.

26. Goal: *Listen to Confirm Your Expectations*

    Listen to short radio advertisements for jobs that are available. Check the job qualifications against your expectations.

27. Goal: *Use Context to Build Expectations. Use Bottom-Up Processing to Recognize Missing Words. Compare Your Predictions to What You Actually Heard*

    Read some telephone messages with missing words. Decide what kinds of information are missing so you know what to listen for. Listen to the information and fill in the blanks. Finally, discuss with the class what strategies you used for your predictions.

Table 15.1 Techniques for teaching listening comprehension (*Continued*)

28. Goal: *Use Incomplete Sensory Data and Cultural Background Information to Construct a More Complete Understanding of a Text*

    Listen to one side of a telephone conversation. Decide what the topic of the conversation might be and create a title for it.

    Listen to the beginning of a conversation between two people and answer questions about the number of participants, their ages, gender, and social roles. Guess the time of day, location, temperature, season, and topic. Choose among some statements to guess what might come next.

FOR ADVANCED LEVEL LEARNERS

Bottom-Up Exercises

29. Goal: *Use Features of Sentence Stress and Volume to Identify Important Information for Note-Taking*

    Listen to a number of sentences and extract the content words, which are read with greater stress. Write the content words as notes.

30. Goal: *Become Aware of Sentence-Level Features in Lecture Text*

    Listen to a segment of a lecture while reading a transcript of the material. Notice the incomplete sentences, pauses, and verbal fillers.

31. Goal: *Become Aware of Organizational Cues in Lecture Text*

    Look at a lecture transcript and circle all the cue words used to enumerate the main points. Then listen to the lecture segment and note the organizational cues.

32. Goal: *Become Aware of Lexical and Suprasegmental Markers for Definitions*

    Read a list of lexical cues that signal a definition; listen to signals of the speaker's intent, such as rhetorical questions; listen to special intonation patterns and pause patterns used with appositives.

    Listen to short lecture segments that contain new terms and their definitions in context. Use knowledge of lexical and intonational cues to identify the definition of the word.

33. Goal: *Identify Specific Points of Information*

    Read a skeleton outline of a lecture in which the main categories are given but the specific examples are left blank. Listen to the lecture and find the information that belongs in the blanks.

Top-Down Exercises

34. Goal: *Use the Introduction to the Lecture to Predict Its Focus and Direction*

    Listen to the introductory section of a lecture. Then read a number of topics on your answer sheet and choose the topic that best expresses what the lecture will discuss.

35. Goal: *Use the Lecture Transcript to Predict the Content of the Next Section*

    Read a section of a lecture transcript. Stop reading at a juncture point and predict what will come next. Then read on to confirm your prediction.

36. Goal: *Find the Main Idea of a Lecture Segment*

    Listen to a section of a lecture that describes a statistical trend. While you listen, look at three graphs that show a change over time and select the graph that best illustrates the lecture.

(*Continued*)

Table 15.1 Techniques for teaching listening comprehension (*Continued*)

Interactive Exercises

37. Goal: *Use Incoming Details to Determine the Accuracy of Predictions about Content*

    Listen to the introductory sentences to predict some of the main ideas you expect to hear in the lecture. Then listen to the lecture. Note whether or not the instructor talks about the points you predicted. If she/he does, note a detail about the point.

38. Goal: *Determine the Main Ideas of a Section of a Lecture by Analysis of the Details in That Section*

    Listen to a section of a lecture and take notes on the important details. Then relate the details to form an understanding of the main point of that section. Choose from a list of possible controlling ideas.

39. Goal: *Make Inferences by Identifying Ideas on the Sentence Level That Lead to Evaluative Statements*

    Listen to a statement and take notes on the important words. Indicate what further meaning can be inferred from the statement. Indicate the words in the original statement. Indicate the words in the original statement that serve to cue the inference.

40. Goal: *Use Knowledge of the Text and the Lecture Content to Fill in Missing Information*

    Listen to a lecture segment for its gist. Then listen to a statement from which words have been omitted. Using your knowledge of the text and of the general content, fill in the missing information. Check your understanding by listening to the entire segment.

41. Goal: *Use Knowledge of the Text and the Lecture Content to Discover the Lecturer's Misstatements and to Supply the Ideas That He Meant to Say*

    Listen to a lecture segment that contains an incorrect term. Write the incorrect term and the term that the lecturer should have used. Finally, indicate what clues helped you find the misstatement.

Classroom Connections

The list of listening techniques in Table 15.1 is quite exhaustive, and possibly exhaust*ing* to read! Choose a few at random at each level and imagine (or script out) how you would implement each technique in a context of your choice. Technique #26, for example, is very briefly described, leaving a lot to the teacher's creativity to implement. What details need to be added?

A SAMPLE LISTENING LESSON

Now that a number of principles and practical pedagogical strategies have been outlined, let's take a look at a sample lesson in listening comprehension and pose some questions about the extent to which the lesson exemplified (or not) the guidelines. This is an outline of a unit from the second of a three-volume series of books on listening comprehension (Bohlke & Rogers, 2011, pp. 85–90). Unit 5, titled "The Whale's Tale," focuses on listening for main ideas, sequences of events, and listening for details.

Unit 5. The Whale's Tale (from Bohlke & Rogers, 2011, pp. 85–90)

A. Warm Up (Photo of diver next to a whale caught in fishing ropes)

[Work with a partner. Discuss the questions.]

- What do you know about whales?
- What do you see in the picture?
- What do you think is happening?

B. Before You Listen

[Match the words. Complete the sentences.]

- Matching exercise, ten vocabulary items, e.g., *rescue, tangled, trap*
- Fill-in-the-blank, ten sentences, using the same vocabulary, e.g., *My headphone cord is always getting* __________. *It's annoying!*

C. While You Listen

First Listening

[Sequence: Number the events in order.]

- Ten sentences, e.g., *A rescue team arrives.*

[Main Idea: Check the statement that best describes the main idea.]

- Four options, e.g., *Divers have to enter cold water to rescue whales.*

Second Listening

[Details: Listen to the talk again. Complete your sentences. One student is A and the other is B. Work in pairs, reading your completed sentences to your partner.]

- Examples of sentences: *They used their* __________ *to call an environmental group. The whale swam in* __________ *around them.*

D. After You Listen

[With your partner use your completed sentences to answer the questions.]

- Ten questions, e.g., *When and where did this event happen?*
  [In groups, discuss these questions.]
- Five questions, e.g., *Do you think the whale was really thanking the rescuers?*

What are some other ways that human activities such as fishing can be dangerous to human life?

To what extent did this unit utilize the guidelines presented in this chapter? Even though you have not been given the complete lesson here, nor do you know exactly what was presented to students, try asking yourself the following questions:

- What *type* of spoken language was featured?
- How did the lesson include student interaction?
- What types of listening performance were used?
- Was the subject matter (as far as you can tell) stimulating and interesting?
- What were the pre-, while-, and post-listening tasks?
- What forms of listener response were used?
- What strategies were students encouraged to use?
- Were students encouraged to use bottom-up and top-town strategies?
- Based on the synopsis above, how would you go about assessing the success of students' performance?

 **CLASSROOM CONNECTIONS**

Judging from what you see above, a synopsis of the "whale" lesson, how effective do you think it was? If you were given this lesson to teach, imagine an appropriate audience, and ask yourself what you would add (perhaps to personalize it). Would you delete anything? Or would you change or modify any of the elements for your presumed audience?

ASSESSING LISTENING IN THE CLASSROOM

Every classroom lesson involves some form of assessment, whether it's in the form of informal, unplanned, and intuitive teacher processing and feedback, or in formal, prepared, scored tests. In order to appropriately call some attention to this very important role that teachers must assume, we offer—in this and the next three chapters on the four skills—a few principles and practical guidelines for assessing those skills in the classroom. For a much more comprehensive treatment of the assessment of the four skills, as well as background research and theory, we refer you to *Language Assessment: Principles and Classroom Practices* (Brown & Abeywickrama, 2010). Buck's (2001) detailed look at the assessment of listening is also very useful.

Disambiguating the Terms *Assessment* and *Test*

Before specifically considering the topic of assessing listening in particular, a word is in order about two commonly used terms. It's tempting at times to simply think that **assessment** and **test** are synonymous, appearing in free variation depending on the whim of the speaker or writer. A glance at some teacher reference books of ten or more years ago could bear out such an assumption. However, in recent years, thankfully, the profession seems to have come to an appropriate consensus that the two terms are, in fact, *not* synonymous.

Tests are a subset of assessment. Assessment is on ongoing pedagogical process that includes a number of evaluative acts on the part of the teacher. When a student responds to a question, offers a comment, or tries out a new word or structure, the teacher subconsciously makes an evaluation of the student's performance. A student's written work, from notes or short answers to essays, is judged by the teacher. In reading and listening activities, students' responses are implicitly evaluated. All that is assessment. Technically it is referred to as **informal assessment**—because it is usually unplanned and spontaneous and without specific scoring or grading formats, as opposed to **formal assessment**, which is more deliberate and usually has conventionalized feedback. Tests fall into the latter category. They are planned sets of tasks or exercises, with designated time frames, often announced in advance, prepared for (and sometimes feared) by students, and they characteristically offer specific scoring or grading formats.

 **CLASSROOM CONNECTIONS**

From your own experience learning an L2 or teaching one, what are some examples of informal and formal assessments? Are there some that fall in between the two? What purposes does each of your examples fulfill?

In considering classroom assessment, then, be prepared to entertain a range of possible pedagogical procedures. In the comments that follow, for the most part more formal aspects of assessment are implied. The informal processes have already been subsumed into the various guidelines and examples of this chapter.

One of the first observations that needs to be made in considering assessment is that listening is *unobservable*. You cannot directly see or measure or otherwise observe either the process or the product of aural comprehension. Oh, yes, we can hear you saying that if you ask someone to close the window, and they close it, you have observed aural comprehension. Or that if someone nods and says, "uh-huh," while you're talking, you have evidence of comprehension. Well, what you have in these cases is indeed *evidence* of comprehension, but you have not actually observed receptors sending messages to the brain, nor of the brain's processing of sound and converting it to meaning. So, when it comes to assessing listening, we're pretty well stuck with reliance on our best *inference* in determining comprehension. How you do that, and remain as accurate in your assessment as possible, is the challenge of assessing listening.

Assessing Types of Listening and Micro- and Macroskills

In this chapter, we have already looked at types of listening, from intensive listening on up to extensive and interactive. We have also considered the micro- and macroskills of listening, from processing tiny bits and pieces of language to strategic, interactive, and complex skills of extended discourse. These two related taxonomies are indispensable to valid, reliable assessment of students' listening comprehension ability. The more closely you can pinpoint exactly *what* you want to assess, the more reliably will you draw your conclusions.

What assessment methods (tasks, item formats) are commonly used at the various levels? Consider the following list of sample tasks (not an exhaustive list, by any means), and for further information consult Brown and Abeywickrama (2010).

The fifth category of listening, interactive tasks, is deliberately omitted from this list since such interaction involves speaking and will be covered in the next chapter. With this brief outline, we hope you can gain a bit of a picture of some assessment possibilities in listening comprehension.

Table 15.2 Tasks for assessing listening

1. Intensive listening tasks
   - distinguishing phonemic pairs (*grass-glass; leave-live*)
   - distinguishing morphological pairs (*miss-missed*)
   - distinguishing stress patterns (*I can go; I can't go*)
   - paraphrase recognition (*I come from Taiwan; I'm Taiwanese*)
   - repetition (S repeats a word)
2. Responsive listening tasks
   - question (*What time is it?* – multiple choice [MC] response)
   - question (*What time is it?* – open-ended response)
   - simple discourse sequences (*Hello. Nice weather. Tough test.*)
3. Selective listening tasks
   - listening cloze (Ss fill in blanks)
   - verbal information transfer (Ss give MC verbal response)
   - picture-cued information transfer (Ss choose a picture)
   - chart completion (Ss fill in a grid)
   - sentence repetition (Ss repeat stimulus sentence)
4. Extensive listening tasks
   - dictation (Ss listen [usually three times] and write a paragraph
   - dialogue (Ss hear dialogue – MC comprehension questions)
   - dialogue (Ss hear dialogue – open ended response)
   - lecture (Ss take notes; summarize; list main points; etc.)
   - interpretive tasks (Ss hear a poem – interpret meaning)
   - stories, narratives (Ss retell a story)

FOR THE TEACHER: ACTIVITIES (A) & DISCUSSION (D)

Note: For each of the "Classroom Connections" in this chapter, you may wish to turn them into individual or pair-work discussion questions.

1. **(A)** Direct pairs to review the difference between language that learners are merely exposed to (input) and language that is *internalized*. Ask them to illustrate with classroom examples how input gets internalized in long-term competence. Ask the pairs to brainstorm ideas or strategies for helping students to internalize language that they are exposed to. Have them report their examples to the class.
2. **(D)** Pick an English language news program and audio-record a two- or three-minute segment (or stream it in video form for the class). In class, ask students to listen to the excerpt and identify "clusters" of words that form thought groups. Then ask students to brainstorm hints they could give to L2 learners to help them to listen to such clusters rather than to each separate word.
3. **(A)** Instruct pairs to specifically identify the redundant words/phrases in the conversation between Matt and Jeff (p. 323), and to brainstorm how they would teach students (a) to use such redundancies for comprehension and (b) to overlook them when comprehension is already sufficient.
4. **(D)** Audio-record (or video on a phone or camera, and feed to a laptop/projector) a casual conversation between two native speakers of English. In class, play the conversation and ask your students to pick out as many "performance variables" as they can. How do these performance variables differ from those of a learner of English? Can L2 learners be taught to overlook or to compensate for such naturally occurring performance variables?
5. **(A)** Divide the taxonomy of listening microskills and macroskills (Table 15.1) among as many pairs as you can in the class, perhaps two per pair. Ask them to come up with an example of their skill. Do the same, in another activity, with the six types of classroom listening performance (pp. 328–330). Ask the pairs to share examples of each and discuss their appropriateness in the classroom.
6. **(A)** As a whole class, review the seven principles for effective listening techniques on pages 330–333. Then, assign to pairs one or two of the 41 techniques outlined in Table 15.2, and have them systematically evaluate the techniques they have been given. Their evaluation should be based on the six principles. Ask them to share their results with the rest of the class.
7. **(D)** One type of listening technique (combined with writing) not considered in this chapter is dictation (only mentioned in the final section on assessment). How useful is dictation? What are the pros and cons of using dictation in a classroom?

FOR YOUR FURTHER READING

Richards, J., & Burns, A. (2012). *Tips for teaching listening: A practical approach*. White Plains, NY: Pearson Education.

A highly practical manual detailing practical classroom techniques for teaching listening, including dozens of handouts and activities for all levels.

Brown, S. (2011). *Listening myths*. Ann Arbor, MI: University of Michigan Press.

An easily understood, practical primer on the nature of L2 listening, focusing on a number of popular misconceptions about listening.

Brown, G. (2010). Listening in a second language. In M. Berns (Ed.), *Concise encyclopedia of applied linguistics* (pp. 157–163). Oxford, UK: Elsevier.

Flowerdew, J., & Miller, L. (2005). *Second language listening: Theory and practice*. Cambridge, UK: Cambridge University Press.

Vandergrift, L., & Goh, C. (2011). *Teaching and learning second language listening: Metacognition in action*. New York, NY: Routledge.

All three resources offer in-depth coverage of research on listening comprehension, as well as practical classroom implications, and include extensive bibliographies.

Brown, H. D., & Abeywickrama, P. (2010). *Language assessment: Principles and classroom practices* (2nd ed.). White Plains, NY: Pearson Education.

A survey of language assessment in general, with Chapter 7 devoted to assessing listening. The material is classroom-based and does not require technical knowledge in the field of assessment to comprehend and apply.

CHAPTER 16

TEACHING SPEAKING

Questions for Reflection

- What are some of the major issues and concepts in pedagogical research that are related to teaching speaking?
- What might make speaking *difficult* for students?
- How can spoken language be classified into microskills, macroskills, and types of classroom speaking performance?
- What are some principles to follow in designing speaking tasks and activities?
- When should teachers treat spoken errors and when should they be ignored, and what are some possibilities in between?
- What are some basic principles and formats for assessing speaking?

In communicative language courses, listening and speaking skills are closely intertwined, often combined as "Oral Communication Skills" or "Listening/Speaking." The interaction between these two modes of performance applies especially strongly to conversation, the most popular discourse category in L2 curricula. And in the classroom even relatively unidirectional types of spoken language input (e.g., speeches, lectures) are usually followed or preceded by various forms of oral production on the part of students.

Some of the components of teaching spoken language were covered in Chapter 15 as we looked closely at teaching listening comprehension: *types* of spoken language, *idiosyncrasies* of spoken language that can be difficult, and *microskills* that are also a factor of oral language. This chapter will build on those considerations as we investigate the teaching of oral communication (OC) skills.

ORAL COMMUNICATION SKILLS IN PEDAGOGICAL RESEARCH

A review of some of the current issues in teaching OC will help to provide some perspective on the more practical considerations that follow in this chapter.

Conversational Discourse

When someone asks you "Do you speak English?" they usually mean, "Can you carry on a *conversation* reasonably competently?" The benchmark of successful language acquisition is almost always the demonstration of an ability to accomplish pragmatic goals through interactive discourse with other speakers of the language. And yet, as Richards (2008b) noted, the conversation class is something of an enigma in language teaching. The goals and the techniques for teaching conversation are extremely diverse, depending on the student, teacher, and overall context of the class. Historically, "conversation" classes have ranged from quasi-communicative drilling to free, open, and sometimes agenda-free discussions among students.

Pedagogical research on teaching conversation has provided some parameters for developing objectives and techniques (McCarthy & O'Keeffe, 2010; Lazaraton, 2014). We have learned to differentiate between transactional and interactional conversation. We have discovered techniques for teaching students conversation rules for topic nomination, maintaining a conversation, turn-taking, interruption, and termination. Our pedagogical storehouse has equipped us with ways to teach sociolinguistic appropriateness, styles of speech, nonverbal communication, and conversational routines (such as "Well, I've gotta go now." "Great weather today, huh?" "Haven't I met you somewhere before?"). Within all these foci, the phonological, lexical, and syntactic properties of language can be attended to either directly or indirectly.

Teaching Pronunciation

There has been some controversy over the role of pronunciation work in a communicative, interactive course of study (Levis, 2005; Setter & Jenkins, 2005; Tarone, 2005; Lane, 2010; Murphy, 2013; Goodwin, 2014). Because the overwhelming majority of adult learners will never acquire an accent-free command of a foreign language, should a language program that emphasizes whole language, meaningful contexts, and automaticity of production focus on these tiny phonological details of language? The answer is "yes," but in a different way from what was perceived to be essential a few decades ago. This topic will be taken up later in the chapter.

Accuracy and Fluency

An issue that pervades all of language performance centers on the distinction between accuracy and fluency (Bailey, 2003; Bohlke, 2014; Lazaraton, 2014). In spoken language the question we face as teachers is: How shall we prioritize the two clearly important speaker goals of *accurate* (clear, articulate, grammatically and phonologically correct) language and *fluent* (flowing, natural) language?

In the mid to late 1970s, egged on by a somewhat short-lived anti-grammar approach, some teachers turned away from accuracy issues in favor of providing a plethora of "natural" language activity in their classrooms. The argument was that adult SLA should simulate the child's L1 learning processes and become the locus of meaningful language involvement (at the expense of focus on forms). Unfortunately, such classrooms so strongly emphasized the importance of fluency—with a de-emphasis on grammar and phonology—that many students managed to produce fairly fluent but barely comprehensible language. Something was lacking.

It's now very clear that fluency and accuracy are both important goals to pursue in CLT and/or TBLT (Lazaraton, 2014). While fluency may in many communicative language courses be an *initial* goal in language teaching, accuracy is achieved to some extent by allowing students to focus on the elements of phonology, grammar, morphosyntax, and discourse in their spoken output. If you were learning to play tennis instead of a second language, this same philosophy would initially get you out on the tennis court to feel what it's like to hold a racquet, hit the ball, serve it, and then have you focus more cognitively on certain fundamentals. Fluency is probably best achieved by allowing the "stream" of speech to "flow"; then, as some of this speech spills over beyond comprehensibility, the "riverbanks" of instruction on some details of phonology, grammar, or discourse can channel the speech on a more purposeful course.

 **CLASSROOM CONNECTIONS**

In your experience learning and/or teaching an L2, what are some of the tasks and activities that may promote the "river" of production to flow? And what are some of the "riverbanks" that a teacher can include to focus on forms (phonology, grammar, discourse) that may need containment, to avoid a "flood" of incomprehensibility?

The fluency/accuracy issue often boils down to the extent to which our techniques should be message oriented (or, as some call it, teaching language *use*) as opposed to language oriented (also known as teaching language *usage*). Current approaches to language teaching lean strongly toward message orientation, with language usage offering a supporting but important role.

Complexity

A related issue that has garnered some attention recently is the extent to which L2 tasks can be graded by **complexity** (Ellis, 2009; Skehan, 2009). Both grammatical and lexical complexity must be taken into account, but the task design itself may fall into a range of cognitive, strategic, and interpersonal complexity. The extent to which a task involves pre- and within-task *planning* has been found to be a major contributor to complexity, and subsequently to both fluency and accuracy of learners' oral production (Skehan, 2009). Complexity also varies according to cognitive operations, abstract thinking, quantity of information, negotiation of meaning, and time pressure, among other factors (Ellis, 2009), all of which could account for accuracy, fluency, and successful completion of a task.

Affective Factors

> "It's better to keep your mouth closed and have others think you are ignorant than to open it and remove all doubt."—Mark Twain

Ah yes, but Mark Twain wasn't talking about language classes! One of the major obstacles learners have to overcome in learning to speak is the anxiety generated over the risks of blurting things out that sound ignorant, embarrassing, or incomprehensible. Because of our language *identity* (Pavlenko & Norton, 2007) that informs others that "you are what you speak," learners tend to be reluctant to put themselves in the situation of being judged by hearers. Language learners must put a new twist on Mark Twain's quip. Our job as teachers is to provide the kind of warm, embracing climate that encourages students to speak, however halting or tentative their attempts may be.

 **CLASSROOM CONNECTIONS**

In what way have your teachers in L2 classes promoted an affective climate that encouraged (or discouraged) oral participation? What are some "dos" and "don'ts" for teachers in setting an embracing atmosphere in the classroom? If a student says something that might make other students laugh, how can a teacher help them to laugh *with* the other student, as opposed to laughing *at* him or her?

The Interaction Effect

The greatest difficulty that learners encounter in attempts to speak is not the multiplicity of sounds, words, phrases, and discourse forms that characterize any language, but rather the interactive nature of most communication. Conversations are collaborative as participants engage in a process of negotiation of meaning. So, for the learner, the matter of what to say—a tremendous task, to be sure—is often eclipsed by conventions of how to say things, when to speak, and other discourse constraints. For example, among the many possible grammatical sentences that a learner could produce in response to a comment, how does that learner make a choice?

Tarone (2005) and Oxford (2011) both noted a crucial role for communication strategies in learning to participate in conversational discourse. A few such strategies are discussed later in this chapter. Nunan (1991b, p. 47) noted yet another complication in interactive discourse: what he calls the interlocutor effect, or the difficulty of a speaking task as gauged by the skills of one's interlocutor. In other words, one learner's performance is always colored by that of the person (interlocutor) with whom he or she is talking.

Intelligibility

A now outdated model of English language teaching assumed that intelligibility should be gauged by whether nonnative speakers are intelligible to native speakers. This "rather arrogant" (Setter & Jenkins, 2005, p. 5) premise has now evolved into much more complex questions, especially because, statistically, most interactions among English speakers are among *non*native speakers. So, materials, technology, and teacher education programs are being challenged to grapple with the issue of intelligibility, and to adopt new standards of "correctness" and new attitudes toward "accent" in order to meet current global realities (Levis, 2005; Derwing & Munro, 2005; McCarthy & O'Keeffe, 2010; Lazaraton, 2014).

Corpus-Based Data on Spoken Language

The intelligibility issue has been revolutionized by a growth of readily available **corpora** of spoken language (McCarthy & O'Keeffe, 2004), one of the key developments in research on teaching oral production. As the size and scope of corpora expand, so our understanding of what people *really* say is informed by empirical evidence. An increasing stockpile of data on *spoken* grammar (as opposed to *written* grammar) has been instrumental in guiding L2 curricula and textbooks and in exposing learners to greater authenticity (Mumford, 2008; McCarthy & O'Keeffe, 2010).

Of special interest to teachers of English worldwide is the wider range of language varieties that are now available through such projects as the International Corpus of English, which contains data from the spoken Englishes of Hong Kong, New Zealand, Singapore, the UK, Nigeria, the Caribbean, and others. These data are spurring the language teaching profession—especially textbook and course developers—to adopt new models that transcend the traditional native-speaker/ nonnative-speaker dichotomy. Our notions of what is correct, acceptable, or appropriate, both phonologically and grammatically, are changing.

Genres of Spoken Language

Finally, research on spoken language has recently attended to a specification of differences among various genres of oral production, and how to teach those variations (Hughes, 2002; Tardy, 2013). What is judged to be acceptable and/or correct varies by contexts, or genres, such as small talk, discussion, and narrative, among others. As research more accurately describes the constraints of such genres on spoken language, we will be better able to pinpoint models of appropriateness for students' specific purposes in learning English.

TYPES OF SPOKEN LANGUAGE

In Chapter 15, several categories were defined for understanding types of spoken language, including monologue versus dialogue, planned versus spontaneous, and interpersonal versus transactional. In beginning through intermediate levels of proficiency, most of the efforts of students in oral production come in the form of conversation, or dialogue. As you plan and implement techniques in your interactive classroom, make sure your students can deal with both interpersonal (sometimes referred to as interactional) and transactional dialogue and that they are able to converse with a total stranger as well as someone with whom they are quite familiar.

WHAT MAKES SPEAKING DIFFICULT?

In Chapter 15 we also outlined some idiosyncrasies of spoken language that make listening skills somewhat difficult to acquire. These same characteristics must be taken into account in the productive generation of speech, but with a slight twist in that the learner is now the producer. Bear in mind that the following characteristics of spoken language can make oral performance easy as well as, in some cases, difficult.

Factors Contributing to Difficulty of Speaking Tasks

1. Clustering

Fluent speech is phrasal, not word by word. Learners can organize their output both cognitively and physically (in breath groups) through clustering.

2. Redundancy

Learners can capitalize on redundancy, a feature of spoken language that allows a speaker to make meaning clearer.

3. Reduced forms

Contractions, elisions, reduced vowels, and other similar characteristics all pose special problems in teaching spoken English (see the section below on Teaching Pronunciation). Students who don't learn colloquial contractions can sometimes develop a stilted, bookish quality of speaking that in turn stigmatizes them.

4. Performance variables

One of the advantages of spoken language is that the process of thinking as you speak allows you to manifest a certain number of performance hesitations, pauses, backtracking, and corrections. Learners can actually be taught how to pause and hesitate. For example, in English our "thinking time" is not silent; we insert certain "fillers" such as *uh, um, well, you know, I mean,* or *like.* One of the most salient differences between native and nonnative speakers of a language is in their hesitation phenomena.

5. Colloquial language

Make sure your students are reasonably well acquainted with the words, idioms, and phrases of colloquial language and that they get practice in producing these forms.

6. Rate of delivery

Another salient characteristic of fluency is rate of delivery. One of your tasks in teaching spoken English is to help learners achieve an acceptable speed along with other attributes of fluency.

7. Stress, rhythm, and intonation

This is the most important characteristic of English pronunciation, as will be explained below. The stress-timed rhythm of spoken English and its intonation patterns convey important messages.

8. Complexity

The complexity of grammatical and discourse structures is an obvious source of difficulty, but *task* complexity can also be a feature that teachers should consider. Tasks that are multidimensional or that have interdependencies may themselves be challenging regardless of linguistic features (Robinson, 2001; Ellis, 2009; Skehan, 2009; Kim & Payant, in press).

9. Interaction

As noted in the previous section, learning to produce strings of language in a vacuum—without interlocutors—would deny spoken language its richest component: the creativity of conversational negotiation.

MICRO- AND MACROSKILLS OF ORAL COMMUNICATION

In Chapter 15, micro- and macroskills for listening comprehension (adapted from Richards, 1983) were presented. Here, many of the same skills apply, but because of major cognitive and physical differences between listening and speaking, some noticeable alterations have been made, as illustrated in the box on page 352.

One implication of such a list is the importance of focusing on both the forms and the functions of language. In teaching OC, we should not *limit* students' attention to the whole picture, even though that whole picture is important. We can also help students to see the pieces—right down to the small parts—of language that make up the whole. Just as you would instruct a novice artist in composition, the effect of color hues, shading, and brush stroke techniques, so language students need to be shown the *details* of how to convey and negotiate the ever-elusive meanings of language.

CLASSROOM CONNECTIONS

What is the difference between the *micro* and *macro* skills listed below? Which skills would more likely be treated in beginning levels of L2 courses? Which ones in advanced levels? How do the first ten microskills build on the last six macroskills?

Micro- and Macroskills of Oral Communication

Microskills

1. Produce chunks of language of different lengths.
2. Orally produce differences among the English phonemes and allophonic variants.
3. Produce English stress patterns, words in stressed and unstressed positions, rhythmic structure, and intonational contours.
4. Produce reduced forms of words and phrases.
5. Use an adequate number of lexical units (words) in order to accomplish pragmatic purposes.
6. Produce fluent speech at different rates of delivery.
7. Monitor your own oral production and use various strategic devices—pauses, fillers, self-corrections, backtracking—to enhance the clarity of the message.
8. Use grammatical word classes (nouns, verbs, etc.), systems (e.g., tense, agreement, pluralization), word order, patterns, rules, and elliptical forms.
9. Produce speech in natural constituents—in appropriate phrases, pause groups, breath groups, and sentences.
10. Express a particular meaning in different grammatical forms.

Macroskills

11. Use cohesive devices in spoken discourse.
12. Accomplish appropriately communicative functions according to situations, participants, and goals.
13. Use appropriate registers, implicature, pragmatic conventions, and other sociolinguistic features in face-to-face conversations.
14. Convey links and connections between events and communicate such relations as main idea, supporting idea, new information, given information, generalization, and exemplification.
15. Use facial features, kinesics, body language, and other nonverbal cues along with verbal language to convey meanings.
16. Develop and use a battery of speaking strategies, such as emphasizing key words, rephrasing, providing a context for interpreting the meaning of words, appealing for help, and accurately assessing how well your interlocutor is understanding you.

TYPES OF CLASSROOM SPEAKING PERFORMANCE

In Chapter 15, six types of listening performance were listed. With the obvious connection between listening and speaking, six similar categories apply to the kinds of oral production that students are expected to carry out in the classroom.

1. Imitative

A very limited portion of classroom speaking time may legitimately be spent generating rehearsed, imitative speech, where, for example, learners practice an intonation contour or try to pinpoint a certain vowel sound. Imitation of this kind is carried out not for the purpose of meaningful interaction, but for focusing on some particular element of language form.

Is *drilling* a legitimate part of the communicative language classroom? The answer is a qualified "yes." Drills offer students an opportunity to listen and to orally repeat certain strings of language that may pose some linguistic difficulty—either phonological or grammatical. Drills are to language teaching what the pitching machine is to baseball. They offer limited practice through repetition. They allow one to focus on one element of language in a controlled activity. They can help to establish certain psychomotor patterns (to "loosen the tongue") and to associate selected grammatical forms with their appropriate context. Here are some useful guidelines:

GUIDELINES FOR SUCCESSFUL DRILLS

- Keep them short (a few minutes of a class hour only).
- Keep them simple (preferably just one point at a time).
- Keep them quick-paced and "snappy."
- Make sure students know why they are doing the drill.
- Limit them to phonological, morphological, or syntactic points.
- Make sure they ultimately lead to communicative goals.
- Don't overuse them.

2. Intensive

Intensive speaking goes one step beyond imitative to include any speaking performance that is designed to practice some phonological or grammatical aspect of language. Intensive speaking can be self-initiated or it can even form part of some pair work activity, where learners are "going over" certain forms of language.

3. Responsive

A good deal of student speech in the classroom is responsive: short replies to teacher- or student-initiated questions or comments. These replies are usually sufficient and do not extend into dialogues (categories 4 and 5). Such speech can be meaningful and authentic:

T: How are you today?
S: Pretty good, thanks; and you?

T: What is the main idea in this essay?
S: The United Nations should have more authority.

S1: So, what did you write for question number one?
S2: Well, I wasn't sure, so I left it blank.

4. Transactional (Dialogue)

Transactional language, carried out for the purpose of conveying or exchanging specific information, is an extended form of responsive language. Conversations, for example, may have more of a negotiative nature to them than does responsive speech:

T: What is the main idea in this essay?
S: The United Nations should have more authority.
T: More authority than what?
S: Than it does right now.
T: What do you mean?
S: Well, for example, the UN should have the power to force a country to destroy its nuclear weapons.
T: You don't think the UN has that power now?
S: I don't think so. Some countries are still manufacturing nuclear bombs.

Such conversations could readily be part of group work activity as well.

Classroom Connections

In conversations such as the one above, how do language users *negotiate* meaning? What conversation strategies were used to negotiate meaning? How effective was the teacher in encouraging the student to clarify or expand ideas? What, if anything, would you have done differently if you were the teacher?

5. Interpersonal (Dialogue)

The other form of conversation mentioned in Chapter 15 was *interpersonal dialogue*, carried out more for the purpose of maintaining social relationships than for the transmission of facts and information. These conversations are a little trickier for learners because they can involve some or all of the following factors:

Characteristics of Interpersonal Conversation

- a casual register
- colloquial language
- emotionally charged language
- slang
- ellipsis
- sarcasm
- hidden meanings that require understanding "between the lines"

For example:

Amy: Hi, Bob, how's it going?

Bob: Oh, so-so.

Amy: Not a great weekend, huh?

Bob: Well, far be it from me to criticize, but I'm pretty miffed about last week.

Amy: What are you talking about?

Bob: I think you know perfectly well what I'm talking about.

Amy: Oh, that . . . How come you get so bent out of shape over something like that?

Bob: Well, whose fault was it, huh?

Amy: Oh, wow, this is great. Wonderful. Back to square one. For crying out loud, Bob, I thought we'd settled this before. Well, what more can I say?

Learners would need to learn how such features as the relationship between interlocutors, casual style, and sarcasm are coded linguistically in this conversation.

Classroom Connections

In the above conversation between Amy and Bob, what are some examples of the seven characteristics of interpersonal conversation listed? The last three—ellipsis, sarcasm, and hidden meaning—are often difficult for learners to discern. How would you go about teaching learners, first, to comprehend these elements, and then to produce them in authentic conversation?

6. Extensive (Monologue)

Finally, students at intermediate to advanced levels are sometimes asked to give extended monologues in the form of oral reports, summaries, or perhaps short speeches. Here the register is more formal and deliberative. These monologues can be planned or impromptu.

PRINCIPLES FOR TEACHING SPEAKING SKILLS

Let's look at some of the foundational principles that should guide your teaching of OC skills.

1. Focus on Both *Fluency* and *Accuracy*, Depending on Your Objective

In our current zeal for interactive language teaching, we can easily slip into a pattern of providing zesty, content-based, interactive activities that don't capitalize on grammatical pointers or pronunciation tips. We need to bear in mind a spectrum of learner needs, from language-based focus on accuracy to message-based focus on interaction, meaning, and fluency. When you do a jigsaw group technique, play a game, or discuss solutions to the environmental crisis, make sure that your tasks have a linguistic (language-based) objective, and seize the opportunity to help students to perceive and use the building blocks of language. At the same time, don't bore your students with lifeless, repetitious drills. As noted above, make any drilling you do as meaningful as possible.

Classroom Connections

Let's say you're leading your students in a task (in small groups) that involves locating buildings on a map and giving directions on how to go from point "A" to point "B". What might be some *language-based* objectives in such a task? How would you make sure your students pursue those objectives? Consider pre-task preparation, and then what would you do *while* students are performing the task, and how might you assess their success?

2. Ascertain That the *Complexity* of Your Techniques Is Appropriate

As we noted above, speaking tasks can range from very simple to extremely complex, depending on linguistic, cognitive, and task-design elements. As you design and carry out techniques, put yourself into the shoes of your learners, ascertaining that the complexity of task is appropriate for your learners' proficiency levels. Sometimes activities may be linguistically simple, for example, but involve task complexity that causes undue difficulty.

3. Provide Techniques That Spark the *Interest* of Students

Try at all times to appeal to students' interests, daily lives outside the classroom, cultural habits, and to what is of genuine relevance to them, and ultimately to continuing their language learning journey. Even in those techniques that don't send students into ecstasy, help them to see how the activity will benefit them. Often students don't know why we ask them to do certain tasks and activities. It doesn't hurt to tell them, as in, "This task will help to be able to order from an online store."

4. Encourage the Use of *Authentic* Language in *Meaningful* Contexts

This theme has been played time and again in this book, but one more reminder shouldn't hurt! It is not easy to keep coming up with meaningful interaction. It's easy to succumb to the temptation to do disconnected grammar exercises when we go around the room calling on students one by one to pick the right answer. It takes energy and creativity to devise authentic contexts and meaningful interaction, but with the help of a storehouse of teacher resource material (see recommended books and articles at the end of this chapter) it can be done. Even drills can be structured to provide a sense of authenticity.

5. Provide Appropriate *Feedback*

In most "foreign" language situations, students are totally dependent on the teacher for useful linguistic feedback. In the context of L2 learning within an L2 speaking culture, they may get such feedback "out there" beyond the classroom, but even then you are in a position to be of great benefit. It is important that you take advantage of your knowledge of the L2 to inject the kinds of feedback that are appropriate for the moment, and that will help students to *notice* elements of language that need work.

CLASSROOM CONNECTIONS

How likely is it that in natural conversations outside the classroom, an L1 hearer will actually correct an L2 speaker's mistakes? Unless speech is totally incomprehensible—which might elicit a "What?" from the hearer—corrective feedback is unlikely. How might a teacher encourage students to *solicit* corrective feedback outside the classroom? What kinds of discourse devices could L2 learners use in that solicitation, without becoming annoying?

6. Capitalize on the Natural *Link* Between Speaking and Listening

Many interactive techniques that involve speaking will also, of course, include listening. Don't lose out on opportunities to integrate these two skills. As you are perhaps focusing on speaking goals, listening goals may naturally coincide, and the two skills can reinforce each other. Skills in producing language are often initiated through comprehension.

7. Give Students Opportunities to *Initiate* Oral Communication

A good deal of typical classroom interaction is characterized by teacher initiation of language. We ask questions, give directions, and provide information, and students have been conditioned only to "speak when spoken to." Part of OC competence is the ability to initiate conversations, to nominate topics, to ask questions, to control conversations, and to change the subject. As you design and use speaking techniques, ask yourself if you have allowed students to initiate language.

8. Encourage the Development of Speaking *Strategies*

The concept of strategic competence (see *PLLT*, Chapters 5 and 8) is one that few beginning language students are aware of. They simply have not thought about developing their own personal strategies for accomplishing oral communicative purposes. Your classroom can be one in which students become aware of, and have a chance to practice, such strategies as the following:

ORAL COMMUNICATION STRATEGIES TO TEACH L2 LEARNERS

- asking for clarification (*What?*)
- asking someone to repeat something (*Huh? Excuse me?*)
- using fillers (*Uh, I mean, Well*) in order to gain time to process
- using conversation maintenance cues (*Uh huh, Right, Yeah, Okay, Hm*)
- getting someone's attention (*Hey, Say, So*)
- using paraphrases for structures one can't produce
- appealing for assistance from the interlocutor (to get a word or phrase, for example)
- using formulaic expressions (at the survival stage) (*How much does ______ cost? How do you get to the ______ ?*)
- using mime and nonverbal expressions to convey meaning

TEACHING CONVERSATION

Research on teaching conversational skills (Tarone, 2005; McCarthy & O'Keeffe, 2010; Lazaraton, 2014) historically describes two major approaches for teaching conversation. The first is an *indirect* approach in which learners are more or less set loose to engage in interaction. The second is a *direct* approach that "involves planning a conversation program around the specific microskills, strategies, and processes that are involved in fluent conversation" (Richards 1990, pp. 76–77).

The indirect approach implies that one does not actually *teach* conversation, but rather that students acquire conversational competence, peripherally, by engaging in meaningful tasks. A direct approach explicitly calls students' attention to conversational rules, conventions, and strategies.

Classroom Connections

In L2 classes that you have taken or taught, have you noticed, in groups or pairs, that students are talking a *lot*, with plenty of give-and-take and no loss for words? When that happens, to what extent is that discourse focused on some specific microskill or grammatical or discourse feature? Is it purposeful to have such stretches of *fluent* conversation with no formal focus? If so, what are those purposes?

While both approaches can be found in language-teaching institutions around the world, recent developments in such models as task-based language teaching (TBLT) have taken the learner well beyond simply using language. Research on SLA strongly suggests the inclusion focus on form, including analysis and practice, as an integral part of every task (Nunan, 2004; Loewen, 2011; Sheen & Ellis, 2011; Spada, 2011). Likewise, Skehan (1998a, p. 131) recommended that communicative tasks "maximize the chances of a focus on form through attentional manipulation." It is clear, upon scanning current English language textbooks, that the prevailing approach to teaching conversation includes the learner's inductive involvement in meaningful tasks as well as consciousness-raising elements of focus on form.

What are some the specific elements of conversation implied in the current research on teaching conversation? We have adapted a list of features from Richards (1990, pp. 79–80) to create the following possible goals:

Potential Goals to Incorporate into Conversation Tasks

- conversing for both transactional and interactional purposes
- producing both short and long turns in conversation
- encouraging strategies for managing turn-taking in conversation
- teaching strategies for opening and closing conversations
- initiating, developing, maintaining, and responding to a range of topics

- using casual, neutral, and formal styles of speaking
- using conversation in different social settings and social encounters
- developing strategies for repairing trouble spots in conversation, including communication breakdowns and comprehension problems
- maintaining fluency in conversation through avoiding excessive pausing, breakdowns, and errors of grammar or pronunciation
- using conversational fillers and small talk
- using conversational routines

Classroom Connections

If you were teaching students to "use conversation in different social settings and social encounters," what are some of those settings and encounters? How does a telephone conversation, for example, differ from face-to-face conversation in a social setting, such as at a party, lunching with a friend, or striking up a conversation with a stranger?

What follows on pages 361–368 are some sample tasks and activities from textbooks that illustrate teaching various aspects of conversation.

- The first (Figure 16.1) is an activity for beginners, and involves conversation about daily schedules, using the simple present tense.
- The second excerpt (Figure 16.2), for an intermediate level, gets students to give advice (imperatives) about things they should try.
- The third example (Figure 16.3) is also for an intermediate level, giving students an opportunity to request information about clothing and to place an order.
- The fourth lesson excerpt (Figure 16.4) is for advanced students, a role play that raises awareness of communication styles.

Figure 16.1 Describe Your Schedule (Saslow & Ascher, 2006, pp. 70–71). Reprinted by permission.

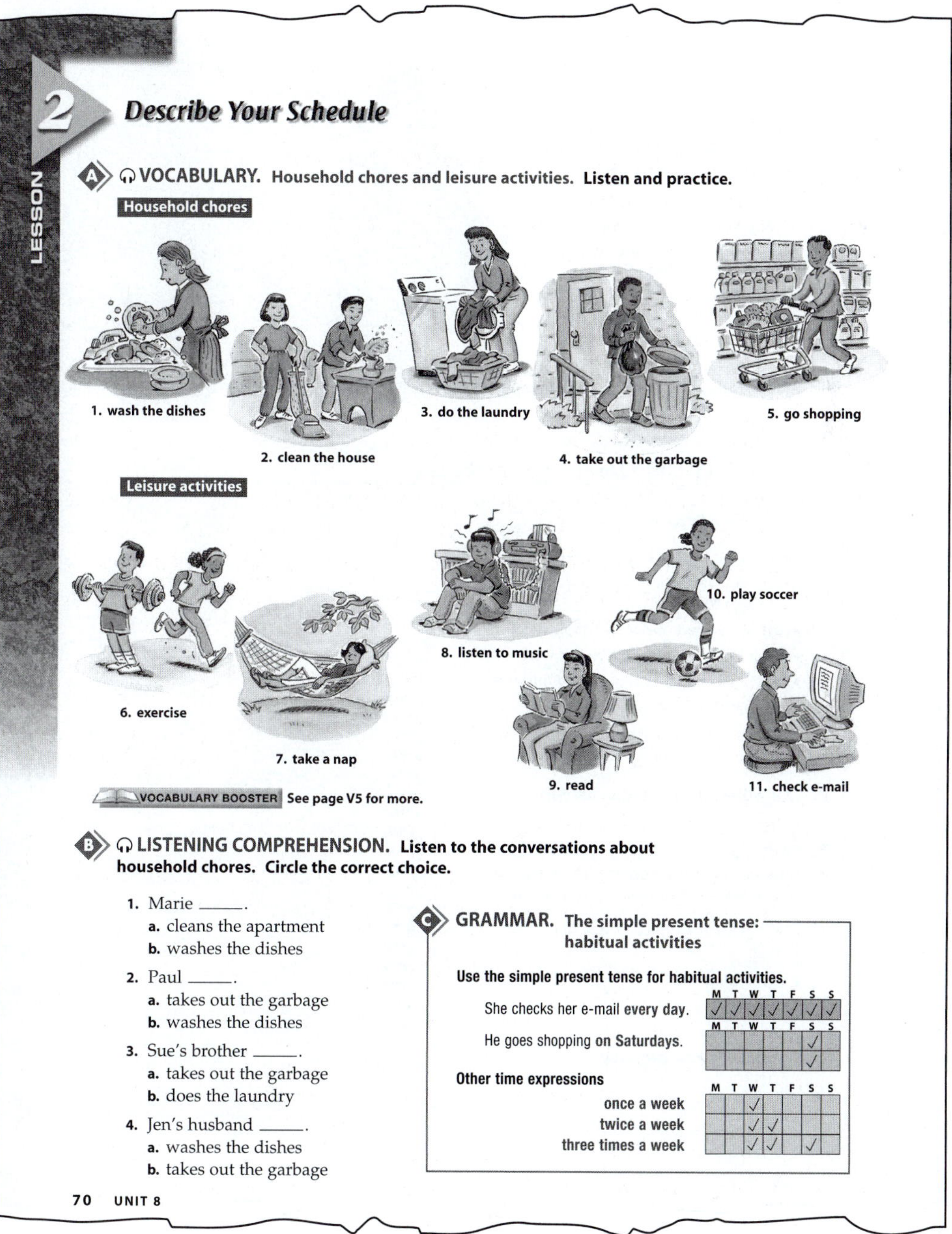

LESSON
2
Describe Your Schedule
A VOCABULARY. Household chores and leisure activities. Listen and practice.
Household chores
1. wash the dishes
2. clean the house
3. do the laundry
4. take out the garbage
5. go shopping
Leisure activities
6. exercise
7. take a nap
8. listen to music
9. read
10. play soccer
11. check e-mail
VOCABULARY BOOSTER See page V5 for more.
B LISTENING COMPREHENSION. Listen to the conversations about household chores. Circle the correct choice.
1. Marie ____.
a. cleans the apartment
b. washes the dishes
2. Paul ____.
a. takes out the garbage
b. washes the dishes
3. Sue's brother ____.
a. takes out the garbage
b. does the laundry
4. Jen's husband ____.
a. washes the dishes
b. takes out the garbage
C GRAMMAR. The simple present tense: habitual activities
Use the simple present tense for habitual activities.
She checks her e-mail every day.
He goes shopping on Saturdays.
Other time expressions
once a week
twice a week
three times a week
M T W T F S S
70 UNIT 8

Figure 16.1 Describe Your Schedule (*Continued*)

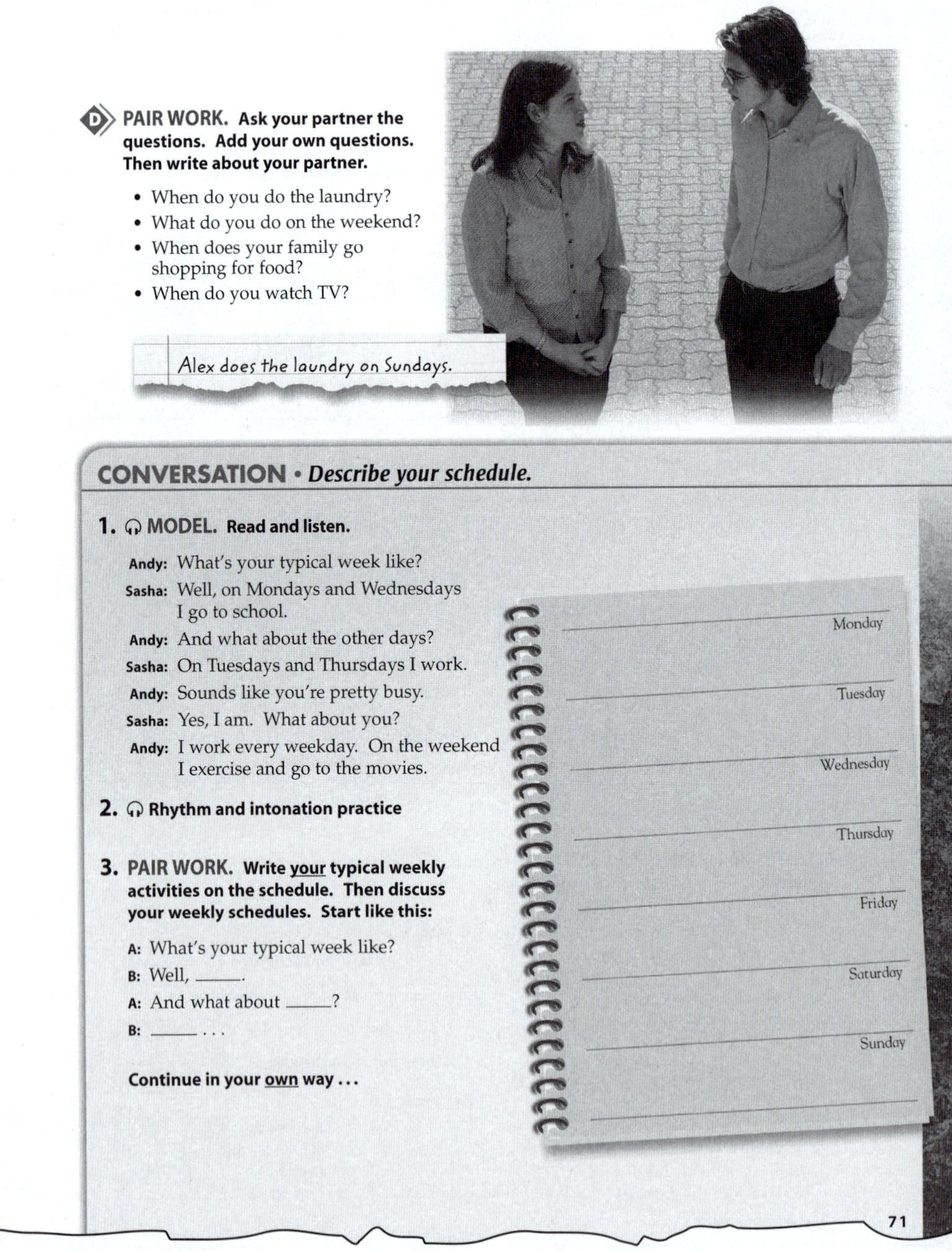

D PAIR WORK. Ask your partner the questions. Add your own questions. Then write about your partner.

- When do you do the laundry?
- What do you do on the weekend?
- When does your family go shopping for food?
- When do you watch TV?

Alex does the laundry on Sundays.

CONVERSATION • *Describe your schedule.*

1. MODEL. Read and listen.

Andy: What's your typical week like?
Sasha: Well, on Mondays and Wednesdays I go to school.
Andy: And what about the other days?
Sasha: On Tuesdays and Thursdays I work.
Andy: Sounds like you're pretty busy.
Sasha: Yes, I am. What about you?
Andy: I work every weekday. On the weekend I exercise and go to the movies.

2. Rhythm and intonation practice

3. PAIR WORK. Write your typical weekly activities on the schedule. Then discuss your weekly schedules. Start like this:

A: What's your typical week like?
B: Well, ______.
A: And what about ______?
B: ______ . . .

Continue in your own way . . .

71

Figure 16.2 How do you stay healthy? (Helgeson, Brown, & Wiltshier, 2010, pp. 28–30). Reprinted by permission.

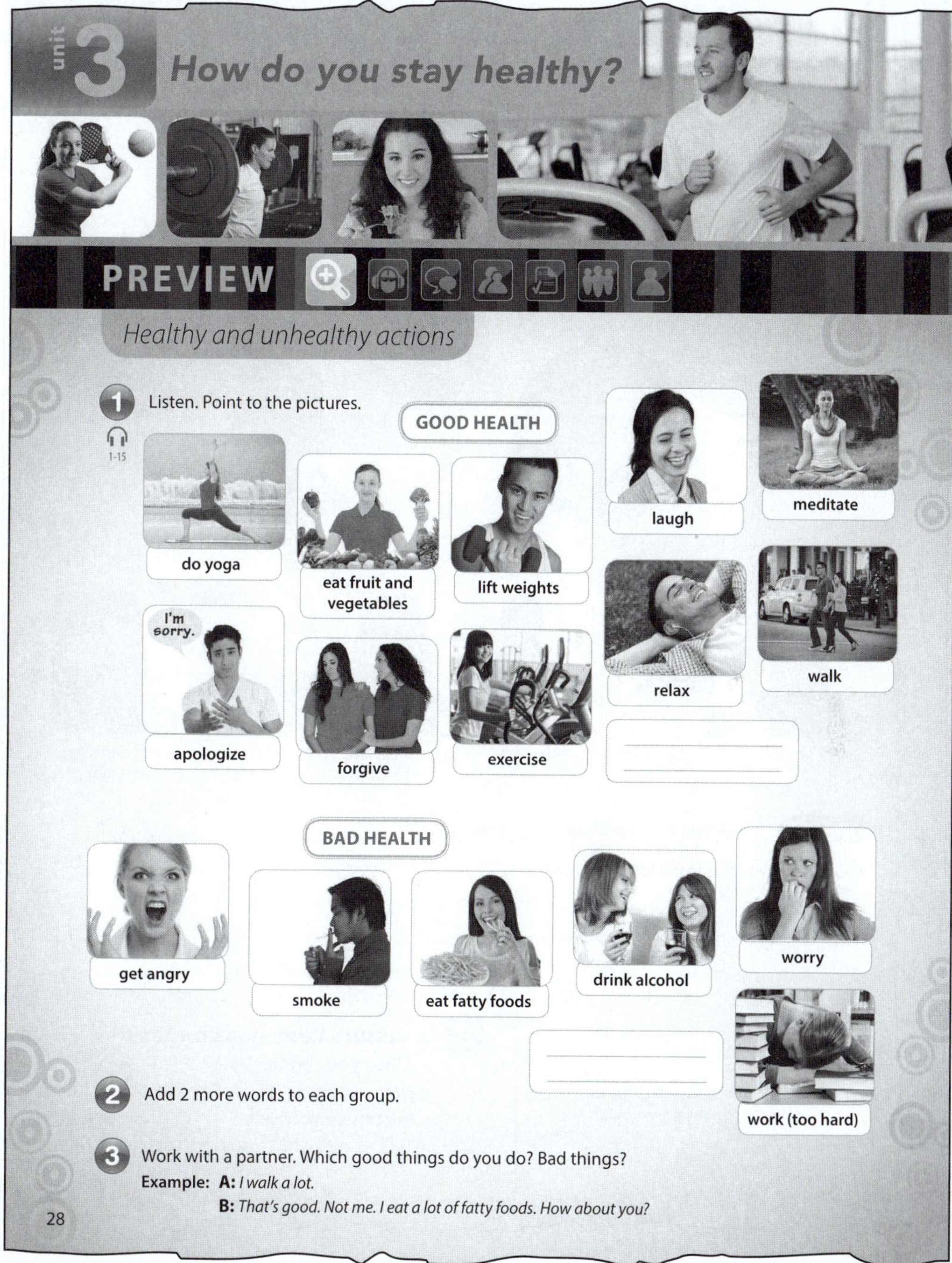

Figure 16.2 How do you stay healthy? (*Continued*)

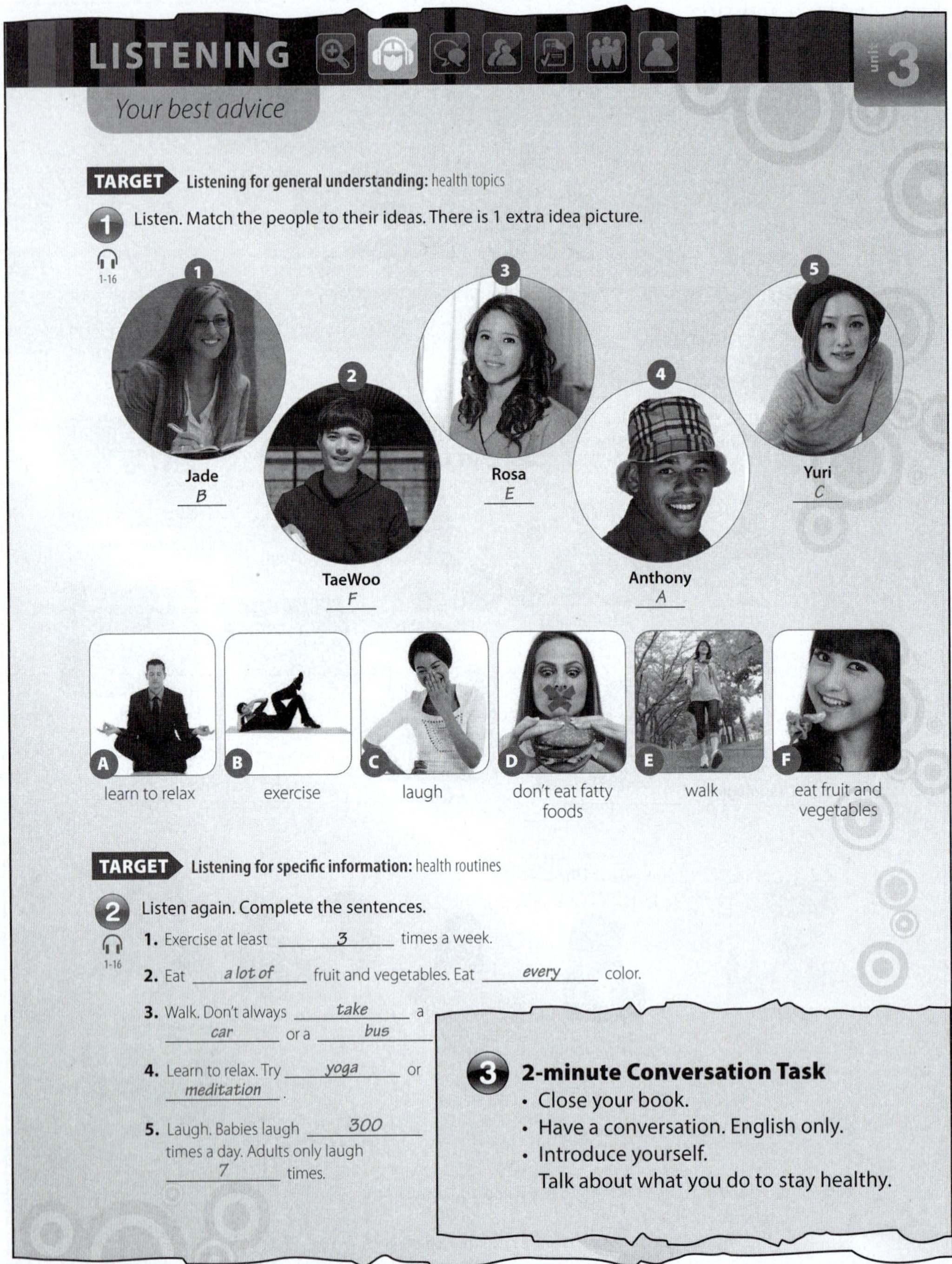

Figure 16.3 Ordering from a catalog (Brown, New Vistas 2, 1999, pp. 131–132)

Information Gap Activity 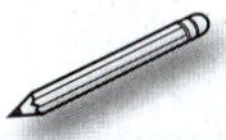 Student A

You are a telephone salesperson for the Best Wear Company. Your partner is a customer. Your partner calls to order some items from your company' s catalog. Take the order and fill out the order form. Make sure you have written the order correctly by asking your partner to confirm it. Don't look at your partner's page!

Ordered by:

Name ______________________

Address ______________________

City ______________________

State ____________ Zip ________

Telephone ______________________

Ship to: (Use only if different from "ORDERED BY")

Name ______________________

Address ______________________

City ______________________

State ____________ Zip ________

Item number	Quantity	Color	Size	Description	Unit price	Total

Merchandise Total	
Shipping and Handling	
Total	

Method of Payment

[ ] store account [ ] credit card
[ ] check [ ] debit card

Useful Language

Answering the telephone:	**Hello, Best Wear Company.**
Asking for information:	**What's the item number (or price)?**
	What color (or size) would you like?
Confirming the order:	**Did you say the item number (or price or color or size) was . . .?**
Ending the conversation:	**Thank you for your order. Good-bye.**

Figure 16.3 Ordering from a catalog (*Continued*)

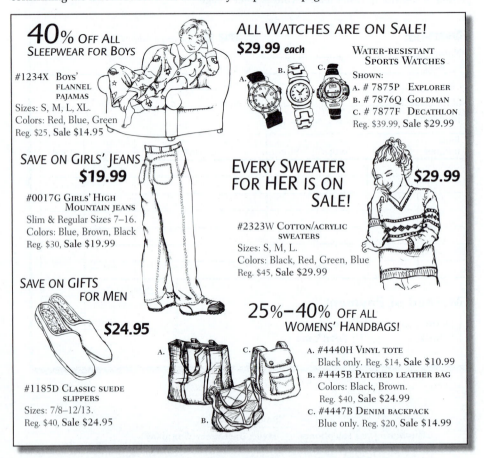

Information Gap Activity 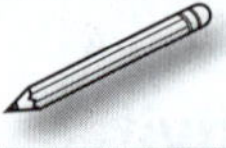 Student B

You want to place a catalog order. Your partner is a telephone salesperson. Look at the catalog page below. Choose two items you want to buy. Call the Best Wear Company and give your order to your partner. Make sure that your partner takes the order correctly by confirming the information. Don't look at your partner's page!

40% Off All Sleepwear for Boys

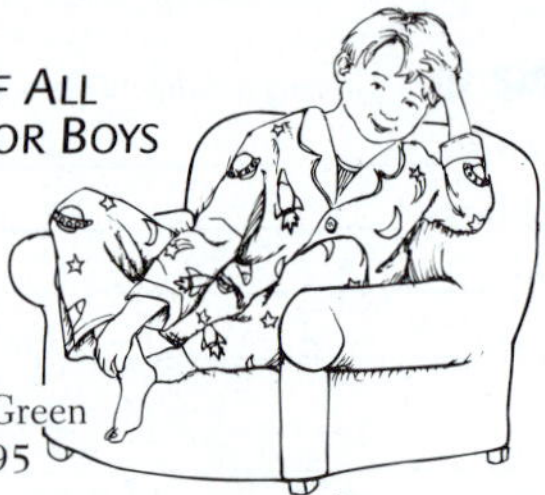

#1234X Boys' flannel pajamas
Sizes: S, M, L, XL.
Colors: Red, Blue, Green
Reg. $25, Sale $14.95

All Watches Are on Sale!

$29.99 each

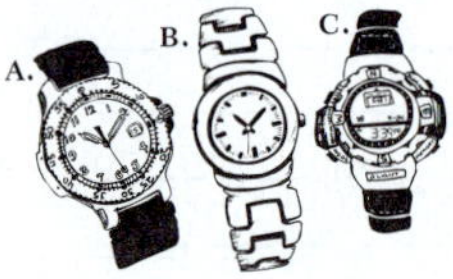

Water-resistant Sports Watches
Shown:
A. # 7875P Explorer
B. # 7876Q Goldman
C. # 7877F Decathlon
Reg. $39.99, Sale $29.99

Save on Girls' Jeans

$19.99

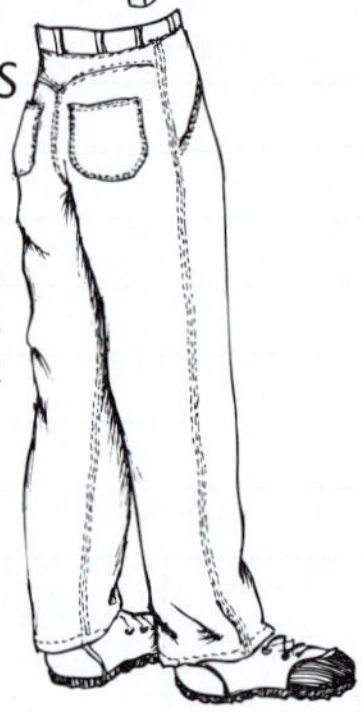

#0017G Girls' High Mountain jeans
Slim & Regular Sizes 7–16.
Colors: Blue, Brown, Black
Reg. $30, Sale $19.99

Every Sweater for HER Is on Sale!

$29.99

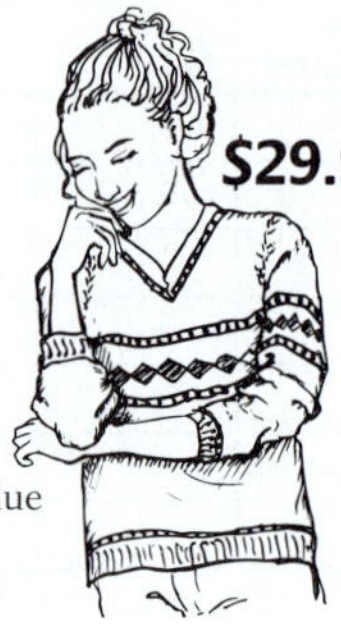

#2323W Cotton/acrylic sweaters
Sizes: S, M, L.
Colors: Black, Red, Green, Blue
Reg. $45, Sale $29.99

Save on Gifts for Men

$24.95

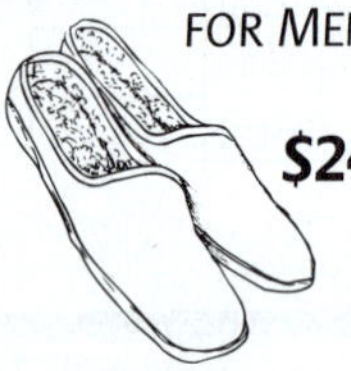

#1185D Classic suede slippers
Sizes: 7/8–12/13.
Reg. $40, Sale $24.95

25%–40% Off All Womens' Handbags!

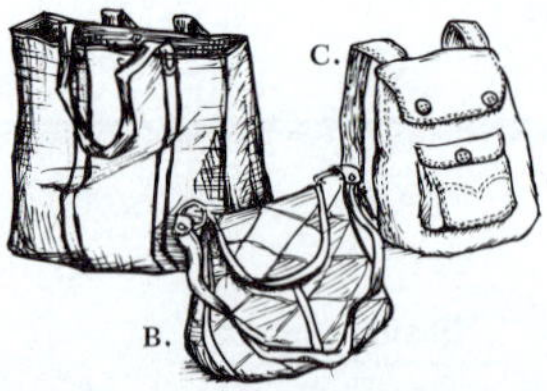

A. #4440H Vinyl tote
Black only. Reg. $14, Sale $10.99
B. #4445B Patched leather bag
Colors: Black, Brown.
Reg. $40, Sale $24.99
C. #4447B Denim backpack
Blue only. Reg. $20, Sale $14.99

Useful Language

Starting the conversation:	**Hello. I'd like to place an order.**
Placing an order:	**I'd like . . . .**
Confirming the order:	**Yes, I said the item number (price or color or size) is . . . .**

Figure 16.4 Direct and indirect communication styles (Dale, 2013, pp. 87–88)

II. Direct and Indirect Communication Styles

In some cultures, people are very direct. They usually tell others exactly how they think or feel about a situation. People from the United States, Canada, Australia, England, Israel, and Germany tend to communicate very directly. In contrast, people from countries like Japan, China, Korea, Thailand, and Mexico often communicate indirectly. They worry about hurting people's feelings if they disagree or show they are unhappy about a situation. They often avoid direct eye contact with their listeners.

ACTIVITY 1 Role-play Direct and Indirect Communication Styles

1 Work with a partner. Choose one of the following situations to role-play.

a. You want to get to know a classmate. You would like to invite him or her for a cup of coffee after class.

b. You have been working for the same company for two years for the same salary. You work very hard. You would like to ask your boss to give you a raise.

c. Your friend borrowed a book from you and hasn't given it back. You need the book to study. You would like your friend to return your book.

d. You just got married. You are shopping for furniture with your spouse. You think the furniture your spouse likes is ugly. You would like to buy different furniture.

e. Your teacher made a mistake grading your exam. She gave you a B instead of a B+. You would like her to correct her mistake.

f. You just had a wonderful lunch in a café with your boyfriend or girlfriend. The waiter brings your bill and has charged you too much for your lunch. You would like the waiter to correct the mistake before you pay.

2 Write a simple dialog about the situation you chose. Think of the words and body language you might use if you have an *indirect* communication style.

EXAMPLE:

Situation: You bought a new portable radio that didn't work properly. You bring it back to the store and show it to the salesman who sold it to you. Your conversation goes like this:

You: I am so sorry to bother you.

Salesman: How can I help you?

You: [*looking down at the floor*] I just bought this radio and it doesn't work.

Salesman: Oh, that's too bad.

You: Isn't there something you can do about this? [*still looking down at the floor*]

Salesman: No, I'm sorry.

You: Thank you anyway. [*You leave the store with the broken radio.*]

3 Now write a dialog about the situation in which you use a *direct* communication style.

EXAMPLE:

You: [*looking directly at the salesman*] Excuse me. I just bought this radio and it doesn't work.

Salesman: Oh, that's too bad.

You: [*still looking directly at the salesman*] I would like a refund, please.

Salesman: I'm sorry, we don't give refunds.

Communicating across Cultures **87**

Figure 16.4 Direct and indirect communication styles (*Continued*)

You: Then I would like to speak to the manager, please. Would you call him?
Manager: What seems to be the problem here?
You: I just bought this radio and it doesn't work. Here is my receipt. I would like a refund, please.
Manager: Of course, I will take care of this for you.
You: Thank you very much.

4 Act out (role-play) your situation in front of the class twice. First use the indirect communication style. Then use the direct one.

5 After all the role plays, discuss the following questions in small groups:

a. Which communication style are you more comfortable with—direct or indirect?
b. Which style is used most often in your culture?
c. How would people from your culture handle the situations in Activity 1?

ACTIVITY 2 Interpret Behaviors

1 Misunderstandings happen when we don't understand why people from different cultures act the way they do. Look at the student behaviors in the chart. List possible reasons why the person is behaving that way. The first item is completed as an example.

Student Behavior	Possible Reasons
1. doesn't look at other people when speaking	-it is rude in the student's culture -student lacks confidence -student is dishonest -student dislikes person she is speaking to
2. constantly apologizes	
3. shrugs shoulders when asked questions	
4. always sits away from everyone else	
5. usually sits way in the back of the classroom	
6. says "yes" to everything	
7. gives opinions without being asked	
8. never gives opinions, even when asked	
9. asks lots of questions	
10. acts embarrassed when called on by the teacher	
11. does not participate in class discussions	

2 Work in small groups. Share the reasons you listed for each behavior in the chart. Then discuss these questions:

a. Were you surprised by your classmates' reasons for a behavior? Why?
b. If there were differences in the reasons you and your classmates listed, were they caused by differences in culture or by something else?

88 Chapter 7

ORAL COMMUNICATION FOR ACADEMIC PURPOSES

Courses that are designed for academic purposes usually entail a specialized set of objectives and tasks, because students are learning the L2 for the purpose of pursuing a degree in the medium of the L2 (Belcher, 2009; Johns & Price, 2014). These courses often target certain disciplines, such as business, medicine, or law, which involve their own unique genres of language in both written and oral modes. In all disciplines, it's safe to say oral production skills in the academy share some commonalities in conventions for discussion and presentations, which we'll touch on briefly here.

Discussions

One of the most difficult aspects of L2 learning is developing the ability to initiate and sustain discussion in the classroom. In an era in which many classrooms around the world—in all disciplines—use a variety of group and pair work, being an active participant is essential. Students can no longer count on an academic course of study that will consist simply of a teacher or professor lecturing from start to finish.

So what are some of the skills that learners need to acquire? In Chapter 13 (page 275) we outlined some classroom language functions (Sarosy & Sherak, 2006) that are involved:

Classroom Language Functions

- interrupting another student (" . . . Excuse me . . . ")
- asking for clarification ("Sorry, what did you mean by ____?")
- asking for more information ("Could you elaborate, please?")
- agreeing and disagreeing politely ("I see your point, but . . . ")
- supporting your opinion ("Let me tell you why . . . ")
- coming to a consensus ("Would you all agree to . . . ?")
- going over exercises with a partner ("Oh, I wrote something different")
- giving oral feedback to peers' written work ("Have you thought about . . . ?")

Figure 16.5 (page 370) is an excerpt from a textbook on academic English (Cassriel & Martinsen, 2010), a lesson that focuses on agreeing and disagreeing with a point of view. Following several exercises in listening and writing, students listen to a radio report in which several interviewees state their opinion.

Figure 16.5 Using waste vegetable oil (Cassriel & Martinsen, 2010, pp. 92–93)

3. *Listen to excerpts from a radio report on using waste vegetable oil to power cars. In the Excerpt column of the chart, take notes on what each person says. Then compare your notes with a partner's. You will use the other columns of the chart later.*

Excerpt	Ideas from the Lecture	Relationship between Ideas (Agree/Disagree)
1. Kent Glass, reporter *WVO=good alternative* *Oil=used twice* *Driving car = better for environment*	Using waste vegetable oil is like turning garbage into gold.	
2. Peter Berger, WVO user	WVO is cheap.	
3. Peter Berger, WVO user	WVO is easy to use.	
4. Kim Wei, environmental studies expert	WVO is a simple and green alternative to petroleum fuel.	

4. *Compare the notes you took on each excerpt with the information in the Ideas from the Lecture column. In the Relationship between Ideas column, write* **Agree** *or* **Disagree** *to describe how the speaker in the excerpt would probably feel about the idea from the lecture.*

5. *Discuss the questions in small groups.*

1. Which green chemistry principles from page 83 does WVO follow?

2. How does WVO compare to other fuels you have learned about? Explain your answers.

   Example

   In my opinion, WVO is better than other biofuels because . . .

3. What are some other solutions to our dependence on petroleum? What can we do as individuals and in our communities?

Three questions are posed for students to discuss, all requiring the use of classroom language.

Classroom Connections

What are some specific phrases that students might use in discussing the questions listed in Figure 16.5, especially in agreeing or disagreeing with a classmate? For question 3, what are some ways a student could introduce some proposed solutions?

Presentations

A second distinguishing characteristic of academic oral communication is the frequent demand for making presentations. These range from brief, informal, quickly prepared monologues to longer "speeches" that are prepared well in advance and are more formal. The former might be less than a minute in duration while the latter could involve much longer stretches of time with potential question-and-answer periods following.

In Figure 16.6 (pages 372–373) we have included part of a unit for advanced students on giving a persuasive speech (Dale & Wolf, 2013). What has preceded this stage of the unit is listening to a speech, learning about presentation aids, pronunciation tips, and how to build on areas of agreement, including dealing with hostile listeners. Note that part of the preparation for giving a presentation involves interviewing classmates.

TEACHING PRONUNCIATION

Views on teaching pronunciation changed dramatically over the last half of the twentieth century (Lane, 2010; Murphy, 2013). In the heyday of the Audiolingual Method and its various behavioristic variants, the pronunciation component of a course or program was a mainstay. But in the 1970s, as the language-teaching profession began to experience revolutionary changes (see Chapter 2), explicit pedagogical focus on linguistic "nuts and bolts" was under siege by proponents of the various nondirective "let-it-just-happen" approaches to language teaching. Pronunciation instruction became somewhat incidental to a course of study.

However, the mid-1980s saw greater attention to grammatical structures as important elements in discourse, and to a balance between fluency and *accuracy*. With a focus on form becoming an accepted and necessary component of communicative approaches, and with convincing research providing support,

Figure 16.6 A speech to persuade (Dale & Wolf, 2103, pp. 199–200). Reprinted by permission.

V. Presentation Project: A Speech to Persuade

Choose a topic that is controversial and about which you feel strongly. Your project is to prepare and present a four- to five-minute speech to persuade. Your goal is to convince your audience to agree with your point of view.

STEP 1 | Formulate a Persuasive Claim

Review Choosing Your Topic on page 181 to refresh your memory on how to choose a topic and formulate a persuasive claim. You may choose any of the sample topics on page 182 or another one.

STEP 2 | Analyze Your Audience

A **Review Analyzing Your Audience on page 185.**

B **Interview as many classmates as possible to learn how they feel about your specific persuasive claim. Use the opinion survey form below to record your findings. If they disagree or are indifferent, ask them why.**

AUDIENCE ANALYSIS FORM

Persuasive Claim: ______________________________

Record how each of your classmates feels about your topic by placing a checkmark in the appropriate column.

Disagree	Indifferent	Agree
✓ ____________	✓ ____________	✓ ____________
____________	____________	____________
Total = ________	Total = ________	Total = ________

If your classmates are indifferent, it is because (check all reasons given):

_____ They don't think your topic affects them.

_____ They have never heard of your topic.

_____ They have never given your topic any thought.

_____ Other: ______________________________

____

If your classmates disagree with your opinion, it is because (write all reasons given):

1. ______________________________
2. ______________________________
3. ______________________________
4. ______________________________
5. ______________________________

Figure 16.6 A speech to persuade (*Continued*)

STEP 3 | Plan Your Speech

A **Review your completed outline of Feng's persuasive speech on page 195. Pay attention to the parts of his speech.**

B **Read the guidelines for organizing your speech.**

Introduction

1. Build on areas of agreement.
2. State your specific persuasive claim.
3. Preview your main persuasive arguments.

Body

1. Include three persuasive arguments to support your claim.
2. Provide evidence.
   - Cite sources.
   - Use examples.
   - Use presentation aids.
3. Include transitions stating the reasons why listeners disagree with your claim and your intention to disprove those reasons.

Conclusion

1. Repeat your persuasive claim in the opening summary sentence. Then summarize your main persuasive points.
2. Conclude with memorable remarks.

C **Read the Useful Language you can use during your persuasive speech. Place a check mark ✓ next to the expressions you like best.**

USEFUL LANGUAGE: BUILDING ON AREAS OF AGREEMENT

______ I'm sure everyone here worries about . . .

______ The majority of people would agree that . . .

______ Most of us know someone who . . .

______ We all love and care about our families and dear friends. Therefore we all hope that...

USEFUL LANGUAGE: TRANSITIONS

______ Many of you disagree with [topic] because. . . . Let me assure you that . . .

______ Some of you don't think [topic] is important. My evidence proves ______ is very important.

______ Many of you were against [topic] because. . . . I have solid proof that shows . . . [the opposite]

200 Chapter 9

it became clear that pronunciation was a key to gaining full communicative competence.

Current approaches to pronunciation contrast starkly with the early approaches (Murphy, 2013). Rather than attempting only to build a learner's articulatory competence from the bottom up, and simply as the mastery of a list of phonemes and allophones, a top-down approach is taken in which the most relevant features of pronunciation—stress, rhythm, and intonation—are given high priority. Instead of teaching only the role of articulation *within* words, or at best, phrases, we teach its role in a whole stream of discourse.

Classroom Connections

How did the prevailing language teaching methods of the mid-twentieth century justify a heavy focus on teaching pronunciation of segmental sounds and words? How does a focus on phonology in current communicative approaches differ? In what way is an approach that features stress, rhythm, and intonation a *top-down* approach?

Three decades ago, Wong (1987, p. 21) reminded us that "contemporary views [of language] hold that the sounds of language are less crucial for understanding than the way they are organized. . . . Rhythm and intonation merit greater priority in the teaching program than attention to individual sounds." Wong's comments reflected an approach that put all aspects of English pronunciation into the perspective of a communicative, interactive view of human speech. Once again, history taught us the lesson of maintaining balance.

Many learners of L2s feel that their ultimate goal in pronunciation should be accent-free speech that is indistinguishable from that of a native speaker. Such a goal is not only unattainable (see *PLLT*, Chapter 3) for virtually every adult learner, but in a multilingual, multicultural world, accents are quite acceptable. With the rapid spread of English as an international language, native accents pose virtually no barrier to cross-cultural communication. Moreover, as the world community comes to appreciate and value people's heritage, one's accent is just another symbol of that heritage.

Our goal as teachers of English pronunciation should therefore be more realistically focused on clear, comprehensible pronunciation. At the beginning levels, we want learners to surpass that threshold beneath which pronunciation detracts from their ability to communicate. At the advanced levels, pronunciation goals can focus on elements that enhance communication: intonation features that go beyond basic patterns, voice quality, phonetic distinctions between registers, and other refinements that are far more important in the overall stream of clear communication than rolling the English /r/ or getting a vowel to perfectly imitate a native speaker.

What are the factors within learners that affect pronunciation, and how can you deal with each of them? Here is a list of variables to consider.

Learner Factors That Affect Pronunciation

1. **Native language.** Clearly, the native language is the most influential factor affecting a learner's pronunciation (see *PLLT*, Chapter 9). If you are familiar with the sound system of a learner's native language, you will be better able to diagnose student difficulties. Many L1–L2 carryovers can be overcome through a focused awareness and effort on the learner's part.
2. **Age.** Generally speaking, children under the age of puberty stand an excellent chance of "sounding like a native" if they have continued exposure in authentic contexts. Beyond the age of puberty, while adults will almost surely maintain a "foreign accent," there is no particular advantage attributed to age (see *PLLT*, Chapter 3). A fifty-year-old can be as successful as an eighteen-year-old if all other factors are equal. Remind your students, especially if your students are older, that "the younger, the better" is a myth.
3. **Exposure.** It is difficult to define exposure. One can actually live in a foreign country for some time but not take advantage of being "with the people." Research seems to support the notion that the quality and intensity of exposure are more important than mere length of time. If class time spent focusing on pronunciation demands the full attention and interest of your students, then they stand a good chance of reaching their goals.
4. **Innate phonetic ability.** Often referred to as having an "ear" for language, some people manifest a phonetic coding ability that others do not. In many cases, if a person has had exposure to a foreign language as a child, this "knack" is present whether the early language is remembered or not. Others are simply more attuned to phonetic discriminations. Some people would have you believe that you either have such a knack, or you don't. Strategies-based instruction (see Chapter 3, pp. 51–55), however, has proven that some elements of learning are a matter of an awareness of your own limitations combined with a conscious focus on doing something to compensate for those limitations. Therefore, if pronunciation

seems to be naturally difficult for some students, they should not despair; with some effort and concentration, they can improve their competence.

5. **Identity and agency.** Yet another influence is one's perception of speakers of the target language and the extent to which the L2 user identifies with those speakers. Learners need to be reminded of the importance of positive attitudes toward the people who speak the language (if such a target is identifiable), but more important, students need to become aware of—and not afraid of—the second identity that may be emerging within them.
6. **Motivation and concern for good pronunciation.** Some learners are not particularly concerned about their pronunciation, while others are. The extent to which learners' intrinsic motivation propels them toward improvement will be perhaps the strongest influence of all six of the factors in this list. If that motivation and concern are high, then the necessary effort will be expended in pursuit of goals. You can help learners to perceive or develop that motivation by showing, among other things, how clarity of speech is significant in shaping their self-image and, ultimately, in reaching some of their higher goals.

Classroom Connections

Language ego has been capsulized in the claim that "you are what you speak." How would that factor *intimidate* a learner who is trying to be as accurate as possible in oral production? On the other hand, how might such a feeling actually *motivate* a learner to keep trying to improve pronunciation? If one's accent is a manifestation of one's *identity*, is it advisable to try to "lose" an accent that might signal one's native language?

All six of the above factors suggest that any learner who really wants to can learn to pronounce English clearly and comprehensibly. You can assist in the process by gearing your planned and unplanned instruction toward these six factors.

On the next few pages you will find excerpts of lessons designed to teach different aspects of English pronunciation, along with some description of meaningful minimal pair exercises. Take note of how those techniques may capitalize on the positive benefits of the six factors above, and the extent to which they reflect a discourse-based view of pronunciation teaching. A significant factor for you in the success of such techniques lies in your ability to instill in your students the motivation to put forth the effort needed to develop clear, comprehensible pronunciation.

Figure 16.7 Listening for pitch changes (Adapted from Wong 1987, p. 61)

Record the following conversation and play it for the students. Establish the participants, the setting, and the event by asking the students to guess who and what they are.

He: Ready? ↗
She: No. ↘
He: Why? ↘
She: Problems. ↘
He: Problems? ↗
She: Yes. ↘
He: What? ↘
She: Babysitter. ↘

After the students have figured out what is going on, you can play the conversation again. This time put the transcription of the conversation on the board or on an overhead projector and ask the students to try to determine for each utterance whether the speaker's voice ends with a rising or falling pitch. Draw arrows next to each utterance and play the conversation once more. To isolate pitch from the words, you can use a kazoo, which can be purchased at a toy store (see Gilbert, 1978). By humming into it, you can demonstrate rising and falling pitch to the amusement and illumination of your students.

Ask the students to explain what each utterance means. Then point out that a change in pitch can indicate a change in meaning (e.g., "Ready?" with a rising pitch means "Are you ready?" but "Ready" with a falling pitch means "I am ready").

Additional practice dialogues are provided here. Make up more for your particular students. Follow the procedure described for the first conversation.

Conversation B

A: Single?
B: Double.
A: Double?
B: Yes.
A: Cone?
B: Cup.

Conversation C

A: Good?
B: Delicious.
A: More?
B: Please.

Conversation D

A: Locked?
B: Locked.
A: Key?
B: Key?
A: Key.
B: Oh-oh.

Figure 16.8 Compound nouns (Lane, 2010, pp. 33–34)

Activity 1.6 ***Compounds: Which came first?***

Level Intermediate/Advanced

Worksheet Page 206

Tip Teach classes of words that have predictable stress patterns.

Description This activity practices compounds in the context of a trivia activity and can be integrated with other work on discoveries/inventions or technology. Students see pairs of compounds (e.g., cell phones, iPods) and decide which came first.

1. Direct students' attention to the compound pairs. Go over meaning if necessary.
2. Select one of the compounds and write it on the board. Write the first word higher than the second, to illustrate the pitch pattern. Model the compound and the isolated stress-pitch pattern (DA da). Ask the class whether the first or second word is pronounced on a higher pitch.

   cell
   phones

3. Students listen to the compounds and repeat them.
4. In pairs, students decide which came first, guessing as needed. For example, cell phones were in use before iPods.
5. After the pair work, ask students to report which came first. Provide feedback on the stress-pitch pattern of the compounds—make sure students pronounce the first word on a higher pitch.

Meaningful Minimal Pairs

Traditional minimal-pair drills, used for decades in language teaching, go something like this:

T: Okay, class, on the board, picture number 1 is a "pen," and picture number 2 is a "pin." Listen: Pen [points to number 1], pin [points to number 2] [several repetitions]. Now, I'm going to say either number 1 or number 2. You tell me which. Ready? [pause] Pin.

Ss: Number 2.

T: Good. Ready. Pin.
Ss: Number 2.
T: Okay. [pause] Pen.
Ss: Number 1.

CLT and TBLT principles prod us to be a little more meaningful. In the following examples you can see that a little contextualization goes a long way:

T: This pen leaks.
S: Then don't write with it.
T: This pan leaks.
S: Then don't cook with it.

T: Where is the White House?
S: In Washington, D.C.
T: Where can I find a white house?
S: Right across the street.

T: The sun is hot on my head!
S: Then get a cap.
T: Oh, no, I missed the bus. I'm going to be late!
S: Then get a cab.

These are examples of drilling techniques that have been modified to bring context, interest, and a modicum of authenticity to what would otherwise be a mechanical task.

 **CLASSROOM CONNECTIONS**

Consider some other minimal pairs, such as sheep/ship, glass/grass, bet/vet, and others. Try to devise a few other exercises, like the above, that add a little meaningfulness.

OTHER ORAL COMMUNICATION TECHNIQUES

The number of techniques for teaching OC skills is almost limitless. For the sake of stimulating your awareness, we'll simply list some of these here, and encourage you to explore the many other possibilities that are available. For some ideas, consult Klippel (1984), Hughes (2002), and Bailey (2005).

Oral Communication Techniques

Oral dialogue journals. Students create audio recordings of thoughts, reactions, questions, and concerns that the teacher can listen and respond to.

Games. Team building and guessing games can be used in pairs, groups, or the whole class.

Role play. Role play offers learners a chance to get "outside themselves," to use their imagination, and at times to voice opinions that may not be their very own beliefs. Role play can be worked into interviews, simulations, and problem-solving activities.

Information gap. Sometimes called "jigsaw" exercises, these tasks require collaboration between or among students to derive the desired information. Activities range from map exercises, to ranking, to problem solving.

Oral form-focused activities. Some OC techniques are designed to elicit certain grammatical forms. In the context of relevant, meaningful communication, such techniques can be very useful practice exercises. (See the next section for examples.)

FOCUS ON FORM AND ERROR TREATMENT

One of the most frequently posed questions by teachers who are new to the trade is: When and how should I correct the speech errors of learners in my classroom? This happens also to be one of the most enigmatic questions in the language teaching profession. I offer some guidelines here, but at the same time urge you to read the last part of Chapter 9 of *PLLT*, where issues surrounding form-focused instruction are described in more detail.

The Role of Feedback

One of the keys to successful L2 learning lies in the feedback that a learner receives from others. Research has shown that the *quality* and *quantity* of feedback given to learners will affect what they eventually incorporate into their linguistic competence (Williams, 2005; Loewen, 2011; Sheen & Ellis, 2011; Spada, 2011).

The quality of feedback lies in what teachers choose to call to learners' attention, how they do it, when they do it, and in what manner. Four decades ago Vigil and Oller (1976) suggested that the *affective* quality of feedback is as important as its *cognitive* elements. So, for example, supportive, encouraging, and affirming verbal (and nonverbal) feedback from a teacher is an almost essential element of the extent to which a learner will be *receptive* to feedback. And a barrage of interruptions and corrections will, of course, lead learners to shut off their attempts at communication. Once a positive affective climate is established, learners will feel encouraged to continue their attempts to communicate orally (Vigil & Oller, 1976).

The cognitive nature of feedback is a little more complicated, as we shall see in our next few sections, and as a stockpile of research has shown (Sheen & Ellis, 2011; Spada, 2011). The quantity of feedback is also relevant. Which errors should teachers treat? Should they supply overt, immediate "correction"? Should they make *incidental* references to form? How can they encourage learners to *notice* errors? Should error treatment be *planned* on the part of the teacher or *spontaneous*? These are issues that are still being addressed, but we do have some positive guidelines in recent research. Let's look at those options.

 **Classroom Connections**

Think of the feedback you give to learners as being "green lights" (positive, affirming) and "red lights" (intimidating, overwhelming). What are some specific ways in which you as a teacher could provide green lights to encourage students to continue communication? Do you think those green lights might be so encouraging that you actually end up reinforcing students' errors? How do you achieve an optimum?

How to Treat Errors

In a very practical article on error treatment, James Hendrickson (1980) advised teachers to try to discern the difference between *global* and *local* errors, that is, errors that cannot be interpreted by the hearer versus errors that are interpretable. When a learner of English describes a quaint old hotel in Europe by saying, "There is a French widow in every bedroom," the local error is clearly—and humorously—recognized. Hendrickson recommended that local errors not be corrected because the message is clear and correction might interrupt a learner's flow of communication.

Global errors need to be treated in some way because the message may otherwise remain garbled. Many utterances are not clearly global or local, and it is difficult to discern the necessity for corrective feedback. A learner once wrote, "The grammar is the basement of every language." In this witty little proclamation the speaker probably meant "basis" rather than "basement," but because of some potential misunderstanding, the error probably warrants treatment.

The matter of *how* to treat errors is complex. It seems quite clear that students in the classroom generally *want* and expect errors to be corrected. However, correcting (or treating) every error is obviously not advisable. We can safely conclude that a sensitive and perceptive language teacher should make the language classroom a happy optimum, which may best be accomplished through a number of different treatment options.

The first choice that a teacher needs to make is to decide whether to *treat* an error or to *ignore* it. Then, if some form of treatment is warranted, consider the following options (adapted from Bailey, 1985, p. 111):

- treat immediately or delay to a more appropriate moment
- treat explicitly or give the student an opportunity to self-correct
- the teacher initiates treatment or defers to others (students)
- if the latter, defer to an individual or to the whole class
- return, or not, to the original error maker after treatment

Then, if some form of treatment is chosen, quite a number of strategies for treatment are possible. Among those are:

- simply indicate (possibly nonverbally) that an error occurred
- point out the location of the error (e.g., "You *go* to the store yesterday?")
- recast, using the correct form (e.g., "Oh, I see, you *went* to the store?")
- indicate the type of error (e.g., "What's the past tense of *go*?")

These basic options and strategies are common and viable modes of error treatment in the classroom. It's important to understand that not all error treatment is error *correction*. Among the strategies listed above, none of them is an *explicit* correction, in which the wrong form is specified and the correct form provided. Error treatment encompasses a wide range of options, one of which—at the extreme end of a continuum—may be considered to be correction.

Research (Williams, 2005; Loewen, 2011; Sheen & Ellis, 2011; Spada, 2011) shows that the best way to help a learner to repair malformed utterances is, first, to assist the learner in *noticing* an incorrect form (through recasts, prompts, and other attention-getting devices), and second, for the learner to initiate repair (with as little prompting as possible from the teacher).

Figure 16.9 illustrates the split-second series of decisions that a teacher makes when a student has uttered a deviant form of English in the classroom. In those few nanoseconds, information is accessed, processed, and evaluated, with a decision forthcoming on what the teacher is going to "do" about the deviant form.

Imagine that you are a teacher and your student has made some sort of "deviant" utterance. Instantly, you run this speech event through a number of nearly simultaneous screens (1–10), not so much systematically as intuitively. You are now ready to decide whether to *treat* or *ignore* the deviation. If you

Figure 16.9 A model for treatment of classroom speech errors

DEVIANT UTTERANCE

1. Type
lexical, phonological, grammatical, discourse, pragmatic, sociocultural

2. Source
L1, L2, teacher-induced, other Ss, outside L2 input, A/V/print/electronic media

3. Linguistic Complexity
intricate & involved or easy to explain/deal with

4. Local or **Global**

5. Mistake or **Error**

6. Learner´s Affective State
language ego fragility, anxiety, confidence, receptiveness

7. Learner´s Linguistic Stage
emergent, presystematic, systematic, postsystematic

8. Pedagogical Focus
immediate task goals, lesson objectives, course goals/purposes

9. Communicative Context
conversational flow factors, individual, group, or whole-class work, S–S or S–T exchange

10. Teacher Style
direct or indirect, interventionist, laissez-faire

TREAT | **IGNORE** → **OUT**

WHEN?	immediately		end of utterance		much later
WHO?	T	another S		whole class	self
HOW? **a. input to S**	fact indicated	location indicated	correction modeled	type/source indicated	metalinguistic explanation
b. manner	indirect/unintrusive				direct/intrusive
c. S´s output	none				rephrase utterance
d. follow-up • **affective**	none	"okay"		"good"	[gush]
• **cognitive**	none	acknowledge	verbalize		further clarification

decide to do nothing, you simply move on. But if you decide to do something in the way of treatment, you have a number of treatment options, as discussed earlier, and as represented in the chart.

Notice that you, the teacher, do not always have to be the person who provides the treatment. Manner of treatment varies according to the input to the student, the directness of the treatment, the student's output, and your follow-up. After one very quick deviant utterance by a student, you have made an amazing number of observations and evaluations that go into the process of error treatment.

CLASSROOM CONNECTIONS

How can you set the stage for students to treat each other's errors? They could stifle their classmates' production with too much correction, especially when another student has actually spoken correctly! How would you control this potentially undesirable level of peer corrections?

ASSESSING SPEAKING IN THE CLASSROOM

Assessing speaking skills in the classroom has one clear advantage over assessing listening: speech is observable, recordable, and measurable. However, once the criterion of your assessment moves beyond the phonological level, this advantage quickly disappears as *acceptable responses* are more difficult to specify reliably.

The prospect of designing classroom assessment procedures for oral production require the same preconsiderations that were outlined in the previous chapter: (1) Specify the category of speaking performance (from imitative to extensive) that is in question; and (2) describe the micro- and/or macroskills that are to be assessed. A further factor should also be taken into account: (3) the genre of spoken language that is being assessed. It's easier said than done, but the more specific you can be in pinpointing these three criteria, the greater the chances are that you will create a valid, reliable assessment procedure.

Item Types and Tasks for Assessing Speaking

So that you can gain an initial glimpse of options for assessing spoken language at the various levels of performance, we have listed some possibilities below. For a further, more comprehensive survey, we refer you to Brown and Abeywickrama (2010), a textbook on language assessment that includes a separate chapter on assessing speaking.

Types of Items and Tasks for Assessing Speaking

1. Imitative speaking tasks

- minimal pair repetition
- word/phrase repetition
- sentence repetition

2. Intensive speaking tasks

- directed response (Tell me he went home; Tell him to come see me.)
- read-aloud (for either pronunciation or fluency)
- oral sentence completion (Yesterday, I ______)
- oral cloze procedure (Yesterday, I ______ to the grocery store)
- dialogue completion (T: May I help you? S: ______)
- directed response (What did you do last weekend?)
- picture-cued elicitation of a grammatical item (e.g., comparatives)
- translation [into the L2] (of a word, phrase, or sentence or two)

3. Responsive speaking tasks

- picture-cued elicitation of response or description
- map-cued elicitation of directions (How do I get to the post office?)
- question and answer – open-ended (How do you like this weather?)
- question elicitation (Ask me about my hobbies and interests.)
- elicitation of instructions (What's the recipe for lasagna?)
- paraphrasing (of a short narrative or phone message)

4. Interactive speaking tasks

- oral interview
- role play
- discussions and conversations
- games

5. Extensive speaking tasks

- oral presentations [in academic or professional contexts]
- picture-cued [extensive] story-telling
- retelling a story or news event
- translation [into the L2] of an extended text (short story, news article)

Evaluating and Scoring Speaking Tasks

The evaluation of oral production performance can get quite complicated. First, you need to be clear in specifying the level of language you are targeting. One or more of at least six possible criteria may be your target:

Criteria for Evaluating Speaking Tasks

- pronunciation
- fluency
- vocabulary
- grammar
- discourse features (cohesion, sociolinguistic appropriateness, etc.)
- task (accomplishing the objective of the task)

Classroom Connections

If you were to devise a scale for evaluating oral production, how much weight would you give to each of the above six criteria? Of course, this would depend on your context and objectives, but are some of the above criteria almost always more "important" than some others?

Some scales add "comprehension" to account for the extent to which a student has comprehended directions or elicitation. This category can be subsumed in the last two criteria above.

Within each of these categories you can judge a student's response(s) to be at one of several possible levels of performance. Typically, we think of beginning, intermediate, and advanced as potential levels. But as we saw in Chapter 7, those categories are quite slippery. Moreover, three levels may not be sufficient for your classroom purposes, and you may wish to score performance on five or six levels, ranging from "novice" or "true beginner" to "superior" or "completely acceptable." Whatever those categories are, it is important to describe them as clearly as possible in order to make reliable evaluations. For more on the issue of specifying scoring criteria, please consult Brown and Abeywickrama (2010).

* * * * *

Listening and speaking are the two skills that are most widely used for classroom interaction. By now, having covered the last two chapters, you have at least encountered many different parameters of these two skills, what they are, types of each, issues, some idea of the kinds of techniques that help to focus on either one or both of them, and may have a few guidelines for assessment.

FOR THE TEACHER: ACTIVITIES (A) & DISCUSSION (D)

Note: For each of the "Classroom Connections" in this chapter, you may wish to turn them into individual or pair-work discussion questions.

1. **(D)** Ask your students to think about the concept of fluency. Is it possible to devise an operational definition (by specifying measurable factors) of fluency through such variables as rate, pronunciation accuracy, colloquial language, errors, clarity, and other factors? What does the operational definition say about what one should teach?
2. **(A)** Ask pairs to review for each other the difference between accuracy and fluency, and discuss which should come first in a curriculum and under what circumstances. Then challenge them to think of some examples of how both fluency and accuracy might get attention within one task or technique.
3. **(D)** On page 348, the interlocutor effect was described. Ask the class to think of some specific examples of this interlocutor effect and share them with the rest of the class. How might this effect help one to formulate certain plans for grouping or pairing students?
4. **(D)** Review the nine factors (pp. 350–351) that make spoken language difficult. Ask your students to speculate on which is more difficult, speaking or listening (compare pp. 323–326). Ask for justifications of their responses.
5. **(A)** Look at the list of features of conversation (pp. 359–360) that need to be attended to in an OC class. Divide up the features among pairs and ask each pair to (a) cite some examples of the feature and (b) speculate on how one would teach that aspect of conversation. Ask pairs to share their conclusions with the rest of the class.
6. **(D)** If possible, obtain a video of an L2 class in which there is a considerable amount of oral activity. Using the list of microskills on page 352 as a checklist, ask your class to take notes on how various microskills manifested themselves. Ask for volunteers to share their ideas.
7. **(A)** Ask students to look again at the conversation between Bob and Amy (p. 355) and, in pairs, to identify as many of the seven factors of interpersonal exchange (cited just prior to the conversation) as possible. Then ask them to discuss how they would teach these factors; then have them share their ideas with the rest of the class.

8. **(A)** In the last section of this chapter, a number of principles of error correction are cited. In pairs, have students make up a short list (three or four) of "error correction maxims," then share their maxims by writing them on the board and sharing them with the class. Through discussion, try to come up with a composite list of maxims.
9. **(A)** Ask small groups, each assigned to one of the five levels of assessment described in the last chapter, to pick one of the suggested tasks and design a short test for a classroom context that the group determines. Then, ask them to design a way to score or evaluate student performance on such a test. Have them report their result to the class.

FOR YOUR FURTHER READING

McCarthy, M., & O'Keeffe, A. (2010). Speaking in a second language. In M. Berns (Ed.), *Concise encyclopedia of applied linguistics* (pp. 212–218). Oxford, UK: Elsevier.

A survey of research on the teaching of speaking with a useful extensive bibliography.

Bailey, K. (2005). *Practical English language teaching: Speaking.* New York, NY: McGraw-Hill.

Richards, J. (2008). *Teaching listening and speaking: From theory to practice.* Cambridge, UK: Cambridge University Press.

Lazaraton, A. (2014). Second language speaking. In M. Celce-Murcia, D. Brinton, & M. A. Snow (Eds.), *Teaching English as a second or foreign language* (4th ed., pp. 106–120). Boston, MA: National Geographic Learning.

All three sources offer extensive surveys of techniques and tasks useful in teaching oral communication skills. They also offer synopses of research along with bibliographies.

Lane, L. (2010). *Tips for teaching pronunciation: A practical approach.* White Plains, NY: Pearson Longman.

Murphy, J. (2013). *Teaching pronunciation.* Alexandria, VA: TESOL.

Goodwin, J. (2014). Teaching pronunciation. In M. Celce-Murcia, D. Brinton, & M. A. Snow (Eds.), *Teaching English as a second or foreign language* (4th ed., pp. 136–152). Boston, MA: National Geographic Learning.

These sources offer synopses of the state of the art in teaching pronunciation along with extensive batteries of practical techniques, covering stress, intonation, rhythm, segmental phonemes, as well as pronunciation within the context of discourse.

CHAPTER 17

TEACHING READING

Questions for Reflection

- What are some of the major issues and concepts in pedagogical research that are related to teaching reading?
- How can the processing of written language (reading) be classified into microskills, macroskills, and types of classroom reading performance?
- What are some principles to follow in designing reading comprehension tasks and activities?
- What are some key strategies for successful reading comprehension?
- What are some guidelines for evaluating the success of reading tasks, activities, and lessons?
- What are some basic principles and formats for assessing reading ability?

The written word surrounds us daily—at times enlightening, amusing, and heart-warming, at other times mystifying, depressing, and saddening. At every turn, we who are members of a literate society are dependent on a couple of dozen or so letters and a sprinkling of other written symbols for significant, even life-and-death, matters in our lives. How do we teach second language learners to master this written code? What do we teach them? What are the issues?

As you read this chapter, keep in mind that once again, interactive, integrated approaches to language teaching emphasize the interrelationship of skills. Reading ability will be developed best in association with writing, listening, and speaking activities. Even in those courses that may be labeled "reading," your goals will be best achieved by capitalizing on the connection between reading and other modes of performance, especially the reading-writing relationship. So, we focus here on reading as a component of general second language proficiency, but ultimately reading must be considered only in the perspective of the whole picture of interactive language teaching.

RESEARCH ON READING IN A SECOND LANGUAGE

By the 1970s, research on reading one's L1 had been flourishing for a couple of decades as solutions were being sought to why some children were not successfully learning to read. But research on reading in an L2 was almost nonexistent.

Then, with Goodman's (1970) seminal article, "Reading: A Psycholinguistic Guessing Game" and other subsequent work, L2 specialists began to tackle the unique issues and questions facing second language reading pedagogy. A glance now through almost five decades of research reveals some significant findings that will affect you and your approach to teaching reading skills. Some of the highlights are reviewed here.

1. Bottom-Up and Top-Down Processing

Led by Goodman's (1970) work, the distinction between bottom-up and top-down processing became a cornerstone of reading methodology for years to come (Eskey, 2005). In *bottom-up processing*, readers must first recognize a multiplicity of linguistic signals (letters, morphemes, syllables, words, phrases, grammatical cues, discourse markers) and use their linguistic data-processing mechanisms to impose some sort of order on these signals. These **data-driven** operations obviously require a sophisticated knowledge of the language itself. From among all the perceived data, the reader selects the signals that make some sense, that cohere, that "mean."

Virtually all reading involves a risk—a guessing game, in Goodman's words—because readers must, through a puzzle-solving process, infer meanings, decide what to retain and not to retain, and move on. This is where a complementary method of processing written text is imperative: *top-down*, or **conceptually driven processing** in which we draw on our own intelligence and experience to understand a text. Nuttall (1996, pp. 16–17) compares bottom-up processes with the image of a scientist with a magnifying glass or microscope examining all the minute details of some phenomenon, while top-down processing is like taking an eagle's-eye view of a landscape below. Such a picture reminds us that field-independent and field-sensitive cognitive styles are analogous to bottom-up and top-down processing, respectively.

A half-century ago, perhaps, reading specialists might have argued that the best way to teach reading is through bottom-up methodology: teach symbols, grapheme–phoneme correspondences, syllables, and lexical recognition first, then comprehension would be derived from the sum of the parts. More recent research on teaching reading (Hedgcock & Ferris, 2009; Grabe & Stoller, 2011, 2014; Anderson, 2014) has shown that a combination of top-down and bottom-up processing, or what has come to be called *interactive reading,* is almost always a primary ingredient in successful teaching methodology because both processes are important. "In practice, a reader continually shifts from one focus to another, now adopting a top-down approach to predict probable meaning, then moving to the bottom-up approach to check whether that is really what the writer says" (Nuttall, 1996, p. 17).

 **CLASSROOM CONNECTIONS**

Consider a specific example of how a reader shifts from top-down to bottom-up processing. For example, when you see a newspaper article and make a decision to read it, what processes, exactly, do you go through to make that decision? Then, once you're reading it, suppose you misread something or don't understand a segment, what psycholinguistic strategies do you adopt for better comprehension? How might you teach those strategies?

2. Schema Theory and Background Knowledge

How do readers construct meaning? How do they decide what to hold on to, and having made that decision, how do they infer a writer's message? These are the sorts of questions addressed by what has come to be known as **schema theory**, the hallmark of which is that a text does not by itself carry meaning (Anderson, 2004; Grabe, 2004, 2009; Eskey, 2005). The reader brings information, knowledge, emotion, experience, and culture—that is, schemata (plural)—to the printed word. Schema theory is not a new construct. Four decades ago, Clarke and Silberstein (1977) captured the essence of schema theory:

> Research has shown that reading is only incidentally visual. More information is contributed by the reader than by the print on the page. That is, readers understand what they read because they are able to take the stimulus beyond its graphic representation and assign it membership to an appropriate group of concepts already stored in their memories. . . . Skill in reading depends on the efficient interaction between linguistic knowledge and knowledge of the world (pp. 136–37).

 **CLASSROOM CONNECTIONS**

It has been said that readers bring more information from the brain to the page than from the page to the brain. What are some examples of this phenomenon? When you're reading a menu in a restaurant, how do you use this two-way communication? How would you help students to become aware of this interaction?

A good example of the role of schemata in reading is found in the following anecdote:

> A fifteen-year-old boy got up the nerve one day to try out for the school chorus, despite the potential ridicule from his classmates. His audition time made him a good fifteen minutes late to the next class. His hall permit clutched nervously in hand, he nevertheless tried surreptitiously to slip into his seat, but his entrance didn't go unnoticed.
>
> "And where were you?" bellowed the teacher.
>
> Caught off guard by the sudden attention, a red-faced Harold replied meekly, "Oh, uh, er, somewhere between tenor and bass, sir."

A full understanding of this story and its humorous punch line requires that the reader intuitively know something about **content** and **formal schemata**. Content schemata include what we know about people, the world, culture, and the universe, while formal schemata consist of our knowledge about language and discourse structure (Grabe & Stoller, 2014).

For the above anecdote, these *content* schemata are a prerequisite to understanding its humor:

- Fifteen-year-old boys might be embarrassed about singing in a choir.
- Hall permits allow students to be outside a classroom during the class hour.
- Teenagers often find it embarrassing to be singled out in a class.
- Choral vocal parts, e.g., *tenor* and *bass*.
- Fifteen-year-old boys' voices are often "breaking."

Formal schemata also reveal some implied connections:

- The chorus tryout was the cause of potential ridicule.
- The audition occurred just before the class period.
- Continuing to "clutch" the permit means he did not give it to the teacher.
- The teacher did indeed notice his entry.
- The teacher's question referred to location, not a musical part.

The widespread acceptance of schema theory by reading researchers has not gone unchallenged. Nassaji (2002) provided an alternative view of the role of background knowledge, appealing to connectionist models of memory. In Nassaji's view, background knowledge is not "pre-stored," but "rather it emerges in the context of the task, and is relatively unstructured as opposed to the highly structured knowledge representations suggested by . . . schema theory" (p. 453). In this "construction-integration" model, the learner is seen to play a more active role in constructing meaning, while reading, than is proposed by schema theory.

3. Teaching Strategic Reading

One of the questions that have been asked about teaching reading has been the extent to which learners will learn to read better in a laissez-faire atmosphere of enriched surroundings than in an instructed sequence of direct attention to the strategies of efficient reading. Most experts in reading research side with the latter (Anderson, 1999, 2004; Grabe, 2004, 2009; Eskey, 2005) and cite research in support of their conclusion. A viable theory of instructed second language acquisition can hardly be sustainable without a solid component of strategic competence.

One of the ongoing themes among researchers and teachers of foreign languages is the tension between what in the last chapter we referred to as direct and indirect approaches to teaching language skills. This continuum of possibilities is highlighted in debates over conscious and subconscious acquisition, explicit and implicit learning, and focal and peripheral processing. Instruction should, of course, provide an optimal mix of each, but Anderson (1999, 2004, 2014; Grabe & Stoller, 2014) advocated a healthy dose of strategy-based instruction, including metacognitive strategies of self-planning, monitoring, and evaluating one's own reading processes. Grabe (2004) stressed the coordinated use of multiple strategies *while* students are reading. Eskey (2005) reminds us of research on pre-reading, while-reading, post-reading, and follow-up strategies for reading, to be discussed later in this chapter.

4. Extensive Reading

On the other hand, there is a place for extensive reading of longer texts with little or no conscious strategic intervention. Researchers agree that, at least for academic purposes, extensive reading is a key to student gains in reading ability, linguistic competence, vocabulary, spelling, and writing (Day & Bamford, 1998; Elley, 2001; Grabe & Stoller, 2014). Further, Green and Oxford (1995) found that reading for pleasure and reading without looking up all the unknown words were both highly correlated with overall language proficiency.

This research suggests that instructional programs in reading should give consideration to the teaching of extensive reading. It does not suggest, of course, that focused approaches to specific strategies for intensive reading ought to be abandoned, but strengthens the notion that an extensive reading component in conjunction with other focused reading instruction is highly warranted.

Classroom Connections

How would you teach students at an intermediate to advanced level to engage in efficient extensive reading? What steps or stages might you go through in helping learners to sustain reading beyond a few minutes? What are some useful strategies that *you* have found useful that you might pass on to your students?

5. Reading Rate, Fluency, and Automaticity

Paralleling the research on other language skills, fluency, or reading rate, has drawn the attention of some research. In L1 reading, fluency and reading rate have long been a concern (Kuhn & Stahl, 2003; Grabe, 2004), and recently more research has appeared supporting the essential role of fluency and reading rate in L2 learning (Grabe, 2009; Grabe & Stoller, 2014). Anderson (2014, p. 172) further notes that "fluency is a combination of both reading rate and reading *comprehension*." He goes on to suggest strategies of skimming, scanning, predicting, and identifying main ideas as approaches to increasing fluency, or what might also be described as *automaticity*.

6. Focus on Vocabulary

In recent years there has been a resurgence of interest in the role of vocabulary knowledge on the acquisition of reading skills (Nation, 2003, 2005; Read, 2004; Grabe & Stoller, 2014), with findings that support a strong relationship between vocabulary knowledge and later reading ability. Principles and classroom practices in teaching vocabulary will be taken up in further detail in Chapter 19 of this book.

CLASSROOM CONNECTIONS

For many decades L2 pedagogy has advocated teaching vocabulary *in context*. What does this mean? If an L2 learner tells you he or she is spending many hours as day memorizing definitions of words, how would you respond? What alternative strategies for word acquisition could you suggest?

7. The Role of Affect and Culture

It's readily apparent from just a cursory survey of research on second language acquisition that affective factors play major roles in ultimate success. Just as language ego, self-esteem, empathy, and motivation undergird the acquisition of spoken discourse, reading is subject to variability within the affective domain. The "love" of reading has propelled many a learner to successful acquisition of reading skills. Instruction has been found to be effective when students' self-esteem is high (Dole, Brown, & Trathen, 1996). The autonomy gained through the learning of reading strategies has been shown to be a powerful motivator (Bamford & Day, 1998), not to mention the affective power of reading itself. Similarly, culture plays an active role in motivating and rewarding people for literacy. We cannot simply assume that cognitive factors alone will account for the eventual success of second language readers (Fitzgerald, 1994).

8. Second Language Literacy

As L2 materials and methods continue to apply both bottom-up and top-down models of reading to programs and curricula, one particularly challenging focus of effort for researchers and teachers has been literacy-level teaching of adults (Devine & Eskey, 2004; August et al., 2006; Ediger, 2014). A significant number of immigrants arriving in various nonnative countries and cultures are nonliterate in their native languages, posing special issues in the teaching of an L2. What are sometimes referred to as "skills-based" (bottom-up) and "strategies-based" (top-down) approaches are both used in adult literacy training. For more information on this specialized field, a particularly good reference is Ediger's (2014) synopsis of research and practice in teaching literacy.

 **CLASSROOM CONNECTIONS**

A significant number of adult L2 learners are *not* literate in their L1, for a variety of circumstantial reasons. How would you feel if you had no reading ability in your L1 and now needed to learn to read in an L2? Overwhelmed? Discouraged? How would a teacher provide both emotional and practical support to such a student?

Aside from the five major issues touched on above, a multitude of other topics are grist for current researchers' mills:

- the role of cognition in reading
- the role of automaticity in word recognition
- reading as sociocultural practice
- effective techniques for activating schemata
- relationships of reading to writing

And the list goes on. At this stage in your professional career when you are learning to teach, rather than immersing you in oceans of research data, it is perhaps more important to lay some basic foundations for the development of an effective teaching approach, which we now turn to.

GENRES OF WRITTEN LANGUAGE

In Chapters 15 and 16 we looked at types of spoken language so that you could identify the kinds of language your listening and speaking techniques should include. Here, we do the same for types, or **genres**, of reading and writing.

In our highly literate society, there are literally hundreds of different types of written texts, a much larger variety than found in spoken texts. Each of the types listed below represents, or is an example of, a *genre* of written language.

Each has certain rules or conventions for its manifestation, and we are thus able immediately to identify a genre and to know what to look for within the text. Consider the following nonexhaustive list:

Genres of Written Language

- nonfiction: reports, editorials, essays, articles, reference (dictionaries, etc.)
- fiction: novels, short stories, jokes, drama, poetry
- letters: personal, business
- electronic: e-mails, tweets, blog posts
- greeting cards
- diaries, journals
- memos (e.g., interoffice memos)
- messages (e.g., phone messages)
- announcements
- newspaper "journalese" reports
- academic writing: short answer test responses, reports, papers, theses, books
- forms, applications
- questionnaires
- directions
- labels
- signs
- recipes
- bills (and other financial statements)
- maps
- manuals
- menus
- schedules (e.g., transportation tables)
- advertisements: commercial, personal
- invitations
- directories (e.g., telephone, yellow pages)
- comic strips, cartoons

And you could no doubt name a few more! It's interesting that every literate adult knows the distinctive features of each of these genres. You can immediately distinguish a menu from a map, an interoffice memo from a telephone message, and a bill from an invitation—well, yes, some bills are "invitations" to pay up!

When you encounter one of the above, you usually know what your purpose is in reading it, and therefore you know what to select and what not to select for short- and long-term memory—in other words, you bring various *schemata* to bear on the message that you have chosen to retain. What would happen if you didn't know some of these differences? That is what your students may encounter when they read an L2, so part of your job as a teacher is to enlighten your students on features of these genres and to help them to develop strategies for extracting necessary meaning from each.

 **Classroom Connections**

Consider several of the genres listed above: memos, directions (for assembling a furniture item), recipes, and e-mails. What are the distinctive features of each? What specifically are the *linguistic* features? What grammatical and discourse features might you teach within any one of these genres?

CHARACTERISTICS OF WRITTEN LANGUAGE

There are quite a number of salient and relevant differences between spoken and written language. Students already literate in their native languages will, of course, be familiar with the broad, basic characteristics of written language; however, some characteristics of English writing, especially certain rhetorical conventions, may be so different from the students' native language that reading efforts are blocked. The characteristics listed below will also be of some help for you in doing the following:

- diagnosing certain reading difficulties arising from the idiosyncrasies of written language,
- pointing your techniques toward specific objectives, and
- reminding students of some of the advantages of written language over spoken.

1. Permanence

Spoken language is fleeting. Once you speak a sentence, it vanishes (unless there is a tape recorder around). The hearer, therefore, is called upon to make immediate perceptions and immediate storage. Written language is permanent (or as permanent as paper and computer files are!), and therefore the reader has an opportunity to return again and again, if necessary, to a word or phrase or sentence, or even a whole text.

2. Processing Time

A corollary to the above is the processing *time* that the reader gains. Many reading contexts allow readers to read at their own rate, especially reading for pleasure (armchair book reading, newspaper reading, etc.). They aren't forced into following the rate of delivery, as in spoken language, and so somewhat "slower" readers are not always at a disadvantage, especially when they are in complete control of the amount of time needed to read a text.

However, there are notable contexts in which an *optimal* reading rate becomes significant. Academic reading assignments usually presuppose the ability to comprehend material within required or scheduled time constraints (Grabe & Stoller, 2014). Tests and other assessments are often timed, requiring a reader to complete a task within a specified period of time. Learners studying in an L2 can feel frustrated by what they feel is an extremely slow rate of reading or the necessity to reread a text multiple times in order to achieve comprehension. In reading for occupational purposes, similar time constraints may pose challenges for an L2 reader.

Teachers are therefore called on to help learners to achieve a fluency rate that will enable them to function adequately within their various contexts. Classroom lessons in reading must account for those contexts and place appropriate emphasis on whatever optimal reading rates are deemed necessary.

Classroom Connections

What might determine "necessary" reading rates? Some have claimed that L2 readers ought to strive for 250–300 words per minute as an ultimate goal. Do you agree? What are some of the varied *contexts* or *genres* of reading that might lead you to consider lower or higher rates as optimal? Do levels of ability (beginning, intermediate, advanced) make a difference in the goals you set for students?

3. Distance

The written word allows messages to be sent across two dimensions: physical distance and temporal distance. The pedagogical significance of this fact centers on interpretation. The task of the reader is to interpret language that was written in some other place at some other time with only the written words themselves as contextual clues. Readers can't confront an author and say, "Now, what exactly did you mean by that?" Nor can they transport themselves back through a time machine and "see" the surrounding context, as we can in face-to-face conversations. This sometimes decontextualized nature of writing is one thing that makes reading difficult.

4. Orthography

In spoken language, most languages have phonemes, stress, rhythm, juncture, intonation, pauses, volume, voice quality settings, and nonverbal cues, all of which enhance the message. In writing we have graphemes—that's it! Yes, sometimes punctuation, pictures, graphics, or charts lend a helping hand. And, yes, a writer can describe the aforementioned phonological cues, as in, "With loud, rasping grunts, punctuated by roars of pain, he slowly dragged himself out of the line of enemy fire." But these written symbols stand alone as the one set of signals that the reader must perceive. Because of the frequent ambiguity that is present in a good deal of writing, readers must do their best to infer, to interpret, and to "read between the lines."

In spite of its reputation for being "irregular," English orthography is highly predictable from its spoken counterpart, especially when one considers morphological information as well. Yet, even for literate learners of English, our spelling system presents difficulties, especially for those whose native languages have quite different systems (Nassaji, 2014). On the other hand, most of the irregularity in English manifests itself in high-frequency words (*of, to, have, do, done, was*, etc.). So, should orthographic processing be an issue in teaching reading? Yes, according to Nassaji (2014, p. 13), who concludes that "limited knowledge of orthographic representations may negatively affect L2 readers' word recognition processes and reading comprehension."

 **CLASSROOM CONNECTIONS**

Among native English speakers, there are "poor" spellers here and there. Why is that? Do you think of English is a "difficult" language to learn, orthographically? How important is it for learners who are literate in their L1 to be explicitly taught English spelling patterns? Or should they just be left to "pick up" spelling rules?

5. Complexity

You might be tempted to say that writing is more complex than speech, but in reality, that would be difficult to demonstrate. Writing and speech represent different modes of complexity, and the most salient difference is in the nature of clauses. Spoken language tends to have shorter clauses connected by more coordinate conjunctions, while writing has longer clauses and more subordination. The shorter clauses are often a factor of the redundancy we build into speech (repeating subjects and verbs for clarity). Look at the following pair:

a. Because of the frequent ambiguity that therefore is present in a good deal of writing, readers must do their best to infer, to interpret, and to "read between the lines."

b. There's frequent ambiguity in a lot of writing. And so, readers have to infer a lot. They also have to interpret what they read. And sometimes they have to "read between the lines."

The cognitive complexity of version (a), the written version, is no greater than version (b), the spoken version. But structurally, four sentences were used in version (b) to replace the one long sentence (with two clauses) of version (a).

Readers—especially second language readers who may be quite adept in the spoken language—have to retool their cognitive perceptors in order to extract meaning from the written code. The linguistic differences between speech and writing are another major contributing cause to difficulty.

6. Vocabulary

It is true that written English typically utilizes a greater variety of lexical items than spoken conversational English. In our everyday give and take with family, friends, and colleagues, vocabulary is limited. Because writing allows the writer more processing time, because of a desire to be precise in writing, and simply because of the formal conventions of writing (see #7 below), lower-frequency words often appear. Such words can present stumbling blocks to learners. However, because the meaning of a good many unknown words can be predicted from their context, and because sometimes the overall meaning of a sentence or paragraph is nevertheless still clear, learners should refrain from the frequent use of a bilingual dictionary.

7. Formality

Writing is quite frequently more formal than speech. What do we mean by that? Formality refers to prescribed *forms* that certain written messages must adhere to. The reason that you can both recognize a menu and decide what to eat fairly quickly is that menus conform to certain conventions. Things are categorized (appetizers, salads, entrees, desserts, etc.) in logical order and subcategorized (all seafood dishes are listed together); exotic or creative names for dishes are usually defined; prices are given for each item; and the menu isn't so long that it overwhelms you.

We have **rhetorical**, or organizational, formality in essay writing that demands a writer's conformity to conventions like paragraph topics. There is usually a logical order for, say, comparing and contrasting something; opening and closing an essay, and a preference for nonredundancy and subordination of clauses, and more. Until a reader is familiar with the formal features of a written text, some difficulty in interpretation may ensue.

MICRO- AND MACROSKILLS FOR READING COMPREHENSION

Below is an adaptation of the models of micro- and macroskills offered in the previous two chapters—a breakdown of what L2 learners need to do to become efficient readers.

Micro- and Macroskills for Reading Comprehension

Microskills

1. Discriminate among the distinctive graphemes and orthographic patterns of English.
2. Retain chunks of language of different lengths in short-term memory.
3. Comprehend written language at an efficient rate of speed to suit the purpose.
4. Recognize a core of words, and interpret word order patterns and their significance.
5. Recognize grammatical word classes (nouns, verbs, etc.), systems (e.g., tense, agreement, pluralization), patterns, rules, and elliptical forms.
6. Recognize that a particular meaning may be expressed in different grammatical forms.

Macroskills

7. Recognize cohesive devices in written discourse and their role in signaling the relationship between and among clauses.
8. Recognize the rhetorical forms of written discourse and their significance for interpretation.
9. Recognize the communicative functions of written texts, according to form and purpose.
10. Infer context that is not explicit by using background knowledge.
11. Infer links and connections between events, ideas, etc., deduce causes and effects, and detect such relations as main idea, supporting idea, new information, given information, generalization, and exemplification.
12. Distinguish between literal and implied meanings.
13. Detect culturally specific references and interpret them in a context of the appropriate cultural schemata.
14. Develop and use a battery of reading strategies such as scanning and skimming, detecting discourse markers, guessing the meaning of words from context, and activating schemata for the interpretation of texts.

STRATEGIES FOR READING COMPREHENSION

For most second language learners who are already literate in a previous language, reading comprehension is primarily a matter of developing appropriate, efficient comprehension strategies. Some strategies are related to bottom-up procedures, and others enhance the top-down processes. Following are ten such strategies, each of which can be practically applied to your classroom techniques.

1. Identify the Purpose in Reading

How many times have you been told to read something, yet you didn't know why you were being asked to read it? You did only a mediocre job of retaining what you "read" and perhaps were rather slow in the process. Efficient reading consists of clearly identifying the purpose in reading something. By doing so, you know what you're looking for and can weed out potential distracting information. Whenever you are teaching a reading technique, make sure students know their purpose in reading something.

 **CLASSSROOM CONNECTIONS**

How would you make sure your students have a purpose in reading an assigned passage? Would you simply tell them? Or ask them, after a quick skim of the passage, what purposes they might have or derive in reading it? How would you help your students connect the principle of identifying purpose to schema theory, discussed above?

2. Use Graphemic Rules and Patterns to Aid in Bottom-Up Decoding

At the beginning levels of learning English, one of the difficulties students encounter in learning to read is making the correspondences between spoken and written English. In many cases, learners have become acquainted with oral language and have some difficulty learning English spelling conventions. They may need hints and explanations about certain English orthographic rules and peculiarities. While you can often assume that one-to-one grapheme–phoneme correspondences will be acquired with ease, other relationships might prove difficult. Consider how you might provide hints and pointers on such patterns as these:

- "short" vowel sound in VC patterns (*bat*, *him*, *leg*, *wish*, etc.)
- "long" vowel sound in VCe (final silent *e*) patterns (*late*, *time*, *bite*, etc.)
- "long" vowel sound in VV patterns (*seat*, *coat*, etc.)
- distinguishing "hard" *c* and *g* from "soft" *c* and *g* (*cat* vs. *city*, *game* vs. *gem*, etc.)

These and a multitude of other *phonics* approaches to reading can prove useful for learners at the beginning level and especially useful for teaching children and nonliterate adults.

3. Use Efficient Silent Reading Techniques for Improving Fluency

If you are teaching beginning level students, this particular strategy will not apply because they are still struggling with the control of a limited vocabulary and grammatical patterns. Your intermediate-to-advanced level students need not be speed readers, but you can help them increase reading rate and comprehension efficiency by teaching a few silent reading rules:

- You don't need to "pronounce" each word to yourself.
- Try to visually perceive more than one word at a time, preferably phrases.
- Unless a word is absolutely crucial to global understanding, skip over it and try to infer its meaning from its context.

Aside from these fundamental guidelines, which if followed can help learners to be efficient readers, reading speed is usually not much of an issue for all but the most advanced learners. Academic reading, for example, is something most learners manage to accomplish by allocating whatever time they personally need in order to complete the material. If your students can read 250 to 300 words per minute, further concern over speed may not be necessary.

4. Skim the Text for Main Ideas

Perhaps the two most valuable reading strategies for learners (as well as native speakers) are skimming and scanning. **Skimming** consists of quickly running one's eyes across a whole text (such as an essay, article, or chapter) for its gist. Skimming gives readers the advantage of being able to predict the purpose of the passage, the main topic, or message, and possibly some of the developing or supporting ideas. This gives them a head start as they embark on more focused reading. You can train students to skim passages by giving them, say, thirty seconds to look through a few pages of material, close their books, and then tell you what they learned.

 **Classroom Connections**

Skimming may not be a familiar process for some students. Beyond just giving them 30 seconds to skim a passage, what are some *specific steps* you can go through to teach skimming? What do learners look for? How do they avoid just retaining only a blur of jumbled ideas?

5. Scan the Text for Specific Information

The second in the most valuable category is **scanning**, or quickly searching for some particular piece or pieces of information in a text. Scanning exercises may ask students to look for names or dates, to find a definition of a key concept, or to list a certain number of supporting details. The purpose of scanning is to extract specific information without reading through the whole text. For academic

English, scanning is absolutely essential. In vocational or general English, scanning is important in dealing with genres like schedules, manuals, or forms.

6. Use Semantic Mapping or Clustering

Readers can easily be overwhelmed by a long string of ideas or events. The strategy of **semantic mapping**, or grouping ideas into meaningful clusters, helps the reader to provide some order to the chaos. Making such semantic maps can be done individually, but they make for a productive group work technique as students collectively induce order and hierarchy to a passage. Early drafts of these maps can be quite messy—which is perfectly acceptable. Figure 17.1, for example, shows a first attempt by a small group of students to draw a semantic map of an article by Rick Gore called "Between Fire and Ice: The Planets," an article about a total solar eclipse as seen through the eyes of villagers in Patuk, Java.

7. Guess When You Aren't Certain

This is an extremely broad category. Learners can use guessing to their advantage to

- guess the meaning of a word
- guess a grammatical relationship (e.g., a pronoun reference)

Figure 17.1 Semantic map

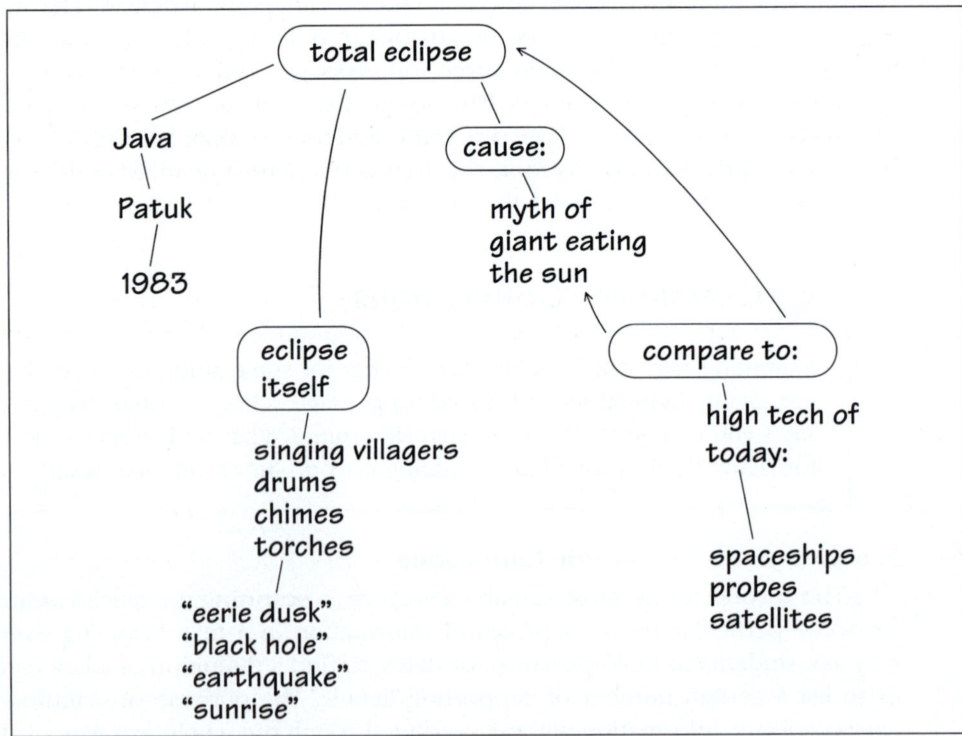

- guess a discourse relationship
- infer implied meaning ("between the lines")
- guess about a cultural reference
- guess content messages.

Now, you of course don't want to encourage your learners to become haphazard readers! They should utilize all their skills and put forth as much effort as possible to be on target with their hypotheses. But the point here is that reading is, after all, a guessing game of sorts, and the sooner learners understand this game, the better off they are. The key to successful guessing is to make it reasonably *accurate*.

Classroom Connections

Guessing may be a very unfamiliar process for many learners, especially those whose education and upbringing have stressed accuracy and the avoidance of error. How might you ease your students into the process of guessing meanings? Are there some guessing games you could introduce that would help them to lose their inhibitions about risk-taking?

You can help learners to become accurate guessers by encouraging them to use effective *compensation* strategies in which they fill gaps in their competence by intelligent attempts to use whatever clues are available to them. Language-based clues include word analysis, word associations, and textual structure. Nonlinguistic clues come from context, situation, and other schemata.

8. Analyze Vocabulary

One way for learners to make guessing pay off when they don't immediately recognize a word is to analyze it in terms of what they know about it. Several techniques are useful here:

Guidelines for Helping Learners to Employ Word Analysis Techniques

- Look for prefixes (*co-*, *inter-*, *un-*, etc.) that may give clues.
- Look for suffixes (*-tion*, *-tive*, *-ally*, etc.) that may indicate what part of speech it is.
- Look for roots that are familiar (e.g., *intervening* may be a word a student doesn't know, but recognizing that the root *ven* comes from Latin "to come" would yield the meaning "to come in between").

- Look for grammatical contexts that may signal information.
- Look at the semantic context (topic) for clues.

9. Distinguish Between Literal and Implied Meanings

This requires the application of sophisticated top-down processing skills. The fact that not all language can be interpreted appropriately by attending to its literal, syntactic surface structure makes special demands on readers. Implied meaning usually has to be derived from processing *pragmatic* information, as in the following examples:

> (1) Bill walked into the frigid classroom and immediately noticed Bob, sitting by the open window, with a heavy sweatshirt on.
>
> "Brrr!" he exclaimed, simultaneously eyeing Bob and the open windows. "It's sure cold in here, Bob."
>
> Bob glanced up from his book and growled, "Oh, all right, I'll close the window."
>
> (2) The policeman held up his hand and stopped the car.
>
> (3) Mary heard the ice cream man coming down the street. She remembered her birthday money and rushed into the house . . . (Rumelhart, 1977, p. 265)

 **CLASSROOM CONNECTIONS**

In each of the above three examples, what is the *implied* information? How would you help your students to recognize (1) indirect requests that are made without forming a question, (2) the effect of the policeman's hand signal, and (3) what the reader *thinks* will happen next. This final example has a surprise ending: "*. . . and locked the door!*"

10. Capitalize on Discourse Markers to Process Relationships

Many discourse markers in English signal relationships among ideas as expressed through phrases, clauses, and sentences. A clear comprehension of such markers can greatly enhance learners' reading efficiency. Table 17.1 enumerates almost one hundred of these markers with which learners of intermediate proficiency levels ought to be thoroughly familiar.

Table 17.1 Types of discourse markers (Mackay, 1987, p. 254)

Notional category/meaning	Marker
1. *Enumerative.* Introduce in order in which points are to be made or the time sequence in which actions or processes took place.	first(ly), second(ly), third(ly), one, two, three / a, b, c, next, then, finally, last(ly), in the first / second place, for one thing / for another thing, to begin with, subsequently, eventually, finally, in the end, to conclude
2. *Additive*	
2.1 Reinforcing. Introduces a reinforcement or confirmation of what has preceded.	again, then again, also, moreover, furthermore, in addition, above all, what is more
2.2 Similarity. Introduces a statement of similarity with what has preceded.	equally, likewise, similarly, correspondingly, in the same way
2.3 Transition. Introduces a new stage in the sequence of presentation of information.	now, well, incidentally, by the way, O.K., fine
3. *Logical Sequence*	
3.1 Summative. Introduces a summary of what has preceded.	so, so far, altogether, overall, then, thus, therefore, in short, to sum up, to conclude, to summarize
3.2 Resultative. Introduces an expression of the result or consequence of what preceded (and includes inductive and deductive acts).	so, as a result, consequently, hence, now, therefore, thus, as a consequence, in consequence
4. *Explicative.* Introduces an explanation or reformulation of what preceded.	namely, in other words, that is to say, better, rather, by (this) we mean
5. *Illustrative.* Introduces an illustration or example of what preceded.	for example, for instance
6. *Contrastive*	
6.1 Replacive. Introduces an alternative to what preceded.	alternatively, (or) again, (or) rather, (but) then, on the other hand
6.2 Antithetic. Introduces information in opposition to what preceded.	conversely, instead, then, on the contrary, by contrast, on the other hand
6.3 Concessive. Introduces information that is unexpected in view of what preceded.	anyway, anyhow, however, nevertheless, nonetheless, notwithstanding, still, though, yet, for all that, in spite of (that), at the same time, all the same

TYPES OF CLASSROOM READING PERFORMANCE

Different kinds of reading performance in the language classroom are derived more from the variety of texts (refer to the list earlier in this chapter) to which you can expose students than from the variety of overt types of performance. Consider the types of performance depicted in Figure 17.2.

Figure 17.2. Types of classroom reading performance

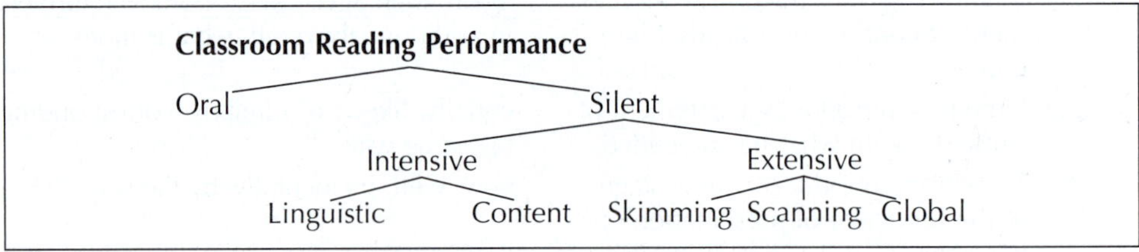

1. Oral and Silent Reading

Occasionally, you will have reason to ask a student to read orally. At the beginning and intermediate levels, oral reading provides some *advantages* as well as disadvantages. Consider the following:

Advantages	**Disadvantages**
1. Oral reading serves as an evaluative check on bottom-up processing skills.	**1.** Oral reading is not a very authentic language activity.
2. It doubles as a pronunciation check.	**2.** While one student is reading, others can easily lose attention (or, if they are reading in turns, be silently rehearsing the next paragraph!).
3. It adds some extra student participation if you want to highlight a certain short segment of a reading passage.	**3.** It may have the outward appearance of student participation when in reality it is mere recitation.

For advanced levels, usually only advantage (3) can be gained by reading orally. As a rule of thumb, you want to use oral reading to serve at least one of the above purposes. On the other hand, the *disadvantages* of too much oral reading also need to be considered when asking students to read aloud.

Silent reading, on the other hand, is essential in order for learners to gain any speed in the process. For extensive reading, explained below, speed is usually an important factor. For intensive reading, learning to read silently may be of less importance, but still remains an ultimate goal.

 **CLASSROOM CONNECTIONS**

When learners are reading on their own, what is the advantage of silent reading? Can you *teach* students to read silently? Or is this a skill they have to pick up with advancing proficiency? What is the advantage—or is there one—of helping students to read without "moving their lips" as they read?

2. Intensive and Extensive Reading

Silent reading may be subcategorized into intensive and extensive reading. **Intensive reading**, analogous to intensive listening (described in Chapter 16), is usually a classroom-oriented activity in which students focus on the linguistic or semantic details of a passage. Intensive reading often calls students' attention to grammatical forms, discourse markers, and other surface structure details for the purpose of understanding literal meaning, implications, rhetorical relationships, and the like.

As a "zoom lens" strategy for taking a closer look at a text, intensive reading also may be a content-related reading strategy initiated because of subject-matter comprehension difficulty. A complex cognitive concept may be "trapped" inside the words of a sentence or paragraph, and a good reader will then very slowly and methodically extract meaning.

Extensive reading is carried out to achieve a general understanding of a usually somewhat longer text (for example, books, long articles, essays). Most extensive reading is performed outside class time. Pleasure reading is often extensive. Technical, scientific, and professional reading can, under certain special circumstances, be extensive when one is striving for global or general meaning from longer passages.

The advantages of extensive reading were discussed in the first section of the chapter. By stimulating reading for enjoyment or reading where all concepts, names, dates, and other details need not be retained, students gain an appreciation for the affective and cognitive window of reading: an entrée into new worlds. Extensive reading can sometimes help learners get away from their tendency to overanalyze or look up words they don't know, and read for understanding as "engaged" readers (Anderson, 2014).

PRINCIPLES FOR TEACHING READING SKILLS

1. In an Integrated Course, Include a Focus on Reading Skills

L2 learners who are literate in their own language are sometimes left to their own devices when it comes to learning reading skills. It's easy for teachers to assume that our students will learn good reading simply by absorption through generous offerings of both intensive and extensive reading opportunities. In reality, there is much to be gained by a strategic focus on reading skills within lessons that cover other skills. Virtually all course materials include the written word, so students are *reading*, even if their reading is incidental to other tasks. But even in those incidental reading moments, you can inject focal moments in which students attend to reading.

CLASSROOM CONNECTIONS

Look at the lesson represented in Figure 17.4 toward the end of this chapter. Identify as many reading skills that are *directly* focused on and that *indirectly* require reading abilities. How appropriate, in this lesson, is it to allow those incidental reading skills to be simply assumed—without focusing specifically on them?

2. Offer Reading on Relevant, Interesting, Motivating Topics

What do you think makes for interesting and relevant reading for your students? Of the long list of texts at the beginning of this chapter, how many will your students encounter in "real life"? Use those texts. What are your students' goals in learning to read English? Focus on those goals. Choose material that is *relevant* to those goals.

One approach to reading instruction is to have students create their *own* material for reading (see Chapter 3 for a description of the Language Experience Approach). Other approaches in which learners are given *choices* in selecting reading material offer the potential of increasing their *investment*. Carefully sequenced readings and instructional strategies that are *success-oriented* give further personal involvement in the process. Further, readings that help learners to form their respective *identities* should help to bolster their sense of *agency*.

CLASSROOM CONNECTIONS

What are some genres or topics that might help a student to understand his or her *identity*? If students read a passage about someone else's personal struggle with adjusting to a new culture, feeling ostracized or inferior in the L2 culture, what kinds of questions or discussion topics might you plan for pre-, while-, and post-reading?

3. Balance Authenticity and Readability in Choosing Texts

By now, the importance of authentic language should be more than clear. But in teaching reading, one issue that has invited some controversy is the advisability of what are called "simplified texts," in which an otherwise authentic text is edited to keep language within the proficiency level of a set of students. In order for you to make a decision on this issue, it is important to distinguish between (a) simple texts and (b) simplified texts and to understand sources of complexity in reading material.

Authentic simple texts can either be devised or located in the real world. From ads to labels to reports to essays, texts are available that are grammatically and lexically simple. Simplifying an existing potential reading selection may not be necessary. Yet if simplification must be done, it is important to preserve the natural redundancy, humor, wit, and other captivating features of the original material.

Second, you might ask yourself what "simplicity" is and then determine if a so-called simplified text is really simpler than its original. Sometimes simplified texts remove so much natural redundancy that they actually become difficult. And what you perceive as textual complexity may be more a product of background schemata than of linguistic complexity. Take another look at the list of characteristics of written language earlier in this chapter and you will no doubt see what it is that makes a text difficult. In light of those criteria, is a simplified text really simpler? The answer may be "no." Richard Day and Julian Bamford (1998, p. 53), in warning against "the cult of authenticity and the myth of simplification," contended that our CLT approach has overemphasized the need for so-called authenticity, and that there is indeed a place for simplified texts in reading instruction.

Nuttall (1996) offered three criteria for choosing reading texts for students:

a. *suitability* of content: material that students will find interesting, enjoyable, challenging, and appropriate for their goals in learning English

b. *exploitability*: a text that facilitates the achievement of certain language and content goals, that is exploitable for instructional tasks and techniques, and that is integratable with other skills (listening, speaking, writing)

c. *readability*: a text with lexical and structural difficulty that will challenge students without overwhelming them.

4. Encourage the Development of Reading Strategies

Already in this chapter, ten different reading strategies have been discussed. To what extent are you encouraging your students to use all these strategies?

5. Include Both Bottom-Up and Top-Down Techniques

In our craze for communicative, authentic language activity in the classroom, we sometimes forget that learners can indeed benefit from studying the fundamentals. Make sure that you give enough classroom time to focusing on the building blocks of written language, geared appropriately for each level.

6. Follow the "SQ3R" Sequence

One effective series of procedures for approaching a reading text has come to be labeled the **SQ3R** technique, a process consisting of the following five steps:

SQ3R Processes

1. **Survey:** Skim the text for an overview of main ideas.
2. **Question:** The reader asks questions about what he or she wishes to get out of the text.
3. **Read:** Read the text while looking for answers to the previously formulated questions.
4. **Recite:** Reprocess the salient points of the text through oral or written language.
5. **Review:** Assess the importance of what one has just read and incorporate it into long-term associations.

This series of techniques, of course, may not fit all classes and contexts, but it serves as a general guide for a reading class.

Classroom Connections

In L2 classes you have taken, do you recall following the SQ3R sequence in your lessons? Have you tried this sequence in your own teaching or lesson planning? How rigidly would you adhere to the sequence—that is, what variations might you employ in approaching a reading text?

7. Design Pre-Reading, While-Reading, and Post-Reading Phases

It's tempting, especially at intermediate and advanced levels, to tell students, "Okay now, class, read the next two pages silently." No introduction, no hints on anything special to do while reading, and nary a thought about something to follow the silent reading period. A good rubric to keep in mind for teaching reading is the following three-part framework:

Tips for Teaching Reading

1. **Before you read:** Spend some time introducing a topic, encouraging skimming, scanning, predicting, and activating schemata. Students can bring the best of their knowledge and skills to a text when they have been given a chance to "ease into" the passage.
2. **While you read:** Not all reading is simply extensive or global reading. There may be certain facts or rhetorical devices that students should take note of while they read. Give students a

sense of purpose for reading rather than just reading because you ordered it.

3. **After you read:** Comprehension questions are just one form of activity appropriate for post-reading. Also consider vocabulary study, identifying the author's purpose, discussing the author's line of reasoning, examining grammatical structures, or steering students toward a follow-up writing exercise.

8. Build Ongoing (Informal) Assessment into Your Techniques

Because reading, like listening comprehension, is totally unobservable (we have to infer comprehension from other behavior), it is as important in reading as it is in listening to be able to accurately assess students' comprehension and development of skills. Consider some of the following overt responses (modeled after the list in Chapter 15 for listening) that indicate comprehension:

Overt Responses That Indicate Comprehension

1. doing—the reader responds physically to a command.
2. choosing—the reader selects from alternatives posed orally or in writing.
3. transferring—the reader summarizes orally what is read
4. answering—the reader answers questions about the passage
5. condensing—the reader outlines or takes notes on a passage
6. extending—the reader provides an ending to a story
7. duplicating—the reader translates the message into the native language or copies it (beginning level, for very short passages only)
8. modeling—the reader puts together a toy, for example, after reading directions for assembly
9. conversing—the reader engages in a conversation that indicates appropriate processing of information

Classroom Connections

The above nine modes offer observable responses that can be informally assessed in the classroom as you teach. For some of the responses, you can fairly easily determine success or comprehension. Others are more "slippery." How would you determine whether responses to numbers 3, 5, and 9 show expected levels of comprehension?

TWO READING LESSONS

On pages 415-421 are excerpts from two different textbooks designed to teach reading skills. In both cases, of course, the other three skills (listening, speaking, writing) are implied in the unfolding of the lesson.

The first excerpt (Figure 17.3) is for a high beginning level of learners, on the topic of fast and healthy foods (Saslow & Ascher, 2011). The lesson gives a pre-reading focus on vocabulary, then, while-reading, guessing word meanings from context, followed by post-reading exercises on inference, note taking, and discussion. This is part of a general-skills textbook.

CLASSROOM CONNECTIONS

What is your overall assessment of the effectiveness of this excerpt (Figure 17.3 on fast and healthy foods) for high beginners? How effectively are the objectives accomplished (vocabulary in adjective forms, understanding from context, and discussing healthy food)? If you were given this lesson to teach, what would you add (or delete) in order to accomplish the objectives? Are the exercises following the reading itself an effective way to process the reading?

The second excerpt (Figure 17.4) is for students at a high-intermediate level preparing for academic reading in English (Böttcher, 2014, pp. 139–146). The topic is laughter and the brain, and objectives focus on main idea, connotations, antonyms, dictionary use, note taking, and critical thinking, among others. The genre, feature writing in a magazine or newspaper, manifests more complexity in discourse structure, vocabulary, and cognition than the first lesson. A number of the principles and strategies cited in this chapter are included. Notice especially the exercise on critical thinking, which requires inference and creativity.

CLASSROOM CONNECTIONS

What is your overall assessment of the effectiveness of this excerpt (Figure 17.4 on laughter and the brain) for advanced students learning English for academic purposes? How effectively are the objectives accomplished? If you were given this lesson to teach, what would you add (or delete) in order to accomplish the objectives? In the critical thinking exercise and the next writing activity, what would you add or change?

Figure 17.3 Fast and healthy foods

LESSON 4 **GOAL** **Discuss food and health**

BEFORE YOU READ

A 2:31 **Vocabulary • *Adjectives to describe the healthfulness of food*** Read and listen. Then listen again and repeat.

healthy / healthful is good for you
unhealthy / unhealthful is bad for you
fatty / high-fat contains a lot of oil
salty contains a lot of salt
sweet contains a lot of sugar
high-calorie can make you fat or overweight
low-calorie is not going to make you fat

B **Warm-up** Do you like to eat at fast-food restaurants? Is it possible to get healthy food there? Use the Vocabulary.

READING 2:32

File Edit View History Bookmarks Tools Help

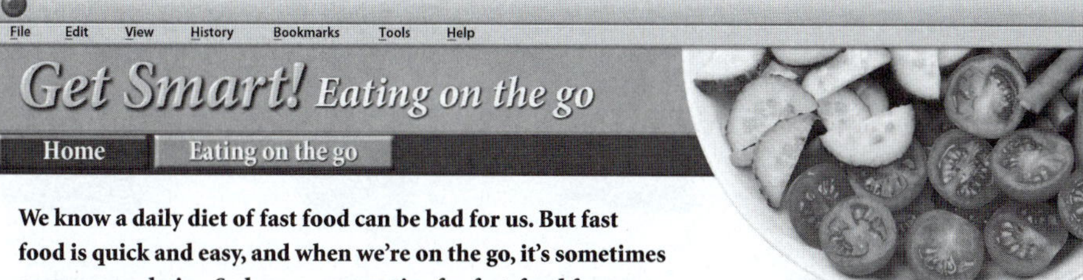

We know a daily diet of fast food can be bad for us. But fast food is quick and easy, and when we're on the go, it's sometimes a necessary choice. So here are some tips for fast-food fans:

Eat more "veggies."

- **Choose the chicken.** Have chicken rather than red meat. When in doubt, order the grilled chicken—not the fried.
- **Go light on the sauce.** Mayo, salad dressings, and other sauces are loaded with calories. Cut down on them, or cut them out altogether!

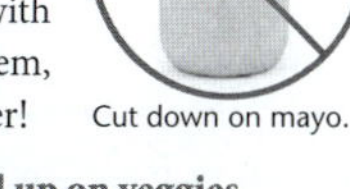

Cut down on mayo.

- **Fill up on veggies.** Ask for tomato, lettuce, onion, or other veggies on your sandwich. These low-calorie choices can help you avoid fries and other high-calorie options.

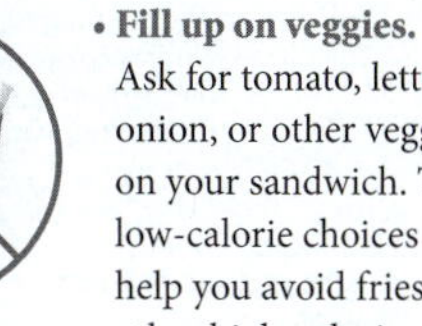

Skip the fries.

- **Go for the regular size,** not the extra-large. Super-size portions can super-size YOU.
- **Skip the sides entirely.** Eating a burger by itself is often enough. If you need a side order of something, consider a fruit cup or a side salad, instead of those fatty, salty french fries. Most fast-food restaurants offer those healthy options now.

Get a side salad.

- **Finally, treat yourself.** When you just have to have something sweet, opt for some delicious low-fat frozen yogurt or fruit ices rather than ice cream or cookies. You won't miss the calories a bit!

Source: fruitsandveggiesmatter.gov

46 **UNIT 4**

Figure 17.3 Fast and healthy foods (*Continued*)

A Understand from context Find the following words and phrases in the Reading and match them with their meanings. Then, on a separate sheet of paper, use the words to write your own sentences.

.... **1** "veggies"	**a** the amount you eat at one time
.... **2** "side order"	**b** not choose
.... **3** "go for"	**c** vegetables
.... **4** "skip" or "avoid"	**d** choice
.... **5** "portion"	**e** something you eat with your main course
.... **6** "option"	**f** choose

B Infer information Which tips on the website can help you cut down on calories? fat? salt? sugar? Explain how.

On your *ActiveBook* Self-Study Disk:
Extra Reading Comprehension Questions

NOW YOU CAN Discuss food and health

A Frame your ideas Write a ✓ next to the foods you think are healthy. Write an X next to the foods you think are not. Then discuss your answers with a partner. Explain why some of the foods are unhealthy.

"French fries are not healthy. They're too fatty."

"I agree."

☐ rice ☐ french fries ☐ hot peppers ☐ ice cream

☐ snacks: nuts, chips ☐ chicken ☐ salad ☐ pasta with sauce

B Notepadding List other foods and drinks you think are good for you and bad for you.

Healthy foods	Unhealthy foods
oranges	*salty foods, like potato chips*

C Discussion Now discuss food and health with your class. Suggest healthy eating tips. Use your lists.

Text-mining (optional)
Underline more language in the Reading on page 46 to use in the Discussion. For example:
"Have ___ rather than ___."

Be sure to recycle this language.

Categories of foods		Adjectives	Verbs
grains	meat	healthy / unhealthy	skip / avoid / cut out
seafood	sweets	good / bad for you	go light on / cut down on
dairy products	fruit	high-calorie / low-calorie	fill up on
vegetables	oils	fatty / salty / sweet / spicy	

47

Figure 17.4 Laughter and the brain

READING TWO: Laughter and the Brain

A Warm-Up

List the ways you think laughter is beneficial. Share your answers with the class.

B Reading Strategy

Predicting Type of Text from the Title

Predicting is a very important pre-reading skill. When you **predict**, you make a guess about something based on the information you have. Predicting helps prepare the reader for the reading experience that is to come. The title of a text can often help you predict the type of text. At the same time it helps you to imagine the situation for which the text was written or prepared.

Look at the title of the reading. Do you think the text contains mostly facts or opinions? Discuss your answer with a partner.

Now read the text to find out if your prediction was correct.

Laughter and the Brain

By Eric H. Chudler

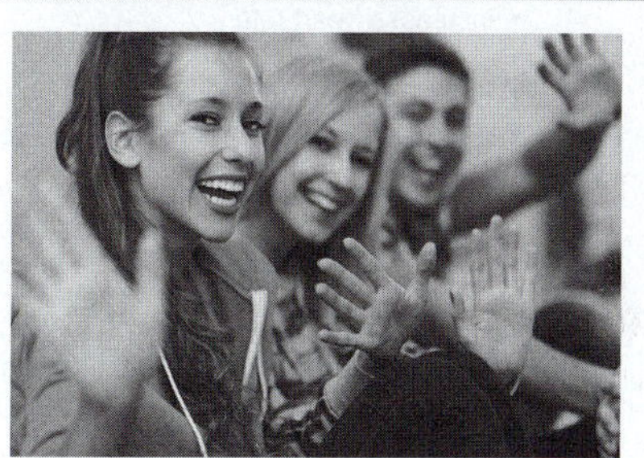

1 Laughter . . . it's fun . . . it's funny . . . but why do we do it? What part of the brain is responsible for laughter and **humor**? There are not many answers to these questions because there have not been very many experiments on laughter. Part of the reason for this is that laughter is not a big medical problem.

2 A paper published in the journal *Nature* (vol. 391, page 650, 1998) called "Electric Current Stimulates Laughter" has provided a bit more information about how the brain is involved with laughter. The paper discussed the case of a 16-year-old girl named "A.K." who was having surgery to control seizures[1] **due to** epilepsy.[2] During surgery, the doctors electrically stimulated[3]

(continued on next page)

[1] ***seizures:*** brief periods when someone is unconscious and cannot control the movements of his/her body

[2] ***epilepsy:*** a medical condition in the brain that can make someone become unconscious or unable to control his/her movements for a short time

[3] ***electrically stimulated:*** used the power carried by wires to get a muscle or group of muscles to move

Figure 17.4 Laughter and the brain (*Continued*)

A.K.'s cerebral cortex to map her brain.[4] Mapping of the brain is done to determine the function of different brain areas and to make sure that brain tissue that will be removed does not have an important function.

3 The doctors found that A.K. always laughed when they stimulated a small 2 cm by 2 cm area on her left superior frontal gyrus (part of the frontal lobe of the brain). This brain area is part of the supplementary motor area.[5] Each time her brain was stimulated, A.K. laughed and said that something was funny. The thing that she said caused her to laugh was different each time. A.K. laughed first, then **made up** a story that was funny to her. Most people first know what is funny, then they laugh.

4 The authors of the paper believe that the area of the brain that caused laughter in A.K. is part of several different brain areas which are important for:

- the emotions produced by a funny situation (emotional part of humor)
- the "**getting it**" part of a joke (cognitive, thinking part of humor)
- moving the muscles of the face to smile (motor part of humor).

5 The physiological study of laughter has its own name: "gelotology." Research has shown that laughing is more than just a person's voice and movement. Laughter requires the **coordination** of many muscles throughout the body. Laughter also:

- **increases** blood pressure
- increases heart rate
- changes breathing
- **reduces** levels of certain hormones.[6]
- provides a **boost** to the immune system.[7]

6 Can laughter improve health? It may be a good way for people to relax because muscle tension is **reduced** after laughing. There are some cases when a good deep laugh may help people with breathing problems. Perhaps laughing can also help heart patients by giving the heart a bit of a workout. Some hospitals even have their own "humor rooms," "**comedy** carts," and clown kids in attempts to speed a patient's recovery and boost **morale**.

[4] ***map her brain:*** to make a visual representation of her brain

[5] ***supplementary motor area:*** a part of the brain that helps control movement

[6] ***hormones:*** substances produced by your body that influence its growth, development, and condition

[7] ***immune system:*** the system by which the body protects itself against disease

140 CHAPTER 10

Figure 17.4 Laughter and the brain (*Continued*)

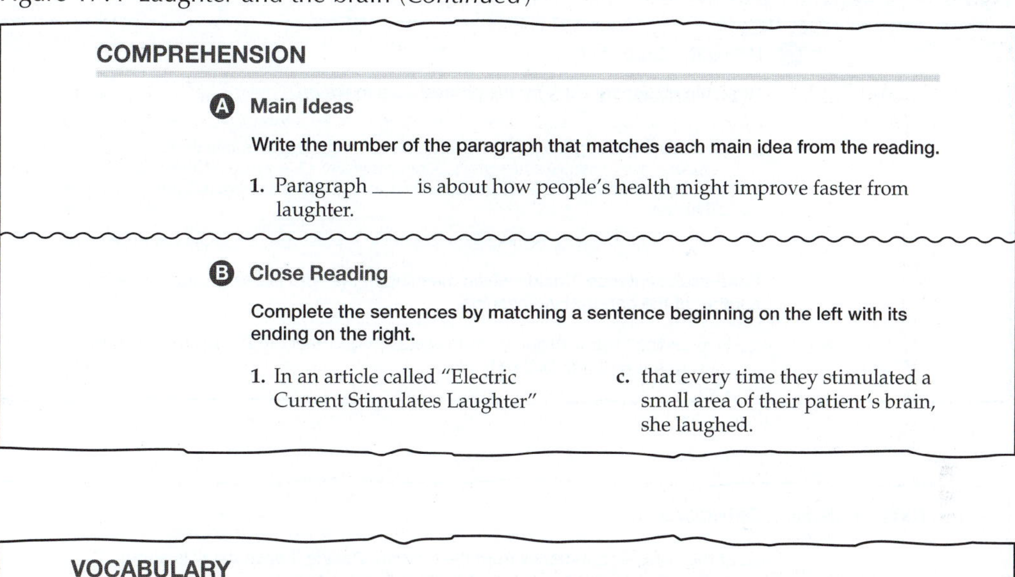

COMPREHENSION

A Main Ideas

Write the number of the paragraph that matches each main idea from the reading.

1. Paragraph ____ is about how people's health might improve faster from laughter.

B Close Reading

Complete the sentences by matching a sentence beginning on the left with its ending on the right.

1. In an article called "Electric Current Stimulates Laughter"	**c.** that every time they stimulated a small area of their patient's brain, she laughed.

VOCABULARY

A Connotations

Some words have **feelings** connected to them depending on how they are used in a sentence. These feelings, or **connotations**, can be **positive** (good or useful) or **negative** (bad or harmful).

Look at each word. Find it in the reading. Decide whether it has a *Positive* or *Negative* meaning. Check the appropriate box. Discuss your answers with a partner.

	Positive	Negative
1. humor	☐	☐

B Antonyms

Underline the antonym (the word that has the opposite meaning) of the word in bold. Compare your answers with a partner.

1. humor funniness seriousness comedy

Figure 17.4 Laughter and the brain (*Continued*)

C Using the Dictionary

Read the dictionary entry for the phrasal verb *make up*.

> **make (something) up** *phr. v.* **1** to invent a story or explanation to deceive someone **2** to produce a new story, song, game, etc. **3** to work at times when you don't usually work because you have not done enough work at some other time

Read each sentence. Decide which meaning of the verb is being used. Write the number of the appropriate meaning.

____ **a.** In the "humor rooms" at hospitals, volunteers **make up** funny stories to get patients to laugh.

NOTE-TAKING: Categorizing

Look at the notes about details from the reading. Decide if each detail is about "laughter" or "the brain" and list each in the correct category.

- a small 2 cm by 2 cm area can be stimulated and cause laughter
- boosts morale
- can be mapped to determine the function of different brain areas
- caused by something funny
- coordinates muscle movements needed to laugh
- helps patients feel more optimistic
- may help breathing problems and heart patients
- may help people recover faster
- more than just a person's voice and movement
- not a medical problem
- reduces muscle tension

Figure 17.4 Laughter and the brain (*Continued*)

CRITICAL THINKING

Discuss the questions in a small group. Be prepared to share your ideas with the class.

1. In paragraph 3, the doctors found that A.K. laughed when they stimulated a small area of her brain and then she made up a funny story to explain her laughter, which is the opposite of how laughter usually occurs. What did this discovery suggest?
2. How has the study of laughter affected the treatment of patients in some hospitals?
3. Why do you think laughter might help people recover faster?
4. Sitcoms are popular around the world. Why do you think these types of television shows are so popular and attract people of all ages and cultures?

AFTER YOU READ

WRITING ACTIVITY

Choose one of the topics and write a paragraph about it. Use at least five of the words and phrases you studied in the chapter.

1. Do you think "humor rooms" and "comedy carts" would be possible in hospitals in your country? Why or why not?
2. Who is the funniest person you know? What makes them so funny?
3. The actor Charlie Chaplin said: "A day without laughter is a day wasted." Do you agree with this quote? Give reasons and examples to support your opinion.

SELF-ASSESSMENT

In this chapter you learned to:

- ❍ Scan a text to answer a question in the title
- ❍ Predict the type of text from the title
- ❍ Understand and use the prefix *un-*
- ❍ Determine whether a word has a positive or negative meaning
- ❍ Identify parts of speech
- ❍ Understand and use synonyms and antonyms
- ❍ Use dictionary entries to learn different meanings of a phrasal verb
- ❍ Categorize notes

What can you do well? ✓

What do you need to practice more? X

ASSESSING READING

The classic principles of classroom assessment apply to your attempts to assess reading comprehension: be specific about which micro- or macroskill(s) you are assessing; identify the genre of written communication that is being evaluated; and choose carefully among the range of possibilities from simply perceiving letters or words all the way to extensive reading. In addition, for assessing reading, some attention should be given to the highly strategic nature of reading comprehension by accounting for which of the many strategies for reading are being examined. Finally, reading assessment implies differentiating bottom-up from top-down tasks, as well as focus on form versus focus on meaning.

In your efforts to design tests at any one or combination of these levels and categories, consider the following taxonomy of tasks (Brown & Abeywickrama, 2010). These are not meant to be exhaustive, but rather to provide an overview of some possibilities.

ITEM TYPES FOR ASSESSING READING

1. **Perceptive reading** (recognition of symbols, letters, words)
   - reading aloud
   - copying (reproduce in writing)
   - multiple choice recognition (including true-false and fill-in-the-blank)
   - picture cued identification
2. **Selective reading** (focus on morphology, grammar, lexicon)
   - multiple-choice grammar/vocabulary tasks
   - contextualized multiple-choice (within a short paragraph)
   - sentence-level cloze tasks
   - matching tasks
   - grammar/vocabulary editing tasks (multiple choice)
   - picture-cued tasks (Ss choose among graphic representations)
   - gap-filling tasks (e.g., sentence completion)
3. **Interactive reading**
   - discourse-level cloze tasks (requiring knowledge of discourse)
   - reading + comprehension questions
   - short answer responses to reading
   - discourse editing tasks (multiple choice)
   - scanning
   - reordering sequences of sentences
   - responding to charts, maps, graphs, diagrams

4. **Extensive reading**
   - skimming
   - summarizing
   - responding to reading through short essays
   - note taking, marginal notes, highlighting
   - outlining

This chapter should serve as an overview of information on the teaching of reading, giving you a grasp of some issues surrounding this challenging task, and a sense of how to go about designing effective tasks and activities. Of further importance is the reading-writing *connection*, the second half of which we turn to in Chapter 18.

FOR THE TEACHER: ACTIVITIES (A) & DISCUSSION (D)

Note: For each of the "Classroom Connections" in this chapter, you may wish to turn them into individual or pair-work discussion questions.

1. **(A)** Find four or five different samples of types (genres) of written language (see pp. 395–396), such as a memo, a newspaper article, a questionnaire, a menu, or a set of directions, and give one each to pairs. Each pair's task is to cite examples of *bottom-up* and *top-down* processing of written material. Ask pairs to report findings to the whole class.
2. **(A)** Ask small groups to think of a funny anecdote or joke (or you might supply each group with a short joke to read), and have one volunteer tell one to their group. Then, direct them to identify examples of *content* and *formal schemata* in the anecdote. Have them report findings back to the class.
3. **(D)** Review the meaning of *skimming* and *scanning*. Ask your students to volunteer examples of the two processes. What purposes does each serve? What suggestions do they have for hints they would give to a learner who doesn't know how to skim a passage?
4. **(A)** Ten reading *strategies* are discussed on pages 401–408. Direct pairs to look at the textbook lesson reprinted in Figure 17.3 beginning on page 415, and (a) note which strategies are being encouraged in each activity, and (b) think of other activities that would fill any gaps.
5. **(A)** Review with the class the purpose of *semantic mapping* (page 404). Ask pairs to skim the reading selection "Laughter and the brain" in Figure 17.4 and to draw a semantic map of it. Then, have pairs compare their maps with others in the class and talk about why they drew theirs the way they did.

6. **(D)** Ask your students to look at the lesson represented in Figure 17.4 on "Laughter and the brain" and use the micro- and macroskills listed on page 401 to analyze which of these skills is being touched on in the lesson, and where. Ask students to volunteer responses as you jot them down on the board.
7. **(A)** Ask small groups to look at the textbook lesson on fast food (Figure 17.3) and to critique it in terms of its adherence to principles of teaching *interactive reading*. What changes would they recommend and why? Have them share their conclusions with the rest of the class. If time permits, ask the groups to outline some additional tasks to include in this lesson to a specified group of advanced beginning students. Have them share those ideas with the rest of the class.
8. **(D)** Ask your class to skim the textbook lesson reprinted in Figure 17.4 at the end of the chapter. Then ask them to evaluate the lesson on the basis of (a) opportunities for learners to acquire strategies of reading and (b) the eight principles for designing interactive techniques (pp. 408–413).

FOR YOUR FURTHER READING

Grabe, W., & Stoller, F. (2011). *Teaching and researching reading* (2nd ed.). White Plains, NY: Pearson Longman.

Hedgcock, J., & Ferris, D. (2009). *Teaching readers of English: Students, texts, and contexts*. New York, NY: Routledge.

Nuttall, C. (1996). *Teaching reading skills in a foreign language* (2nd ed.). Oxford, UK: Heinemann.

These three teacher reference books offer comprehensive treatments of research issues and classroom practice in teaching reading skills, with extensive bibliographic references.

Eskey, D. (2005). Reading in a second language. In E. Hinkel (Ed.), *Handbook of research in second language teaching and learning* (pp. 563–579). Mahwah, NJ: Lawrence Erlbaum Associates.

Grabe, W., & Stoller, F. (2014). Teaching reading for academic purposes. In M. Celce-Murcia, D. Brinton, & M. A. Snow (Eds.), *Teaching English as a second or foreign language* (4th ed., pp. 189–205). Boston, MA: National Geographic Learning.

For a more concise overview of the teaching of reading and supporting research, these two chapter/article length pieces are excellent sources to consult.

Nation, I. S. P. (2005). Teaching and learning vocabulary. In E. Hinkel (Ed.), *Handbook of research in second language teaching and learning* (pp. 581–595). Mahwah, NJ: Lawrence Erlbaum Associates.

Read, J. (2004). Research in teaching vocabulary. *Annual Review of Applied Linguistics, 24*, 146–161.

These two articles survey issues in vocabulary acquisition and teaching, with useful bibliographic references.

Ediger, A. (2014). Teaching second/foreign language literacy to school-age learners. In M. Celce-Murcia, D. Brinton, & M. A. Snow (Eds.), *Teaching English as a second or foreign language* (4th ed., pp. 154–169). Boston, MA: National Geographic Learning.

This chapter provides an overview of issues and practices in teaching literacy to L2 learners.

Alderson, J. C. (2000). *Assessing reading.* Cambridge, UK: Cambridge University Press.

Read, J. (2000). *Assessing vocabulary.* Cambridge, UK: Cambridge University Press.

These two volumes in a series on language assessment report on research, issues, theoretical foundations, and practical applications in their respective areas.

CHAPTER **18**

TEACHING WRITING

Questions for Reflection

- What are some of the major issues and concepts in pedagogical research that are related to teaching writing?
- What are some of the unique difficulties involved in learning to write effectively?
- How can the microskills and macroskills of written language be used to teach writing?
- What are some types of writing performance?
- What are some principles to follow in designing writing tasks and activities?
- What are some keys to evaluating the success of writing tasks, activities, and lessons?

The psycholinguist Eric Lenneberg (1967) once noted, in a discussion of "species specific" human behavior, that human beings universally learn to walk and to talk, but that swimming and writing are culturally specific, learned behaviors. We learn to swim if there is a body of water available and usually only if someone teaches us. We learn to write if we are members of a literate society, and usually only if someone teaches us.

Just as there are nonswimmers, poor swimmers, and excellent swimmers, so it is for writers. Why isn't everyone an excellent writer? What is it about writing that blocks so many people, even in their own native language? Why don't people learn to write "naturally," as they learn to talk? How can we best teach L2 learners how to write? What should we be trying to teach? Let's look at these and many other related questions as we tackle the last of the "four skills."

RESEARCH ON SECOND LANGUAGE WRITING

Trends in the teaching of L2 writing have, not surprisingly, coincided with those of the teaching of other skills, especially listening and speaking (Cumming, 2012; Weigle, 2014). You will recall from earlier chapters that as communicative language teaching gathered momentum in the 1980s, teachers learned more and more about how to teach fluency, not just accuracy, how to use authentic texts and contexts in the classroom, how to focus on the purposes of linguistic communication, and how to capitalize on learners' *investment* in learning. Those same trends and the principles that undergirded them also applied to advances in the teaching of writing in L2 contexts.

Over the past few decades of research on teaching writing to L2 learners, a number of issues have appeared, some of which remain controversial in spite of reams of data on second language writing. Here is a brief look at some of those issues.

1. Composing

A simplistic view of writing would assume that written language is simply the graphic representation of spoken language, and that written performance is much like oral performance, the only difference lying in graphic instead of auditory signals. Fortunately, no one holds this view today. The process of writing requires an entirely different set of competencies and is fundamentally different from speaking in ways that have already been reviewed in the last chapter. The *permanence* and *distance* of writing, coupled with its unique rhetorical conventions, indeed make writing as different from speaking as swimming is from walking.

Classroom Connections

In what ways have you felt that it was helpful to have information in written form? And under what circumstances have you felt that preserving something in writing (that would otherwise be spoken or nonverbal) diminishes its impact? In what way does writing represent *distant* communication? How might these characteristics influence the way you would teach writing?

One major theme in pedagogical research on writing is the nature of the **composing** process of writing (O'Brien, 2004; Silva & Brice, 2004; Leki, Cumming, & Silva, 2008; Silva, 2010). Written products are often the result of thinking, drafting, and revising procedures that require specialized skills—skills that not every speaker develops naturally. Further, students exhibit a number of different styles and preferences in their composing processes (Chen, 2005). The upshot of the compositional nature of writing has produced writing pedagogy that focuses students on how to generate ideas, how to organize them coherently, how to use discourse markers and rhetorical conventions to put them cohesively into a written text, how to revise text for clearer meaning, how to edit text for appropriate grammar, and how to produce a final product.

We must insert an important caveat here. Our treatment of writing and composing in this chapter applies to *academic* writing and most *traditional* writing genres. Most of our discussion (with the exception of an example, at the end of the chapter, of a lesson that uses blogging) does not apply to electronic communications such as e-mailing, texting, and blogging. These communications, of course, comprise a popular set of genres, with varying characteristics and functions.

 **CLASSROOM CONNECTIONS**

With so many genres of writing now in use in electronic social media, what would you say are some of the conventions of *texting*? Are there socially accepted "rules" of when and how to text someone? What sort of *revision* is involved in texting? Would you teach students how to text? What about blogging and e-mailing? Or would you simply leave it to students to "pick up" whatever conventions they need?

2. Process and Product

Recognition of the compositional nature of writing has changed the face of writing classes. Half a century ago, writing teachers were mostly concerned with the final **product** of writing: the essay, the report, the story, and what that product should "look" like. Compositions were supposed to meet standards of English rhetorical style, reflect accurate grammar, and be structurally and cohesively well organized. A good deal of attention was placed on "model" compositions that students would emulate and on how well a student's final product measured up against a list of criteria that included content, organization, vocabulary use, grammatical use, and mechanical considerations such as spelling and punctuation.

There is nothing inherently "wrong" with attention to any of the above criteria. They are still the concern of writing students and teachers. But in due course of time, we became better attuned to the advantage given to learners when they were seen as *composers* of language, when they were allowed to focus on content and message, and when their own individual intrinsic motives were put at the center of learning. We began to develop what is now termed the **process** approach to writing instruction.

Hedgcock (2005, pp. 604–605) described the essence of process writing as one that engages learners in *meaningful* writing, encourages stages of multiple drafts and revisions, and provides formative feedback through conferencing. You may know from personal experience what it's like to try to come up with a "perfect" final product without the above process. You may have experienced "writer's block" or experienced anxiety building within you as you felt the pressure to write an in-class essay that would be judged by the teacher, graded, and returned with no chance of future revision. The process approach is an attempt to take advantage of the *planned* potential of writing to give students a chance to think as they write. Another way of putting it is that writing is indeed a *thinking process*.

 **CLASSROOM CONNECTIONS**

Have you ever felt "writer's block," when you just can't seem to get started or make any headway in writing something? Think about one or two of these instances and ask yourself why you "froze up." How would you then help students to "unfreeze" as they attempt to compose in their L2?

The current emphasis on process writing must, of course, be seen in the perspective of history (Hedgcock, 2005; Silva, 2010; Hinkel, 2011; Ferris & Hedgcock, 2014). As in most language-teaching approaches, it is quite possible for you to go to an extreme in emphasizing process to the extent that the final product diminishes in importance. Try not to let this happen! The product is, after all, the ultimate goal; it is the reason that we go through the process of prewriting, drafting, revising, and editing. Without that final product firmly in view, we could quite simply drown ourselves in a sea of revisions. Process is not the end; it is the means to an end.

We'll provide more detail on the process approach later in this chapter.

3. Intercultural Rhetoric

Kaplan's (1966) article on *contrastive rhetoric* has been the subject of debate for five decades. Kaplan's thesis was that languages (and their cultures) have their own unique patterns of written discourse. English discourse, according to Kaplan (p. 14), was schematically described as proceeding in a straight line, Semitic writing in a zigzag formation, Oriental [*sic*] written discourse in a spiraling line, and so forth.

A half-century of subsequent research has shown that L2 learners do indeed bring with them certain predispositions from their native languages and cultures about how to organize writing. While some generalizations apply, it's now clear that not only were Kaplan's diagrams simplistic (Connor, 2002; Casanave, 2004), but his conclusions were based on intuition rather than sound research. Further, the diagrams were overgeneralized in promoting stereotypes that may or may not hold for individual writers.

Nevertheless, there was and still is a ring of truth to Kaplan's claims, as both Kaplan (2005) himself and Connor (2002) noted. No one can deny the effect of one's native culture, or one's predispositions that are the product of perhaps years of schooling, reading, writing, thinking, asserting, arguing, and defending, a concept that became known as **contrastive rhetoric**. As teachers attend carefully to their students' schemata, L1 patterns of thinking and writing cannot be ruled out. A balanced position on this issue, then, would remind teachers to consider a student's cultural/literary schemata as a possible source of difficulty, but not to predict those patterns *a priori* (Matsumoto & Juang, 2013).

Classroom Connections

Reflecting on some cultures you are familiar with, do you feel that there are rhetorical conventions that predictably apply? So, for example, are there typical "American," "Chinese," or "Arabic" characteristics of writing? If so, how would that information influence your approach to teaching writing to one of these cultures? How would you help students appreciate and negotiate both their L1 traditions and new rhetorical conventions of L2 culture?

In recent years the issue of contrastive rhetoric has re-emerged in the redefined form of **intercultural rhetoric** to more appropriately "account for the richness of rhetorical variation of written texts and the varying contexts in which they are constructed" (Connor, Nagelhout, & Rozycki, 2008, p. 9). From a social constructivist perspective, we now recognize that many languages have genres of writing, and even within, say, an academic genre, disciplines vary in their views of acceptable writing. Writing contexts (who is writing, to whom, and for what purpose) and specific conventions within subgroups of genres (e.g., a scientific laboratory report; a personal narrative essay) may prove to be far more important for learners to attend to than a possible *contrasting* native language convention (Connor, 2011).

4. Differences Between L1 and L2 Writing

In the 1970s, research on L2 writing was strongly influenced by previous research on L1 writing. Assumptions were made that the composing processes in both instances were similar if not identical. But it is imperative for teachers to understand that there are in fact many differences between the two, as Silva (1993) noted: L2 writers do less planning, are less fluent (used fewer words), less accurate (made more errors), and less effective in stating goals and organizing material. Differences in using appropriate grammatical and rhetorical conventions and lexical variety were also cited as significant factors.

Current research on differences between L1 and L2 writing (Hedgcock, 2005; Hinkel, 2011; Weigle, 2014) highlight some pedagogical principles:

Pedagogical Principles for L2 Writing

- Consider L1 *rhetorical conventions* as an important factor in determining what and how you teach.
- Factor in the L1 sociocultural *context* of your students as you enable them to participate in one or more *discourse communities* (Weigle, 2014).
- Focus on the ultimate purposes of your students in learning to write (in some cases, these could *specific purposes* (occupational, professional, academic) that have marked L1–L2 contrasts.
- As much as possible, embed writing instruction into *content-based* and *genre-based* approaches, which may have significant cultural ramifications (Hinkel, 2011, p. 527).
- In *assessing* writing, students may need to be gently persuaded to adopt a *process approach* that differs markedly from their L1 cultural norms.

5. Authenticity

How authentic are the classroom writing exercises that we ask students to perform? Perhaps this question is best answered with another question: how much *writing* do most people in today's high-tech world actually do? If we enumerate those genres, we may begin to approach the issue of authenticity (Hedgcock, 2005; Weigle, 2014). For a huge proportion of educated people around the world, writing consists of filling out forms, making lists, texting, e-mailing, sending "wish you were here" post cards from your vacation, and dashing off a "post-it" note to your kids to clean up their room when they get home from school. We are less and less called upon to *compose*.

So, why do we want students to write? In school, without some ability to express yourself in writing, you don't pass the course. In writing for academic purposes, writing ranges from short phrases (as in fill-in-the-blank tests), to brief paragraphs (as in essay question exercises and tests), to reports of many different kinds, to research papers. In vocational-technical L2 courses, students need to fill out forms, write simple messages, write reports (for example, a bid on a contract, an inspection report), and for some, write brief business letters. In adult education and survival English classes, authenticity may be found in filling out simple forms and questionnaires. This leaves the "academy" as the major locus of writing pedagogy that concerns itself with the *composing* process: development of ideas, argument, logic, cause and effect (Paltridge, 2004).

Another way to look at the authenticity issue in classroom writing is to distinguish between **real writing** and **display writing**. Real writing occurs when the reader doesn't know the answer and genuinely wants information

(Raimes, 1991). In many academic/school contexts, however, if the instructor is the sole reader, writing is primarily for the display of a student's knowledge. Written exercises, short answer essays, and other writing in test situations are instances of display writing.

Classroom Connections

What are some examples of display writing that you remember doing in learning an L2? Is it realistic to convert *every* writing assignment for your students into completely authentic real writing? What are some examples of writing techniques or exercises that might fall somewhere in between real and display? Is there still some benefit in such writing?

Should we as teachers incorporate more real writing in our classrooms? In some ways, yes. If L2 courses strive to be more content-based, theme-based, or task-based, students are more likely to be given the opportunity to convey genuine information on topics of intrinsic interest. But display writing is not totally unjustified. Writing to display one's knowledge is a fact of life in the classroom, and by encouraging your students to perform well in display writing exercises, they can learn skills that will help them to succeed in further academic pursuits.

6. Content- and Genre-Based Writing Pedagogy

An excellent way to involve students in more real writing is through *content-based instruction*, in which writing (along with reading) plays a central role and the purposes of writing are embedded into the overall goals of the program. Through "thematically-selected readings, the teaching of L2 writing can address matters of discourse structuring and information flow" (Hinkel, 2011, p. 533). As more and more L2 instruction is specialized in a number of *specific purposes*, writing can—beyond the early stages of learning the mechanics of writing—focus on the central interests of students.

Likewise, *genre-based* writing, besides its natural fit with integrated approaches, offers an opportunity to focus on the discourse features of various writing genres. Ranging from e-mail, to memos, to reports, to research papers and more, genre-based pedagogy enables students to appreciate the subtleties of discourse and syntactic conventions (Martin, 2012; Tardy, 2013). What is conventional and acceptable in one genre may not be the case for another. Formal academic research writing, for example, differs considerably from informal news reports.

7. Responding to Student Writing

The gradual recognition of writing as a process of thinking and composing was a natural byproduct of CLT. With its emphasis on learner-centered instruction, student–student negotiation, and strategies-based instruction that values the variability of learners' pathways to success, CLT is an appropriate locus for process writing. As students are encouraged (in reading) to bring their own schemata to bear on understanding texts, and (in writing) to develop their own ideas, offer their own critical analysis, and find their own voice (see #7 below), the role of teacher must be one of facilitator and coach, not an authoritative director and arbiter.

This facilitative role of the writing teacher has inspired research on the role of the teacher as a responder to students' writing (Ferris & Hedgcock, 2005, 2014; Goldstein, 2010; Ferris, 2011; Weigle, 2014). In a process approach, the teacher offers guidance in helping students to engage in the thinking process of composing but, in a spirit of respect for student opinion, should guard against imposing on, or in Reid's (1994) terminology, "appropriating," a student text. In this role, responding to content normally precedes dealing with linguistic issues such as spelling, grammar, and discourse. Further, Ferris (1997) found that when teachers requested *specific* information from students, more substantive revisions ensued than when teachers simply made positive comments.

 **CLASSROOM CONNECTIONS**

Why would requesting specific information from a student result in better revising? What are some examples of specific information? Given Ferris's (1997) finding, should you avoid giving a student generalized *positive comments* like, "Good essay! Nice job on this. You've improved a lot." Under what circumstances might positive comments still be pedagogically sound?

8. Form-Focused Feedback

In Chapter 19 we will offer detailed pedagogical comments on error treatment, but for the moment, this topic deserves a comment. Approaches to teaching writing have varied between minimal, highly indirect feedback to direct, focused feedback that provides corrections (Ferris, 2012). Researchers have also looked at the efficacy of providing feedback on content as opposed to form, on how to stimulate revisions, on particular grammatical and rhetorical features, and on students' preferences for feedback (Sheen, 2007; Hartshorn et al., 2010; Sheen & Ellis, 2011).

The somewhat cautious conclusion from a variety of studies is that all skill acquisition can benefit from "coaching," and learning to write in an L2 is no exception. However, writing, unlike speaking, is a learned, and not acquired skill, and even native users of a language exhibit extreme diversity of abilities. Researchers (Ferris, 2011, 2012; Frodesen, 2014; Weigle, 2014) generally agree that error treatment is important within an optimum range—that is, don't overcorrect to the point of discouraging an L2 writer, but offer enough feedback to keep students challenged. Many learners progress through intermediate stages of writing unaware of persistent errors, and we do a disservice not to help students to *notice* those errors.

9. Identity and Voice

Weaving in and out of several of the above topics is the issue of how to preserve the cultural and social *identities* of students but at the same time to teach English language writing conventions. This issue is especially acute in the case of academic writing programs where a major goal is for students to write acceptable academic prose in their respective subject matter fields (Paltridge, 2004). In other writing courses, however, the problem is also significant, as course designers and instructors must attend to "the socially and politically *situated contexts* of writing and how these contexts influence both how writing gets done and the end products of writing" (Casanave, 2004, p. 84).

A related issue is the question of preserving the **voice** of a writer. Once L2 writers progress to intermediate and advanced stages of writing, and become capable of expressing and transacting an identity in their writing, their writing takes on personal and unique styles of expression. The question for teachers is when and how, if at all, to intervene. Writing can be as personal as speaking, and when L2 writers demonstrate a unique idiolect, it may not be your place to try to change that voice.

One of the international students in Lee's (2013) study, Seong-jin (whom we mentioned in Chapter 8) struggled to balance his identities as a creative writer on the one hand, and as a student trying to learn academic writing conventions on the other. His fear of losing his creative voice in writing an essay made him resistant to follow the norms demanded by his ESL writing teacher. An important question we need to consider here is "what kinds of textual possibilities can institutions [and teachers] envision for international students" (Lee & Maguire, 2011, p. 367) like Seong-jin, so we can be responsive to their identity and personal aspirations?

Classroom Connections

What genres of writing are "as personal as speaking"? In most classroom writing assignments, in what way is the student's *voice* a factor? Beyond very basic instruction in the mechanics of writing, what are some specific ways that you can show respect for that voice?

TYPES OF WRITTEN LANGUAGE

In Chapter 17, on pages 395–397, we listed many types of written language genres. As you consider an L2 class that you might be teaching, how many of these types of writing will your students be likely to produce themselves? Those types that they will indeed need, either for further study of English or for their ultimate academic/vocational goals, should then become the prime focus of "real" writing in your classroom.

CHARACTERISTICS OF WRITTEN LANGUAGE: A WRITER'S VIEW

In Chapter 17, some characteristics of written language from the perspective of a reader were set forth. Let's revisit those from a writer's viewpoint.

1. Permanence

Once something is written down and delivered in its final form to its intended audience, the writer abdicates a certain power: the power to change, to clarify, to withdraw. That prospect is perhaps the most significant contributor to making writing a scary operation! Student writers often feel that the act of releasing written work to an instructor puts them in a vulnerable if not helpless state. Therefore, whatever you can do as a teacher, guide, and facilitator to help your students to revise and refine their work before final submission will help give them confidence in their work.

2. Production Time

The good news is that, given appropriate stretches of time, a writer can indeed become a "good" writer by developing efficient processes for achieving the final product. The bad news is that many educational contexts demand student writing within time limits, or "writing for display" as noted previously (examination writing, for example). So, one of your goals, especially if you are teaching in an academic context, would be to train your students to make the best possible use of such time limitations. This may mean sacrificing some process time, but with sufficient training in process writing, combined with practice in display writing, you can help your students deal with time limitations.

3. Distance

One of the major problems writers face is anticipating their audience. That anticipation ranges from general audience characteristics to how specific words, phrases, sentences, and paragraphs will be interpreted. The distance factor requires what might be termed "cognitive" empathy, in that good writers can "read" their own writing from the perspective of the mind of the targeted audience. Writers need to be able to predict the audience's general knowledge, cultural and literary schemata, specific subject-matter knowledge, and how their choice of language will be interpreted.

4. Orthography

Everything from simple greetings to extremely complex ideas is captured through the manipulation of a few dozen letters and other written symbols. Sometimes we take for granted the mastering of the mechanics of English writing by our students. If students are nonliterate in their L1, you must begin at the very beginning with fundamentals of reading and writing (Olshtain, 2014). For literate students, if their L1 system is not alphabetic, new symbols have to be produced (or keyboarded) that may differ from their familiar system. If the L1 has a different phoneme–grapheme system (most do!), then some attention is due here.

Classroom Connections

English spelling is popularly thought to be "irregular." However, many data-driven studies have shown English to be more rule-governed than we suspect, with a high percentage of predictable orthography, especially when morphological factors are considered. How would you help students learning *English* as an L2 not to despair over what are actually just a few irregularities?

5. Complexity

In Chapter 17, the complexity of written—as opposed to spoken—language was illustrated. Writers must learn the discourse features of the written L2 (which may not jibe with their L1 rhetorical tradition), how to create syntactic and lexical variety, how to combine sentences, and more. Sentence combining can pose some difficulty for learners of English, for example, as the shorter sentences and clauses typical of spoken language may not be appropriate in the written mode. Learning to use coordinating and subordinating clauses effectively in writing poses a challenge even for native English users.

6. Vocabulary

As was noted in Chapter 17, written language places a heavier demand on vocabulary use than does speaking. Good writers will learn to take advantage of the richness added in a wide variety of word choices. Adding that lexical diversity extends well beyond simply looking up synonyms to an appreciation of the nuances of meaning, or connotations, of words in context.

7. Formality

Whether a student is texting a friend or writing an academic essay, the conventions of written forms are not always easily mastered. For L2 students, the most complex conventions occur in academic writing where students have to learn how to describe, explain, compare, contrast, illustrate, defend, criticize, and argue, all within certain prescribed styles.

Classroom Connections

What are some of the *formalities* of academic writing such as a lab report, an abstract of an article, a book review, an argument, a narrative, or a proof of a theorem? Are those formalities rhetorical or grammatical, or both? Must students simply learn them by noticing examples and models?

MICRO- AND MACROSKILLS FOR WRITING

Utilizing the format from the previous three chapters, we offer the following list of micro- and macroskills for writing production.

Micro- and Macroskills for Writing

Microskills

1. Produce graphemes and orthographic patterns of English.
2. Produce writing at an efficient rate of speed to suit the purpose.
3. Produce an acceptable core of words and use appropriate word order patterns.
4. Use acceptable grammatical systems (e.g., tense, agreement, pluralization), patterns, and rules.
5. Express a particular meaning in different grammatical forms.

Macroskills

6. Use cohesive devices in written discourse.
7. Use the rhetorical forms and conventions of written discourse.
8. Appropriately accomplish the communicative functions of written texts according to form and purpose.
9. Convey links and connections between events and communicate such relations as main idea, supporting idea, new information, given information, generalization, and exemplification.
10. Distinguish between literal and implied meanings when writing.
11. Correctly convey culturally specific references in the context of the written text.
12. Develop and use a battery of writing strategies, such as accurately assessing the audience's interpretation, using prewriting devices, writing with fluency in the first drafts, using paraphrases and synonyms, soliciting peer and instructor feedback, and using feedback for revising and editing.

TYPES OF CLASSROOM WRITING PERFORMANCE

While various genres of written texts abound, classroom writing performance is, by comparison, limited. Consider the following five major categories of classroom writing performance:

Imitative or Mechanical Writing

At the beginning level of learning to write, students will simply "write down" English letters, words, and short sentences in order to learn the conventions of the orthographic code. Several types of classroom technique are commonly used at this stage.

Recognition Techniques

Common tasks for beginning *readers* include the identification of the features of letters, and for *writers* the same prerequisite ability applies. Techniques include: find the letter that is different; letter and word matching; circle all the _______ you can find; and matching capital and lowercase letters (Olshtain, 2014, p. 214).

Copying

Learning to write by hand is as much a psychomotor and kinesthetic challenge as it is cognitive. Students who can recognize letter differences may nevertheless have difficulty producing them, so copying remains an old-fashioned but effective practice in small doses. With the surge of digital-keyboarding technologies, handwriting is, according to some, becoming a lost art (Hensher, 2013). Still, handwriting no doubt will prevail as a ready means of writing for decades to come.

Sound-Spelling Practice

Matching phonemes to graphemes is a basic writing skill that applies to all alphabetic writing systems. For learners whose L1 writing is nonalphabetic (Chinese, Japanese, etc.) a new system could pose difficulty, but early research on cross-linguistic influence suggested that "subtle" L1–L2 differences might cause as much difficulty as great differences (Oller & Ziahosseiny, 1970). Thus, a Spanish L1 speaker may have more issues with English as an L2 than one might expect.

Dictation

One effective technique for practicing sound–spelling correspondences as well as reinforcing grammatical and discourse features is dictation. Dictations typically involve the teacher reading (aloud) a short passage, rereading it in segments, pausing for students to write what they hear, reading it through a third time, and then checking written responses for accuracy.

Classroom Connections

Some research has shown that dictation is a remarkably accurate indicator of overall language proficiency, with dictation performance correlating well with both receptive and productive abilities (Buck, 2001). Why is that? What abilities or skills, beyond simply writing what you hear and spelling it correctly, are required to succeed in dictation?

Intensive or Controlled Writing

Writing is sometimes used as a production mode for learning, reinforcing, or testing grammatical concepts. This intensive writing typically appears in controlled, written grammar exercises. This type of writing does not allow much, if any, creativity on the part of the writer.

A common form of **controlled** writing is to present a paragraph to students in which they have to alter a given structure throughout. So, for example, they may be asked to change all present tense verbs to past tense; in such a case, students may need to alter other time references in the paragraph.

Guided writing loosens the teacher's control but still offers a series of stimulators. For example, the teacher might get students to tell a story just viewed on a videotape by asking them a series of questions: Where does the story take place? Describe the principal character. What does he say to the woman in the car?

Yet another form of controlled writing is a **dictocomp**. Here, a paragraph is read at normal speed, usually two or three times; then the teacher asks students to rewrite the paragraph to the best of their recollection of the reading. In one of several variations of the dictocomp technique, the teacher, after reading the passage, puts key words from the paragraph, in sequence, on the chalkboard as cues for the students.

Self-Writing

A significant proportion of classroom writing may be devoted to self-writing, or writing with only the self in mind as an audience. The most salient instance of this category in classrooms is note-taking, where students take notes during a lecture for the purpose of later recall. Other note-taking may be done in the margins of books, through digital notes and highlights, as portfolio entries, and simply on notepaper filed for easy access later on.

Diary or journal writing also falls into this category. However, in many circumstances a **dialogue journal**—in which a student records thoughts, feelings, and reactions and which an instructor reads and responds to—while ostensibly written for oneself, has two audiences.

 **CLASSROOM CONNECTIONS**

What are some advantages/benefits of assigning an ongoing dialogue journal to your students? Disadvantages or drawbacks? How would you overcome some of the drawbacks in order to capitalize on the benefits? In Figure 18.1, in the teacher's comments, would you add (or delete) anything?

Figure 18.1 is an entry from a journal written by an advanced ESL student from China, followed by the teacher's response (contributed by Lauren Vanett and Donna Jurich).

Display Writing

It was noted earlier that writing within the school curricular context is a way of life. For all language students, short answer exercises, essay examinations, and even research reports will involve an element of display. For academically bound ESL students, one of the academic skills that they need to master is a whole array of display writing techniques.

Real Writing

While virtually every classroom writing task will have an element of display writing in it, some classroom writing aims at the genuine communication of messages to an audience in need of those messages. The two categories of real and display writing are actually two ends of a continuum, and in between the two extremes lies a combination of display and real writing. Three subcategories illustrate how reality can be injected:

Academic

Group problem-solving tasks, especially those that relate to specific disciplinary themes along with personally relevant topics, may have a writing component in which information is genuinely sought and conveyed. Peer-editing work adds to what would otherwise be an audience of one (the instructor) and provides real writing opportunity. In many academic courses, students may exchange new information (that they have written about) with each other, and/or present findings from written work to the rest of the class, adding the reality of an audience.

Vocational/Technical

Quite a variety of real writing can take place in classes of students studying an L2 for advancement in their occupation. Real letters can be written; genuine directions for some operation or assembly might be given; and actual forms can be filled out. These possibilities are even greater in workplace language courses, where an L2 is offered within companies and corporations.

Figure 18.1 Journal entry—advanced student from China

Journal Entry:

Yesterday at about eight o'clock I was sitting in front of my table holding a fork and eating tasteless noodles which I usually really like to eat but I lost my taste yesterday because I didn't feel well. I had a headache and a fever. My head seemed to be broken. I sometimes felt cold, sometimes hot. I didn't feel comfortable standing up and I didn't feel comfortable sitting down. I hated everything around me. It seemed to me that I got a great pressure from the atmosphere and I could not breath. I was so sleepy since I had taken some medicine which functioned as an antibiotic.

The room was so quiet. I was there by myself and felt very solitary. This dinner reminded me of my mother. Whenever I was sick in China, my mother always took care of me and cooked rice gruel, which has to cook more than three hours and is very delicious, I think. I would be better very soon under the care of my mother. But yesterday, I had to cook by myself even though I was sick, The more I thought, the less I wanted to eat, Half an hour passed. The noodles were cold, but I was still sitting there and thinking about my mother, Finally I threw out the noodles and went to bed.

MingLing

Teacher's Response:

This is a powerful piece of writing because you really communicate what you were feeling. You used vivid details, like "...eating tasteless noodles . . . ", "my head seemed to be broken . . ." and ". . . rice gruel, which has to cook more than three hours and is very delicious." These make it easy for the reader to picture exactly what you were going through. The other strong point about this piece is that you bring the reader full circle by beginning and ending with "the noodles."

Being alone when you are sick is difficult. Now, I know why you were so quiet in class.

If you want to do another entry related to this one, you could have a dialogue with your "sick" self. What would your "healthy" self say to the "sick" self? Is there some advice that could be exchanged about how to prevent illness or how to take care of yourself better when you do get sick? Start the dialogue with your "sick" self speaking first.

Personal

In virtually any L2 class, diaries, letters, post cards, notes, personal messages, and other informal writing can take place, especially within the context of an interactive classroom. While certain tasks may be somewhat contrived, nevertheless the genuine exchange of information can happen.

PRINCIPLES FOR TEACHING WRITING SKILLS

Out of all of these characteristics of the written word, along with microskills, macroskills, and research issues, a number of specific principles for designing writing techniques emerge.

1. Incorporate Practices of "Good" Writers

This first guideline is sweeping. But as you contemplate devising a technique that has a writing goal in it, consider the various things that effective writers do, and see if your pedagogy includes some of the practices listed below.

Guidelines for Helping Students to Write Effectively

Good writers . . .

- carefully attend to the specific, assigned writing task.
- focus on a goal or main idea.
- perceptively gauge their audience.
- spend some time (but not too much!) planning to write.
- easily let their first ideas flow onto the paper.
- follow a general organizational plan as they write.
- solicit and utilize feedback on their writing.
- are not wedded to certain surface structures.
- revise their work willingly and efficiently.
- patiently make as many revisions as needed.

Classroom Connections

What other characteristics of successful writers would you add to this list? How would you "translate" or reword these characteristics into steps that a student could take in writing effectively?

2. Balance Process and Product

Because writing is a composing process and usually requires multiple drafts before an effective product is created, make sure that students are carefully led through appropriate stages in the process of composing. This includes careful attention to your own role as a guide and as a responder (see #8). At the same time, don't get so caught up in the stages leading up to the final product that you lose sight of the ultimate attainment: a clear, articulate, well-organized, effective piece of writing. Make sure students see that everything leading up to this final creation was worth the effort.

3. Account for Cultural/Literary Backgrounds

Make sure that your techniques do not assume that your students know English rhetorical conventions. If there are some apparent contrasts between students' native traditions and those that you are trying to teach, try to help students to understand what it is, exactly, that they are accustomed to and then, by degrees, bring them to the use of acceptable English rhetoric.

4. Connect Reading and Writing

Clearly, students learn to write in part by carefully observing what is already written. That is, they learn by observing, or reading, the written word. By reading and studying a variety of relevant types of text, students can gain important insights both about how they should write and about subject matter that may become the topic of their writing.

5. Provide as Much Authentic Writing as Possible

Whether writing is real writing or for display, it can still be authentic in that the purposes for writing are clear to the students, the audience is specified overtly, and there is at least some intent to convey meaning. Sharing writing with other students in the class is one way to add authenticity. Publishing a class newsletter, writing letters to people outside of class, writing a script for a skit or dramatic presentation, writing a resume, writing advertisements—all these can be seen as authentic writing.

6. Design Prewriting, Drafting, and Revising Stages of Writing

Process approaches generally involve three drafts but as many as seven phases, as described in Table 18.1.

The first *prewriting* stage encourages the generation of ideas, which, as noted in Table 18.1, can happen in numerous ways. One technique that may be somewhat difficult to catch on to is **brainstorming**. This involves an open-minded, rapid-fire voluntary listing of ideas with no debate or judgment made by anyone. It allows students to "get their creative juices flowing," then in subsequent stages, ideas that are deemed pertinent can be further explored while others are set aside.

 **CLASSROOM CONNECTIONS**

Let's say you have conducted a brainstorming exercise with your students on the topic of "conserving our daily use of water in the home." Your students have come up with a dozen different ideas. What would you do next to put the ideas into use in a writing assignment?

Table 18.1 Process approaches to teaching L2 writing (adapted from Weigle, 2014, p. 227)

Phases	Techniques
1. **Prewriting:** Activities provide background information, stimulate interest	Readings, videos, discussion, whole-class, group or pair work, researching, brainstorming
2. **First draft:** Students sketch out ideas without much preplanning	Freewriting, little or no emphasis on form (grammar, spelling), focus on content
3. **Commenting:** Peer or teacher reads first draft and comments	Peer reviews (pair work), teacher conferences, feedback on content
4. **Second draft:** Students look at whole essay, use peer/instructor feedback, rethink, revise	Learner reorganizes, restructures, adds details, clarifies
5. **Third draft:** Learner edits, attends to writing conventions, rhetoric, grammar, vocabulary	Checklists, grammar logs, proofreading practice, dictionary checks
6. **Postwriting:** Students share finished products	Discussion, pair/group work following up on topics covered, share products online, enter product into portfolio
7. **Evaluation:** Self, peer, and teacher assessment of the final written product	Using rubrics, teacher-student conferences, self-assessment

In the first draft stage, **freewriting**, like brainstorming, is a useful way for students to simply start the "flow" of writing, unfettered by the potential of being judged for ungrammaticalities, incorrect spelling, or fuzzy thinking.

The drafting and revising stages are the core of process writing. In traditional approaches to writing instruction, students either are given timed in-class compositions to write from start to finish within a class hour, or they are given a homework writing assignment. This method gives no opportunity for systematic drafting, and too often assumes that students would learn the essentials of good writing on their own. In a process approach, drafting is viewed as an important and complex set of strategies, the mastery of which takes time, patience, and trained instruction.

Several strategies or skills are implied in the three drafting stages in Table 18.1:

STRATEGIES TO ENCOURAGE IN DRAFTING STAGES OF WRITING

- generating ideas in a trial-and-error process
- monitoring of one's own writing without premature diverted attention to wording, grammar, etc.
- accepting/using classmates' and teacher's feedback and comments
- editing, restructuring, repairing one's written work
- proofreading for grammatical and spelling errors

Evaluation of the final written product, especially peer- and self-assessment, could prove to be a complex process for students who feel that the instructor is the authority. But even instructor assessment is tricky. The purpose of such an evaluation needs to be clear. In periodic written assignments during term, the evaluation should at the very least be *formative* in suggesting ways to improve one's writing the next time around.

7. Strive to Offer Techniques That Are as Interactive as Possible

It is no doubt already apparent that a process-oriented approach to writing instruction is, by definition, interactive (as students work in pairs and groups to generate ideas and to peer-edit), as well as learner-centered (with ample opportunities for students to initiate activity and exchange ideas). Writing techniques that focus on purposes other than compositions (such as letters, forms, memos, directions, short reports) are also subject to the principles of interactive classrooms. Group collaboration, brainstorming, and critiquing are as easily and successfully a part of many writing-focused techniques. Don't buy into the myth that writing is a solitary activity! Some of it is, to be sure, but a good deal of what makes a good writer can be most effectively learned within a community of learners.

8. Be a Facilitator, Not a Judge, in Responding to Students' Writing

In Chapter 16, some principles of error correction were suggested for dealing with learners' speech errors. Earlier in this chapter we also commented on form-focused feedback. Because writing, unlike speaking, often includes an extensive planning stage, error treatment can begin in the drafting and revising stages, during which time it is more appropriate to consider errors among several features of the whole process of responding to student writing. When you respond to an error, remember to allow students to *notice* their errors and then to self-correct.

 **CLASSROOM CONNECTIONS**

If your students have some difficulty viewing you as something other than an authoritative judge, how could you help them to think of you as a facilitator instead? What would you say and do to help establish your position as a coach as opposed to someone who has all the right answers?

As you respond to your students' writing, you are an ally and guide, a facilitator (Ferris, 2011, 2012). After the final work is turned in, you may indeed have to assume the position of judge and evaluator (see below for some comments on evaluation), but until then, the role of consultant will be the most productive way to respond. Ideally, your responses—or at least some of them—will be both *oral* and written as you hold a conference, however short, with a student. Under less than ideal conditions, written comments may have to suffice.

Here are some guidelines for responding to the first draft.

Guidelines for Responding to a First Draft

- Resist the temptation to treat minor (local) grammatical errors.
- Major (global) errors may be indicated either directly (say, by underlining) or indirectly (for example, by a check next to the line in which an error occurs).
- Resist the temptation to rewrite a student's sentences.
- Comment holistically, in terms of the clarity of the overall thesis, main idea, and the general structural organization.
- Comment on (or question) features that appear to be irrelevant.
- Question clearly inadequate word choices and awkward expression within those paragraphs/sentences that are relevant to the topic.

For the subsequent drafts, your responses may change slightly, because the student has now had an opportunity to see and process your comments on the first draft. Your focus will now include more attention to the *form* of the essay.

Guidelines for Commenting on Second and Third Drafts

- Minor (local) grammatical and mechanical (spelling, punctuation) errors should be indicated, but not corrected by you.
- Comment on the specific clarity and strength of main ideas, supporting ideas, and on argument and logic.
- Comment on word choices and expressions that may not be as clear or direct as they could be.
- Check cohesive devices within and across paragraphs.
- For academic papers, comment on documentation, citing sources, evidence, and other support.
- Comment on the adequacy and strength of the conclusion.

9. Explain Rhetorical, Formal Conventions of Writing

Each genre of writing has its formal properties. Don't just assume that students will pick these up by absorption. Make them explicit. A reading approach to writing is very helpful here. For academic writing, for example, some of the features of English rhetorical discourse that writers use to explain, propose solutions, debate, and argue are listed below.

Academic Writing Conventions to Teach L2 Learners

- Provide a clear statement of the thesis or topic or purpose
- Use main ideas to develop or clarify the thesis
- Use supporting ideas
- Support by "telling": describing
- Support by "showing": giving evidence, facts, statistics, etc.
- Support by linking cause and effect
- Support by using comparison and/or contrast

Classroom Connections

If your curriculum called for a unit on *news writing* (journalistic writing), what would the list of conventions for that genre be? Or suppose you asked your students to write an *advertising brochure* to entice customers to buy a product—what would be the essential components of that particular genre?

TWO WRITING LESSONS

Some of the principles for designing writing lessons, along with an integration of skills, are exemplified in the two writing lessons that follow. In the first (Figure 18.2 on pages 448–450), Blanchard (2013) introduces blogs to intermediate L2 writers, acquaints them with the unique features of blogging, and gives students a chance to write some of their own blogs. Notice that the lesson involves pair work as students collaborate with classmates to complete the objectives of the lesson.

Interesting, isn't it, how blogging can incorporate so many principles of learning to write in an L2? Some educators have found blogging to be popular with elementary school age children. In a website called *Kidblog* kidblog.org learners are able to develop basic writing skills (including typing). Teachers can also use the blogging platform as a tool to help students develop their *voice* and ownership while exercising *agency* as bloggers (McGrail & Davis, 2011).

Classroom Connections

Look at the lesson on blogging in Figure 18.2, and imagine a classroom with students at the appropriate intermediate level. How would you teach this lesson? What would you add or delete from the material you see? Would you extend this topic beyond blogging?

Figure 18.2 Writing blogs

What Is a Blog?

A **blog** is a place to share information online. The word *blog* is short for "web log." A blog is a special type of website. You can read, write, and share information on a blog. The information is called an entry or a post. A blog usually has many posts. The newest post is at the top of the page.

Blogs are different from other types of websites. On a blog, readers "discuss" the information. They write their ideas and opinions about the blog. Everyone can read their writing. So blogs are another type of social writing.

WRITING TASK

Write a blog about your favorite day.

A. ***Prepare for writing. Read the blog post.***

http://manuel's.blog.com

MANUEL'S BLOG: MY FAVORITE DAY

Oct. 22
Friday is my favorite day of the week. I like Friday. It's the last day of the school week. Friday is usually an easy day for me. I only have two classes on Friday, and they are both in the afternoon. I usually get up at 9 o'clock, and I meet my friends for coffee at around 10. We talk about our homework and make plans for the weekend. Then I go to my classes. I have English Writing at 12:00 and Art History at 2:30. After my classes, I often go to the gym. I go back to my apartment around 5:00. Sometimes I take a nap. Then I get ready to go out. I usually meet my friends at 8:00 and the weekend begins!

Leave a Reply

B. ***Write a short comment to Manuel in the blank*** **Leave a Reply** ***box.***

Figure 18.2 Writing blogs (*Continued*)

C. ***Complete your own blog about your favorite day.***

http://__________.blog.com

__________ **BLOG: MY FAVORITE DAY**

____
(date)

__________ is my favorite day of the week. It's usually a __________ day for me. I __________ get up __________ and then I __________. After __________, I often __________. Sometimes, I like to __________. In the evening, I like to __________. I usually go to bed around __________.

SOCIAL

D. ***Work with a partner. Share your posts. Write a comment to your partner's post on a separate sheet of paper.***

Check Your Writing

A. ***Read your blog in the Writing Task. Use this form to check your writing.***

Blog Checklist

Every sentence in this blog . . .

- begins with a capital letter. ☐
- includes correct punctuation. ☐
- uses contractions where possible. ☐
- uses capital letters for names of people, days, months, cities, and states. ☐

B. ***Correct any errors in your writing. Then write your blog again.***

Figure 18.2 Writing blogs (*Continued*)

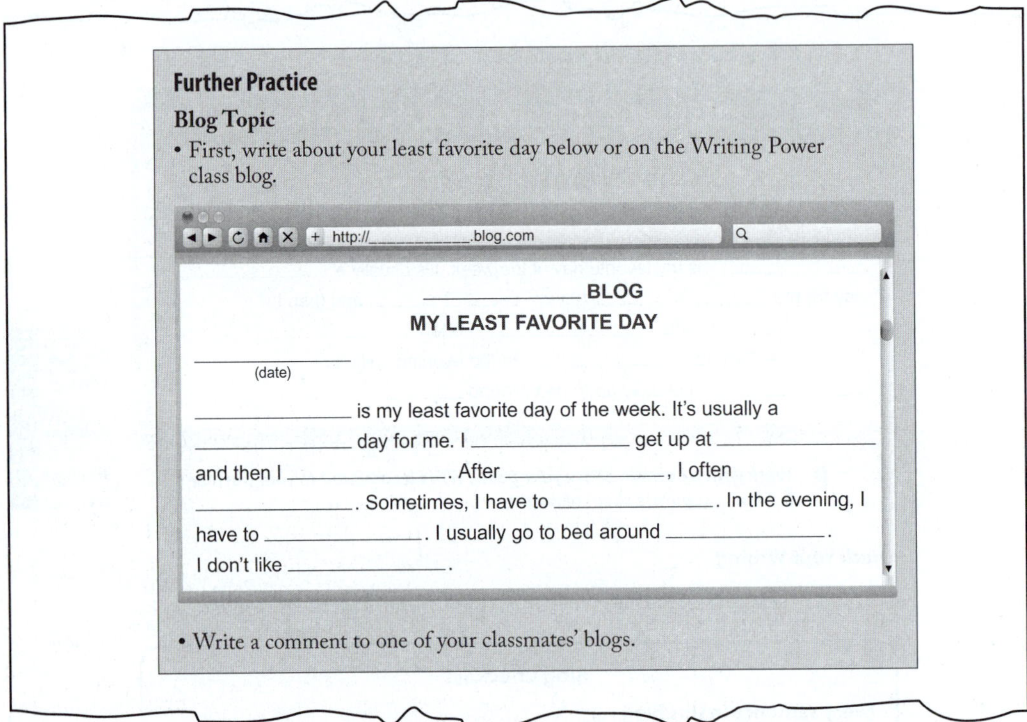
Further Practice

Blog Topic

- First, write about your least favorite day below or on the Writing Power class blog.

- Write a comment to one of your classmates' blogs.

In the second example (Figure 18.3 on pages 451–455), Cassriel and Martinsen (2010) continue the lesson that we excerpted (to show an example of a listening focus) in Chapter 16 (see Figure 16.5, pp. 370–371). Now, as the same unit continues, the focus shifts to writing, yet with integration of reading and pair work. As the authors center on a real-world problem, the proliferation of plastic bags in landfills, students are focused on a variety of factors: comprehension of a reading passage, the structure of a problem-solution essay, processing information in lists and charts, and a class discussion of their own unique proposed solutions.

Classroom Connections

Look at the lesson on green chemistry in Figure 18.3, and imagine a classroom with students at the appropriate high intermediate level. How would you teach this lesson? What would you add or delete from the material you see? How would you extend this topic, in the class hours that follow, to perhaps project-based teaching or to an oral presentation?

Figure 18.3 Writing a problem-solution paragraph

4

Building Academic Writing Skills

In this section, you will practice writing problem-solution paragraphs. Then you will write a paragraph about a modern problem related to green chemistry. You will synthesize information and use vocabulary from the readings and the lecture.

For online assignments, go to

myacademicconnectionslab

Before You Write

Writing a Problem-Solution Paragraph

A problem-solution paragraph describes a problem. Then it explains a solution or possible solutions to the problem. A problem-solution paragraph typically includes three parts:

- a topic sentence with a description of the problem
- a body with a description of (a) possible solution(s)
- a conclusion with an explanation of how the solution is helpful

Read a transcript from a talk given by Martyn Poliakoff, a chemist at the University of Nottingham. Then answer the questions on page 94.

Taking Green Chemistry to the Developing World

Recently I was asked to introduce the ideas of green chemistry to a group of high school students and teachers at Wachamo Comprehensive High School in Hossana, Ethiopia. The problem was that I wasn't sure of the best way to explain green chemistry simply. My solution was to use an example of a plastic bag that I got two days earlier at the town's market. They make bags like these from petroleum from other countries because Ethiopia does not have much petroleum of its own. After people use these bags, they throw them away. On the road I counted 12 bags that people had thrown away in just 100 meters on my way to the school. By contrast, Ethiopia produces a lot of sugarcane. If people there made the bags from sugarcane, then Ethiopia would not have to buy its bags—or oil to make bags—from other countries. More

(continued on next page)

Figure 18.3 Writing a problem-solution paragraph (*Continued*)

importantly, cows would be able to eat the used bags in the street! This simple example helped me explain the goals of green chemistry to everyone. Making bags from sugarcane needs new chemistry—it needs green chemistry.[1]

Children collecting plastic bags in Hossana

[1] Together with Proctor and Gamble and Ethiopian chemists, Poliakoff is developing plastic bags made from local sugarcane.

Poliakoff, M., & Noda, I. (2004.) Plastic bags, sugar cane and advanced vibrational spectroscopy: taking green chemistry to the Third World. *Green Chemistry, 6.*

1. What problem does the topic sentence introduce?
2. What is the proposed solution? According to the paragraph, why is it a good solution? Give details.
3. What is the conclusion? How is it connected to the topic sentence?
4. What is your opinion about Poliakoff's solution? Do you think it is a good one? Why or why not?

Focused Writing

Introducing Problems and Solutions

When writing a problem-solution paragraph, you can use certain expressions to make your points clear.

To introduce a problem:

The problem is/was _______.

_______ is one of the main problems.

One difficulty is _______.

To introduce a solution:

His/Her/Their/My solution is/was _______.

One way to solve this problem is _______.

_______ is a great way to solve the problem of _______.

Figure 18.3 Writing a problem-solution paragraph (*Continued*)

1. *Read the transcript from Martyn Poliakoff's talk on pages 93–94 again. Underline the expressions he uses to introduce the problem and solution.*

2. *In his talk, Poliakoff describes the plastic bag problem in Ethiopia. Follow the instructions to write a short paragraph about the problem.*

1. Complete the chart using the information from Poliakoff's presentation.

Plastic Bag Problem	Solution to Plastic Bag Problem

2. Write your paragraph. Be sure to include:
   - the problem
   - the proposed solution(s)
   - a conclusion
   - expressions to introduce problems and solutions
3. Work with a partner. Exchange paragraphs. Use the questions to comment on each other's paragraph.
   - Does the topic sentence introduce the problem?
   - Does the body explain the proposed solution?
   - Does the conclusion explain how the solution is helpful?
   - Did your partner use expressions to introduce problems and solutions?

Integrated Writing Task

You have listened to a lecture and read texts about green chemistry and the modern problem of plastic bags. You will now use your knowledge of the unit content, topic vocabulary, synthesizing information, and writing a problem-solution paragraph to write a paragraph answering this question: **What is the best solution to solve the worldwide plastic bag problem?**

Figure 18.3 Writing a problem-solution paragraph (*Continued*)

Follow the steps to write your paragraph.

Step 1: Read more about the global plastic bag problem. Check (✓) the facts that are most important to you.

Fast Facts about Plastic Bags

- ○ Each year, people around the world use about 500 billion to 1 trillion plastic bags.
- ○ Plastic bags are made from petroleum, and the used bags cause a lot of pollution.
- ○ Each year, people throw away 4 billion plastic bags.
- ○ Animals that eat plastic bags can die from the toxins.
- ○ Plastic bags pollute the dirt and water in the ground as they break down into smaller and smaller pieces.
- ○ It takes plastic 450 years to break down in water.
- ○ It takes plastic 1,000 years to break down on land.

Step 2: Many countries are trying to solve the plastic bag problem. Read the possible solutions. Consider the pros (positive reasons) and cons (negative reasons). Choose the solution that you think is best. You may also choose your own solution based on the principles of green chemistry. (Note: Your solution must be different from Poliakoff's solution on pages 93–94.)

SOLUTION 1: Change waste plastic back into oil. **PRO:** Plastics don't have to be clean. Waste plastic goes through a process under heat and is then turned into valuable diesel fuel. **CON:** Only certain plastics can be used. If the wrong plastic is mixed in, the diesel fuel cannot be sold. The process of changing plastic into oil causes pollution and puts many toxins in the air.	**SOLUTION 2: Use plastic made of plants.** **PRO:** These bags break down more quickly than bags made from petroleum, and they are made from renewable resources. **CON:** The process of growing plants to make this plastic uses pesticides, land, and freshwater, and this harms the environment.
SOLUTION 3: Recycle used bags to make new ones. **PRO:** It keeps bags out of landfills.[1] **CON:** Only certain plastic bags can be reused, and it is hard to separate them. It is more expensive to recycle plastic bags than to make new plastic bags.	**SOLUTION 4:** (choose your own) **PRO:** **CON:**

[1] **landfill** *n* a place where waste is buried in large amounts

Figure 18.3 Writing a problem-solution paragraph (*Continued*)

Step 3: Work with a partner. Look for connections among the plastic bag issue, the green chemistry principles, and the concepts and ideas in this unit. Discuss the questions and take notes.

- How is the plastic bag problem similar to problems related to petroleum fuel and biofuel use?
- Are there any similarities between the solution you chose and the solutions of biofuel and WVO offered for the petroleum problem? Does the solution you chose have possible negative consequences?
- Which green chemistry principles relate to your proposed solution?

Step 4: Complete the chart with ideas you want to write about in your paragraph. To support your ideas, make connections to ideas from the listenings and readings in this unit.

Topic sentence (describe the problem)	
Body (describe the solution or possible solutions)	
Conclusion (explain how the solution is or would be helpful)	

Step 5: Use your notes from Step 4 to write a problem-solution paragraph about plastic bags. Use the vocabulary and skills you learned in this unit, including expressions that introduce problems and solutions.

Step 6: Exchange paragraphs with a partner. Use the checklist for feedback.

Feedback Checklist	Yes	No
Does the topic sentence introduce the problem?		
Does the body explain the proposed solution?		
Does the conclusion explain how the solution is/could be helpful?		
Did your partner use expressions to introduce the problem?		
Did your partner use expressions to introduce the solution?		

Step 7: Rewrite your paragraph based on your partner's feedback.

Step 8: Discuss your proposed solutions as a class. Do you agree with other classmates' solutions? Which solution do you think is best? Why?

ASSESSING WRITING IN THE CLASSROOM

The assessment of writing, especially in a process-oriented classroom, is a complex issue (Brown & Abeywickrama, 2010; Ferris & Hedgcock, 2014). If you are a guide and facilitator of students' performance in the ongoing process of developing a piece of written work, can you also be the judge? The answer is one of the primary dilemmas of all teachers. Juggling this dual role requires wisdom and sensitivity. The key to being a judge is fairness and explicitness (reliability) in what you take into account in your evaluation.

Evaluation Checklists

One way to view writing assessment is through various rating checklists or grids that can indicate to students their areas of strength and weakness, and in many cases such taxonomies are scoring rubrics. Following is a typical list of categories that may form a set of **rubrics** for the evaluation of student writing.

In your evaluation of student writing, the most instructive evaluative feedback you can give is your comments. The preceding six-category list can serve as the basis for such evaluations.

If numerical scores are either pedagogically or administratively important to you, then you can establish a point scale (perhaps 0 to 5) for each of the categories and return papers with six different scores on them. By avoiding a single overall score, you can help students to focus on aspects of writing to which they need to give special attention.

If you still need to assign a single "grade" or score to each paper, how can you assign points for each element? Writing specialists disagree somewhat on the system of weighting each of the above categories. However, treating the categories as rubrics for assessment, consider weighting the first few categories more heavily. You can thereby emphasize the *content-based* nature of your evaluation. Such a weighting scale might look like this:

SUGGESTED WEIGHTING SCALE FOR EVALUATION OF WRITING

Category	Points
Content	0–24
Organization	0–20
Discourse	0–20
Syntax	0–12
Vocabulary	0–12
Mechanics	0–12
TOTAL	100

 **Classroom Connections**

The weighting scale above is one of many possible distributions of point systems. There are disadvantages to these systems. In the one above, a student might hypothetically have an essay that's riddled with mechanical errors, for example—so mechanically flawed that the student earns zero points on mechanics. But if everything else is really *great*, he or she might still get close to an 88% score. Does that make sense? What could you do to guard against such drawbacks?

Table 18.2 Categories for evaluating writing (adapted from J. D. Brown, 1991)

Content
- thesis statement
- related ideas
- development of ideas (personal experience, illustration, facts, opinions)
- use of description, cause/effect, comparison/contrast
- consistent focus

Organization
- effectiveness of introduction
- logical sequence of ideas
- conclusion
- appropriate length

Discourse
- topic sentences
- paragraph unity
- transitions
- discourse markers
- cohesion
- rhetorical conventions
- reference
- fluency
- economy
- variation

Syntax

Vocabulary

Mechanics
- spelling
- punctuation
- citation of references (if applicable)
- neatness and appearance

A key, of course, to successful evaluation is to get your students to understand that your grades, scores, and other comments are varied forms of feedback from which they can benefit. The final evaluation on one composition simply creates input to the learner for the next composition.

Writing Assessment Tasks

Writing an essay in successive drafts, with checklists to guide evaluation, is one general category of writing assessment. There are many more. Hedgcock (2005) describes over fifty different writing techniques, all of which can have an assessment component. Consider the following writing tasks (Brown & Abeywickrama, 2010), listed according to their level of linguistic complexity, which may stimulate your own creativity.

Item Types for Assessing Writing

1. **Imitative writing**
   - exercises in handwriting letters, words, and punctuation
   - keyboarding (typing) exercises
   - copying
   - listening cloze selection tasks (listen and write)
   - picture-cued writing exercises
   - completing forms and questionnaires
   - converting numbers and abbreviations to words and phrases
   - spelling tasks
   - one-word dictation tasks
2. **Intensive (controlled) writing**
   - dictation of phrases and simple sentences
   - dictocomp (rewrite a story just heard)
   - grammatical transformation exercises
   - picture description tasks
   - use vocabulary in a sentence
   - ordering tasks (reorder a list of words in random order)
   - short answer tasks
   - sentence completion tasks
3. **Responsive writing**
   - paraphrasing
   - guided writing (e.g., question and answer)
   - paragraph construction tasks (topic sentence, main idea, etc.)
   - responding to a reading or lecture

4. **Extensive writing**
   - essay writing tasks
   - tasks in types of writing (narrative, description, argument, etc.)
   - tasks in genres of writing (lab report, opinion essay, research paper)

It is, of course, of paramount importance to be absolutely clear, in your designing of assessment tasks in writing, about *what* you are trying to assess and *why* you are testing written performance. The concept of **formative** assessment is prominent in a course that uses a process approach to writing: our assessments should serve the purpose of facilitating improvement in a student's written work, and judgment of the final product should occur only when such **summative** evaluation is warranted.

★ ★ ★ ★ ★

Writing instruction in a communicative, interactive language course should be deeply rooted in the eight principles of language learning and teaching that have formed a train of thought throughout this book. As you think about each principle, you can make the connections. *Automaticity*, for example, is gained as students develop fluency in writing, which can best be promoted through the multiple stages of a process writing approach. *Self-regulation* and *autonomy* are important as students develop a strategic approach to writing. *Agency* is paramount as your students become capable of expressing their *voice* in the written mode, develop their *identities*, and seize their own *empowerment*.

FOR THE TEACHER: ACTIVITIES (A) & DISCUSSION (D)

Note: For each of the "Classroom Connections" in this chapter, you may wish to turn them into individual or pair-work discussion questions.

1. **(D)** Review with your students what is meant by a *process approach* to teaching writing. Do they think there are any cross-cultural issues involved in teaching writing as a process? Are there feasible *variations* to a process approach? How would a teacher's process approach differ depending on the content or specific purpose of the L2 course?
2. **(A)** Ask small groups to review Kaplan's diagrams on contrastive rhetoric (p. 429). Ask them to share how writing conventions differ between or among cultures that they are familiar with? Then ask the groups to pick two cultures and sketch out salient differences, if any, between the two sets of rhetorical conventions? Have groups report back to the whole class, then discuss any implications for teaching.

3. **(D)** Ask your students what it means to recognize and respect a student's *voice* and sociocultural *identity*. Have any students experienced, in their prior L2 classes, writing assignments or assessment systems that violate their sense of cultural or personal identity? If so, what might the teacher have done to change these situations into more authentic, respectful experiences?
4. **(A)** Ask pairs to turn back to pages 395–397 in Chapter 17 and review the genres of written language listed there. Then have them pick several familiar audiences or contexts and decide which of the genres their students might actually need to produce. Finally, ask them to prioritize those genres and share their conclusions with the rest of the class.
5. **(D)** On page 442, some specific steps for guiding students through stages of drafting and revising a composition are listed. Try a *role-play* in which you demonstrate (with a student volunteer and his or her essay) a teacher-student conference in which you follow the guidelines. Ask your class to notice the interaction between student and teacher, and to comment on what you were doing. (If your classroom has projection equipment, the task could be enhanced by showing the essay and writing your comments—for your class to see—as you conduct the conference.)
6. **(A)** Ask pairs to carefully look through the guidelines on methods of *responding to written work* (page 446). Supply them with a sample first draft and ask them to sketch out some written responses that would stimulate the writer to make some appropriate revisions. Have the pairs share some of their results with the rest of the class. (If your classroom has projection equipment, the final (sharing) stage of the task could be enhanced by showing the essay and writing comments for your class to see.)
7. **(A)** There are numerous scales and inventories for rating and scoring written work. The one presented here (p. 456) lists *suggested* elements. Can students think of things they would add to the inventory? Distribute to pairs an actual student's composition and ask them to rate the student's performance on the basis of the taxonomy. To do so, pairs might want to experiment with assigning a numerical weighting scale (p. 456). Facilitate the comparison of the various "diagnoses," and discuss how well the scale served its purpose. (Again, projection equipment could enhance the processing of this task.)

FOR YOUR FURTHER READING

Hinkel, E. (2011). What research on second language writing tells us and what it doesn't. In E. Hinkel (Ed.), *Handbook of research in second language teaching and learning, Volume II.* (pp. 523–538). New York, NY: Routledge.

Leki, I., Cumming, A., & Silva, T. (2008). *A synthesis of research on second language writing*. London, UK: Routledge.

Silva, T. (2010). Writing in a second language. In M. Berns (Ed.), *Concise encyclopedia of applied linguistics* (pp. 233–240). Oxford, UK: Elsevier.

These three sources summarize research on L2 writing both historically and in recent years, offering extensive bibliographic references.

Ferris, D. (2011). *Treatment of error in L2 student writing* (2nd ed.) Ann Arbor, MI: University of Michigan Press.

Ferris, D. (2012). Written corrective feedback in second language acquisition and writing studies. *Language Teaching, 45*, 446–459.

Frodesen, J. (2014). Grammar in second language writing. In M. Celce-Murcia, D. Brinton, & M. A. Snow (Eds.), *Teaching English as a second or foreign language* (4th ed., pp. 238-253). Boston, MA: National Geographic Learning.

The two Ferris sources summarize findings on the effectiveness of corrective feedback and error treatment in L2 writing. Frodesen offers practical techniques for attending to grammatical form in writing instruction.

Ferris, D., & Hedgcock, J. (2014). *Teaching L2 composition: Purpose, process, and practice* (3rd ed.). New York, NY: Routledge.

Weigle, S. (2014). Considerations for teaching second language writing. In M. Celce-Murcia, D. Brinton, & M. A. Snow (Eds.), *Teaching English as a second or foreign language* (4th ed., pp. 222–237). Boston, MA: National Geographic Learning.

Both sources offer classroom-based practicalities such as syllabus and task design while also providing synopses of research on second language writing.

Hedge, T. (2005). *Writing*. Oxford, UK: Oxford University Press.

Over fifty different writing activities are described—categorized into sections on communication, composing, crafting, and improving—in this practical, teacher-friendly book.

Brown, H. D., & Abeywickrama, P. (2010). *Language assessment: Principles and classroom practices* (2nd ed.). White Plains, NY: Pearson Education.

See Chapter 10 for a detailed description of classroom assessment of writing, including how to design and score assessment tasks.

CHAPTER **19**

TEACHING GRAMMAR AND VOCABULARY

Questions for Reflection

- What is grammar?
- Why is it important to consider discourse in teaching and learning grammar?
- What are some of the approaches to teaching grammar and vocabulary?
- How can learners' errors be treated effectively?
- What are some classroom techniques for promoting students' language awareness?
- What are some strategies for strengthening vocabulary and lexicogrammar?

> I read [Hong's autobiography] when I was in high school back in Korea. [In the book] he said, on the first day of his new school [in the United States], he said to the class, "Hello, I'm Hong J. W. from Korea, it's nice to meet you." Then his classmates were laughing at him because of his awkward English pronunciation. So, he decided to study English very hard and thought that the only way to master English is through memorizing everything about English grammar and vocabulary. Thereafter, he studied very hard every day and night. He usually stayed up until 2 to 3 a.m. in order to study [the books of English grammar and vocabulary]. He said he used to memorize more than 100 English words per day. I was so impressed. So, I tried to do like him. I tried to memorize 100 English words everyday, and seriously, I did it! I put my watch right in front of me on the desk, and checked frequently if I was getting one word per three second. One word per three second! . . . I still have the book with me in my room here in Canada. I am still studying like him.

In this interview excerpt, Seong-jin, a student in an intensive English program at a Canadian university, talks about how he has been studying English since he went to Canada to improve his English skills. According to Seong-jin, Hong's autobiography illustrates how rigorously Hong studied in order to overcome the barrier of language when he arrived in the United States as a teenager, and how he was finally able to enter Harvard University and become one of the top graduates.

What's interesting here is that Seong-jin adopted a very traditional approach to studying English—form-focused memorization and individual study—even though he had traveled all the way to Canada to enroll in an intensive English program. Why would he still continue to believe that is the best way to "master" grammar and vocabulary? What did English grammar and vocabulary mean to him?

GRAMMAR

Whether you are a language learner or teacher, *grammar* may mean many different things. One common idea to all of us may be that it is something significant we need to tackle by exerting a great deal of time and effort in order to "master" the language. Nevertheless, many learners and teachers often struggle with grammar, figuring out how to just "pick it up" or how best to instruct it. Michael Halliday (1978) says, "Language is as it is because of what it has to do" (p. 19). Understanding and explaining grammar may seem complex, and it is indeed complex because it has "to do all the things we make it do for us" (Halliday, 2004, p. 5). As discussed earlier in Chapter 5, drawing on the principle of agency, we view language not as something we possess inside the head; it is something that we *do*. Language is a complex and dynamic entity that we *use* "to say things, do things, and be things" (Gee, 2011, p. 3).

This view of language has complex consequences for teaching grammar. Let's look at some of those complexities.

Three Dimensions of Grammar

Diane Larsen-Freeman (2003, 2014) argues that in order to help language learners use language accurately, meaningfully, and appropriately, we need to explain the three interconnected and nonhierarchal dimensions of grammar: form, meaning, and use.

- The **form** dimension refers to observable structural components such as phonemes, graphemes, inflectional morphemes, and syntactic patterns.
- **Meaning** refers to the semantic level of the structural items including lexical and grammatical meaning.
- The **use** dimension accounts for meanings of utterances across different contexts and cohesion in discourse.

Consider this example: The modal *must* is placed in front of a verb to mean obligation or necessity. However, if an English learner tells an American friend, "I must take my baby to the doctor," the friend might find the sentence awkward, as it sounds too formal in the context (Savage, 2010, p. 8). Thus, in order to fully understand how to use the language correctly and appropriately, learners need to be aware of the *use* dimension of the target structure.

Let's look at another example: "That is enough." In regard to *form*, the utterance consists of three single morphemes, where the verb *be* is inflected for the third person singular form *is*. The pronunciation would be [ðæt ɪz əˈnəf], though a common variation in speech would contract the first two words and it would be pronounced as [ðæts əˈnəf]. In the *meaning* dimension, *that* is a demonstrative pronoun referring to a preceding word. The copula *is* has the meaning of "having a particular state or quality" and shows the relationship between *that* and *enough*. The third word in the utterance, *enough*, is an adjective in the predicate position meaning "adequate or sufficient." In the *use* dimension the social function can vary depending on the tone used and what the antecedent of *that* is in the larger discourse. For instance, if a parent wants to reprimand a crying child, yelling "That is enough" is a command for the child to be quiet. If a waiter is filling your water glass, "That's enough" signals that you have a sufficient amount to drink and want him to stop pouring more water.

The three dimensions are interconnected in the sense that a change in one dimension could change the other two (Larsen-Freeman, 2003). In the example above, "That is enough," whether the form is contracted and how each word is pronounced will affect the meaning. In a classroom of rowdy students, emphasizing each individual word to bring the class to order will be very different than the contracted form *that's enough* when notifying the person pouring water that you have enough in your glass. Furthermore, when political activists put up a sign saying *that's enough*, it is an indication that they want to take an action in order to stop a particular social injustice.

Traditionally, language teaching methodology has focused on one dimension while ignoring others. The Grammar Translation Method and the Audiolingual Method focus on form, somewhat on meaning, but ignore use almost completely. The Natural Approach on the other hand, focuses on use and meaning, but mostly ignores the form dimension. Learners of any language must learn *all three* of these components. Grammar is not only about form; it is about "what forms mean and when and why they are used" (Larsen-Freeman, 2014, p. 269).

Grammar and Discourse

Form, meaning, and use of language are context-sensitive and are co-constructed by the members of a particular discourse. Therefore, teaching language through discourse is inevitable. Celce-Murcia and Olshtain (2014) define **discourse** as "an instance of spoken or written language with describable internal relationships of form and meaning (e.g., words, structures, cohesion) that relate coherently to an external communicative function or purpose and a given audience or interlocutor" (p. 427) in a particular context. In other words, context defines the way we use the language, and we need to take into account such factors as:

- who the speaker/writer is,
- who the audience is,
- where the communication takes place,
- what communication takes place before and after a sentence in question,
- implied versus literal meanings,
- styles and registers,
- the alternative forms among which a producer can choose.

It's important to grasp the significance of the interconnectedness of all features of discourse, as the patterns of language forms emerge out of discourse and are shaped by an ongoing process (Hopper, 1998; Bybee, 2006; Ellis & Larsen-Freeman, 2009).

CLASSROOM CONNECTIONS

What are some ways that English speakers compensate for the fact that the second-person pronoun *you* does not allow them to distinguish between singular and plural? If some or all of the L1s represented in your class distinguish the forms of singular and plural *you*, how would you teach a lesson that helps learners to use English words and phrases that disambiguate (when necessary) the two meanings?

Emergent Grammar

According to Hopper (1998), the patterns of language emerge through repeated use and become "sedimented" (p. 158) as fixed or semi-fixed patterns that may look stabilized. From this perspective, grammar is not the source of understanding and communication but "a byproduct of it" (p. 156). Earlier, Hopper (1988) argued that grammar is "a real-time activity, whose regularities are always provisional and continuously subject to negotiation, renovation, and abandonment" (p. 120). We are tentatively making meaning and making sense with patterns that have been previously used and that are familiar to us. Therefore, the patterns of linguistic rules are based on *frequency* (Bybee, 2006; N. Ellis, 2012). For instance, originally, the proper noun *Google* was used to refer to the online search engine, and now also functions as a verb to mean "to look up information online." We often hear people saying, "Why don't you google the word so that we know what it is." In the Chinese language, a similar linguistic phenomenon has happened with the name of the company 百度 [baidu].

To capture this dynamic, complex, and adaptive nature of language, Larsen-Freeman (2003) proposed the term *grammaring*, which shifts the focus from the product of learning static grammar rules to the process of using grammar in real world communicative contexts. The notion of grammaring helps us move away from the usual traditions of teaching grammar as a body of knowledge and instead treats grammar as a *skill* to develop. Grammaring also refers to the organic process of using "grammar constructions accurately, meaningfully, and appropriately" (Larsen-Freeman, 2003, p. 264).

 **CLASSROOM CONNECTIONS**

Have you noticed ways in which English is changing these days? What are some examples, say, of new words or expressions that have become accepted usage? At what point does "incorrect" grammar eventually become "correct," and how do you draw the line between the two? How would you explain to your students the widespread use (by L1 speakers of English) of utterances such as "Between you and I . . ." and "Me and my buddy went to the ballgame"?

APPROACHES TO FORM-FOCUSED INSTRUCTION

R. Ellis (2012) defines **form-focused instruction** (FFI) as "any planned or incidental instructional activity that is intended to induce language learners to pay attention to linguistic form" (p. 271). FFI approaches vary from traditional structure-based focusing primarily on form to more communicative approaches with attention to form while students are engaged in activities that are meaning-focused.

A glance through the last century of language-teaching practices reveals mixed opinions about the place of teaching language **forms**, depending on the method or era. In the Grammar Translation and Audiolingual Methods (see Chapter 2), formal aspects of language received central attention. In the Direct Method and the Natural Approach, overt focus on form was almost forbidden. Some manifestations of CLT, especially indirect approaches, advocated only a brief attention to form, while other proponents of CLT injected healthy doses of form-focused techniques into a communicative curriculum.

Nowadays only a handful of language-teaching experts advocate *no* focus on form ("zero option") at all, a prime proponent of which is Krashen (1997) with his **input hypothesis** (see *PLLT*, Chapters 9 and 10). Current views of L2 classroom methodology are almost universally agreed on the importance of some **form-focused instruction** within the communicative framework, ranging from **explicit** treatment of rules, to **noticing** and **input enhancement** (Polio, 2007; Nassaji & Fotos, 2011; R. Ellis, 2012), to **implicit** techniques for structuring input to learners. This consensus, of course, still leaves open a wide range of options from which you must choose, depending on your students, their purposes, and the context. In other words, we need to consider an *informed eclectic* approach to form-focused instruction (Savage, 2010).

Explicit Presentation of Forms

Explicit instruction attempts to help learners develop metalinguistic awareness of a rule that can be carried out *deductively* or *inductively* (Ellis, 2014). In a deductive explicit presentation, the teacher begins a lesson by announcing the grammar focus: "Today we're going to learn about the present progressive." The teacher might then write examples of the target structure on the board or show a grammar chart or table in the textbook (e.g., "I *am* look*ing* for my cellphone." "She *is* buy*ing* a house."). Afterwards, the teacher would follow up with an explicit explanation of the rule in detail, including the form, meaning, and use, saying something like: "The present progressive tense is formed with a present form of *be* (i.e., *am*, *is*, or *are*) and the present participle of the main verb. The present progressive is used to mean ongoing action at the time of speaking or for future events" (Cowan, 2008, pp. 362–363).

When providing an explicit presentation *inductively*, the teacher tries to elicit information from the students by presenting example sentences, sometimes by using input enhancement techniques such as **consciousness-raising** (e.g., highlighting or bolding the target forms):

It **is** rain**ing** now.

You **are** study**ing** English now.

She **is** sleep**ing** now.

They **are** hav**ing** lunch now.

Teacher: Can you see how we can form the present progressive tense?

Students: Use is, are, + verb –ing.

T: What time words do we use with this tense?

Ss: This moment, right now.

In addition to deduction and induction, *abduction* can be another approach to obtaining linguistic knowledge. Introduced by C. S. Peirce at the end of 19th century, *abduction* refers to the exploratory process of trying out tentative solutions to problems or facts to figure out what may happen, to see if they work, or to experience something new (Cunningham, 2002). According to van Lier (2007), unlike *inductive* (i.e., data-driven, extracting rules and patterns from examples) or *deductive* (i.e., rule-driven, from rule-learning to rule application) reasoning, in abductive learning learners come to understand hidden rules of language use through the process of exploring hypotheses and inferences.

Language teachers can start with abduction, taking experiential and exploratory approaches (e.g., puzzle-based learning) and then move on to either inductive or deductive tasks as relevant, followed with further exploration at a wider or deeper level. Consider the following example (adapted from van Lier, 2011a, p. 13):

Abduction in the L2 classroom

1. Choose an authentic text that incorporates some features you want to highlight. *Possible option: Input enhancement, relative clauses* (see p. 477 for an example)

2. Design an activity that focuses on these features. *Example: Relative clauses embedded into an information-gap map activity.*
3. Students work in groups and note the grammatical features or patterns they observe.
4. Students report their findings to the class.

Expansion:

5. Inductive: Students collect further examples illustrating the pattern(s) found and formulate a general rule.
6. Deductive: Teacher and students formulate a rule, check it in a grammar book, and look at examples that illustrate the rule.

The use of grammatical explanation and terminology must be approached with care. Following a few rules of thumb may enhance any grammatical explanations you undertake:

Suggestions for Enhancing Grammatical Explanations

- Keep your explanations brief and simple. Use the students' L1, if your context permits it, to help students to comprehend more easily.
- Use charts and other visuals whenever possible to graphically depict grammatical relationships.
- Illustrate with clear, unambiguous examples.
- Do not get yourself (and students!) tied up in knots over so-called "exceptions" to rules.
- If you don't know how to explain something (for instance, if a student asks you about a point of grammar and you are not sure of the rule), do not risk giving false information (that you may have to retract later, which will cause even more embarrassment). Rather, tell students you will research that point and bring an answer back the next day.

Classroom Connections

Reflecting upon your learning experience of a second or foreign language, what are some examples of encountering particular linguistic items of the target structure in deductive, inductive, and abductive ways? How would you modify the procedure of presenting the target rules if you were to teach them in the future?

Implicit Presentation of Forms

In an implicit approach to grammar instruction, the teacher does not employ structural analysis or technical terms to explain the linguistic rules. Instead, the target form is used in the utterances made to communicate with the students. The context of the utterances helps them to understand the meaning and sustain the communication (Savage, 2010). Consider the following examples provided in authentic context drawing on (a) the teacher's and students' current actions, (b) their personal lives, or (c) visuals (Savage, 2010):

a. I am speaking now. I am not reading.
Suji is sitting on a chair now, not standing on it.
We are studying English now. We are not watching TV.

b. I am living in the U.S. now. I was living in Canada before.
Tom is taking a cooking class these days.

c. In this picture, what is this little girl doing now?
Is she running or swimming?
In this movie, to whom is the man speaking?
Is the man speaking to the police or to his friend?

Focus on Form

A **focus on form** (FonF) approach attempts to induce learners' incidental learning by drawing their attention to target forms while they are engaged in communicative activities. The emphasis is on the learners' noticing their knowledge about grammatical features, which is necessary for successful target language use and has been influential in task-based approaches to grammar instruction.

Noticing refers to "the process of the learner picking out specific features of the target language input which she or he hears or reads, and paying conscious attention to them so that they can be fed into the learning process" (Cullen, 2012, p. 260). Noticing is a natural process, but one considered to be essential to language acquisition (Schmidt, 1990) when learners are exposed to sufficient input.

A FonF approach can be considered more appropriate because:

- it is more in keeping with natural language acquisition (where rules are absorbed subconsciously with little or no conscious focus).
- it conforms more easily to the concept of interlanguage development in which learners progress, on variable timetables, through stages of rule acquisition.
- it allows students to get a communicative "feel" for some aspect of language before possibly being overwhelmed by grammatical explanations.
- it builds more intrinsic motivation by allowing students to discover rules rather than being told them.

FonF usually occurs reactively when difficulties of the learner's performance are identified after or during the completion of a given task in which students use the grammatical knowledge available to them rather than particular grammatical points preselected and pre-presented by the teacher. The post-task stage is an important part of the process of acquiring necessary forms because it is this stage where learners compare their performance with correct forms such as in a reading text, or a transcript of a conversation.

Then it becomes the consciousness-raising (Sharwood-Smith, 1981) stage of the lesson: the teacher's role at this stage is to help students notice and pay attention to the gaps between their utterances and the correct forms by giving corrective feedback with further explanation, exemplification, and follow-up practice as required. A variety of tasks can be implemented for this stage such as dictogloss, jigsaw, and text-reconstruction tasks, which are exemplified later in this chapter.

Feedback on Errors

Existing research on corrective feedback supports the importance of feedback for successful acquisition of oral communicative competence. The practical question is determining which specific type of error correction is most beneficial and under what circumstances, the answer to which is unclear and has not been resolved (Loewen, 2012). Therefore, it is desirable to employ a variety of feedback options such as recasting, self-correction, and metalinguistic explanation (Loewen, 2012; R. Ellis, 2012; Larsen-Freeman, 2014). (See *PLLT*, Chapter 9 for an overview of error treatment in SLA and Chapter 16 of this book for a discussion of the treatment of spoken errors.) The important point to keep in mind is that we should adhere to principles of maintaining communicative flow, of maximizing student self-correction, and of sensitively considering the affective state and linguistic stage of the learner.

The treatment of grammatical (and discourse) errors in writing is a different matter. In process writing approaches, overt attention to **local** grammatical and rhetorical (discourse) errors is normally delayed until learners have completed one or two drafts of a paper. **Global** errors that impede meaning must, of course, be attended to earlier in the process. Studies have shown (Ferris & Hedgcock, 2014) that certain attention to errors does indeed make a difference in final written products.

Aljaafreh and Lantolf (1994) developed a 12-point regulatory scale ranging from implicit to explicit strategies for writing tutoring sessions. As shown in Table 19.1, this scale describes a range of corrective feedback strategies differing in their degree of explicitness with different degrees of scaffolding. A teacher begins by asking students to identify errors in their own writing and then gradually moves to offering concrete examples of the correct sentences if the students fail to correct the errors by themselves. The goal here is to achieve self-regulation through the learners' self-correction.

Table 19.1 Regulatory scale—implicit to explicit (Aljaafreh & Lantolf, 1994, p. 471)

0. Tutor asks the learner to read, find the errors, and correct them independently, prior to the tutorial.
1. Construction of a "collaborative frame" prompted by the presence of the tutor as a potential dialogic partner.
2. Prompted or focused reading of the sentence that contains the error by the learner or the tutor.
3. Tutor indicates that something may be wrong in a segment (for example, sentence, clause, line) – "Is there anything wrong in this sentence?"
4. Tutor rejects unsuccessful attempts at recognizing the error.
5. Tutor narrows down the location of the error (for example, tutor repeats or points to the specific segment which contains the error).
6. Tutor indicates the nature of the error, but does not identify the error (for example, "There is something wrong with the tense marking here").
7. Tutor identifies the error ("You can't use an auxiliary here").
8. Tutor rejects learner's unsuccessful attempts at correcting error.
9. Tutor provides clues to help the learner arrive at the correct form (for example, "It is not really past but something that is still going on").
10. Tutor provides the correct form.
11. Tutor provides some explanation for use of the correct form.
12. Tutor provides examples of the correct pattern when other forms of help fail to produce an appropriate responsive action.

Classroom Connections

If you were tutoring or conferencing with a student and were asked to provide feedback on the student's essay, how would you use the 13-point regulatory scale developed by Aljaafreh and Lantolf (1994)? What are some factors you need to keep in mind before using the scale?

A Lexicogrammatical Approach

The term **lexicogrammar**, originally coined by Michael A. Halliday, represents a view that lexis and grammar are two inherently connected parts of a single entity and should not be treated separately. Grammar is considered as "a meaning-making resource and to describe grammatical categories by reference to what they mean" (Halliday, 2004, p. 10). From this view a grammatical structure may be lexically bound and lexical items also have grammatical features (Liu, 2013). This approach has been supported by corpus research, which illustrates strong connection between contextual patterns.

Figure 19.1 Sample of corpus-based lexicogrammatical error worksheet (Liu & Jiang, 2009, p. 66)

Computer Lab Worksheet (Assignment #2) **Name**____________________
English Composition 2 **Spring 2006**

A. Write down the problems noted on your paper.

1. Crazy mobs who contributed to ostracize her
2. bored and boring
3. interested and interesting

B. Find a sentence on the corpus that uses the word/phrase (for each of the sentences you wrote above) in the desired way. Write the sentence below.

1. Levin makes a special case for Debord as a film-maker whose aim was to contribute to the ultimate destruction of cinema as a spectacularist medium.
2. I'm bored Wasn't that a damn boring game!
3. Helen is not interested in making lists about her life.
   Informal admissions are also interesting.

C. Describe how this word/phrase is used.

1. After the phrase "contribute to": most of sentence has noun, not a verb
2. If something needs to be bored, it should be in passive position.
   However, being accompanies something active.
3. Same pattern applies to "Interested" and "Interesting."
   "Interested" for a passive thing and "Interesting" for a active thing.

D. Rewrite your sentences using the information that you learned from the corpus

1. Crazy mobs who contributed to ostracizing her.
2. The students are bored because of boring class.
3. The audiences were interested after the singer made the show interesting.

The sample activity in Figure 19.1 was used in Liu and Jiang's study (2009) in composition classes at an American university to help students recognize lexicogrammatical errors in their writing. A worksheet was provided for students to complete as shown in the sample. Students then followed the procedures below (Liu & Jiang, 2009, p. 65):

- List the lexicogrammatical problems that his/her instructor has marked.

- Find examples from an electronic corpus (e.g., the British National Corpus [BNC], the Corpus of Contemporary American English [COCA]) that use each lexicogrammatical item in the desired way and write one example down on the worksheet.
- Rewrite his/her original sentence using the information learned from the corpus.

In this sample worksheet the target linguistic forms were the use of proposition "to" in "contribute to," and the difference between present and past participles used as adjectives as in "bored and boring" and "interested and interesting." The worksheet shows that the student was able to address the problems successfully using the corpus information.

PRINCIPLES FOR TEACHING GRAMMAR

As discussed so far, varied opinions on how to teach grammar can be found in the literature on language teaching. The overall consensus in recent communicative methodology is that judicious attention to grammatical form is not only helpful, if appropriate techniques are used, but essential to a speedy learning process (Loewen, 2011; Nassaji & Fotos, 2011; Ellis, 2014). The question is what the optimal conditions are for teaching grammar, and what degree of overt attention should be included in such form-focused instruction. van Lier (2011a) noted that "grammar activities can be along a continuum from implicit to explicit, and at any point along the continuum inductive and/or deductive work may be carried out" (p. 13). A lesson may start with a more implicit focus, which may then shift to becoming more explicit, or vice versa.

Following are some principles that underlie effective grammar teaching, taken from the current literature (Loewen, 2011; Nassaji & Fotos, 2011; van Lier, 2011a; Ellis, 2014).

Principles for Teaching Grammar

- All three dimensions of grammar—form, meaning, and use—should be emphasized.
- Take a lexicogrammatical approach to presenting new linguistic items to students (see Chapter 12 for sample activities to raise such awareness of language using corpus data).
- Learners need to have the opportunity to practice and use forms in communicative tasks.
- Attend to both input-based (comprehension) and output-based (production) grammar and vocabulary.
- Deductive, inductive, and abductive approaches can all be useful, depending on the goals and emergent needs of the learner in a particular context.

- Incidental focus on form is valuable in that it treats errors that occur while learners are engaged in meaningful communication.
- Corrective feedback can facilitate acquisition if it involves a mixture of implicit and explicit feedback.
- Explicit grammar lessons and implicit grammar integrated into communicative activities (FonF) are both viable, depending on the context and learners' needs.
- Instruction needs to consider learners' individual differences. Try to cater to their different needs by involving a variety of learning activities. Make use of learner-training materials to help make them aware of their own approaches to learning and encourage them to alternate different strategies.

 **CLASSROOM CONNECTIONS**

What are some of the possible individual differences you might encounter among students in their preferences for learning the forms of language? If some students lean toward analytical, deductive styles and others prefer inductive, incidental learning, what would you do?

GRAMMAR TECHNIQUES

Following are some sample techniques for teaching grammar, especially for helping learners notice and pay attention to grammatical features they need for the completion of given tasks.

1. Charts, Objects, Maps, and Drawings

Some practices for calling students' attention to grammatical forms have been around for decades and still serve as effective devices (Thornbury, 2006; Azar & Hagen, 2011; Saslow & Ascher, 2011). There is always a useful place for a *chart*, for example, that requires a student to notice and check off certain forms. In Figure 19.2, frequency adverbs are the focus.

Likewise, *objects* (or pictures of objects), *maps*, and other *illustrations* help to make focus on grammatical forms somewhat concrete. A page full of common articles of clothing, for example, could aid in the noticing of possessives:

This is *my* jacket.

These are *Oscar's* glasses.

Are these *your* shoes? No, they are *Lucy's*.

Figure 19.2 Frequency adverbs (Brown, 1992, p. 99)

EXERCISE 1

Read the paragraphs on page 98 again. Then choose the appropriate adverb of frequency.

	never	seldom	sometimes	often	usually	always
1. Keiko works hard.						✔
2. She is on time for work.						
3. She is late or sick.						
4. She is early for work.						
5. She types letters.						
6. She files.						
7. She makes copies.						
8. She makes mistakes when she types.						
9. She answers the phone politely.						
10. She is angry.						

Now say the complete sentences.

1. Keiko always works hard.
2. She is always on time for work.
3. ____________
4. ____________
5. ____________
6. ____________
7. ____________
8. ____________
9. ____________
10. ____________

Maps are traditionally favorite aids in introducing and reinforcing certain grammatical and lexical features of language. Asking for directions ("Where is the post office?") and responding ("Go down this street, turn right, walk about half a block, and it will be on your left") are among a number of possible formal elements that can be included.

2. Dialogues and Conversations

For over half a century *dialogues* have been successfully used to focus learners on form and meaning simultaneously. For beginners, they provide models for practice while injecting some meaning and reality, even if *all* the lexical and grammatical components are not completely understood. For intermediate learners, dialogues and other conversations give learners a chance to confidently produce language, and then to vary the models with their own creative additions.

In Figure 19.3 (page 476), a conversation is presented to students. They can listen to it on an audio recording, read it, repeat it to get the "flow" of the conversation, practice it with different partners, and eventually (as their level permits) expand on it to share their *own* vacation plans. The focus is on the present progressive used for future planned events.

Figure 19.3 Present progressive, future events

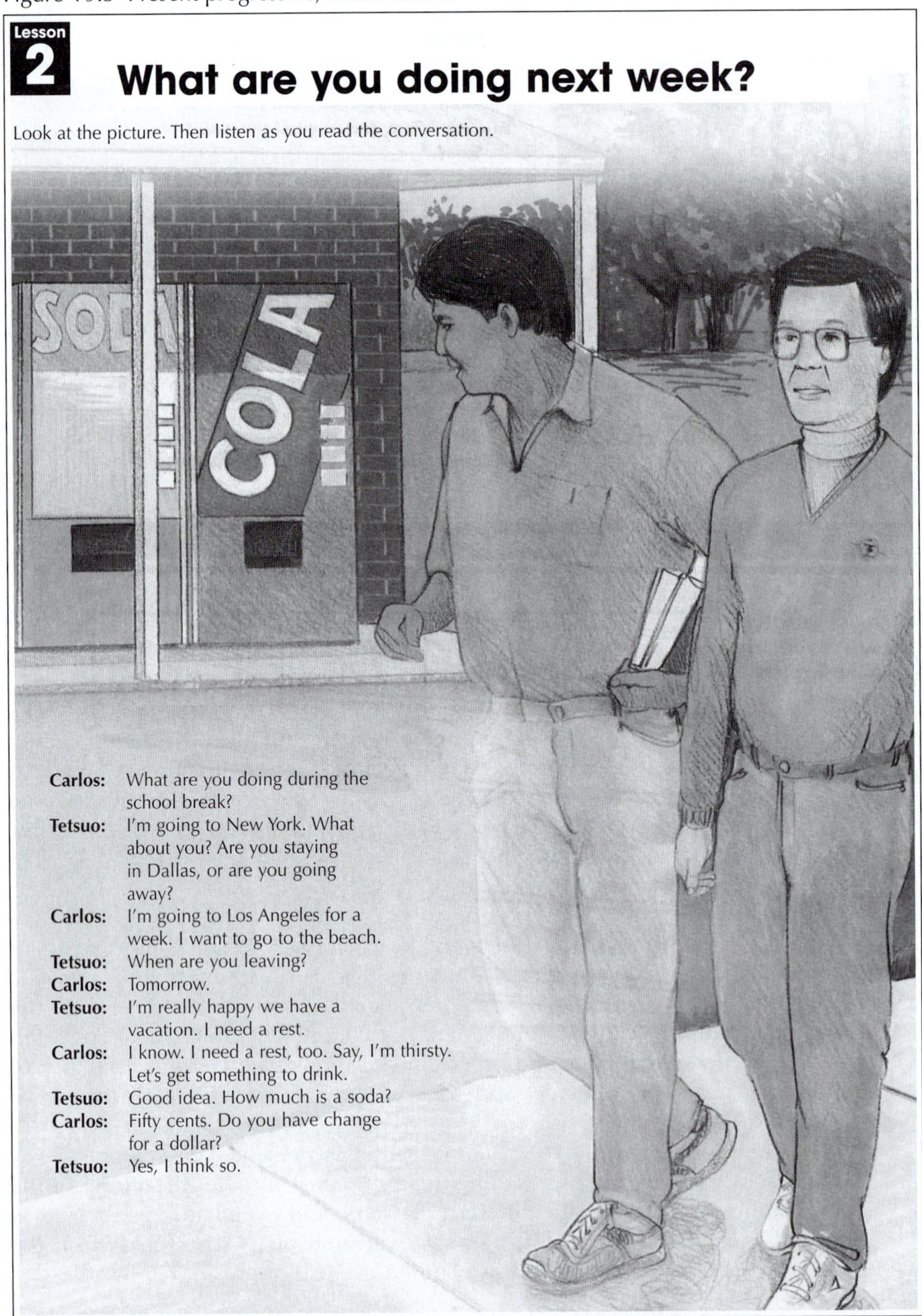

Lesson 2

What are you doing next week?

Look at the picture. Then listen as you read the conversation.

Carlos: What are you doing during the school break?
Tetsuo: I'm going to New York. What about you? Are you staying in Dallas, or are you going away?
Carlos: I'm going to Los Angeles for a week. I want to go to the beach.
Tetsuo: When are you leaving?
Carlos: Tomorrow.
Tetsuo: I'm really happy we have a vacation. I need a rest.
Carlos: I know. I need a rest, too. Say, I'm thirsty. Let's get something to drink.
Tetsuo: Good idea. How much is a soda?
Carlos: Fifty cents. Do you have change for a dollar?
Tetsuo: Yes, I think so.

Classroom Connections

Suppose your intermediate students have practiced the dialogue in Figure 19.3. How would you expand on the forms that have been practiced? What specific tasks or activities could you ask them to perform that would build communicatively on the dialogue?

3. Input Enhancement

A more recent common technique involves highlighting (or boldfacing) certain target grammatical forms in a reading text or stressing (or slowing down, or using hand gestures) certain forms when speaking. Consider the example text in Figure 19.4.

Figure 19.4 Input enhancement in written texts (Nassaji & Fotos, 2011, p. 46)

Classroom Activity

Instructions: Please read the following text. Then in groups of two, discuss the following questions:

The teacher ***has told*** me that I have homework today. It will have to be completed by tomorrow. I ***have looked*** at it, and it looks very difficult. I have asked my brother if he ***has*** ever ***worked*** on homework like this. He ***has*** never ***seen*** an assignment like this before. This will be the first time that I ***have needed*** help!

Questions for Discussion

1. Has anything like this ever happened to you as a student?
2. What do you think the problem with the student's homework has been?
3. Do you think homework is useful?
4. Do you think homework will help learners to study harder?

Input enhancement in oral texts:

Example (Nassaji & Fotos, 2011, p. 42)
Student: And she catched her.
Teacher: She CAUGHT her? [Enhanced with added stress]
Student: Yeah, caught her.

4. Input Flood

Another technique presents texts that contain a target structure that appears frequently or repeatedly, and is therefore more salient. This may trigger syntactic priming, as speakers tend to "produce a previously spoken or heard structure" (Mackey & Gass, 2006, p. 173). Figure 19.5 (page 478) is an example.

Figure 19.5 Input flood, definite and indefinite articles (Nassaji & Fotos, 2011, p. 43)

To the teacher:

The target forms below are the English definite and indefinite articles. The sample text includes frequent instances of these target forms. It should be noted that the target forms should not be textually enhanced.

A chipmunk sat on some branches in a great big tree. It was very hungry, so it decided to leave the tree and look for food. It climbed off the branches and reached the trunk of the tree, and went down the trunk to the ground below. The chipmunk saw lots of grass, and in the grass lay many acorns! The chipmunk, in its delight, took as many acorns as it could, put them in its mouth, and ran back up the tree trunk to its nest. There the chipmunk had a very good meal.

CLASSROOM CONNECTIONS

In Figure 19.5, an example of Input Flood is given. Suppose your high beginning students have just read the sample passage. What could you do next to help them to *notice* definite and indefinite articles? What kinds of tasks or activities would help them to move from this text to producing (orally or in writing) a text that includes articles?

5. Input Processing

Because it may be difficult for learners to attend to meaning and form in the input at the same time, a more explicit technique, input processing, was proposed by VanPatten (1996). It is important that the text used for input remain reasonably natural, and that the learners make the necessary connections between form and function in authentic contexts of L2 use. Consider the following exercise in Figure 19.6.

Figure 19.6 Input processing, present and past tenses (Nassaji & Fotos, 2011, pp. 30–31)

Instructions: Listen to the following sentences and decide whether they describe an action that was done before or is usually done.

1. The teacher corrected the essays.	*Now* ( )	*Before* ( )
2. The man cleaned the table.	*Now* ( )	*Before* ( )
3. I wake up at 5 in the morning.	*Now* ( )	*Before* ( )
4. The train leaves the station at 8 am.	*Now* ( )	*Before* ( )
5. The writer finished writing the book.	*Now* ( )	*Before* ( )
6. The trees go green in the spring.	*Now* ( )	*Before* ( )

Figure 19.7 Dictogloss technique (Nassaji & Fotos, 2011, p. 113)

To the teacher:

You intend to teach or practice the use of relative clauses. You may choose a text such as the following, in which several instances of this structure occur.

Friendship

We are always looking for good friends. These days it is hard to find true friends whom we can trust. Certainly, it is important to be considerate of those who care for us. However, a true friend is someone who is sincere and loyal, and is with us through tough times. We don't have to wonder if a friend, who is busy with a new partner and three kids, will have time to comfort us after a bad day. However, a true friendship is like a bridge that is built with planks of loyalty and fastened with nails of sincerity. It is that kind of connection that binds us together.

Procedures for completing the task:

1. **Preparation and warm-up:** discuss the importance of friendship and the different ways in which someone can be a friend. Examine the different characteristics of a good friend. Also, tell the class that they are going to hear a text on friendship. Ask them what they guess the text would include. Explain difficult vocabulary such as *trust, loyalty, sincerity,* and *considerate*.
2. **Dictation:** read the text at a normal pace. Ask learners to jot down the words related to the content as you read.
3. **Reconstruction:** ask learners to form groups of two or three and pool their resources to reconstruct the text as closely as possible to the original.
4. **Analysis and correction:** when they finish, ask learners to analyze and compare their versions. Go around the class and help learners to correct their errors. Do not show learners the original text until after the text has been compared and analyzed.

6. Dictogloss

Dictogloss, a variation on the *dictocomp* technique described in Chapter 18, is a task-based procedure designed to help L2 learners internalize certain grammatical elements that are built into a text (Wajnryb, 1990). Through the reconstruction of a text, students come to notice certain grammatical features. In Figure 19.7, students are not asked to notice relative clauses, even though they are embedded in the text. Only at the last stage of the procedure will students possibly become aware of using relative clauses.

Classroom Connections

From what you have learned in this chapter about teaching grammar, in the last phase of the dictogloss technique above, how would you "go around the class and help learners to correct their errors"? How would you "correct" them, or in some way help them to *notice* errors?

TEACHING VOCABULARY

The other "half" of form-focused instruction is vocabulary—the thousands of lexical building blocks that are available to the average user of a language. As we consider vocabulary teaching, be reminded again that lexical items are basic to all of the four skills, and so vocabulary is not a "skill" as we normally use the term. The skill comes in the efficient storage (competence) and adept retrieval (performance) of those units. How vocabulary should be taught has stimulated some controversies over time, which we'll first take a brief look at here.

Historical Perspectives

While traditional language-teaching methods highlighted vocabulary study with lists, definitions, written and oral drills, and flash cards, there was a period of time when "the teaching and learning of vocabulary [were] undervalued" (Zimmerman, 1997, p. 5). In the zeal for natural, authentic classroom tasks and activities, vocabulary focus was swept under the rug. Further, as teachers increasingly perceived their role as facilitators and guides, they became more reluctant to take the directive and sometimes intrusive steps to turn students' focus to lexical form.

Toward the end of the twentieth century, we saw a revival of systematic attention to vocabulary learning across a number of proficiency levels and contexts. Ranging from very explicit focus, such as that found in Michael Lewis's (1993, 1997, 2000) Lexical Approach, to more indirect approaches in which vocabulary is incorporated into communicative tasks, attention to lexical forms is now more central to the development of language curricula (Nation, 2001, 2003, 2005; Read, 2004).

One of the recent "hot topics" in vocabulary teaching is whether learners are better served in the long run with **incidental** exposure to lexical items (that is, as a by-product of communicative activities), or with **intentional**, explicit focus on vocabulary. In the earlier years of CLT approaches, "the concept of incidental learning offered the seductive prospect that, provided the learners had access to sufficient comprehensible input, L2 vocabulary acquisition would largely take care of itself" (Read, 2004, p. 147). However, Schmitt (2008) observes that many features of vocabulary require deliberate attention, as learners may not notice the features of use if they are focusing on the meaning of task. In fact, research shows that intentional vocabulary focus accounts for significant gains in acquisition (Laufer, 2003; Read, 2004).

A further development in vocabulary teaching is the rapid growth of **corpus linguistics** and the volumes of raw data that are now available in corpora that encompass spoken and written language, genres of each, as well as data from a number of varieties of world Englishes. Researchers (e.g., Conrad, 2005; Liu & Jiang, 2009; Reppen, 2010) have described numerous ways in which corpus linguistics has improved our collective capacity to expose learners to real-world language. We have ready access not just to statistics such as word frequency counts, but more important, **collocations** (words that tend to appear in the company of other words). **Concordancing** enables learners (and textbook writers) to see words in context (McCarthy, 2004). And these voluminous corpora provide data banks through which we can more closely examine and appreciate associations between grammatical and lexical units (Hunston & Francis, 2000).

Current practices in teaching vocabulary, especially in view of the technology of corpus linguistics, are clearly not simply a rebirth of the same methods of half a century ago. Rather than viewing vocabulary items as a long and boring list of words to be defined and memorized, lexical forms are seen in their central role in contextualized, meaningful language. Learners can be guided in specific ways to internalize these important building blocks of language.

Strategies for Teaching Vocabulary

Below are some guidelines for the communicative treatment of vocabulary instruction:

1. Allocate Specific Class Time to Vocabulary Learning

In the hustle and bustle of our interactive classrooms, sometimes we get so caught up in lively group work and meaningful communication that we don't pause to devote some attention to words. Noting the incremental nature of word learning (Zimmerman, 2014), it is important to have students meet target words several times. Webb and Nation (2013) note that at least somewhere between 7–16 encounters of any new word are required for gaining necessary knowledge. Furthermore, the spacing between the repetitions is also important to keep in mind. For example, spreading 20 minutes across a few days at progressive intervals will be much more effective for long-term recall than spending 20 minutes all at once (Webb & Nation, 2013).

2. Help Students to Learn Vocabulary in Context

The best internalization of vocabulary comes from encounters (comprehension or production) with words within the context of surrounding discourse. Data from linguistic corpora can provide real-world actual language that has been printed or spoken. Rather than isolating words and/or focusing on dictionary definitions, learners can benefit from attending to vocabulary within a communicative framework in which items appear. Students will then associate new words with a meaningful context to which they apply. For example, for a beginning level of students, pictures, realia, and gestures can be used to describe meaning in context. For a more advanced level of students, encourage them to consult online corpora (e.g., the British National Corpus, or the Corpus of Contemporary American English: COCA) to gain knowledge of patterned sequences, particularly collocations or words that go together (Liu & Jiang, 2009).

The concordance examples in Figure 19.8 (page 482) show the use of the word *interesting* in context from the COCA.

Figure 19.8 Concordance examples of the use of *interesting* from the Corpus of Contemporary American English (COCA)

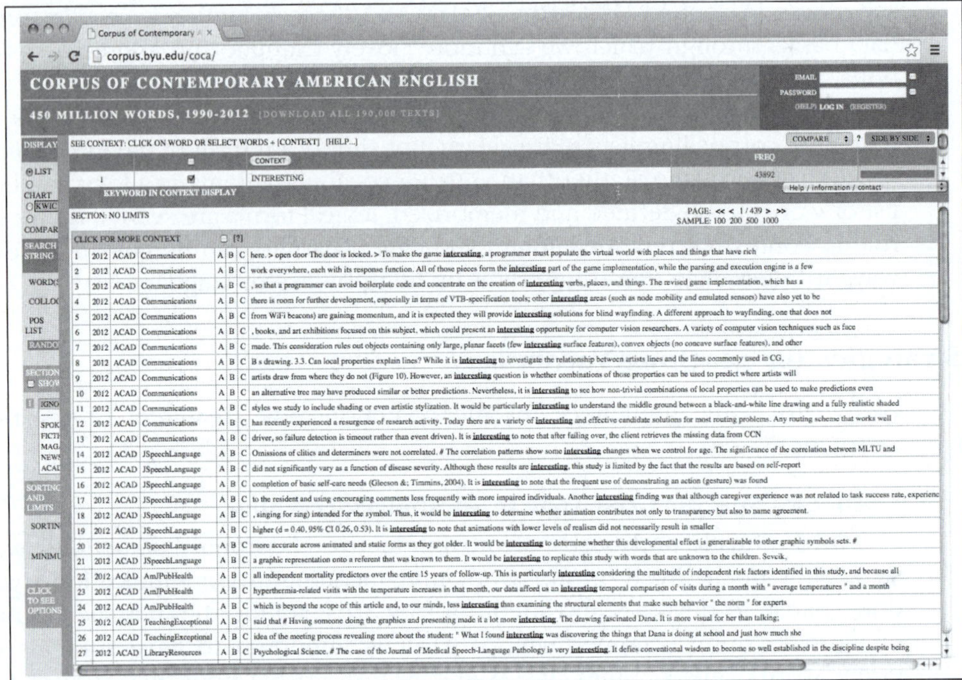

These samples of concordance can provide students with instances of "real language use, helping learners to know how to use language that is appropriate in different contexts" (Reppen, 2010, p. 20).

Classroom Connections

Search the Internet for a major *corpus* of English or another language of interest (e.g., for English, try the Corpus of Contemporary American English or the British National Corpus). Look up a somewhat uncommon word and notice its most frequent *collocations*. How might you use those collocations in teaching the use and meaning of the word in its contexts?

Learner's dictionaries also offer good resources for clear definitions and examples sentences drawing on a limited number of words. Unlike commonly used online/electronic dictionaries designed for native speakers, good learner's dictionaries (e.g., the *Oxford Basic American Dictionary for Learners of English* or *Merriam-Webster's Learner's Dictionary*) additionally include information about collocation, grammatical forms, register, word parts, and so on (Zimmerman, 2014).

3. Engage in "Unplanned" Vocabulary Teaching

In all likelihood, most of the attention you give to vocabulary learning will be unplanned: those moments when a student asks about a word or when a word has appeared that you feel deserves some attention. These impromptu moments are very important. Sometimes, they are simply brief little pointers; for example, the word "clumsy" once appeared in a paragraph students were reading and the teacher volunteered:

T: Okay, "clumsy." Does anyone know what that means? [*writes the word on the board*]

Ss: [*silence*]

T: No one? Okay, well, take a look at the sentence it's in. "His clumsy efforts to imitate a dancer were almost amusing." Now, was Bernard a good dancer? [*S1 raises her hand.*] Okay, Mona?

S1: Well, no. He was very bad dancer . . . we see this in next sentence.

T: Excellent! So, what do you think "clumsy" might mean?

S2: Mmm, . . . not graceful?

T: Good, what else? Anyone?

S3: Not smooth, eh, . . . uncoordinated?

T: Great! Okay, so "clumsy" means awkward, ungraceful, uncoordinated. [*writes synonyms on the board*] Is that clear now?

Ss: [*most Ss nod in agreement*]

Sometimes, such impromptu moments may be extended: the teacher gives several examples and/or encourages students to use the word in other sentences. Make sure that such unplanned teaching, however, does not detract from the central focus of activity by drifting into a long and possibly irrelevant tangent.

4. Encourage Students to Develop Word-Learning Strategies

Included in the discussion of teaching reading in Chapter 17 were such strategies as guessing vocabulary in context. A number of clues are available to learners to develop word-attack strategies. Consider the following examples (Kruse, 1987; Ur, 2012).

SUGGESTIONS FOR TEACHING VOCABULARY DEVELOPMENT (ADAPTED FROM KRUSE, 1987; UR, 2012)

1. Word building

a. *Suffixes*, examples: good*ness*, famili*ar*, happi*ly*
Practice word formation through exercises in which the student adds and subtracts suffixes

b. *Prefixes*, examples: *in*formal, *un*natural, *inter*national
Substitute various root stems with prefixes (*inter*+action);
Add prefixes (violent → *non*violent)

c. *Roots*, examples: *help* + ful, extra + *ordinary*

2. Definition clues

a. *Parentheses*, example: We saw a panther (large black cat) on the Safari.

b. *Synonyms* and *antonyms*, example: A birthday is an observance, that is, a remembrance of someone's day of birth.

c. *Superordinates*, example: *animal* is the superordinate of *dog, lion, mouse*

3. Inference clues

a. *Specific*, example: Peru is trying to *restore* some of its deteriorated monuments. Machu Picchu is being partly rebuilt by curators.

b. *Restatement*, example: Some products are designed to stop *perspiration*, but this bodily secretion of salty liquid can actually help to cool you.

c. *Contextual cues*, example: The old dog *snuffled* and *moped* as he sadly walked from room to room.

4. Word associations

a. *Linking meaning*, example: fat + pig, tall + tree

b. *Collocations*, example: tell the truth, make a copy

Considering that only a small fraction of the word list can be covered inside the classroom, it is necessary for students to develop effective strategies for learning vocabulary on their own. Word-learning strategies refer to "the planned approaches that a word-learner takes as an agent of his or her own word learning" (Zimmerman, 2014, p. 297). Once they encounter unknown words, they can try to figure out how the words are used by asking questions such as:

- Is the word countable or uncountable?
- Is there a particular preposition that follows it?
- Is it a formal word?
- Does it have positive or negative connotations? (Zimmerman, 2014, p. 298)

An effective way to encourage word-learning is to urge students to use *vocabulary notebooks* to enter new words, and to review them daily, once they identify their learning goals. Studies show that in order to understand television shows learners need to know about 3,000 word families and have knowledge of proper nouns (Web & Rodgers, 2009). If they wish to read novels and newspapers comfortably, they need to have a vocabulary size of 8,000–9,000 word families (Nation, 2006). The fact that increasing vocabulary size will influence the degree to which they can understand and use language may motivate them to be determined to expand their vocabulary notebooks.

★ ★ ★ ★ ★

Unfortunately, professional pendulums have a disturbing way of swinging too far one way or the other, and sometimes the only way we can get enough perspective to see these overly long arcs is through hindsight. Hindsight has now taught us that there was some overreaction to the almost exclusive attention that grammar and vocabulary received in the first two-thirds of the twentieth century. So-called "natural" approaches in which grammar was considered damaging were equally overreactive. Advocating the "absorption" of grammar and vocabulary with no overt attention whatsoever to language forms went too far. We now seem to have a healthy respect for the place of form-focused instruction—attention to those basic "bits and pieces" of a language—in an interactive curriculum. And now we can pursue the business of finding better and better techniques for getting these bits and pieces into the communicative repertoires of our learners.

FOR THE TEACHER: ACTIVITIES (A) & DISCUSSION (D)

Note: For each of the "Classroom Connections" in this chapter, you may wish to turn them into individual or pair-work discussion questions.

1. **(A)** Tell pairs to look at the following:
   - **a.** "Oh! That's just great!" [falling intonation]
   - **b.** "Good to see you again, Helen. You've lost some weight, haven't you?"
   - **c.** "Brrrr! It's sure cold in this house!"

   The "surface" grammatical meaning differs from potential "deep" structure meanings. Ask the pairs to identify those meanings, and, if possible, to think of other examples. Then have them devise a few techniques that could be used to teach such pragmatic aspects of English, and share their ideas with the rest of the class.
2. **(A)** Have students observe a class in which the teacher uses some form-focused instruction. Evaluate the effectiveness of the class using the six criteria on pages 467–468. Ask them to share their observations with the whole class.
3. **(A)** Assign a separate, different grammar "point" to every *two* pairs and have them do the following: one pair figures out how to teach that point with a *deductive* approach and describes students for which such an approach is justified; the other pair is directed to do the same with an inductive approach. Pairs then present their suggestions to the whole class for comparison.
4. **(D)** Review the section on error treatment in Chapter 16 (pp. 380–384). Observe a class and try to determine which principles of error correction were followed. How *explicitly* did the teacher treat grammatical (as opposed to vocabulary, pronunciation, etc.) errors?
5. **(A)** Six grammar-focusing techniques are illustrated in this chapter (pp. 474–479). Tell groups or pairs, each assigned to one technique, to

demonstrate (peer-teach) that technique to the rest of the class. Ask the class to offer collective critiques of what worked well, what didn't, and why.

6. **(A/D)** Ask students to think of one particular grammar point in English that is challenging to explain. List the points on the board and then assign them to pairs (one point for each pair). Ask them to analyze it in terms of the *three dimensions* of Larsen-Freeman's grammar model (p. 463).

FOR YOUR FURTHER READING

Loewen, S. (2011). Focus on form. In E. Hinkel (Ed.), *Handbook of research in second language teaching and learning*: Volume II (pp. 576–592). New York, NY: Routledge.

Larsen-Freeman, D. (2014). Teaching grammar. In M. Celce-Murcia, D. Brinton, & M.A. Snow (Eds.), *Teaching English as a second or foreign language* (4th ed., pp. 256–270). Boston, MA: National Geographic Learning.

Spada, N., & Lightbown, P. (2008). Form-focused instruction: Isolated or integrated? *TESOL Quarterly*, *42*, 181–207.

These three articles offer comprehensive surveys of research on form-focused instruction, with an emphasis on the teaching grammar. Extensive bibliographies are included.

Nassaji, H., & Fotos, S. (2011). *Teaching grammar in second language classrooms: Integrating form-focused instruction in communicative context.* New York, NY: Routledge.

A comprehensive overview on the topic of L2 grammar instruction with thoughtful integration of theory, research findings, and many practical examples and classroom activities.

Larsen-Freeman, D. (2003). *Teaching language: From grammar to grammaring.* Boston, MA: Heinle/Cengage.

An insightful framework for a reconceptualization of grammar and the way it is taught, featuring grammar as a dynamic complex system.

Thornbury, S. (2006). *Grammar.* Oxford, UK: Oxford University Press.

A comprehensive collection of practical classroom techniques, activities, and worksheets for teaching grammar to secondary and adult students. It covers three levels of grammar in use: word, sentence, and text levels.

Reppen, R. (2010). *Using corpora in the language classroom.* New York, NY: Cambridge University Press.

An excellent volume including the overview of corpus linguistics and clear explanations, instructions, and examples about how to use corpora and corpus tools for classroom applications.

PART V

ASSESSING LANGUAGE SKILLS

Assessment is an integral aspect of the pedagogical process of designing lessons, implementing them, and evaluating their success. This section addresses concepts, issues, and practicalities of assessment in the classroom. It is intended to serve simply as an introduction to the complex field of language assessment—enough to supply you with some useful tools for creating or adapting your own assessment procedures.

For a comprehensive treatment of language assessment, we recommend reading our companion textbook, *Language Assessment: Principles and Classroom Practices* (Brown & Abeywickrama, 2010).

- **Chapter 20, Language Assessment: Principles and Issues,** surveys principles and basic concepts in language assessment, takes a brief look at large-scale and standards-based testing, and summarizes some of the critical ethical issues involved in assessment.
- **Chapter 21, Classroom-Based Assessment,** is focused directly on the classroom, and on what you as a teacher can do to develop principled, effective, informative assessments in your teaching process.

CHAPTER **20**

LANGUAGE ASSESSMENT: PRINCIPLES AND ISSUES

Questions for Reflection

- What is the difference between *assessment* and *testing*?
- What are some basic principles of language assessment and how can they be applied to practical, classroom-based tests and other assessment procedures?
- What are the various genres of tests?
- How did historical developments in language testing lead up to some current issues?
- How does one analyze the effectiveness of large-scale standardized tests?
- What do we mean by *critical* language testing, and what are some of the moral and ethical issues involved in large-scale commercial testing?

So far, if you have been reading this book chapter by chapter from the beginning, you have a grasp of principles underlying a sound approach to L2 teaching, contextual considerations, lesson design, classroom management, teaching language skills, and form-focused instruction. In all these discussions, the notion of language assessment has emerged implicitly on a number of occasions, and explicitly at the end of each of the chapters on the four skills, but not to the point of taking a broad look at the field of language assessment and the principles and issues involved.

This and the next chapter offer a survey of language assessment, a look at designing language tests, and a primer on classroom alternatives in assessment. These two chapters should acquaint you with some basic tools for considering the role of assessment in your classroom. Obviously, in a field so complex and diverse, a comprehensive understanding of language assessment will require more reading. For the latter, in a book-length treatment of language assessment, we refer you to the second edition of *Language Assessment: Principles and Classroom Practices* (Brown & Abeywickrama, 2010).

DEFINING *TEST* AND *ASSESSMENT*

Before launching into a description of the language assessment field, it's important to define some frequently misunderstood terms. The word *assessment* has, in recent years, become a popular word for educators—in much the same way that *communicative* or *interactive* have gained widespread acceptance in language teaching circles. You are said to be on the cutting edge if you *assess* your students in lieu of *testing* them. This is a misunderstanding.

On the one hand, sometimes you find writers using *test* and *assessment* synonymously, which should not be the case. A **test** is a method of measuring a person's ability or knowledge in a given domain, with an emphasis on the concept of *method* and *measuring*. Tests are instruments that are (usually) carefully designed, and that have identifiable scoring methods. Tests are prepared administrative procedures that (almost always) occupy specified time periods in which student performance is systematically measured.

Assessment, on the other hand, is an ongoing process that encompasses a much wider domain. Whenever a student responds to a question, offers a comment, or tries out a new word or structure, the teacher subconsciously makes an assessment of the student's performance. Written work—from a jotted-down phrase to a formal essay—is performance that ultimately gets assessed by self, teacher, and possibly other students. Reading and listening activities usually require some sort of productive performance that the teacher implicitly judges. A good teacher never ceases to assess students, whether those assessments are *incidental* or *intentional*.

In this view of these two concepts, tests are *subsets* of assessment. They can be useful devices, but are only one among many procedures and tasks that teachers can ultimately use to assess students. But you might be thinking, if I make assessments every time I teach something in the classroom, does all *teaching* involve assessment? Are teachers constantly assessing students with no room for interaction that is assessment-free?

The answer depends on your perspective. For optimal learning to take place, students must have the freedom in the classroom to experiment, to try out their own hypotheses about language without feeling that their overall competence is being "judged." In the same way that, say, tournament tennis players must, before a tournament itself begins, have the freedom to *practice* their skills with no implications for their final placement on that day of days, so also must your learners have ample opportunities to "play" with language in your classroom without being formally graded. Teaching, in part, sets up the practice games of language learning, the opportunities for learners to listen, think, take risks, set goals, and process feedback from the "coach" and then recycle through whatever it is that they are trying to set in place.

At the same time, during these practice activities, teachers (and tennis coaches) are indeed observing students' performance and making various evaluations of the learner: How did the performance compare to previous performance? Which aspects of the performance were better than others? Is the learner performing up to an expected potential? How does the performance compare to that of others in the same learning community? And, in the ideal classroom, all these observations then feed into the way the teacher provides instruction to each student.

What you're doing when you're "coaching" your students and giving them feedback is essentially **informal assessment**: incidental, unplanned comments and responses like "Nice job!" "Did you say *can* or *can't*?" "You *go* to the movies yesterday?" or a marginal comment on a paper. A good deal of a teacher's informal assessment is embedded in classroom tasks designed to elicit performance but *not* with the intent of recording results and making fixed judgments about a student's competence.

On the other hand, **formal assessment** includes exercises or procedures specifically designed to tap into a storehouse of skills and knowledge. They are systematic, planned sampling techniques constructed to give teacher and student an appraisal of student achievement. To extend the tennis analogy, formal assessments are like the occasional matches that periodically occur during a season, or in classroom terms, those student performances that are noted in a teacher's gradebook.

Is formal assessment the same as a test? We can say that all tests are formal assessments, but not all formal assessment is testing. For example, you might use a student's journal or portfolio of materials as a formal assessment of the attainment of certain course objectives, but it is problematic to call those two procedures "tests." A systematic set of observations of a student's frequency of oral participation in class is certainly a formal assessment, but it too is hardly what anyone would call a test. Tests are usually relatively time-constrained (usually spanning a class period or at most several hours) and draw on a limited sample of behavior.

Classroom Connections

In your own L2 learning, recall the kinds of exercises that you did that were "graded" by the teacher in the form of a letter grade or score in the teacher's record book. What specifically was the nature of those exercises? Did you feel "tested"? What exactly was the difference between those exercises and formal *tests* that you took periodically?

PRINCIPLES OF LANGUAGE ASSESSMENT

Whether you are focusing on testing or assessing, a finite number of principles can be named that serve as guidelines for the design of a new test or assessment and for evaluating the efficacy of an existing procedure. I offer five such principles here. They represent a synthesis of what various assessment specialists cite as priorities for the design of language assessments. As I explain each principle, I will use the term *test* here as a generic term for both *test* and *formal assessment*, because all the principles apply to both.

Practicality

A good test is **practical**. It is within the means of financial limitations, time constraints, ease of administration, and scoring and interpretation. A test that is prohibitively expensive is impractical. A test of language proficiency that takes a student ten hours to complete is impractical. A test that requires individual one-to-one proctoring is impractical for a group of 500 people and only a handful of examiners. A test that takes a few minutes for a student to take and several hours for an examiner to evaluate is impractical for most classroom situations. A test that can be scored only by computer is impractical if the test takes place a thousand miles away from the nearest computer. The value and quality of a test are dependent upon such nitty-gritty, practical considerations.

The extent to which a test is practical sometimes hinges on whether a test is designed to be **norm-referenced** or **criterion-referenced**. In norm-referenced tests, each test-taker's score is interpreted in relation to a mean, median, standard deviation, and/or percentile rank. The purpose in such tests is to place test-takers along a mathematical continuum in rank order. Typical of norm-referenced tests are standardized tests intended to be administered to large audiences, with results quickly disseminated to test-takers. Such tests must have fixed, predetermined responses in a format that can be electronically scanned. Practicality is a primary issue.

Criterion-referenced tests, on the other hand, are designed to give test-takers feedback on specific course or lesson objectives, that is, the "criteria." Classroom tests involving smaller numbers, and connected to a curriculum, are typical of criterion-referenced testing. Here, more time and effort on the part of the teacher (test administrator) are usually required in order to deliver the feedback. One could say that criterion-referenced tests may, in the opinion of some, consider practicality as a secondary issue in the design of the test; teachers may sacrifice time and effort in order to offer students appropriate and useful feedback—the instructional value of a test. Testing (assessing) and teaching are interrelated, as noted already in this chapter.

Reliability

A **reliable** test is consistent and dependable. A number of sources of *un*reliability may be identified:

- the test itself (its construction), known as *test reliability*
- the administration of a test
- the test taker, known as student-related reliability
- the scoring of the test, known as rater (or scorer) reliability

A test might be unreliable if, for example, items are not well calibrated for difficulty, poorly designed, or unfairly distributed. Measures of test reliability are rarely the province of classroom-based assessment, but rather of statistical psychometric research.

More practically, in routine classroom tests, you may have experienced a test administration in which noise (from a street outside), temperature (overheating or cooling), or light (a burned-out light fixture) impaired some students but not all students equally. Those are cases of test administration unreliability. Sometimes a test yields unreliable results because of factors beyond the control of the test writer, but within the test taker, such as illness, a "bad day," or no sleep the night before (student-related reliability).

Scorer reliability sometimes refers to the consistency of scoring by two or more scorers, but for classroom teachers and your own classroom-based assessment, it's rare that you will have the luxury of a second scorer or grader. So, how does scorer reliability enter into the picture when you are the only scorer? Unclear scoring criteria, fatigue, carelessness, or a bias toward "good" and "bad" students can all play a part in our own unreliability. If subjective techniques or fuzzy scoring criteria are employed in the grading of a test, reliability can suffer. Or let's say you have 40 tests to evaluate before morning and it's late at night and you're very tired: application of your criteria for judgment could become inconsistent. If scoring directions are clear and specific as to the exact details that you should attend to, then such scoring can become reasonably consistent and dependable.

Validity

By far the most complex criterion of a good test is **validity**, the degree to which the test actually measures what it is intended to measure. A valid test of reading ability is one that actually measures reading ability and not, say, 20/20 vision, previous knowledge of a subject, or some other variable of questionable relevance. To measure writing ability, one might conceivably ask students to write as many words as they can in fifteen minutes, then simply count the words for the final score. Such a test would be easy to administer (practical), and the scoring quite dependable (reliable). But it would hardly constitute a valid test of writing ability unless some consideration is given to the communication and organization of ideas, among other factors.

Some have felt that standard language proficiency tests, with their context-reduced, CALP (cognitive academic language proficiency) oriented language and limited stretches of discourse, are not valid measures of language "proficiency" because they do not appear to tap into the communicative competence of the learner. There is good reasoning behind such criticism; nevertheless, what such proficiency tests lack in validity, they gain in practicality and reliability. We will return to the question of large-scale proficiency later in this chapter.

Classroom Connections

"That's a very reliable test!" your friend exclaims, actually meaning that it's *valid*, in that it tested exactly what it proposed to test. It's easy to confuse reliability and validity, partly because the two principles are interconnected. Can you think of a test (or a test administration) of an L2 skill that is reliable but not valid? Is the converse also true—can a test be valid but unreliable? In your own teaching, how can you work toward creating valid tests?

How does one establish the validity of a test? Statistical correlation with other related measures is a standard method. But ultimately, validity can be established only by observation and theoretical justification. There is no final, absolute, and objective measure of validity. We have to ask questions that give us convincing evidence that a test accurately and sufficiently measures the test-taker for the particular objective, or criterion, of the test. If that evidence is there, then the test may be said to have criterion validity.

In tests of language, validity is supported most convincingly by subsequent personal observation by teachers and peers. The validity of a high score on the final exam of a foreign language course will be substantiated by "actual" proficiency in the language. A classroom test designed to assess mastery of a point of grammar in communicative use will have validity if test scores correlate either with observed subsequent behavior or with other communicative measures of the grammar point in question.

How can teachers be somewhat assured that a test, whether it is a standardized test or one constructed for classroom use, is indeed valid? Three types of validation are important in your role as a classroom teacher: content validity, face validity, and construct validity.

Content Validity

If a test actually samples the subject matter about which conclusions are to be drawn, if it requires the test-taker to perform the behavior that is being measured, it can claim **content validity**. You can usually determine content validity, observationally, if you can clearly define the achievement that you are measuring. A test of tennis competency that asks someone to run a 100-yard dash lacks content validity. If you are trying to assess a person's ability to speak a second language in a conversational setting, a test that asks the learner to answer paper-and-pencil multiple choice questions requiring grammatical judgments does not achieve content validity. A test that requires the learner actually to speak within some sort of authentic context does.

Classroom Connections

In many contexts a *renewal* of a driver's license occasionally demands responding to multiple choice questions about safe distances, speeds, turns, stop signs, and the like. Pass that test plus maybe an eye test, pay your money, and you're licensed to drive for a few more years! Does the multiple-choice test have *content* validity (without a behind-the-wheel test)? How do motor vehicle agencies justify giving you a renewed license on the basis of such a test? In your own learning or teaching of an L2, can you think of language test methods that are low on content validity?

In most human situations, we are best tested in something when we are required to perform a sampling of the criterion behavior. But there are a few highly specialized and sophisticated testing instruments that do not have high content validity yet are nevertheless valid. Projective personality tests are a prime example. The Thematic Apperception Test and the Rorschach "inkblot" tests have little content validity, yet they have been shown to be accurate in assessing certain types of deviant personality behavior. A test of field independence as a prediction of language success in the classroom may have potentially good criterion validity but poor content validity in that the ability to detect an embedded geometric figure bears little direct resemblance to the ability to speak and hear a language. As already noted, standard proficiency tests often don't get high scores on content validity.

Face Validity

A concept that is very closely related to content validity is **face validity**, which asks the question, "Does the test, on the 'face' of it, appear from the learner's perspective to test what it is designed to test?" To achieve "peak" performance on a test, a learner needs to be convinced that the test is indeed testing what it claims to test. Here's a case in point: A *dictation* test and a *cloze* test were once administered as a *placement* test for an experimental group of learners of English as a second language. Some learners were upset because such tests, on the *face* of it, did not appear to them to test their true abilities in English. In reality, the dictation + cloze proved to be an excellent device; only one or two out of 40 students had to be reassigned to a new level. Face validity is almost always perceived in terms of content: if the test samples the actual content of what the learner has achieved or expects to achieve, then face validity will be perceived.

 **Classroom Connections**

Sometimes face validity is the most important type of validity for classroom assessment. Why is that? Have you ever taken a test that you *thought* was unfair or irrelevant to the proposed criterion? If there are tests that you use in the L2 classroom that you think might be incorrectly perceived, what can you do as a teacher to help your students understand its overall validity?

Construct Validity

A third category of validity that teachers must be aware of in considering language tests is **construct validity**. One way to look at construct validity is to ask the question "Does this test actually tap into the theoretical construct as it has been defined?" "Proficiency" is a construct. "Communicative competence" is a construct. "Self-esteem" is a construct. Virtually every issue in language learning and teaching involves theoretical constructs. Tests are, in a manner of speaking, operational definitions of such constructs in that they operationalize the entity that is being measured (Bachman & Palmer, 2010; Chapelle & Plakans, 2013; Kunnan & Grabowski, 2014).

A teacher needs to be satisfied that a particular test is an adequate definition of a construct. Let's say you have been given a procedure for conducting an oral interview. The scoring analysis for the interview weighs several factors into a final score: pronunciation, fluency, grammatical accuracy, vocabulary use, and sociolinguistic appropriateness. The justification for these five factors lies in a theoretical construct that claims those factors as major components of oral proficiency. So, on the other hand, if you were asked to conduct an oral proficiency interview that accounted only for pronunciation and grammar, you could be justifiably suspicious about the construct validity of such a test.

Most of the tests that you will encounter as a classroom teacher can be validated adequately through content; if the test samples the outcome behavior, then validity will have been achieved. But when there is low, or questionable, content validity in a test, it becomes very important for a teacher to be assured of its construct validity. Standardized tests designed to be given to large numbers of students might have low content validity but demonstrate high construct validity. For example, until recently a number of highly respected worldwide tests of English ability did not sample oral production, yet through statistical analyses were able to show high construct validity.

There are other forms of validity that you might want to consider (Brown & Abeywickrama, 2010, pp. 34–36; McNamara, 2010; Chapelle, 2011), but these three are the most relevant to classroom-based assessment, and are at the same time indispensable to your understanding of what makes a "good" test.

Authenticity

A fourth major principle of language testing is **authenticity**, a concept that is a little slippery to define, especially within the art and science of evaluating and designing tests. Bachman and Palmer (1996, p. 23) define authenticity as "the degree of correspondence of the characteristics of a given language test task to the features of a target language task," and then suggest an agenda for identifying those target language tasks and for transforming them into valid test items.

Essentially, when you make a claim for authenticity in a test task, you are saying this is a task that is likely to be enacted in the "real world." Many test item types fail to simulate real-world tasks. They may be contrived or artificial in their attempt to target a grammatical form or a lexical item. The sequencing of items that bear no relationship to one another lacks authenticity. One does not have to look very long to find reading comprehension passages in proficiency tests that hardly reflect a real-world passage.

Classroom Connections

Many teachers say the more you try to include authentic material in an assessment, the more difficult it is to make sure you're testing your intended objectives, and the design of tasks is complicated. Why is this so? Let's say your curriculum lists 20 vocabulary items that students should "know." How might you create an authentic test of reading that includes those very items while maintaining both authenticity and validity?

In a test, authenticity may be present in the following ways:

Criteria for Designing an Authentic Test

- The language in the test is as natural as possible.
- Items are contextualized rather than isolated.
- Topics and situations are interesting, enjoyable, and humorous.
- Thematic organization to items is provided (e.g., through a storyline).
- Tasks represent, or closely approximate, real-world tasks.

The authenticity of test tasks in recent years has increased noticeably. Two or three decades ago, unconnected, contrived items were accepted as a necessary by-product of testing. Things have changed. It was once assumed that large-scale testing could not stay within budgetary constraints and include performance of the productive skills, but now many such tests offer speaking and writing components. In the Internet version (iBT) of the TOEFL, for example, some tasks involve reading + listening + speaking or reading + listening + writing (Kunnan & Grabowski, 2014). Elsewhere, reading passages are selected from real-world sources that test-takers are likely to have encountered or will encounter someday. Listening comprehension sections feature natural language with hesitations, white noise, and interruptions. More and more tests offer items that are "episodic" in that they are sequenced to form meaningful units, paragraphs, or stories.

Washback

When students take a test, ideally they will receive information (feedback) about their competence, based on their performance. That feedback should "wash back" to them in the form of useful diagnoses of strengths and weaknesses. **Washback** also includes the effects of an assessment on teaching and learning prior to the assessment itself, that is, on preparation for the assessment. Informal assessment is by nature more likely to have built-in washback effects, because the teacher is usually providing interactive feedback. Formal tests can also have positive washback, but they are also subject to an absence of washback if students simply receive a letter grade or a single overall numerical score.

The challenge to teachers is to create classroom tests that serve as learning devices through which washback is achieved. Students' incorrect responses can become windows of insight into further work. Their correct responses may need to be praised, especially when they represent accomplishments in a student's interlanguage. Teachers can suggest strategies for success as part of their "coaching" role. Washback enhances a number of basic principles of language acquisition: autonomy, self-confidence, identity, and investment, among others.

One way to enhance washback is to comment generously and specifically on test performance. Many teachers, in our overworked (and underpaid!) lives, return tests to students with a single letter grade or numerical score on them, and consider our job done. In reality, letter grades and a score showing the number right or wrong give absolutely no information of intrinsic interest to the student. Grades and scores reduce a mountain of linguistic and cognitive performance data to an absurd molehill. At best, they give a relative indication of a formulaic judgment of performance as compared to others in the class—which fosters competitive, not cooperative learning.

Classroom Connections

In your own L2 learning, recall tests that you took in which you received little or no beneficial washback. Let's say a teacher returned a reading/grammar test with only check marks next to the wrong answers. How would you transform that into a more beneficial washback-giving experience?

With this in mind, when you return a written test or a data sheet from an oral production test, consider giving more than a number, grade, or phrase as your feedback. Even if your evaluation is not a neat little paragraph appended to the test, at least you can respond to as many details throughout the test as time will permit. Give praise for strengths—the "good stuff"—as well as constructive criticism of weaknesses. Give strategic hints on how a student might improve certain elements of performance. In other words, take some time to make the test performance a fulfilling experience through which a student will feel a sense of accomplishment.

A little bit of washback may also accrue to students through a specification to the student of the numerical scores on the various subsections of the test. A section on verb tenses, for example, that yields a relatively low score may serve the diagnostic purpose of showing the student an area of challenge.

Washback also implies that students have ready access to you to discuss the feedback and evaluation you have given. You may have known teachers in your life with whom you wouldn't dare "argue" about a grade. In an interactive, cooperative, collaborative classroom, one could hardly promote such an atmosphere. For learning to continue, students need to have a chance to "feed back" on your feedback, to seek clarification of any issues that are fuzzy, and to appropriately set new goals for themselves for the days and weeks ahead.

Washback may also imply the benefit learners experience in their preparation for a test, before the fact. (We might playfully call this "wash *forward*.") By using appropriate strategies for reviewing, synthesizing, and consolidating of material before taking a test, students may find that the preparation time is as beneficial as the feedback received after the fact. Sometimes, preparation and reviewing before a test is even *more* instructive than the test itself! You can be a facilitator in this process by helping to direct your students toward productive and relevant reviewing techniques.

You now have five basic principles for designing effective tests and assessments in your classroom, as illustrated in the summary in Table 20.1.

If in your language teaching you can attend to these principles in evaluating or adapting existing procedures, or in designing new ones on your own, then you are well on the way to making accurate judgments about the competence of the learners with whom you are working.

Table 20.1 Principles of assessment

Principle	Associated Concepts
1. Practicality	clear administrative details
2. Reliability	consistency
3. Validity	assessment of intended objective
a. content	test tasks involve performance of the objective
b. face	test appears valid to the test taker
c. construct	support through statistical and other research
4. Authenticity	natural, real-world tasks
5. Washback	positive, useful feedback to test taker

KINDS OF TESTS

There are many kinds of tests, each with a specific purpose and a particular criterion to be measured. Below you will find descriptions of five test types that are in common use in language curricula. Explanations here are only for the purpose of helping you to identify and differentiate among types, not to serve as a manual for designing such tests.

Proficiency Tests

If your aim in a test is to tap global competence in a language, then you are, in conventional terminology, testing proficiency. A **proficiency test** is not intended to be limited to any one course, curriculum, or single skill in the language. Proficiency tests have traditionally consisted of standardized multiple-choice items on grammar, vocabulary, reading comprehension, aural comprehension, and sometimes a sample of writing. Such tests often have content validity weaknesses as already noted above, but after several decades of construct validation research, some great strides have been made toward constructing communicative proficiency tests.

 **Classroom Connections**

You are no doubt among millions who have taken *high stakes* standardized tests, the results of which had a monumental impact on your life. College entrance exams, for example, rely on a few hours of your performance to determine your future in higher education. How could you help your students to receive beneficial washback (or "wash forward") from such an anticipated moment coming up in their lives?

Typical examples of standardized proficiency tests are the *Test of English as a Foreign Language* (TOEFL), now in Internet format (iBT), and the *International English Language Testing System* (IELTS). Together, they are used by thousands of educational institutions as an indicator of a prospective student's ability to undertake academic or professional work in an English medium. Both TOEFL and IELTS consist of performance on all four skills and both are computer-based. The comprehension sections (listening and reading) of virtually all large-scale proficiency tests are computer-scorable for rapid turnaround and cost effectiveness. Production performance (speaking and writing) usually demands human scorers.

Diagnostic Tests

A **diagnostic test** is designed to diagnose a particular aspect of a language. A diagnostic test in pronunciation might have the purpose of determining which phonological features of English are difficult for a learner and should therefore become a part of a curriculum. Usually, such tests offer a checklist of features for the administrator (often the teacher) to use in pinpointing difficulties. A writing diagnostic would first elicit a writing sample from students. Then, the teacher would identify, from a list of rhetorical features that are already present in a writing course, those on which a student needs to have special focus. It is not advisable to use a general achievement test (see below) as a diagnostic, because diagnostic tests need to be specifically tailored to offer information on student need that will be worked on imminently. Achievement tests are useful for analyzing the extent to which students have acquired language features that have already been taught.

Placement Tests

Certain proficiency tests and diagnostic tests can act in the role of **placement tests**, whose purpose is to place a student into an appropriate level or section of a language curriculum or school. A placement test typically includes a sampling of material to be covered in the curriculum (that is, it has content validity), and it thereby provides an indication of the point at which the student will find a level or class to be neither too easy nor too difficult, but appropriately challenging

Achievement Tests

An **achievement test** is related directly to classroom lessons, units, or even a total curriculum. Achievement tests are limited to particular material covered in a curriculum within a particular time frame, and are offered after a course has covered the objectives in question. Achievement tests can serve as indicators of features that a student needs to work on in the future, but the primary role of an achievement test is to determine acquisition of course objectives at the end of a period of instruction.

Aptitude Tests

Finally, we need to consider the type of test that is given to a person *prior* to any exposure to the second language, a test that predicts a person's future success. A language aptitude test is designed to measure a person's capacity or general ability to learn a foreign language and to be successful in that undertaking (DeKeyser & Koeth, 2011). Aptitude tests are considered to be independent of a particular language.

Two standardized aptitude tests were once in popular use—the *Modern Language Aptitude Test* (MLAT) (Carroll & Sapon, 1958) and the *Pimsleur Language Aptitude Battery* (PLAB) (Pimsleur, 1966). Both are English language tests and require students to perform such tasks as memorizing numbers and vocabulary, listening to foreign words, and detecting spelling clues and grammatical patterns. The validity of both tests rested on correlations between such tasks and subsequent performance in foreign language courses.

This genre of aptitude test is seldom used today. Research has not yet pinpointed exactly what the components of aptitude are and how they might interact with each other. DeKeyser and Koeth (2011) claim that the only ability so far that has promise of predicting language success is *working memory*, with a good deal of research yet to be done "to come to a fuller understanding of the exact role working memory plays in the learning process" (p. 402). More disturbing is an ethical issue: If you could actually predict a learner's ultimate success in learning an L2 *a priori*, what would you do with that information?

Classroom Connections

In the 1960s and 1970s, some institutions used results of the MLAT to place high-scoring MLAT takers into "accelerated" levels of L2 classes, and, of course, those that were lower scoring were presumed to be less capable of learning the language. How do you think it affected the teacher to know that his or her students were *predicted* to be "high" or "low" achievers? Is it educationally, psychologically, and ethically appropriate to use aptitude tests to predict (before the fact) ultimate success?

A better tack is to probe the relationship between the strategic abilities of would-be language learners and their eventual success in natural, real-world input generation, interaction, and output performance (Robinson, 2005). Any test that claims to *predict* success in learning a language is undoubtedly flawed, because we now know that, with appropriate self-knowledge, active strategic involvement in learning, and/or strategies-based instruction, virtually everyone can succeed eventually.

ISSUES IN LANGUAGE ASSESSMENT

Historically, language testing trends and practices have followed the changing winds and shifting sands of methodology described earlier in this book (Chapter 2). For example, in the mid-twentieth century, an era marked by the popularity of behavioral psychology and structural linguistics, special attention was given to phonological, grammatical, and lexical contrasts between two languages, and to specific language elements. This emphasis bolstered what was known as **discrete point testing**, which assumed that language could be broken down into its component parts, and those parts could be adequately tested.

In the 1970s and 1980s, communicative approaches to language teaching ushered in a more **integrative** view of testing in which assessment specialists claimed that "the whole of the communicative event was considerably greater than the sum of its linguistic elements" (Clark, 1983, p. 432). Research began to show that language ability could not be captured in additive tests of grammar, reading, vocabulary, and other discrete points of language (Cziko, 1982; Savignon, 1982). A more valid form of assessment, argued Bachman (1990) and others, was the incorporation of the tenets of communicative competence (Canale & Swain, 1980) into **communicative language testing**.

Today, test designers are still challenged in their quest for more authentic, content-valid instruments that simulate real-world interaction while still meeting reliability and practicality criteria (Leung & Lewkowicz, 2006). And with the "social turn" in SLA research and pedagogy, language assessment is further challenged to account for culture, identity, social interaction, and agency as important factors in the learning of an L2 (Chapelle, 2011).

In recent years, some giant strides have been taken to improve the construction, delivery, and scoring of assessments. From an era not too many decades ago when virtually all tests were thought to necessitate decontextualized linguistic stimuli of dubious authenticity, we have emerged into a new world of more communicative, authentic, performance-based assessment. Nevertheless, many challenges remain—in the world of commercial production of language tests and in the language classroom. Let's look at a few of those highlights.

Large-Scale Tests of Language Ability

The first issue that springs into the mind of most of us when "language testing" is mentioned is our global obsession over **high stakes** standardized tests, mass produced by corporations and government agencies, hailed as empirically validated, thought to provide accurate measures of ability, and used to make crucial decisions about one's future path. Are such tests valid? Are they authentic? To what use are they put? What are the *consequences* for the test takers? The accumulated research on language testing in the last decade or two witnessed its share of challenges as well as accomplishments in creating large-scale, standardized tests (Kunnan, 2013).

In order to test tens if not hundreds of thousands, the principle of practicality is always foremost. The following challenges, among many others, must be met:

- in a world of commercial competition, costs must be within reach of customers
- assessing multitudes of test takers requires intricate procedures to protect the security of items and forms
- tasks need to be designed to mirror language tasks of the real world, yet allow for rapid (computer-based) scoring at a marketable cost.

Among recent accomplishments (McNamara, 2010; Chapelle, 2011; Kunnan, 2013) are:

- increased focus on the *communicative* components of assessment
- inclusion of sociolinguistic and *sociocultural* factors in test tasks
- recognition of *varieties* of L2s, especially important in the case of English (Leung & Lewkowicz, 2006)
- greater attention to designing tests for *specific purposes* (Douglas, 2005)
- utilizing results of research in *corpus linguistics*, now with comprehensive corpora in both written and oral form (Conrad, 2005)
- unparalleled sophistication in *online* delivery and scoring of instruments (Jamieson, 2005)

CLASSROOM CONNECTIONS

To what extent have you seen evidence of the above list of "accomplishments" in recent standardized tests? How significant is *practicality* in the design, administration, and scoring of such tests? How can teachers effectively influence the large corporations and agencies that create standardized tests that don't measure up to this list of six accomplishments?

Authenticity

A second and related current issue in language assessment is authenticity. Earlier in this chapter you were introduced to authenticity as one of five major underlying principles of language assessment. The focus in language pedagogy on communication in real-world contexts has spurred many attempts to create more communicative assessment procedures. Current approaches (Leung, 2005; Chapelle, 2011; Kunnan, 2013) reveal that assessment specialists *and* classroom teachers are addressing the issues named above, including an emphasis on authenticity.

One of the keystones of language ability is the interactive nature of language, which means that tests should involve people in actually performing the behavior that we want to measure. Paper-and-pencil or computer-delivered multiple-choice tests certainly do not involve test-takers in speaking, requesting, responding, interacting, or in combining listening and speaking, or reading and writing. Interactive testing involves students in all of the above rather than relying on the assumption that a good paper-and-pencil test-taker is a good overall language performer.

Several decades ago Mueller (1987, p. 124) proposed taking "the audacious step of making testing truly interactive: . . . a lively exchange of stimulating ideas, opinions, impressions, reactions, positions or attitudes. Students can be actively involved and interested participants when their task is not restricted to providing the one and only correct answer."

Creating authentic tasks within formal assessment procedures presents some dilemmas. Authentic tasks can be complex and lack practicality (Alderson & Banerjee, 2002; Kunnan, 2013). They are difficult to create and even more difficult to evaluate because they often involve reliability issues. An oral interview can go a long way toward authenticity, but the possibility of unpredictable responses from test takers could mean making a "judgment call" that could be inconsistent. Another problem raised by authentic assessment tasks is how to judge the difficulty of a task, an important factor in standardized testing (Leung & Lewkowicz, 2006). Authentic tasks are rarely confined to one simple level of difficulty across phonological, syntactic, discourse, and pragmatic planes.

Finally, authenticity almost always means the integration of two or more skills, and so how is an evaluator to judge, say, both the listening competence and the speaking competence of a learner on an interview task? They are interdependent skills, and so, for example, a speaking error may actually stem from a listening error.

Performance-Based Assessment

Closely related to the issue of authenticity is what has come to be called **performance-based assessment**. An authentic task in any assessment implies that the test taker (or classroom student) must engage in actual performance of the specified linguistic objective. In educational settings around the world, test designers and classroom teachers are now tackling this new agenda (Leung, 2005; Katz, 2014). Instead of just offering single-answer tests of possibly hundreds of discrete items, performance-based testing of typical school subjects involves

- open-ended problem solving tasks
- hands-on projects
- student portfolios and journals
- experiments
- tasks in various genres of writing
- group projects

 **CLASSROOM CONNECTIONS**

All six of the items listed above seem like common techniques used frequently in communicative L2 classrooms. Why do they appear in this list as performance-based *test* tasks? What is the difference between treating these as teaching techniques and as testing techniques?

To be sure, such testing is time-consuming and therefore expensive, but the losses in practicality are made up for in higher validity. Students are tested as they actually perform the behavior itself. In technical terms, higher content validity is achieved as learners are measured in the process of performing the objectives of a lesson or course.

In the context of L2 classrooms, performance-based testing means that you may have a difficult time distinguishing between formal and informal testing. If you do a little less setting aside of formally structured techniques labeled as "tests" and a little more formative evaluation during students' performance of various tasks, you will be taking some steps toward meeting some of the goals of performance-based testing.

Expanding the "IQ" Concept of Intelligence

Intelligence was once viewed strictly as the ability to perform linguistic and logical-mathematical problem solving. This "IQ" concept of intelligence has for decades permeated educational contexts worldwide. Because "smartness" in general is measured by timed, discrete-point tests consisting of many little items, then why shouldn't every field of study be so measured? Today we still live in a world of standardized, norm-referenced tests that are timed, multiple-choice, tricky, long, and artificial.

Research on intelligence by psychologists like Gardner (1983, 1999), Sternberg (1985, 1997), and Goleman (1995) challenged the traditional psychometric orthodoxy. Standard theories of intelligence, on which standardized IQ (and other) tests are based, were expanded to include inter- and intra-personal, spatial, kinesthetic, contextual, and emotional intelligences, among others. (For a summary of these theories of intelligence, see *PLLT*, Chapter 4.)

These new conceptualizations of intelligence coincided with a sense of both freedom and responsibility in our testing agenda. We are somewhat freed from exclusive reliance on timed, discrete-point, analytical tests in measuring language. We are being liberated from the "tyranny" of objectivity and its accompanying impersonal treatment of learners whose identities and agency are at stake. But we are also assuming the responsibility for tapping into multiple language skills, learning processes, and most importantly the social consequences (McNamara, 2010) of language testing.

Classroom Connections

The concept of multiple intelligences has been quite popular among teachers. Why is that so? Do you feel that inter- and intra-personal, spatial, kinesthetic, contextual, and emotional abilities are part of what you would call *intelligence*? What are some ways that *teaching* techniques tasks might incorporate the various intelligences? How about *testing* tasks?

Alternatives in Classroom-Based Assessment

Implied in some of the above discussions are two interconnected current challenges. Performance-based assessment that embodies a learner-centered, authentic approach to designing assessment tasks goes hand in hand with an increasing recognition (and celebration) of classroom teachers as wholly capable professionals who can design their own classroom-based procedures with confidence (Jamieson, 2011; Katz, 2014). In the "old" days, teachers labored under the impression that test design must be left to the experts and it was the teacher's job to simply trust those experts and administer their tests. There was something wrong with this picture!

Current practice sees a great deal of action by teachers more and more involved in the creation of their own instruments and/or the willing adaptation of published tests for their own classroom context. In what has come to be known as **classroom-based assessment** (Leung, 2005; Jamieson, 2011; Katz, 2014), a number of current challenges and issues merge: authentic assessment, performance-based assessment, formative assessment (designed to facilitate a student's continued *formation* of language competence), informal assessment, and alternatives in assessment.

Let's make something clear: *alternatives* in assessment are not the same as *alternative* assessment, a term that conveys the wrong message. To speak of *alternative* assessment implies something that is on the periphery or "exempt from the requirements of responsible test construction" (Brown & Hudson, 1998, p. 657). Instead, alternatives in assessment recognize that tests are one of many possible methods or designs within the superordinate concept of assessment. Table 20.2 highlights how such alternatives differ from traditional tests.

It should be noted here that traditional testing offers significantly higher levels of practicality. Considerably more time and higher institutional budgets

Table 20.2 Traditional tests and alternatives in assessment

Traditional Tests	Alternatives in Assessment
One-shot, standardized exams	Continuous long-term assessment
Timed, multiple-choice format	Untimed, free-response format
Decontextualized test items	Contextualized tasks
Scores suffice for feedback	Formative, interactive feedback
Norm-referenced scores	Criterion-referenced scores
Focus on the "right" answer	Open-ended, creative answers
Summative	Formative
Oriented to product	Oriented to process
Non-interactive performance	Interactive performance
Fosters extrinsic motivation	Fosters intrinsic motivation

are usually required to administer and evaluate assessments that require more subjective evaluation, more individualization, and more interaction in the process of offering feedback. The payoff for the latter, however, comes with more useful washback to students, better possibilities for individualization, recognition of students' identity formation, and ultimately greater validity.

Classroom Connections

Why do the "alternatives" listed here have lower levels of *practicality* than traditional tests? Do they make up for that in higher *validity*? Which, if any, of the traditional characteristics here would you say are good models for *teaching*? What could you do to make your classroom assessment process more like the alternatives and less like the traditional?

We'll say more about alternatives in assessment in Chapter 21. Meanwhile, you may also want to consult Brown and Abeywickrama (2010), Chapter 6, for a complete treatment of alternatives in assessment.

The "Social Turn" and Language Assessment

Recent theoretical positions on SLA have brought to the foreground what has come to be called the "social turn" in accounting for L2 development (Block, 2003; Ortega, 2009; Duff, 2012; Norton, 2013; Pavlenko, 2013). In Chapters 4 and 5 of this book, we explored the importance of *agency* for a learner of an L2, that is, "people's ability to make choices, take control, self-regulate, and thereby pursue their goals as individuals, leading potentially to personal or social transformation" (Duff, 2012, p. 417). When learners capitalize on their role as an agent, they can make specific efforts to take on new roles and identities within their communities of practice and sociocultural milieu.

Does this social perspective apply to language assessment? In short, yes. First, we have already noted the incorporation of pragmatic, sociolinguistic, and cultural dimensions of language into test *tasks*. Authenticity, which must account for the social, cultural, and political milieu of test takers, cannot be achieved if social dimensions are ignored (Ross, 2011; Kunnan, 2013). The test form used for test takers in Japan may differ considerably from a form of the same test used in Brazil, thus involving a possibly difficult but necessary process of equating the two forms.

A further implication of the social turn in language testing involves direct attention to the *consequences* of tests, which may also be seen as *washback*, but usually on a larger scale than classroom instruction alone. Two decades before SLA researchers talked about a social turn, Messick (1989) referred to *validity* as "the degree to which empirical evidence and theoretical rationale support the *adequacy and appropriateness of inferences and actions* based on test scores" (p. 13). His statement shows "a concern for the social and political function of language tests [and] the social consequences of test use" (McNamara, 2010, p. 109).

For more on this topic, see Brown and Abeywickrama (2010), Chapters 4 and 5.

Critical Language Assessment

Closely related to the social nature of assessment is the timely issue of **critical language assessment**. One of the byproducts of a rapidly growing testing industry is the danger of an abuse of power. "Tests represent a social technology deeply embedded in education, government, and business; as such they provide the mechanism for enforcing power and control. Tests are most powerful as they are often the single indicators for determining the future of individuals" (Shohamy, 1997, p. 2). Test designers, and the corporate sociopolitical infrastructure that they represent, have an obligation to maintain certain standards as specified by their client educational institutions. These standards bring with them certain ethical issues surrounding the **gate-keeping** nature of high-stakes standardized tests (Ross, 2011).

Assessment experts (Shohamy, 2001; Bachman, 2005; McNamara, 2010; Ross, 2011) have shown an increasing interest in the ethics of testing as a case of critical language testing (see Chapter 23 for a discussion of critical language pedagogy in general). Critical language testing research asks incisive questions about possible bias in large-scale testing, and claims in some cases that such tests are the "agent of cultural, social, political, educational, and ideological agendas that shape the lives of individual participants, teachers, and learners" (Shohamy, 1997, p. 3). The issues of critical language testing are numerous:

- Psychometric traditions are challenged by interpretive, individualized procedures for predicting success and evaluating ability.
- Test designers have a responsibility to offer multiple modes of performance to account for varying styles and abilities among test-takers.
- Tests are deeply embedded in culture and ideology.
- Test-takers are political subjects in a political context.

These issues are not new. As long ago as the 19th century, British educator F. Y. Edgeworth (1888) challenged the potential inaccuracy of contemporary qualifying examinations for university entrance. But in recent years, the debate has heated. More than a century later researchers continue to probe issues of critical language testing worldwide (Gould, 1996; Shohamy, 2000; Garrison, 2009; Ross, 2011; Kunnan & Grabowski, 2014).

Classroom Connections

Do you think the standardized testing industry wields too much power over students? And if it does, how might you as a teacher or teachers' organization begin to persuade those in "power" to refrain from pushing "ideological agendas"? What, if any, are the alternatives to these highly efficient, practical, computer scored and generated tests capable of testing massive numbers of people?

One of the problems of critical language testing is the widespread belief that standardized tests designed by reputable test manufacturers are infallible in their predictive validity. Universities, for example, will deny admission to a student whose test scores fall below the requisite score, even though that student, if offered other measures of language ability, might demonstrate abilities necessary for success in a university program. One standardized test is deemed to be sufficient; follow-up measures are considered to be too costly.

A further problem with a test-oriented culture lies in the agendas of those who design and those who utilize the tests. Here are a few examples:

- Tests are used in some countries to deny citizenship (Shohamy, 2001).
- Tests may be culture-biased and therefore may disenfranchise members of a non-mainstream value system.
- Test producers tend to be in a position of power over test-takers and therefore can impose social and political ideologies on test-takers through standards of acceptable and unacceptable items (Garrison, 2009).

- Tests may promote the notion that answers to real-world problems have unambiguous right and wrong answers with no "shades of gray."
- Tests usually reflect an appropriate core of common knowledge and acceptable behavior; therefore, the test-taker must buy into such a system of beliefs in order to pass the test (Ross, 2011).

As a language teacher, you might be able to exercise some influence in the ways tests are used and interpreted in your own context. Perhaps, if you are offered a variety of choices in standardized tests, you could choose a test that offers the least degree of *culture bias*. Or can you encourage the use of *multiple measures* of performance (varying item types, oral and written production, for example) even though this may cost more money? Furthermore, you might be instrumental in establishing an institutional system of evaluation that places less emphasis on standardized tests and more emphasis on the ongoing process of *formative evaluation* you and your co-teachers can offer. In so doing, you might offer educational opportunity to a few more people who would otherwise be eliminated from contention.

FOR THE TEACHER: ACTIVITIES (A) & DISCUSSION (D)

Note: For each of the "Classroom Connections" in this chapter, you may wish to turn them into individual or pair-work discussion questions.

1. **(A)** In groups each assigned to one of the four skills, have students brainstorm some techniques, activities, or tasks in about two minutes or less. Then, ask the groups to discuss the extent to which selected techniques have an *assessment* component to them, either explicit or implicit. Then have them report back to the class.
2. **(D)** Find a published classroom test (many textbook series include ready-made tests) and scan it for projection to the class or photocopy it for distribution of paper copies. With the class, analyze it according to each of the five principles described in this chapter. How does it measure up to each principle?
3. **(D)** Review with your class the distinction between content and construct validity. Then ask your students: If content validity is absent, why does construct validity assume greater importance? Why is there no final, absolute, and objective measure of validity? Why does validity ultimately go back to the rather subjective opinion of testers and theorists?
4. **(A)** Ask pairs or small groups to share experiences from their past experiences in L2 classes about tests that they thought had *high* or *low* face validity. Why is face validity important? Have pairs share their examples with the rest of the class.
5. **(A)** Review some of the problems of designing and using the results of language aptitude tests. Then, ask pairs to discuss the following issue: In

light of the discussion at the end of this chapter about ethical issues in language testing, is aptitude testing ethical? Why or why not? Have pairs briefly share their thoughts with the rest of the class.

6. **(D)** Solicit comments from students in the class on any experiences they have had taking large-scale standardized language tests (TOEFL, IELTS, TOEIC, etc.). To what extent can they be argued to be "communicative" as explained in this chapter? Were they authentic? Performance-based? What were the scores used for? Were specific purposes represented in the test?
7. **(A)** One of the current issues discussed here is authenticity. In pairs, have students brainstorm kinds of tests or other more informal assessments (in any or all skill areas) that fit into two categories: authentic and *in*authentic. Have pairs list their findings on the board, then share their thoughts with the rest of the class.
8. **(D)** Review the discussion of alternative views of intelligence. List several columns on the board: interpersonal, intrapersonal, spatial, contextual, emotional. Ask students to volunteer some *assessment tasks* that would tap into one or more of the intelligences. Write them on the board and then ask students to justify their position in a column or columns.
9. **(D)** Review with the class the notion that tests serve as "gatekeepers" in society. Among familiar standardized tests, what ethical issues might emerge? Does the testing industry promote a widening of gaps between educated and uneducated, rich and poor, "haves" and "have nots"?

FOR YOUR FURTHER READING

Brown, H. D., & Abeywickrama, P. (2010). *Language assessment: Principles and classroom practices* (2nd ed.). White Plains, NY: Pearson Education.

This might well be considered a "companion" volume to Teaching by Principles, with its comprehensive description of principles of assessment and an emphasis on classroom assessment.

Chapelle, C., & Plakans, L. (2013). Assessment and testing: Overview. In C. Chapelle (Ed.), *The encyclopedia of applied linguistics* (pp. 241–244). West Sussex, UK: Blackwell Publishing Ltd.

Kunnan, A., & Grabowski, K. (2014). In M. Celce-Murcia, D. Brinton, & M. A. Snow (Eds.), *Teaching English as a second or foreign language* (4th ed., pp. 304–319). Boston, MA: National Geographic Learning.

These two sources provide a survey of issues in language assessment. Both have useful bibliographic references to research in the field.

Kunnan, A. (2013). *The companion to language assessment.* Volumes 1, 2, 3, 4. Malden, MA: Wiley-Blackwell.

This literally voluminous reference (four volumes) provides virtually everything one would want to know about language assessment, some of it quite technical. The fourth volume (assessment around the world) is of the most practical use to the teacher.

DeKeyser, R., & Koeth, J. (2011). Cognitive aptitudes for second language learning. In E. Hinkel (Ed.), *Handbook of research in second language teaching and learning*: Volume II (pp. 395–406). New York, NY: Routledge.

An update on where we stand in measuring language aptitude. The bibliography is a useful set of references.

Shohamy, E. (2001). *The power of tests: A critical perspective on the use of language tests.* Harlow, UK: Pearson Education.

An excellent discussion of the way political and governmental agencies exert their power through large-scale mandatory language testing. An eye opener for the naïve.

CHAPTER 21

CLASSROOM-BASED ASSESSMENT

Questions for Reflection

- How do norm-referenced and criterion-referenced tests differ?
- How can one apply some principles for designing tests to the creation of classroom-based tests and other assessment procedures?
- What are some steps to creating revised, modified versions of existing tests that adhere to principles of authenticity and beneficial washback?
- To what extent can "alternatives" in assessment—portfolios, journals, conferences, observations, and self- and peer-assessment—become a standard part of L2 courses?
- How can teachers work toward treating assessment and teaching as *partners* in the learning process?

Tests have become a way of life in the educational world. In every learning experience there comes a time to pause and take stock, to put focal processes to their best use, and to demonstrate accumulated skills or knowledge. From pop quizzes to final exams to standardized entrance exams, tests are crucial milestones in the journey to success.

It's unfortunate, however, that learners all too often view tests as dark clouds hanging over their heads, upsetting them with lightning bolts of anxiety as they anticipate a hail of questions they can't answer and, worst of all, a flood of disappointment if they don't make the grade. Students tend to feel "prodded, jostled, or dragged by an establishment bent on spoiling what might otherwise be a pleasant student life" (Mueller, 1987, p. 124).

Tests have so pervaded students' lives that *cheating* has become a hot issue globally. Test takers have been known to pay high prices to clandestine "brokers" of answers to tests (Cizek, 1999). Internet sites offer "custom" made research papers on thousands of topics—for a price. To counteract the impulse to cheat, and try to get away with it, some researchers have documented hundreds of cheating methods that students have used (Cizek, 1999; Anderson, 2013), and offered advice to teachers and professors on how to prevent cheating.

Within this atmosphere, can tests be positive experiences? Can they build a person's confidence? Can they be part of an ongoing interaction between teacher and learners? Can they bring out the *best* in students? The answer is an encouraging *yes* when teachers and other educators understand the *benefits* of tests and their place within the larger domain of assessment.

In this chapter, we turn from the macro-issues and challenges of language assessment as a discipline to the day-to-day micro-issues that you face as a classroom teacher. The discussion in this chapter is designed to briefly acquaint you with some principles for designing your own tests, some steps to take in that process, and more details on some of the alternatives in assessment that were mentioned in the previous chapter. The underlying theme of this exploration is an emphasis on assessment as a positive, motivating, feedback-giving element of second language learning in the classroom.

NORM-REFERENCED AND CRITERION-REFERENCED TESTS

Before proceeding directly to the process of designing and implementing tests in your classroom, a few words are necessary in order to make one more distinction. The dichotomy between norm- and criterion-referenced testing is not just another technical construct that you can soon forget once you've read this chapter. Rather, the two concepts help to resolve a misunderstanding that teachers have had (Jamieson, 2011). Sometimes teachers think that every classroom test, quiz, or exercise should be mathematically scored, charted, and assigned percentiles or quartiles. Not so! Nor should a large-scale proficiency test be expected to be responsive to some of the criteria demanded of classroom tests.

In **norm-referenced** tests, each test-taker's score is interpreted in relation to a mean (average score), median (middle score), standard deviation (extent of variance in scores), and/or percentile rank. The purpose in such tests is to place test-takers along a mathematical continuum in rank order, and little else. If test takers are *differentiated* through their performance on the instrument, the mission of a norm-referenced test has virtually been accomplished. Scores are usually reported back to the test-taker in the form of a numerical score (e.g., 230 out of 300) and/or a *percentile* rank (e.g., 84%, which means that the test-taker's score was better than 84% of the total number of test-takers, but below 16% of the test-takers).

Typical of norm-referenced tests are standardized tests like the Scholastic Aptitude Test (SAT), Graduate Record Examination (GRE), and the Test of English as a Foreign Language (TOEFL and iBT), intended to be administered to large audiences, with results efficiently disseminated to test-takers. Such tests usually have fixed, predetermined responses in a format that can be quickly scored at minimum expense. Money and efficiency are important concerns in these tests. Therefore, the principles of practicality, reliability, and validity are primary.

Criterion-referenced tests, on the other hand, are designed to give test-takers feedback on specific course or lesson *objectives*, or the *criteria* of the course. Classroom achievement tests involving just the students in one class, and connected to a curriculum, are typical of criterion-referenced testing. Here, there is a significant responsibility on the part of the teacher (as the test administrator) to deliver useful, appropriate feedback to students, or "instructional value" (Oller, 1979, p. 52). Such tests help teachers to "target feedback, . . . to reinforce successful learning and to identify learning errors and misconceptions" (Jamieson, 2011, p. 769).

In a criterion-referenced test, the distribution of students' scores across a continuum may be of little concern, as long as the instrument assesses appropriate objectives. In the following sections of this chapter, with its emphasis on classroom-based assessment (as opposed to standardized, large-scale testing), criterion-referenced testing emerges as a more significant focus. The principle of practicality still remains important to you, but authenticity and especially washback are of primary concern.

 **CLASSROOM CONNECTIONS**

In simple terms, *criterion* is another word for objective, aim, or goal. With that in mind, what are some objectives of, let's say, a lesson in a beginning course on pronunciation of English word stress patterns? What would a few sample *criterion-referenced* test tasks look like?

So, the next time you're perplexed about why a large-scale test doesn't provide washback, or why students' scores on your biweekly quizzes don't adhere to a normal curve, or why it takes such a long time to evaluate your students' essays, or why a multiple-choice test may not elicit actual language performance from students in your classroom, you might find answers in the nature of criterion-referenced versus norm-referenced testing. For the remainder of this chapter, we'll be looking strictly at the former: tests and assessments in your classroom designed to elicit performance on the specific criteria, or objectives, of your course.

SOME PRACTICAL STEPS TO TEST CONSTRUCTION

If you haven't already had an occasion to create and administer a classroom test, your time is coming soon! Now that you have read about testing issues in this and the previous chapter, you may be thinking that tests can only be designed by "experts." Not so! Yes, it takes some practice and experience, but there's no time like the present to dive into your own test creation.

Your best tack as a new teacher is to work within the guidelines of accepted, known testing techniques, and you can still work to create a valid, reliable test that's practical enough for your needs. And you can give it an authentic, interesting flavor. Slowly, with experience, you will get bolder in your attempts—which we'll talk about in the next section of the chapter. In that spirit, here are some practical steps to take in constructing classroom tests.

1. Test Toward Clear, Unambiguous Objectives

In Chapters 9 and 10, you were strongly advised to state clear, specific objectives for courses and lessons. Doing so enables you to focus clearly on such objectives (or criteria) when it comes to either informal or formal assessment. Likewise, for a test that you design, make sure that students actually perform the criterion objectives that your test was designed to assess. You *don't* want your students to say after a test, "I don't see a connection between your test and what we studied."

You need to know as specifically as possible what it is you want to test. Sometimes teachers give tests only because it's Friday or it's the third week of the course. After hasty glances at the chapter(s) covered during the period, they dash off some test items so the students will have something to do during the class period. This is no way to approach a test! Instead, carefully list everything that you think your students should "know" or be able to "do," based on the material the students are responsible for.

Your "objectives" can, for testing purposes, be as simple as the following list of grammatical structures and communicative skills in a unit that, let's say, you have recently taught:

Grammar

Tag questions
Simple past tense in negative statements and information questions
Irregular past-tense verbs
Who as subject
Anyone, someone, and *no one*
Conjunctions *so* and *because*

Communication Skills

Stating guesses about what happened
Asking about who did something
Talking about family and friends
Talking about famous people and events
Giving reasons
Asking for confirmation

Classroom Connections

The target grammar points listed above are not stated in the form of *performance* (what the student is expected to *do*). How would you incorporate some of those grammatical items into statements about what students are expected to *do* (to perform) in the communication skills (also listed above)?

2. From Your Objectives, Draw Up Test Specifications

Now, this sounds like you're supposed to have a Ph.D. in psychometrics! Wrong. Test specifications for classroom use can be a simple and practical outline of your test. Let's say you are testing the above unit. Your specifications should indicate what skills you will test, what the items or tasks will look like, how many items will be included in each section, and how you will divide up the total time set aside for the test:

Guidelines for Designing Test Specifications

- topics (objectives) to be covered
- item types to be used in the test
- approximate number of items in each section
- time allocations for each section

For the above mentioned unit, your "specs" for a 45-minute test may look something like this:

Listening (15 Minutes)

Part 1: Minimal sentence pairs (choose the sentence that you think you hear) [10 pairs, 2 themes]

tag questions
negative statements
guessing what happened
finding out who did something

Part 2: Conversation (choose the correct answer) [5 items]
- information questions
- talking about family and friends

Multiple Choice (10 minutes) [15 items in a storyline (cloze) format]
- simple past tense
- past irregular verbs
- *anyone, someone,* and *no one*

Writing production (15 minutes) [topic: Why I liked/didn't like a recent movie]
- affirmative and negative statements
- conjunctions *so* and *because*
- giving reasons

Notice that a couple of communication skills and one grammatical structure are not tested—this may be a decision based on the time you devoted to these objectives, or only on the finite number of minutes available to administer the test. Notice, too, that this course quite likely has a good deal of oral production in it, but for reasons of practicality (perhaps oral testing was done separately?), oral production is also not included on this test.

3. Draft Your Test

A first draft will give you a good idea of what the test will look like, how students will perceive it (face validity), the extent to which authentic language and contexts are present, the length of the listening stimuli, how well a storyline comes across, how things like the cloze testing format will work, and other practicalities. Your items may look like these:

Listening, Part 1 (theme: last night's party)

1. Teacher says: We did make a mess last night, didn't we?

Student reads:

(a) We didn't make a mess last night, did we?

(b) We did make a mess last night, didn't we?

Listening, Part 2 (theme: still at the party)

2. Voice A. Mary, who was that gorgeous man I saw you with at the party?

Voice B. Oh, Nancy, that was my brother!

Student reads:

(a) Mary's brother is George.
(b) Nancy saw Mary's brother at the party.
(c) Nancy's brother is gorgeous.

Multiple choice (theme: still at the party)

Student reads:

Then we ____ 3 ____ the loudest thunder you have ever heard! And of course right away lightning ____ 4 ____ right outside the house!

3. (a) heared **(b)** did hear **(c)** heard
4. (a) struck **(b)** stricken **(c)** strack

Ideally, for the sake of authenticity, you should enlist the aid of a colleague and make a recording in which each of you reads a different part so that students will readily perceive that two people are speaking. If time, equipment, and colleagues don't permit this, make sure that if you read the two parts, you differentiate clearly (with voice and also by bodily facing in two different directions) between the two characters.

As you can see, these items are quite traditional. In fact, you could justifiably object to them on the grounds that they ask students to rely on short-term memory and on spelling conventions. But the thematic format of the sections, the authentic language, and the contextualization add face validity, interest, and intrinsic motivation to what might otherwise be a mundane test. And the essay section adds some creative production to help compensate for the lack of an oral production component.

4. Pilot the Test in a "Trial Run"

All your carefully designed techniques may not be perfect! In an ideal situation, you would try out your test on some *students* before actually administering them. But practically, piloting a test with your students is virtually impossible, and so you must do what you can to bring to your students an instrument that is, to the best of your ability, practical, reliable, and valid.

The solution may be to do a "trial run" of the test *yourself*, as if you are one of your students. Go through each set of directions and all items slowly and deliberately, timing yourself as you do so. Often we underestimate the time students will need to complete a test. If the test needs to be shortened or lengthened, make the necessary adjustments. An alternative is to ask a colleague to do this for you (and reciprocate by taking your colleague's test), and you'll then have another pair of eyes and ears checking for items, timing, or other elements that might need revision.

Classroom Connections

Is it absurd to suggest that you take your own test? After all, you know the answers ahead of time! Can you put yourself "in the shoes" of one of your students? What can you learn from taking your own test, beyond the suggestions about timing mentioned above?

5. Revise Your Test

At this stage, you will work through all the items you have devised and ask a number of important questions:

Checklist for Revision of a Classroom Test

1. Are the directions to each section absolutely clear?
2. Is there an example item for each section?
3. Does each item measure a specified objective?
4. Is each item stated in clear, simple language?
5. Does each multiple-choice item have appropriate distracters, that is, are the wrong items clearly wrong and yet sufficiently "alluring" that they aren't ridiculously easy?
6. Does the difficulty of each item seem to be appropriate for your students?
7. Do the sum of the items and test as a whole adequately reflect the learning objectives?

Your own answers to these questions should uncover any problems you did not see in the previous four stages, and lead to minor revisions.

6. Finalize the Test

A final edit is now in order. In your final editing of the test, make sure your test is neat and uncluttered on the page (or on a computer screen), reflecting all the care and precision you have put into its construction. If your test has a listening component, make sure your script is clear and that any audio equipment you will use is in working order. If a computer, laptop, or other technology is involved, make sure everything is up and running smoothly.

 **CLASSROOM CONNECTIONS**

Tests are prominent among all the *technology* available to aid teachers in our daily pedagogy. Most textbooks now come with digital or web-based supplementary quizzes and tests. An Internet search readily comes up with quizzes indexed by grammatical or discourse categories. How would technological media aid *you* in helping students review for tests, or in your own delivering of classroom tests?

7. Utilize Your Feedback after Administering the Test

After you give the test, you will have some information about how easy or difficult it was, about the time limits, and about your students' reactions to it and their general performance. Take note of these forms of feedback and use them for making your next test.

8. Provide Ample Washback

As you evaluate the test and return it to your students, your feedback should reflect the principles of *beneficial* washback discussed earlier. Use the information from the test performance as a springboard for review and/or for moving on to the next unit.

TRANSFORMING AND ADAPTING EXISTING TESTS

For many language learners, the mention of the word *test* evokes images of walking into a classroom after a sleepless night of anxiously sitting hunched over a test page while a clock ticks ominously, and of a mind suddenly gone empty as they vainly attempt to "multiple guess" their way through the ordeal. How can you, as a classroom teacher and designer of your own tests, change this image?

Now that you have considered standard steps for creating a somewhat traditional classroom test, let's go a little further. Consider the following five guidelines for converting what might be ordinary, traditional tests into authentic, interesting, appropriately challenging, washback-giving learning opportunities designed for learners' best performance and for optimal feedback.

1. Facilitate Strategic Options for Test-Takers

The first principle is to offer your learners appropriate, useful strategies for taking the test. With some preparation in test-taking strategies, learners can allay some of their fears and put their best foot forward during a test. Through strategies-based test-taking, they can avoid miscues due to the format of the test alone. They should also be able to demonstrate their competence through an optimal level of performance.

Swain (1984) referred to the principle of "bias for best" as an important goal for teachers in designing tests. In other words, design, prepare, administer, and evaluate tests in such a way that the *best* performance of your students will be elicited! One of the ways to bias your test for best performance is by encouraging before-, during-, and after-test options, as listed below.

Before-, During-, and Post-Test Strategies

Before the Test

1. Give students all the information you can about the test. Exactly what will the test cover? Which topics will be the most important? What kind of items will be included? How long will it be?
2. Encourage students to do a systematic review of material. For example: skim the textbook and other material, outline major points, write down examples, etc.
3. Give them practice tests or exercises, if available.
4. Facilitate formation of a study group, if possible.
5. Caution students to get a good night's rest before the test.
6. Remind students to get to the classroom early.

During the Test

7. As soon as the test is distributed, tell students to quickly look over the whole test in order to get a good grasp of its different parts.
8. Remind them to mentally figure out how much time they will need for each part.
9. Advise them to concentrate as carefully as possible.
10. Alert students a few minutes before the end of the class period so that they can proofread their answers, catch careless errors, and still finish on time.

After the Test

11. When you return the test, include feedback on specific things the student did well, what he or she did not do well, and if possible, the reasons for such a judgment on your part.
12. Advise the student to pay careful attention in class to whatever you say about the test results.
13. Encourage questions from students.
14. Advise students to make a plan to pay special attention in the future to points that they are weak on.

Classroom Connections

Let's say you have helped your students adopt the above strategies for taking an upcoming test. Now, as the teacher, what other ways can you "bias" the test for "best" performance by the student? What other hints can you give them for optimal performance? On the other hand, how do you balance difficult and easy items so that the test will be a *challenge*?

2. Establish Face Validity

Sometimes students don't know what is being tested when they tackle a test. Sometimes they feel, for a variety of possible reasons, that a test isn't testing what they feel it was intended to test. Face validity, as we saw in the previous chapter, means that in the students' perception, the test is valid. You can help to foster that perception in the following ways:

Guidelines for Ensuring the Face Validity of a Test

- Provide a carefully constructed, well-thought-out format.
- Make sure the test can be completed within the allotted time limit.
- Design items that are clear and uncomplicated.
- Make all your directions crystal clear—unambiguous.
- Design tasks that are familiar and relate to students' course work.
- Gauge a difficulty level that is appropriate for your students.

3. Design Authentic Tasks

Make sure that the language in your test is as natural and authentic as possible. Also, try to give language some context so that items aren't just a string of unrelated language samples. Thematic organization of items may help in this regard. Or consider a storyline that may run through your items.

Also, the tasks themselves need to be tasks in a form that students have practiced and feel comfortable with. A classroom test is not the time to introduce brand-new tasks because you won't know if student difficulty is a factor of the task itself or of the language you are testing.

4. Distinguish between Summative and Formative Assessment

A few of your classroom tests will be **summative**: they will serve the purpose of "summing up" what students can perform. Placement tests, final exams, and end-of-unit tests are typical of this category. Other tests will very clearly have a **formative** purpose: they help students to "check" progress, to discern areas that need improvement, and to give them some future goals to pursue. They will help students to *form* their language learning process in the coming days or weeks. And of course, they will help *you* to tailor your instruction toward areas of need.

It's important to understand that "assessment tools in and of themselves are not summative or formative. It is the *purpose* to which they are put that determines how assessments are characterized" (Katz, 2014, p. 322). As the teacher, you will need to make the purposes clear, so that students can direct their efforts accordingly. There usually is more *washback* pertaining to formative assessment, as students will use the feedback from their performance to guide future pathways of learning.

CLASSROOM CONNECTIONS

What do you think is the difference in a *student's* mind between a test that he or she is taking that's summative versus one that's formative? In a test that's designed to serve a formative purpose, what kinds of feedback (written, verbal, a conference, notes, scores, etc.) can you give in order for students to gain the most washback from their performance?

5. Work for Beneficial Washback

Washback, described in Chapter 20, is the effect that tests have on prior preparation and on learning as the result of having taken the test. Washback, as we saw earlier, can be positive (beneficial) or negative (detrimental), and our mission as teachers is to accentuate the positive!

When students take a test, they should be able, within a reasonably short period of time, to utilize the information about their competence that test feedback offers. Formal tests should therefore be learning devices through which students can receive a diagnosis of areas of strength and weakness. Their incorrect responses can become windows of insight about further work. Your prompt return of written tests with your feedback is therefore very important to your students' motivation.

One way to enhance beneficial washback is to provide a generous number of specific comments on test performance. We teachers, in our overworked (and underpaid!) lives, can slip into the habit of returning tests to students with a letter grade or number score on them, and consider our job completed. In reality, letter grades and a score showing the number right or wrong give absolutely no information of intrinsic interest to the student. Grades and scores reduce a mountain of linguistic and cognitive performance data to an absurd minimum. At best they give a relative indication of a formulaic judgment of performance as compared to others in the class—which fosters competitive, not cooperative, learning.

So, when you return a written test, or even a data sheet from an oral production test, consider giving more than a number or grade or phrase as your feedback. Even if your evaluation is not a neat little paragraph, at least you can respond to as many details in the test as time permits. Give praise for strengths—the "good stuff"—as well as constructive criticism of weaknesses. Give strategic hints on how a student might improve certain elements of performance. In other words, take some time to make the test performance an experience through which a student will feel a sense of accomplishment and challenge. In so doing, you will be "linking assessment to learning" (Katz, 2014, p. 324).

Another way to increase *investment* among students is to involve them in the design and review process (what we've called the "wash forward" effect in Chapter 20), and in the evaluation of responses afterward. Depending on a number of contextual variables in your plan to assess students, peer feedback can be an excellent way for learners to gain washback from the test.

 **Classroom Connections**

What are some advantages to involving students in designing their own tests and in self- or peer-evaluation? What are some drawbacks to this kind of student-centered pedagogy? To what extent would you have to maintain some control or restriction over the process? How would you do that?

Finally, washback also implies that students have ready access to *you* to discuss the feedback and evaluation you have given. We're sure you have known teachers with whom you wouldn't dare argue about a grade. Such a tyrannical atmosphere is out of place in an interactive, cooperative, intrinsically motivating classroom. For learning to continue, learners need to have a chance to respond to your feedback, to seek clarification on any fuzzy issues, and to set new appropriate goals for themselves for the days and weeks ahead.

ALTERNATIVES IN ASSESSMENT

So far in this chapter, the focus has been on the administration of formal tests in the classroom. It was noted earlier that *assessment* is a broad term covering any conscious effort on the part of a teacher or student to draw some conclusions on the basis of performance. Tests are a special subset of the range of possibilities within assessment; of course, they constitute a very salient subset, but not all assessment consists of tests.

In recent years language teachers have stepped up efforts to develop non-test assessment options that are nevertheless carefully designed and that adhere to the criteria for adequate assessment (Law & Eckes, 2007). Sometimes such innovations are referred to as *alternative* assessment, if only to distinguish them from *traditional* formal tests. However, as you saw in Chapter 20, we're opting for Brown and Hudson's (1998) phrase, *alternatives in assessment*, which emphasizes the responsibility to apply all assessment principles to such options, and *not* to treat them as strange aberrations of normal assessment practices.

Several alternatives in assessment will be briefly discussed here. For a more detailed description and analysis of these options, consult our companion text, *Language Assessment: Principles and Classroom Practices* (Brown & Abeywickrama, 2010), Chapter 6.

Portfolios

One of the most popular forms of alternative assessment within a communicative framework is the construction of portfolios (Brown, 1998). A portfolio is "a purposeful collection of students' work that demonstrates to students and others their efforts, progress, and achievements in given areas" (Genesee & Upshur, 1996, p. 99). Portfolios include essays, compositions, poetry, book reports, art work, video or audio recordings of a student's oral production, journals, and virtually anything else one wishes to specify. In earlier decades of our history, portfolios were thought to be applicable only to younger children who assembled a portfolio of art and written work for presentation to a teacher and/or a parent. But now, learners of all ages and in all fields of study are benefiting from the tangible, hands-on nature of portfolio development.

Following are some hints for using portfolios as a form of classroom-based assessment:

Guidelines for Portfolio Use

- Specify to students what the purpose of the portfolio is (to emphasize accomplishments, to offer tangible material for feedback from the teacher, etc.).
- Give clear directions to students on how to get started (many students will never have compiled a portfolio before and may be mystified about what to do). Showing a sample portfolio from a previous student might help to stimulate thoughts on what to include.
- Give guidelines on acceptable material to include.
- Collect portfolios on pre-announced dates and return them promptly.
- Be clear yourself on the principal purpose of the portfolio and make sure your feedback speaks to that purpose.

- Help students to process your feedback and show them how to respond to your responses. This processing might take place in a conference, or simply through written feedback.
- If feasible, utilize *web-based* or *online* opportunities for portfolio compilation and sharing. Many teachers now have class websites that give teacher and students easy access to announcements, supplementary materials, discussions, and posting of student-generated material.

Classroom Connections

You are no doubt quite familiar with the many ways that the *social media* (through smart phones, tablets, and other portable technology) open up vistas of opportunity for communications that can be shared instantly with any number of people you wish. What are some of the ways you could bring *web-based* technology into productive forms of assessment in your L2 class?

Journals

Usually one thinks of journals simply as opportunities for learners to write relatively freely without undue concern for grammaticality. Journals can have a number of purposes: language learning logs; grammar discussions; responses to readings; self-assessment; and reflections on attitudes and feelings about oneself. Recently, the assessment qualities of journal writing have assumed an important role in the teaching–learning process. Because journal writing is a dialogue between student and teacher, journals afford a unique opportunity for a teacher to offer various kinds of feedback to learners. A carefully specified, systematic approach is important:

Using Journals as Assessment Instruments

- Specify to students what the purpose of the journal is (response to reading, learning log, grammar commentary, etc.).
- Give clear directions to students on how to get started (many students will never have written a journal before and may be mystified about what to do). Sometimes an abbreviated model journal entry helps.
- Give guidelines on length of each entry and any other format expectations.

- Collect journals on pre-announced dates and return them promptly. If using *online* technology, adhere to promised time lines.
- Be clear yourself on the principal purpose of the journal and make sure your feedback speaks to that purpose.
- Help students to process your feedback, and show them how to respond to your responses. If feedback and student response is online, make sure your students are clear about the process.

Conferences

For a number of years, conferences have been a routine part of language classrooms, especially courses in writing. Conferencing can serve a number of possible functions; among them are the following:

Advantages of Conferencing

- commenting on drafts of essays and reports
- reviewing portfolios
- responding to journals
- advising on a student's plan for a paper or presentation
- exploring compensatory strategies to overcome weaknesses
- giving feedback on the results of performance on a test
- setting learning goals for the near future

Conferencing has become a standard part of the process approach to teaching writing, as the teacher, in a conversation about a draft, facilitates the improvement of the written work. Such interaction has the advantage of allowing one-on-one communication between teacher and student such that the specific needs of a student can receive direct feedback. Conferences can be *in-person* (for maximum exchange of ideas) or *computer-based* through blogs and other online media.

Classroom Connections

In your L2 learning, have you ever had a conference with your teacher? Perhaps over a draft of an essay or an oral performance? Were you anxious about those moments, one-on-one with your teacher? How would you help your students to approach a conference with low anxiety and the feeling that they are not so much being judged as "coached"?

Through conferences, a teacher can assume the role of a facilitator and guide, rather than a master controller and deliverer of final grades. In this embracing atmosphere, students can feel that the teacher is an ally who is encouraging self-reflection. It's important to consider a conference as a dialogue that is *not* to be graded. Conferences are by nature formative, not summative; formative assessment points students toward further development, rather than offering a final summation of performance.

Observations

One of the characteristics of an effective teacher is the ability to *observe* students as they perform. Teachers are constantly engaged in a process of taking students' performance and intuitively assessing it and using those evaluations to offer feedback. Without ever administering a test or a quiz, teachers know a lot about their students. In fact, experienced teachers are so good at this almost subliminal process of assessment that their estimates of a student's competence are often highly correlated with actual independently administered test scores.

On the other hand, teachers' intuitions about students' performance are not infallible, and certainly both the reliability and face validity of their feedback to students can be increased with the help of empirical means of observing their language performance. Observations can become systematic, planned procedures for real-time, almost surreptitious recording of student verbal and nonverbal behavior. One of the objectives of such observation is to assess students as much as possible without their awareness (and possible consequent anxiety) of the observation, so that the naturalness of their linguistic performance will be maximized. Checklists, charts, rating scales, systematic note-taking, and teachers' journals can all help to support our intuitive observations and to provide a source of identifiable feedback to students.

What kinds of student performance can be the subject of such observations? Consider a few possibilities:

Observations: Suggestions for What to Look For

- sentence-level oral production micro- and macroskills
- interaction with classmates (cooperation, frequency of oral production)
- frequency of student-initiated responses (whole class, group work)
- quality of teacher-elicited responses
- evidence of listening comprehension (questions, clarifications, attention giving verbal and nonverbal behavior)
- evidence of attention span issues, learning style preferences, etc.

- use of strategic options in comprehension or production (use of communication strategies, avoidance, etc.)
- culturally specific linguistic and nonverbal factors (kinesics, proxemics, use of humor, slang, metaphor, etc.)

In order to carry out classroom observation, it is, of course, important to be clear about why you are observing, what you are observing, how you will observe (what system you will use), and how you will convey your perceptions to your students. Checklists and grids are a common form of recording observed behavior. In Spada and Fröhlich's (1995) system, grids capture such variables as whole-class, group, and individual performance, formal versus functional errors, and which one of the four skills is involved. The observer identifies performance and checks appropriate boxes in the grid. Checklists need not be that elaborate. Simpler options—noting occurrences of student errors in certain grammatical categories, or "action zones" in the classroom, for example—may be more realistic.

Rating scales have also been suggested for recording observations. One type of rating scale asks teachers to indicate the frequency of occurrence of target performance on a separate frequency scale (always = 5; never = 1). Rating scales may be appropriate for recording observations after the fact – on the same day but after a class period, for example. Specific quantities of occurrences may be difficult to record while teaching a lesson and managing a classroom, but immediate subsequent evaluations might offer some data on observations that will certainly fade from memory by the next day or so.

Classroom Connections

Have you been a student in an L2 class in which you and your classmates were being observed? How did you feel about that? What kinds of feedback would you like to receive from an observer as you're learning an L2? How could your own observations of L2 students be made as useful as possible, for students as well as the teacher?

You will probably find moderate practicality and reliability in observations, especially if the objectives are kept simple. Face validity and content validity are likely to get high marks because observations are likely to be integrated into the ongoing process of a course. Authenticity is high because, if an observation goes relatively unnoticed by the student, then there is little likelihood of contrived situations. Washback can be high if you take the time and effort to help a student to become aware of your data on their performance.

Self- and Peer-Assessments

A conventional view of language pedagogy might consider self- and peer-assessment to be an absurd reversal of the teaching–learning process. After all, how could learners who are still in the process of acquisition, especially the early processes, be capable of rendering an accurate assessment of their own performance? But a closer look at the acquisition of any skill reveals the importance, if not the necessity, of self-assessment and the benefit of peer-assessment. What successful learner has not developed the ability to monitor his or her own performance and to use the data gathered for adjustments and corrections? Successful learners extend the learning process well beyond the classroom and the presence of a teacher or tutor, autonomously mastering the art of self-assessment. And where peers are available to render assessments, why not take advantage of such additional input?

Research has shown (O'Malley & Pierce, 1996; Brown & Hudson, 1998; Alderson & Banerjee, 2001) a number of advantages of self and peer-assessment: speed, direct involvement of students, the encouragement of autonomy, and increased motivation because of self-involvement in the process of learning. Of course, the disadvantage of *subjectivity* (which leads to unreliability) looms large, and must be considered whenever you propose to involve students in self- and peer-assessment.

Classroom Connections

What, besides subjectivity, are some other disadvantages of self- and peer-assessment? In your own classroom, how would you help to minimize the risk of widely varying standards, which then threatens reliability? To what extent do you rely on students' honesty and goodwill in undertaking self- or peer-assessment?

Following are some ways in which self- and peer-assessment can be implemented in language classrooms.

Implementing Self- and Peer-Assessment Across the Four Skills

- Oral production: student self-checklists; peer checklists; offering and receiving a holistic rating of an oral presentation; listening to tape-recorded oral production to detect pronunciation or grammar errors; in natural conversation, asking others for confirmation checks; setting goals for creating opportunities to speak

- Listening comprehension: listening to TV or radio broadcasts and checking comprehension with a partner; in pair or group work, asking when you don't understand something; listening to an academic lecture and checking yourself on a "quiz" of the content; setting goals for increasing opportunities for listening
- Writing: revising written work on your own; revising written work with a peer (peer-editing); proofreading; setting goals for increasing opportunities to write
- Reading: reading textbook passages followed by self-check comprehension questions; reading and checking comprehension with a partner; vocabulary quizzes; self-assessment of reading habits; setting goals

SCRUTINIZING THE ALTERNATIVES

As you consider using some of the alternatives that have just been described, two factors deserve your attention and application: maximizing practicality and reliability in your procedures, and focusing on your students' actual language performance.

Maximizing Practicality and Reliability

The classroom-based tests described in the first part of this chapter, as well as the alternatives in assessment, are contextualized to a specific curriculum, referenced to criteria (objectives) of a course or module, offer greater potential for both authenticity and washback, and, in the case of the "alternatives," are open-ended in their response format and time orientation. This is a very different picture from large-scale standardized tests structured for computer delivery and rapid machine scoring.

One way of looking at this contrast poses a rather tantalizing challenge to you as a teacher and test designer. Formal standardized tests are almost by definition highly practical, reliable instruments. They are designed to minimize time and money on the part of test designer and test-taker, and to be painstakingly accurate in their scoring. Alternatives such as portfolios, or conferencing with students on drafts of written work, or observations of learners over time, all require considerable time and effort on the part of the teacher and the student.

Even more time must be spent if the teacher hopes to offer an evaluation that is *reliable*—within students across time, as well as across students (taking care not to favor one student or group of students). But the latter techniques also offer markedly greater washback, are superior formative measures, and, because of their authenticity, usually carry greater face validity.

Classroom Connections

Maintaining *reliability* in some of the alternatives in assessment is often a challenge for teachers. Even for "grading" traditional tests, reliability can become a factor: you grow tired of "marking" the same test over and over; you subconsciously are biased favorably toward some students. In instruments like portfolios and journals, your reliability must be consistent across weeks and months. How do you achieve that?

Does this mean that multiple-choice formats are inevitably devoid of authenticity and washback? And that the more open-ended, long-term alternatives are by nature unreliable and will forever cost teachers sleepless nights? We hope not. The challenge that faces us all as conscientious teachers and assessors in our profession is to change this perception. With some creativity and effort, we can transform otherwise inauthentic and negative-washback-producing tests into more pedagogically fulfilling learning experiences by doing the following:

Balancing Principles of Assessment

- Build as much authenticity as possible into multiple-choice task types and items.
- Design classroom tests that have both objective-scoring sections and open-ended response sections: varying the performance tasks.
- Turn multiple-choice test results into diagnostic feedback on areas of needed improvement.
- Maximize the preparation period before a test to elicit performance relevant to the ultimate criteria of the test.
- Teach test-taking strategies.
- Help students to see beyond the test: Don't "teach to the test."
- Triangulate information on a student before making a final assessment of competence.

The flip side of this challenge is to understand that the alternatives in assessment are not by nature destined to flounder in a quagmire of impracticality and unreliability. As we look at alternatives in assessment in this chapter, we must be mindful of Brown and Hudson's (1998) admonition to scrutinize the practicality, reliability, and validity of those alternatives at the same time that we celebrate their face validity, washback potential, and authenticity. It is easy to fly out of the cage of traditional testing rubrics, but it is tempting in doing so to flap our wings aimlessly accepting virtually any classroom activity as a viable alternative. Assessments that are proposed to serve as triangulating measures of competence imply a responsibility to be rigorous in determining objectives, response modes, and criteria for evaluation and interpretation.

Performance-Based Assessment

A second interesting factor at play in the alternatives in assessment is a recognition of the importance of **performance-based assessment**, sometimes merely called *performance assessment* (Leung & Lewkowicz, 2006; Katz, 2014). The push toward more performance-based assessment is part of the same general educational reform movement that has raised strong objections to using standardized test scores as the only measures of student competencies (Kohn, 2000). The argument, as you can guess, is that standardized tests, to some extent, do not elicit actual performance on the part of test-takers.

CLASSROOM CONNECTIONS

Large-scale standardized tests often benefit from substantial research that validates test tasks and test takers' results. If you found over the years that a *cloze* test (reading, fill in the blank) was *highly* indicative of students' writing ability, would you feel justified in using this very practical (easily and quickly scored) test method as a final "exam"? You would certainly feel confident about its *validity*. What's wrong with this reasoning?

Performance-based assessment implies productive, observable skills, such as speaking and writing, of content-valid tasks. Such performance usually, but not always, brings with it an air of authenticity—real-world tasks that students have had time to develop. They often imply an integration of language skills, perhaps all four skills in the case of portfolios and conferencing. Because the tasks that students perform are consistent with course goals and curriculum, students and teachers are likely to be more motivated to perform them, as opposed to a set of multiple-choice questions about grammaticality or reading comprehension.

O'Malley and Valdez-Pierce (1996, p. 5) considered performance-based assessment to be a subset of authentic assessment, with the following characteristics:

Authenticity in Performance-Based Assessment

- Students make a constructed response.
- They engage in higher-order thinking (analyzing, evaluating, applying, creating) with open-ended tasks.
- Tasks are meaningful and engaging.
- Tasks call for the integration of language skills.
- Both process and product are assessed.
- The depth of a student's mastery is emphasized over breadth.

Performance-based assessment needs to be approached with care. It is tempting for teachers to assume that if a student is *doing* something, then the process has fulfilled its own goal, and the evaluator needs only to make a check mark in the grade book next to a particular competency. In reality, performances as assessment procedures need to be treated with the same rigor as traditional tests. This implies that teachers would benefit from the following guidelines.

Guidelines for Performance-Based Assessment

- State the overall goal of the performance.
- Specify the objectives (criteria) of the performance in detail.
- Prepare students for performance in stepwise progressions.
- Use an evaluation form, checklist, or rubric to give students specific feedback (Brown & Abeywickrama, 2010, p. 129).
- Treat performances as opportunities for giving feedback and provide that feedback systematically.
- If possible, utilize self- and peer-assessments judiciously.

We hope that it's obvious by now that assessment is an integral part of the teaching-learning cycle. In fact, in an interactive, communicative curriculum, assessment is almost constant. Tests, as a subset of all assessment processes, are in keeping with many of the foundational principles that have been thematic in this book. And we like to think that all forms of assessment are partners in our pedagogical pursuits.

Assessment and teaching: Principled partners

- Assessments can spur learners to *notice* some of their linguistic development, and give *attention* to areas of needed development.
- Assessments encourage *retention* of information through the *rewarding* feedback they give to learners.
- Periodic assessments, both formal and informal, can increase *self-determination*, as they serve as milestones of student progress.
- Assessments can encourage students' *self-regulation*, as they develop *strategies* for success.
- Assessments can spur students to greater *investment* in their learning, and spur them to set *autonomous* goals for themselves.
- Assessments can, in many cases, involve *collaboration* and interaction, increasing students' sense of their *community in practice.*
- Assessments can promote student *empowerment* and *agency* as they confirm progress, growth, areas of strength, and what a learner can *do* with the language.

FOR THE TEACHER: ACTIVITIES (A) & DISCUSSION (D)

Note: For each of the "Classroom Connections" in this chapter, you may wish to turn them into individual or pair-work discussion questions.

1. **(A)** Teachers are called upon to play dual roles in the classroom. One is the role of a coach or guide, and the other is the role of a judge who administers tests and assigns grades. Ask pairs to discuss whether these two roles are conflicting. Then ask them to brainstorm some ways that a teacher can lessen the potential conflict such that one can play both roles. Then, have them share their ideas with the rest of the class.
2. **(D)** Review the distinction between norm- and criterion-referenced testing. Then ask the class for examples of each and for a justification of placing a test in one or the other category. Can a test fulfill both categories?
3. **(A)** This one might take up a full class hour to complete, or it could be an extra-class assignment. Ask pairs to design a relatively simple, brief classroom test for a specified purpose and an audience that they are familiar with, following the practical steps for test design in this chapter. On completion of the task, ask the class to describe any difficulties they had.
4. **(A)** Five guidelines were offered in this chapter (pp. 521–524) for turning traditional tests into more authentic, washback-giving, formative

experiences. Find several existing classroom tests (paper-based or web-based), print or digitally distribute them to groups, and ask the groups to *redesign* aspects of the test to fit some or all of the principles. Then have them share their results with the rest of the class.

5. **(D)** Ask your class to look again at the lists of strategies for test-takers and ask them the extent to which they used or didn't use those strategies in their own educational experiences. Which ones were the most useful?
6. **(D)** It was mentioned in this chapter that technology has become a key "player" in L2 classrooms. Ask your students to describe their experiences with computer-based large-scale testing. Did they find those experiences to be rewarding? Scary? Authentic? Ask them for pros and cons on computer-based or online testing.
7. **(A)** Ask groups to review the five different alternatives in assessment described in this chapter. Then have them (a) tell each other about any examples of any of the five that they have experienced in a previous L2 class, and (b) evaluate their success. Have groups share their findings with the rest of the class.
8. **(A)** Ask half of your class, in pairs, to brainstorm specific ways, with examples from tests that they know, in which standardized tests might be made to be more *authentic* and *washback giving*. Then ask the other half, also in pairs, to describe ways that the alternatives could become more *practical* (less time consuming to evaluate) and *reliable* (consistent evaluation criteria). Have them share their thoughts with the whole class.

FOR YOUR FURTHER READING

Brown, H. D., & Abeywickrama, P. (2010). *Language assessment: Principles and classroom practices* (2nd ed.). White Plains, NY: Pearson Education.

Brown, J. (2005). *Testing in language programs: A comprehensive guide to English language assessment.* New York, NY: McGraw-Hill.

Hughes, A. (2003). *Testing for language teachers* (2nd ed.). Cambridge, UK: Cambridge University Press.

All three of these books are practical in their attention to classroom testing techniques. Teachers are given numerous examples of tests covering varying skills and proficiency levels, along with guidelines and principles.

Brown, J. (1998). *New ways of classroom assessment.* Alexandria, VA: TESOL.

Law, B., & Eckes, M. (2007). *Assessment and ESL: An alternative approach.* Winnipeg, Canada: Portage & Main Press.

These books describe many different classroom assessment procedures, including portfolios, journals, conferences, and self- and peer-asessment.

Jamieson, J. (2011). Assessment of classroom language learning. In E. Hinkel (Ed.), *Handbook of research in second language teaching and learning, Volume II* (pp. 768–785). New York, NY: Routledge.

Katz, A. (2014). Assessment in second language classrooms. In M. Celce-Murcia, D. Brinton, & M. A. Snow (Eds.), *Teaching English as a second or foreign language* (4th ed., pp. 320–337). Boston, MA: National Geographic Learning.

Both of these book chapters summarize issues and provide practical examples of classroom-based assessment.

PART VI

LIFELONG LEARNING

Every effective teacher knows that the pursuit of excellence is a lifelong journey. From the first days of apprenticeship and training to the final stretches of experience perhaps decades later, we're in a constant state of change. This final section addresses the need for us as teachers to engage in the kind of reflection and "teacher-learning" that will continue to sharpen our senses and to improve our craft.

- **Chapter 22, Teacher Development,** outlines a number of suggestions for optimal development of your talents and skills. Suggestions are made for creative ways to engage in collaborative teacher development and in individual development.
- **Chapter 23, Teachers for Social Responsibility,** strikes at the "heart" of teaching: what beliefs, convictions, and personal ambitions drive you and challenge you in this profession of service to others? By examining the concept of social responsibility and critical pedagogy, we urge you to explore how you can be an agent of change in a world that longs for communication, understanding, healing, and peace.

CHAPTER **22**

TEACHER DEVELOPMENT

Questions for Reflection

- What are some of the qualities of "peak performers" in general?
- What are some key characteristics of successful language teachers in particular?
- What some potential personal goals one can set for optimal performance as a teacher?
- How can one insightfully observe other teachers in the process of teaching and apply those insights to oneself?
- What are some potential classroom-based research projects that one could engage in, for greater insight into the effectiveness of teaching?
- What are some guidelines for collaboration with one's colleagues in an effort to improve professional expertise?
- What are some avenues of individualized professional development?

One of the most invigorating things about teaching is that you never stop learning. The complexity of the dynamic triangular interplay among teachers and learners and subject matter continually gives birth to an endless number of questions to answer, problems to solve, issues to ponder. Every time you walk into a classroom to teach, you face some of those issues, and if you're a growing teacher, you learn something new yourself. You find out how well a technique works, how a student processes language, how classroom interaction can be improved, how to assess a student's competence, how emotions enter into learning, or how your teaching style affects learners. The discoveries go on and on—for a lifetime.

As you embark on this journey into the teaching profession, how can you best continue to grow professionally? How can you most fruitfully meet the challenges that lie ahead? Are there some practical goals that you can pursue? So far, as you have worked through the material of this book, you have already begun your own teacher development. Richards and Farrell (2005, pp. 6–7) frame this developmental process in terms of four conceptualizations of teacher learning:

Developmental Processes of Teacher Learning

1. **Skill learning**. Teachers develop basic skills (such as those addressed in this book, e.g., lesson design, classroom management, and performance assessment).
2. **Cognitive process**. Teachers formulate assumptions about SLA that stem from their background, experience, and knowledge.
3. **Personal construction**. Through an ongoing process of reorganization and reconstruction, teachers actively construct knowledge as new learning and experiences form a personal framework.
4. **Reflective practice**. Teachers critically examine and reflect on their own teaching experiences, leading to improvement and further development.

One of the major themes that continues to be expressed in current research on teacher development is a constructivist approach to development that highlights the active and responsible role of teachers to forge their own personal frameworks within their respective *situated contexts* (Bailey, Curtis, & Nunan, 2001; Hedgcock, 2002; Freeman, 2002; Borg, 2003b; Mann, 2005; Richards & Farrell, 2005; Johnson, 2006; Mullock, 2006; Richards & Farrell, 2011; Crandall & Miller, 2014).

Teachers are trained and continue their training in what Hedgcock (2002, 2009) described as **communities of practice** (Lave & Wenger, 1991) in which teachers of varying degrees of experience carry out their roles as practicing professionals who learn from each other. We best fulfill the goal of professional development *not* through a "transmission" model of education in which knowledge is simply deposited into the brains of teachers, but through a process model in which teachers learn and continue to develop their skill in dialogue with a professional community (Freire, 1970; Johnson, 2006).

Classroom Connections

If you have taught before, to what extent did you feel a part of a community of practice in which you and your colleagues were in dialogue with each other? If you have not taught, in what way does the methodology class you are now in act as that community? How might you enhance or expand that dialogue?

If you are a novice teacher reading and studying this book, your dialogue is just beginning. You have perhaps begun to move through the first two (skill learning, cognitive process) of the four elements of teacher development cited by Richards and Farrell (2005). Continuing to strengthen those two factors and moving into stages of personal construction and reflective practice (Murphy, 2014) is a process that will demand your patience and perseverance. Don't expect to become a "master" teacher overnight!

Right now, as you begin your teaching career, you can set some realistic, practical goals that you can focus on without being overwhelmed by everything you have to attend to when you teach. Just as beginning language learners are able to manage only a few bits of information at a time with capacity-limited systems, so it is with your teaching. If you try to focus on everything in the classroom (the management issues, techniques, delivery, body language, feedback, individual attention, lesson goals, mid-lesson alterations) all at once, you may end up doing nothing well. In due course of time, however, the abundance of cognitive/emotional phenomena in the classroom will be sufficiently automatic that you will indeed manage to operate on many planes simultaneously.

As you read on here, you will find some ideas that you can immediately put to work and others that may apply to you after you have gained some experience.

PEAK PERFORMERS

Are you doing the *best* you can do? Are you "being all that you can be"? Or are you satisfied with getting by? In the stressful (but rewarding) world of teaching, it's easier than you might imagine to slip into a pattern of just keeping one step ahead of your students as you struggle through long working hours and with large classes. This pattern is the beginning of a downward spiral that you should avoid at all costs. How do you do that? In part by practicing the behaviors of peak performers, people who are reaching their fullest potential and who therefore, in turn, reap success.

 **CLASSROOM CONNECTIONS**

In other endeavors you have undertaken—besides teaching—what did you do to become a *peak performer*? If you have been on a successful sports team, acted in a play, sung in a chorus, or become a really great cook, what were the "secrets" of your success? How do those same secrets apply to teaching?

Consider the following five maxims (among many) of peak performers (adapted from Covey, 1990, and others) that you might apply to yourself, even at this early stage in your career:

1. Believe in Yourself

Teaching is no easy profession. It requires deep dedication, a willingness to work long hours, a genuine desire to help other people, a commitment sometimes to "walk the second mile" in facilitating students' best performance, cognizance of a professional core of knowledge, an ability to be "on tap" in front of students many hours in a day, and more. Are you up to the (possibly) daunting prospect of being a teacher? Almost every "formula" for success begins with the importance of believing that you are fully capable of undertaking the task(s) at hand. So, at the outset, you need to be convinced that you can indeed be a teacher and be an excellent one!

2. Set Realistic Goals

Peak performers know their limitations and strengths and their feelings and needs, and then set goals that will be realistic within this framework. They set their own goals and don't let the world around them (colleagues, supervisors, or friends) dictate goals to them. If you have a sense of overall purpose in your career as a mission, then this mission will unfold in the form of daily, weekly, monthly, or annual goals.

It's always a good idea to write down some short-term and long-term goals. Be realistic in terms of what you can accomplish. Be specific in your statements. Here are some examples to get the wheels turning.

Guidelines for Setting Professional Goals

- Read *x* number of teacher resource books this year.
- Design my next test to be more authentic, biased for best, with maximum washback.
- Observe five other teachers this semester.
- Monitor my error treatments in the classroom.
- Attend two professional conferences/workshops this year.

3. Set Priorities

It's crucial that you have a sense of what is most important, what is least important, and everything in between, in your professional goals and tasks. If you don't, you can end up spending too much time on low-priority tasks that rob you of the time you should be spending on higher priorities. Priority-setting requires a sense of your whole professional and personal life, and how you are going to use your waking hours.

CLASSROOM CONNECTIONS

What are some of your priorities as you consider becoming a better, more skilled, more successful L2 teacher? Which of those would you place high on your list? Which should receive lower priority? Why did you place your priorities in that order?

4. Take (Calculated) Risks

Peak performers don't play it safe all the time. They are not afraid to try new things. Nor are they put off by limiting circumstances: what cannot be done, or "the way" things are done. They don't linger in the safety of a "comfort zone"; instead, they reach out for new challenges.

The key to risk-taking as a peak performance strategy, however, is not simply in taking the risks. It's in learning from your "failures." When you risk a new technique in the classroom, try a new approach to a difficult student, or make a frank comment to a supervisor, you must be willing to accept possible "failure" in your attempt. Then, you assess all the facets of that failure and turn it into an experience that teaches you something about how to calculate the next risk.

5. Reduce and Manage Stress Factors

Contrary to some perceptions from outside our profession, teaching is a career with all the makings for high-stress conditions. Think of some of the sources of stress in this business: long hours, large classes, low pay, pressure to "perform" in the classroom, high student expectations, professional demands outside the classroom, emotional connections with students' lives, sometimes parents of your students, bureaucracies, pressure to keep up with a rapidly changing field, and information overload. Wow! That's a lot to contend with. Managing those potential stress factors is an important key to keeping yourself fresh, creative, bright, and happy.

Here are few guidelines for stress management, some of which have been mentioned above:

STRESS MANAGEMENT GUIDELINES

- Set priorities.
- Know your limitations.
- Learn how to say "no" when you can. Don't take on too much.

- Balance your personal and professional time. Take time to "smell the roses"—read a novel; take a walk; go out to eat; see a movie; sing in a chorus; develop a hobby.
- Open up emotionally with a few people close to you. Don't bottle up feelings of frustration, anger, or sadness.
- Nurture fulfilling personal relationships with friends, significant others, and family.

Classroom Connections

Whether or not you are currently teaching, what are some of your stresses? How might you effectively take things in stride, and lessen the stress in your life? What are some other ways you could "smell the roses" in your life?

As you begin a teaching career, you may feel the weight of heavy demands. And teaching is not one of those careers where you can necessarily leave all the cognitive and emotional load in the office. But in the midst of all your professional demands, try to balance your life, and take everything in perspective.

EFFECTIVE LANGUAGE TEACHERS

One way to begin setting goals and priorities is to consider the qualities of an effective language teacher. Numerous experienced, seasoned teachers have come up with their lists of attributes, and they all differ in a variety of ways. Consider the following down-to-earth list of characteristics of language teachers who are successful in their art and craft (Allen, 1980; Pennington, 1990):

Characteristics of Effective Language Teachers

- competent preparation and knowledge of L2 pedagogical principles
- experience in teaching and ability to reflect on your practice
- a love of language
- critical thinking ability and analytical skills to assess your teaching
- willingness to take pedagogical risks in the classroom
- readiness to go the extra mile for your students
- cultural adaptability and openness to change

- interpersonal communication skills
- excitement to engage in professional development
- a feeling of being energized after teaching a class

Now, take a look at another list of successful language-teaching characteristics, a synthesis of several unpublished sources. You may wish to use this list as a self-check to earmark some areas for continued professional growth, to prioritize those areas, and to articulate some specific goals to pursue.

The items on both lists make a substantive list of challenges for your professional growth. However, they are not prescriptions! The key to healthy teacher development is to take a reflective approach, which "requires that teachers have the opportunities to observe, evaluate, and reflect systematically on their classroom practices in order to promote understanding and self-awareness and to make changes when necessary" (McDonough, 2006, p. 33). So, treat such lists as suggestions, possibilities, and perhaps mental prods to stimulate some further growth.

Characteristics of a Successful Language Teacher

Background Knowledge

1. Understands organizational, pragmatic, and sociocultural systems of the English language.
2. Comprehensively grasps basic principles of language learning and teaching.
3. Has fluent competence in speaking, writing, listening to, and reading English.
4. Knows through experience what it is like to learn a foreign language.
5. Understands the close connection between language and culture.
6. Keeps up with the field through regular reading, collaboration with others, and conference/workshop attendance.

Pedagogical Skills

7. Has a comprehensive, informed approach to language teaching.
8. Efficiently designs and executes lesson plans.
9. Understands and appropriately uses a variety of techniques.
10. Monitors lessons as they unfold and makes effective mid-lesson alterations.
11. Effectively perceives students' linguistic and personal needs, along with their various styles, preferences, strengths, and weaknesses.

12. Gives optimal feedback to students.
13. Stimulates interaction, cooperation, and teamwork in the classroom.
14. Uses appropriate principles of classroom management.
15. Uses effective, clear presentation skills.
16. Creatively adapts textbook material and other audio, visual, and technological aids.
17. Innovatively creates brand-new materials when needed.
18. Uses authentic, washback-giving techniques to assess students.

Interpersonal Skills

19. Is aware of cross-cultural differences and is sensitive to students' cultural traditions.
20. Enjoys people; shows enthusiasm, warmth, rapport, and appropriate humor.
21. Values the opinions and abilities of students.
22. Is patient in working with students of lesser ability.
23. Offers challenges to students of exceptionally high ability.
24. Cooperates harmoniously and candidly with colleagues, including seeking opportunities to share thoughts, ideas, and techniques.

Personal Qualities

25. Is well organized, conscientious in meeting commitments, and dependable.
26. Is flexible when things go awry.
27. Engages in regular self-reflection on teaching practices and strives to learn from those reflective processes.
28. Maintains an inquisitive mind in trying out new ways of teaching.
29. Sets short-term and long-term goals for continued professional growth.
30. Maintains and exemplifies high ethical and moral standards.

 **CLASSROOM CONNECTIONS**

Using the above list of 30 items as a checklist, rate yourself on a scale of 5 (yes, I do this consistently) to 1 (I need to do a lot of work on this one) for each item. What do you think? How can you make the lower-scoring items into a list of goals for yourself?

CLASSROOM OBSERVATION

One of the most neglected areas of professional growth among teachers is the mutual exchange of classroom observations. Once you establish a teaching routine, it's very difficult to make time to go and see other teachers and to invite the same in return. Too often, teachers tend to view observations as necessary while "in training" but unnecessary thereafter unless a supervisor is forced by regulations to visit their class in order to write up a recommendation for rehiring. If one of your colleagues comes up to you and says, "Hey, guess what? I was observed today," your answer might be something like "Oh, no! How bad was it?"

Fortunately, in an era of classroom-based research (see the next section in this chapter), the prevailing attitude toward observations is changing. Teachers are coming to understand that seeing their actions through another's eyes is an indispensable tool for classroom research as well as a potentially enlightening experience. Before you get into the habit of filling your time with everything else, why not carve out some time in your work schedule to visit other teachers and to invite reciprocity? As long as such visits pose no undue complication in schedules and other institutional constraints, you will reap rewarding benefits as you gain new ideas, keep fresh, and sharpen your own skills.

A second form of observation, which can be very effective in different ways, is self-observation. Actually, self-observation is no more than a systematic process of monitoring yourself, but it's the *systematic* part that is crucial. It requires discipline and perseverance, but the results are worth it. How do you go about observing yourself?

STEPS TO SELF-OBSERVATION OF TEACHING

1. **a.** One option is to select an element of your teaching to "keep an eye out for" as you teach. Examples include teacher talk, eye contact, teaching predominantly to one side of the classroom, and board work, among others. Limit yourself to just one or two elements.

   b. A second option is to use an observation checklist (see Figures 22.1 and 22.2 on pages 549–554, for suggested items to observe).
2. Preferably, video-record yourself for later viewing. Perhaps a colleague can manage the recording for close-ups and following action zones. While recording, monitor your focus element.
3. Later, view the recording and assess your success. You might then reflect on the experience in a personal journal. Better yet, partner with a colleague on all this, and then you can reciprocate.
4. Synthesize your reflections into a set of personal objectives for the near future.

Figure 22.1 Teacher observation form: observing other teachers

Circle or check each item in the column that most clearly represents your evaluation: 4 = excellent, 3 = above average, 2 = average, 1 = unsatisfactory, N/A = not applicable. You may also write comments in addition to or in lieu of checking a column.

I. Preparation

1. The teacher was well-prepared and well-organized in class. 4 3 2 1 N/A
   Comment:

2. The lesson reviewed material and looked ahead to new material. 4 3 2 1 N/A
   Comment:

3. The prepared goals/objectives were apparent. 4 3 2 1 N/A
   Comment:

II. Presentation

4. The class material was explained in an understandable way. 4 3 2 1 N/A
   Comment:

5. The lesson was smooth, sequenced, and logical. 4 3 2 1 N/A
   Comment:

6. The lesson was well-paced. 4 3 2 1 N/A
   Comment:

7. Directions were clear and concise and students were able to carry them out. 4 3 2 1 N/A
   Comment:

8. Material was presented at the students' level of comprehension. 4 3 2 1 N/A
   Comment:

9. An appropriate percentage of the class was student production of the language. 4 3 2 1 N/A
   Comment:

10. The teacher answered questions carefully and satisfactorily. 4 3 2 1 N/A
    Comment:

11. The method(s) was(were) appropriate to the age and ability of students. 4 3 2 1 N/A
    Comment:

12. The teacher knew when the students were having trouble understanding. 4 3 2 1 N/A
    Comment:

13. The teacher showed an interest in, and enthusiasm for, the subject taught. 4 3 2 1 N/A
    Comment:

(Continued)

Figure 22.1 Teacher observation form: observing other teachers (*Continued*)

III. Execution/Methods

14. There were balance and variety in activities during the lesson. 4 3 2 1 N/A
Comment:

15. The teacher was able to adapt to unanticipated situations. 4 3 2 1 N/A
Comment:

16. The material was reinforced. 4 3 2 1 N/A
Comment:

17. The teacher moved around the class and made eye contact with students. 4 3 2 1 N/A
Comment:

18. The teacher knew students' names. 4 3 2 1 N/A
Comment:

19. The teacher positively reinforced the students. 4 3 2 1 N/A
Comment:

20. Student responses were effectively elicited (i.e., the order in which the students were called on). 4 3 2 1 N/A
Comment:

21. Examples and illustrations were used effectively. 4 3 2 1 N/A
Comment:

22. Instructional aids or resource material was used effectively. 4 3 2 1 N/A
Comment:

23. Drills were used and presented effectively. 4 3 2 1 N/A
Comment:

24. Structures were taken out of artificial drill contexts and applied to the real contexts of the students' culture and personal experiences. 4 3 2 1 N/A
Comment:

25. Error perception. 4 3 2 1 N/A
Comment:

26. Appropriate error correction. 4 3 2 1 N/A
Comment:

IV. Personal Characteristics

27. Patience in eliciting responses. 4 3 2 1 N/A
Comment:

Figure 22.1 Teacher observation form: observing other teachers (*Continued*)

28. Clarity, tone, and audibility of voice. 4 3 2 1 N/A
    Comment:

29. Personal appearance. 4 3 2 1 N/A
    Comment:

30. Initiative, resourcefulness, and creativity. 4 3 2 1 N/A
    Comment:

31. Pronunciation, intonation, fluency, and appropriate and acceptable use of language. 4 3 2 1 N/A
    Comment:

V. Teacher/Student Interaction

32. Teacher encouraged and assured full student participation in class. 4 3 2 1 N/A
    Comment:

33. The class felt free to ask questions, to disagree, or to express their own ideas. 4 3 2 1 N/A
    Comment:

34. The teacher was able to control and direct the class. 4 3 2 1 N/A
    Comment:

35. The students were attentive and involved. 4 3 2 1 N/A
    Comment:

36. The students were comfortable and relaxed, even during intense intellectual activity. 4 3 2 1 N/A
    Comment:

37. The students were treated fairly, impartially, and with respect. 4 3 2 1 N/A
    Comment:

38. The students were encouraged to do their best. 4 3 2 1 N/A
    Comment:

39. The teacher was relaxed and matter-of-fact in voice and manner. 4 3 2 1 N/A
    Comment:

40. The teacher was aware of individual and group needs. 4 3 2 1 N/A
    Comment:

41. Digressions were used positively and not overused. 4 3 2 1 N/A
    Comment:

Figure 22.2 Teacher self-observation form (adapted from Christison & Bassano, 1984)

Thoughtfully consider each statement. Rate yourself in the following way:

3 = Excellent 2 = Good 1 = Needs Improvement 0 = Not Applicable

Write your ratings in the blanks. When you've finished, give overall consideration to the various areas.

I. Learning Environment

A. Relationship to Students

_____ 1. I establish good eye contact with my class. I do not talk over their heads, to the chalkboard, or to just one person.

_____ 2. If I tend to teach predominantly to one area of the classroom, I am aware of this. I make a conscious effort at all times to pay attention to all students equally.

_____ 3. I divide my students into small groups in an organized and principled manner. I recognize that these groups should differ in size and composition, varying with the objective of the group activity.

B. The Classroom

_____ 1. If possible, I arrange the seating in my class to suit the class activity for the day.

_____ 2. I consider the physical comfort of the room, such as heat and light.

_____ 3. When I need special materials or equipment, I have them set up before the class begins.

C. Presentation

_____ 1. My handwriting on the chalkboard and charts is legible from all locations in the classroom. It is large enough to accommodate students with vision impairments.

_____ 2. I speak loudly enough to be heard in all parts of the classroom, and I enunciate clearly.

_____ 3. I vary the exercises in class, alternating rapid and slow-paced activities to keep up the maximum interest in the class.

_____ 4. I am prepared to give a variety of explanations, models, or descriptions for all students.

_____ 5. I help the students form working principles and generalizations.

_____ 6. Students use new skills or concepts long enough so that they are retained and thus future application is possible.

_____ 7. I plan for "thinking time" for my students so they can organize their thoughts and plan what they are going to say or do.

D. Culture and Adjustment

_____ 1. I am aware that cultural differences affect the learning situation.

_____ 2. I keep the cultural background(s) of my students in mind when planning daily activities and am aware of cultural misunderstandings that might arise from the activities I choose.

_____ 3. I promote an atmosphere of understanding and mutual respect.

Figure 22.2 Teacher self-observation form (*Continued*)

II. The Individuals

A. Physical Health

_____ 1. I know which students have visual or aural impairments and seat them as close to my usual teaching positions as possible.

_____ 2. I am aware that a student's attention span varies from day to day, depending on mental and physical health and outside distractions. I pace my class activities to accommodate the strengths. I don't continue with an activity that may exhaust or bore them.

_____ 3. I begin my class with a simple activity to wake students up and get them working together.

_____ 4. I am sensitive to individual students who have bad days. I don't press a student who is incapable of performing at the usual level.

_____ 5. I try to challenge students who are at their best.

_____ 6. If I am having a bad day and feel it might affect my normal teaching style, I let my students know it so there is no misunderstanding about my feelings for them.

B. Self-Concepts

_____ 1. I treat my students with the same respect that I expect them to show me.

_____ 2. I plan "one-centered" activities that give all students an opportunity at some point to feel important and accepted.

_____ 3. I like to teach and have a good time teaching—on most days.

C. Aptitude and Perception

_____ 1. I am aware that my students learn differently. Some students are visual-receptive, some are motor-receptive, and others are audio-receptive.

_____ 2. My exercises are varied; some are visual, aural, oral, and kinesthetic. I provide models, examples, and experiences to maximize learning in each of these areas.

_____ 3. I know basic concepts in the memory process. When applicable, I use association to aid students in rapid skills acquisition.

D. Feedback

_____ 1. I tell students when they have done well, but I don't let praise become mechanical.

_____ 2. I finish my class period in a way that will review the new concepts presented during the class period. My students can immediately evaluate their understanding of those concepts.

_____ 3. My tests are well-planned and produced.

_____ 4. I make my system of grading clear to my students so that there are no misunderstandings of expectations.

E. Development

_____ 1. I keep up to date on new techniques in the ESL profession by attending conferences and workshops and by reading pertinent professional articles and books.

_____ 2. I realize that there is no one right way to present a lesson. I try new ideas where and when they seem appropriate.

_____ 3. I observe other ESL teachers so that I can get other ideas and compare them to my own teaching style. I want to have several ideas for teaching one concept.

(*Continued*)

Figure 22.2 Teacher self-observation form (*Continued*)

III. The Activity

A. Interaction

_____ 1. I minimize my role in conducting the activities.
_____ 2. I organize the activities so they are suitable for real interactions among students.
_____ 3. The activities maximize student involvement.
_____ 4. The activities promote spontaneity or experimentation on the part of the learner.
_____ 5. The activities generally transfer attention away from "self" and outward toward a "task."
_____ 6. The activities are organized to ensure a high success rate, leaving enough room for error to make the activity challenging.
_____ 7. I am not always overly concerned with error correction. I choose the appropriate amount of correction for the activity.

B. Language

_____ 1. The activity is focused.
_____ 2. The content of the skill presented will be easily transferrable for use outside the class.
_____ 3. The activity is geared to the proficiency level of my class or slightly beyond.
_____ 4. The content of the activity is not too sophisticated for my students.
_____ 5. I make the content of the activity relevant and meaningful to my students' world.

CLASSROOM CONNECTIONS

Would you like to try a self-observation of your teaching? If so, what would like to "keep an eye out for"? Consider making a list of elements of your teaching on which you would like to get some feedback, and then make plans to carry out the observation, and then set some personal goals based on your findings.

CLASSROOM-BASED "ACTION" RESEARCH

Research is a scary word for some. We are happy to leave it in someone else's hands because it involves statistics, experimental design, and the interpretation of results, which we (mistakenly) think only "experts" can do. Even so, leaving all the research in the hands of certified psychometricians is an upside-down policy, as the L2 teaching profession has increasingly stressed the importance of teachers doing their own research in their classrooms (Spada, 2012; Bailey, 2014).

Actually, research doesn't have to be a frightening prospect at all. You're researching ideas all the time, whether you know it or not. If, as a growing teacher, you have a goal to improve the quality of your teaching, then you'll ask some relevant questions, hypothesize some possible answers or solutions, put the solutions to a practical tryout in the classroom, look for certain results, and weigh those results in some manner to determine whether your hypothesized answer held up. Such a process is quite formal in following classic steps for experimental research. It may not be a habitual practice for you.

CLASSROOM CONNECTIONS

What ideas are teachers "researching all the time"? Does the prospect of conducting research scare you? If so, what exactly about it is frightening? Is it the amount of work involved? Designing the project? Scoring or tabulating results? Writing or presenting a report? What would allay these fears?

A good deal of classroom research is an informal, everyday occurrence for you. You divide up small groups in a different way to stimulate better exchange of ideas; you modify your usual nondirective approach to getting students to study harder and take a bold, direct, no-nonsense approach; you try a videotape as a conversation stimulus; you try a deductive approach to presenting a grammar point instead of your usual inductive approach. Other classroom research may be more of a long-term process that covers a term or more. In this mode, still in an informal manner, you may try out some learner strategy training techniques to see if students do better at conversation skills; you may do a daily three-minute pronunciation drill to see if students' pronunciation improves; you may assign specific extra-class reading to see if reading comprehension improves.

This kind of classroom-based research has commonly been called **action research**, which is "more than simply research conducted by teachers in the classroom" (Bailey, 2014, p. 602). The purpose of action research is "to investigate a social environment (e.g., classroom) in which researchers (e.g., teachers) perceive a situation in which a gap exists between the 'actual' and the 'ideal'" (Burns, 2011, p. 238). Participants in an L2 class are thus personally involved in a systematic process of inquiry that addresses their own practical concerns (Burns, 2005).

Action research may be carried out not so much to publish a journal article as to improve your own understanding of the teaching–learning process in the classroom. The payoff for treating your teaching-learning questions seriously is, ultimately, your becoming a better teacher. And, yes, you might also find that what you have learned is worth sharing with other teachers, either through informal conversations in the teacher's lunchroom or through a conference presentation.

Here are some possible questions, divided into four categories, that might form the focus of some action research (adapted from Nunan, 1989b, p. 36, and Bailey, 2014):

Suggestions for Action Research

Linguistic features of learners' language

1. What kind of classroom *discourse features* (such as holding the floor, bringing in another speaker) do learners use when doing problem solving tasks in small groups?
2. Do learners more easily learn *similar* vocabulary items when these are presented in the *same* lesson, as opposed to when they are taught separately over a period of time?

Interactive features of classroom language

3. Under what conditions do English learners feel reticent to use oral English in classes in non–English-speaking countries?
4. Do learners involve themselves in greater interaction when discussing controversial topics (in which *opinions* must be ventured) than when topics are more factual or scientifically based?

Tasks

5. What kinds of tasks stimulate more interaction?
6. Which tasks work best with mixed-ability groups?

Strategies

7. Is there better oral production when the teacher encourages students' preferred strategies as opposed to encouraging less preferred strategies?
8. Do more successful learners share certain strategy preferences that distinguish them from less efficient learners?

One of the possible benefits of action research is its stimulus for collaboration among teachers. The following scenario, taken from Doug's personal notes, is a case in point.

> To discover the effect of error treatment on the performance of ESL students, two matched sections of the same low-intermediate intensive English course were selected for investigation over a seven-week period. An oral pre-test was designed by a group of teachers and administered to each student. In one section, teachers deliberately withheld any treatment of present tense, present progressive, and third person singular speech errors committed by the students. In the other section, teachers attempted to treat overtly all such errors that they noticed.

During the seven-week period, teachers observed each other, and other members of the research group not teaching those sections also came in to observe, mostly to check up on the extent to which teachers were carrying out their respective charge. At the end of the seven-week period, the pretest was re-administered as a post-test, and gain scores were calculated.

The statistical findings of the study were disappointing: no significant difference between the two sections! But the pedagogical gains accrued by the collaboration among eight teachers were more than worth the effort. In the process of investigating a potentially interesting instructional variable, teachers did the following, all collaboratively: they formulated research hypotheses; they designed the study; they designed a test; they observed and gave feedback to each other; they were sensitized to the complexities of error treatment; and they lowered their fear of performing research!

Why do you suppose there were no differences between the two sections of students? What could have contaminated the experiment? What are some possible action research projects that *you* and/or your colleagues might undertake? What do you think you could gain from the experience, regardless of the final results?

You still may be feeling a little queasy about labeling some of your teacher inquisitiveness as *research*. Can I really ask the "right" questions? How do I know if my research methodology is sound? How will I deal with numerical results (statistics)? Will my conclusions be valid?

Good questions. First of all, we recommend that you consult a teacher resource book on classroom research (Freeman, 1998; Wallace, 1998; Edge, 2001; Burns, 2010). Second, consider the following pointers to get yourself started on some simple but potentially effective action research.

1. Convert Your "Ideas" into Specific Questions

You may have quite a few "ideas" about things that you could investigate in the classroom. That's good; keep those creative juices flowing. But in order to be able to draw conclusions, your ideas have to be converted into questions that you can answer. Sometimes those questions are too broad: Is communicative language teaching effective? How useful is reading aloud in class? Does process writing work?

So, make sure that your questions are specific enough that you can look back after your investigation and really come up with an answer. The questions do not have to be long and drawn out, just specific, like the eight questions listed earlier. As an example here, let's consider the following question:

> *Given a selection of six commonly used techniques, how do they compare with each other in terms of stimulating interaction?*

2. Operationally Define the Elements of Your Question

Next, take your question and operationally define all the elements in it. "Operational" means that you have a measurable means for determining something. So, in the example question above, we'll assume that each group has *four* students in it, and that you have stated the following limitations:

> **Techniques:** *(A) information gap—find out each other's birthday, hobbies, etc.; (B) jigsaw—map; (C) role-play; (D) scanning a reading passage to find a list of details; (E) brainstorming; (F) opinion exchange*
>
> **Interaction:** *the total number of turns taken in each group; total number of minutes of student talk (vs. silence)*

3. Determine How You Will Answer Your Question

Now you are ready to launch the investigation. How will you answer the question? Your research methodology may call for a multiple number of data-gathering instances and, in this particular case, some audio recorders, because you will not be able to record data for several small groups at once and monitor the techniques as well. For each of the six designated techniques, you will have a recorder placed in each small group and running during the entire task.

You will (perhaps with the help of a colleague?) then listen to each recording and tally the number of turns within each group plus the number of minutes of student talk. Assuming that you have allowed all the groups an equal number of total minutes within each technique, you can assign a grand total of turns and minutes of student talk.

Rank order will be determined by the total number of turns in each group of four students.

4. Interpret Your Results Appropriately

According to your findings (see below), technique *A* stimulates the most interaction, *B* is next, and so on. But your conclusion may not be so simple. Every research study has its necessary caveats, so before you make a sweeping generalization about your findings, it will help to state, even if only for yourself, some of the limitations on your results. Here are the results you found:

Technique	Turns	Minutes Student Talk/Total Time
A	137	73/90
B	133	85/90
C	116	79/90
D	114	69/90
E	102	71/90
F	91	79/90

Now, can you be sure that Technique *A* stimulated significantly more turns than Technique *B*? And *B* more than *C*, and so forth? One solution to this dilemma is to divide the total number of turns by the total time, but that doesn't seem logical does it? The number of minutes of student talk didn't correspond with rank order of turns, meaning that in some techniques (*A*, for example) there was some relatively rapid turn-taking interspersed with student silence, and in other techniques (*F*, for example) certain students talked for longer stretches of time. This may cause you to redefine interaction or at least to interpret your results.

 **CLASSROOM CONNECTIONS**

In this example of classroom research, what further difficulties do you think might have arisen? From the statement of the specific question, to the design, to the gathering of results, are there measures you might have taken to avoid further problems?

Further, the results need to be seen in terms of other limitations in the study itself: the choice and number of tasks, the operational definitions chosen, and your particular groups of students. You may, for example, be tempted to generalize results of classroom research to the world at large. Beware. Your safest conclusion is one that reports what you found for your class, and to invite others to replicate your study if they wish to see whether similar results are obtained.

Classroom-based research is ideally suited to current practice in language teaching. Our communicative, interactive approach implies that every teacher assesses his or her own classroom of students and designs instructional techniques that work under those *particular* conditions, and with learners who are pursuing a number of possible purposes for learning an L2.

Action research is an excellent way to promote teacher development within a framework that values the personal construction of teacher knowledge as opposed to a transmission model (Burns, 2011; Bailey, 2014). It fosters a spirit of understanding of one's own beliefs, knowledge, and experience. It forces teachers to look at their own situated context. And, almost inevitably, action research encourages collaborative relationships among teachers (Freeman, 2002; Burns, 2005, 2011; Mann, 2005).

TEACHER COLLABORATION: LEARNING FROM EACH OTHER

The process of continuing to develop your professional expertise as a teacher is sometimes difficult to manage alone. The challenges of teaching in a rapidly changing profession almost necessitate collaboration with other teachers in order to stay on the cutting edge (Murphey & Sato, 2005). Can you successfully collaborate with other teachers to fulfill your expectations? Besides action research, described above, we suggest five other forms of collaboration—of teachers learning from each other—that have worked for others and that may work for you.

1. Peer Coaching

Already in this chapter you have been given some guidelines for observation of both yourself and other teachers. *Peer coaching* is a systematic process of collaboration in which one teacher observes and gives feedback to another teacher, usually with some form of reciprocity. Kate Kinsella (1994, p. 5) defines and elaborates as follows:

> Peer coaching is a structured process by which faculty members voluntarily assist each other in enhancing their teaching within an atmosphere of collegial trust and candor, through: (1) development of individual instructional improvement goals and clear observation criteria; (2) reciprocal, focused, nonevaluative classroom observations; and (3) prompt constructive feedback on those observations.

Observers need not technically be "peers" in every sense of the word, but as colleagues, observer and teacher engage in a cooperative process of mutual communication about the actual teaching–learning process as directly observed in the classroom. Feedback is classified as **formative** rather than **summative**. It is offered and received as information for the enhancement of one's future teaching, not as data for summing up one's competencies as a teacher.

Peer coaching can be especially helpful if you focus on certain aspects of your teaching. If you've been concerned, say, about the quantity of teacher talk versus student talk in your teaching, a peer observer may be able to give you some feedback that could lead you to make some adjustments. Among topics that peer-coaching programs have centered on are distribution of student participation across the classroom; teacher speech mannerisms, patterns, eye contact, and nonverbal distracters; group and pair work management; and transitions from one activity to the next, to the next, and so on.

Classroom Connections

Is there a downside to peer coaching? What might interfere with a successful peer coaching experience and how would you propose to avoid, if possible, such interfering elements? Would you be willing to initiate a peer coaching arrangement with a colleague?

Peer coaching can offer a personalized opportunity for growth (Dove & Honigsfeld, 2010). Both sides of the team benefit: the observer is called upon to carefully analyze another's teaching and thereby sharpen his or her own metacognitive ability to reflect on the teaching process; the teacher being observed is nudged out of what might otherwise be some complacency into a heightened awareness of his or her own areas of strength and weakness.

2. Team Teaching

To the extent that the structure and budget of your program permit, team teaching can be an extraordinarily rewarding experience. Several models of team teaching are common: (1) two teachers are overtly present throughout a class period, but divide responsibility between them; (2) two teachers take different halves of a class period, with one teacher stepping aside while the other performs; and (3) two or more teachers teach different consecutive periods of one group of learners, and must collaborate closely in carrying out and modifying curricular plans.

The first two models are less frequently found among English language programs not because of absence of reward for student and teacher, but because of budgetary limitations. The third model is extremely common in the English language–teaching world, especially whenever a group of learners compose an intact set of students across two or more class periods. Within this model, the importance of collaboration is sometimes underestimated. Teachers may be too ready to assume that a curriculum spanning a whole term of, say, ten to fifteen weeks will simply proceed as planned, only to discover that another teacher has not been able to follow the time-plan, throwing off the expected sequencing of material.

The advantages of team teaching, especially in the first two models, parallel those of peer coaching. Teachers are encouraged to collaborate, to consider respective strengths, and to engage in reflective practice. In the third model, teachers must develop a pattern of frequent communication and exchange, the fruits of which often are greater professional growth.

3. Collaborative Curriculum Development and Revision

The process of curriculum development and revision warrants a similar collaborative effort. In the same way that teachers are sometimes all too happy to turn over research to the experts, so we are tempted to get curriculum specialists to do course and program development. Growing, dynamic language programs are a product of an ongoing creative dialogue between teachers and among teachers and those that are assigned to compile curricula. Not to involve teachers in the process is to run the risk of programs that are generated in a vacuum of sorts, devoid of a dynamic interaction among student, teacher, and administrator.

Classroom Connections

The American Language Institute at San Francisco State University is a "teaching" institution. Curriculum supervisors are in daily communication with novice teachers and interns. As teachers consult with their supervisors on lesson design, textbook adaptation, and pedagogical innovations, new curriculum is born every day. This kind of collaboration results in teacher contributions—even from novice teachers—to course syllabuses, which are then adapted and incorporated into established, revised curricula. Thus, the curricula for courses are always in a slow but constant state of creative change.

To what extent do you think teacher collaboration leads to (or might lead to) curriculum change over time in an institution you are familiar with? How might you go about suggesting such collaboration if it doesn't already happen?

4. Presenting at a Professional Conference

In quite a number of graduate Master of Arts programs in TESOL, an annual or semiannual conference is planned, in which graduates make professional presentations. Graduates find that this is an excellent training ground for planning to present at a professional gathering of teachers, and that it forces them to prepare and deliver a high-quality presentation on a topic of professional interest. A number of those presentations are co-presented, giving the presenters an opportunity to collaborate and pool their efforts.

We include the suggestion of conference presentations here because it's difficult *not* to collaborate in some way on such events. Even if you do a solo presentation, some collaboration is often involved in the preparation, critiquing, and, of course, in interacting with one's audience. A conference presentation is a superb opportunity to develop some of your own ideas and to share them with the professional community at large. It gives you an impetus to focus on some background reading, to systematically pull together an idea or topic, to present it clearly and enthusiastically, and ultimately to establish new professional connections beyond your own institution. It's also an excellent addition to your resumé!

Some Ideas for Conference Presentations

- a task or activity that demonstrates a principle or theme (e.g., environmental action)
- a set of tasks or activities (e.g., a project involving all four skills) focused on a theme

- a study of students' language development in a specific area (e.g., relative clauses, verb tenses)
- a curriculum or module that you created for a course
- a focus on a learning principle (e.g., anxiety) with background research and practical examples for facilitating learning
- report on some teacher development projects (e.g., formation of a support group, peer coaching)
- a focus on an age group (e.g., very young learners) with examples of classroom tasks and activities
- a cross-cultural analysis of a subtopic within education with practical classroom examples

This list could continue for pages, as a glance at any conference handbook will reveal. By organizing your thoughts clearly and carefully following directions for submitting a proposal for a presentation, you have an excellent chance of having your proposal accepted. I can guarantee you that it will be a very rewarding experience!

5. Joining a Professional Association of Teachers

Closely linked to the above suggestion of presenting at a professional conference is one of the most rewarding, lifelong modes of professional development: joining a professional association of teachers. Teachers' associations are in every country and virtually in every "corner of the earth." The best way to stay in touch with the field, to join with others in your profession, and to experience the stimulation and education of your professional partners is to participate in such an organization.

Virtually all these organizations hold periodic local or national conferences, and "there is perhaps no single experience with more potential for educating and refreshing a professional than an international . . . conference" (Crandall & Miller, 2014, p. 633). However experienced or inexperienced you are as a teacher, there is so much to gain from these energizing occasions. And, of course, they are a lot of fun, too!

6. Informal Local Teacher Support Groups

Finally, collaboration can take the form of gatherings of teachers in your school or neighborhood or city (Murphey & Sato, 2005). At the local level of the day-to-day routine that we all find ourselves in, the importance of purposeful gatherings of teachers cannot be too strongly stressed. Even if agendas are rather informal—empathetic support will readily be found even within informal agendas—it is important to have times when a staff of teachers gets together to cover a number of possible issues: student behavior problems, teaching tips, curricular issues, and even difficulties with administrative bureaucracy. When teachers talk together, there is almost always a sense of solidarity and purpose, and ultimately a morale boost.

 **Classroom Connections**

Are there local teacher support groups available to you? If so, how useful are they? Do they offer the support and inspiration you would like? If not, how might you either start such a group or improve communications within one that you are already in?

FURTHER AVENUES OF PROFESSIONAL DEVELOPMENT

So far in this chapter, we've looked at teacher development in the form of observations and action research, and then in the section above, several methods of collaborative development. The latter endeavors, but to some extent the former two as well, involve *collaboration* with fellow teachers, which in many circumstances may be difficult to arrange in a language teacher's hectic schedule and pace. Other effective ways to continue your professional growth include efforts that you can *individually* make on your own timetable and pace (Bailey, Curtis, & Nunan, 2001). We'll conclude this chapter with some thoughts about these rewarding possibilities.

1. Reflective Teaching Journals

The use of student-generated journals in our classrooms has already been discussed in previous chapters. Journal-writing has in recent years evolved from simply a matter of keeping a diary into a potentially integral aspect of a learner's process of acquisition. Now, in the burgeoning field of teacher development, teacher journal-writing has been prominently featured (Mann, 2005; Richards & Farrell, 2005, 2011; Crandall & Miller, 2014).

Journals enable a teacher to record events, observations, questions, and feelings more or less immediately, before recollections fade in the memories of our busy minds. Teacher journals serve much the same purpose that student journals serve in enabling the writer to focus more clearly on relevant phenomena, to reflect on them, and to resolve to take action on goals that are derived from the insights that accrue.

Richards and Farrell (2005) suggest that the primary audience for such journals is the writer, but that at times journals can be fruitfully shared with other teachers or a supervisor. Crandall and Miller (2014) note the added benefit of electronic journal-writing that can be shared if you desire, and also easily imported digitally into other writings that you might put together at a later date.

A key to successful journal writing lies in commitment: set goals; address specific questions; set aside a regular time for writing; and review and evaluate your entries in order to learn something from them.

Classroom Connections

Have you ever written an ongoing reflective journal on your learning or teaching of an L2? If so, what did you gain from it? If not, why not? Personal journal writing might not be your "cup of tea." And if not, would it help to make *oral* recordings of your reflections? Perhaps you could talk with a friend who is a journal writer and solicit some suggestions for getting started and making it a fruitful process?

2. Teaching Portfolios

The creation of a professional portfolio is a second method of individual development that one can accomplish without the difficulty imposed by collaborative efforts. Although you are ultimately likely to want to share your portfolio with someone else, much of it can be assembled on your own time. A portfolio is an assembly of your professional handiwork, thoughts and reflections, beliefs and principles, and personal data (Constantino & De Lorenzo, 2002; Tanner, 2003; Crandall & Miller, 2014).

A portfolio might take on a summative nature by serving as a demonstration of your professional qualifications for, say, a job that you're interviewing for, or it can play a more formative role in putting together a personally-oriented set of documents that show your progress in selected areas of concern. Like a journal, a portfolio can be an instrument for reflection and goal-setting.

In quite a number of L2 education programs around the world, graduating students create a professional portfolio as part of their culminating experience in the program (Crandall & Miller, 2014). Your portfolio could consist of the following elements:

Suggested Components of a Teaching Portfolio

- introduction
- résumé (suggestion: Keep it brief—one or at most two pages.)
- statement of your philosophy of education (beliefs about teaching and learning—one to three pages)
- annotated bibliographies on selected topics of your interest

- one or two sample (revised) academic papers from your program
- one or two lesson plans with reflections on each
- samples of your students' work (if you have taught)
- an annotated list (from your résumé) of your professional presentations, articles, and other writing (if applicable)

These portfolios may then be used for imminent job applications and interviews, but their greatest value is in the process of synthesizing two or more years of graduate study.

Teacher educators emphasize the usefulness of keeping an *e-portfolio*, given the ubiquitous presence of electronic hardware among L2 learners worldwide (Cambridge, Cambridge, & Yancey, 2009). Online platforms are able to give teachers a ready opportunity to "capture and reflect on your learning through the inclusion of various multimedia artifacts (e.g., text, photos, audio-recordings, and videos)" (Crandall & Miller, 2014, p. 643).

CLASSROOM CONNECTIONS

Are you compiling a teaching portfolio? Even if you haven't taught before, you're steadily learning, observing, gathering materials, and talking with classmates. How are those experiences entering into the making of a portfolio? To what extent would an e-portfolio be a fulfilling, interesting project?

3. Professional Reading on Your Own

In a teacher's busy daily life, it's all too often the case that you simply "run out of time" for things like reading professional journals and books. At the end of the day—literally—you end up being mentally spent and your body craves some physical exercise, a good meal, a friendly conversation, or anything but more reading! By then it's late at night, you need some sleep, and the cycle starts over. There's no question that selective reading to "keep up with the field," and simply to discover what other people are thinking and doing, is essential to the growing, dynamic teacher (Borg, 2003a; Hedgcock, 2009). So what's the solution?

One possible avenue that can fit into the corners of your busy day is to skim through an occasional professional newsletter, many of which are free to members and available online. TESOL offers an online *English Language Bulletin*; ACTFL disseminates the *ACTFL SmartBrief*; the Center for Applied Linguistics has online briefs, digests, and other resources including a periodic newsletter; the *Linguist List* makes available research summaries, discussions, journal table of contents, and other useful information.

It's often difficult to maintain a discipline of *regular* reading and study. We may put these sorts of professional activities off until summertime, a spring break, or some other block of time. Instead, it might be better to force the issue by trying to do some of the following:

Guidelines for Personal Professional Reading

- Set goals for directing your reading. The L2 teaching profession has an overwhelming number of possible subfields, and you can't tackle them all.
- Designate times during the day or week for catching up on professional reading.
- Make use of "empty" periods of time during the day (waiting for a bus; riding a commuter train; sitting in the doctor's waiting room).
- When a professional journal comes, flag items of interest and put them on a list of "things to do."
- Use skimming and scanning strategies. Read abstracts and note titles of articles or presentations; then, later, you can read the research in detail.
- Devise a system of note-taking for future retrieval, such as index cards, folders, computer-based files, spreadsheets, electronic notes, etc.

4. Writing for Publication

One of the most rewarding endeavors in a teacher's life is professional writing for publication. Your reading, action research, journal writing, or curriculum development projects, among many other possibilities, can become a potentially useful, interesting, and innovative addition to professional literature in the field of language teaching. With a huge variety of journals in our field, in addition to newsletters, local professional booklets, and a growing number of web-based opportunities for writing (Murphey et al., 2005), you should by all means consider this creative outlet for your energies. Consider the following possibilities:

Suggestions for Professional Writing

- a professional journal article on some action research you have done
- a response to a recent journal article that particularly interested you

- a review of a book that you recently read
- a "teaching tip" on a task you developed in your class
- writing a curriculum for your institution (Seymour, 2003)
- publishing a student textbook
- compiling a teacher's manual for a student textbook
- editing a textbook for a publisher
- reviewing a manuscript for a publisher
- creating web-based blogs or other electronic resources
- compiling an annotated bibliography of references on a specific topic

 **CLASSROOM CONNECTIONS**

The following is a first-person account from Doug.

My first journal article was an outgrowth of what I thought was a minor research project for a linguistics class. It was a study of native and nonnative English speakers' intuitions about spelling (Brown, 1970). I did background reading, devised a hypothesis, set up the research methodology, gathered data, and came up with some interesting results. I never dreamed that my "little" study was worthy of publication in a "big" journal, but at the encouragement of others, I edited the piece, submitted it, and much to my surprise at the time, it was accepted!

What are some or your own research ideas that you have explored for a course project? How about converting something into a potential professional publication?

It's tempting for teachers to assume that professional writing must be undertaken by "experts" (PhDs and professors and the like), and certainly not by "ordinary" teachers. Nonsense! In the same way that research is not the exclusive province of highly trained psychometricians, as we noted above, professional writing is (or should be) equally shared by classroom teachers. Many teachers find that professional writing is not only an excellent motivating experience, but also a rewarding one that opens up new personal and professional vistas.

THE MULTIPLE ROLES OF A LANGUAGE TEACHER

In Chapter 13, we outlined several roles of an interactive teacher: controller, manager, facilitator, among others. We're revisiting the concept here, but from a different perspective—from a more overarching view of expectations placed upon teachers, and not just language teachers. As an educator, leader, and sometimes "model" person, just what are those many roles that you must be prepared to assume?

We're suggesting seven such components of a teacher's *professional identity* here, with thanks to Joseph Lee (2014) for contributing these valuable thoughts. Perhaps these attributes can be who you want to *be* or *become* as a language teacher?

Roles of a Language Teacher (Adapted from J. Lee, 2014)

Language specialist. Being/becoming a language specialist means continuously developing your declarative and procedural knowledge about the language (its form, meaning, and use), being/becoming proficient in using the language (in various registers and genres), and knowing how to teach the language.

Craftsperson. Being/becoming a craftsperson means continuously working to expand and fine-tune your craft in order to make principled choices and selections of skills and strategies to realize particular curricular ends.

Artist. Being/becoming a craftsperson suggests mostly externally imposed skills through technical training that may be shared by the broader teacher community, but being/becoming an artist implies a particular personal dimension that recognizes the uniqueness of an individual teacher. Thus, it entails drawing on the available community resources to mature and continuously refine one's taste of the art of teaching as an educational performer, critic, and connoisseur.

Intellectual. Being/becoming an intellectual is not about basing your practice on only "official" knowledge in the field. It is about reflecting and theorizing about language, language learning, and language teaching, constantly forming and reforming your personal theories through various interactions with students, peers, readings, and other educational discourse; thus, it is about being/becoming an active thinker who develops grounded theories in practice and experience, though also informed by others' theories.

Researcher. Related to being/becoming an intellectual is being/becoming a researcher, which means carefully, intentionally, and systemically inquiring about and exploring classroom life. Through collecting data, documenting experiences in and outside of the classroom, reflecting on and creating written records of insights, and sharing findings (thus making them visible to others), teachers move from being passive recipients of sanctioned knowledge toward becoming active producers of knowledge.

Learner. Implied in all of the above (and the final role below) is being/becoming a learner of teaching. All growth and change involves learning, and as you develop your craft and practice your art, as you raise questions and discover more about language and teaching, and as you benefit from the wisdom of your own students, you learn.

Transformative reflectivist. Being/becoming a transformative reflectivist means constantly engaging in critical reflection of your own practice; that is, actively, intentionally, and recursively "problematizing practice" (Pennycook, 2001) with the explicit desire for, commitment toward, and purpose of transforming your thoughts and practices. Such teachers seek out critical moments in their practice when they dare to reach out and embrace those opportunities to make a meaningful difference in the lives of their students.

In our next and final chapter, we'll explain in much greater detail what it means to be a transformative teacher engaged in critical pedagogy.

★ ★ ★ ★ ★

You can now see that teacher development is a lifelong process. If you're just starting out in the profession, you have many adventures ahead of you, and the best way to fully appreciate those adventures is to keep growing. As you do so, remember that there's no single, ideal, model teacher that you need to aspire to. Every teacher is unique, with individual experiences, knowledge, and beliefs, and you are now forming your own construction of yourself as a teacher. Proceed with pride in who you *are* already and with dedication to who you will *become*.

FOR THE TEACHER: ACTIVITIES (A) & DISCUSSION (D)

Note: For each of the "Classroom Connections" in this chapter, you may wish to turn them into individual or pair-work discussion questions.

1. **(A)** If students have been systematically reading and studying the chapters of this book, they have by now picked up a reasonably comprehensive picture of principles and issues in language teaching and how they apply to the classroom. With that background information, ask pairs to go back now to Chapter 1 and look through the lesson that was described there in 18 numbered segments. Then, have them look at the

18 questions/comments posed in the subsequent section ("Beneath the Lesson," pp. 4–8). Dividing the questions among pairs or small groups, direct them to discuss the questions and propose answers. What aspects of this class hour should one change, and why? Have the groups present their responses and rationale for changes to the whole class.

2. **(A)** Ask pairs to look again at the eight principles of language learning and teaching outlined in Chapter 4 and summarized in Table 4.1 on page 85. Then ask each person in the pair to choose *one* principle that they would like to "develop" in their teaching expertise. It may be a principle that is particularly challenging for them to pursue. Then have them share with each other some specific, concrete ways that they could infuse their pedagogy with a greater awareness of the principle they have chosen. If time permits, have a few volunteers present their resolutions.
3. **(D)** Ask your students to brainstorm ways that they could become more of a "peak performer" as a teacher. List their ideas on the board and suggest that individuals select a few of the ideas to put into practice. They could then enter those thoughts into individual journals, which could perhaps form blogs or otherwise shared online.
4. **(A)** Using the information provided in the section Characteristics of a successful language teacher (pp. 546–547), ask pairs to pick just *one* item and talk about how they could implement the item in their context. Then have them share their thoughts with the rest of the class.
5. **(A)** (For class members who are *not* currently teaching) Use observation form A in Figure 22.1 to observe a language class. After the observation, cluster them in pairs or small groups to assess the usefulness of the form for identifying significant elements of the class and the teacher's methodology. Then ask them to report their findings to the class
6. **(A)** (For class members who *are* currently teaching) Use the self-observation form B (Figure 22.2.) the next time they teach. If possible, have them pair up to exchange observations of each other. What did they learn? In pairs or small groups have them reflect on the benefits and drawbacks of the experience, then report back to the whole class.
7. **(A)** (For class members who are *not* currently teaching) In assigned groups, using the list of research questions on page 556 as a starting point, ask them to brainstorm some other researchable ideas. (Use a chalkboard or poster paper to write the ideas down.) Pick several ideas that the groups might carry out collaboratively. Help your students to make plans (using steps 1 through 4 in this chapter) for some *action research* that they might someday carry out. Ask groups to share their ideas with the rest of the class.
8. **(A)** (For class members who *are* currently teaching) Form groups of three or four people each. Have them brainstorm some forms of collaboration that would work in their institution(s) and write down the ideas that are

generated. Ask them to share their thoughts with the rest of the class, and to make a resolution to make this plan actually happen in the near future.

9. **(D)** Refer your students back to the example of an action research project (page 556) on error treatment. Ask your students the questions that were posed on that page: Why do you suppose there were no differences between the two sections of students? What could have contaminated the experiment? What would you have done differently, to avoid pitfalls?
10. **(D)** Engage the class in a discussion of the feasibility of the collaborative methods of teacher development and the individual means that were suggested on pp. 559–568. If members of the class have tried any of these, they could share their experiences with the class and offer comments on what worked and what did not work.
11. **(D)** In the last section of this chapter, roles of a growing, developing teacher were presented. Ask your class to assess the feasibility of taking on these roles. Which ones seem to be more easily accomplished and which ones the most difficult or complex?

FOR YOUR FURTHER READING

Richards, J., & Farrell, T. (2005). *Professional development for language teachers: Strategies for teacher learning*. Cambridge, UK: Cambridge University Press.

Crandall, J., & Miller, S. (2014). Effective professional development for language teachers. In M. Celce-Murcia, D. Brinton, & M. A. Snow (Eds.), *Teaching English as a second or foreign language* (4th ed., pp. 630–648). Boston, MA: National Geographic Learning.

Both offer practical suggestions for a number of professional development options for teachers, including such topics as teacher support groups, teaching journals, peer observation, portfolios, and action research. The Crandall and Miller chapter lists language teacher associations, journals, and web references.

Murphy, J. (2014). Reflective teaching: Principles and practices. In M. Celce-Murcia, D. Brinton, & M. A. Snow (Eds.), *Teaching English as a second or foreign language* (4th ed., pp. 613–629). Boston, MA: National Geographic Learning.

Richards, J., & Farrell, T. (2011). *Practice teaching: A reflective approach*. Cambridge, UK: Cambridge University Press.

Two resources for how to creatively reflect on your teaching, with useful bibliographies.

Bailey, K. (2014). Classroom research, teacher research, and action research in language teaching. In M. Celce-Murcia, D. Brinton, & M. A. Snow (Eds.), *Teaching English as a second or foreign language* (4th ed., pp. 601–612). Boston, MA: National Geographic Learning.

Burns, A. (2010). *Doing action research in English language teaching: A guide for practitioners*. New York, NY: Routledge.

Burns, A. (2011). Action research in the field of second language teaching and learning. In E. Hinkel (Ed.), *Handbook of research in second language teaching and learning, Volume II.* (pp. 237–253). New York, NY: Routledge.

These three sources summarize developments in action research with examples of classroom-based projects, along with suggestions for conducting research in your language classroom.

Egbert, J. (Ed.). (2003). *Becoming contributing professionals*. Alexandria, VA: Teachers of English to Speakers of Other Languages.

Murphey, T. (Ed.). (2003). *Extending professional contributions*. Alexandria, VA: Teachers of English to Speakers of Other Languages.

Byrd, P., & Nelson, G. (2003). *Sustaining professionalism*. Alexandria, VA: Teachers of English to Speakers of Other Languages.

Murphey, T., & Sato, K. (2005). *Communities of supportive professionals*. Alexandria, VA: Teachers of English to Speakers of Other Languages.

This series of short books (125–150 pages each) describes useful ideas for professional development, with contributions from classroom teachers around the world.

CHAPTER **23**

TEACHERS FOR SOCIAL RESPONSIBILITY

Questions for Reflection

- What are the challenges to becoming a socially responsible teacher?
- What are widely held interpretations of what it means to engage in critical pedagogy? How might teachers put such principles into practice?
- How does a teacher introduce controversial issues into classroom activities and treat them sensitively, while respecting students' beliefs and cultural values?
- What are some of the moral dilemmas of taking up the challenge to be an *agent for change*?
- How might one articulate a set of *ethics for language teaching* that is consonant with one's personal beliefs?

> "You must be the change you want see in the world." – Mohandas Gandhi
>
> "The fundamentally spiritual nature of life . . . inspires me to struggle for a better world, meaningful teaching, and ethical and caring relationships." — Suresh Canagarajah
>
> "We exist briefly as identifiable, self-aware organisms in a continuing dance of cosmic energy/matter. Joy." — Julian Edge
>
> "I am committed to opposing those who wish to promote their vision of the world to the exclusion of others, and to try to understand how it is that different understandings of the world are constructed." — Alastair Pennycook
>
> "My nomadic life is guided by intercultural tolerance, an agnostic appreciation of diversity, and a wish to combat injustice that is man-made and therefore can be counteracted by ethically impelled humans." — Robert Phillipson

In this final chapter we'll address an aspect of language teaching that penetrates well below the surface of the professional and technical skills implied in effective teaching. The *critical* nature of language learning and teaching can in many ways be pervasive in your professional life.

The quotes above are from notable language educators (Wong & Canagarajah, 2009, pp. xi–xiv). Well yes, of course, one of them is from the venerable Mahatma Gandhi! They represent an eloquent set of convictions, that which drives them, stirs their souls, and impels them to continue to be better and better *critical* educators.

Ask yourself what, in the deepest foundations of your heart and mind, *drives* you in your chosen profession. What convictions and beliefs directed you into the profession? What sense of purpose continues to propel you through hours and days and weeks of teaching, possibly at a fairly low wage? What is it that somehow prods you to wake up every Monday morning, a bit blurry-eyed perhaps, but ready to face new challenges and opportunities?

Somewhere in those profound recesses of your mind and emotion you are guided by a sense of mission, purpose, and dedication to a profession in which you believe you can make a difference. Your sense of **social responsibility** directs you to be an "agent for change." You're driven by convictions about what this world should look like, how its people should behave, how its governments should control that behavior, and how its inhabitants should be partners in the stewardship of the planet. In the words of Giroux and McLaren (1989, p. xiii), you strive to "embody in [your] teaching a vision of a better and more humane life."

CRITICAL PEDAGOGY

These fundamental moral principles within us have been examined in recent years in what educational professionals have called **critical pedagogy** (Freire, 1970, 1974; Crookes, 2009, 2013; Tollefson, 2011). Canagarajah (2005) shied away from a direct, empirical definition of critical pedagogy, but noted that it implies a way of "doing" learning and teaching, motivated by our beliefs about education and its place in society:

> Critical students and teachers are prepared to situate learning in the relevant social contexts, unravel the implications of power in pedagogical activity, and commit themselves to transforming the means and ends of learning, in order to construct more egalitarian, equitable, and ethical educational and social environments (p. 932).

Critical pedagogy implies that as language teachers we are more than facilitators of communication; we are charged with the responsibility to help our students to "be all that they can be," to seize their agency, to be Earth's stewards, to seek justice, and, through language, to be peacemakers. Let's look at some of the ramifications of this responsibility.

Teaching as a Subversive Activity

The call for teachers to act critically, as agents for change, is not a new one. Almost half a century ago, Postman and Weingartner (1969) shook some educational foundations with their best seller, *Teaching as a Subversive Activity*. In their stinging critique of the American educational establishment, they challenged teachers to enable their students to become "crap" detectors:

- those who will push beyond the facades of convention and correctness, and make major *changes* in our social, economic, and political systems
- those who will cut through burgeoning *bureaucracies*, which are repositories of conventional assumptions and standard practices
- those who will find ways to release us from the stranglehold of the *media*, which often creates its own version of censorship

Classroom Connections

Think about this story from an English teacher in Egypt:

In Egypt, a culture where equal opportunities and rights of women are abridged, an English teacher tells of teaching a class with both men and women in it in which students discussed "bills of rights" from various countries. Then, her culminating activity asked her students collaboratively to write up a "bill of rights" for women in Egypt. Some students questioned why they "must" do this activity, but accepted the task, and after the final activity, agreed that they learned something!

Was this teacher "subversive"? In what ways did she help to make changes in a system? To question standard practices? Would you be willing to be as courageous? How do you suppose her students reacted?

The call for subversive teaching is not unlike the challenge to English language teachers today to engage in critical pedagogy. Those of us who teach languages may indeed have a special responsibility to "subvert" attitudes and beliefs and assumptions that ultimately impede the attainment of such goals as equality, justice, freedom, and opportunity.

Some educators, notably Edge (2003), McLaren (2005), and Giroux (2006), have taken a "strong" interpretation of the implications of critical pedagogy. The title alone of McLaren's (2005) book, *Capitalists and Conquerors: A Critical Pedagogy Against the Empire*, provides a picture of its contents: a call to teachers for classroom practices that assertively direct students toward becoming critical thinkers (and doers) in the face of war, violence, corruption, imperialism, greed, and waste of natural resources.

Some Cautionary Observations

Debates over the means and ends of carrying out critical pedagogies bring with them some warnings. We are reminded that our learners must be free to be themselves, to think for themselves, to behave intellectually without coercion from a powerful elite (Clarke, 1990, 2003), to cherish their beliefs and traditions and cultures without the threat of forced change (Edge, 1996; Benesch, 2001; Norton & Toohey, 2004; Wong & Canagarajah, 2009).

In our classrooms, where "the dynamics of power and domination permeate the fabric of classroom life" (Auerbach, 1995, p. 9), we are alerted to a possible "covert political agenda [beneath our] overt technical agenda" (Phillipson, 1992, p. 27). Julian Edge (2003, p. 705) cautions against those who might teach English out of a religious "conversion-motivated" zeal, lest the very act of teaching English create its own hegemony, a theme echoed by Scollon (2004), Kubota (2009), and Tollefson (2011).

Classroom Connections

The following is taken from Doug's personal journal:

In an office-hour conversation, my student confessed that she wanted to be a language teacher because it was the best way, she thought, to spread the Christian gospel. She suggested including in her lessons Christian teachings and biblical passages, so that her students would know about Jesus Christ, and ultimately accept him as Lord and Savior. I drew a deep breath and praised her for having strong convictions. But I reminded her that teaching in a government-sponsored, taxpayer-funded university obligated her to embody constitutional affirmations of religious liberty and equal treatment of all faiths. I suggested that in our California state institution, the classroom could be a podium but not a pulpit.

How do you reconcile what may perhaps be your strong religious convictions with the call to affirm your students' right to have their own religious beliefs, which may differ markedly from yours? How do you draw lines of distinction between *podium* and *pulpit* in your classroom?

What has come to be known as **liberation education** (Freire, 1970; Clarke, 1990, 2003), must no doubt be tempered with some cautionary observations. Some have recently argued that our ostensibly benign assumptions about teaching methodology (Holliday, 1994; Pennycook, 2001; Canagarajah, 2005) have an element of controversy in them. Are student-centered, collaborative approaches to the classroom universally accepted by all cultures and all educational traditions? Probably not. Gadd (1998), for example, cautioned *against* viewing ourselves as a "nurturer of souls . . ." because this "inappropriate and oppressive role . . . does not encourage or permit the students' intellectual and cognitive development."

The counterpoint to this rallying of teachers to change a world mired in bureaucracies is epitomized, in what Skutnabb-Kangas and Phillipson (1994) called **linguicism**. Phillipson (1992) argued that, historically at least, worldwide English language teaching has served to "legitimize . . . an unequal division of power and resources," as "the dominant language [English] is glorified, [and] dominated languages are stigmatized" (p. 27). Now, while Holliday (1994) argues that Phillipson's stance "implies a conspiracy view of English language teaching which is over-simplistic and naive" (p. 99), nevertheless perhaps all of us need to take heed lest we become the inadvertent perpetuators of a widening of the gap between haves and have-nots. Language is power, and the unequal distribution of language programs across the world surely could contribute to the ultimate unequal distribution of power (Macedo, Dendrinos, & Gounari, 2003; Norton & Toohey, 2004).

Is there a middle ground? Some writers suggest that there is (Snow, 2001; Clarke, 2003; Edge, 2003; Johnston, 2003; Canagarajah, 2005, 2009; Edge, 2009). In the face of current mounting threats from warring nations, polarized ideologies, and even crises in climate change, we are in dire need of information, understanding, and communication. Such educative processes must be undertaken with the utmost care (Dewaele, 2004).

Your own language classroom is an excellent place to begin the quest for a more humane world. Our classrooms can themselves become models of mutual respect across cultural, political, and religious boundaries. As we take up Julian Edge's (2006, 2009) challenge to engage in nonjudgmental discourse in our classrooms, we begin the journey. Can English language teachers facilitate the formation of classroom communities of learners who critically examine moral, ethical, and political issues surrounding them, and do so sensitively, without pushing a personal subversive agenda? In the next section, we offer some guidelines for teaching, along with some examples of engaging in critical pedagogy while respecting the values and beliefs of our students.

CONTROVERSIAL ISSUES IN THE LANGUAGE CLASSROOM

A number of the topics that we address in our classrooms (e.g., nonviolence, human rights, gender equality, racial/ethnic discrimination, health issues, environmental action, and political activism) are controversial. They demand critical thinking, and they are sensitive to students' value systems. They cannot, in any context, be simply thrown into a classroom routine without risking alienation, anger, or resentment on the part of students.

Consider three guiding principles for engaging in teaching with social responsibility, that is, critical pedagogy that fully respects the values and beliefs of your students.

1. Keeping an Open Mind

Give students opportunities to learn about important social, moral, or ethical issues and to analyze all sides of an issue. A language class is an ideal locus for offering information on topics of significance to students. The objectives of a curriculum are not limited to linguistic factors alone, but also include developing the art of critical thinking. Complex issues (religious fundamentalism or sexual orientation, for example) can become the focus of relevant, meaningful content-based language learning.

Classroom Connections

Some have suggested that teachers should never express their personal opinion on a controversial topic, and that they should therefore remain neutral and balanced in equally treating both (or all) sides of a touchy issue. Consider this situation:

A student in a class discussion of "people I admire in history" once said, "I admire Hitler because of his courage to stand up for his beliefs and his strong leadership."

What would you do next? Would you remain *completely* neutral in your response to such a comment? Or might your response ultimately convey your own opinion about what Hitler's "courage and leadership" did to millions of innocent people?

2. Respect

Create an atmosphere of respect for each other's opinions, beliefs, and ethnic or cultural diversity. The classroom becomes a model of the world as a context for tolerance and for the appreciation of diversity. Discourse structures such as "I see your point, but . . ." are explicitly taught and used in classroom discussions and debates. Students learn how to disagree without imposing their own beliefs or opinions on others. In all this, it is important that the teacher's personal opinions or beliefs remain sensitively covert, lest a student feel coerced into thinking something because the teacher thinks that way.

Pratt (1991) proposed the concept of "contact zones" in classrooms, which she referred to as "social spaces where cultures meet, clash, and grapple with each other, often in contexts of highly asymmetrical relations of power, such as colonism, slavery, or their aftermaths as they are lived out in many parts of the world today" (p. 34). She goes on to note that we sometimes presume our personal values and beliefs to be beyond reproach, an attitude worthy of continued self-examination.

Classroom Connections

This is an excerpt from Doug's personal journal:

I received an email last week from an instructor of Arabic who referred to a previous edition of Teaching by Principles, and asked about my comparing language learners (and their varying styles and strategies) to participants in an elaborate wine-tasting party. She noted that in her culture the analogy was not appropriate, since "we do not drink wine." I responded with thanks for her sensitivity, and promised the analogy would be removed in the next edition. That analogy has been expunged!

What are some of the inadvertent offensive cultural assumptions that you might make in your teaching? Is it possible to remove all mention of everything that could offend a student? If you do offend someone, how should you treat it?

3. Morality and Ethics

Maintain a threshold of morality and ethics in the classroom climate. Occasionally a teacher needs to exercise some discipline when students show disrespect or hatred based on, say, race, religion, ethnicity, or gender. Teachers should ascertain that "universal" moral principles (love, equality, tolerance, freedom) are manifested in the classroom. This guideline is, in effect, a paradox because it presupposes certain values to be beyond reproach. Such a presupposition violates the very principle of respect captured in the guideline (#2) above. Nevertheless, this is where one's pedagogy becomes "critical" in that the teacher's vision of "a better and more humane life" is usually predicated on such basic values.

Classroom Connections

Here's an excerpt from Doug's journal:

One English teacher had students study censorship and suppression of free speech in another country—not their own—calling for critical analysis of the roots and remedies of what he personally believed was a denial of freedom. Without espousing any particular point of view, and under the guise of offering criticism of another country's practices, the teacher led students to examine alternative points of view—and subliminally, to look at their own country's practices in reporting political and ideological news stories.

To what extent might certain topics be frowned upon (or forbidden) in your educational and cultural context? Suppose you were asked to teach a unit on same-sex marriage, abortion rights, or "death with dignity" (the right of terminally ill patients to take their own lives)? How would you approach such a topic?

A number of presentations and publications show that educators are increasingly taking bold steps to incorporate global concerns and social responsibility in their classrooms. In the TESOL organization, a fast-growing Interest Section is *Teachers for Social Responsibility*. At a recent TESOL convention, the following presentations were made:

- Fostering sustainability: Bringing the environment into the language classroom
- Confronting intolerance: Teaching English in a culture of respect
- Motivating performers and audience to combat prejudice through readers' theater
- Gender bias in the Moroccan ELT guidelines
- From cross-cultural curriculum to socially responsible students

Interest groups in other organizations and conferences are embracing presentations on controversial and other critical issues (Garfield, 2004; Givner, 2004; Sampedro & Hillyard, 2004; Graybill & Shehan, 2006). In Japan, a quarterly publication, *Global Issues in Language Education Newsletter*, has a worldwide readership.

 **Classroom Connections**

Can you engage in "sensitive" critical pedagogy in your classroom? What are some activities you can do that would respect students' points of view yet stir them to a higher consciousness of their own role as *agents of change*? The little differences here and there that you make can add up to fulfilling visions of a better and more humane world.

MORAL DILEMMAS AND MORAL IMPERATIVES

The process of engaging in a socially responsible approach in which we teachers take up the challenge of being agents for change brings with it some moral dilemmas (Wong & Canagarjah, 2009). How far should we push our own personal beliefs and agendas in our zeal for realizing visions of a better world and for creating critically thinking future leaders among our students? Do you have the right to subversively push your vision of the ideal world out there?

Intertwined in these kinds of questions are a number of *moral dilemmas*, but each dilemma carries with it what we're calling a *moral imperative*. Consider the following dilemmas, and their corollaries in the form of imperatives, that call us to action as socially responsible teachers (H. D. Brown, 2009).

1. Cultural Biases of Communicative Approaches

Our widely accepted communicative approach to language teaching (CLT), which aims to empower and value students, may itself reflect a cultural bias that is not universally embraced. Not all educational traditions value the learner-centered, interactive approaches that could—in the mind of a teacher—usurp the teacher's authority (and power) in the classroom. We believe such a dilemma can be resolved in the following moral imperative:

> Respect the diversity of cultural patterns and expectations among our students, while utilizing the best methodological approaches available to accomplish course goals and objectives.

Classroom Connections

Suppose you were offered a well-paying position to teach in an institution that frowned upon group and pair work, that felt that students should speak only when asked to, that required students to face the teacher at all times, and that promoted a lot of individual memorization. You need the job and the money, so you accept it. How would you approach the administration to allow you to take a communicative, student-centered approach to your teaching?

2. *Dis*empowerment

In the case of English as a global language, altruistic "agendas" for bringing English to the world at large might have the potential of legitimizing an unequal division of power and resources. As noted above, the very act of teaching English may have the residual effect of widening the gap between "haves" and "have nots" by enabling an elite class to distinguish itself from a less powerful group by the ability to use English. Here's a possible moral imperative that may resolve this:

> Help students to claim their own power and resources, and to bridge the gaps that separate countries, political structures, religions, and values through a unifying language, but to do all we can to celebrate indigenous heritage languages and cultures.

Classroom Connections

In Brazil, a curriculum for children takes them on an adventure trip using "magic glasses," which—they discover—enables them to "see" a world in which native cultures of Brazil are held in high esteem, people of different races are treated equally, and family heritages are celebrated.

In this curriculum, children at a young age are taught certain values that may not be *universal*. Does it appear that *all* sides of the issues are being taught? Probably not. But is it okay to teach children what we see as highly positive values without presenting opposing values? Remember, they are children, but are they being "indoctrinated"?

3. Balancing Perspectives

In our curricular materials, our choices of topics and issues present us with opportunities to stimulate critical thinking but also to offend and polarize students. But those materials risk being very bland and uninteresting if everything that has a remote potential of being offensive is deleted. Perhaps some middle ground can be achieved in this moral imperative:

> Sensitively, with due attention to the potential for students to be offended and polarized, approach critical, relevant, and informative issues in appropriate pedagogical contexts with as balanced a perspective as possible, and with the particular cultural sensitivities of your students well in mind.

Classroom Connections

Here's an excerpt from Doug's journal:

I was shocked when, with my team of writers, the publisher said "no" to our unit on HIV/AIDS education and prevention of sexually transmitted diseases. It was, we thought, a sensitive unit that raised much needed awareness. The publisher said they would never be able to market the book with that unit in it. It was too "offensive."

Was the publisher (from a marketing viewpoint) justified in their decision? Is there a line between being too offensive (and upsetting students) and being so bland in our topics and issues that students lose interest? How can you introduce controversial topics in a sensitive way?

4. Maintaining Neutrality?

Our discussions, debates, group work activities, essays, and other classroom tasks offer opportunities for us to be agents for change, but does our zeal for realizing our own vision of a better world stand in the way of *genuinely* equal, balanced treatment of all sides of controversial issues? Is it realistic to think that a teacher can completely hide his or her own beliefs on such fundamental issues as racial hatred, nonviolence, gender equality, gay rights, environmental stewardship, or freedom of expression, to name a few? Students have an uncanny ability to "psych out" their teachers, and it's difficult for you to remain staunchly neutral on issues about which you feel very passionately. Perhaps this dilemma can be at least partially resolved in the following resolution:

Guided by a clear vision of your own mission as a teacher, promote critical thinking on complex issues, remain as neutral as possible in the process, but be fully aware that you are almost certainly promoting a set of values in your classroom, even if somewhat covertly or "subversively."

 **Classroom Connections**

Here's an excerpt from Doug's journal:

In a recent teacher workshop, the topic of "hate groups" was suggested as a possible set of readings, discussions, and debates for an advanced L2 class. When it was suggested that <u>*all sides*</u> *of an issue—pro's and con's—should be presented, one teacher responded, "I'm never going to present or tolerate anything positive about hate groups, racial, religious, or otherwise. We can discuss why people hate, but I would never ask a student to represent anything 'good' about it."*

How would you respond to this teacher? Was she justified in drawing the line where she did? Can you justify her refusal to "tolerate" intolerance? How would you approach the same ethical issue?

AGENTS FOR CHANGE

No doubt all of the above dilemmas are commonly experienced among teachers around the world. However, if we're too daunted by the dilemmas, we risk becoming passive supporters of a status quo that may be in dire need of change.

If we shrink from our responsibility as change agents, surely we will have lost the opportunity to act on the imperatives that can drive us as teachers. We will have lost the chance, in Gandhi's words at the beginning of this chapter, to *be* the change we want to see in the world!

Can you take a bold step forward and at the same time respect the beliefs and attitudes of your students? What are some activities you can do that would respect students' points of view yet stir them to a higher consciousness of their own role as agents of change? How would you respond to statements from students that seem to support hate, violence, or intolerance? The little differences here and there that you make can add up to fulfilling visions of better and more humane world.

Your role as a socially responsible teacher highlights the fact that you're not merely a *language* teacher. You're much more than that! Our professional commitment drives us to help the inhabitants of this planet to communicate with each other, to negotiate the meaning of peace, of goodwill, and of survival on this fragile globe. You're an agent for change in a world in desperate need of change: change from competition to cooperation, from war to peace, from powerlessness to empowerment, from conflict to resolution, from prejudice to understanding.

FOR THE TEACHER: ACTIVITIES (A) & DISCUSSION (D)

Note: For each of the "Classroom Connections" in this chapter, you may wish to turn them into individual or pair-work discussion questions.

1. **(D)** Ask your students to volunteer definitions, in their *own* words, of *critical pedagogy*, and to provide one or two illustrative classroom examples that they have either experienced in their own teaching or seen other teachers carry out. Then suggest that they share their examples in a blog or on a class website.
2. **(D)** Ask students their opinion of Phillipson's claim that English language teaching can lead to what he called *linguicism*. What examples or counterexamples might students have? (Note these on the board.) What are some suggestions for circumventing the possible outcome that knowledge of English could create a further gap between socioeconomic classes?
3. **(A)** Pair up your students and ask them to brainstorm some current controversial issues in local, national, or world news. Then ask them to report to the rest of class their top three issues. Write them on the board. Then put the pairs into groups of four, and ask them to choose any *one* topic on the board and outline a *task* that could be built round the topic. What lexical, grammatical, or discourse objectives would the task seek to highlight?

4. **(A)** Here's an account of one teacher's experience with critical pedagogy:

   A language teacher recounted a unit in which students had to create an ethical marketing and advertising campaign for a product. Cases of Colgate's widening the mouth of toothpaste tubes and of Revlon's making the glass on nail polish bottles a little thicker led students to debate ethical business issues. Students then sent their findings to various companies by email and web links.

   Ask pairs to brainstorm some instances of similar marketing ploys to make people think they are getting *more* of a product or that the product is *superior*. Then ask them to state specific steps in a lesson that could have their students address the issue and take action beyond the classroom. What linguistic elements might such a task feature?
5. **(D)** Three guidelines were offered here for treating controversial issues in the classroom (pages 579–581). To what extent do your students agree that these guidelines are useful? Would they add to or change any of them?
6. **(D)** Ask your students to do some research to find information on organizations, Internet sources, or print media that promote social responsibility and the treatment of global and/or controversial issues. Then have them bring the information back to class for discussion or post their findings on a class website.
7. **(A)** Four moral dilemmas and imperatives were proposed in this chapter. Assign one dilemma/imperative to a pair or group and have them discuss (a) the extent of their agreement or disagreement with the dilemma as stated, (b) any additional information they would add to the statement of the dilemma, (c) personal experiences either learning or teaching a language that any have had that illustrate the dilemma, and (d) any cautionary statements they would add to the "moral imperative" that was stated here. Then ask them to report back to the whole class.
8. **(D)** At the beginning of the chapter, five quotes were given that represent a "vision of a better and more humane life." Ask individuals to freewrite their own personal "vision" or convictions regarding their role as a language teacher. Then, *only if they want to*, ask some of them to share their statement with the rest of the class. They might also opt to post their thoughts as a blog for the rest of the class.

FOR YOUR FURTHER READING

Canagarajah, A. S. (2005). Critical pedagogy in L2 learning and teaching. In E. Hinkel (Ed.), *Handbook of research in second language teaching and learning* (pp. 931–949). Mahwah, NJ: Lawrence Erlbaum Associates.

Crookes, G. (2013). Critical pedagogy in language teaching. In C. Chapelle (Ed.), *The encyclopedia of applied linguistics* (pp. 1511–1514). West Sussex, UK: Blackwell Publishing Ltd.

Two different surveys of developments, research, and controversies in critical pedagogy. Extensive bibliographies are included in each.

Norton, B., & Toohey, K. (Eds.). (2004). *Critical pedagogies and language learning.* Cambridge, UK: Cambridge University Press.

An anthology of different international perspectives on critical pedagogy in English language teaching contexts.

Wong, M., & Canagarajah, S. (Eds.). (2009). *Christian and critical English language educators in dialogue: Pedagogical and ethical dilemmas.* New York, NY: Routledge.

A stimulating anthology of 30 chapters written by educators describing and analyzing their perception of the "spiritual" nature of critical pedagogy. Some of the chapters are responses, thus comprising a fascinating dialogue among educators.

Johnston, B. (2003). *Values in English language teaching.* Mahwah, NJ: Lawrence Erlbaum Associates.

An analysis of personal and moral issues that arise in the process of language teaching, with a balance in treating the controversies.

Tollefson, J. (2011). Ideology in second language education. In E. Hinkel (Ed.), *Handbook of research in second language teaching and learning, Volume II.* (pp. 801–816). New York, NY: Routledge.

An analysis of the manner in which ideology—power and power relationships, assumptions, beliefs—shape societies as well as educational institutions.

Sampedro, R., & Hillyard, S. (2004). *Global issues.* Oxford, UK: Oxford University Press.

A description of classroom activities that focus on global issues, indexed by awareness raising, personal experience, global issues, music, and drama.

Some useful websites for your reference:

Educators for Social Responsibility:

esrnational.org

Global Issues Newsletter (Japan):

gilesig.org

Peace Education Foundation:

www.peace-ed.org

TESOL Social Responsibility Interest Section:

www.tesol.org/connect/interest-sections/social-responsibility

BIBLIOGRAPHY

Aebersold, J., & Field, M. (1997). *From reader to reading teacher: Issues and strategies for second language classrooms.* Cambridge, UK: Cambridge University Press.

Agar, M. (1994). *Language shock: Understanding the culture of conversation.* New York, NY: William Morrow and Company, Inc.

Agger, M. (2008). Lazy eye: How we read online. *Slate.* Retrieved from http://www.slate.com/articles/technology/the_browser/2008/06/lazy_eyes.html

Ahearn, L. (2001). Language and agency. *Annual Review of Anthropology, 30,* 109–137.

Alderson, J. C. (2000). *Assessing reading.* Cambridge, UK: Cambridge University Press.

Alderson, J. C., & Banerjee, J. (2001). Language testing and assessment (Part 1). *Language Teaching, 34,* 213–236.

Alderson, J. C., & Banerjee, J. (2002). Language testing and assessment (Part 2). *Language Teaching, 35,* 79–113.

Aljaafreh, A., & Lantolf, J. (1994). Negative feedback as regulation and second language learning in the zone of proximal development. *Modern Language Journal, 78,* 465–483.

Allen, H. (1980, April). What it means to be a professional in TESOL. Lecture presented at the conference of TEXTESOL.

Allwright, D., & Hanks, J. (2009). *The developing language learner: An introduction to exploratory practice.* New York, NY: Palgrave MacMillan.

Alsagoff, L. (2012). Identity and the EIL learner. In L. Alsagoff, S. McKay, G. Hu, & W. Renandya (Eds.), *Principles and practices for teaching English as an international language* (pp. 104–122). New York, NY: Routledge.

Alsagoff, L., McKay, S., Hu, G., & Renandya, W. (Eds.). (2012). *Principles and practices for teaching English as an international language.* New York, NY: Routledge.

American Council on the Teaching of Foreign Languages. (2012). *ACTFL proficiency guidelines 2012—speaking.* Alexandria, VA: American Council on the Teaching of Foreign Languages.

Anderson, B. (1991). *Imagined communities: Reflections on the origin and spread of nationalism.* New York, NY: Verso.

Anderson, N. (1999). *Exploring second language reading: Issues and strategies.* Boston, MA: Heinle & Heinle.

Anderson, N. (2003a). L2 learning strategies. In E. Hinkel (Ed.), *Handbook of research in second language teaching and learning* (pp. 757–771). Mahwah, NJ: Lawrence Erlbaum Associates.

Anderson, N. (2003b). Reading. In D. Nunan (Ed.), *Practical English language teaching* (pp. 67–86). New York, NY: McGraw-Hill Contemporary.

Anderson, N. (2004). Metacognitive reading strategy awareness. *CATESL Journal, 16,* 11–27.

Anderson, N. (2014). Developing engaged second language readers. In M. Celce-Murcia, D. Brinton, & M. A. Snow (Eds.), *Teaching English as a second or foreign language* (4th ed., pp. 170–188). Boston, MA: National Geographic Learning.

Anderson, V. (2013). *How to cheat on college papers and tests*. Seattle, WA: Amazon Digital Services, Inc.

Anthony, E. (1963). Approach, method, and technique. *English Language Teaching, 17,* 63–67.

Armstrong, T. (1994). *Multiple intelligences in the classroom*. Philadelphia, PA: Association for Curriculum Development.

Arnold, J. (Ed.). (1999). *Affect in language learning*. Cambridge, UK: Cambridge University Press.

Arnold, J., & Murphey, T. (Eds.). (2013). *Meaningful action: Earl Stevick's influence on language teaching*. Cambridge, UK: Cambridge University Press.

Asher, J. (1977). *Learning another language through actions: The complete teacher's guidebook*. Los Gatos, CA: Sky Oaks Productions.

Atkinson, D. (2003). L2 writing in the post-process era: Introduction. *Journal of Second Language Writing, 12,* 3–15.

Atkinson, D. (2010). Extended, embodied cognition and second language acquisition. *Applied Linguistics, 31,* 599–622.

Atkinson, D. (2011). A sociocognitive approach to second language acquisition. In D. Atkinson (Ed.), *Alternative approaches to second language acquisition* (pp. 143–166). New York, NY: Routledge.

Auerbach, E. (1995). The politics of the ESL classroom: Issues of power in pedagogical choice. In J. Tollefson (Ed.), *Power and inequality in language education* (pp. 9–33). Cambridge, UK: Cambridge University Press.

August, D., Shanahan, T., Christian, D., & Beck, I. (2006). *Developing literacy in second-language learners: A report of the national literacy panel on language minority children and youth*. Washington, DC: Center for Applied Linguistics.

Ausubel, D. (1963). Cognitive structure and the facilitation of meaningful verbal learning. *Journal of Teacher Education, 14,* 217–221.

Ausubel, D. (1968). *Educational psychology: A cognitive view*. New York, NY: Holt, Rinehart & Winston.

Aydin, Z., & Yildiz, S. (2014). Using wikis to promote collaborative EFL writing. *Language Learning & Technology, 18,* 160–180.

Azar, B., & Hagen, S. (2011). *Fundamentals of English grammar* (4th ed.). White Plains, NY: Pearson Education ESL.

Bachman, L. (1990). *Fundamental considerations in language testing*. New York, NY: Oxford University Press.

Bachman, L. (2005). Building and supporting a case for test use. *Language Assessment Quarterly, 2,* 1–34.

Bachman, L., & Palmer, A. (1996). *Language testing in practice*. New York, NY: Oxford University Press.

Bachman, L., & Palmer, A. (2010). *Language assessment in practice*. Oxford, UK: Oxford University Press.

Baetens Beardsmore, H. (2009). Language promotion by European supra-national institutions. In O. Garcia & H. Baetens Beardsmore (Eds.), *Bilingual education in the 21st century: A global perspective* (pp. 197–217). Malden, MA: Wiley-Blackwell.

Bailey, K. (1985). Classroom-centered research on language teaching and learning. In M. Celce-Murcia, *Beyond basics: Issues and research in TESOL* (pp. 96–121). Rowley, MA: Newbury House.

Bailey, K. (2003). Speaking. In D. Nunan (Ed.), *Practical English language teaching* (pp. 47–66). New York, NY: McGraw-Hill Contemporary.

Bailey, K. (2005). *Practical English language teaching: Speaking.* New York, NY: McGraw-Hill.

Bailey, K. (2014). Classroom research, teacher research, and action research in language teaching. In M. Celce-Murcia, D. Brinton, & M. A. Snow (Eds.), *Teaching English as a second or foreign language* (4th ed., pp. 601–612). Boston, MA: National Geographic Learning.

Bailey, K., Curtis, A., & Nunan, D. (2001). *Pursuing professional development: The self as source.* Boston, MA: Heinle & Heinle.

Baker, C. (2011). *Foundations of bilingual education and bilingualism* (5th ed.). Clevedon, UK: Multilingual Matters.

Bakhtin, M. (1981). *The dialogic imagination: Four essays.* Austin, TX: University of Texas Press.

Bamford, J., & Day, R. (1998). Teaching reading. *Annual Review of Applied Linguistics, 18,* 124–141.

Banathy, B., Trager, E., & Waddle, C. (1966). The use of contrastive data in foreign language course development. In A. Valdman (Ed.), *Trends in Language Teaching* (pp. 35–56). New York, NY: McGraw-Hill.

Bandura, A. (1986). *Social foundations of thought and action: A social cognitive theory.* Englewood Cliffs, NJ: Prentice-Hall.

Bandura, A. (1997). *Self-efficacy: The exercise of control.* New York, NY: Freeman.

Bandura, A. (2000). Exercise of human agency through collective efficacy. *Current Directions in Psychological Science, 9,* 75–78.

Bandura, A. (2001). Social cognitive theory: An agentic perspective. *Annual Review of Psychology, 52,* 1–26.

Barrett, L. (2009). Variety is the spice of life: A psychological construction approach to understanding variability in emotion. *Cognition and Emotion, 23,* 1284–1306.

Bassano, S., & Christison, M. A. (1984). Teacher self-observation. *TESOL Newsletter, 18,* 17–19.

Bax, S. (2003). The end of CLT: A context approach to language teaching. *ELT Journal, 57,* 278–287.

Beare, K. (2010). How many people learn English globally? Retrieved December 7, 2013 from http://esl.about.com/od/englishlearningresources/f/f_eslmarket.htm

Belcher, D. (Ed.). (2009). *English for specific purposes in theory and practice.* Ann Arbor, MI: University of Michigan Press.

Belcher, D., & Lukkarila, L. (2011). Identity in ESP context: Putting the learner in front and center in needs. In D. Belcher, A. Johns, & B. Paltridge (Eds.), *New directions for ESP research.* Ann Arbor, MI: University of Michigan Press.

Bell, D. (2003). Method and postmethod: Are they really so incompatible? *TESOL Quarterly, 37,* 325–336.

Bell, D. (2007). Do teachers think that methods are dead? *ELT Journal, 61*, 135–143.

Bell, J. (2012). Teaching mixed level classes. In A. Burns & J. Richards (Eds.), *The Cambridge guide to pedagogy and practice in second language teaching* (pp. 86–94). Cambridge, UK: Cambridge University Press.

Benesch, S. (2001). *Critical English for academic purposes.* Mahwah, NJ: Lawrence Erlbaum Associates.

Benson, P. (2001). *Teaching and researching autonomy in language learning.* London, UK: Longman.

Benson, P. (2003). Learner autonomy in the classroom. In D. Nunan (Ed.), *Practical English language teaching* (pp. 289–308). New York, NY: McGraw-Hill Contemporary.

Benson, P. (2007). Autonomy in language teaching and learning. *Language Teaching, 40*, 21–40.

Berlitz, M. (1887). *Méthode Berlitz*. New York, NY: Berlitz and Company.

Biber, D., & Conrad, S. (2001). Quantitative corpus-based research: Much more than bean counting. *TESOL Quarterly, 35*, 331–336.

Blackwell, A., & Naber, T. (2006). *Open forum: Academic listening and speaking.* New York, NY: Oxford University Press.

Blake, R. J. (2013). *Brave new digital classroom: Technology and foreign language learning* (2nd ed.). Washington, DC: Georgetown University Press.

Blanchard, L. (2013). *Writing Power 1*. White Plains, NY: Pearson Education.

Blattner, G., & Fiori, M. (2011). Virtual social network communities: An investigation of language learners' development of sociopragmatic awareness and multiliteracy skills. *CALICO Journal, 29*, 24–43.

Bley-Vroman, R. (1983). The comparative fallacy in interlanguage studies: The case of systematicity. *Language Learning, 33*, 1–17.

Block, D. (2003). *The social turn in second language acquisition*. Washington, DC: Georgetown University Press.

Block, D. (2007). The rise of identity in SLA research: Post Firth and Wagner (1997). *The Modern Language Journal, 91*, 863–876.

Blommaert, J. (2010). *The sociolinguistics of globalization*. Cambridge, UK: Cambridge University Press.

Blommaert, J. (2013). Citizenship, language, and superdiversity: Towards complexity. *Journal of Language, Identity, and Education, 12*, 193–196.

Bohlke, D. (2014). Fluency-oriented second language teaching. In M. Celce-Murcia, D. Brinton, & M. A. Snow (Eds.), *Teaching English as a second or foreign language* (4th ed., pp. 121–135). Boston, MA: National Geographic Learning.

Bohlke, D., & Rogers, B. (2011). *Listening power 2*. White Plains, NY: Pearson Longman.

Borg, S. (2003a). Pulp fiction? The research journal and professional development. In T. Murphey (Ed.), *Extending professional contributions* (pp. 39–46). Alexandria, VA: Teachers of English to Speakers of Other Languages.

Borg, S. (2003b).Teacher cognition in language teaching: A review of research on what language teachers think, know, believe, and do. *Language Teaching, 36,* 81–109.

Böttcher, E. (2014). *Longman academic reading series 1: Reading skills for college.* White Plains, NY: Pearson Education.

Bourdieu, P. (1991). *Language & symbolic power.* Cambridge, UK: Polity Press.

Bowen, J. D., Madsen, H., & Hilferty, A. (1985). *TESOL techniques and procedures.* Rowley, MA: Newbury House.

Braine, G. (1999). *Nonnative educators in English language teaching.* Mahwah, NJ: Lawrence Erlbaum Associates.

Breen, M., & Candlin, C. (1980). The essentials of a communicative curriculum in language teaching. *Applied Linguistics, 1,* 89–112.

Brinton, D. (2003). Content-based instruction. In D. Nunan (Ed.), *Practical English language teaching* (pp. 199–224). New York, NY: McGraw-Hill Contemporary.

Brinton, D. (2013). Content-based instruction in English for specific purposes. In C. Chapelle (Ed.), *The encyclopedia of applied linguistics* (pp. 897–906). West Sussex, UK: Wiley-Blackwell.

Brinton, D., Snow, M. A., & Wesche, M. (1989). *Content-based second language instruction.* Rowley, MA: Newbury House.

Brock, C. (1986). The effects of referential questions on ESL classroom discourse. *TESOL Quarterly, 20,* 47–59.

Brophy, J. (1981). Teacher praise: A functional analysis. *Review of Educational Research, 51,* 5–32.

Brown, G. (2010). Listening in a second language. In M. Berns (Ed.), *Concise encyclopedia of applied linguistics* (pp. 157–163). Oxford, UK: Elsevier.

Brown, H. D. (1970). Categories of spelling difficulty in speakers of English as a first and second language. *Journal of Verbal Learning and Verbal Behavior, 9,* 232–236.

Brown, H. D. (1973). Affective variables in second language acquisition. *Language Learning, 23,* 231–244.

Brown, H. D. (1991). *Breaking the language barrier.* Yarmouth, ME: Intercultural Press.

Brown, H. D. (1993). After method: Toward a principled strategic approach to language teaching. In J. Alatis (Ed.), *Proceedings of the Georgetown University round table on languages and linguistics* (pp. 509–520). Washington, DC: Georgetown University Press.

Brown, H. D. (1999). *New vistas: An interactive course in English.* Getting started, Books 1 and 2. Upper Saddle River, NJ: Prentice Hall Regents.

Brown, H. D. (2000). *New vistas: An interactive course in English.* Book 3. White Plains, NY: Pearson Education.

Brown, H. D. (2001). *New vistas: An interactive course in English.* Book 4. White Plains, NY: Pearson Education.

Brown, H. D. (2002a). English language teaching in the "post-method" era: Toward better diagnosis, treatment, and assessment. In J. Richards & W. Renandya (Eds.), *Methodology in language teaching* (pp. 9–18). Cambridge, UK: Cambridge University Press.

Brown, H. D. (2002b). *Strategies for success: A practical guide to learning English.* White Plains, NY: Pearson Education.

Brown, H. D. (2009). Imperatives, dilemmas, and conundrums in spiritual dimensions of ELT. In M. Wong & S. Canagarajah (Eds.), *Christian and critical English language educators in dialogue: Pedagogical and ethical dilemmas* (pp. 265–271). New York, NY: Routledge.

Brown, H. D. (2014). *Principles of language learning and teaching* (6th ed.). White Plains, NY: Pearson Education.

Brown, H. D., & Abeywickrama, P. (2010). *Language assessment: Principles and classroom practices* (2nd ed.). White Plains, NY: Pearson Longman.

Brown, J. (1991). Do English faculties rate writing samples differently? *TESOL Quarterly, 25,* 587–603.

Brown, J. (1995). *The elements of language curriculum: A systematic approach to program development.* Boston, MA: Heinle & Heinle.

Brown, J. (1998). *New ways of classroom assessment.* Alexandria, VA: TESOL.

Brown, J. (2005). *Testing in language programs: A comprehensive guide to English language assessment.* New York, NY: McGraw-Hill.

Brown, J. (2010). Second language curriculum development. In M. Berns (Ed.), *Concise encyclopedia of applied linguistics* (pp. 341–349). Amsterdam, The Netherlands: Elsevier.

Brown, J., & Hudson, T. (1998). The alternatives in language assessment. *TESOL Quarterly, 32,* 653–675.

Brown, S. (2011). *Listening myths.* Ann Arbor, MI: University of Michigan Press.

Brumfit, C., & Johnson, K. (1979). *The communicative approach to language teaching.* Oxford, UK: Oxford University Press.

Bruner, J. (1962). *On knowing: Essays for the left hand.* Cambridge, MA: Harvard University Press.

Bruner, J. (1961). The act of discovery. *Harvard Educational Review, 31*, 21–32.

Buck, G. (2001). *Assessing listening*. Cambridge, UK: Cambridge University Press.

Burns, A. (2005). Action research. In E. Hinkel (Ed.), *Handbook of research in second language teaching and learning* (pp. 241–256). Mahwah, NJ: Lawrence Erlbaum Associates.

Burns, A. (2010). *Doing action research in English language teaching: A guide for practitioners.* New York, NY: Routledge.

Burns, A. (2011). Action research in the field of second language teaching and learning. In E. Hinkel (Ed.), *Handbook of research in second language teaching and learning*, Volume II. (pp. 237–253). New York, NY: Routledge.

Bybee, J. (2006). From usage to grammar: The mind's response to repetition. *Language, 82,* 711–733.

Bygate, M., Skehan, P., & Swain, M. (Eds.). (2001). *Researching pedagogic tasks: Second language learning, teaching, and testing*. London, UK: Longman.

Byram, M. (2000). Assessing intercultural competence in language teaching. *Sprogforum, 18,* 8–13. Retrieved on 20 October 2013 from http://inet.dpb.dpu.dk/infodok/sprogforum/Espr18/byram.html

Byrd, P., & Nelson, G. (2003). *Sustaining professionalism*. Alexandria, VA: Teachers of English to Speakers of Other Languages.

Byrd, P., & Schuemann, C. (2014). English as a second/foreign language textbooks: How to choose them—how to use them. In M. Celce-Murcia, D. Brinton, & M. A. Snow (Eds.), *Teaching English as a second or foreign language* (4th ed., pp. 380–393). Boston, MA: National Geographic Learning.

Cambridge, D., Cambridge, B., & Yancey, K. B. (2009). *Electronic portfolios 2.0: Emergent research on implementation and impact.* Sterling, VA: Stylus.

Campbell, R. (1978). Notional-functional syllabuses 1978: Part I. In C. H. Blatchford & J. Schachter (Eds.), *On TESOL 78: EFL policies, programs, practices* (pp. 15–19). Washington, DC: Teachers of English to Speakers of Other Languages.

Canagarajah, S. (2005). Critical pedagogy in L2 learning and teaching. In E. Hinkel (Ed.), *Handbook of research in second language teaching and learning* (pp. 931–949). Mahwah, NJ: Lawrence Erlbaum Associates.

Canagarajah, S. (2004). Subversive identities, pedagogical safe houses, and critical learning. In B. Norton & K. Toohey (Eds.), *Critical pedagogies and language learning* (pp. 116–37). New York, NY: Cambridge University Press.

Canagarajah, S. (2007). Lingua franca English, multilingual communities, and language acquisition. *The Modern Language Journal, 91*, 923–939.

Canagarajah, S. (2009). New possibilities for the spiritual and the critical in pedagogy. In M. Wong & S. Canagarajah (Eds.), *Christian and critical English language educators in dialogue: Pedagogical and ethical dilemmas* (pp. 1–18). New York, NY: Routledge.

Canagarajah, S. (2013). *Translingual practice: Global Englishes and cosmopolitan relations.* New York, NY: Routledge.

Canale, M. (1983). From communicative competence to communicative language pedagogy. In J. Richards & R. Schmidt (Eds.), *Language and communication* (pp. 2–27). London, UK: Longman Group, Ltd.

Canale, M., & Swain, M. (1980). Theoretical bases of communicative approaches to second language teaching and testing. *Applied Linguistics, 1,* 1–47.

Carroll, J., & Sapon, S. (1958). *Modern language aptitude test.* New York, NY: Psychological Corporation.

Casanave, C. (2004). *Controversies in second language writing.* Ann Arbor, MI: University of Michigan Press.

Cassriel, B., & Martinsen, M. (2010). *Academic connections: 1.* White Plains, NY: Pearson Longman.

Celce-Murcia, M., & Olshtain, E. (2014). Teaching language through discourse. In Celce-Murcia, M., Brinton, D., & Snow, M.A. (Eds.), *Teaching English as a second or foreign language* (4th ed.) (pp. 424–437). Boston, MA: National Geographic Learning.

Celce-Murcia, M., Brinton, D., & Snow, M. A. (Eds.). (2014). *Teaching English as a second or foreign language* (4th ed.). Boston, MA: National Geographic Learning.

Celik, S. (2012). Internet-assisted technologies for English language teaching in Turkish universities. *Computer Assisted Language Learning, 26*, 468–483.

Chamot, A. (2005). Language learning strategy instruction: Current issues and research. *Annual Review of Applied Linguistics, 25,* 112–130.

Chamot, A., & McKeon, D. (1984). *Second language teaching.* Rosslyn, VA: National Clearinghouse for Bilingual Education.

Chamot, A., O'Malley, M., & Kupper, L. (1992). *Building bridges: Content and learning strategies for ESL.* Books 1–3. New York, NY: Heinle & Heinle.

Chan, W., Chin, K., & Suthiwan, T. (Eds.). (2011). *Foreign Language Teaching in Asia and Beyond: Current Perspectives and Future Directions.* Amsterdam, The Netherlands: de Gruyter Mouton.

Chapelle, C. (2011). Validation in language assessment. In E. Hinkel (Ed.), *Handbook of research in second language teaching and learning, Volume II* (pp. 717–730). New York, NY: Routledge.

Chapelle, C. (2013). Instructional computer-assisted language learning. In C. Chapelle (Ed.), *The encyclopedia of applied linguistics* (pp. 2718–2721). West Sussex, UK: Wiley-Blackwell.

Chapelle, C., & Jamieson, J. (2008). *Tips for teaching with CALL: Practical approaches to computer-assisted language learning.* White Plains, NY: Pearson Education, Inc.

Chapelle, C., & Plakans, L. (2013). Assessment and testing: Overview. In C. Chapelle (Ed.), *The encyclopedia of applied linguistics* (pp. 241–244). West Sussex, UK: Blackwell Publishing Ltd.

Chen, H. (2013). Identity practices of multilingual writers in social networking spaces. *Language Learning & Technology, 17,* 143–170. Retrieved from http://llt.msu.edu/issues/june2013/chen.pdf

Chen, K. (2005). Preferences, styles, behavior: The composing processes of four ESL students. *CATESOL Journal, 17,* 19–37.

Chiu, L., & Tulley, M. (1997). Student preferences of teacher discipline styles. *Journal of Instructional Psychology, 24,* 168–175.

Christenbury, L., & Kelly, P. (1983). *Questioning: A path to critical thinking.* Urbana, IL: National Council of Teachers of English.

Christison, M. A. (2005). *Multiple intelligences and language learning.* San Francisco, CA: Alta Book Center Publishers.

Christison, M.A., & Bassano, S. (1984, August). Teacher self-observation. *TESOL Newsletter,* pp. 17–19.

Chun, D. (2008). Computer-mediated discourse in instructed environments. In S. Magnan (Ed.), *Mediating discourse online* (pp. 15–44). Amsterdam, The Netherlands: John Benjamins.

Cizek, G. (1999). *Cheating on tests: How to do it, detect it, and prevent it.* New York, NY: Routledge.

Claire, E. (1988). *ESL teacher's activities kit.* Englewood Cliffs, NJ: Prentice-Hall.

Clark, H., & Clark, E. (1977). *Psychology and language: An introduction to psycholinguistics.* New York, NY: Harcourt Brace Jovanovich.

Clark, J. L. D. (1983). Language testing: Past and current status—directions for the future. *Modern Language Journal, 67,* 431–443.

Clarke, M. (1990). Some cautionary observations on liberation education. *Language Arts, 67,* 388–398.

Clarke, M. (1994). The dysfunction of the theory/practice discourse. *TESOL Quarterly, 28*, 9–26.

Clarke, M. (2003). *A place to stand: Essays for educators in troubled times.* Ann Arbor, MI: University of Michigan Press.

Clarke, M., & Silberstein, S. (1977). Toward a realization of psycholinguistic principles for the ESL reading class. *Language Learning, 27,* 135–154.

Cohen, A. (2011). *Strategies in learning and using a second language.* Harlow, UK: Pearson Education.

Coleman, A. (1929). *The teaching of modern foreign languages in the United States: A report prepared for the modern language study.* New York, NY: Macmillan.

Comas-Quinn, A., Mardomingo, R., & Valentine, C. (2009). Mobile blogs in language learning: making the most of informal and situated learning opportunities. *ReCALL, 21*, 96–112.

Connor, U. (1996). *Contrastive rhetoric: Cross-cultural aspects of second language writing.* Cambridge, UK: Cambridge University Press.

Connor, U. (2002). New directions in contrastive rhetoric. *TESOL Quarterly, 36,* 493–510.

Connor, U. (2011). *Intercultural rhetoric in the writing classroom.* Ann Arbor, MI: University of Michigan Press.

Connor, U., Nagelhout, E., & Rozycki, W. (Eds.). (2008). *Contrastive rhetoric: Reaching to intercultural rhetoric.* Amsterdam, The Netherlands: John Benjamins.

Conrad, S. (2005). Corpus linguistics and L2 teaching. In E. Hinkel (Ed.), *Handbook of research in second language teaching and learning* (pp. 393–409). Mahwah, NJ: Lawrence Erlbaum Associates.

Constantino, P., & De Lorenzo, M. (2002). *Developing a professional teaching portfolio.* Boston, MA: Allyn & Bacon.

Cook, V. (1999). Going beyond the native speaker in language teaching. *TESOL Quarterly, 33*, 185–209.

Cook, V. (2013). Multicompetence. In C. A. Chapelle (Ed.), *The encyclopedia of applied linguistics* (pp. 3768–3774). West Sussex, UK: Blackwell Publishing Ltd.

Council of Europe. (2001). *Common European framework of reference for languages: Learning, teaching, assessment.* Cambridge, UK: Cambridge University Press.

Covey, S. (1990). *The seven habits of highly effective people: Powerful lessons in personal change.* New York, NY: Simon & Schuster.

Cowan, R. (2008). *The teacher's grammar of English.* Cambridge, UK: Cambridge University Press.

Crandall, J. (1999). Cooperative language learning and affective factors. In J. Arnold (Ed.), *Affect in language learning* (pp. 226–245). Cambridge, UK: Cambridge University Press.

Crandall, J., & Miller, S. (2014). Effective professional development for language teachers. In M. Celce-Murcia, D. Brinton, & M. A. Snow (Eds.), *Teaching English as a second or foreign language* (4th ed., pp. 630–648). Boston, MA: National Geographic Learning.

Crandall, J., & Shin, J. (2013). *Teaching young learners English.* Boston, MA: Heinle ELT.

Creese, A., & Blackledge, A. (2010). Translanguaging in the bilingual classroom: A pedagogy for learning and teaching? *The Modern Language Journal, 94*, 103–115.

Crookes, G. (2009). The practicality and relevance of second language critical pedagogy. *Language Teaching, 43*, 333–48.

Crookes, G. (2013). Critical pedagogy in language teaching. In C. Chapelle (Ed.), *The encyclopedia of applied linguistics* (pp. 284–290). London, UK: Blackwell Publishing Ltd.

Crookes, G., & Chaudron, C. (1991). Guidelines for classroom language teaching. In M. Celce-Murcia, *Teaching English as a second or foreign language* (2nd ed., pp. 46–66). New York, NY: Newbury House.

Cullen, R. (2012). Grammar instruction. In A. Burns & J. Richards (Eds.), *The Cambridge guide to pedagogy and practice in second language teaching* (pp. 258–266). New York, NY: Cambridge University Press.

Cumming, A. (2012). Writing development in second language acquisition. In C. Chapelle (Ed.), *The encyclopedia of applied linguistics* (pp. 6254–6258). West Sussex, UK: Blackwell Publishing Ltd.

Cummins, J. (2001). *Negotiating identities: Education for empowerment in a diverse society* (2nd ed.). Los Angeles, CA: California Association for Bilingual Education.

Cummins, J. (2007). Rethinking monolingual instructional strategies in multilingual classrooms. *Canadian Journal of Applied Linguistics, 10*, 221–240.

Cunningham, D. (2002). Semiotic inquiry in education. *Teaching and Learning, 17*, 19–24.

Cunningsworth, A. (1995). *Choosing your coursebook*. Oxford, UK: Heinemann.

Curran, C. (1972). *Counseling-learning: A whole person model for education*. New York, NY: Grune & Stratton.

Curran, C. (1976). *Counseling-learning in second languages*. Cliffside Park, NJ: Counseling-Learning Institutes.

Curtain, H., & Dahlberg, C. (2010). *Languages and children—making the match: New languages for young learners* (4th ed.). White Plains, NY: Pearson.

Cziko, G. (1982). Improving the psychometric, criterion-referenced, and practical qualities of integrative language tests. *TESOL Quarterly, 16*, 367–379.

Dale, P. (2013). *Speech Communication made simple: 1*. White Plains, NY: Pearson Longman.

Dale, P., & Wolf, J. (2013). *Speech communication made simple: 2*. White Plains, NY: Pearson Longman.

Damasio, A. (1994). *Descartes' error: Emotion, reason and the human brain*. New York, NY: Avon Books.

Damasio, A. (2003). *Looking for Spinoza: Joy, sorrow and the feeling brain*. New York, NY: Harcourt Brace.

Day, R., & Bamford, J. (1998). *Extensive reading in the second language classroom*. Cambridge, UK: Cambridge University Press.

Deci, E. (1975). *Intrinsic motivation*. New York, NY: Plenum Press.

Deci, E., & Ryan, R. (1985). *Intrinsic motivation and self-determination in human behavior*. New York, NY: Plenum Publishing Co.

Deci, E., & Ryan, R. (Eds.). (2002). *Handbook of self-determination research.* Rochester, NY: The University of Rochester Press.

DeKeyser, R., & Criado, R. (2013). Automatization, skill acquisition, and practice in second language acquisition. In C. Chapelle (Ed.), *The encyclopedia of applied linguistics* (pp. 323–331). London, UK: Blackwell Publishing Ltd.

DeKeyser, R., & Koeth, J. (2011). Cognitive aptitudes for second language learning. In E. Hinkel (Ed.), *Handbook of research in second language teaching and learning, Volume II* (pp. 395–406). New York, NY: Routledge.

Demouy, V., & Kukulska-Hulme, A. (2010). On the spot: Using mobile devices for listening and speaking practice on a French language programme. *Open Learning, 25,* 217–232.

Derwing, T., & Munro, M. (2005). Second language accent and pronunciation teaching: A research-based approach. *TESOL Quarterly, 39,* 379–397.

Desjarlais R. (1997). *Shelter blues: Sanity and selfhood among the homeless.* Philadelphia, PA: University of Pennsylvania Press.

Devine, J., & Eskey, D. (2004). Literacy as sociocultural practice: Comparing Chinese and Korean readers. *CATESOL Journal, 16,* 81–96.

Dewaele, J. (2004). Slaying the dragon on fanaticism through enlightenment. *Modern Language Journal, 88,* 620–622.

Dewey, J. (1896). The reflex arc concept in psychology. *Psychological Review, 3,* 357–370.

Dole, J., Brown, K., & Trathen, K. (1996). The effects of strategy instruction on the comprehension performance of at-risk students. *Reading Research Quarterly, 31,* 62–88.

Dörnyei, Z. (2001). *Motivational strategies in the language classroom.* Cambridge, UK: Cambridge University Press.

Dörnyei, Z. (2005). *The psychology of the language learner: Individual differences in second language acquisition.* Mahwah, NJ: Lawrence Erlbaum Associates.

Dörnyei, Z. (2009). The L2 motivational self system. In Z. Dörnyei & E. Ushioda (Eds.), *Motivation, language identity and the L2 self* (pp. 9–42). Bristol, UK: Multilingual Matters.

Dörnyei, Z., & Murphey, T. (2003). *Group dynamics in the language classroom.* Cambridge, UK: Cambridge University Press.

Dörnyei, Z., & Skehan, P. (2003). Individual differences in L2 learning. In C. Doughty & M. Long (Eds.), *The handbook of second language acquisition* (pp. 589–630). Malden, MA: Blackwell Publishing.

Dörnyei, Z., & Ushioda, E. (2011). *Teaching and researching motivation* (2nd ed.). Harlow, UK: Pearson Education, Ltd.

Dörnyei, Z., & Ushioda, E. (Eds.). (2009). *Motivation, language identity and the L2 self.* Bristol, UK: Multilingual Matters.

Dorr, R. (2006). Something old is new again: Revisiting Language Experience. *The Reading Teacher, 60,* 138–146.

Douglas, D. (2005). Testing languages for specific purposes. In E. Hinkel (Ed.), *Handbook of research in second language teaching and learning* (pp. 857–868). Mahwah, NJ: Lawrence Erlbaum Associates.

Dove, M., & Honigsfeld, A. (2010). ESL coaching and collaboration: Opportunities to develop teacher leadership and enhance student learning. *TESOL Journal, 1*, 3–23.

Duff, P. (2002). The discursive co-construction of knowledge, identity, and difference: An ethnography of communication in the high school mainstream. *Applied Linguistics, 23*, 289–322.

Duff, P. (2012). Identity, agency, and SLA. In A. Mackey & S. Gass (Eds.), *Handbook of second language acquisition* (pp. 410–426). London, UK: Routledge.

Dunkel, P. (1991). Listening in the native and second/foreign language: Toward an integration of research and practice. *TESOL Quarterly, 25,* 431–457.

Echevarria, J., Vogt, M., & Short, D. (2012). *Making content comprehensible for English learners: The SIOP model* (4th ed.). White Plains, NY: Pearson Education.

Edelsky, C. (1993). Whole language in perspective. *TESOL Quarterly, 27,* 548–550.

Edge, J. (1996). Cross-cultural paradoxes in a profession of values. *TESOL Quarterly, 30,* 9–30.

Edge, J. (2003). Imperial troopers and servants of the Lord: A vision of TESOL for the 21st century. *TESOL Quarterly, 37,* 701–709.

Edge, J. (2006, March). *Daring not to evaluate.* Paper presented at TESOL, Tampa, FL.

Edge, J. (2009). Non-judgmental steps on a road to understanding. In M. Wong & S. Canagarajah (Eds.), *Christian and critical English language educators in dialogue: Pedagogical and ethical dilemmas* (pp. 21–34). New York, NY: Routledge.

Edge, J. (Ed.). (2001). *Action research.* Alexandria, VA: Teachers of English to Speakers of Other Languages.

Edgeworth, F. Y. (1888). The statistics of examinations. *Journal of the Royal Statistical Society, 51,* 599–635.

Ediger, A. (2014). Teaching second/foreign language literacy to school-age learners. In M. Celce-Murcia, D. Brinton, & M. A. Snow (Eds.), *Teaching English as a second or foreign language* (4th ed., pp. 154–169). Boston, MA: National Geographic Learning.

Egbert, J. (Ed.). (2003). *Becoming contributing professionals.* Alexandria, VA: Teachers of English to Speakers of Other Languages.

Elley, W. (2001). Literacy in the present world: Realities and possibilities. In L. Verhoeven & C. Snow (Eds.), *Literacy and motivation: Reading engagement in individuals and groups* (pp. 225–242). Mahwah, NJ: Lawrence Erlbaum Associates.

Ellis, N. (2012). Frequency-based accounts of second language acquisition. In S. M. Gass & A. Mackey (Eds.), *The Routledge handbook of second language acquisition* (pp. 193–210). New York, NY: Routledge.

Ellis, N., & Collins, L. (2009). Input and second language acquisition: The role of frequency, form, and function. *The Modern Language Journal, 93, 329–335.*

Ellis, R. (2003). *Task-based language teaching and learning.* Oxford, UK: Oxford University Press.

Ellis, R. (2009). The differential effects of three types of task planning on the fluency, complexity, and accuracy in L2 oral production. *Applied Linguistics, 30,* 474–509.

Ellis, R. (2012). *Language teaching research and language pedagogy.* Malden, MA: Wiley-Blackwell.

Ellis, R. (2014). Principles of instructed second language learning. In Celce-Murcia, M., Brinton, D. M., & Snow, M. A. (Eds.), *Teaching English as a second or foreign language* (4th ed.) (pp. 31–45). Boston, MA: National Geographic Learning.

Eskey, D. (2005). Reading in a second language. In E. Hinkel (Ed.), *Handbook of research in second language teaching and learning* (pp. 563–579). Mahwah, NJ: Lawrence Erlbaum Associates.

Eyring, J. (1991). Experiential language learning. In M. Celce-Murcia (Ed.), *Teaching English as a second or foreign language* (2nd ed., pp. 346–359). New York, NY: Newbury House.

Eyring, J. (2014). Adult learners in English as a second/foreign language settings. In Celce-Murcia, M., Brinton, D. M., & Snow, M.A. (Eds.), *Teaching English as a second or foreign language* (4th ed.) (pp. 568–583). Boston, MA: National Geographic Learning.

Facebook. (2014). Newsroom. *Statistics: Facebook.* Retrieved from http://newsroom.fb.com/company-info.

Ferris, D. (1997). The influence of teacher commentary on student revision. *TESOL Quarterly, 31,* 315–339.

Ferris, D. (2011). *Treatment of error in L2 student writing* (2nd ed.) Ann Arbor, MI: University of Michigan Press.

Ferris, D. (2012). Written corrective feedback in second language acquisition and writing studies. *Language Teaching, 45,* 446–459.

Ferris, D., & Hedgcock, J. (2005). *Teaching ESL composition: Purpose, process, and practice* (2nd ed.). Mahwah, NJ: Lawrence Erlbaum Associates.

Ferris, D., & Hedgcock, J. (2014). *Teaching L2 composition: Purpose, process, and practice* (3rd ed.). New York, NY: Routledge.

Finocchiaro, M., & Brumfit, C. (1983). *The functional-notional approach: From theory to practice.* New York, NY: Oxford University Press.

Fitzgerald, J. (1994). How literacy emerges: Foreign language implications. *Language Learning Journal, 9,* 32–35.

Flowerdew, J. (Ed.). (1994). *Academic listening: Research perspectives.* Cambridge, UK: Cambridge University Press.

Flowerdew, J., & Miller, L. (2005). *Second language listening: Theory and practice.* Cambridge, UK: Cambridge University Press.

Flowerdew, J., & Miller, L. (2014). Dimensions of academic listening. In M. Celce-Murcia, D. Brinton, & M. A. Snow (Eds.), *Teaching English as a second or foreign language* (4th ed., pp. 90–103). Boston, MA: National Geographic Learning.

Fogle, L. (2012). *Second language socialization and learner agency: Adoptive family talk.* Bristol, UK: Multilingual Matters.

Freeman, D. (1998). *Doing teacher research: From inquiry to understanding.* Boston, MA: Heinle & Heinle.

Freeman, D. (2002). The hidden side of the work: Teacher knowledge and learning to teach. *Language Teaching, 35,* 1–13.

Freire, P. (1970). *Pedagogy of the oppressed.* New York, NY: Seabury Press.

Freire, P. (1974). Education: The practice of freedom. In P. Freire, *Education for critical consciousness*. London, UK: Sheed & Ward. (Original work published 1967)

Fries, C. (1945). *Teaching and learning English as a foreign language*. Ann Arbor, MI: University of Michigan Press.

Frodesen, J. (2014). Grammar in second language writing. In M. Celce-Murcia, D. Brinton, & M. A. Snow (Eds.), *Teaching English as a second or foreign language* (4th ed., pp. 238–253). Boston, MA: National Geographic Learning.

Gadd, N. (1998). Point and counterpoint: Towards less humanistic English teaching. *English Language Teaching Journal, 52*, 223–234.

García, O. (2009). *Bilingual education in the 21st century: A global perspective*. Malden, MA: Wiley-Blackwell.

García, O. (2013). Bilingual education. In C. Chapelle (Ed.), *The encyclopedia of applied linguistics* (pp. 425–429). West Sussex, UK: Wiley-Blackwell.

García, O., & Sylvan, C. (2011). Pedagogies and practices in multilingual classrooms: Singularities in pluralities. *The Modern Language Journal, 95*, 385–400.

Gardner, H. (1983). *Frames of mind: The theory of multiple intelligences*. New York, NY: Basic Books.

Gardner, H. (1999). *Intelligence reframed: Multiple intelligences for the 21st century*. New York, NY: Basic Books.

Gardner, H. (2004). *Frames of mind: The theory of multiple intelligences* (2nd ed.). New York, NY: Basic Books.

Gardner, H. (2011). *Frames of mind: The theory of multiple intelligences* (3rd ed.). New York, NY: Basic Books.

Gardner, R. (1985). *Social psychology and second language learning: The role of attitudes and motivation*. London, UK: Edward Arnold.

Gardner, R., & Lambert, W. (1972). *Attitudes and motivation in second language learning*. Rowley, MA: Newbury House.

Garfield, M. (2004, December). Students' attitudes toward controversial social issues in the ESL classroom. Paper presented at the MATESOL conference, San Francisco State University, San Francisco.

Garinger, D. (2002). *Textbook selection for the ESL classroom*. Washington, DC: Center for Applied Linguistics. (Available online at www.cal.org)

Garrison, M. (2009). *A measure of failure: The political origins of standardized testing*. Albany, NY: SUNY Press.

Garton, S., Copland, F., & Burns, A. (2011). *Investigating global practices in teaching English to young learners*. London, UK: British Council.

Gattegno, C. (1972). *Teaching foreign languages in schools: The silent way* (2nd ed.). New York, NY: Educational Solutions.

Gebhard, J. (2006). *Teaching English as a second or foreign language: A self-development and methodology guide* (2nd ed.). Ann Arbor, MI: University of Michigan Press.

Gee, J. (2011). *An introduction to discourse analysis: Theory and method* (3rd ed.). New York, NY: Routledge.

Genesee, F., & Upshur, J. (1996). *Classroom-based evaluation in second language education*. Cambridge, UK: Cambridge University Press.

Gibbons, J. (1985). The silent period: An examination. *Language Learning, 35,* 255–267.

Gibbs, R. (2006). *Embodiment and cognitive science.* New York, NY: Cambridge University Press.

Giroux, H. (2006). *America on the edge: Henry Giroux on politics, culture, and education.* New York, NY: Palgrave Macmillan.

Giroux, H., & McLaren, P. (1989). *Critical pedagogy, the state, and cultural struggle.* Albany, NY: State University of New York Press.

Givner, K. (2004, May). *The use of socially controversial topics in the academic ESL classroom.* Paper presented at the MATESOL conference, San Francisco State University, San Francisco.

Goh, C. (2014). Second language listening comprehension: Process and pedagogy. In M. Celce-Murcia, D. Brinton, & M. A. Snow (Eds.), *Teaching English as a second or foreign language* (4th ed., pp. 72–89). Boston, MA: National Geographic Learning.

Goldstein, L. (2010). Finding "theory" in the particular: An "autobiography" of what I learned and how about teacher feedback. In S. Tony & P. Matsuda (eds.), *Practicing theory in second language writing* (pp. 106–126). West Lafayette, IN: Parlor Press.

Goleman, D. (1995). *Emotional intelligence.* New York, NY: Bantam Books.

Goodman, K. (1970). Reading: A psycholinguistic guessing game. In H. Singer & R. B. Ruddell (Eds.), *Theoretical models and processes of reading* (pp. 497–508). Newark, DE: International Reading Association.

Goodwin, J. (2014). Teaching pronunciation. In M. Celce-Murcia, D. Brinton, & M. A. Snow (Eds.), *Teaching English as a second or foreign language* (4th ed., pp. 136–152). Boston, MA: National Geographic Learning.

Goodwin, M. (1990). *He-said-she-said: Talk as social organization among black children.* Bloomington, IN: Indiana University Press.

Gor, K., & Long, M. (2009). Input and second language processing. In W. Ritchie & T. Bhatia (Eds.), *The new handbook of second language acquisition* (pp. 445–472). Bingley, UK: Emerald Group Publishing, Ltd.

Gouin, F. 1880. *L'art d'enseigner et d'étudier les langues.* Paris, France: Librairie Fischbacher. Translation by H. Swan & V. Bétis (1892), *The art of teaching and studying languages.* London, UK: Philip.

Gould, S. (1996). *The mismeasure of man.* New York, NY: W.W. Norton & Company.

Grabe, W. (2004). Research on teaching reading. *Annual Review of Applied Linguistics, 24,* 44–69.

Grabe, W. (2009). *Reading in a second language: Moving from theory to practice.* New York, NY: Cambridge University Press.

Grabe, W., & Stoller, F. (2011). *Teaching and researching reading* (2nd ed.). White Plains, NY: Pearson Longman.

Grabe, W., & Stoller, F. (2014). Teaching reading for academic purposes. In M. Celce-Murcia, D. Brinton, & M. A. Snow (Eds.), *Teaching English as a second or foreign language* (4th ed., pp. 189–205). Boston, MA: National Geographic Learning.

Graddol, D. (2006). *English next: Why global English may mean the end of "English as a Foreign Language."* London, UK: British Council.

Graves, K. (1996). *Teachers as course developers.* Cambridge, UK: Cambridge University Press.

Graves, K. (2000). *Designing language courses: A guide for teachers.* Boston, MA: Heinle & Heinle.

Graves, K. (2014). Syllabus and curriculum design for second language teaching. In M. Celce-Murcia, D. Brinton, & M. A. Snow (Eds.), *Teaching English as a second or foreign language* (4th ed., pp. 46–62). Boston, MA: National Geographic Learning.

Graybill, R., & Shehane, M. (2006, May). *Using global topics in the ESL classroom.* Paper presented at the MATESOL conference, San Francisco State University, San Francisco, CA.

Green, J., & Oxford, R. (1995). A closer look at learning strategies, L2 proficiency, and gender. *TESOL Quarterly, 29,* 261–297.

Guiora, A., Brannon, R., & Dull, C. (1972). Empathy and second language learning. *Language Learning, 22,* 111–130.

Gurung, B., & Rutledge, D. (2014). Digital learners and the overlapping of their personal and educational digital engagement. *Computers & Education*, 77, 91–100.

Hall, G., & Cook, G. (2012). Own language use in language teaching and learning. *Language Teaching, 45,* 271–308.

Halliday, M. A. K. (1978). *Language as social semiotic: The social interpretation of language and meaning.* Baltimore: University Park Press.

Halliday, M. A. K. (2004). *An introduction to functional grammar* (3rd ed.). London, UK, & New York, NY: Hodder Arnold.

Hamp-Lyons, L. (2011). English for academic purposes. In E. Hinkel (Ed.), *Handbook of research in second language teaching and learning: Volume II* (pp. 89–105). New York, NY: Routledge.

Harklau, L. (2000). From the "good kids" to the "worst": Representations of English language learners across educational settings. *TESOL Quarterly, 34,* 35–67.

Harmer, J. (2001). *The practice of English language teaching.* (3rd ed.). Harlow, UK: Pearson Education Ltd.

Harmer, J. (2003). Popular culture, methods, and context. *ELT Journal, 57,* 288–294.

Harmer, J. (2007). *The practice of English language teaching.* (4th ed.). Harlow, UK: Pearson Longman.

Hartshorn, K. J., Evans, N., Merrill, P., Sudweeks, R., Strong-Krause, D., & Anderson, N. (2010). Effects of dynamic corrective feedback on ESL writing accuracy. *TESOL Quarterly, 44,* 84–109.

Harwood, N. (Ed.). (2010). *English language teaching materials: Theory and practice.* Cambridge, UK: Cambridge University Press.

Haught, J., & McCafferty, S. (2008). Embodied language performance: Drama and the ZPD in the second language classroom. In J. Lantolf & M. Poehner (Eds.), *Sociocultural theory and the teaching of second languages* (pp. 139–162). London, UK, & Oakville, CT: Equinox.

Healey, D., Hanson-Smith, E., Hubbard, P., Ioannou-Georgiou, S., Kessler, G., & Ware, P. (2011). *TESOL technology standards: Description, implementation, integration*. Alexandria, VA: TESOL International Association.

Hedgcock, J. (2002). Toward a socioliterate approach to second language teacher education. *Modern Language Journal, 86,* 299–317.

Hedgcock, J. (2005). Taking stock of research and pedagogy in L2 writing. In E. Hinkel (Ed.), *Handbook of research in second language teaching and learning* (pp. 597–613). Mahwah, NJ: Lawrence Erlbaum Associates.

Hedgcock, J. (2009). Acquiring knowledge of discourse conventions in teacher education. In A. Burns & J. Richards (Eds.), *The Cambridge guide to second language teacher education* (pp. 144–152). Cambridge, UK: Cambridge University Press.

Hedgcock, J., & Ferris, D. (2009). *Teaching readers of English: Students, texts, and contexts*. New York, NY: Routledge.

Hedge, T. (2005). *Writing*. Oxford, UK: Oxford University Press.

Heift, T., & Chapelle, C. (2012). Language learning through technology. In S. M. Gass & A. Mackey (Eds.), *The Routledge handbook of second language acquisition* (pp. 555–569). New York, NY: Routledge.

Helgesen, M., & Brown, S. (2007). *Practical English language teaching: Listening*. New York, NY: McGraw-Hill.

Helgesen, M., Brown, S., & Wiltshier, J. (2009). *English firsthand. Book 1*. Hong Kong, China: Pearson Education Asia.

Helgesen, M., Brown, S., & Wiltshier, J. (2010). *English firsthand: Success*. Hong Kong, China: Pearson Longman Asia ELT.

Hendrickson, J. (1980). Error correction in foreign language teaching: Recent theory, research, and practice. In K. Croft (Ed.), *Readings on English as a second language* (2nd ed., pp. 153–173). Cambridge, MA: Winthrop.

Hensher, P. (2013). *The missing link: The lost art of handwriting*. London, UK: Faber & Faber.

Higgins, C. (2003). "Ownership" of English in the outer circle: An alternative to the NS-NNS dichotomy. *TESOL Quarterly*, 37, 615–644.

Hinkel, E. (2006). Current perspectives on teaching the four skills. *TESOL Quarterly, 40*, 109–131.

Hinkel, E. (2011). What research on second language writing tells us and what it doesn't. In E. Hinkel (Ed.), *Handbook of research in second language teaching and learning, Volume II*. (pp. 523–538). New York, NY: Routledge.

Hinkel, E. (2014). Culture and pragmatics in language teaching and learning. In Celce-Murcia, M., Brinton, D., & Snow, M. A. (Eds.), *Teaching English as a second or foreign language* (4th ed.) (pp. 394–408). Boston, MA: National Geographic Learning.

Hofstede, G. (1986). Cultural differences in teaching and learning. *International Journal of Intercultural Relations, 10*, 301–320.

Holliday, A. (1994). *Appropriate methodology and social context*. Cambridge, UK: Cambridge University Press.

Hollinger, D. (1995). *Postethnic America: Beyond multiculturalism*. New York, NY: Basic Books.

Holloway, L. (2013). *Hotel English, teacher's edition* (2nd ed.). Las Vegas, NV: Workplace ESL Solutions.

Hopper, P. (1988). Emergent grammar and the a priori grammar postulate. In D. Tannen (Ed.), *Linguistics in context: Connecting observation and understanding* (pp. 117–134). Norwood, NJ: Ablex Publishing Corporation.

Hopper, P. (1998). Emergent grammar. In M. Tomasello (Ed.), *The new psychology of language: Cognitive and functional approaches to language structure* (pp. 155–175). Mahwah, NJ: Lawrence Erlbaum.

Hornberger, N. (2005). Opening and filling up implementational and ideological spaces in heritage language education. *The Modern Language Journal, 89*, 605–609.

Hubbard, P. (2014, March). Interpreting and integrating the TESOL technology standards in a CALL mini-course. Paper presented at the TESOL convention, Portland, Oregon.

Hughes, A. (2003). *Testing for language teachers* (2nd ed.). Cambridge, UK: Cambridge University Press.

Hughes, R. (2002). *Teaching and researching speaking*. London, UK: Pearson Education.

Huhta, A. (2013). Common European framework of reference. In C. Chapelle (Ed.), *The encyclopedia of applied linguistics* (pp. 740–746). West Sussex, UK: Wiley-Blackwell.

Hunston, S., & Francis, G. (2000). *Pattern grammar: A corpus-driven approach to the lexical grammar of English*. Amsterdam, The Netherlands: John Benjamins.

Hyland, K. (2004). *Genre and second language writing*. Ann Arbor, MI: University of Michigan Press.

Hymes, D. (1972). On communicative competence. In J. Pride & J. Holmes (Eds.), *Sociolinguistics* (pp. 269–293). Harmondsworth, UK: Penguin Books.

Hymes, D. (1996). *Ethnography, linguistics, narrative inequality: Toward an understanding of voice*. London, UK, & Bristol, PA: Taylor & Francis.

Iida, A. (2010). Developing voice by composing haiku: A social-expressivist approach for teaching haiku writing in EFL contexts. *English Teaching Forum, 1*, 28–34.

Immordino-Yang, M., & Damasio, A. (2007). We feel, therefore we learn: The relevance of affective and social neuroscience to education. *Mind, Brain, and Education, 1*, 3–10.

James, M. (2006). Transfer of learning from a university content-based EAP course. *TESOL Quarterly, 40*, 783–806.

James, M. (2010). An investigation of learning transfer in English-for-general-academic-purposes writing instruction. *Journal of Second Language Writing, 19*, 183–206.

James, M. (2012). An investigation of motivation to transfer second language learning. *The Modern Language Journal, 96*, 51–69.

Jamieson, J. (2005). Trends in computer-based second language assessment. *Annual Review of Applied Linguistics, 25*, 228–242.

Jamieson, J. (2011). Assessment of classroom language learning. In E. Hinkel (Ed.), *Handbook of research in second language teaching and learning, Volume II* (pp. 768–785). New York, NY: Routledge.

Jarvis, S. (2013). Cross-linguistic influence and multilingualism. In C. Chapelle (Ed.), *The encyclopedia of applied linguistics* (pp. 291–298). West Sussex, UK: Wiley-Blackwell.

Jarvis, S., & Pavlenko, A. (2008). *Crosslinguistic influence in language and cognition*. New York, NY: Routledge.

Jenkins, J. (2009). English as a lingua franca: Interpretations and attitudes. *World Englishes, 28*, 200–207.

Jenkins, J. (2011). Accommodating (to) ELF in the international university. *Journal of Pragmatics, 43*, 926–936.

Johns, A. (2010). Pedagogy of languages for specific purposes. In M. Berns (Ed.), *Concise encyclopedia of applied linguistics* (pp. 318–323). Amsterdam, The Netherlands: Elsevier.

Johns, A. (Ed.). (2002). *Genre in the classroom: Multiple perspectives*. Mahwah, NJ: Lawrence Erlbaum Associates.

Johns, A., & Price, D. (2014). English for specific purposes: International in scope, specific in purpose. In M. Celce-Murcia, D. Brinton, & M. A. Snow (Eds.), *Teaching English as a second or foreign language* (4th ed., pp. 471–487). Boston, MA: National Geographic Learning.

Johnson, K. (2006). The sociocultural turn and its challenges for second language teacher education. *TESOL Quarterly, 40*, 235–257.

Johnston, B. (2003). *Values in English language teaching*. Mahwah, NJ: Lawrence Erlbaum Associates.

Jones, L. (2007). *The student-centered classroom*. New York, NY: Cambridge University Press. Available online: http://www.brettwilkin.com/phocadownload/StudentCentredClassroom/jones-student-centered.pdf

Kachru, B. (1992). *The other tongue: English across cultures*. Urbana, IL: University of Illinois Press.

Kachru, B. (2010). World Englishes. In M. Berns (Ed.), *Concise encyclopedia of applied linguistics* (pp. 521–528). Oxford, UK: Elsevier

Kaplan, R. (1966). Cultural thought patterns in intercultural education. *Language Learning, 16*, 1–20.

Kaplan, R. (2005). Contrastive rhetoric. In E. Hinkel (Ed.), *Handbook of research in second language teaching and learning* (pp. 375–391). Mahwah, NJ: Lawrence Erlbaum Associates.

Katz, A. (2014). Assessment in second language classrooms. In M. Celce-Murcia, D. Brinton, & M. A. Snow (Eds.), *Teaching English as a second or foreign language* (4th ed., pp. 320–337). Boston, MA: National Geographic Learning.

Keck, C. (2013). Corpus linguistics in language teaching. In C. Chapelle (Ed.), *The encyclopedia of applied linguistics* (pp. 1373–1376). London, UK: Blackwell Publishing Ltd.

Kim, Y. (2009). The effects of task complexity on learner-learner interaction. *System, 37*, 254–268.

Kim, Y., & Payant, C. (in press). Impacts of task complexity on the development of L2 performance over time. *International Review of Applied Linguistics in Language Teaching*.

Kinsella, K. (1991, September). Promoting active learning and classroom interaction through effective questioning strategies. Workshop presented at San Francisco State University, San Francisco.

Kinsella, K. (1994). Developing communities of reflective ESL teacher-scholars through peer coaching. *CATESOL Journal, 7,* 31–49.

Kiphart, M., Auday, B., & Cross, H. (1988). Short-term haptic memory for three-dimensional objects. *Perceptual and Motor Skills, 66,* 79–91.

Kirkpatrick, A. (2007). Setting attainable and appropriate English language targets in multilingual settings: A case for Hong Kong. *International Journal of Applied Linguistics, 17,* 376–391.

Klimanova, L., & Dembovskaya, S. (2013). L2 identity, discourse, and social networking in Russian. *Language Learning & Technology, 17,* 69–88.

Klippel, F. (1984). Keep talking: Communicative fluency activities for language teaching. Cambridge, UK: Cambridge University Press.

Kohn, A. (1990, June 21). Rewards hamper creativity. *San Francisco Chronicle,* pp. B3–B4.

Kohn, A. (2000). *The case against standardized testing.* Westport, CT: Heinemann.

Kramsch, C. (2006). From communicative competence to symbolic competence. *Modern Language Journal, 90,* 249–252.

Kramsch, C. (2009). *The multilingual subject. What language learners say about their experience and why it matters.* Oxford: Oxford University Press.

Kramsch, C. (2013). Teaching culture and intercultural competence. In C. Chapelle (Ed.), *The encyclopedia of applied linguistics* (pp. 2895–2898). West Sussex, UK: Blackwell Publishing Ltd.

Krashen, S. (1985). *The input hypothesis.* London, UK: Longman.

Krashen, S. (1997). *Foreign language education: The easy way.* Culver City, CA: Language Education Associates.

Krashen, S., & Terrell, T. (1983). *The natural approach: Language acquisition in the classroom.* Oxford, UK: Pergamon Press.

Kroon, S., & Vallen, T. (2010). Immigrant languages. In M. Berns (Ed.), *Concise encyclopedia of applied linguistics* (pp. 130–133). Amsterdam, The Netherlands: Elsevier.

Kruse, A. (1987). Vocabulary in context. In M. Long & J. Richards (Eds.), *Methodology in TESOL: A book of readings.* (pp. 312–317). New York, NY: Newbury House.

Kubota, R. (2009). Spiritual dimensions in language teaching: A personal reflection. In M. Wong & S. Canagarajah (Eds.), *Christian and critical English language educators in dialogue: Pedagogical and ethical dilemmas* (pp. 225–234). New York, NY: Routledge.

Kuhn, M., & Stahl, S. (2003). Fluency: A review of development and remedial practices. *Journal of Educational Psychology, 95,* 3–21.

Kukulska-Hulme, A. (2013). Mobile-assisted language learning. In C. Chapelle (Ed.), *The encyclopedia of applied linguistics* (pp. 3701–3709). Oxford, UK: Wiley-Blackwell.

Kukulska-Hulme, A., & Bull, S. (2009). Theory-based support for mobile language learning: Noticing and recording. *International Journal of Interactive Mobile Technologies, 3,* 12–18.

Kumaravadivelu, B. (2001). Toward a postmethod pedagogy. *TESOL Quarterly, 35,* 537–560.

Kumaravadivelu, B. (2006a). TESOL methods: Changing tracks, challenging trends. *TESOL Quarterly, 40*, 59–81.

Kumaravadivelu, B. (2006b). *Understanding language teaching: From method to postmethod.* Mahwah, NJ: Lawrence Erlbaum Associates.

Kumaravadivelu, B. (2012). Individual identity, cultural globalization, and teaching English as an international language: The case for an epistemic break. In L. Alsagoff, S. L. McKay, G. Hu, & W. A. Renandya (Eds.), *Principles and practices for teaching English as an international language* (pp. 9–27). New York, NY: Routledge.

Kunnan, A. (2013). *The companion to language assessment.* Volumes 1, 2, 3, 4. Malden, MA: Wiley-Blackwell.

Kunnan, A., & Grabowski, K. (2014). Large-scale second language assessment. In M. Celce-Murcia, D. Brinton, & M. A. Snow (Eds.), *Teaching English as a second or foreign language* (4th ed., pp. 304–319). Boston, MA: National Geographic Learning.

Kurtz, J. (2011). Breaking through the communicative cocoon: Improvisation in secondary school foreign language classrooms. In R. K. Sawyer (Ed.), *Structure and improvisation in creative teaching* (pp. 133–161). New York, NY: Cambridge University Press.

LaForge, P. (1971). Community language learning: A pilot study. *Language Learning, 21,* 45–61.

Lamb, M. (2004). Integrative motivation in a globalizing world. *System, 32,* 3–19.

Lamb, T. (2011). Future selves, motivation, and autonomy in long-term EFL learning trajectories. In G. Murray, X. Gao, & T. Lamb (Eds.), *Identity, motivation, and autonomy in language learning.* Bristol, UK, Buffalo, NY: Multilingual Matters.

Lan, Y., Sung, Y., & Chang, K. (2007). A mobile-device-supported peer-assisted learning system for collaborative early EFL reading. *Language Learning & Technology, 11*, 130–151.

Lane, L. (2010). *Tips for teaching pronunciation: A practical approach.* White Plains, NY: Pearson Longman.

Lantolf, J. (2011). The sociocultural approach to second language acquisition. In D. Atkinson (Ed.), *Alternate approaches to second language acquisition* (pp. 24–47). New York, NY: Routledge.

Lantolf, J., & Thorne, S. L. (2006). *Sociocultural theory and the genesis of second language development.* Oxford, UK: Oxford University Press.

Larsen-Freeman, D. (2003). *Teaching language: From grammar to grammaring.* Boston, MA: Heinle & Heinle.

Larsen-Freeman, D. (2012). Complex, dynamic systems: A new transdisciplinary theme for applied linguistics? *Language Teaching, 45,* 202–214.

Larsen-Freeman, D. (2014). Teaching grammar. In M. Celce-Murcia, D. Brinton, & M. A. Snow (Eds.), *Teaching English as a second or foreign language* (4th ed., pp. 256–270). Boston, MA: National Geographic Learning.

Larsen-Freeman, D., & Anderson, M. (2011). *Techniques and principles in language teaching* (3rd ed.). New York, NY: Oxford University Press.

Laufer, B. (2003). Vocabulary acquisition in a second language: do learners really acquire most vocabulary by reading? Some empirical evidence. *Canadian Modern Language Review, 59*, 567–587.

Lave, J., & Wenger, E. (1991). *Situated learning: Legitimate peripheral participation.* Cambridge, UK: Cambridge University Press.

Law, B., & Eckes, M. (2007). *Assessment and ESL: An alternative approach.* Winnipeg, Canada: Portage & Main Press.

Lazaraton, A. (2014). Second language speaking. In M. Celce-Murcia, D. Brinton, & M.A. Snow (Eds.), *Teaching English as a second or foreign language* (4th ed., pp. 106–120). Boston, MA: National Geographic Learning.

Lee, H. (2008). Learner agency and identity in second language writing. *ITL International Journal of Applied Linguistics, 156*, 109–128.

Lee, H. (2013, March). Rethinking writing struggles in a study abroad context: Two international students' narratives. Paper presented at the American Association of Applied Linguistics, Dallas, TX.

Lee, H., & Maguire, M. (2011). International students and identity: Resisting dominant ways of writing and knowing in academe. In D. Starke-Meyerring, A. Paré, N. Artemeva, M. Horne, & L. Yousoubova (Eds.), *Writing in the knowledge society* (pp. 351–370). West Lafayette, IN: Parlor Press and WAC Clearinghouse.

Lee, J. (2014). Roles of language teachers. (Personal communication.)

Lee, J., Hill-Bonnet, L., & Raley, J. (2011) Examining the effects of language brokering on student identities and learning opportunities in dual immersion classrooms. *Journal of Language, Identity & Education, 10,* 306–326.

Legutke, M. (2012). Teaching teenagers. In A. Burns & J. Richards (Eds.), *The Cambridge guide to pedagogy and practice in second language teaching* (pp. 112–127). New York, NY: Cambridge University Press.

Leki, I., Cumming, A., & Silva, T. (2008). *A synthesis of research on second language writing*. London, UK: Routledge.

Lenneberg, E. (1967). *The biological foundations of language.* New York, NY: J. Wiley & Sons.

Leow, R. (2013). Attention, noticing, and awareness in second language acquisition. In C. Chapelle (Ed.), *The encyclopedia of applied linguistics* (pp. 58–64). West Sussex, UK: Wiley-Blackwell Publishing Ltd.

Leu, D., Everett-Cacopardo, H., Zawilinski, L., McVerry, J. G., & O'Byrne, W. I. (2013). New literacies of online reading comprehension. In C. Chapelle (Ed.), *The encyclopedia of applied linguistics* (pp. 4239–4247). Oxford, UK: Wiley-Blackwell.

Leung, C. (2005). Classroom teacher assessment of second language development: Construct as practice. In E. Hinkel (Ed.), *Handbook of research in second language teaching and learning* (pp. 869–888). Mahwah, NJ: Lawrence Erlbaum Associates.

Leung, C., & Lewkowicz, J. (2006). Expanding horizons and unresolved conundrums: Language testing and assessment. *TESOL Quarterly, 40*, 211–234.

Levis, J. (2005). Changing contexts and shifting paradigms in pronunciation teaching. *TESOL Quarterly, 39*, 369–377.

Lewis, M. (1993). *The lexical approach*. Hove, UK: Language Teaching Publications.

Lewis, M. (1997). *Implementing the lexical approach: Putting theory into practice.* Hove, UK: Language Teaching Publications.

Lewis, M. (2000). *Teaching collocation: Further developments in the lexical approach.* London, UK: Language Teaching Publications.

Li, Z., & Hegelheimer, V. (2013). Mobile-assisted grammar exercises: Effects on self-editing in L2 writing. *Language Learning & Technology, 17,* 135–156. Retrieved from http://llt.msu.edu/issues/october2013/lihegelheimer.pdf

Lindstromberg, S., & Boers, F. (2005). From movement to metaphor with manner-of-movement verbs. *Applied Linguistics, 26,* 241–261.

Linn, M. (2003). Technology and science education: Starting points, research programs, and trends. *International Journal of Science Education, 26,* 727–758.

Linse, C. (2005). *Practical English language teaching: Young learners.* New York, NY: McGraw-Hill.

Littlewood, W. (1981). *Communicative language teaching: An introduction.* Cambridge, UK: Cambridge University Press.

Littlewood, W. (2011). Communicative language teaching: an expanding concept for a changing world. In E. Hinkel (Ed.), *Handbook of research in second language teaching and learning: Volume II* (pp. 541–557). New York, NY: Routledge.

Liu, D. (2013). Teaching grammar. In C. Chapelle (Ed.), *The encyclopedia of applied linguistics* (pp. 5572–5578). West Sussex, UK: Blackwell Publishing Ltd.

Liu, D., & Jiang, P. (2009). Using a corpus-based lexicogrammatical approach to grammar instruction in EFL and ESL contexts. *The Modern Language Journal, 93,* 61–78.

Llurda, E. (2009). The decline and fall of the native speaker. In V. Cook & L. Wei (Eds.), *Contemporary applied linguistics (Vol. 1): Language teaching and learning* (pp. 37–53). London, UK, and New York, NY: Continuum.

Lo Bianco, J. (2013). Language policy and planning: Overview. In C. Chapelle (Ed.), *The encyclopedia of applied linguistics* (pp. 3094–3101). West Sussex, UK: Blackwell Publishing Ltd.

LoCastro, V. (2001). Large classes and student learning. *TESOL Quarterly, 35,* 493–496.

Loewen, S. (2011). Focus on form. In E. Hinkel (Ed.), *Handbook of research in second language teaching and learning*: Volume II (pp. 576–592). New York, NY: Routledge.

Loewen, S. (2012). The role of feedback. In S. M. Gass & A. Mackey (Eds.), *The Routledge handbook of second language acquisition* (pp. 24–40). New York, NY: Routledge.

Long, M. (1985). Input and second language acquisition theory. In S. Gass & C. Madden (Eds.), *Input in second language acquisition* (pp. 377–393). Rowley, MA: Newbury House.

Long, M. (1996). The role of the linguistic environment in second language acquisition. In W. C. Ritchie & T. K. Bhatia (Eds.), *Handbook of second language acquisition* (pp. 413–468). San Diego, CA: Academic Press.

Long, M. (2007). *Problems in SLA.* New York, NY: Lawrence Erlbaum Associates.

Long, M., & Porter, P. (1985). Group work, interlanguage talk, and second language acquisition. *TESOL Quarterly, 19,* 207–228.

Lowe, P. (1988). The unassimilated history. In P. Lowe & C. Stansfield (Eds.), *Second language proficiency assessment: Current issues* (pp. 11–51). Englewood Cliffs, NJ: Prentice Hall Regents.

Lozanov, G. (1979). *Suggestology and outlines of suggestopedy*. New York, NY: Gordon and Breach Science Publishers.

Lund, R. (1990). A taxonomy for teaching second language listening. *Foreign Language Annals, 23,* 105–115.

Lys, F. (2013). The development of advanced learner oral proficiency using iPads. *Language Learning & Technology, 17,* 94–116. Retrieved from http://llt.msu.edu/issues/october2013/lys.pdf

Macedo, D., Dendrinos, B., & Gounari, P. (2003). *The hegemony of English*. Boulder, CO: Paradigm.

MacIntyre, P., Baker, S., Clément, R., & Conrod, S. (2001). Willingness to communicate, social support, and language-learning orientations of immersion students. *Studies in Second Language Acquisition, 23,* 369–388.

MacIntyre, P., Burns, C., & Jessome, A. (2011). Ambivalence about communicating in a second language: A qualitative study of French immersion students' willingness to communicate. *The Modern Language Journal, 95,* 81–96.

MacIntyre, P., Clément, R., Dörnyei, Z., & Noels, K. (1998). Conceptualizing willingness to communicate in a L2: A situational model of L2 confidence. *Modern Language Journal, 82,* 545–562.

Mackay, R. (1987). Teaching the information-gathering skills. In M. Long & J. Richards (Eds.), *Methodology in TESOL: A book of readings* (pp. 248–256). New York, NY: Newbury House.

Mackey, A., & Gass, S. (Eds.). (2006). Pushing the methodological boundaries in interaction research (special issue). *Studies in Second Language Acquisition* (vol. 28).

Maloney, E. (2007). What Web 2.0 can teach us about learning. *The Chronicle of Higher Education, 53,* Retrieved from http://chronicle.com/article/What-Web-20-Can-Teach-Us/8332.

Mann, S. (2005). The language teacher's development. *Language Teaching, 38,* 103–118.

Marckwardt, A. (1972). Changing winds and shifting sands. *MST English Quarterly, 21,* 3–11.

Marshall, T. (1989). *The whole world guide to language learning*. Yarmouth, ME: Intercultural Press.

Martin, J. (2012). Writing and genre studies. In C. Chapelle (Ed.), *The encyclopedia of applied linguistics* (pp. 6258–6266). West Sussex, UK: Blackwell Publishing Ltd.

Martin-Jones, M., Blackledge, A., & Creese, A. (Eds.). (2012). *The Routledge handbook of multilingualism.* New York, NY: Routledge.

Marzano, R., & Marzano, J. (2003). The key to classroom management. *Educational Leadership, 61,* 6–13.

Maslow, A. (1970). *Motivation and personality* (2nd ed.). New York, NY: Harper & Row.

Master, P. (2005). English for specific purposes. In E. Hinkel (Ed.), *Handbook of research in second language teaching and learning* (pp. 99–115). Mahwah, NJ: Lawrence Erlbaum Associates.

Matsumoto, D., & Juang, L. (2013). *Culture and psychology* (5th ed.). Stamford, CT: Wadsworth Publishing.

Matthews, P. (2010). Factors influencing self-efficacy judgments of university students in foreign language tutoring. *The Modern Language Journal, 94*, 618–635.

McArthur, T. (2001). World English and world Englishes: Trends, tensions, varieties, and standards. *Language Teaching, 34*, 1–20.

McBride, K. (2009). Social networking sites in foreign language classes: Opportunities for re-creation. In L. Lomicka & G. Lord (Eds.), *The next generation: Social networking and online collaboration in foreign language learning* (pp. 35–58). San Marcos, TX: CALICO.

McCafferty, S., Jacobs, G., & DaSilva, C. (Eds.). (2006). *Cooperative learning and second language teaching*. Cambridge, UK: Cambridge University Press.

McCarthy, M. (2004). *Touchstone: From corpus to course book.* Cambridge, UK: Cambridge University Press.

McCarthy, M., & O'Keeffe, A. (2004). Research in the teaching of speaking. *Annual Review of Applied Linguistics, 24,* 26–43.

McCarthy, M., & O'Keeffe, A. (2010). Speaking in a second language. In M. Berns (Ed.), *Concise encyclopedia of applied linguistics* (pp. 212–218). Oxford, UK: Elsevier.

McDonough, K. (2004). Learner-learner interaction during pair and small group activities in a Thai EFL context. *System, 32,* 207–224.

McDonough, K. (2006). Action research and the professional development of graduate teaching assistants. *Modern Language Journal, 90*, 33–47.

McEnery, T., & Xiao, R. (2011). What corpora can offer in language teaching and learning. In E. Hinkel (Ed.), *Handbook of research in second language teaching and learning: Volume II* (pp. 364–380). New York, NY: Routledge.

McGrail, E., & Davis, A. (2011). The influence of classroom blogging on elementary student writing. *Journal of Research in Childhood Education, 25*, 415–437.

McGroarty, M., & Fitzsimmons-Doolan, S. (2014). Approaches to school-based bilingual education. In M. Celce-Murcia, D. Brinton, & M. A. Snow (Eds.), *Teaching English as a second or foreign language* (4th ed., pp. 501–515). Boston, MA: National Geographic Learning.

McKay, S. (2002). *Teaching English as an international language: Rethinking goals and approaches.* Oxford, UK: Oxford University Press.

McKay, S. (2006). *Researching second language classrooms.* Mahwah, NJ: Lawrence Erlbaum Associates.

McKay, S. (2012). Principles of teaching English as an international language. In L. Alsagoff, S. McKay, G. Hu, & W. Renandya (Eds.), *Principles and practices for teaching English as an international language* (pp. 28–46). New York, NY: Routledge.

McKay, S., & Wong, S. (1996). Multiple discourses, multiple identities: Investment and agency in second language learning among Chinese adolescent immigrant students. *Harvard Educational Review, 66*, 577–608.

McLaren, P. (2005). *Capitalists and conquerors: A critical pedagogy against the empire.* Lanham, MD: Rowman & Littlefield.

McLaughlin, B. (1990). "Conscious" versus "unconscious" learning. *TESOL Quarterly, 24,* 617–634.

McNamara, T. (2010). Assessment of second language proficiency. In M. Berns (Ed.), *Concise encyclopedia of applied linguistics* (pp. 105–112). Oxford, UK: Elsevier.

McNamara, T., & Roever, C. (2006). *Language testing: The social dimension*. Hoboken, NJ: Wiley-Blackwell.

Mendelsohn, D. (1998). Teaching listening. *Annual Review of Applied Linguistics, 18,* 81–101.

Messick, S. (1989). Validity. In R. Linn (Ed.), *Educational measurement* (pp. 13–103). New York, NY: Macmillan.

Mills, N. (2011). Situated learning through social networking communities: The development of joint enterprise, mutual engagement, and a shared repertoire. *CALICO Journal, 28,* 345–368.

Minogue, J., & Jones, M. (2006). Haptics in education: Exploring an untapped sensory modality. *Review of Educational Research, 76,* 317–348.

Mitchell, R., Myles, F., & Marsden, E. (2013). *Second language learning theories* (3rd ed.). Oxford, UK: Routledge.

Morley, J. (1991a). Listening comprehension in second/foreign language instruction. In M. Celce-Murcia (Ed.), *Teaching English as a second or foreign language* (2nd ed., pp. 81–106). New York, NY: Newbury House.

Morley, J. (1991b). The pronunciation component in teaching English to speakers of other languages. *TESOL Quarterly, 25,* 481–520.

Mueller, M. (1987). Interactive testing: Time to be a test pilot. In W. M. Rivers (Ed.), *Interactive language teaching*. New York, NY: Cambridge University Press.

Mullock, B. (2006). The pedagogical knowledge base of four TESOL teachers. *Modern Language Journal, 90,* 48–66.

Mumford, S. (2008). An analysis of spoken grammar: The case for production. *ELT Journal, 63,* 137–144.

Murphey, T. (Ed.). (2003). *Extending professional contributions*. Alexandria, VA: Teachers of English to Speakers of Other Languages.

Murphey, T., & Sato, K. (2005). *Communities of supportive professionals*. Alexandria, VA: Teachers of English to Speakers of Other Languages.

Murphey, T., Connolly, M., Churchill, E., McLaughlin, J., Schwartz, S., & Krajka, J. (2005). Creating publishing communities. In T. Murphey (Ed.), *Extending professional contributions* (pp. 105–118). Alexandria, VA: Teachers of English to Speakers of Other Languages.

Murphy, J. (2013). *Teaching pronunciation*. Alexandria, VA: TESOL

Murphy, J. (2014). Reflective teaching: Principles and practices. In M. Celce-Murcia, D. Brinton, & M. A. Snow (Eds.), *Teaching English as a second or foreign language* (4th ed., pp. 613–629). Boston, MA: National Geographic Learning.

Murphy, J., & Byrd, P. (Eds.). (2001). *Understanding the courses we teach: Local perspectives on English language teaching*. Ann Arbor, MI: University of Michigan Press.

Nassaji, H. (2002). Schema theory and knowledge-based processes in second language reading comprehension: A need for alternative perspectives. *Language Learning, 52,* 439–481.

Nassaji, H. (2014). The role and importance of lower-level processes in second language reading. *Language Teaching, 47,* 1–37.

Nassaji, H., & Fotos, S. (2011) *Teaching grammar in second language classrooms: Integrating form-focused instruction in communicative context.* New York, NY: Routledge.

Nation, I. S. P. (2001). *Learning vocabulary in another language.* Cambridge, UK: Cambridge University Press.

Nation, I. S. P. (2003).Vocabulary. In D. Nunan (Ed.), *Practical English language teaching* (pp. 129–152). New York, NY: McGraw-Hill Contemporary.

Nation, I. S. P. (2005). Teaching and learning vocabulary. In E. Hinkel (Ed.) *Handbook of research in second language teaching and learning* (pp. 581–595). Mahwah, NJ: Lawrence Erlbaum Associates.

Nation, I. S. P. (2006). How large a vocabulary is needed for reading and listening? *The Canadian Modern Language Review, 63,* 59–82.

Nation, I. S. P., & Macalister, J. (2010). *Language curriculum design.* New York, NY: Routledge.

Nayar, P. (1997). ESL/EFL dichotomy today: Language politics or pragmatics? *TESOL Quarterly, 31,* 9–37.

Nelson, M., & Kern, R. (2012). Language teaching and learning in the *postlinguistic* condition? In L. Alsagoff, et al. (Eds.), *Principles and practices for teaching English as an international language* (pp. 47–66). New York, NY: Routledge.

Norton, B. (2000). *Identity and language learning: Gender, ethnicity and educational change.* London, UK: Pearson/Longman.

Norton, B. (2013). Identity and second language acquisition. In C. Chapelle (Ed.), *The encyclopedia of applied linguistics* (pp. 2587–2954). West Sussex, UK: Wiley-Blackwell.

Norton, B., & Gao, Y. (2008). Identity, investment, and Chinese learners of English. *Journal of Asian Pacific Communication, 18,* 109–120.

Norton, B., & Toohey, K. (Eds.). (2004). *Critical pedagogies and language learning.* Cambridge, UK: Cambridge University Press.

Norton Peirce, B. (1995). Social identity, investment, and language learning. *TESOL Quarterly, 29,* 9–31.

Nunan, D. (1988). *The learner-centered curriculum.* Cambridge, UK: Cambridge University Press.

Nunan, D. (1989a). *Designing tasks for the communicative classroom.* Cambridge, UK: Cambridge University Press.

Nunan, D. (1989b). *Understanding language classrooms: A guide for teacher-initiated action.* Englewood Cliffs, NJ: Prentice-Hall.

Nunan, D. (1991a). Communicative tasks and the language curriculum. *TESOL Quarterly, 25,* 279–295.

Nunan, D. (1991b). *Language teaching methodology: A textbook for teachers.* New York, NY: Prentice-Hall.

Nunan, D. (2004). *Task-based language teaching.* Cambridge, UK: Cambridge University Press.

Nunan, D. (2005). *Practical English language teaching: Grammar.* New York, NY: McGraw-Hill.

Nunan, D. (2014). Task-based teaching and learning. In M. Celce-Murcia, D. Brinton, & M. A. Snow (Eds.), *Teaching English as a second or foreign language* (4th ed., pp. 455–470). Boston, MA: National Geographic Learning.

Nunan, D. (Ed.). (2003). *Practical English language teaching.* New York, NY: McGraw-Hill Contemporary.

Nuttall, C. (1996). *Teaching reading skills in a foreign language* (2nd ed.). Oxford, UK: Heinemann.

O'Brien, T. (2004). Writing in a foreign language: Teaching and learning. *Language Teaching, 37*, 1–28.

O'Malley, J. M., & Pierce, L. (1996). *Authentic assessment for English language learners: Practical approaches for teachers.* White Plains, NY: Addison-Wesley.

Oller, J. (1979). *Language tests at school: A pragmatic approach.* London, UK: Longman.

Olshtain, E. (2014). Practical tasks for mastering the mechanics of writing and going just beyond. In M. Celce-Murcia, D. Brinton, & M. A. Snow (Eds.), *Teaching English as a second or foreign language* (4th ed., pp. 208–221). Boston, MA: National Geographic Learning.

Oostendorp, M. (2012). New perspectives on cross-linguistic influence: Language and cognition. *Language Teaching, 45*, 389–398.

Ormiston, M. (2011). *Creating a digital-rich classroom: Teaching in a web 2.0 world.* Bloomington, IN: Solution Tree Press.

Ortega, L. (2009). *Understanding second language acquisition.* London, UK: Hodder Education.

Oxford, R. (1990). *Language learning strategies: What every teacher should know.* New York, NY: Newbury House.

Oxford, R. (1997). Cooperative learning, collaborative learning, and interaction: Three communicative strands in the language classroom. *Modern Language Journal, 81,* 443–456.

Oxford, R. (2011). *Teaching and researching language learning strategies.* Harlow, UK: Pearson Education.

Oxford, R., Tomlinson, S., Barcelos, A., Harrington, C., Lavine, R., Saleh, A., et al. (1998). Clashing metaphors about classroom teachers: Toward a systematic typology for the language teaching field. *System, 26,* 3–50.

Paltridge, B. (2001). *Genre and the language learning classroom.* Ann Arbor, MI: The University of Michigan Press.

Paltridge, B. (2004). Academic writing. *Language Teaching, 37*, 87–105.

Paltridge, B., & Starfield, S. (2011). Research in English for specific purposes. In E. Hinkel (Ed.), *Handbook of research in second language teaching and learning: Volume II* (pp. 106–121). New York, NY: Routledge.

Parrish, B. (2004). *Teaching adult ESL: A practical introduction.* New York, NY: McGraw Hill.

Pasfield-Neofitou, S. (2011). Online domains of language use: Second language learners' experiences of virtual community and foreignness. *Language Learning & Technology, 15*, 92–108. Retrieved from http://llt.msu.edu/issues/june2011/pasfieldneofitou.pdf

Paulston, C., & Bruder, M. (1976). *Teaching English as a second language: Techniques and procedures*. Cambridge, MA: Winthrop.

Pavlenko, A. (2005). *Emotions and multilingualism*. New York, NY: Cambridge University Press.

Pavlenko, A. (2013). The affective turn in SLA: From "affective factors" to "language desire" and "commodification of affect." In D. Gabrys-Barker & J. Brelska (Eds.), *The affective dimension in second language acquisition* (pp. 3–28). Clevedon, UK: Multilingual Matters.

Pavlenko, A., & Blackledge, A. (Eds.). (2004). *Negotiation of identities in multilingual contexts*. Clevedon, UK: Multilingual Matters.

Pavlenko, A., & Driagina, V. (2007). Russian emotion vocabulary in American learners' narratives. *The Modern Language Journal, 91*, 213–234.

Pavlenko, A., & Norton, B. (2007). Imagined communities, identity, and English language learners. In J. Cummins & C. Davison (Eds.), *International handbook of English language teaching* (pp. 669–680). New York, NY: Springer.

Pavlik, C. (2004). *Grammar sense*. Oxford, UK: Oxford University Press.

Pawan, F., & Sietman, G. (Eds.). (2008). *Helping English language learners succeed in middle and high schools*. Alexandria, VA: TESOL.

Payne, S., & Whitney, P. (2002). Developing L2 oral proficiency through synchronous CMC: Output, working memory, and interlanguage development. *CALICO Journal, 20*, 7–32.

Pennington, M. (1990). A professional development focus for the language teaching practicum. In J. Richards & D. Nunan (1990) (Eds.), *Second language teacher education* (pp. 132–152). New York, NY: Cambridge University Press.

Pennycook, A. (1994). *The cultural politics of English as an international language*. Harlow, UK: Longman.

Pennycook, A. (2001). *Critical applied linguistics: A critical introduction*. Mahwah, NJ: Lawrence Erlbaum Associates.

Pham, H. (2007). Communicative language teaching: Unity within diversity. *ELT Journal, 61*, 193–201.

Phillipson, R. (1992). *Linguistic imperialism*. Oxford, UK: Oxford University Press.

Phillipson, R., & Skutnabb-Kangas, T. (1996). English only worldwide or language ecology? *TESOL Quarterly, 30*, 429–452.

Piaget, J. (1955). *The language and thought of the child*. New York, NY: Meridian.

Piaget, J. (1970). *The science of education and the psychology of the child*. New York, NY: Basic Books.

Piaget, J. (1972). *The principles of genetic epistemology*. New York, NY: Basic Books.

Pimsleur, P. (1966). *Pimsleur language aptitude battery*. New York, NY: Harcourt, Brace & World.

Pinter, A. (2006). *Teaching young language learners*. Oxford, UK: Oxford University Press.

Polio, C. (2007). A history of input enhancement: Defining an evolving concept. In C. Gascoigne (Ed.), *Assessing the impact of input enhancement in second language education* (pp. 1–18). Stillwater, OK: New Forums Press.

Postman, N., & Weingartner, C. (1969). *Teaching as a subversive activity*. New York, NY: Dell Publishing Company.

Prator, C., & Celce-Murcia, M. (1979). An outline of language teaching approaches. In M. Celce-Murcia & L. McIntosh (Ed.), *Teaching English as a second or foreign language* (pp. 3–5). New York, NY: Newbury House.

Pratt, M. (1991). Art of the contact zone. *Profession, 91*, 33–40.

Prensky, M. (2001). Digital natives, digital immigrants. *On the Horizon, 9*, 1–6.

Prensky, M. (2010). *Teaching digital natives: Partnering for real learning*. Thousand Oaks, CA: Corwin Press.

Purgason, K. (2014). Lesson planning in second/foreign language teaching. In M. Celce-Murcia, D. Brinton, & M. A. Snow (Eds.), *Teaching English as a second or foreign language* (4th ed., pp. 362–369). Boston, MA: National Geographic Learning.

Purpura, J. (2014). Language learning strategies and styles. In M. Celce-Murcia, D. Brinton, & M. A. Snow (Eds.), *Teaching English as a second or foreign language* (4th ed., pp. 532–549). Boston, MA: National Geographic Learning.

Raimes, A. (1991). Out of the woods: Emerging traditions in the teaching of writing. *TESOL Quarterly, 25,* 407–430.

Ranalli, J. (2013). Online strategy instruction for integrating dictionary skills and language awareness. *Language Learning & Technology, 17, 75–99.*

Read, J. (2000). *Assessing vocabulary.* Cambridge, UK: Cambridge University Press.

Read, J. (2004). Research in teaching vocabulary. *Annual Review of Applied Linguistics, 24,* 146–161.

Reid, J. (1994). Responding to students' texts: The myths of appropriation. *TESOL Quarterly, 28,* 273–292.

Reppen, R. (2010). *Using corpora in the language classroom*. Cambridge, UK: Cambridge University Press.

Ricento, T. (2005). Considerations of identity in L2 learning. In E. Hinkel (Ed.), *Handbook of research in second language teaching and learning* (pp. 895–910). Mahwah, NJ: Lawrence Erlbaum Associates.

Richard-Amato, P. (2010). *Making it happen: From interactive to participatory language teaching* (4th ed.). White Plains, NY: Pearson Education, Inc.

Richards, J. (1983). Listening comprehension: Approach, design, procedure. *TESOL Quarterly, 17,* 219–239.

Richards, J. (1990). *The language teaching matrix. Cambridge*, UK: Cambridge University Press.

Richards, J. (2001). *Curriculum development in language teaching*. Cambridge, UK: Cambridge University Press.

Richards, J. (2002). Theories of teaching in language teaching. In J. Richards & W. Renandya (Eds.), *Methodology in language teaching: An anthology of current practice* (pp. 19–25). Cambridge, UK: Cambridge University Press.

Richards, J. (2008a). *Moving beyond the plateau: From intermediate to advanced levels in language learning*. Cambridge, UK: Cambridge University Press.

Richards, J. (2008b). *Teaching listening and speaking: From theory to practice.* Cambridge, UK: Cambridge University Press.

Richards, J., & Bohlke, D. (2011). *Creating effective language lessons.* Cambridge, UK: Cambridge University Press.

Richards, J., & Burns, A. (2012). *Tips for teaching listening: A practical approach*. White Plains, NY: Pearson Education.

Richards, J., & Farrell, T. (2005). *Professional development for language teachers: Strategies for teacher learning*. Cambridge, UK: Cambridge University Press.

Richards, J., & Farrell, T. (2011). *Practice teaching: A reflective approach*. Cambridge, UK: Cambridge University Press.

Richards, J., & Rodgers, T. (2001). *Approaches and methods in language teaching* (2nd ed.). Cambridge, UK: Cambridge University Press.

Richards, J., & Rodgers, T. (1982). Method: Approach, design, and procedure. *TESOL Quarterly, 16,* 153–168.

Richards, J., & Schmidt, R. (2002). *Longman dictionary of language teaching and applied linguistics*. London, UK: Pearson Education Limited.

Rigg, P. (1991). Whole language in TESOL. *TESOL Quarterly, 25,* 521–542.

Rivers, W. (1964). *The psychologist and the foreign language teacher*. Chicago, IL: University of Chicago Press.

Robinson, P. (2001). Task complexity, task difficulty, and task production: Exploring interactions in a componential framework. *Applied Linguistics, 22,* 27–57.

Robinson, P. (2005). Aptitude and second language acquisition. *Annual Review of Applied Linguistics, 25,* 46–73.

Robinson, P. (2009). Syllabus design. In M. Long & C. Doughty (Eds.), *Handbook of language teaching* (pp. 294–310). Malden, MA: Blackwell.

Robinson, P. (2011). *Second language task complexity: Researching the cognition hypothesis of language learning and performance*. Amsterdam, The Netherlands: John Benjamins Publishing.

Rogers, C. (1951). *Client-centered therapy*. Boston, MA: Houghton Mifflin.

Rogers, C. (1983). *Freedom to learn for the eighties*. Princeton, NC: Merrill Publishing Company.

Rosell-Aguilar, F. (2013). Podcasting for language learning through iTunes U: The learner's view. *Language Learning & Technology, 17,* 74–93. Retrieved from http://llt.msu.edu/issues/october2013/rosellaguilar.pdf

Ross, S. (2011). The social and political tensions of language assessment. In E. Hinkel (Ed.), *Handbook of research in second language teaching and learning, Volume II* (pp. 786–797). New York, NY: Routledge.

Rost, M. (2002). *Worldview*. Level 1. White Plains, NY: Pearson Education.

Rost, M. (2005). L2 listening. In E. Hinkel (Ed.), *Handbook of research in second language teaching and learning* (pp. 503–527). Mahwah, NJ: Lawrence Erlbaum Associates.

Rubin, J. (1975). What the "good language learner" can teach us. *TESOL Quarterly, 9,* 41–51.

Rubin, J. (1994). A review of second language listening comprehension research. *Modern Language Journal, 78,* 199–221.

Rubin, J., & Thompson, I. (1982). *How to be a more successful language learner*. Boston, MA: Heinle & Heinle.

Rubin, J., & Thompson, I. (1994). *How to be a more successful language learner* (2nd ed.). Boston, MA: Heinle & Heinle.

Rueda, R., & Moll, L. C. (1994). A sociocultural perspective on motivation. In H. F. O'Neil, Jr. & M. Drillings (Eds.), *Motivation: Theory and research* (pp. 117–137). Hillsdale, NJ: Erlbaum.

Rumelhart, D. (1977). Toward an interactive model of reading. In S. Dornic (Ed.), *Attention and performance IV* (pp. 722–750). New York, NY: Academic Press.

Ryan, R. (2007). Motivation and emotion: A new look and approach for two reemerging fields. *Motivation and Emotion, 31*, 1–3.

Ryan, R., & Deci, E. (2000). Intrinsic and extrinsic motivations: Class definitions and new directions. *Contemporary Educational Psychology, 25*, 54–67.

Sampedro, R., & Hillyard, S. (2004). *Global issues.* Oxford, UK: Oxford University Press.

Samuda, V., & Bygate, M. (2008). *Tasks in second language learning.* New York, NY: Palgrave Macmillan.

Sanou, B. (2014). ICT facts and figures. International Telecommunication Union, Geneva Switzerland. Retrieved from: http://www.itu.int/en/ITU-D/Statistics/Documents/facts/ICTFactsFigures2013-e.pdf

Sarkisian, E. (2010). *How people function in groups.* Boston, MA: Derek Bok Center for Teaching and Learning, Harvard University.

Sarosy, P., & Sherak, K. (2006). Lecture ready: Strategies for academic listening, notetaking, and discussion. New York, NY: Oxford University Press.

Saslow, J., & Ascher, A. (2006). *Top notch: English for today's world. Fundamentals; Book 2.* White Plains, NY: Pearson Education.

Saslow, J., & Ascher, A. (2011). *Top notch: English for today's world* (2nd ed.). White Plains, NY: Pearson Education.

Sathian, K. (1998). Perceptual learning. *Current Science, 75,* 451–456.

Savage, K. L. (2010). *Grammar matters: Teaching grammar in adult ESL programs.* New York, NY: Cambridge University Press.

Savignon, S. (1982). Dictation as a measure of communicative competence in French as a second language. *Language Learning, 32,* 33–51.

Savignon, S. (1983). *Communicative competence: Theory and classroom practice.* Reading, MA: Addison-Wesley.

Savignon, S. (1991). Communicative language teaching: State of the art. *TESOL Quarterly, 25,* 261–277.

Savignon, S. (2005). Communicative language teaching: Strategies and goals. In E. Hinkel (Ed.), *Handbook of research in second language teaching and learning* (pp. 635–651). Mahwah, NJ: Lawrence Erlbaum Associates.

Savignon, S. (2007). Beyond communicative language teaching: What's ahead? *Journal of Pragmatics, 39,* 207–220.

Savignon, S., & Berns, M. (Eds.). (1984). *Initiatives in communicative language teaching: A book of readings.* Reading, MA: Addison-Wesley.

Scherer, K. (2009). The dynamic architecture of emotion: Evidence for the component process model. *Cognition and Emotion, 23,* 1307–1351.

Schieffelin, B. (1990). *The give and take of everyday life: Language socialization of Kaluli children.* Cambridge, UK: Cambridge University Press.

Schiffler, L. (1992). *Suggestopedic methods and applications.* Philadelphia, PA: Gordon and Breach Science Publishers.

Schleppegrell, M. (2004). *The language of schooling: A functional linguistics perspective.* Mahwah, NJ: Erlbaum.

Schmenk, B. (2005). Globalizing learner autonomy. *TESOL Quarterly, 39,* 107–118.

Schmidt, R. (1990). The role of consciousness in second language learning. *Applied Linguistics, 11,* 129–158

Schmitt, N. (2008). Instructed second language vocabulary learning. *Language Teaching Research, 12,* 329–363.

Schunk, D. (1991). Self-efficacy and academic motivation. *Educational Psychologist, 26,* 207–231.

Schunk, D. (1996). Goal and self-evaluative influences during children's cognitive skill learning. *American Educational Research Journal, 33,* 359–382.

Scollon, R. (2004). Teaching language and culture as hegemonic practice. *Modern Language Journal, 88,* 271–274.

Scovel, T. (1978). The effect of affect on foreign language learning: A review of the anxiety research. *Language Learning, 28,* 129–142.

Scovel, T. (1979). Review of suggestology and outlines of suggestopedy by Georgi Lozanov. *TESOL Quarterly, 13,* 255–266.

Scovel, T. (2001). *Learning new languages: A guide to second language acquisition.* Boston, MA: Heinle & Heinle.

Scrivener, J. (2012). *Classroom management techniques.* Cambridge, UK: Cambridge University Press.

Seidlhofer, B. (2004). Research perspectives on teaching English as a lingua franca. *Annual Review of Applied Linguistics*, 24, 209–239.

Seidlhofer, B. (2011). *Understanding English as a lingua franca.* Oxford, UK: Oxford University Press.

Setter, J., & Jenkins, J. (2005). Pronunciation. *Language Teaching, 38,* 1–17.

Seymour, S. (2003). Sabbatical projects can make a difference: A tale of curriculum revision. Creating a teaching portfolio. In P. Byrd & G. Nelson (Eds.), *Sustaining professionalism* (pp. 89–96). Alexandria, VA: Teachers of English to Speakers of Other Languages.

Shamim, F. (2012). Teaching large classes. In A. Burns & J. Richards (Eds.), *The Cambridge guide to pedagogy and practice in second language teaching* (pp. 95–102). Cambridge, UK: Cambridge University Press.

Sharwood-Smith, M., (1981). Consciousness-raising and the second language learner. *Applied Linguistics 2,* 159–168.

Sheen, Y. (2007). The effect of focused written corrective feedback and language aptitude on ESL learners' acquisition of articles. *TESOL Quarterly, 41,* 255–283.

Sheen, Y., & Ellis, N. (2011). Corrective feedback in language teaching. In E. Hinkel (Ed.), *Handbook of research in second language teaching and learning: Volume II* (pp. 593–610). New York, NY: Routledge.

Shin, J. (2014). Teaching young learners in English as a second/foreign language. In M. Celce-Murcia, D. Brinton, & M. A. Snow (Eds.), *Teaching English as a second or foreign language* (4th ed., pp. 550–567). Boston, MA: National Geographic Learning.

Shoemaker, C., & Shoemaker, F. (1991). *Interactive techniques for the ESL classroom.* New York, NY: Newbury House.

Shohamy, E. (1997, March). Critical language testing and beyond. Paper presented at the American Association of Applied Linguistics, Orlando, FL.

Shohamy, E. (2000). Fairness in testing. In A. Kunnan (Ed.), *Fairness and validation in language assessment: Selected papers from the 19th Language Testing Research Colloquium*, Orlando, FL (pp. 15–19). Cambridge, UK: Cambridge University Press.

Shohamy, E. (2001). *The power of tests: A critical perspective on the use of language tests.* Harlow, UK: Pearson Education.

Silberstein, S. (2011). Constrained but not determined: Approaches to discourse analysis. In E. Hinkel (Ed.), *Handbook of research in second language teaching and learning: Volume II* (pp. 274–290). New York, NY: Routledge.

Silberstein, S., Dobson, B., & Clarke, M. (2002). *Reader's choice* (4th ed.). Ann Arbor, MI: University of Michigan Press.

Silva, T. (1993). Towards an understanding of the distinct nature of L2 writing: The ESL research and its implications. *TESOL Quarterly, 27,* 657–677.

Silva, T. (2010). Writing in a second language. In M. Berns (Ed.), *Concise encyclopedia of applied linguistics* (pp. 233–240). Oxford, UK: Elsevier.

Silva, T., & Brice, C. (2004). Research in teaching writing. *Annual Review of Applied Linguistics, 24,* 70–106.

Silva, T., & Leki, I. (2004). Family matters: The influence of applied linguistics and composition studies on second language writing studies—past, present, and future. *Modern Language Journal, 88,* 1–13.

Singleton, D., & Muñoz, C. (2011). Around and beyond the critical period hypothesis. In E. Hinkel (Ed.), *Handbook of research in second language teaching and learning: Volume II* (pp. 407–425). New York, NY: Routledge.

Singleton, D., & Ryan, L. (2004). *Language acquisition: The age factor* (2nd ed.). Clevedon, UK: Multilingual Matters.

Skehan, P. (1998a). *A cognitive approach to language learning.* Oxford, UK: Oxford University Press.

Skehan, P. (1998b). Task-based instruction. In W. Grabe (Ed.), *Annual review of applied linguistics (1998)* (pp. 268–286). New York, NY: Cambridge University Press.

Skehan, P. (2003). Task-based instruction. *Language Teaching, 36,* 1–14.

Skehan, P. (2009). Modeling second language performance: Integrating complexity, accuracy, fluency, and lexis. *Applied Linguistics, 30,* 510–532.

Skinner, B. F. (1938). *Behavior of organisms: An experimental analysis.* New York, NY: Appleton-Century-Crofts.

Skutnabb-Kangas, T., & Phillipson, R. (Eds.). (1994). *Linguistic human rights: Overcoming linguistic determination.* Berlin, Germany: Mouton de Gruyter.

Slagter, P., Surface, E., & Mosher, A. (2009). *ACTFL guidelines and the European CEFR in learning, teaching, and testing.* Symposium presented at ACTFL Convention, San Diego, CA.

Slavin, R. (2011). *Educational psychology: Theory and practice* (10th ed.). White Plains, NY: Pearson Education.

Smith, A., & Strong, G. (Eds.). (2009) *Adult language learners: Context and innovation.* Alexandria, VA: TESOL.

Smith, B. (2004). Computer-mediated negotiated interaction and lexical acquisition. *Studies in Second Language Acquisition, 26*, 365–98.

Smith, F. (1975). *Comprehension and learning: A conceptual framework for teachers.* New York, NY: Holt, Rinehart & Winston.

Snow, D. (2001). *English teaching as Christian mission.* Scottdale, PA: Herald Press.

Snow, M. A. (2014). Content-based and immersion models of second/foreign language teaching. In M. Celce-Murcia, D. Brinton, & M. A. Snow (Eds.), *Teaching English as a second or foreign language* (4th ed., pp. 438–454). Boston, MA: National Geographic Learning.

Sokolik, M. (2014). Digital technology in language teaching. In M. Celce-Murcia, D. Brinton, & M. A. Snow (Eds.), *Teaching English as a second or foreign language* (4th ed., pp. 409–421). Boston, MA: National Geographic Learning.

Spada, N. (2007). Communicative language teaching: Current status and future prospects. In J. Cummins & C. Davison (Eds.), *International handbook of English language teaching* (pp. 271–288). Boston, MA: Springer Science and Business Media.

Spada, N. (2011). Beyond form-focused instruction: Reflections on past, present and future research. *Language Teaching, 44*, 225–236.

Spada, N. (2012). Classroom research. In C. Chapelle (Ed.), *The encyclopedia of applied linguistics* (pp. 626–628). West Sussex, UK: Wiley-Blackwell.

Spada, N., & Fröhlich, M. (1995). *Communicative orientation of language teaching observation schemes.* Sydney, Australia: National Centre for English Teaching and Research, Macquarie University.

Spada, N., & Lightbown, P. (2008). Form-focused instruction: Isolated or integrated? *TESOL Quarterly, 42,* 181–207.

Spalding, D. (2013). *How to teach adults.* Oakland, CA: Self-published.

Spolsky, B. (1989). *Conditions for second language learning.* Oxford, UK: Oxford University Press.

Spolsky, B. (1997). The ethics of gatekeeping tests: What have we learned in a hundred years? *Language Testing, 14,* 242–247.

Sternberg, R. (1985). *Beyond IQ: A triarchic theory of human intelligence.* New York, NY: Cambridge University Press.

Sternberg, R. (1997). *Successful intelligence: How practical and creative intelligence determine success in life.* New York, NY: Plume.

Sternberg, R. (2007). *Wisdom, intelligence, and creativity synthesized.* New York, NY: Cambridge University Press.

Stoller, F. (2004). Content-based instruction: Perspectives on curriculum planning. *Annual review of applied linguistics, 24*, 261–283.

Stoller, F. (2006). Establishing a theoretical foundation for project-based learning. In G. Beckett and P. Miller (Eds.), *Project-based second and foreign language education* (pp. 19–40). Greenwich, CT: Information Age Publishing.

Storch, N. (2013). Collaborative language learning. In C. Chapelle (Ed.), *The encyclopedia of applied linguistics* (pp. 725–730). West Sussex, UK: Wiley-Blackwell.

Street, B. (1994). What is meant by local literacies? *Language and Education, 8*, 9–17.

Swain, M. (1984). Large-scale communicative language testing. In S. Savignon & M. Berns (Eds.), *Initiatives in communicative language teaching: A book of readings* (pp. 185–201). Reading, MA: Addison-Wesley.

Tanner, R. (2003). Outside in, inside out: Creating a teaching portfolio. In P. Byrd & G. Nelson (Eds.), *Sustaining professionalism* (pp. 19–25). Alexandria, VA: Teachers of English to Speakers of Other Languages.

Tapscott, D. (1998). *Growing up digital: The rise of the net generation.* New York, NY: McGraw-Hill.

Tapscott, D. (2009). *Growing up digital: How the net generation is changing your world.* New York, NY: McGraw Hill.

Tardy, C. (2013). Genre-based language teaching. In C. Chapelle (Ed.), *The encyclopedia of applied linguistics* (pp. 2278–2281). West Sussex, UK: Wiley-Blackwell.

Tarone, E. (2005). Speaking in a second language. In E. Hinkel (Ed.), *Handbook of research in second language teaching and learning* (pp. 485–502). Mahwah, NJ: Lawrence Erlbaum Associates.

Tedick, D., Christian, D., & Fortune, T. (Eds.). (2011). *Immersion education: Practices, policies, possibilities.* Clevedon, UK: Multilingual Matters.

Thornbury, S. (2005). *Uncovering grammar.* Oxford, UK: Macmillan.

Thornbury, S. (2006). *Grammar.* Oxford: Oxford University Press.

Thornton, P., & Houser, C. (2005). Using mobile phones in English education in Japan. *Journal of Computer Assisted Learning, 21,* 217–228.

Tollefson, J. (2011). Ideology in second language education. In E. Hinkel (Ed.), *Handbook of research in second language teaching and learning, Volume II* (pp. 801–816). New York, NY: Routledge.

Tomlinson, B. (2011). *Materials development in language teaching* (2nd ed.). Cambridge, UK: Cambridge University Press.

Tse, L. (1996). Who decides? The effect of language brokering on home-school communication. *Journal of Educational Issues of Language Minority Students, 16,* 225–233.

Tyler, A. (2008). Cognitive linguistics and second language instruction. In P. Robinson & N. Ellis (Eds.), *Handbook of cognitive linguistics and second language acquisition* (pp. 456–488). New York, NY: Routledge.

Underhill, N. (1987). *Testing spoken language: A handbook of oral testing techniques.* Cambridge, UK: Cambridge University Press.

Underwood, M. (1991). *Effective class management.* London, UK: Longman.

Ur, P. (1984). *Teaching listening comprehension.* Cambridge, UK: Cambridge University Press.

Ur, P. (2012). *A course in English language teaching* (2nd ed.). Cambridge, UK: Cambridge University Press.

Ushioda, E. (2009). A person-in-context relational view of emergent motivation, self and identity. In Z. Dörnyei & E. Ushioda (Eds.), *Motivation, language identity and the L2 self* (pp. 215–228). Bristol, UK: Multilingual Matters.

Ushioda, E. (2013a). Motivation in second language acquisition. In C. Chapelle (Ed.), *The encyclopedia of applied linguistics* (pp. 3763–3768). West Sussex, UK: Wiley-Blackwell.

Ushioda, E. (2013b). Motivation matters in mobile language learning: A brief commentary. *Language Learning & Technology, 17*, 1–5. Retrieved from http://llt.msu.edu/issues/october2013/commentary.pdf

Van Allen, R., & Allen, C. (1967). *Language experience activities.* Boston, MA: Houghton Mifflin.

Van den Branden, K. (2006). *Task-based language education: From theory to practice.* Cambridge, UK: Cambridge University Press.

Van Ek, J., & Alexander, L. (1975). *Threshold level English.* Oxford, UK: Pergamon Press.

van Lier, L. (1996). *Interaction in the language curriculum: Awareness, autonomy and authenticity.* London, UK: Longman.

van Lier, L. (2000). From input to affordance: Social-interactive learning from an ecological perspective. In J. P. Lantolf (Ed.), *Sociocultural theory and second language learning* (pp. 245–260). Oxford: Oxford University Press.

van Lier, L. (2004). *The ecology and semiotics of language learning: A sociocultural perspective.* Boston, MA: Kluwer.

van Lier, L. (2007). Action-based teaching, autonomy and identity. *Innovation in Language Learning and Teaching, 1*, 46–65.

van Lier, L. (2008). Agency in the classroom. In J. Lantolf & M. Poehner (Eds.), *Sociocultural theory and the teaching of second languages* (pp. 163–186). London, UK: Equinox.

van Lier, L. (2009). Internet and language education. In M. Berns (Ed.), *Concise encyclopedia of applied linguistics* (pp. 287–292). Oxford, UK: Elsevier.

van Lier, L. (2011a). Green grammar: Ways of languaging. *Taiwan Journal of TESOL, 8*, 1–21.

van Lier, L. (2011b). Language learning: An ecological-semiotic approach. In E. Hinkel (Ed.), *Handbook of research in second language teaching and learning Volume II* (pp. 383–394). New York, NY: Routledge.

Vandergrift, L. (2003). Orchestrating strategy use: Toward a model of the skilled second language listener. *Language Learning, 53*, 463–496.

Vandergrift, L. (2004). Listening to learn or learning to listen? *Annual Review of Applied Linguistics, 24*, 3–25.

Vandergrift, L. (2006). Second language listening: Listening ability or language proficiency? *Modern Language Journal, 90*, 6–18.

Vandergrift, L. (2013). Teaching listening. In C. Chapelle (Ed.), *The encyclopedia of applied linguistics* (pp. 1169–1176). West Sussex, UK: Wiley-Blackwell.

Vandergrift, L., & Goh, C. (2011). *Teaching and learning second language listening: Metacognition in action.* New York, NY: Routledge.

Vanett, L., & Jurich, D. (1985, April). The missing link: Connecting journal writing to academic writing. Paper presented at the conference of CATESOL.

VanPatten, B. (1996). *Input processing and grammar instruction: Theory and research.* Norwood, NJ: Ablex Publishing.

Vertovec, S. (2007). Super-diversity and its implications. *Ethnic and Racial Studies, 29*, 1024–1054.

Vigil, N., & Oller, J. (1976). Rule fossilization: A tentative model. *Language Learning, 26*, 281–295.

Villanueva, C., & Buriel, R. (2010). Speaking on behalf of others: A qualitative study of the perceptions and feelings of adolescent Latina language brokers. *Journal of Social Issues, 66*, 197–210.

Vygotsky, L. (1962). *Thought and language.* Cambridge, MA: MIT Press.

Vygotsky, L. (1978). *Mind in society: The development of higher psychological processes.* Cambridge, MA: Harvard University Press.

Wajnryb, R. (1990). *Grammar dictation.* Oxford, UK: Oxford University Press.

Walker, B. (2012). *English vocabulary for academic success.* Eugene, OR: Bill Walker.

Wallace, M. (1998). *Action research for language teachers.* Cambridge, UK: Cambridge University Press.

Walsh, S. (2011). *Exploring classroom discourse: Language in action.* New York, NY: Routledge.

Wang, S., & Smith, S. (2013). Reading and grammar learning through mobile phones. *Language Learning & Technology, 17*, 117–134. Retrieved from http://llt.msu.edu/issues/october2013/wangsmith.pdf

Ware, P., & Kramsch, C. (2005). Toward an intercultural stance: Teaching German and English through telecollaboration. *Modern Language Journal, 89*, 190–205.

Warschauer, M., & Grimes, D. (2008). Audience, authorship, and artifact: the emergent semiotics of Web 2.0. *Annual Review of Applied Linguistics, 27*, 1–23.

Warschauer, M., & Healey, D. (2009). Computers and language learning. In P. Hubbard (Ed.), *Computer assisted language learning: Critical concepts in linguistics* (pp. 79–107). London, UK, and New York, NY: Routledge.

Warschauer, M., & Kern, R. (2000). *Network-based language teaching: Concepts and practice.* Cambridge, UK: Cambridge University Press.

Webb, S., & Nation, P. (2013). Teaching vocabulary. In C. Chapelle (Ed.), *The encyclopedia of applied linguistics* (pp. 5670–5677). West Sussex, UK: Wiley-Blackwell.

Weigle, S. (2002). *Assessing writing.* Cambridge, UK: Cambridge University Press.

Weigle, S. (2014). Considerations for teaching second language writing. In M. Celce-Murcia, D. Brinton, & M. A. Snow (Eds.), *Teaching English as a second or foreign language* (4th ed., pp. 222–237). Boston, MA: National Geographic Learning.

Weimer, M. (2013). *Learner-centered teaching: Five key changes to practice.* San Francisco, CA: Jossey-Bass.

Wenden, A. (1998). Metacognitive knowledge and language learning. *Applied Linguistics, 19*, 515–537.

Wenden, A. (2002). Learner development in language learning. *Applied Linguistics, 23*, 32–55.

Wesch, M. (2007). What is Web 2.0? What does it mean for anthropology? Lessons from an accidental viral video. *Anthropology News, 48*, 30–31.

Whitman, R., & Jackson, K. (1972). The unpredictability of contrastive analysis. *Language Learning, 22*, 29–41.

Widdowson, H. (1978). *Teaching language as communication.* Oxford, UK: Oxford University Press.

Wiley, T. (2013). English-only movement. In C. Chapelle (Ed.), *The encyclopedia of applied linguistics* (pp. 1970–1976). West Sussex, UK: Wiley-Blackwell.

Wilkins, D. (1976). *Notional syllabuses.* London, UK: Oxford University Press.

Williams, J. (2005). Learning without awareness. *Studies in Second Language Acquisition, 27*, 269–304.

Wintergerst, A., & McVeigh, J. (2011). *Tips for teaching culture: Practical approaches to intercultural communication*. White Plains, NY: Pearson Longman.

Wong, L., & Nunan, D. (2011). The learning styles and strategies of effective language learners. *System, 39,* 144–163.

Wong, L.-H., Chin, C.-K., Tan, C.-L., & Liu, M. (2010). Students' personal and social meaning making in a Chinese idiom mobile learning environment. *Educational Technology & Society, 13,* 15–26.

Wong, M., & Canagarajah, S. (Eds.). (2009). *Christian and critical English language educators in dialogue: Pedagogical and ethical dilemmas*. New York, NY: Routledge.

Wong, R. (1987). *Teaching pronunciation: Focus on English rhythm and intonation*. Englewood Cliffs, NJ: Prentice Hall Regents.

Woodward, T. (2001). *Planning lessons and courses*. Cambridge, UK: Cambridge University Press.

Wright, T. (2005). *Classsroom management in language education*. New York, NY: Palgrave Macmillan.

Xie, K., DeBacker, T. K., & Ferguson, C. (2006). Extending the traditional classroom through online discussion: The role of student motivation. *Journal of Educational Computing Research, 34*, 68–78.

Xie, K., Yu, C., & Bradshaw, A. (2014). Impacts of role assignment and participation in asynchronous discussions in college-level online classes. *Internet and Higher Education, 20*, 10–19.

Yang, C., & Xie, Y. (2013). Learning Chinese idioms through iPads. *Language Learning & Technology, 17*, 12–23. Retrieved from http://llt.msu.edu/issues/june2013/yangxie.pdf

Yashima, T. (2002). Willingness to communicate in a second language: The Japanese EFL context. *Modern Language Journal, 86*, 54–66.

Yashima, T. (2013). Agency in second language acquisition. In C. Chapelle (Ed.), *The encyclopedia of applied linguistics* (pp. 49–56). West Sussex, UK: Wiley-Blackwell.

Zimmerman, B. (1990). Self-regulated learning and academic achievement. *Educational Psychologist, 25*, 3–17.

Zimmerman, C. (1997). Historical trends in second language vocabulary instruction. In J. Coady & T. Huckin (Eds.). *Second language vocabulary acquisition: A rationale for pedagogy* (pp. 5–19). Cambridge, UK: Cambridge University Press.

Zimmerman, C. (2014). Teaching and learning vocabulary for second language learners. In M. Celce-Murcia, D. Brinton, & M. A. Snow (Eds.), *Teaching English as a second and foreign language* (4th ed., pp. 288–302). Boston, MA: National Geographic Learning.

GLOSSARY

achievement test an instrument used to determine whether course objectives have been met—and appropriate knowledge and skills acquired—by the end of a given period of instruction

action research the systematic investigation of an issue, problem, or pedagogical question in a "live" classroom setting with students, and reporting on the findings of the investigation

activity a reasonably unified set of student behaviors, limited in time, preceded by some direction from the teacher, with a particular objective

additive bilingualism context in which the native language is held in prestige by the community or society

adjunct model (of content-based language teaching) linking subject-matter teachers and language teachers in content-based courses

affect emotion or feeling

affordances opportunities for meaningful action that a situation leads to; a reciprocal relationship between a person and a particular feature of the environment that signals a possibility for action

agency a person's ability to make choices, take control, self-regulate, and thereby pursue goals as an individual, leading potentially to personal or social transformation

approach theoretical positions and beliefs about teaching, language, language learning, learners, institutional and societal factors, purposes of a course, and the applicability of all to a specific educational context

assessment an ongoing process ranging from formal tests to informal evaluation (see **test**)

Audiolingual Method (ALM) a language teaching method that emphasized oral production, pattern drills, and conditioning through repetition

authenticity (of a test) the degree of correspondence of the characteristics of a given language test task to the features of the actual target language task

automaticity the act of processing input and giving output without deliberation or hesitation in real-time speed

autonomy individual effort and action through which learners initiate language, problem solving, strategic action, and the generation of linguistic input

basic interpersonal communication skills (BICS) abilities that enable language users to function in everyday personal exchanges; context-embedded performance

bilingual education classroom instruction in two languages for the same group of students; students receive some of their instruction in one language and some in the other, in varying proportions according to program type, instructional goals, and contextual influences

bilingualism ability in two or more languages

bottom-up processing a focus on the "bits and pieces" of language, breaking language into component parts and giving them central focus, eventually working toward meaning

brainstorming open-ended, rapid-fire voluntary oral or written listing of ideas with no debate or evaluation by others

CALL (Computer Assisted Language Learning) the subfield of applied linguistics concerned with the use of computers for teaching and learning a second language

Classical Method a language teaching method in which the focus is on grammatical rules, memorization of vocabulary and other language forms, translation of texts, and performing written exercises

classroom language academic discourse typical of linguistic exchanges in classrooms between teacher and students and among students (e.g., in small group work), often involving directions, questions, discussions, agreeing and disagreeing

classroom management the process of ensuring that classroom lessons run smoothly considering a wide range of factors from the physical arrangement of a classroom, to teaching styles and philosophy, to classroom energy

classroom-based assessment instruments either created or adapted to assess classroom/course objectives

cognitive academic language proficiency (CALP) ability of language users to function in such academic contexts as test-taking, writing, analyzing, and reading academic texts

collaboration the process of learners working together (as opposed to individually) with their classmates in reaching goals of a task, solving problems, practicing language, etc.

collocation a sequence of words or terms that co-occur more often than would be expected by chance, such as "iron will," "zero tolerance," and "sugar and cream"

communicative student responses are meaningful, real-world related, open-ended, and unpredictable

communicative competence (CC) the cluster of abilities that enable humans to convey and interpret messages and to negotiate meanings interpersonally within specific contexts

Communicative Language Teaching (CLT) an approach to language teaching methodology that emphasizes authenticity, interaction, student-centered learning, task-based activities, and communication for real-world, meaningful purposes

communicative language test assessment that incorporates authentic, meaningful, real-world tasks

Community Language Learning (CLL) language teaching method that emphasizes interpersonal relationships, inductive learning, and views the teacher as a "counselor"

community of practice (CoP) group of people who share a common interest in a particular domain, characterized by mutual engagement, joint enterprise, and shared repertoire

composing the thinking, drafting, and revising procedures involved in planned writing

computer-mediated communication (CMC) communication through the use of two or more electronic devices such as computers, tablet PCs, and smart phones. Commonly used formats are e-mail, video, audio, or text chatting supported by social software (applications)

conceptually driven processing same as top-down processing

concordancing indexing of words that enables one to reference words in the multiple possible contexts in which they appear in spoken or written language

consciousness-raising drawing students' attention to formal elements of language within the context of meaningful communication and tasks

construct validity (of a test) the extent to which a test actually taps into the theoretical construct that it proposes to assess

content schemata what we know about people, the world, culture, and the universe

content validity (of a test) the extent to which test tasks actually sample the subject matter about which conclusions are to be drawn

content-based language teaching (CBLT) an umbrella term for a multifaceted approach to L2 language teaching that integrates language teaching aims with content instruction

contrastive rhetoric L1 schemata and patterns of thinking and writing can carry over into L2 writing (see **intercultural rhetoric)**

controlled writing teachers typically present a short text to students in which they must alter a given structure throughout (e.g., convert present to past tense)

cooperative learning model of education in which students work together in pairs and groups, share information, and come to each other's aid, as opposed to teacher-centered instruction (see **learner-centered instruction**)

corpora plural of corpus (see **corpus linguistics**)

corpus linguistics an approach to linguistic research that relies on computer analyses of a collection, or corpus, of texts—written, transcribed speech, or both—stored in electronic form and analyzed with digital software

corpus-based teaching using corpora to inform curriculum and lesson designs (see **corpus linguistics)**

course a unified series of classes over a determined period of time, centered on a particular subject in an educational institution

course management system (CMS) a software application for administering, documenting, tracking, reporting, and delivering e-learning education courses or training programs

criterion-referenced test designed to give test-takers feedback on specific course or lesson objectives

critical language assessment the recognition that tests represent a social technology deeply embedded in education, government, and business, and as such, they provide the mechanism for enforcing power and control (see **critical pedagogy**)

critical pedagogy a view of learning and teaching as deeply embedded in social, political, and ideological mores, and motivated by our beliefs about education and its place in society

cross-linguistic influence (CLI) a concept that recognizes the significance of the role of the L1 and subsequent languages in learning an additional language, but with an emphasis on both the facilitating and interfering effects the two languages have on each other

curriculum a course of study that includes specifications of topics, forms, assignments, and schedules for completion; also, a *group* of separate courses within a program (see **syllabus)**

data-driven processing same as bottom-up processing

diagnostic test an assessment instrument designed to analyze a test-taker's strengths and weaknesses in terms of grammar, pronunciation, fluency, discourse, or other targeted linguistic features

dialogical cosmopolitanism the ideology that persons can belong to a single community through mutual collaboration and acceptance of all members' varying cultures, ideas, values, etc.

dialogue journal a student records thoughts, feelings, and reactions and an instructor reads and responds

dictocomp a paragraph is read at normal speed 2–3 times, then students rewrite the paragraph to the best of their recollection

Direct Method a language teaching method popular in the early twentieth century that emphasized direct target language use, oral communication skills, and inductive grammar, without recourse to translation from the first language

directive (approaches to teaching) the teacher is more in control of lessons than students

discourse an instance of spoken or written language with describable internal relationships of form and meaning (e.g., words, structures, cohesion) that relate coherently to an external communicative function or purpose and a given audience or interlocutor

discovery learning the concept that when learners are spurred to induce language or other content, as opposed to being told by the teacher, greater retention results

discrete point testing assessment on the assumption that language could be broken down into its component parts and those parts adequately tested

display question an attempt to elicit information already known by the teacher

display writing primarily for the display of a student's knowledge, as opposed to **real writing**

drill a mechanical technique focusing on a minimal number of language forms through repetition

dynamic systems theory (DST) an amalgamation of claims, based on chaos theory and complexity theory, that language acquisition is a dynamic process involving nonlinear individual variations

embodied cognition the concept that an organism's sensorimotor capacities, body, and environment play crucial roles in the development of cognitive and linguistic abilities

enabling objectives interim steps within a lesson that build upon each other and ultimately lead to a terminal objective

English for academic purposes (EAP) see **languages for specific purposes**

English for specific purposes (ESP) see **languages for specific purposes**

environment analysis see **situation analysis**

experiential learning instruction that highlights giving students concrete experiences in which they must use language in order to fulfill the objectives of a lesson

explicit (treatment of form) drawing learners' focal attention to formal elements of language, as opposed to **implicit** treatment

extensive reading the process of achieving a general understanding of a relatively long text (book, long article, or essay, etc.)

extra-class work assignments that a student is given to do outside the regular class hours, commonly called "homework"

extrinsic motivation choices made and effort expended on activities in anticipation of a reward from outside and beyond the self

face validity (of a test) the extent to which a test, on the "face" of it, appears from the learner's perspective to test what it is designed to test

fluency the unfettered flow of language production or comprehension, usually without focal attention on language forms

focus on form (FonF) an approach that attempts to induce learners' incidental learning by drawing their attention to target forms while they are engaged in communicative activities (see **form-focused instruction**)

foreign language (context) the target language is not readily accessible outside the classroom; for example, German (as the L2) in Australia

form (of language) unit of language, such as morphemes, words, grammar rules, discourse rules, and other organizational elements of language

form-focused instruction (FFI) any planned or incidental instructional activity that is intended to include language learners to pay attention to linguistic form

formal assessment deliberate, planned assessment using scoring and grading criteria and usually with conventionalized feedback

formal schemata knowledge about language and discourse structure

formative assessment ongoing informal evaluation serving the purpose of facilitating improvement in a student's performance

freewriting writing simply to start the "flow" of writing, with little thought to grammaticality, spelling, logical thinking, or organization

function (of language) a meaningful, interactive purpose within a social (pragmatic) context, which we accomplish with forms of language

Functional Syllabus see **Notional-Functional Syllabus**

gate-keeping the extent to which tests control entry and exit into and from educational, political, social, and commercial entities

genre a category of discourse characterized by similarities in form, style, or subject matter (e.g., academic essay, poem, business letter)

genre-based pedagogy a focus on discipline-specific genres, such as laboratory reports, travel brochures, financial reports, essays, or newspaper articles

goal the overall purpose toward which a course or a lesson is directed and is intended to achieve

Grammar Translation Method a language teaching method in which the central focus is on grammatical rules, paradigms, and vocabulary memorization as the basis for translating from one language to another

group dynamics the way that two or more students behave with each other in a particular classroom environment, which also influences how they relate to each other and how effectively communicate and work together

group work a variety of techniques in which two or more students are assigned a task that involves collaboration and self-initiated language

guided writing teachers provide a series of stimulators (e.g., asking students a series of questions), which enables them to tell a story just viewed on a videotape

haptics any form of nonverbal communication involving touch, also known as kinesthetics

high stakes (standardized tests) instruments used to make crucial decisions about one's future path (e.g., college entrance, employment, certification)

identity the extent to which L2 learners do not perceive themselves merely as individual entities, but more importantly, as an integral and constitutive part of the social world to which they are connected

imagined communities a community as perceived by a learner, or the mental image of a socially constructed community

immersion educational model that typically provides the majority of subject-matter content through the medium of the L2

implicit (treatment of form) incorporation of formal elements of language without overt focal attention to forms, as opposed to **explicit** treatment of form

incidental learning acquisition without intention to learn or focal awareness of elements of language, as opposed to **intentional learning**

informal assessment incidental, unplanned evaluation usually embedded in classroom tasks, and usually designed to elicit improved performance (see **formal assessment**)

input enhancement highlighting, boldfacing, or otherwise calling attention to certain target grammatical forms in a reading text

input hypothesis the claim that linguistic input is sufficient for L2 acquisition

instrumental orientation acquiring a language as a means for attaining instrumental goals, such as acquiring a degree or certificate in an academic institution, furthering a career, reading technical material, translation, etc.

integrative orientation learning a language in order to integrate oneself into the culture of a second language group and become involved in social interchange in that group

integrative testing a view of testing that incorporated the whole of a communicative event, considered to be greater than the sum of its linguistic elements

intensive reading usually a classroom-oriented activity in which students focus on the linguistic or semantic details of a passage.

intentional learning see **explicit** (treatment of form)

interaction the collaborative exchange of thoughts, feelings, or ideas between two or more people; in an L2 classroom, face-to-face communication (usually orally) involving pair/group work, meaningful communication, and spontaneous conversations and discussions

interaction hypothesis the claim that language competence is the result not only of input, but also of interaction between a learner's input and output

intercultural competence ability to understand, empathize with, and/or function in a culture or cultures other than one's L1 culture

intercultural rhetoric accounting for the richness of rhetorical variation of written texts, the varying contexts in which they are constructed, and the cultural characteristics of writing (see **contrastive rhetoric**)

interference negative transfer in which a previous item is incorrectly transferred or incorrectly associated with an item to be learned

interlanguage learner language that emphasizes the separateness of a second language learner's system, a system that has a structurally intermediate status between the native and target languages

interlingual transfer the effect of one language on another

interpersonal existing or happening between people

intralingual transfer the effect of forms, patterns, and discourse conventions of one language (usually the L2) on other forms, patterns, and discourse conventions *within* the same language

intrinsic motivation choices made and effort expended on activities for which there is no apparent reward except the activity itself

investment commitment and motivation to accomplish major goals (such as language learning); learners are seeking to increase the "value" of their cultural capital

languaculture the inseparability of language and culture; the "langua" is about discourse, not just about words and sentences, and the "culture" is about meanings that include, but go well beyond, what the dictionary and grammar offer

language ego the identity a person develops in reference to the language he or she speaks

Language Experience Approach (LEA) an integrated-skills approach initially used in teaching native language reading skills, but more recently adapted to second language learning contexts

language policy official statements by governmental or educational institutions that declare the status, use, and teaching of a language within a political or geographical entity

languages for specific purposes (LSP) instruction in which students learn to interact with the language as it is spoken or written in specific disciplines being pursued by students.

LCTLs (Less Commonly Taught Languages) all languages other than English and the commonly taught European languages of French, German, and Spanish

learner-centered instruction model of education with a focus on learners' needs and goals and individual differences in a supportive atmosphere that offers students choices and some control

learning style cognitive, affective, and physiological traits that are relatively stable indicators of how learners perceive, interact with, and respond to the learning environment

lesson a single class or part of a course of instruction

Lexical Approach a language teaching method that emphasized the importance of words (vocabulary) in SLA

lexicogrammar a view that lexis and grammar are two inherently connected parts of a single entity and should not be treated separately

liberation education teaching to enable learners to think critically, to be freed from oppressive doctrines and systems, to believe in themselves, and to "pull themselves up by their own bootstraps"

linguicism the belief that language has the potential to legitimize an unequal division of power and resources in which a dominant language is held in high esteem and dominated languages are stigmatized

macroskills skills that are technically at the discourse level

MALL (Mobile Assisted Language Learning) the use of mobile technologies (e.g., smart phones, tablets) for language learning, especially in situations where device portability offers particular advantages

manipulative pertaining to techniques totally controlled by the teacher and requiring a predicted response from the student(s)

meaning the semantic level of structural items including lexical and grammatical meaning

meaningful drills techniques with a predicted or a limited set of possible responses relating to some form of reality

meaningful learning anchoring and relating new items and experiences to knowledge that exists in the cognitive framework

mechanical drills techniques that require only one correct response from a student without connection with reality

mediation utilizing a concept or idea to act as an intermediary between otherwise difficult or unrelatable cognitive/linguistic constructs in order to achieve meaning or communicative goals; the process of assisting learning through scaffolding and other means that help learners to reach their goals

method a coherent, prescribed group of activities and techniques for language teaching, unified by a homogeneous set of principles or foundations; sometimes claimed to be suitable for all L2 teaching contexts

methodology pedagogical practices in general, including theoretical underpinnings and related research

microskills skills that are at the sentence level

motivation the anticipation of reward, whether internally or externally administered; choices made about goals to pursue and the effort exerted in their completion

multilingualism ability to use two or more languages

multimodal communication sending and receiving messages through several modes, such as text, visuals, audio, and touch, that are available when creating ePortfolios, websites, visual presentation slides, research posters, and other materials

multiple intelligences the hypothesis that intelligence is not limited to traditional concepts of verbal, logical, and mathematical ability, but has multiple modes including spatial, emotional, musical, contextual, and interpersonal

native English-speaking teachers (NESTs) teachers whose L1 is English

Natural Approach a language teaching method that simulates child language acquisition by emphasizing communication, comprehensible input, kinesthetic activities, and virtually no grammatical analysis

needs assessment a systematic process for determining and addressing needs, overall purposes, or "gaps" that the course is intended to fill, and the opinions of both course designers and students about their reasons for developing/taking the course

negotiation the act or process of reaching an agreement, usually involving linguistic exchanges, as in the give-and-take of conversation

nondirective using more inductive, student-centered approaches

nonnative English-speaking teachers (NNESTs) teachers whose L1 is not English

norm-referenced test instrument in which each test-taker's score is interpreted in relation to a mean, median, standard deviation, and/or percentile rank

noticing the learner's paying attention to specific linguistic features in input

Notional-Functional Syllabus a language course that attends primarily to functions as organizing elements of a foreign language curriculum

objective explicit statement of what students will gain from a lesson and their expected performance, which will demonstrate achievement of learning outcomes

orientation one's personal perspective on a culture other than one's own, and the extent to which that perspective influences the intensity of motivation to understand or adapt to that culture and/or the language of the culture

overgeneralization the process of generalizing a particular rule or item in the second language, irrespective of the native language, beyond conventional rules or boundaries

pacing the comfort level of a lesson in terms of rhythm and speed

pair work group work in groups of two, but usually involves less complex and briefer tasks

pedagogical tasks any of a sequence of techniques designed ultimately to teach students to perform the target task.

performance-based assessment the test taker (or classroom student) must engage in actual performance of the specified linguistic objective

placement test an assessment instrument specifically designed to determine test takers' levels of ability among two or more course levels in an educational program

postmethod a concept that arose around the turn of the twenty-first century that described the need to put to rest the limited concept of method as it was used in the previous century

practicality (of a test) extent to which an instrument is within desirable financial limitations, time constraints, and ease of administration, scoring, and interpretation

procedure a series of actions that are performed either by a teacher or students in a certain order during the lesson

process a progression of procedures (steps, stages, strategies, milestones) in learners' language development (versus the end **product**)

product the ultimate or end result of a set of learning efforts; for example, a final "paper" or the summation of abilities at the end of a course of study (versus the **process** of progressive achievement of that end)

proficiency test an assessment of one's general language ability, irrespective of any one course or curriculum

program a collection of classes or courses offered within a single institution that lead to a certificate or degree

project-based learning see **experiential learning**
real writing the reader does not know the answer (to a question or problem) and genuinely wants information, as opposed to **display writing**
referential question request for information not known by the questioner
reliability (of a test) the consistency and dependability of an assessment instrument
rhetorical formality (in writing) organizational conventions in writing for connecting sentences, showing relationships, opening paragraphs, using subordination, and so on, that extend beyond the sentence level
role-play giving a role to one or more members of a group and assigning an objective or purpose that participants must accomplish
roles functions or positions that a teacher or students have in a particular activity or in the classroom
rote learning acquiring and storing information in discrete categories unrelated to existing cognitive structure (e.g., by memorization or repetition)
rubrics specified categories, which break down a skill into several components, for scoring or evaluating language performance
scaffolding the process of supporting learners' progression toward goals by providing hints, clues, reminders, examples, steps to solving a problem, encouragement, and other aids
scanning quickly searching for a particular piece or pieces of information in a text
schema theory the concept that information is stored in long-term memory in networks of connected facts, concepts, and structures, which learners bring to bear on comprehension and production of language
schemata background information that a language user brings to bear on a text
second language (context) the target language is spoken outside the classroom, for example, Chinese (as the L2) in China (see **foreign language** context)
self-actualization reaching the pinnacle of one's potential; the culmination of human attainment
self-determination one's own choice to make an effort because of what he or she will gain, either in the short term or long run
self-efficacy belief in one's own capabilities to perform a specific activity
self-regulation deliberate goal-directed attempts to manage and control efforts to learn the L2
semantic mapping grouping ideas from a text into meaningful clusters, connecting those clusters in a visual diagram
Series Method language teaching method in which learners practiced a number of connected "series" of sentences, which together formed a meaningful story or sequence of events
sheltered models the deliberate separation of L2 students from native speakers of the target language for the purpose of content instruction
Silent Way a language teaching method that encouraged inductive learning, engaging in problem solving, and relating (mediating) physical objects to the new language
simulations group role-plays or games in which characters and/or situations are assigned in advance to students (players), with the task of acting out the situation
situated cognition see **embodied cognition**

situation analysis a study of information about the target educational setting, characteristics of class, faculty, and students, governance of course content and materials, and assessment methods

skimming quickly running one's eyes across a whole text (such as an essay, article, or chapter) for its gist

social networking sites (SNSs) web-based communities such as Facebook and Twitter in which individuals can develop and maintain social ties, both online and offline, through participation in a multifaceted and multisensory environment

social responsibility the obligation to act to benefit society at large, to promote the collective and common good for all, and to perform so as to maintain a balance between the economy and the ecosystems

SQ3R a pedagogical set of procedures for approaching a reading text involving (in sequential order): survey, question, read, recite, review

strategic investment a certain degree of investment of one's time and effort into using effective strategies for accomplishing L2 goals

strategies-based instruction (SBI) teaching learners with an emphasis on the strategic options that are available for learning; usually implying the teacher's facilitating awareness of those options in the learner and encouraging strategic action

strategy a specific method or technique for approaching a problem or task; a mode of operation for achieving a particular end; a planned design for controlling and manipulating certain information

styles consistent and enduring tendencies or preferences within an individual; general characteristics of intellectual and emotional functioning that differentiate one person from another

subtractive bilingualism contexts in which a target language is held in relatively high esteem while home, native, or heritage languages are devalued

Suggestopedia a language teaching method that contended that the human brain could process great quantities of material in a (suggested) state of relaxation and yielding control to the teacher

summative assessment evaluation of the final products, performances, and usually end-of-course or end-of-unit overall evaluation

superdiversity a diversification of diversity due to the multilateral flow of people, goods, and ideas across borders

syllabus a curriculum; also specifications of topics, forms, assignments, and schedules for completion of a course

target tasks uses of language in the world beyond the classroom that become the focus of classroom instruction

task a classroom activity in which meaning is primary, there is a problem to solve, a relationship to real-world activities, and an objective that can be assessed in terms of an outcome

Task-Based Language Teaching (TBLT) an approach to language instruction that focuses on tasks (see **task**)

teacher-centered instruction the teacher controls everything; students speak only when asked to; the teacher is an authority who is not to be questioned

teaching styles particular preferences of a teacher's performance that reflects his or her personality, values, and beliefs and that can vary greatly from individual to individual

technical school an institution dedicated to the occupation related training ranging from art, fashion design, and architecture, to carpentry, automotive mechanics, etc.

techniques any of a wide variety of exercises, activities, procedures, or tasks used in the language classroom for realizing lesson objectives

terminal objective final learning outcome

test a method (usually an instrument) that systematically measures a person's ability or knowledge in a given domain

theme-based instruction an organizing framework for a language course that transcends formal or structural requirements in a curriculum and focuses on meaningful topics as organizing elements of units and lessons

top-down processing activation of schemata to deriving meaning, global understanding, and interpretation of a text

topic-based see **theme-based instruction**

Total Physical Response (TPR) a language teaching method relying on physical or kinesthetic movement accompanied by language practice

trade school see **technical school**

transactional dialogue two or more speakers' exchanges to convey propositional or factual information

transfer the carryover of previous performance or knowledge to previous or subsequent learning

translanguaging code-switching or translating in reading, writing, discussing, note-taking, or singing, a strategy in which bilingual students and teachers engage in multiple discursive practices in order to make sense of meanings and functions of target forms

translingual meshing two or more languages in transformative ways, generating new forms, meanings, or uses through situated interactions

transnational reaching beyond the boundaries and interests of a single nation

use meanings of utterances across different contexts and cohesion in discourse

validity (of a test) the degree to which a test actually measures what it is intended to measure

Vocational English as a Second Language (VESL) see **vocational L2 instruction**

vocational L2 instruction part of an adult education program that provides pre-employment language training, typically including basic academic language skills along with specialized occupational contexts

voice infusing one's words with one's own feelings, thoughts, and identity

washback the effects, both beneficial and detrimental, of an assessment on teaching and learning prior to and after the assessment itself

Web 1.0 use of the World Wide Web only to search for information and read it; the users of the tools are simply viewers of such content

Web 2.0 use of the World Wide Web in which social experience, in the form of blogs, wikis, or forums, plays a more important role than simply accessing information; websites allow people to "read-write," connect with each other, and *create* content

whole language education an emphasis on the interconnections between oral and written language and the integration of all four skills

willingness to communicate (WTC) a state of readiness to engage in the L2, the culmination of processes that prepare the learner to initiate L2 communication with a specific person at a specific time

workplace L2 instruction tailoring language to the specific linguistic needs of carrying out one's duties "on the job"

zone of proximal development (ZPD) the distance between a learner's existing developmental state and his or her potential development

NAME INDEX

Page references followed by *f*, *t*, or *n* refer to a figure, table, or source note.

SUBJECT INDEX

CREDITS

Photo Credits

Page 6 Pearson Education; **p. 115** Jelena Ivanovic/Fotolia; **p. 230** (A) digidreamgrafix/Fotolia, (B) Tom Hirtreiter/Fotolia, (C) LeNi/Shutterstock, (D) Tund/Shutterstock, (E) Anna Sedneva/Shutterstock, (F) Denise Kappa/Shutterstock, (G) andrej_sv/Shutterstock, (H) scanrail/123RF, (I) Adam Gilchrist/Shutterstock, (J) M. Unal Ozmen/Shutterstock, (K) Viktor/Fotolia, (L) Joe Gough/Fotolia, (M) Nataliya Peregudova/Shutterstock, (N) Mara Zemgaliete/Fotolia, (O) sss615/Fotolia; **p. 249** (top) Felix Mizioznikov/Fotolia, (bottom) ptnphotof/Fotolia; **p. 254** (left) .shock/Fotolia, (right) Maridav/Fotolia; **p. 362** Pearson Education; **p. 363** (top left) cunaplus/Fotolia, (top middle left) Tyler Olson/Fotolia, (top middle right) asife/Fotolia, (top right) Andres Rodriguez/Fotolia, (yoga) byheaven/Fotolia, (eat) Ljupco Smokovski/123RF, (lift) Jason Stitt/Fotolia, (laugh) Gabriela/Fotolia, (meditate) SolisImages/Fotolia, (apologize) PathDoc/Shutterstock, (forgive) Gelpi/Fotolia, (exercise) DragonImages/Fotolia, (relax) Minerva Studio/Fotolia, (walk) Phase4Studios/Shutterstock, (angry) Voyagerix/Fotolia, (smoke) Stuart Miles/Fotolia, (eat fatty) Gennadiy Poznyakov/Fotolia, (drink) Masson/Fotolia, (worry) PathDoc/Shutterstock, (work) Kzenon/Shutterstock; **p. 364** (1) Click Images/Fotolia, (2) LIUSHENGFILM/Shutterstock, (3) George Wada/Fotolia, (4) bst2012/Fotolia, (5) yo/Fotolia, (A) michaeljung/Fotolia, (B) underdogstudios/Fotolia, (C) michaeljung/Fotolia, (D) xalanx/Fotolia, (E) studiopure/Fotolia, (F) Odua Images/Fotolia; **p. 415** (top right) Nitr/Fotolia, (left) johnfoto18/Shutterstock, (middle) Feng Yu/Fotolia, (right) valery121283/Fotolia; **p. 417** Edyta Pawlowska/Fotolia; **p. 452** ISSOUF SANOGO/AFP/Getty Images; **p. 454** bikeriderlondon/Shutterstock.

Text Credits

Page 6 Used by Permission of Pearson Education, Inc.; **pp. 114–116** © Vera Chen. Used with permission; **p. 119** Used by Permission of Pearson Education, Inc.; **pp. 122–127** Reprinted with permission of Claire Joy Ballon Arnett; **p. 132** Used with permission of Interagency Language Roundtable; **p. 133** IELTS: Jointly owned by British Council, IDP: IELTS Australia and Cambridge English Language Assessment. Used with permission; **p. 134** American Council on Teaching Foreign Languages, ACFTL Guidelines, Listening; **pp. 134–135** American Council on the Teaching of Foreign Languages, ACTFL Guidelines, Speaking: Intermediate Level, http://www.actfl.org/sites/default/files/pdfs/public/ACTFLProficiencyGuidelines2012_FINAL.pdf; **p. 137** From the Common European Framework of Reference for Languages: Learning, Teaching, Assessment, © Council of Europe. Language Policy Unit, Strasbourg, www.coe.int/lang CEFR; **p. 138** (top) From the Common European Framework of Reference for Languages: Learning, Teaching, Assessment, © Council of Europe. Language Policy Unit, Strasbourg, www.coe.int/lang CEFR; **p. 138** (bottom) IELTS: Jointly owned by British Council, IDP: IELTS Australia and Cambridge English Language Assessment. Used with permission; **pp. 144–145** Helgeson, M., Brown, S., & Wiltshier, J. (2010). *English Firsthand, Book 1.* Hong Kong: Pearson Education Asia; **pp. 209–215** © Safa Lateef. Used with permission; **p. 215** Appendix E: Reproduced by permission of Oxford University Press, from *Grammar Sense Student's Book Level 1,* by Cheryl Pavlik © Oxford University Press, 2003; **pp. 230–231** Used by Permission of Pearson Education, Inc.; **p. 241** Interpreting and integrating the TESOL technology standards in a CALL mini course. Paper presented at the TESOL 2014 Convention, Portland, Oregon; reprinted with permission from TESOL Technology Standards: Description,

Implementation, Integration, © 2014 by TESOL International Association. All rights reserved; **p. 249** From "Situated learning through social networking communities: The development of joint enterprise, mutual engagement, and a shared repertoire," by N. Mills (2011) in *CALICO Journal*, 28(2),354. © Equinox Publishing Ltd, 2011; **p. 254** Republished with permission of University of Hawaii Press, from "Learning Chinese idioms through iPads." *Language Learning & Technology*, 17(2), 12–23, by C. Yang & Y. Xie; 2013; permission conveyed through Copyright Clearance Center, Inc.; **pp. 361–362** Used by Permission of Pearson Education, Inc.; **pp. 363–364** Helgeson, M., Brown, S., & Wiltshier, J. (2010). *English Firsthand, Book 1*. Hong Kong: Pearson Education Asia; **pp. 365–366** Used by Permission of Pearson Education, Inc.; **pp. 367–368** Used by Permission of Pearson Education, Inc.; **p. 370** Used by Permission of Pearson Education, Inc.; **pp. 372–373** Used by Permission of Pearson Education, Inc.; **p. 377** Excerpted from *Teaching Pronunciation: Focus on English Rhythm and Intonation*, pages 61–64, by Rita Wong. 1987. Prentice Hall and Center for Applied Linguistics. Used by permission; **p. 378** Used by Permission of Pearson Education, Inc.; **p. 407** From Long & Richards, *Methodology in TESOL, 1E*. © 1987 Heinle/ELT, a part of Cengage Learning, Inc. Reproduced by permission. www.cengage.com/permissions; **pp. 415–416** Used by Permission of Pearson Education, Inc.; **p. 417** Used by Permission of Pearson Education, Inc.; **pp. 417–421** Used with permission of Dr. Eric H. Chudler, University of Washington; **pp. 448–450** Used by Permission of Pearson Education, Inc.; **pp. 451–455** Republished with permission of the Royal Society of Chemistry, from "Plastic Bags, Sugar Cane and Advanced Vibrational Spectroscopy: Taking Green Chemistry to the Third World," *Green Chemistry, Volume 6*, by M. Poliakoff & I. Noda, 2004; permission conveyed through Copyright Clearance Center, Inc.; **pp. 451–455** Used by Permission of Pearson Education, Inc.; **p. 471** Republished with permission of John Wiley & Sons, from "Negative feedback as regulation and second language learning in the zone of proximal development," *Modern Language Journal*, 78, 465–483; permission conveyed through Copyright Clearance Center, Inc.; **p. 472** Republished with permission of John Wiley & Sons, from "Using a corpus based lexicogrammatical approach to grammar instruction in EFL and ESL contexts," *Modern Language Journal*, 93, 61–78; permission conveyed through Copyright Clearance Center, Inc.; **pp. 477–479** Republished with permission of Taylor & Francis LLC, from *Teaching Grammar in Second Language Classrooms: Integrating Form-Focused Instruction in Communicative Context*, by H. Nassaji & S. Fotos, 2011; permission conveyed through Copyright Clearance Center, Inc.; **p. 482** http://corpus.byu.edu/coca/; **pp. 552–554** Republished with permission of Teachers of English to Speakers of Other Languages, from "Teacher self observation," TESOL Newsletter, 8, 17–19 by Christison, M., & Bassano, S., 1984; permission conveyed through Copyright Clearance Center, Inc.; **pp. 569–570** © Joseph Lee. Used with permission.